THE CAMBRIDGE BIBLE COMMENTARY
NEW ENGLISH BIBLE

GENERAL EDITORS
P. R. ACKROYD, A. R. C. LEANEY,
J. W. PACKER

I KINGS

THE FIRST BOOK OF
KINGS

COMMENTARY BY

J. ROBINSON
Canon of Canterbury

CAMBRIDGE
AT THE UNIVERSITY PRESS
1972

Published by the Syndics of the Cambridge University Press
Bentley House, 200 Euston Road, London NW1 2DB
American Branch: 32 East 57th Street, New York, N.Y.10022

© Cambridge University Press 1972

Library of Congress Catalogue Card Number: 72-80592

ISBNS:
0 521 08619 1 hard cover
0 521 09734 7 paperback

Printed in Great Britain
at the University Printing House, Cambridge
(Brooke Crutchley, University Printer)

GENERAL EDITORS' PREFACE

The aim of this series is to provide the text of the New English Bible closely linked to a commentary in which the results of modern scholarship are made available to the general reader. Teachers and young people have been especially kept in mind. The commentators have been asked to assume no specialized theological knowledge, and no knowledge of Greek and Hebrew. Bare references to other literature and multiple references to other parts of the Bible have been avoided. Actual quotations have been given as often as possible.

The completion of the New Testament part of the series in 1967 provides a basis upon which the production of the much larger Old Testament and Apocrypha series can be undertaken. The welcome accorded to the series has been an encouragement to the editors to follow the same general pattern, and an attempt has been made to take account of criticisms which have been offered. One necessary change is the inclusion of the translators' footnotes since in the Old Testament these are more extensive, and essential for the understanding of the text.

Within the severe limits imposed by the size and scope of the series, each commentator will attempt to set out the main findings of recent biblical scholarship and to describe the historical background to the text. The main theological issues will also be critically discussed.

Much attention has been given to the form of the volumes. The aim is to produce books each of which will be read consecutively from first to last page. The introductory material leads naturally into the text, which itself leads into the alternating sections of the commentary.

The series is accompanied by three volumes of a more general character. *Understanding the Old Testament* sets out to provide the larger historical and archaeological background, to say something about the life and thought of the people of the Old Testament, and to answer the question 'Why should we study the Old Testament?'. *The Making of the Old Testament* is concerned with the formation of the books of the Old Testament and Apocrypha in the context of the ancient near eastern world, and with the ways in which these books have come down to us in the life of the Jewish and Christian communities. *Old Testament Illustrations* contains maps, diagrams and photographs with an explanatory text. These three volumes are designed to provide material helpful to the understanding of the individual books and their commentaries, but they are also prepared so as to be of use quite independently.

P. R. A.

A. R. C. L.

J. W. P.

CONTENTS

☆   ☆   ☆   ☆   ☆   ☆   ☆   ☆   ☆   ☆   ☆   ☆   ☆

CONTENTS

LIST OF MAPS AND TIME CHART

THE FOOTNOTES TO THE
N.E.B. TEXT

The footnotes to the N.E.B. text are designed to help the reader either to understand particular points of detail – the meaning of a name, the presence of a play upon words – or to give information about the actual text. Where the Hebrew text appears to be erroneous, or there is doubt about its precise meaning, it may be necessary to turn to manuscripts which offer a different wording, or to ancient translations of the text which may suggest a better reading, or to offer a new explanation based upon conjecture. In such cases, the footnotes supply very briefly an indication of the evidence, and whether the solution proposed is one that is regarded as possible or as probable. Various abbreviations are used in the footnotes.

(1) Some abbreviations are simply of terms used in explaining a point: *ch(s)*., chapter(s); *cp*., compare; *lit*., literally; *mng*., meaning; *MS(S)*., manuscript(s), i.e. Hebrew manuscript(s), unless otherwise stated; *om*., omit(s); *or*, indicating an alternative interpretation; *poss*., possible; *prob*., probable; *rdg*., reading; *Vs(s)*., version(s).

(2) Other abbreviations indicate sources of information from which better interpretations or readings may be obtained.

Aq.   Aquila, a Greek translator of the Old Testament (perhaps about A.D. 130) characterized by great literalness.

Aram.   Aramaic–may refer to the text in this language (used in parts of Ezra and Daniel), or to the meaning of an Aramaic word. Aramaic belongs to the same language family as Hebrew, and is known from about 1000 B.C. over a wide area of the Middle East, including Palestine.

Heb.   Hebrew – may refer to the Hebrew text or may indicate the literal meaning of the Hebrew word.

Josephus   Flavius Josephus (A.D. 37/8–about 100), author of the *Jewish Antiquities*, a survey of the whole history of his people, directed partly at least to a non-Jewish audience, and of various other works, notably one on the *Jewish War* (that of A.D. 66–73) and a defence of Judaism (*Against Apion*).

Luc. Sept.   Lucian's recension of the Septuagint, an important edition made in Antioch in Syria about the end of the third century A.D.

Pesh.   Peshitta or Peshitto, the Syriac version of the Old Testament. Syriac is the name given chiefly to a form of Eastern Aramaic used by the Christian community. The translation varies in quality, and is at many points influenced by the Septuagint or the Targums.

Sam.   Samaritan Pentateuch – the form of the first five books of the Old Testament as used by the Samaritan community. It is written in Hebrew in a special form of the Old Hebrew script, and preserves an important form of the text, somewhat influenced by Samaritan ideas.

Scroll(s)   Scroll(s), commonly called the Dead Sea Scrolls, found at or near Qumran from 1947 onwards. These important manuscripts shed light on the state of the Hebrew text as it was developing in the last centuries B.C. and the first century A.D.

Sept.   Septuagint (meaning 'seventy'); often abbreviated as the Roman numeral (LXX), the name given to the main Greek version of the Old Testament. According to tradition, the Pentateuch was translated in Egypt in the third century B.C. by 70 (or 72) translators, six from each tribe, but the precise nature of its origin and development is not fully known. It was intended to provide Greek-speaking Jews with a convenient translation. Subsequently it came to be much revered by the Christian community.

Symm.   Symmachus, another Greek translator of the Old Testament (beginning of the third century A.D.), who tried to combine literalness with good style. Both Lucian and Jerome viewed his version with favour.

Targ.   Targum, a name given to various Aramaic versions of the Old Testament, produced over a long period and eventually standardized, for the use of Aramaic-speaking Jews.

Theod.   Theodotion, the author of a revision of the Septuagint (probably second century A.D.), very dependent on the Hebrew text.

Vulg.   Vulgate, the most important Latin version of the Old Testament, produced by Jerome about A.D. 400, and the text most used throughout the Middle Ages in western Christianity.

[...]   In the text itself square brackets are used to indicate probably late additions to the Hebrew text.

(Fuller discussion of a number of these points may be found in *The Making of the Old Testament* in this series)

THE FIRST BOOK OF

KINGS

✻   ✻   ✻   ✻   ✻   ✻   ✻   ✻   ✻   ✻   ✻   ✻   ✻

WHAT THE BOOK IS ABOUT

The book of Kings, printed in our English Bible in two
volumes which we call 1 Kings and 2 Kings, was originally one
book. The division into two was made when the book was
translated from the original Hebrew into Greek, probably for
the very practical reason that the Greek translation was longer
and took up more space than the Hebrew.

The whole book tells the story of the Hebrews from the
beginning of Solomon's reign to the destruction of Jerusalem
by the Babylonians, when the story of the Hebrew people as
an independent nation came to an end. 1 Kings takes the story
from the accession of Solomon to the death of Ahab, king of
Israel, about 850 B.C. The earlier part of the story of the
Hebrews has already been told in the other books which precede Kings in the Bible. The story of the Hebrew tribes
crossing the Jordan and settling in Palestine is told in the book
of Joshua. Their struggle to survive and win a place for themselves among the other inhabitants of the country is told in
Judges, and then follows in the two volumes of Samuel the
account of the transformation of the twelve tribes into a
kingdom, and of how the second king, David, by military
prowess and clever diplomacy, established the Hebrews as the
rulers of Palestine and overlords of most of the neighbouring
peoples. This was the time when the power and influence of
the Hebrews was at its zenith, and later generations of Hebrews
always looked back on the reign of David as the most glorious
period of their history.

Solomon, David's son, who followed him as king, was a

I

disappointment. He set himself up in great splendour as an oriental monarch, but the consequences of this, such as his demand from his subjects for slave labour, alienated the loyalty of the great majority of them. After his death ten tribes withdrew their allegiance to his successor and set up a rival parallel kingdom. It is the story of Solomon's kingdom and the two kingdoms which sprang from it which the two volumes of the book of Kings recount. Solomon's successors continued to rule the southern part of the country from Jerusalem. They were known as kings of Judah. The new kingdom's territory occupied the central and northern part of the land. It was known as Israel or Ephraim.

The fact that the northern kingdom was called Israel can cause confusion since the name 'Israel' can mean more than one thing. It can, as here, refer to the northern kingdom. Also, during the time of David and Solomon the whole kingdom was at times referred to as Israel, or All Israel. Then, too, there is a third use. The Hebrews as the covenant people of God, a community created by God at the Red Sea crossing and living ever afterwards in conscious allegiance to him by obeying the law he had given to them, are also called Israel. The word Israel is used in Kings in each of these senses, and the reader needs to take note in what sense the word Israel is being used each time he meets it.

The capital city of the new state of Israel was at first Shechem and then Tirzah. Finally, one of its kings, Omri, built a new capital, Samaria. Israel was larger, richer and more powerful than Judah. At first there was hostility between the two states but this soon passed into uneasy friendship and, in the time of Omri, an alliance in which Israel was the dominant partner. Not that Israel could be dominant over much more than Judah. The two states were only a small part of the wider world of the Near East, and in the Near East great political changes were taking place. A great nation, Assyria, was increasing its power more and more, and, with its power, its ambitions. In the end it sought to control the whole of the

Near East. In time Assyria declined but then Babylon took its place. The states in Palestine inevitably became involved in these ambitions. To understand the issues we need to know something more of the history of the Near East.

THE NEAR EASTERN BACKGROUND

Civilization had originally begun in the Near East in the Nile valley in Egypt, and in the land bounded by the Tigris and the Euphrates in Mesopotamia. From the earliest times there had been contact between these two centres, and between both and Asia Minor, along the line of the river systems and through Syria and Palestine. This area, a strip of territory fertile by reason of the regularity of its water supply, has been called because of its shape 'the Fertile Crescent'. Such contact was probably at first the friendly contact of trade, but soon became, as the value of the control of the wealthy trade routes was appreciated, the hostile contact of rival armies vying with each other for effective control of the area. Palestine was part of the Fertile Crescent, in many ways the most important part. The Sinai peninsula is the land bridge between Asia and Africa, between Egypt and Mesopotamia, but this land is desert. It is Egypt's natural barrier against any invasion from Asia. The nearest part of the Fertile Crescent to Egypt is Palestine, and this simple geographical fact gave Palestine a military signifi- cance out of all proportion to its size. It was, perhaps, the greatest single factor determining its history in the whole of the Old Testament period. It was always in the interest of Egypt to control Palestine because then she was able to main- tain a buffer state to absorb the force of any hostile advance from Mesopotamia. Moreover, control of Palestine was essen- tial to Egypt if she was to have access to the forests of Lebanon which provided the timber for her ships.

Equally any expansionist Mesopotamian power, with its eye fixed on the rich granaries of Egypt, needed to be master of Palestine if it was to move successfully across the Sinai desert to attack the cities of the Nile valley. Palestine was, for almost the whole of the time during which the Hebrew tribes lived there, a cockpit in which the great powers of the Near East fought for the mastery. Its position was not unlike that of Belgium in nineteenth-century Europe. Palestine is small – it is not much larger than Wales – but it was never able to stand aside in splendid isolation from the quarrels of the great powers. It was drawn into their struggles and intrigues and used as a pawn in their military and diplomatic games.

In view of this situation, it may seem strange that the Hebrews ever had the opportunity to establish themselves so strongly in Palestine as to form kingdoms. This was possible because the Hebrews entered the land at one of those infrequent times when no great power was strong enough to exercise effective control beyond the range of its own territory. In the latter part of the thirteenth century, when it is generally assumed that the Hebrews settled in Palestine, Egypt, which was the titular overlord, was growing weaker and by the twelfth and eleventh centuries had become quite ineffective. The Hittite empire in Asia Minor was collapsing under the attacks of the new, vigorous Mesopotamian power, the Assyrians, but the Assyrians were not yet ready to exploit to the full the benefits of their victories. The vassal city states of Palestine were weak, divided and quarrelling among themselves, and the land was ripe for invasion. There were groups of pastoral peoples living in the desert on the edge of the settled country who were always ready to invade and pillage the richer settled country when they had the opportunity. If they were strong enough to do so, they remained permanently in those areas, either by driving out the inhabitants or by living alongside them and gradually, through intermarriage, fusing with them. In this particular time of weakness many semi-nomadic groups did move into the settled areas and among them were the Hebrews. They settled in the hill country of Palestine and, once established there, expanded throughout the whole country. This expansion brought them into contact with

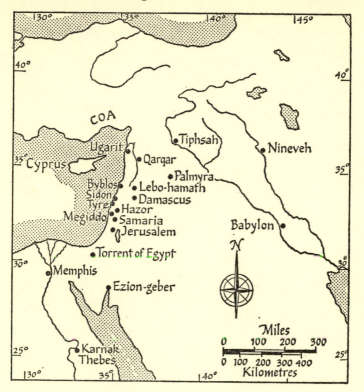

1. The Near East in the time covered by 1 Kings

another people who had also settled in a part of Palestine at the same time but from a completely different direction. These were the Philistines, a people whose place of origin is unknown. They came across the sea from somewhere in the Aegean area and settled on the southern part of the coastal plain of Palestine. They were joined by other groups who had tried unsuccessfully to settle in Egypt. They established some city states there, and also wished to expand and take control of Palestine. So the two peoples, the Hebrews and the Philistines, struggled with each other for control of the land without interference from the great powers. The story of this conflict is traced in some parts of 1 and 2 Samuel.

The greatness of David lay in the fact that he confined the Philistines to their cities on the coastal plain, and held control himself over Palestine and the trade routes. But this greatness was not to last. Solomon's hold was much weaker, if outwardly more splendid. After his death Palestine reverted, alongside the areas to the north ruled by the Aramaeans, to its earlier mode of existence as several small, rival, hostile kingdoms, each trying whenever and wherever possible, by war and diplomacy, to become more powerful than its neighbours. Israel and Judah, whose fortunes are the subject of the two books of Kings, were two of these states.

THE RISE OF ASSYRIA

The kingdoms were not left long to squabble and intrigue against each other. As soon as Assyria felt strong enough to expand, she began to turn her attention to the conquest of the states lying along the Fertile Crescent so as to be able to attack Egypt. The first such drive to the west came in the reign of the Assyrian emperor, Shalmaneser III, who reigned from 859 to 842 B.C. The small kingdoms realized their peril and joined together in a grand military alliance. Their combined forces met the Assyrian armies at Qarqar on the river Orontes in 853 B.C. Although Ahab, king of Israel at the time, contributed troops to this alliance, no mention is made of it in Kings. Our knowledge of the battle comes from Assyrian sources, which is all the stranger since the allies clearly gained the victory. In the Assyrian annals Shalmaneser characteristically claimed a great victory, but after the battle, he went home and did not move west again for five years. The first book of Kings ends with the death of King Ahab, but we need to know the outline of the story told in 2 Kings because it is necessary to understand how the whole of Kings came to be written.

The Assyrians were defeated at Qarqar, but only for a time. After a century of relatively minor attacks, Assyria mounted a full-scale invasion under another great emperor, Tiglath-pileser III, and his successors, Shalmaneser V and Sargon II. This time the small kingdoms were picked off one by one, and were so jealous of each other that they do not seem to have had the capacity to see the threat which menaced them all, until it became the turn of each individual state to face the Assyrians. By then it was too late.

Israel's chief rival was the state of Aram with its capital at Damascus, the neighbour immediately to the north. Assyrian pressure on Aram led to a lightening of pressure from Aram on Israel's northern frontier and a consequent increase in prosperity for Israel – for a time. It did not last. Damascus fell to the Assyrians in 732 B.C. and then came Israel's turn. Samaria fell in 721 B.C. and the northern kingdom came to an end for ever. Judah was invaded in 701 B.C. but was not destroyed and continued to exist as a vassal of Assyria.

So involvement with the Assyrians led to the destruction of the kingdom of Israel, with the consequence that the Hebrew tradition, and especially its religious faith, was passed on to the future through Judah and Jerusalem. Some faithful Hebrews remained in the north but they had little influence. This fact has no small bearing on the form taken by the two volumes of the book of Kings, and the judgements expressed in them. They view the history of the Hebrews from the point of view of Judah, and from Judah at a time when she could rightly claim to be the only state which worshipped Yahweh as its God (see p. 18). The temple at Jerusalem alone maintained the true worship of Yahweh and guarded his teaching. Such a religious claim was easily mingled with nationalism to become the most powerful influence in Judah for the remaining years of its existence.

Assyrian power did not last long. A new rival power, Babylon, arose there to compete with Assyria for the mastery of Mesopotamia. After some years of struggle Assyria was defeated. Nineveh, the Assyrian capital, fell to the Babylon-ians in 612 B.C. and the Assyrian empire came to an end. In the years during which this struggle was taking place, the Assyrian hold on Palestine was weak. The king of Judah at the time, Josiah, saw himself as a second David who could once more bring all Palestine under the control of Jerusalem and her king. Josiah was a nationalist, a patriot, and a firm supporter of the temple at Jerusalem. The book of Kings depicts him as a devout follower of Yahweh the national God, doing what he did out of simple religious faith, but this view may well be the oversimplification of historians who were eager to transform the various greys of human experience into sharp blacks and whites. At all events Josiah used Assyrian weakness to extend his territory and act more independently than Assyria would wish for, or, when more powerful, allow.

JOSIAH'S REFORM

King Josiah carried out in 621 B.C. a great religious reform. He purified the worship of the temple at Jerusalem by remov-ing religious objects and customs which had been taken over by the Hebrews from pagan neighbours. This reform had both political and religious meaning. As a religious act it declared that Yahweh, the god of the Hebrews, was so different from the gods of the surrounding nations that he could not be worshipped in the same manner. As a political act, it was a declaration of independence. Josiah's act was, in effect, an act of rebellion against the overlordship of Assyria. Clearly, both political and religious motives were involved in Josiah's reform. In Kings only the religious aspect is noticed; the political aspect is ignored. This is an oversimplification, but even so Josiah's action was, at least in part, a genuine religious reform and was supported as such by many of his subjects. It reflected the teaching of an influential group of theologians of the time whose distinctive ideas are expressed in the book of Deuteronomy. Because of this, Josiah's work has usually been called the deuteronomic reform. The deuteronomists, as these theologians are called, were concerned with much more than the purging of pagan influences from the temple. They had worked out a comprehensive theological system which is important for our purpose, because the book of Kings was compiled by an editor or editors who were theologians of that school. Jewish tradition has claimed that Jeremiah was the author of Kings, but this is no more than guesswork, and very unlikely guesswork at that. The book of Kings is the work of more than one author, and the man who settled its final shape is best described as an editor who took the writings of other men and assembled them together with his own editorial comments. It is impossible to say just how many men took part in the writing and editing of Kings. The one thing which links them all together is enthusiasm for deuteronomic theology. It seems best, therefore, to refer to them simply as deuteronomists.

THE DEUTERONOMISTS

The deuteronomists looked upon the Hebrews as being first and foremost the covenant people of Yahweh. For them the name Israel meant that first of all. The political states which the Hebrews developed, whether the united monarchy under David and Solomon, or the two kingdoms of Israel and Judah which succeeded, were only important to them as the political form which the covenant people had to accept in order to live in the conditions of those times. Israel was to them a holy nation, distinct from all other nations in that it lived by the law given to it by God. Because Israel was also a political entity living side by side with other nations, it was always in danger of growing like them and losing its own distinctive character. So to the deuteronomists, the neighbouring peoples, and especially the Canaanites – the people with whom the Hebrews came most into contact since they were already living in large areas of Palestine at the time that the Hebrews settled there – were a dangerous moral and spiritual influence. The only way in which Israel could be sure of being free of their influence was by living apart from them. So to the deuteronomists Israel could only be the covenant people of God as it resisted all influence from non-Israelite neighbours.

JOSIAH'S DEATH

Josiah's kingdom came to a violent end. For Josiah over-reached himself and came to disaster. When the Assyrian empire was in its death throes, Pharaoh Necho of Egypt, fearful of the rising power of Babylon, sent an army along the Fertile Crescent to give support to the Assyrians. Josiah intervened. He ranged his army at the pass of Megiddo to prevent the Egyptians passing through. He was defeated and killed, and with him died the last hope of an independent Judah. His successors were mostly vassals of Babylon, but only rarely loyal ones. The Egyptians tried to hold off the Babylonians by fomenting disaffection and even open rebellion in Judah and other vassal states. They were only too successful, and finally Nebuchadnezzar, the Babylonian emperor, in 587 B.C. destroyed Jerusalem, brought the state of Judah to an end, and carried off the king and most of the nobility to Babylon as exiles.

This is the story which the book of Kings tells. The last incident narrated is the account of how Evil-merodach, king of Babylon, released Jehoiachin, the exiled and imprisoned king of Judah, in 562 B.C. and made him a pensioner of his court (2 Kings 25:27-30). We are not sure whether or not the book was compiled during this exile. Some scholars have suggested that it was compiled earlier and then, at a later time, extra narratives were added to bring the story up to date.

THE WRITING OF HISTORY

The point of such discussion is that all history writing reflects its own age and the outlook of the author or authors. This is not to say that historians set out deliberately to distort facts.

The historian is not a propagandist, but he does have to select the events which he wishes to include in his narrative, and, sometimes even more significantly, the events which he chooses to omit as unworthy of attention. The historian like any other writer has a point of view. Certain aspects of the life of the people or the individual with whom he is dealing seem to him more important, and therefore deserving of greater prominence in his work, than others. In such ways the historian reveals his attitudes and his values. The difference between good and bad historians is not between those who have and those who do not have values, for all have values, but in their capacity to deal fully and fairly with all the evidence, and in their refusal to construct theories which ignore or distort evidence. Now the purpose of the deuteronomists who edited the book of Kings was to tell the story of the Hebrews as the covenant people of God. To them this aspect of Israel's life was far more important than the political history of the kingdoms. So they only included political details when those details illuminated their theme. Other incidents which were very important politically were omitted. Thus they tell how Pharaoh Shishak invaded Judah because his invasion affected the temple at Jerusalem. The fact that he also invaded the state of Israel is never mentioned, though politically that invasion was more important than the other.

THE SOURCES USED IN THE BOOK

Some parts of Kings show much more enthusiasm for deuteronomic points of view than other parts. Many scholars have concluded from this that all could not be the work of one author or editor. Of course, the author like other historians has used written sources. Three of these he mentions in his work. They are, 'the annals of Solomon', 'the annals of the kings of Israel', and 'the annals of the kings of Judah'. The last two are each mentioned many times. Perhaps these sources have been acknowledged because they were official; other sources seem to have been used without acknowledgement. The stories about Elijah and Elisha may originally have been an independent unit. They are not so hostile to the northern kingdom as the rest of Kings is, and Elijah's offering of sacrifice to God on Mount Carmel, seemingly with Yahweh's approval, completely contradicts the deuteronomic rule that insists that sacrifice ought to be offered to Yahweh only at the temple in Jerusalem.

THE PURPOSE OF THE EDITORS

Mention of a deuteronomic rule brings us to the heart of the problem. It is clear to even the most casual reader of Kings that the editors saw great significance in the reform carried out by King Josiah. That reform is recorded in detail and with obvious approval. King Josiah is one of the great heroes of the book. The contrast between the treatment of the reform and the lack of any mention of the battle of Qarqar, or the very brief treatment given to King Omri of Israel, is very marked. Omri was one of the most powerful and successful kings of Israel but he receives only a bare mention in Kings (1 Kings 16: 23–8). The reason for this is because, as stated earlier, the editors were principally interested in the Hebrews as the covenant people of God. God had made them a people by delivering them from slavery in Egypt. He had guided them through the wilderness and given them the land of Palestine. The people were bound to their God in gratitude for all his past goodness and ought to show their gratitude by living their corporate life in strict obedience to the law which he had laid upon them through Moses at Mount Sinai. After their settlement in Palestine many of the Hebrews had abandoned the worship of Yahweh as no longer applicable to the new conditions of their lives, or attempted to combine the worship of Yahweh with the worship of the gods of their Canaanite neighbours in such a way that most of its distinctive character was lost. The deuteronomists saw Josiah's reform as an attempt to assert the impossibility of linking the worship of Yahweh with the worship of the gods of any other nation. Yahweh was different in character from all other gods and demanded a different kind of worship and corporate life.

To support their view the deuteronomists told the story of their people to show that their views alone were true to God's original purpose in creating Israel. God had tried to guide his people by rewarding them with blessing and prosperity when they lived according to the deuteronomic ideal, and punishing with great severity all those who strayed from that ideal. So no king of the northern kingdom is ever mentioned without condemnation. The verdict on Nadab, the second king, is, 'He did what was wrong in the eyes of the LORD and followed in his father's footsteps, repeating the sin which he had led Israel to commit' (1 Kings 15: 26). This is a typical example of the judgement on all the northern kings. The 'what was wrong in the eyes of the LORD' always meant that the king at least tolerated the northern religious sanctuaries and did not admit the exclusive position of the Jerusalem temple. Equally, only two kings of Judah, Hezekiah and Josiah, are spoken of with complete approval, and that because they carried out reforms in the Jerusalem temple.

HOW AND WHEN THE BOOK WAS WRITTEN

One way to account for these differences of emphasis is to see the present book as a second, revised edition of an earlier book. The first edition told the story of the covenant people and showed how the division of the kingdom led to apostasy in the north. The result was that the northern kingdom was destroyed. Judah also was seduced by the Canaanites but Josiah with his reform brought the nation back to its true allegiance. Josiah is the hero of this book which was written during his reign, probably sometime between the years 621 and 609 B.C.

The death of Josiah and the story of his unhappy and unsuccessful successors, whose folly led to the destruction of

Jerusalem and the temple, was added in the second edition. This was compiled in the exile sometime after 562 B.C. In this edition the apostasy of Judah is shown to have been just as bad as that of Israel, and the cause of the death of Josiah and the destruction of the kingdom of Judah. The Elijah–Elisha stories refer to the northern kingdom but may well have been added to the book at the time that this revision was made in the exile. They are anti-Canaanite without being pro-Judah and so do not fit easily into the purpose of the first edition of the book.

THE LARGER HISTORY

One further probability ought to be mentioned. The second edition prepared in the exile might not have been confined to the book of Kings alone. All the books from Joshua to Kings, called in the Hebrew Bible the Former Prophets, are really chapters in one story. They tell the continuous story of the Hebrew settlement in Palestine and all that happened to the people until, as independent kingdoms, they ceased to exist. The story is told to show how disobedience to God's will led to suffering, disasters and, in the end, national extinction. What was created in the exile soon after 560 B.C. was probably not just a second edition of Kings but a comprehensive history of the nation whose purpose was to warn, exhort and comfort the disconsolate exiles. God still had a purpose for them, and, if they were obedient and walked in his ways, they need have no fears for their future.

THE WITNESS OF ARCHAEOLOGY

The deuteronomists, in telling the story of their people, did not write history as it is written now. They wrote from their own point of view and wrote about the things in the story of their people which they thought were important. Their purpose was to use history to teach a lesson to their readers, namely that if they wished to prosper and if they wished the nation to prosper, then they must take their obligations as the covenant people of God with the utmost seriousness. For them writing history had only one purpose, to teach moral and religious lessons. The modern reader frequently approaches their work with a great deal of suspicion. We have been taught by modern historians that moralizing is a very dangerous occupation for any historian to indulge in. The moralist has so strong a desire to teach his lessons that only too often has he succumbed to the temptation to distort his facts in order to improve his lesson. Have the deuteronomists fallen into this trap? We have seen that they selected some events to include in their story and omitted others. Can we be sure that they have not distorted facts in order to make them fit in with their theories? The answer to the question must be a personal judgement which each reader must make for him or herself, but the work and findings of the archaeologists do give us some confidence in claiming that the deuteronomists respected facts. Much has come to light from Egypt and Mesopotamia which enables us to form a comprehensive picture of the great empires which existed in those places. If we know less of conditions in Palestine it is because Palestine was less important in those times and has less evidence to yield. We can say that the background of world events as depicted in Kings is of a piece with what we know from archaeology. The story of the Hebrew kingdoms did happen much as Kings shows it to have happened. The lessons that the editors of Kings have drawn from that story are their own. To make a judgement on those, we must first decide how true the theological views are which they held with such conviction and intensity.

THE CHRONOLOGY OF KINGS

One historical issue is of particular importance. It is the chronology which is such a prominent feature of the book. On first reading the dates given in Kings seem very thorough and impressive. The length of the reign of each king, of both the kingdoms of Israel and Judah, is given, and there is a clear system of cross-referencing to fit the beginning of a new reign in one kingdom with the chronology of the other kingdom. Thus, 'It was in the thirty-first year of Asa king of Judah that Omri became king of Israel and he reigned twelve years, six of them in Tirzah' (1 Kings 16: 23). What better evidence could there be that we are dealing with a careful and exact historian? Unfortunately, further study seems to confirm the opposite, for the length of the reigns and the cross-referencing are inconsistent. The numbers do not add up and the author as a historian must be careless or incompetent, even when it is remembered that numbers can be changed or omitted in copying manuscripts more easily than words.

On the basis of evidence taken from archaeology it seems likely that the editor has used a complex system of reckoning which we have not sufficient knowledge to follow. We do know that methods of reckoning these matters in the ancient world were complex and varied. The year was sometimes counted as beginning in the autumn in the month Tishri, and at other times in the spring in the month Nisan. The first year of the reign of a king could be reckoned as the remaining part of the year in which he succeeded to the throne, or these months could be ignored and his first year reckoned from the first New Year's day of his reign. An aged or sick king could have his son as co-monarch for some years before his death, and then the length of the son's reign could be reckoned as the years in which he was sole monarch or could include the longer period in which he was co-monarch. Equally, methods of reckoning may have varied at times, particularly in Judah, as Assyrian influence was strong or weak. To abandon the Assyrian method of reckoning may well have been a mark of national independence. Such variants can produce a considerable discrepancy in a chronological system, and there are scholars who maintain that by taking such variants into account the chronological system of Kings can be seen to be accurate, and indeed, witness to the editor's determination to stick to his sources even at the cost of some confusion. This is a technical, and, to some degree, a controversial matter. It is best to place complete reliance only on such dates as can be confirmed from Assyrian and Babylonian sources. But confusion in the chronology does not automatically convict the editors of being indifferent historians. They may have kept rigidly to their sources without attempting to harmonize them.

UNDERSTANDING THE NOTES TO THE TRANSLATION

In several places a footnote has been added to the N.E.B. text to offer an alternative translation, and also frequently to explain the reason for the two translations. These notes are very brief. An explanation here may help readers to understand them.

When the Old Testament was first written in Hebrew on manuscripts, only the consonants were written. It was not thought necessary to add the vowels for many hundreds of years. Those who studied the Old Testament were taught to learn it by heart. The manuscript was simply a help for the memory. To this day the manuscripts of the Law which are used in the synagogues of the orthodox Jews do not have any vowels. When vowels were written in Hebrew manuscripts, they indicated the way in which the written words were traditionally pronounced. Some words could be pronounced with different vowels and have a quite different meaning. Thus the word YM when pronounced with an O as YOM means 'day', but when pronounced with an A as YAM means 'sea'. In most places the meaning of a word is obvious from the context, but there are some places in the Old Testament where it is difficult to be sure of the meaning. In 1 Kings 10: 29 the same verb can mean 'import' or 'export' according to which vowels are used with the consonants.

Another case of difficulty is that some letters in Hebrew can easily be confused. D and R differ only very slightly in shape.

The words for Edom and Aram, when written in Hebrew without vowels, only differ by the single consonant D or R. So the one word can at times have been mistaken for the other.

Because of these kinds of difficulties, groups of Jewish biblical scholars, called Massoretes, began from the end of the fifth century A.D. to make copies of the Hebrew Bible with vowels to fix the pronunciation of words. The name Massorete comes from the Hebrew word for 'tradition'. One important group of these worked in Tiberias in Galilee in the eighth century. They created the system of vowels which is still used today. Their intention was to make a standard edition of the Hebrew Bible which would be used everywhere, a kind of Authorized Version. They believed that they were collecting the best traditions and using them in their edition of the Bible. Even they found problems which they could not resolve, and in places where they thought that the consonants were wrong they substituted another word in the margin, and wrote in the text the vowels of their word with the consonants which they found and did not wish to change. In this way we have received the name Jehovah of the English Authorized Version. The Massoretes added the vowels of Adonai, the Hebrew word for Lord, to the consonants YHWH. We do not know how the name of God was pronounced. Usually it is written Yahweh, which is a likely guess. These corrections of the Massoretes have a name. The word for the consonants in the text is the *Kethib*, meaning 'what is written'. The word they wished to substitute, i.e. the word for which they have provided vowels, is called the *Qere*, meaning 'what is to be read'.

A special difficulty is caused when the meaning of the Hebrew text of the Massoretes is not the same as the meaning implied by one or more of the early translations. The earliest translations were made before the Massoretes had done their work and so could well have used a Hebrew text which the Massoretes rejected or even did not know about. 'The footnotes to the N.E.B. text' on pp. x–xi will help the reader to understand the abbreviations used in the footnotes, and what the various translations were. Readers who wish to pursue the subject further should consult *The Making of the Old Testament* in this series.

✻   ✻   ✻   ✻   ✻   ✻   ✻   ✻   ✻   ✻   ✻   ✻

The death of David and accession of Solomon

The book of Kings begins with the accession of Solomon to the throne of the united kingdom of Israel and Judah, created by his father David. The first two chapters of I Kings are most probably the continuation of the 'Succession Narrative' – the story of the intrigues among David's sons to determine who should succeed David as king – which now forms part of 2 Samuel, as chapters 9–20. So this book of Kings is continuing a story whose beginning has already been told. Yet, with the accession of Solomon to the throne, something new begins, and this is a very good place to mark a break in the history of the people by beginning a new volume. We are here beginning the history of the kings, because, although Solomon was not the first king, he was the first of a new kind of kings.

The story of how Solomon became king rather than Adonijah, who seemed to have a stronger claim, shows clearly the changes that David had brought about in the Hebrew state by his life and work. Both Saul and David had become kings of Israel by virtue of their strong personalities and proved capacity for leadership in battle. Saul had wished to create a dynasty. He had wanted his son, Jonathan, to succeed him, but this was not to be. David had succeeded because the Hebrews were still at that stage of development when they needed, above all else, a strong, military leader who could both defend the people against their enemies, and also hold them together by loyalty to his person. When David became king, the whole life and prosperity of the kingdom depended on the personality of the monarch. David's greatness lay in the fact that he so developed the kingdom that it became independent of the personality of the king. The personality of the king still mattered, but not in the same way. It was no longer the only factor in the prosperity of the people, as it had been. The institution of kingship had become more important than the personality of particular kings. So David did create a dynasty. Solomon became king because he was one of David's sons; not the son most successful in battle, but the son most successful in palace intrigue. Solomon was the first example of the new kind of leader who fulfilled the role of kingship in society.

In bringing about this change, David had made his people adopt more closely the way of life of the Canaanites among whom they had settled, and over whom they ruled by right of military conquest. The Hebrew tribes had entered Canaan as semi-nomadic herdsmen living off their flocks. The Canaanites were agriculturalists, tilling the fertile land and living a settled life in fortified cities. Their way of life was more rigidly structured than that of the Israelites and based upon a class-system. Their society contained labourers who tilled the fields, soldiers who protected the cities, craftsmen, merchants, and a priesthood whose duties were administrative as well as strictly religious. It was a society geared to the efficient exploitation of the wealth of the land. Its well-being depended upon and was measured by fertility; the fertility of crops, of animals, and of men. Besides all the work of the various members of society, fertility required divine blessing and so religion held society together. The visible expression of the cohesive force of religion which held Canaanite society together and gave it its unity and sense of purpose was kingship. The king was the chief priest who conveyed the benefits of divine favour to society, and exacted obedience from it. His function was to ensure that the fertility upon which the well-being of the whole society depended, was maintained year by year. The king's participation in the annual fertility rites guaranteed the blessing of the gods. In return, he demanded and received absolute obedience from all members of society. The Canaanite state was, thus, one of those dedicated to economic efficiency and material affluence, as religious ideals, and it was prepared to sacrifice all individual liberty to achieve its ends. We can understand what this meant when we realize that in those days affluence for some meant slavery for others.

The Israelite society which came into Canaan from the wilderness was much less regimented. There was much less centralized control. The society was made up of tribal units which were economically self-sufficient. They were held together in a loose federal form of unity. What all the tribes had in common was their religion, and what they all needed was allies to help them defend themselves against the attacks of their enemies. A society of this kind could only maintain a standard of living which was economically much lower than that of the Canaanites. When the Israelites entered Canaan, it soon became obvious to some of their leaders that they must adopt enough of the Canaanite way of life in order to be able to maintain their independence of the Canaanites. Thus they needed an army as well trained and professional as those of the Canaanite cities. The Israelite monarchy was the outward sign of Israel's adapting its way of life and institutions to compete successfully with Canaan. Monarchy implied an hierarchical, structured society which was foreign to the Israelite tribes. David naturalized monarchy so successfully in Israel that his successor could be a different kind of man, and chosen in a way which differed from the way he himself had been chosen. Israel now needed a man to fulfil the functions of kingship more than a leader of great personal magnetism.

The relationship between the spirit of a people and their institutions is always subtle and complex. Canaanite societies were content to seek economic prosperity even though that meant an absence of personal freedom for the individual members of society. Israel had been a society economically poor, but containing much greater opportunity for free expression for ordinary members of society. How far, by accepting Canaanite institutions, did Israel accept the Canaanite spirit and ideals of society? It is difficult to give a clear, simple answer. Certainly some in Israel accepted, as others opposed, the spirit of Canaanite society, but with regard to leaders such as David and Solomon the evidence is not clear. Solomon may have sought to use Canaanite institutions without abandoning Israelite ideals.

How far, by accepting Canaanite institutions, did Israel accept Canaanite religion? Canaan worshipped idols, and the idols were personifications of power. Each member of the Canaanite group of gods and goddesses, the pantheon as it is called, was a personification of some aspect of the natural forces which were believed to control the lives and destinies of the people: gods of war, storm, corn and so on. Israel's god, Yahweh, who had revealed himself to his people at the Red Sea crossing, and who had chosen Israel to be his people and made them into a community by that choice, was no personification of the powers of nature. Yahweh was a person. He had made himself known in and through personal acts, and in them showed Israel that personality itself was the supreme value. Israelite religion subordinated power to personality: Canaanite religion exalted power above personality. The result was two very different kinds of society with opposed moral and spiritual values. The problem is to what degree did Israel by adopting the Canaanite structure of society, and especially the institution of kingship, accept also the ethical and spiritual values which went with it? Clearly the editors of Kings thought that Ahab, king of Israel, went most, if not all, the way with Canaan. But did Solomon? The evidence is less clear and more than one opinion can be held. Solomon can be interpreted as a king who tried, like Ahab, to turn Israel into a purely Canaanite society. His reign was marked by the erection of splendid buildings and the establishment of an elaborate court which needed a slave society to support it. Equally, he can be seen as a king who accepted such Canaanite institutions as were necessary to ensure Israel's survival in the new conditions of her life in Canaan, but attempted always to modify those institutions so that they harmonized with the older ideals of Israelite life and religion.

Either of these views may be held, and, because of the way in which the editors of Kings have presented the evidence, it is impossible to exclude completely either the one or the other. For the editors, Solomon was first the king who founded the temple at Jerusalem, and, because of the place that the temple came to hold in deuteronomic theology, he was a great and good king. But after Solomon's death, misfortune overtook his empire. Most of his subjects rebelled and his descendants, the guardians of the temple, ruled over only the rump of the empire. Jerusalem as the capital of the kingdom of Judah was rather like Vienna as the capital of Austria, after the dissolution of the old Austro-Hungarian empire. Such misfortune, according to deuteronomic theology, was the direct consequence of sin. So Solomon was presented as a sinner, a king led astray to false worship by his love of women and multitude of foreign wives. The division of the kingdom after Solomon's death was God's just punishment for this apostasy.

Where lies the truth about Solomon? Was he strong or weak, successful or a failure? He was probably something of both. A king who could do what Solomon did must have been a strong and complex personality, a much more three-dimensional person than the cardboard figure who is presented to us in the book of Kings. With him, as with all real people, motives and purposes were likely to have been mixed and involved.

DAVID IS PROVED
UNFIT TO REMAIN KING

1
2
KING DAVID WAS NOW a very old man and, though they wrapped clothes round him, he could not keep warm. So his household said to him, 'Let us find a young virgin for your majesty, to attend you and take care of **3** you; and let her lie in your bosom, sir, and make you warm.' So they searched all over Israel for a beautiful **4** maiden and found Abishag, a Shunammite, and brought her to the king. She was a very beautiful girl, and she took care of the king and waited on him, but he had no intercourse with her.

✻ David is here described as senile; all the vigour of manhood has left him. This is in marked contrast to the picture of Moses given at the end of Deuteronomy, where Moses is said to have kept all his powers and faculties, and therefore his capacity to exercise authority, until his death.

2. The provision of a *virgin* may have had a medical purpose. There is some evidence that this expedient was practised in the ancient world; the proximity of youth (and here of virginity) was thought to reinvigorate age.

3. *Abishag* was from the northern village of Shunem (see map 4, p. 119).

4. *he had no intercourse with her:* the mention of this suggests that in fact Abishag was brought to David as a young concubine, and in that case David is here proved to be impotent. Since the fertility of the land and the crops was thought to be bound up with the king's virility, impotence deposed a king. The request of Adonijah to Solomon that he might have Abishag as wife (cp. on 2: 13–25) also suggests that she had been David's concubine since the request is seen as an attempt at gaining the throne.

The incident related here is designed to show that God had declared David's unfitness to remain king. A successor needed to be found. ✳

ADONIJAH'S HOPES

Now Adonijah, whose mother was Haggith, was 5 boasting that he was to be king; and he had already provided himself with chariots and horsemen[a] and fifty out-runners. Never in his life had his father corrected him or 6 asked why he behaved as he did. He was a very handsome man, too, and was next in age to Absalom. He talked with 7 Joab son of Zeruiah and with Abiathar the priest, and they gave him their strong support; but Zadok the priest, 8 Benaiah son of Jehoiada, Nathan the prophet, Shimei, Rei, and David's bodyguard of heroes, did not take his side. Adonijah then held a sacrifice of sheep, oxen, and 9 buffaloes at the stone Zoheleth beside En-rogel, and he invited all his royal brothers and all those officers of the household who were of the tribe of Judah. But he did not 10 invite Nathan the prophet, Benaiah and the bodyguard, or Solomon his brother.

✳ Adonijah, the eldest living son, seems to have been accepted as heir-apparent by David who had allowed him to gather a band of soldiers around himself. He had the support of the older, conservative elements in society.

5. *with chariots and horsemen*: the N.E.B. footnote has the singular because the word *rekeb* can be used as either a singular or collective noun, i.e. chariot or chariotry. The second Hebrew word *parashim* can mean horses or horsemen. It seems more likely that Adonijah was equipping himself with a private armed force rather than a single chariot.

[a] *Or* a chariot and horses.

7. *Joab* was David's nephew and the commander of the national army, a kind of territorial army that could be called out in times of national emergency. *Abiathar* was the sole remaining priest of Nob who had escaped when Saul had killed all the others (I Sam. 22: 20).

8. The men who represented the new element in David's kingdom did not support Adonijah. *Zadok* had probably been a priest of the Jebusite sanctuary at Jerusalem which David had captured. At this time he shared the priesthood at Jerusalem with *Abiathar*. Later, his family alone became the hereditary priests there. *Benaiah* was the leader of the *bodyguard of heroes*, a body of professional troops, not unlike the Praetorian Guard of Imperial Rome, who owed loyalty only to the sovereign. *Nathan* was the prophet who had come to prominence after rebuking David for his seduction of Bathsheba and murder of her husband, Uriah (cp. 2 Sam. 12: 1-14).

9. *the stone Zoheleth:* the name *Zoheleth* may mean 'Serpent Rock'. On this basis *En-rogel* has been identified with the 'Dragon Spring' mentioned by Nehemiah (Neh. 2: 13). The rock could equally well have got its name from a landslide, i.e. the sliding stone. It is more likely that *En-rogel* was the well, now called Job's well, in the southern part of the Kidron valley. Those who accepted the invitation committed themselves to supporting Adonijah's bid for the throne. *buffaloes:* previous translations have used the word 'fatling', i.e. a particularly valuable calf. Here the word is taken to mean a different kind of animal, but *buffaloes* is misleading. The word does not refer to North American bison but humped cattle.

10. Solomon was seen as a rival who could not be placated. ✳

THE RESPONSE TO ADONIJAH'S CHALLENGE

11 Then Nathan said to Bathsheba, the mother of Solomon, 'Have you not heard that Adonijah son of Haggith

12 has become king, all unknown to our lord David? Now

come, let me advise you what to do for your own safety and for the safety of your son Solomon. Go in and see 13 King David and say to him, "Did not your majesty swear to me, your servant, that my son Solomon should succeed you as king; that it was he who should sit on your throne? Why then has Adonijah become king?" Then while you 14 are still speaking there with the king, I will follow you in and tell the whole story.'

So Bathsheba went to the king in his private chamber; 15 he was now very old, and Abishag the Shunammite was waiting on him. Bathsheba bowed before the king and 16 prostrated herself. 'What do you want?' said the king. She answered, 'My lord, you swore to me your servant, 17 by the LORD your God, that my son Solomon should succeed you as king, and that he should sit on your throne. But now, here is Adonijah become king, all unknown to 18 your majesty. He has sacrificed great numbers of oxen, 19 buffaloes, and sheep, and has invited to the feast all the king's sons, and Abiathar the priest, and Joab the commander-in-chief, but he has not invited your servant Solomon. And now,*a* your majesty, all Israel is looking to 20 you to announce who is to succeed you on the throne. Otherwise, when you, sir, rest with your forefathers, my 21 son Solomon and I shall be treated as criminals.' She was 22 still speaking to the king when Nathan the prophet arrived. The king was told that Nathan was there; he 23 came into the king's presence and prostrated himself with his face to the ground. 'My lord,' he said, 'your majesty 24 must, I suppose, have declared that Adonijah should succeed you and that he should sit on your throne. He has 25

[a] And now: *so many MSS.; others* And you.

today gone down and sacrificed great numbers of oxen,
buffaloes, and sheep, and has invited to the feast all the
king's sons, Joab the commander-in-chief,[a] and Abiathar
the priest; and at this very moment they are eating and
drinking in his presence and shouting, "Long live King
26 Adonijah!" But he has not invited me your servant,
Zadok the priest, Benaiah son of Jehoiada, or your
27 servant Solomon. Has this been done by your majesty's
authority, while we[b] your servants have not been told who
should succeed you on the throne?'

☀ Adonijah's public claim to the kingship could only be
answered if David could be persuaded to express his wishes,
and if they could be supported by action.

11. The action is initiated by *Nathan* who turns to *Bathsheba*
as the favourite wife (cp. the story of the marriage in 2 Sam.
11–12) and *mother of Solomon*. *Nathan's* action is not easy to
understand. He must have accepted Solomon as a supporter of
the old traditions. At Solomon's birth *Nathan* called him
Jedidiah which means 'Beloved of the LORD' (cp. 2 Sam.
12: 24f.). Underlying the story is a palace intrigue, but the
editor is concerned to stress the divine choice of Solomon. So
he shows the initiative for Solomon being taken by a prophet.

12. *your own safety:* rivals to a newly crowned king were
often eliminated (cp. Solomon's actions described in chapter
2).

13. We have no knowledge of the making of a promise to
Bathsheba. It is described as a solemn oath, though we might
think it to have been the kind of thing that a king would say
to his favourite wife.

[a] Joab the commander-in-chief: *so Luc. Sept.; Heb.* the commanders
of the army.
[b] Has this...while we: *or* If this has been done by your majesty's
authority, then we...

15. Bathsheba goes first to the king, to be followed, as arranged, by Nathan who will 'tell the whole story' (verses 14, and 23–7).

18 f. The story of Adonijah's action, already told in verses 5–10, is repeated, and yet again in verses 24–6; repetition is a common device of a Hebrew story-teller.

20. The alternative translation, 'And you' (N.E.B. footnote) comes from a common scribal mistake. The Hebrew words for 'now' and 'you' sound very much alike, and are only slightly different in spelling, as 'heir' and 'hair' in English.

21. To *rest with your forefathers* indicates the kind of family grave in which there would be a number of caves, or a number of spaces, cut in the rock, so that a man could be said to 'sleep' with the previous members of his family. *criminals* translates a word usually meaning 'sinners'. It is an example of a word gaining a particular shade of meaning from its context: Bathsheba and her son would be treated as offenders in a political not a theological sense.

25. *commander-in-chief* is from Lucian's Septuagint text (cp. p. x). The Hebrew and the other versions have 'the commanders of the army', but there was only one commander of the army, namely *Joab*; the leaders of the royal guards supported Solomon (cp. verse 10).

27. The syntax of the Hebrew is ambiguous; either translation, as a question or as a conditional sentence, is possible. ✷

BATHSHEBA'S RUSE IS SUCCESSFUL

Thereupon King David said, 'Call Bathsheba', and she 28 came into the king's presence and stood before him. Then 29 the king swore an oath to her: 'As the LORD lives, who has delivered me from all my troubles: I swore by the 30 LORD the God of Israel that Solomon your son should succeed me and that he should sit on my throne, and this day I give effect to my oath.' Bathsheba bowed low to 31 the king and prostrated herself; and she said, 'May my lord King David live for ever!'

✻ 28. *Call Bathsheba* because she had withdrawn from the king's presence when Nathan was announced. Now Nathan withdraws, and she returns to hear the king's decision.

31. '*May my lord King David live for ever*' was the conventional court response. David would live, and his state would prosper, as his will was obeyed and his own chosen successor sat on his throne. ✻

SOLOMON IS MADE KING

32 Then King David said, 'Call Zadok the priest, Nathan the prophet, and Benaiah son of Jehoiada.' They came
33 into the king's presence and he gave them these orders: 'Take the officers of the household with you; mount my son Solomon on the king's mule and escort him down to
34 Gihon. There Zadok the priest and Nathan the prophet shall anoint him king over Israel. Sound the trumpet and
35 shout, "Long live King Solomon!" Then escort him home again, and he shall come and sit on my throne and reign in my place; for he is the man that I have appointed
36 prince over Israel and Judah.' Benaiah son of Jehoiada answered the king, 'It shall be done. And may the LORD,
37 the God of my lord the king, confirm it! As the LORD has been with your majesty, so may he be with Solomon; may he make his throne even greater than the throne of my
38 lord King David.' So Zadok the priest, Nathan the prophet, and Benaiah son of Jehoiada, together with the Kerethite and Pelethite guards went down and mounted Solomon on King David's mule and escorted him to

Gihon. Zadok the priest took the horn of oil from the 39
Tent of the LORD[a] and anointed Solomon; they sounded
the trumpet and all the people shouted, 'Long live King
Solomon!' Then all the people escorted him home in 40
procession, with great rejoicing and playing of pipes, so
that the very earth split with the noise.

✻ Since Solomon was the first Hebrew king to be crowned in
this way, the pattern was probably the traditional one taken
over from the Jebusites who had ruled Jerusalem before David
captured the city.

33. *Gihon* was the spring, now known as the Virgin's Fount,
in the Kidron valley below the city, which was the source of
Jerusalem's water supply. It is likely to have served the
purpose of a city square. The people would visit it daily and
much larger numbers could gather in the valley than in the
constricted streets of the city. So the ceremony would be most
public there. Water may have been used in the ceremony,
though there is no mention of this. The source of the city's
water supply may have been thought to be the right place for
king-making since the king was thought to guarantee life and
prosperity to the city as water did to the earth.

35. *prince over Israel and Judah:* David was anxious to make
sure that Solomon was made king of the two kingdoms of
Israel and Judah. He himself had become king of Judah first.
Only several years later was he accepted as king by the northern
tribes, Israel, and one of the chief aims of his reign had been to
fuse the two kingdoms into one under his own dynasty. He
had not been entirely successful. The rebellions of Absalom and
Sheba had been made possible because of discontent or
disaffection among some of the northern tribes (cp. 2 Sam.
15: 1–6 and 20: 1–22). Adonijah may have appealed to the same
elements. David's concern for the unity of the kingdom
may explain his use of the word *prince* rather than king. The

[a] *Lit.* the tent, *cp. 2: 28.*

31

word for prince, *nagid*, had much deeper roots in Hebrew tradition than the word king. It described that particular kind of military and personal leadership which had brought David himself to the throne. David may have meant that he was designating a leader to continue and uphold the old tribal traditions, even though that leader must now be a king.

38. The main elements in the coronation ritual are clearly stated. Solomon was placed on the royal *mule* and led by the officers to *Gihon*. The *Kerethite and Pelethite guards* were mercenaries who formed part of the king's bodyguard. Both were probably Philistines (see p. 5). *Pelethites* may mean Philistines, and *Kerethites* may mean Cretans.

39. *and anointed Solomon:* anointing with oil was a solemn religious act which set a man apart as God's man. He was believed to be endowed with the spirit of God for his office, and his person was sacrosanct. So David had expressed horror and revulsion when told by Saul's murderer that Saul was dead, even though that death was clearly advantageous to him (cp. 2 Sam. 1: 14–16). *Tent of the LORD:* the translators have used this phrase for clarity rather than 'the tent' which the Hebrew reads here. The fuller description is found later at 2: 28. David must have pitched the tent which housed the Ark near to Gihon since *Zadok* brought the *horn of oil* from it without difficulty. Some scholars have wished to omit the references to *Nathan the prophet* from the anointing on the grounds that a prophet would have had no part to play in the ceremony, and that his name must have been added later to give greater authority to the anointing. There is no textual evidence for such an omission. The presence of prophet and priest underlines the total loyalty to Solomon which it was the author's (and perhaps David's) intention to indicate. *they sounded the trumpet:* this told all present, including those who could not see the ceremony, that the new king had been anointed. *Long live King Solomon:* by this the people acknowledged Solomon as king. The people did not appoint the king, but it was important that they should approve the choice made for them.

40. *escorted him home in procession:* Solomon was probably seated on the throne and received the homage of the great officers of state. He seems to have joined David as a co-king with rights of succession, rather than to have replaced him (cp. verses 47-8 below). ✳

ADONIJAH HEARS THE NEWS

Adonijah and his guests had finished their banquet when 41 the noise reached their ears. Joab, hearing the sound of the trumpet, exclaimed, 'What is all this uproar in the city? What has happened?' While he was still speaking, 42 Jonathan son of Abiathar the priest arrived. 'Come in', said Adonijah. 'You are an honourable man and bring good news.' 'Far otherwise,' Jonathan replied; 'our lord 43 King David has made Solomon king and has sent with 44 him Zadok the priest, Nathan the prophet, and Benaiah son of Jehoiada, together with the Kerethite and Pelethite guards; they have mounted him on the king's mule, and 45 Zadok the priest and Nathan the prophet have anointed him king at Gihon, and they have now escorted him home rejoicing, and the city is in an uproar. That was the noise you heard. More than that, Solomon has taken his seat on 46 the royal throne. Yes, and the officers of the household 47 have been to greet our lord King David with these words: "May your God make the name of Solomon your son more famous than your own and his throne even greater than yours", and the king bowed upon his couch. What is 48 more, he said this: "Blessed be the LORD the God of Israel who has set a successor[a] on my throne this day while I am still alive to see it."'

[a] *Sept. adds* of my seed.

* 41. *when the noise reached their ears:* Adonijah's party was also meeting in the Kidron valley, about half a mile south of Solomon's party and thus farther away from the city. The valley is narrow and winding, but the quick ears of *Joab* the soldier heard the voices which indicated that something unusual was happening.

42. *Jonathan son of Abiathar* has already been met with as a royal messenger (cp. 2 Sam. 15: 36). He tells all the news about Solomon's coronation as though he had been an eye-witness. *honourable man:* the word here translated *honourable* means basically 'strength'. A man can be strong physically; or economically, because of the possession of land and property. Such a man was likely to be a man of independent judgement – no time-server. Adonijah's use of the word may carry the implication that the court was surrounded by time-servers, the new men who belonged to Solomon's party. The fact that Jonathan was the messenger had raised his hopes that the news he brought was favourable to his own cause.

47. *the king bowed upon his couch* in worship to God to associate himself with the sentiments expressed.

48. *a successor* 'of my seed': the fuller text of the Septuagint should be read. The point of David's thanksgiving is not just that a successor had been found, but that the dynastic principle had been accepted. David's own son, chosen by himself, had been set firmly but peacably upon the throne. In the light of what had happened to the family of Saul, this was a matter for great thanksgiving. *

ADONIJAH MAKES PEACE WITH SOLOMON

49 Then Adonijah's guests all rose in panic and scattered.
50 Adonijah himself, in fear of Solomon, sprang up and went
51 to the altar and caught hold of its horns. Then a message was sent to Solomon: 'Adonijah is afraid of King Solomon; he has taken hold of the horns of the altar and

has said, "Let King Solomon first swear to me that he will not put his servant to the sword."' Solomon said, 52 'If he proves himself a man of worth, not a hair of his head shall fall to the ground; but if he is found to be trouble-some, he shall die.' Then King Solomon sent and had him 53 brought down from the altar; he came in and prostrated himself before the king, and Solomon ordered him home.

＊ What had happened so far could well have been the prelude to civil war. In fact, once Adonijah's friends heard the news, they melted away. This is the best possible testimony to the authority that kingship had gained among the Hebrews during the reign of David. No one now dared oppose an anointed king.

50. *Adonijah...went to the altar* which probably stood in front of the Tent of the Lord. His action was the recognized formal method of claiming sanctuary. *horns* were protuber-ances on the four corners of the altar. They may have looked like bull's horns. They provided an anchorage for the ropes with which the sacrifices were tied to the altar and were regarded as the holiest part of the altar, as when the prophet Ezekiel spoke of sacrificial blood being rubbed on the horns of the altar (cp. Ezek. 43: 20).

52. *a man of worth:* it is interesting that Solomon, in speaking of Adonijah, used the same phrase that Adonijah himself had used of Jonathan in verse 42. In the N.E.B. Adonijah calls Jonathan *an honourable man,* while Solomon calls Adonijah *a man of worth.* The Hebrew is the same on both occasions. Solomon's condition was that Adonijah should act like a gentleman.

53. *ordered him home:* the phrase has a wealth of meaning. Adonijah was to retire from public life. ＊

DAVID'S DEATH

2 When the time of David's death drew near, he gave this
2 last charge to his son Solomon: 'I am going the way of all
3 the earth. Be strong and show yourself a man. Fulfil your
duty to the LORD your God; conform to his ways, observe
his statutes and his commandments, his judgements and
his solemn precepts, as they are written in the law of
Moses, so that you may prosper in whatever you do and
4 whichever way you turn, and that the LORD may fulfil
this promise that he made about me: "If your descendants
take care to walk faithfully in my sight with all their
heart and with all their soul, you shall never lack a successor
5 on the throne of Israel." You know how Joab son of
Zeruiah treated me and what he did to two commanders-
in-chief in Israel, Abner son of Ner and Amasa son of
Jether. He killed them both, breaking the peace by bloody
acts of war; and with that blood he stained the belt about
6 my*a* waist and the sandals on my*a* feet. Do as your wisdom
prompts you, and do not let his grey hairs go down to the
7 grave*b* in peace. Show constant friendship to the family of
Barzillai of Gilead; let them have their place at your
table; they befriended me when I was a fugitive from your
8 brother Absalom. Do not forget Shimei son of Gera, the
Benjamite from Bahurim, who cursed me bitterly the day I
went to Mahanaim. True, he came down to meet me at
the Jordan, and I swore by the LORD that I would not
put him to death. But you do not need to let him go
unpunished now; you are a wise man and will know how

[a] *So Luc. Sept.; Heb.* his.
[b] *Heb.* Sheol.

to deal with him; bring down his grey hairs in blood to the grave.'[a]

So David rested with his forefathers and was buried in 10 the city of David, having reigned over Israel for forty 11 years, seven in Hebron and thirty-three in Jerusalem; and 12 Solomon succeeded his father David as king and was firmly established on the throne.

✳ 1–4. This *last charge* of David was, in effect, his will. Were the words really spoken by David, or were they written by the editors? Some have held strongly that the latter is the case, and certainly the language with which the speech begins is strongly reminiscent of the style of the deuteronomists. The phrase, *statutes, commandments, judgements,* and *solemn precepts,* is typically deuteronomic, and the reference to a written *law of Moses* probably refers to the laws in the book of Deuteronomy. The opening phrases of the speech are like the words with which Moses commended the people to Joshua (cp. Josh. 1: 6–7).

If the speech is the work of the editors, it seems to have two purposes. First, David is made to approve of the principle that God had promised the throne to his descendants only in so far as they rendered willing obedience to the religious obligations laid upon them. They must *walk faithfully in my sight.* The story of all the kings, as recorded in this history, is told according to this principle; how God approved and blessed those who were faithful, and disapproved of those who were not faithful, even when he was merciful to them.

Secondly, the demand for revenge against *Joab* and *Shimei* has been put into David's mouth to show that Solomon's treatment of these two men was simply the fulfilment of his father's will, laid upon him in the most solemn manner. Solomon is thereby exonerated from all moral blame.

Yet, even if the editors wrote the words of the speech –

[a] *Heb.* Sheol.

perhaps they wished to use it to stress the parallel between Moses and Joshua on the one hand, and David and Solomon on the other – there seems to be no point in denying that the content expresses David's directions. David was as greatly respected by the deuteronomists as Solomon. The real root cause of the objection has been the unwillingness to admit that David, the great hero of Israel, could utter such sentiments on his death-bed. But David was a man of his time. His moral sensitivity was that of a man of his age, not of ours. Nor was he concerned with unworthy personal or family revenge. In the case of the three men whom he mentioned to Solomon, the well-being of the dynasty, if not that of the state itself, was involved. Thus David's will was a lesson in statecraft which he bequeathed to his successor; and not only in its content. The very fact that David had given this charge would protect Solomon against the accusation of paying off personal scores.

5. *Joab* had been a faithful servant of David and the commander-in-chief of the army of Judah, but, when David by skilful diplomacy was bringing together the two hostile kingdoms, and Israel was on the point of making him king, Joab came near to wrecking David's efforts because of his pursuit of a personal, family vendetta (cp. 2 Sam. 3: 22–34). This action left behind a residue of suspicion and hostility which remained alive throughout David's reign. Adonijah, in his bid for the throne, had drawn support from one side of this old quarrel. So the issue was still alive and would menace the stability of Solomon's kingdom, unless he took action to remove it. *my waist:* the translators have rightly preferred the first person pronoun of the Greek versions. The point is that David was implicated by Joab's action.

6. 'Sheol' (N.E.B. footnote) is paraphrased as *the grave*. Sheol, the place of the shades, was thought by the Hebrews at this time to be a cavern beneath the earth into which men descended after death to endure a dreary expanse of eventless existence.

7. *Barzillai* had remained loyal to David when he seemed to

be the victim of a successful coup (cp. 2 Sam. 19: 31–2). His family needed to be honoured to show that loyalty was rewarded no less than treachery. 'A place at table' seems to have been the equivalent of receiving a pension.

8. *Shimei* was again a special case. He had cursed David, and therefore broken both a primitive taboo and also Israelite law (cp. Exod. 22: 28). While Shimei was allowed to live, it might be thought that the curse was effective, and so he was a threat to the security of Solomon. David had been bound by oath to spare his life, but any leniency on the part of Solomon was likely to be interpreted as weakness and proof of the continuing efficacy of the oath.

10. David was buried within the city of Jerusalem because it was his own personal possession by right of conquest. His tomb was remembered for centuries. In the first century A.D. a tomb of David was known (cp. Acts 2: 29), though whether genuine or not we cannot say. The site now shown as David's tomb on the south-western hill, now called Mount Sion, is certainly not genuine. Jerusalem in David's day occupied the crest of the south-eastern hill, Mount Ophel. There is no sure evidence that the south-western hill was included within the city until the New Testament period. A number of tombs have been discovered at the southern point of Mount Ophel. This may have been the burial place of the Judaean kings and have contained the tomb of David. Unfortunately, the area was used as a stone quarry in the Roman period and so much evidence has been destroyed that positive identification is impossible.

The N.E.B. marks this off as the end of the first part of the book. Solomon has become king remarkably smoothly in spite of the opposition of Adonijah. To the deuteronomists, this was a sign of God's approval. They believed that God had prepared a great work for Solomon to do. On the other hand, it is possible to regard the end of chapter 2 as the end of the first section since the rest of the chapter tells how Solomon carried out the charge laid upon him. ✻

The reign of Solomon

✳ As we should expect, great stress will be laid on those aspects of the reign which interested the deuteronomists. They were concerned to explain an apparent contradiction: that Solomon was a truly great king, and yet his empire broke up at his death. ✳

THE END OF ADONIJAH

13 THEN ADONIJAH son of Haggith came to Bathsheba, the mother of Solomon. 'Do you come as a friend?'
14 she asked. 'As a friend,' he answered; 'I have something to
15 say to you.' 'Tell me', she said. 'You know', he went on, 'that the throne was mine and that all Israel was looking to me to be king; but I was passed over and the throne has
16 gone to my brother; it was his by the LORD's will. And now I have one request to make of you; do not refuse me.'
17 'What is it?' she said. He answered, 'Will you ask King Solomon (he will never refuse you) to give me Abishag
18 the Shunammite in marriage?' 'Very well,' said Bath-
19 sheba, 'I will speak for you to the king.' So Bathsheba went in to King Solomon to speak for Adoniajh. The king rose to meet her and kissed*a* her, and seated himself on his throne. A throne was set for the king's mother and
20 she sat at his right hand. Then she said, 'I have one small request to make of you; do not refuse me.' 'What is it,
21 mother?' he replied; 'I will not refuse you.' 'It is this, that Abishag the Shunammite should be given to your
22 brother Adonijah in marriage.' At that Solomon answered

[a] *So Sept.; Heb.* prostrated himself to...

his mother, 'Why do you ask for Abishag the Shunammite as wife for Adonijah? you might as well ask for the
throne, for he is my elder brother and has both Abiathar
the priest and Joab son of Zeruiah on his side.' Then King 23
Solomon swore by the LORD: 'So help me God, Adonijah
shall pay for this with his life. As the LORD lives, who has 24
established me and set me on the throne of David my
father and has founded a house for me as he promised, this
very day Adonijah shall be put to death!' Thereupon 25
King Solomon gave Benaiah son of Jehoiada his orders,
and he struck him down and he died.

✱ The story of the death of Adonijah is susceptible of more
than one interpretation. Abishag had been one of David's
concubines, and Solomon interpreted Adonijah's request to
marry her as a veiled claim to the throne. So he ordered
Adonijah's execution. Laying claim to a king's concubine
seems to have been a recognized method of publicly claiming
the throne (cp. 2 Sam. 16: 21). Did Adonijah make his request
in this spirit? Did Solomon see a real threat to his throne, or a
good excuse for the removal of a dangerous rival? It is
impossible to give a certain answer to either question. But
would Adonijah have made a claim to the throne in such a
clumsy fashion? Perhaps he genuinely fell in love with
Abishag, and enlisted Bathsheba's help so that his intentions
would not be misunderstood. Then, what was Bathsheba's
part? Did she, when Adonijah approached her, see an opportunity to bring about his death? The initiative she had taken in
bringing her son to the throne shows that she was both interested and experienced in politics. It is difficult to believe
that she did not realize that the request would be seen as
inspired more by politics than by love. If Adonijah was
innocent, then the end of the story is tragic indeed. This
aspect of the story was hidden from the deuteronomists. They

saw it as an opportunity provided by God for Solomon to remove his rival.

15. *I was passed over:* these words gave Solomon good grounds for his action. *it was his by the LORD's will:* this is the point of view of the editors. Perhaps they put the words into Adonijah's mouth.

19. *and kissed her:* here the N.E.B. follows the Septuagint. The Hebrew reads 'and prostrated himself to her' as the footnote indicates. Prostration was a sign of reverence, even of worship, and the Hebrew has been set aside as an overstatement. The queen mother was the most important woman in the kingdom and wielded great authority. (The Hebrew word translated 'queen mother', *gebirah*, means literally 'the great lady'.) There is no reason why the king should not have shown her the greatest sign of respect. It may have been ignorance of the position and authority of the queen mother on the part of the Greek translators which led them to use the word kiss. So the Hebrew may well give the correct reading. ∗

ABIATHAR DISMISSED

26 Abiathar the priest was told by the king to go off to Anathoth to his own estate. 'You deserve to die,' he said, 'but in spite of this day's work I shall not put you to death, for you carried the Ark of the Lord GOD[a] before my father David, and you shared in all the hardships that
27 he endured.' So Solomon dismissed Abiathar from his office as priest of the LORD, and so fulfilled the sentence that the LORD had pronounced against the house of Eli in Shiloh.

∗ 26. *Abiathar the priest* was greatly respected, and therefore dangerous. His father Ahimelech had been one of the priests at the sanctuary at Nob. The whole community there, with the

[a] the Ark...GOD: *so Heb.; but probably read* the ephod.

single exception of Abiathar, had been slaughtered by order of Saul for helping David. Abiathar had escaped and joined himself to David. He had become a leading priest in the kingdom. His support for Adonijah may have owed something to the support given to Solomon by Zadok his chief rival. *Anathoth* was a village some three miles north of Jerusalem (see map 4 on p. 119). There are later references to the priests there. The prophet Jeremiah probably came from this family. *carried the Ark of the Lord GOD:* the translators have suggested in the footnote that 'the ephod' should be read in place of *the Ark of the Lord GOD* because the Ark was in the possession of the Philistines during the period when David was a fugitive. 'The ephod' was an outer garment worn by a priest as a sign of his office. If *Ark* is read, then Solomon's words must refer to the period when David ruled in Jerusalem, after he had brought the Ark to his new capital from Kirjath-jearim. David certainly had hardships in the latter part of his life, but the reference more naturally seems to belong to the days when he was a fugitive.

27. *the sentence* referred to can be found in 1 Sam. 2: 27–36. The reference to it here is editorial comment. The deuteronomists saw the disgrace and banishment of Abiathar as pointing to the superiority of the Jerusalem line of priests, represented at this time by Zadok. ✷

JOAB'S DEATH

News of all this reached Joab, and he fled to the Tent of 28 the LORD and caught hold of the horns of the altar; for he had sided with Adonijah, though not with Absalom. When King Solomon learnt that Joab had fled to the Tent 29 of the LORD and that he was by the altar, he sent[a] Benaiah son of Jehoiada with orders to strike him down. Benaiah 30

[a] *Sept. adds* to Joab, saying, 'What has come upon you that you fled to the altar?' And Joab said, 'I was afraid of you; so I fled to the LORD.' So King Solomon sent...

came to the Tent of the LORD and ordered Joab in the king's
name to come away; but he said, 'No; I will die here.'
31 Benaiah reported Joab's answer to the king, and the king
said, 'Let him have his way; strike him down and bury
him, and so rid me and my father's house of the guilt for
32 the blood that he wantonly shed. The LORD will hold him
responsible for his own death, because he struck down
two innocent men who were better men than he, Abner
son of Ner, commander of the army of Israel, and Amasa
son of Jether, commander of the army of Judah, and ran
them through with the sword, without my father David's
33 knowledge. The guilt of their blood shall recoil on Joab
and his descendants for all time; but David and his
descendants, his house and his throne, will enjoy perpetual
34 prosperity from the LORD.' So Benaiah son of Jehoiada
went up to the altar and struck Joab down and killed him,
and he was buried in his house on the edge of the wilder-
35 ness. Thereafter the king appointed Benaiah son of
Jehoiada to command the army in his place, and installed
Zadok the priest in place of Abiathar.

* 28. *Joab* was the military leader who had supported
Adonijah. He sought sanctuary by standing by the altar where
he felt secure even from the king's authority.

29. The Septuagint has a much longer text, given in the
footnote, which may well be original. The word *sent* occurs
twice. A scribe copying from a manuscript could have read
the second occurrence of *sent* as the first and accidentally
omitted all the words in between. This kind of mistake is
known as haplography. If the longer version is read, it makes
the point even clearer that it was fear of Solomon which caused
Joab to seek sanctuary.

32. Solomon was too clever for Joab. The king invoked the old law that sanctuary was the right only of a man accused of manslaughter, but not of murder (cp. Exod. 21: 12–14). On the ground that Joab was a proved murderer, Solomon ordered him to be put to death even in the holy place. This also fulfilled the last charge of his father David. So two good reasons are given to justify Solomon's action.

35. It was the security of the throne which was the real reason for Joab's execution and Abiathar's banishment. With these two powerful, independent men out of the way, Solomon could place his own nominees, Benaiah and Zadok, in the principal offices of state without fear of opposition. ✳

SHIMEI'S DEATH

Next the king sent for Shimei and said to him, 'Build 36 yourself a house in Jerusalem and stay there; you are not to leave the city for any other place. If ever you leave it 37 and cross the gorge of the Kidron, you shall die; make no mistake about that. Your blood will be on your own head.' And Shimei said to the king, 'I accept your sentence; 38 I will do as your majesty commands.' So for a long time Shimei remained in Jerusalem; but three years later two of 39 his slaves ran away to Achish son of Maacah, king of Gath. When Shimei heard that his slaves were in Gath, he 40 immediately saddled his ass and went there to Achish in search of his slaves; he came to Gath and returned with them. When King Solomon was told that Shimei had 41 gone from Jerusalem to Gath and back, he sent for him and 42 said, 'Did I not require you to swear by the LORD? Did I not give you this solemn warning: "If ever you leave this city for any other place, you shall die; make no mistake about it"? And you said, "I accept your sentence; I

43 obey." Why then have you not kept the oath which you swore by the LORD, and the order which I gave you?
44 Shimei, you know in your own heart all the mischief you did to my father David; the LORD is now making that
45 mischief recoil on your own head. But King Solomon is blessed and the throne of David will be secure before the
46 LORD for all time.' The king then gave orders to Benaiah son of Jehoiada, and he went out and struck Shimei down; and he died. Thus Solomon's royal power was securely established.

* With Shimei's death, all that David had laid upon Solomon in his last charge had been done. Since Shimei virtually committed suicide no further blood feud was created. Shimei was not a person of national importance as were Abiathar and Joab. He is only mentioned here because of David's last charge. He had cursed David as 'you man of blood' at the time of the revolt of Absalom when David retreated from Jerusalem (cp. 2 Sam. 16: 5–8). The editors may have used him as an example of the fate of those who rebel against a reigning king.

36. The order cut Shimei off from his lands, servants and friends, and thus made him of little danger politically. It was an irksome restriction for a wealthy man. Jerusalem at this time was very small, very little larger than a large city square. Its area was a little under 11 acres.

39. The estates were being badly managed because of the permanent absence of the owner.

40. Shimei demanded the extradition of his runaway slaves.

42. His exit from Jerusalem put Shimei at the mercy of Solomon. He had forfeited his life. The editors saw this as purposely willed by God to punish Shimei without bringing any reproach upon Solomon. God was showing through events whom he blessed and whom he cursed.

46. *Thus Solomon's royal power was securely established:* the

N.E.B. understands this sentence as a summary of what has gone before. It could just as easily be the opening words of the following paragraph. In that case the sign of the firmness of Solomon's power was his marriage alliance with a daughter of Pharaoh. ✻

THE WISDOM OF SOLOMON

✻ Solomon's reign is dealt with in Kings at very great length, and two aspects of it are particularly stressed. The greatest emphasis is placed upon the fact that he built the temple. To the deuteronomists that made Solomon a very great king indeed, and the other aspect of the reign which receives such emphasis may also be dependent upon it. Solomon is presented as the founder of the temple and the wisest of all Hebrew monarchs. Certainly some at least of the stories which are told to demonstrate his wisdom give every indication of being legends and many legends gathered around the figure of Solomon in later Jewish tradition. Yet for the Hebrews, and for their neighbours, wisdom did not mean abstract thinking and philosophizing. It consisted of the capacity to get the most out of life: exploiting to the full whatever advantages came one's way, and extracting oneself with least damage from situations of adversity and suffering. A wise king was, there-fore, a strong, astute ruler, skilled in statecraft and the arts of diplomacy. There is no reason to doubt that in this sense Solomon was wise, at least at the beginning of his reign.

How, then, has the tradition of Solomon, the philosopher king, arisen? His marriage to Pharaoh's daughter probably supplies the answer to the question. Such a marriage was an alliance between two sovereign states, and Solomon sought this particular marriage, not only because Egypt was a great power, but also because, in his shaping of the Hebrew monarchy, he wished to use the Egyptian empire as his model. His building programme at Jerusalem was designed to make that city the worthy capital of a great empire. He established a court with permanent officials. And he very probably, again on the model of Egypt, established a Wisdom School. The purpose of such a school was to educate the sons of the upper classes to enable them to take their place in society, and fulfil adequately the tasks which would fall to them in the royal civil and diplomatic services. Such is probably the origin of Solomon's reputation for wisdom. The editors of Kings added to this reputation religious wisdom – had he not founded the temple? – and the tradition began which was later to ascribe almost all Israelite wisdom literature to Solomon. In later Hebrew tradition he was accepted as the author of the books of Proverbs and The Wisdom of Solomon.

In chapter 3 we shall be told the origins of Solomon's wisdom. Here the historical and legendary are so interwoven that it is by no means easy to separate the two. The account of Solomon's marriage to a daughter of Pharaoh seems to be plain history, but even that narrative is used by the editors for a didactic purpose. ✻

SOLOMON'S MARRIAGE ALLIANCE

3 Solomon allied himself to Pharaoh king of Egypt by marrying his daughter. He brought her to the City of David, until he had finished building his own house and 2 the house of the LORD and the wall round Jerusalem. The people however continued to sacrifice at the hill-shrines, for till then no house had been built in honour of the name 3 of the LORD. Solomon himself loved the LORD, conforming to the precepts laid down by his father David; but he too slaughtered and burnt sacrifices at the hill-shrines.

✻ 1. There is no reason to doubt the historicity of this marriage, though the name of the pharaoh is not given. Because Solomon received the great fortress of Gezer as a wedding present (cp. 9: 16), it has been suggested that the pharaoh was Shishonk I, the Shishak of Kings (cp. 14: 25). However, Shishonk only began to reign when Solomon was an old man. Here the marriage is said to have taken place before the palace was built. If this is accurate, the marriage must have taken place early in Solomon's reign, and his wife must have been a daughter of one of the weak pharaohs of the XXI Dynasty which came to an end with the reign of Shishonk. *City of David:* Solomon greatly enlarged the city which he had inherited from his father David. Since the city was built on the spur of a hill, the only expansion could be to the north where the spur was joined to the larger hill. Solomon built his palace and temple to the north of David's city which meant that the centre of the city moved to the north. This explains the distinction, first made here, between the City of David and Jerusalem, i.e. the city which David captured had now become part of a larger city.

2. By mentioning this marriage at this particular place in the narrative, the editors wished to link marriage with a foreign wife with disloyalty to the true religious traditions of Israel. They will return to this theme later in the story. *no house had been built:* this explains why Solomon's dream (verses 4–15 *a*) occurred at Gibeon, after a religious ceremony there, and not at Jerusalem.

3. *hill-shrines:* the Hebrew has previously been translated as 'high places'. They were open-air sanctuaries, situated on the tops of hills, where fertility rites were practised. ✳

SOLOMON'S DREAM

Now King Solomon went to Gibeon to offer a sacrifice, 4 for that was the chief hill-shrine, and he used to offer a thousand whole-offerings on its altar. There that night the 5*a* LORD God appeared to him in a dream and said, 'What shall I give you? Tell me.' And Solomon answered, 'Thou 6

[a] *Verses 5–14: cp. 2 Chr. 1: 7–12.*

didst show great and constant love to thy servant David my father, because he walked before thee in loyalty, righteousness, and integrity of heart; and thou hast maintained this great and constant love towards him and hast now given him a son to succeed him on the throne.

7 Now, O LORD my God, thou hast made thy servant king in place of my father David, though I am a mere child,
8 unskilled in leadership. And I am here in the midst of thy people, the people of thy choice, too many to be numbered
9 or counted. Give thy servant, therefore, a heart with skill to listen, so that he may govern thy people justly and distinguish good from evil. For who is equal to the task of
10 governing this great people of thine?' The Lord was well
11 pleased that Solomon had asked for this, and he said to him, 'Because you have asked for this, and not for long life for yourself, or for wealth, or for the lives of your enemies, but have asked for discernment in administering
12 justice, I grant your request; I give you a heart so wise and so understanding that there has been none like you before
13 your time nor will be after you. I give you furthermore those things for which you did not ask, such wealth and
14 honour*a* as no king of your time can match. And if you conform to my ways and observe my ordinances and commandments, as your father David did, I will give you
15 long life.' Then he awoke, and knew it was a dream.

⁂ Here a further and decisive indication is given that Solomon was the legitimate successor of David. God himself declared it in a dream, and dreams were then accepted as one of the certain means of divine revelation (cp. 1 Sam. 28: 6).

4. *Gibeon* was a city a few miles north of Jerusalem in the

[a] *Or* riches.

territory of the northern tribes (see map 4 on p. 119). Solomon may have sought a dream there to authenticate his claim to the throne among the northern tribes upon whom he had least claim for personal loyalty. *thousand* may mean no more than 'a great many'.

5. *the LORD God appeared to him in a dream:* dreams are found as vehicles of divine revelation mostly in the 'E' Source of the Pentateuch – those passages which use the Hebrew word *Elohim* to refer to God, rather than the proper name Yahweh. The 'E' Source had close associations with the northern tribes. So the choice of the location of Solomon's dream was a sign of genuine political astuteness. There is evidence from outside Israel, from Egypt and other places, that rulers were granted dreams by the gods. That does not mark Solomon's dream as a forgery, but rather substantiates it by showing that it was a fairly common practice for a king to look for divine guidance through dreams. Dreams experienced at sanctuaries had especial authority, as the dream to Jacob at Bethel shows (cp. Gen. 28: 10-17).

6. *constant love:* the Hebrew word *ḥesed* which is translated by this phrase is very difficult to translate. It always indicates loyalty to a person or relationship which has been freely undertaken. *righteousness* was used to describe conduct which adhered to a rule or standard. For Israel the standard was the law which God had given to his people. David was righteous in that he had established a community which lived by that law. So God had shown *constant love* to him.

9. Solomon asked that the same constant love given to his father David be also given to him. In his case its outward mark would be a facility in the exercise of judgement. The king needed to give judgements to his people and settle disputes between them. Solomon's wisdom would be shown in that his judgements built up rather than detracted from the *righteousness* of his people. *a heart with skill to listen:* the Hebrews regarded the heart as the seat of understanding and decision. The ideal of kingship presented here approximates closely to that

expressed in the Messianic passages of Isaiah (cp. Isa. 9 and 11). Isaiah may have been faithfully reproducing a tradition received from Solomon's time as easily as the editor of Kings may have been imposing a late Isaianic tradition on Solomon. Neither Solomon nor his successors lived up to the ideal expressed here, but that does not deny that there was such an ideal in existence in their time.

13. *honour:* the Hebrew word means literally 'outward splendour'. So either *honour* or 'riches', as in the footnote, is a possible translation.

15 *a. it was a dream:* this emphasizes Solomon's recognition of it as a means of divine revelation. Whether the dream happened as described here or not, it has its chief value as a classic statement of the true religious ideal of Israelite kingship. The Hebrews had taken over kingship from Canaan, but in so doing they needed to change its content to bring it into harmony with the older traditions of the covenant people. The king would be maintained by God and his dynasty assured as he and his successors exhibited a quality of kingship which maintained the moral and spiritual qualities of a community in covenant with God. David, it was claimed, had done this by walking before God 'in loyalty, righteousness, and integrity of heart'. Here is expressed an ideal of kingship in marked contrast to that displayed in Canaanite practice. If it was Solomon's early ideal, then he fell farther and farther from it as his reign progressed. But the ideal remained in Israel, and when the prophets sought to describe a future Israel in which there would be complete loyalty to the nation's covenant obligation to God, they could think of no better way of doing it than by describing this same ideal of kingship. *

SOLOMON OFFERS SACRIFICE AT JERUSALEM

15*b* Solomon came to Jerusalem and stood before the Ark of the Covenant of the Lord; there he sacrificed whole-

offerings and brought shared-offerings, and gave a feast
to all his household.

✷ 15 *b*. It has frequently been suggested that this verse is not
historical. If so, then it was inserted by the deuteronomic
editor to redeem Solomon's reputation, after he had offered
sacrifice at Gibeon. But it may be based on fact. If the visit to
Gibeon and the dream were meant to show that the northern
tribes had accepted Solomon as king, then the event would be
a cause of rejoicing and occasion for sacrifice and festivity
when Solomon returned to Jerusalem. The two principal
kinds of sacrifice are mentioned. *whole-offerings*, which have
been called in other translations 'burnt offerings', were
sacrifices in which a whole animal was burnt upon the altar as
a sacrifice to God. The worshipper's readiness to destroy a
valuable object was the outward indication of the strength of
his devotion. *shared-offerings* were communion sacrifices in
which part of the animal was burnt on the altar and part was
eaten by the priest and worshippers. The purpose was to
integrate together the lives of all who shared in the sacrifice:
God, priest and worshippers. Since the Hebrew word for peace
means the integration of lives together in harmony and mutual
fulfilment, it was used of these sacrifices, and they have often
been called 'peace offerings'. ✷

AN EXAMPLE OF SOLOMON'S WISDOM

Then there came into the king's presence two women 16
who were prostitutes and stood before him. The first said, 17
'My lord, this woman and I share the same house, and I
gave birth to a child when she was there with me. On the 18
third day after my baby was born she too gave birth to a
child. We were quite alone; no one else was with us in the
house; only the two of us were there. During the night 19
this woman's child died because she overlaid it, and she 20

got up in the middle of the night, took my baby from my
side while I, your servant, was asleep, and laid it in her
21 bosom, putting her dead child in mine. When I got up in
the morning to feed my baby, I found him dead; but
when I looked at him closely, I found that it was not the
22 child that I had borne.' The other woman broke in, 'No;
the living child is mine; yours is the dead one', while the
first retorted, 'No; the dead child is yours; mine is the
living one.' So they went on arguing in the king's presence.
23 The king thought to himself, 'One of them says, "This is
my child, the living one; yours is the dead one." The
other says, "No; it is your child that is dead and mine that
24 is alive."' Then he said, 'Fetch me a sword.' They brought
25 in a sword and the king gave the order: 'Cut the living
child in two and give half to one and half to the other.'
26 At this the woman who was the mother of the living
child, moved with love for her child, said to the king,
'Oh! sir, let her have the baby; whatever you do, do not
kill it.' The other said, 'Let neither of us have it; cut it in
27 two.' Thereupon the king gave judgement: 'Give the
living baby to the first woman; do not kill it. She is its
28 mother.' When Israel heard the judgement which the king
had given, they all stood in awe of him; for they saw that
he had the wisdom of God within him to administer
justice.

* The purpose of this story is to show how the promise that
God made to Solomon in the dream at Gibeon was implemented. It is very likely legendary; a stock example of
judicial wisdom. Similar stories were told of other rulers of
the period. Yet the story does accurately indicate the nature
of the wisdom with which Solomon was believed to have been

endowed. It was the capacity to give sound judgements to his people, and thus fulfil in the highest way the first duty of a king. All subjects had the right of entry to the king to place their cases before him. So a king's success, or lack of success, in administering justice was soon known throughout the kingdom.

26. *moved with love for her child:* the Hebrew underlying this phrase means, when translated literally, 'her bowels were fermented'. The Hebrews attached all the psychological aspects of life to the various parts of the body. The bowels were thought to be the seat of the emotions. This idiom was taken literally into the Greek of the New Testament, hence the 'bowels of compassion' of the Authorized Version in the first letter of John (1 John 3: 17). The N.E.B. paraphrases with 'heart'. *

SOLOMON'S CABINET

King Solomon reigned over Israel. His officers were as **4** 1, 2*a*
follows:

In charge of the calendar:*b* Azariah son of Zadok the priest.

Adjutant-general:*c* Ahijah son*d* of Shisha.   3

Secretary of state: Jehoshaphat son of Ahilud.

Commander of the army: Benaiah son of Jehoiada.   4

Priests: Zadok and Abiathar.

Superintendent of the regional governors: Azariah son 5
of Nathan.

King's Friend: Zabud son of Nathan.*e*

Comptroller of the household: Ahishar.   6

[a] *Verses 2–6: cp. 2 Sam. 8: 16–18; 20: 23–26; 1 Chr. 18: 15–17.*
[b] *In...calendar: prob. rdg.; Heb.* Elihoreph.
[c] *Prob. rdg., cp. 1 Chr. 18: 16; Heb.* Adjutants-general.
[d] *Prob. rdg.; Heb.* sons.
[e] *So Sept.; Heb. adds* priest.

Superintendent of the forced levy: Adoniram son of Abda.

✻ This list of the chief officers in Solomon's administration might be called his cabinet. This is not the first time that such a list has been given. The footnote refers to three passages where a similar list of David's officers is given. The Hebrew is not clear in places and the clarity of the translation has only been achieved as a result of some emendation in the text.

1. *Israel* both here and in verse 7 below is not strictly correct. The Hebrew in both places has 'All Israel', which refers to the united kingdom of Israel and Judah.

2. *In charge of the calendar* in place of the name 'Elihoreph' is a conjecture, but a very probable one. The name Elihoreph is never found in any other place, and is, in fact, an impossible Hebrew name. Literally it would mean 'My God is autumn'. By a slight change of the Hebrew the word can mean, 'Over the autumn', i.e. Over the year, since the New Year began in the autumn. Solomon seems to have had an official, as did the rulers of other empires at that period, whose duty it was to regulate the seasons. Such an official would come from a priestly family. The title must have been understood as a name at a later time when the office was no longer in use, probably in the post-exilic period.

3. At the same time the Hebrew words in this verse would have been changed into plurals, cp. the footnotes.

4. *Priests: Zadok and Abiathar:* this looks suspiciously like an addition from the earlier list in Samuel (2 Sam. 8: 17). Neither Zadok nor Abiathar is given a patronymic, a father's name (i.e. family name), as are the rest of the officials with the one exception of *Ahishar* who occupied a relatively lowly office and may have been a foreigner. It hardly seems likely that *Abiathar* was reinstated as priest after his banishment to Anathoth. If these words are omitted, then the Hebrew text as given in the footnote should be accepted in verse 5.

5. *Zabud son of Nathan* is 'priest' (N.E.B. footnote) as

well as *King's Friend*. This is the last reference to the title of *King's Friend*, i.e. adviser and close associate. It has been met before in David's reign (2 Sam. 15: 37), and is also known from Egyptian sources. It is never met in Israel or Judah after the reign of Solomon. ✳

SOLOMON'S PROVINCIAL ADMINISTRATION

Solomon had twelve regional governors over Israel and 7 they supplied the food for the king and the royal household, each being responsible for one month's provision in the year. These were their names: 8

Ben-hur in the hill-country of Ephraim.

Ben-dekar in Makaz, Shaalbim, Beth-shemesh, Elon, 9 and Beth-hanan.[a]

Ben-hesed in Aruboth; he had charge also of Socoh and 10 all the land of Hepher.

Ben-abinadab, who had married Solomon's daughter 11 Taphath, in all the district of Dor.

Baana son of Ahilud in Taanach and Megiddo, all 12 Beth-shean as far as Abel-meholah beside Zartanah, and from Beth-shean below Jezreel as far as Jokmeam.

Ben-geber in Ramoth-gilead, including the tent- 13 villages of Jair son of Manasseh in Gilead and the region of Argob in Bashan, sixty large walled cities with gate-bars of bronze.

Ahinadab son of Iddo in Mahanaim.   14

Ahimaaz in Naphtali; he also had married a daughter of 15 Solomon, Basmath.

Baanah son of Hushai in Asher and Aloth.   16

[a] Elon, and Beth-hanan: *so some MSS.; others* Elon-beth-hanan.

17   Jehoshaphat son of Paruah in Issachar.

18   Shimei son of Elah in Benjamin.

19   Geber son of Uri in Gilead, the land of Sihon king of
      the Amorites and of Og king of Bashan.

      In addition, one governor over all the governors[a] in the
      land.

✻ The chief duty of the regional governors was to collect the
king's taxes. The system adopted was quite simple. The kingdom was divided up into twelve administrative areas, each
under a regional governor who was responsible for the upkeep
of the royal palace and all charges upon it for one month in the
year. In the list twelve names are given together with the
areas they controlled. The N.E.B. has only been able to
present this clear and simple picture by emending the Hebrew
text.

8. On the list, many of the names seem to be missing. *Ben-hur*,
named as the governor of Ephraim, means 'son of Hur'. One
explanation is that the manuscript from which the names were
copied was old and frayed on the right edge. The beginning
of some of the names would then have been torn off. Unlike
English, Hebrew is written from right to left. Alternatively,
it may be that in some areas the governorship belonged to a
particular family by hereditary right. Then in such cases, as
Ephraim, only the family name was given.

13. *Ben-geber in Ramoth-gilead* may be the same person and
district as *Geber son of Uri in Gilead* in verse 19. If this is so,
then the twelfth district must be Judah (see note on verse 19
below), and the Hebrew 'All Israel' of the title in verse 7 is
correct.

19. *one governor over all the governors in the land:* the Hebrew
actually reads, 'and there was one governor in the land'. The
N.E.B. has taken this phrase to be a further reference to
Azariah son of Nathan who appeared in the cabinet list as

[a] over. . . governors: *prob. rdg.; Heb. om.*

Superintendent of the regional governors. This is a conjecture, though it is what Josephus, the Jewish historian who wrote in the 1st century A.D., and the early Jewish commentators understood the Hebrew to mean. The words *over all the governors* have been added by the translators to clarify a difficult passage. Without them it would seem that there were thirteen regional governors given in the list.

The N.E.B. way of dealing with the problem is not the only way. There is no mention of Judah in the list of tax districts. It has been suggested that Solomon exempted Judah from his fiscal demands, and that this exemption greatly contributed to the resentment of the northern tribes against his rule. Such a privilege for Judah was very unlikely. Solomon was in too great a need of money to exempt so large a territory as Judah. The resentment of the northern tribes was real, but more likely due to the fact that in the latter part of his reign Solomon imposed a levy of forced labour upon them. In the earlier part of the reign, such a levy was demanded only of the Canaanites living in the kingdom. Why then is there no reference to Judah in this list? The answer is that there probably was a reference but it has been misunderstood. Judah was, from the royal point of view, the homeland, 'the land'. The last sentence in the list was no part of the original list but an addition to it. It tells that as well as the twelve governors appointed to administer the various districts of the north, there was also in addition 'one governor in the land', i.e. over Judah.

The addition of Judah seems to confuse the meaning of the list. It seems to make thirteen regions, which contradicts the number given at the head of the list and also the system of taxation as explained there. Actually confusion is due to misunderstanding. The reference to Judah was not inserted as a part of the list but as an addition to it to give a fuller picture of the way Solomon's kingdom was administered. Israel and Judah were two kingdoms united under one monarch, rather like England and Scotland. Their tax systems were independent.

Here we have a list of the twelve tax districts of Israel to which a note has been added that there was also a tax system in Judah. Judah may in fact have been divided up into twelve districts in much the same way. The fact that there are two original lists, one for Israel and the other for Judah, may be indicated by the name given to Solomon's kingdom in the headings to the two lists in verses 1 and 7 (see note on verse 1 above).

It may seem odd that such a detailed list should be given of the regions of Israel when only the briefest mention is made of Judah. The reason may be that the regions of Judah remained unaltered in Solomon's time, but during his reign a new regional system was brought into operation for Israel. This would have been necessary to incorporate the Canaanite cities, which formed no part of the old tribal groups, into his system. The list dates from the later part of the reign since two of the governors are said to have been his sons-in-law. *

THE WORK OF THE GOVERNORS

27 The regional governors, each for a month in turn, supplied provisions for King Solomon and for all who came to his table; they never fell short in their deliveries.
28 They provided also barley and straw, each according to his duty, for the horses and chariot-horses where it was required.

* This description of the work of the governors originally followed immediately after the list of names so it seems best to read it there. As it stands in the text it is part of a eulogy on Solomon which was added later.

28. The stress laid upon the provision for the horses was because of the growing importance of chariot warfare. *

THE EULOGY OF SOLOMON

The remaining part of chapter 4 was added by an editor after the main part of the narrative had been written. It gives an idealized and romantic picture of Solomon's glories. The reasons for suggesting that it is a late addition to the narrative are these. First, it contains the phrase, 'west of the river', in verse 24. This means 'west of the Euphrates'. It was the title given to Syria and Palestine in the time of the Assyrian, Babylonian and Persian empires. It is used in the same sense in the book of Nehemiah. Secondly, the boundaries of Solomon's empire, as given here, have been greatly enlarged. He was the ruler of Palestine and Syria – Damascus had not yet become a serious rival – but his empire never extended to the limits given here. Thirdly, in the description given of his wisdom, Solomon has become the philosopher of later tradition rather than the wise ruler of chapter 3.

HIS REIGN

The people of Judah and Israel were countless as the 20 sands of the sea; they ate and they drank, and enjoyed life. Solomon ruled over all the kingdoms from the river 21[a] Euphrates to Philistia and as far as the frontier of Egypt; they paid tribute and were subject to him all his life.

Solomon's provision for one day was thirty kor of 22 flour and sixty kor of meal, ten fat oxen and twenty oxen 23 from the pastures and a hundred sheep, as well as stags, gazelles, roebucks, and fattened fowl. For he was para- 24 mount over all the land west of the Euphrates from Tiphsah to Gaza, ruling all the kings west of the river; and he enjoyed peace on all sides. All through his reign Judah 25

[a] 5: 1 *in Heb.*

and Israel continued at peace, every man under his own vine and fig-tree, from Dan to Beersheba.

26   Solomon had forty thousand chariot-horses in his stables and twelve thousand cavalry horses.

* 20. The Hebrew text regards this verse as a summary of the description of Solomon's administration.

21. The Hebrew text begins its chapter 5 at this verse. English Bibles begin the new chapter with the introduction of Hiram king of Tyre. The system of numbering chapters and verses was only added to the text at the end of the medieval period. We are dealing, therefore, with two alternative ways of paragraphing. The English method seems preferable since the introduction of Hiram starts a new subject, the building of the temple.

24. The limits of Solomon's rule are marked by great cities on the trading route between Mesopotamia and Egypt. *Tiphsah* was the city, later known as Thapsakis, on the Euphrates at the river's most western point (see map 1 on p. 5). *Gaza* was the last city in the south of Palestine before the Sinai desert (see map 5 on p. 148). *

HIS WISDOM

29   And God gave Solomon depth of wisdom and insight, and understanding as wide as the sand on the sea-shore,
30   so that Solomon's wisdom surpassed that of all the men of
31   the east and of all Egypt. For he was wiser than any man, wiser than Ethan the Ezrahite, and Heman, Kalcol, and Darda, the sons of Mahol; his fame spread among all the
32   surrounding nations. He uttered three thousand proverbs,
33   and his songs numbered a thousand and five. He discoursed of trees, from the cedar of Lebanon down to the marjoram that grows out of the wall, of beasts and birds, of reptiles

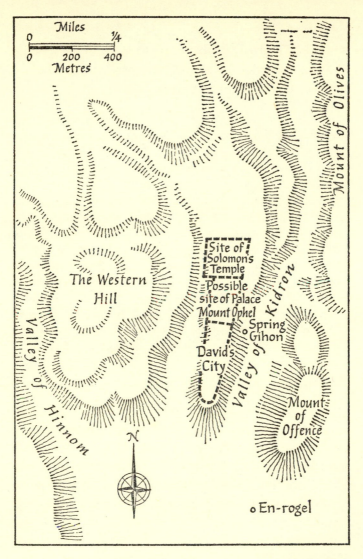

2. Plan of Jerusalem in the time of Solomon. Solomon's palace may have been in the northern extension which joined the city to the temple. The western hill has been known since Josephus' time as Mount Sion.

34 and fishes. Men of all races came to listen to the wisdom
of Solomon, and from all the kings of the earth who had
heard of his wisdom he received gifts.[a]

* 30. *the men of the east and of all Egypt:* evidence of the existence of wisdom schools at times much earlier than the reign
of Solomon has been found in both Mesopotamia and Egypt.
   31. The names of the wise men occur again in Chronicles
(1 Chron. 2: 6).
   33. In Egypt and Mesopotamia there were classified lists of
natural phenomena which were used in training young
scribes. The mention here of Solomon's knowledge of trees,
birds and animals may be based on similar material used in
Hebrew wisdom schools. *marjoram* has in other translations
been called 'hyssop'. The contrast is between the cedar, noted
for its height and beauty, and a very small, humble shrub.
   34. *he received gifts:* these words are not present in the Hebrew.
They are found in two of the Greek versions, and seem to be a
reference to the visit of the queen of Sheba. *

SOLOMON'S NEGOTIATIONS WITH HIRAM

5 1[b] When Hiram king of Tyre heard that Solomon had been
anointed king in his father's place, he sent envoys to him,
2[c] because he had always been a friend of David. Solomon
3 sent this answer to Hiram: 'You know that my father
David could not build a house in honour of the name of the
LORD his God, because he was surrounded by armed
4 nations until the LORD made them subject to him. But
now on every side the LORD my God has given me peace;
5 there is no one to oppose me, I fear no attack. So I pro-
pose to build a house in honour of the name of the LORD

[a] he received gifts: *so Luc. Sept.; Heb. om.*
[b] 5: 15 *in Heb.*   [c] *Verses 2–11: cp. 2 Chr. 2: 3–16.*

my God, following the promise given by the LORD to my
father David: "Your son whom I shall set on the throne
in your place will build the house in honour of my name."
If therefore you will now give orders that cedars be felled 6
and brought from Lebanon, my men will work with
yours, and I will pay you for your men whatever sum you
fix; for, as you know, we have none so skilled at felling
timber as your Sidonians.'

✳ The editors of Kings thought that the building of the
temple was the most important act of Solomon's reign. This
is shown by the prominence they have given to it. Here we
learn how the project was planned.

1. *Hiram* is an abbreviated form of Ahiram. Evidence of a
king of that name ruling in Byblos and the neighbouring city
of *Tyre* has been found. *Tyre* was one of the Phoenician
settlements which had grown up along the Syrian coast. The
city was built on an island, approximately half a mile offshore.
It was regarded as an impregnable fortress until Alexander the
Great captured it in 333 B.C. by building a mole which joined
the island to the mainland. Hiram had been *a friend of David* in
that he had established an alliance with him. This was sensible
in that the interests of the two rulers were complementary.
David established a land empire and controlled the trade
routes through Palestine. Tyre was a sea power. Hiram *sent
envoys* to Solomon to re-affirm the alliance.

3. The text of the message in this and the following verses
has been edited by the deuteronomists. It may be based upon
the original words but it now also contains words which the
editors added to emphasize their theological ideas. An example
is, *my father David could not build a house in honour of the name of
the LORD his God*. These words echo the speech of the
prophet Nathan when David expressed a wish to build a
temple at Jerusalem (cp. 2 Sam. 7: 1–16). The deuteronomists

made great use of the phrase 'the name of God'. In Deuteronomy itself, the temple is always referred to as 'the place which the LORD your God will choose out of all your tribes to receive his Name that it may dwell there' (cp. Deut. 12: 5). The Name, for them, indicated the abiding presence of God and avoided the problems posed by worshippers who believed that God actually lived in the temple. Thus the temple emphasized both God's presence and also that the people among whom God lived, and especially the king who ruled over them, had to respond to that presence by living as God would have them live. *subject to him:* this phrase catches the sense of the Hebrew but hides a graphic metaphor. The Hebrew says that the Lord placed them 'beneath the soles of his feet'. A conquered king lay on the ground while the conqueror placed his foot on his neck as a sign of conquest. Illustrations of this ceremony appear on bas-reliefs of Assyrian emperors.

5. *Your son...will build the house:* the reference is to 2 Sam. 7: 13. In that chapter use is made of the ambiguity of the word 'house': i.e. temple or dynasty.

6. *my men:* Solomon insisted on forced labour from his subjects. It was an accepted part of the Canaanite political system that subjects on royal land were serfs who owed part of their labour to their master the king. So Solomon could rightly demand such service from his tenants, and also from Canaanites living in his territories. His need for labour became so great that, as time went on, he tried to apply the system to native-born Israelites. This was one of the chief reasons for his unpopularity at the end of his reign. ✳

HIRAM REPLIES FAVOURABLY, AND THE WORK BEGINS

7 When Hiram received Solomon's message, he was greatly pleased and said, 'Blessed be the LORD today who has given David a wise son to rule over this great people.'

And he sent this reply to Solomon: 'I have received your 8
message. In this matter of timber, both cedar and pine, I
will do all you wish. My men shall bring down the logs 9
from Lebanon to the sea and I will make them up into
rafts to be floated to the place you appoint; I will have
them broken up there and you can remove them. You,
on your part, will meet my wishes if you provide the food
for my household.' So Hiram kept Solomon supplied with 10
all the cedar and pine that he wanted, and Solomon sup- 11
plied Hiram with twenty thousand kor of wheat as food
for his household and twenty kor of oil of pounded olives;
Solomon gave this yearly to Hiram. (The LORD had given 12
Solomon wisdom as he had promised him; there was
peace between Hiram and Solomon and they concluded
an alliance.)

∗ 7. *a wise son* (and 'wisdom' in verse 12 below) refers to
Solomon's political astuteness in making the agreement.
Hiram's reply created a treaty of friendship between the two
countries. This involved much more than peace in the sense
of absence of war. It meant friendship and co-operation on the
basis of allied interests. Lebanon was noted for its fine timber
which was in great demand for many purposes and formed
the basis of a thriving trade.

8. *cedar and pine:* other translations have thought that
cypress was meant rather than *pine*. The same Hebrew word
was used for both. Cypress trees are not indigenous to the
Lebanon so *pine* is the more probable meaning.

9. *rafts* floated down the coast were the obvious way of
transporting timber. The Chronicler has added the detail that
they were landed at the port of Joppa (2 Chron. 2: 15).

11. The amounts given here are very large, as comparison
with the provisions for Solomon's own household, which

themselves were intended to be on a grand scale, show (cp. 4: 22–3 above). If the figures given here are to be trusted, much of what Solomon sent to Hiram would be exported and *for his household* means, in our terms, 'for his exchequer'. *kor* used of oil is probably a mistake for *bath*. A *kor* was a dry meas- ure, *bath* was the liquid measure. *pounded olives* means oil of the first quality. Olive oil made by crushing olives between mill-stones contained a certain amount of stone dust. The finest oil was hand-made by the use of a pestle and mortar. ✳

SOLOMON'S FORCED LEVY

13 King Solomon raised a forced levy from the whole
14 of Israel amounting to thirty thousand men. He sent them to Lebanon in monthly relays of ten thousand, so that the men spent one month in Lebanon and two at home; Adoniram was superintendent of the whole levy.
15 Solomon had also seventy thousand hauliers and eighty
16 thousand quarrymen, apart from the three thousand three hundred foremen in charge of the work who super-
17 intended the labourers. By the king's orders they quarried huge, massive blocks for laying the foundation of the
18 Lord's house*a* in hewn stone. Solomon's and Hiram's builders and the Gebalites shaped the blocks and pre- pared both timber and stone for the building of the house.

✳ King Hiram provided the skilled workmen; Solomon sent unskilled labourers from Israel.

   13. *a forced levy* (see the comment on 5: 6 above): according to the account of the levy given later in the book (9: 20–2), native-born Israelites were exempt. Only Canaanites living in

[*a*] the Lord's house: *lit.* the house.

Israelite territory were compelled. What is written here contradicts that account, and the attitude of the Israelites to Rehoboam after the death of Solomon (12: 4) would lead us to conclude that this account is the true one.

15–16. These two verses are a later addition to the narrative. They were added to show Solomon's importance by giving the numbers of his workmen. These numbers have been inflated. In chapter 9 below, the number of foremen is given as 550 (9: 23). The N.E.B. represents Solomon as employing these workmen in Lebanon, but the translators have omitted the last Hebrew word from verse 15. This makes plain that the men were occupied 'in the hill country', i.e. in Judah.

17. If this verse follows verse 14 then the *they* is impersonal. This is a way in which Hebrew expresses the passive. It means, 'stones were quarried'. This is also the first mention of Phoenician craftsmen being employed at Jerusalem. There are, beneath the old city of Jerusalem, extensive caves which tradition points to as the place where the stone was cut for the temple. They are still called Solomon's quarries.

18. *Gebalites* were inhabitants of the Phoenician port of Byblos. Why were they in Jerusalem? There is no good reason for regarding Byblos as a source of specially talented stone-masons, nor were they subjects of Hiram. For these reasons many scholars have thought that the word is a corruption of a similar sounding word which has been lost through inaccurate copying of manuscripts. In the Greek versions a verb and not a noun is found at this place in the text. So the original Hebrew may have had a verb, not unlike *Gebalites* in sound, which described the way the stone masons worked, shaping the edges of the stones so that they were more regular and easy to use in building. Archaeology has demonstrated that this was a characteristic Phoenician building technique. But this suggestion is a conjecture and masons from Byblos may well have formed part of Solomon's work-team. ✳

THE TEMPLE

6 ¹ ᵃ ᵇ   It was in the four hundred and eightieth year after the
Israelites had come out of Egypt, in the fourth year of
Solomon's reign over Israel, in the second month of that
year, the month of Ziv, that he began to build the house
of the LORD.

✵ The beginning of the construction of the temple was such
an important event to the deuteronomists that it needed to be
dated accurately, and in such a way as would underline the
significance of the occasion. They saw a real parallel between
the exodus and the building of the temple. Both marked
spiritually creative moments in the history of Israel. In the
first, God attached Israel to himself as his own people: in the
second, he declared that his presence was always with them in
the house built for him. It is noteworthy that the temple is
usually referred to as 'the house', or 'the house of the LORD'.

For the date we are given two cross-references: *the four
hundred and eightieth year after the Israelites had come out of
Egypt*, and *the fourth year of Solomon's reign over Israel*. If
Solomon began to reign in 961 B.C., then the temple was begun
in the year 957 B.C. The exodus would seem to have taken
place in 1437 B.C. There is some archaeological evidence for
such a date in the fifteenth century B.C., but just as much, if not
more, for a date in the thirteenth century. Recent scholarly
opinion has been almost unanimous in favour of the thirteenth
century. If a date in that century is accepted, then the 480
years of this verse cannot be accurate. It is an artificial date
that means no more than 'a long time ago'. How was it
reckoned? The Hebrews counted forty years a generation, as
in the forty years' wandering in the wilderness (Ps. 95: 10),
and 480 is 40 × 12, i.e. one generation for each of the tribes

[a] *In chs. 6 and 7 there are several Hebrew technical terms whose meaning is
not certain and has to be determined, as well as may be, from the context.*
[b] *Verses 1–3: cp. 2 Chr. 3: 2–4.*

which formed the tribal league. *the month of Ziv*, April–May, was the most appropriate time to begin building when the rainy season was over and the harvest had been gathered.

This temple was not the first Israelite sanctuary. There had been in earlier days movable sanctuaries in which the Ark had been kept, and possibly even a permanent house at Shiloh which may have survived until the sixth century (cp. 1 Sam. 1–3 and Jer. 7: 12). What was new about Solomon's temple was its splendour, and the way it fused together the idea of God's dwelling with his people and the royal dynasty of David's house at Jerusalem. From this time there was a very close link between the temple and the Davidic dynasty as was indicated by the play on words in 2 Sam. 7. There David is said to have wanted to build a house (temple) for God, because God had built a house (dynasty) for him. The tradition of the covenant people as it has come down to us in the Old Testament is the tradition as it was known in Judah. There, both the temple of Solomon and the royal house of David became important theological symbols, the one epitomizing the abiding presence of God with his people, and the other the ideal rule of God over the whole world. Later Jesus in the gospels was presented as both the true temple, and also the Messiah, the son of David.

All this still lay in the future. Solomon was concerned to build at Jerusalem a capital worthy of a great emperor and able to stand comparison with the capital cities of other empires. Since for Israel religious faith was the one great unifying force holding together the tribes, a splendid temple which would become a religious centre for the tribes and a place of pilgrimage seemed a political masterstroke. It would link the Davidic dynasty with the religious traditions of the tribes. For the deuteronomic editors this significance was even greater. King Josiah in his reform in 621 B.C. outlawed and attempted to abolish all religious sanctuaries in Judah other than the temple at Jerusalem. His motives were probably mixed. He may well have been seeking to assert his political independence of the Assyrian emperor, but for the deuteronomists the issue was simple. The sanctuaries which Josiah sought to destroy were centres of the influence of the religion of Canaan which they abhorred. Josiah's aim was to them simply religious reform whose purpose was to detach the covenant people from their involvement with Canaan. It made the temple at Jerusalem the ideal of all true Yahwist faith and practice. This accounts both for the great concentration here upon the building of the temple, and also for the theological significance that the temple came to have in the post-exilic period. ✳

THE DESCRIPTION OF THE TEMPLE

2 The house which King Solomon built for the LORD was sixty cubits long by twenty cubits broad, and its height 3 was thirty[a] cubits. The vestibule in front of the sanctuary was twenty cubits long, spanning the whole breadth of the house, while it projected ten cubits in front of the 4, 5 house; and he furnished the house with embrasures. Then he built a terrace against its wall[b] round both the sanctuary 6 and the inner shrine. He made arcades all round: the lowest arcade[c] was five cubits in depth, the middle six, and the highest seven; for he made rebates all round the outside of the main wall so that the bearer beams[d] might 7 not be set into the walls. In the building of the house, only blocks of undressed stone direct from the quarry were used; no hammer or axe or any iron tool whatever was heard in the house while it was being built.

8 The entrance to the lowest[e] arcade was in the right-hand corner of the house; there was access by a spiral

[a] *Or, with Sept.,* twenty-five.
[b] *So Sept.; Heb. adds* round the walls of the house.
[c] *So Sept.; Heb.* platform.
[d] the bearer beams: *so Targ.; Heb. om.*   [e] *So Sept.; Heb.* middle.

stairway from that to the middle arcade, and from the
middle arcade to the highest. So he built the house and 9–10
finished it, having constructed the terrace five cubits high
against the whole building, braced the house with struts
of cedar and roofed it with beams and coffering of cedar.

---

* Since Solomon wished his buildings to mark the splendour
of his reign, he naturally turned to the best and most up-to-
date builders, the Phoenicians, and the temple was built to a
Phoenician plan. From what has been learned, through
archaeology, of other temples in Syria and Palestine, we know
that Solomon's temple did follow a common pattern. It was
an oblong structure divided into three rooms. There was only
one entrance. To get to the second room one had to pass
through the first, and similarly it was necessary to pass through
the second to get to the third room. The entrance was on the
east side so that the whole complex was built on an east–west
axis.

The first room was named the *Ulam*, which has been
translated here as the vestibule. The second room was called
the *Hekal*, here translated the sanctuary. The third room, the
Debir, is called the inner shrine, or the Most Holy Place. This
is the part of the temple which has often been referred to as the
Holy of Holies, which is a literal translation of a Hebrew
idiom which expresses the superlative (cp. 'Song of Songs'
meaning 'The Best Song').

The description given of the building is not clear. It would
be impossible to reconstruct it from this description with
complete accuracy. The vestibule was on the east side of the
sanctuary. Presumably it was at least 30 cubits high although
its height is not stated. It must have been as high as the rest of
the temple, but it could very well have been higher. The
sanctuary was built out of the west wall of the vestibule. It
was 20 cubits wide, 40 cubits long and 30 cubits high. The
Most Holy Place was a continuation of the sanctuary. It was a

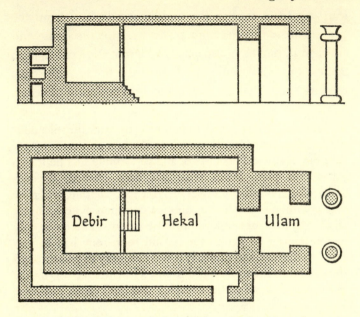

3. Père Roland de Vaux' plan of the temple. The *Ulam* is the vestibule, the *Hekal* is the sanctuary and the *Debir* is the inner shrine, or alternatively, the Most Holy Place.

perfect cube, 20 cubits long, wide and high. Its roof may have been 10 cubits lower than the roof of the sanctuary, but, more probably, there was one continuous roof and the Most Holy Place was raised from the ground 10 cubits higher than the sanctuary. This is quite high, so the figures given in the Greek version, where the Most Holy Place is said to have been 25 cubits high and thus only 5 cubits higher than the sanctuary, may well be correct.

2. The cubit was approximately 18 inches. It was the length from a man's elbow to the tip of his middle finger. So the temple was overall 150 feet long, 30 feet wide and 45 feet high.

4. High in the wall of the sanctuary, higher than the arcades

74

which were built against the wall, was a row of openings, to let light into the sanctuary. The N.E.B. calls them *embrasures*, i.e. openings cut into the stone. The Hebrew is difficult. It might mean windows covered with lattice work.

6. All around the sanctuary and the Most Holy Place were *arcades* built against the walls. They went around three sides of the building from the place on the south side where the vestibule wall began to the corresponding place on the north side. The *arcades* were built in three storeys, each storey being one cubit wider than the one beneath. The lower part of the outer side of the temple wall was made in three steps, each one cubit wide. The beams which formed the floors and roofs of the three storeys were laid on these steps and not set into the temple walls. The *arcades* provided three sets of rooms which were used as stores for temple treasures and other necessary materials. Some of the priests and other temple officials may well have lived in them. They served the same purpose as vestries do for churches.

7. This verse interrupts the narrative. It was added to the description by an editor to make clear that in the building of the temple the deuteronomic regulations were not infringed (Deut. 27: 5).

8. The position of *The entrance to the lowest arcade* is uncertain. (*lowest* is the translation of the Greek Septuagint. The Hebrew 'middle' is due to the confusion of two very similar words.) The Hebrew is ambiguous. It can mean *right-hand*, in which case the entrance was on the north side. It may equally well mean 'south', in which case the entrance was on the other side of the building. The means of communication between the arcades is also uncertain. The Hebrew word describing it is only found here in the Bible. The versions understood it to mean *a spiral stairway*, and one example of such a *stairway* in a temple has been discovered. In later Hebrew the word means 'trap door', and some have preferred that meaning here also.

10. *the terrace* may have been built to accommodate worshippers. Alternatively, it may be another reference to the

lowest of the arcades. The building was roofed with cedar *beams* placed along and across. There were thus hollow squares or rectangles between the beams, and these were covered with panels, i.e. coffered.

The temple was a comparatively small building. The great hall of the palace was much larger (cp. 7: 2). This fact has caused many scholars to describe the temple as a chapel royal (cp. Amos 7: 13), rather than the national shrine which it later became. There may be some truth in this but it can easily be exaggerated. Since the temple was built to house the Ark, it was always, from the beginning, a national shrine. It was small because its purpose was to be the home of such sacred objects as the Ark. Worship, for the most part, did not take place inside the building but in the open air, in front of the building and around it. Thus the altar of Whole Offering was set in the open air to the east of the temple. ✻

AN EDITORIAL ADDITION

11 Then the word of the LORD came to Solomon, saying,
12 'As for this house which you are building, if you are obedient to my ordinances and conform to my precepts and loyally observe all my commands, then I will fulfil my promise to you, the promise I gave to your father
13 David, and I will dwell among the Israelites and never forsake my people Israel.'

✻ This paragraph has been inserted by the editors between the account of the building of the temple and the account of its interior decoration. It is not found in the Greek versions. Its purpose is to underline once more the basic condition upon which God established David's house, namely obedience to his will. It is an example of the way in which the deuteronomists fulfilled their purpose of using the history of their people to teach moral and spiritual lessons. ✻

THE INTERIOR DECORATION OF THE TEMPLE

So Solomon built the LORD's house and finished it. He 14,15
lined the inner walls of the house with cedar boards,
covering the interior from floor to rafters[a] with wood;
the floor he laid with boards of pine. In the innermost 16
part of the house he partitioned off a space of twenty
cubits with cedar boards from floor to rafters[a] and made
of it an inner shrine, to be the Most Holy Place. The 17
sanctuary in front of this[b] was forty cubits long. The cedar 18
inside the house was carved with open flowers and
gourds; all was cedar, no stone was left visible.

He prepared an inner shrine in the furthest recesses of 19
the house to receive the Ark of the Covenant of the LORD.
[c]This inner shrine was twenty cubits square and it stood 20
twenty cubits high; he overlaid it with red gold and
made[d] an altar of cedar. And Solomon overlaid the inside 21
of the house with red gold and drew a Veil[e] with golden
chains across in front of the inner shrine.[f] The whole house 22
he overlaid with gold until it was all covered; and the
whole of the altar by the inner shrine he overlaid with
gold.

* This account of the interior decoration of the temple is
confused as is shown by repetition and confusion in the
Hebrew text. The translators have preferred the Greek text to
the Hebrew in several places and have also inserted 'the Veil' in

[a] rafters: *so Sept.; Heb.* walls.
[b] The sanctuary in front of this: *so Sept.; Heb.* The house, that is the
sanctuary, before me.
[c] *So Vulg.; Heb. prefixes* Before.
[d] *So Sept.; Heb.* overlaid.   [e] a Veil: *prob. rdg.; Heb. om.*
[f] *Prob. rdg.; Heb. adds* and overlaid it with gold.

verse 21, from 2 Chron. 3: 14, in an attempt to clarify the meaning. However, the general sense of the passage is not difficult to follow.

15. *rafters:* the Greek translators had a slightly different Hebrew word in the text they used, than the word which is now found in the Massoretic text. They read *rafters* from the Hebrew *qoroth*. The Massoretic text has *qiroth* meaning walls. In this instance the Greek translators seem to have had a more accurate text than we have.

18. *open flowers and gourds:* the versions read 'lilies' for *open flowers*, and this ancient tradition is very likely accurate. Stone decorated with lilies has been found at Megiddo. *gourds* probably refers to the egg decoration which is still in common use today.

19. *to receive the Ark of the Covenant of the LORD:* in this way the temple was linked with all the old Yahwist traditions of the tribal league which were associated with the Ark. The temple was built to a Canaanite design but its function was firmly rooted in the old Israelite traditions. It was to be the contemporary expression of the old covenant faith of Israel. There was always a danger that these traditions might be ousted from the temple. Some kings were eager to make changes which would bring the temple practices more in line with the customs of Canaan. The deuteronomic editors condemn many kings, Manasseh in particular, as religious apostates. Yet the presence of the Ark ensured that, even in the worst times, the temple could never be completely divorced from the religious tradition of Israel.

20. *red gold* means gold of the best quality. The *altar of cedar* is probably the altar referred to elsewhere as the altar of incense.

21. The Chronicler adds that *a Veil* was suspended from the *chains*. The translators have accepted that purpose for the *chains* and added *Veil* here. The Most Holy Place had also olive-wood doors; cp. verse 31.

22. *The whole house he overlaid with gold* may be an exaggera-

tion. The cedar walls of the sanctuary could have been decorated with inlaid gold. Such inlaid decoration in ivory has been
found at Samaria. ✶

THE INNER SHRINE – THE MOST HOLY PLACE

In the inner shrine he made two cherubim of wild olive, 23[a]
each ten cubits high. Each wing of the cherubim was five 24
cubits long, and from wing-tip to wing-tip was ten
cubits. Similarly the second cherub measured ten cubits; 25
the two cherubim were alike in size and shape, and each 26
ten cubits high. He put the cherubim within the shrine at 27
the furthest recesses and their wings were outspread, so
that a wing of the one cherub touched the wall on one
side and a wing of the other touched the wall on the other
side, and their other wings met in the middle; and he 28
overlaid the cherubim with gold.

✶ 23. The *two cherubim* were made from *wild olive*, a tree very
like the olive in appearance, whose fruit is not edible. From
the description of the cherubim given in Exodus (25: 18–20),
they have been shown generally as the guardians of the Ark.
However, the Exodus description is from the priestly source of
the Pentateuch which was much influenced by the religious
ideas of Babylon with which the Hebrews were in contact
during the exile. In Mesopotamia temples were guarded by
massive stone figures of winged animals. There are some
examples of carvings of such figures from Assyrian temples in
the British Museum. Such an understanding of the function of
the cherubim imposes a much later interpretation on Solomon's
work. The cherubim of his temple are to be interpeted against
a Phoenician rather than a Mesopotamian background. In
Phoenicia, as at Byblos where archaeologists have discovered

[a] *Verses 23–28: cp. 2 Chr. 3: 10–13.*

an example, winged creatures were the supporters of the royal throne. Such a function seems to fit the cherubim described here much better than that of guardians. The *two cherubim* stood with outstretched wings which filled the whole width of the inner sanctuary and provided a throne for the invisible God who had promised to make his dwelling there. In several places in the Old Testament God is described as enthroned on the cherubim (cp. Isa. 37: 16; Ps. 80: 1).

27–8. *He* probably refers to the king. It is emphasized that the cherubim were not made within the temple but put there when finished. ✻

MORE DETAILS

29 Round all the walls of the house he carved figures of cherubim, palm-trees, and open flowers, both in the inner
30 chamber*a* and in the outer. The floor of the house he overlaid with gold, both in the inner chamber*a* and in
31 the outer. At the entrance to the inner shrine he made a double door of wild olive; the pilasters and the*b* door-posts
32 were pentagonal.*c* The doors were of wild olive, and he carved cherubim, palms, and open flowers on them, over-laying them with gold and hammering the gold upon the
33 cherubim and the palms. Similarly for the doorway of the
34 sanctuary he made a square*d* frame of wild olive and a double door of pine, each leaf having two swivel-
35 pins. On them he carved cherubim, palms, and open flowers, overlaying them evenly with gold over the carving.

36   He built the inner court with three courses of dressed stone and one course of lengths of cedar.

[*a*] inner chamber: *so Sept.; Heb*. inwards.
[*b*] and the: *prob. rdg.; Heb. om.*
[*c*] *So Sept.; Heb*. fifth.   [*d*] *So Sept.; Heb*. from with a fourth...

* 29-30. These details have been regarded generally as later
additions to the narrative and of doubtful historical vaue. The
overlaying of the temple floor with gold probably grew out of
the later traditions of the splendour of Solomon's temple.

30. *both in the inner chamber and in the outer* understands the
description to be of the decoration of the inner walls of both
the inner shrine and the sanctuary. This is not certain. The
Hebrew simply reads 'both inside and outside', which could
mean that the decoration was on the inside and outside of the
wall of the inner shrine. Many temples were decorated in this
fashion but much of the outside wall of Solomon's temple was
obscured by the arcades, so the N.E.B. interpretation is more
likely.

31. This description of the door is an attempt to make sense
of a corrupt Hebrew text. A picture of a similar door has been
found at Byblos, though the picture is from a later period. It
was a common custom to cover doors with decoration of
precious metal.

34-5. The door into *the sanctuary* had an horizontal lintel. It
was a large double door with each leaf folding so that only
part of the door need be opened on ordinary occasions.

36. *the inner court* was the open space in front of the temple
where worshippers gathered. *three courses of dressed stone and
one course of lengths of cedar* seems to be a description of the
method of building. It was also used for the walls (cp. 7: 12),
and in the second temple which was built after the return from
exile (Ezra 6: 4). Evidence of such a method of building has
been found in many places in the Middle East. The purpose of
the timber could have been to bond the stones together and so
minimize the effects of earthquakes. *

THE FORMAL RECORD

In the fourth year of Solomon's reign the foundation of 37
the house of the LORD was laid, in the month of Ziv; and 38
in the eleventh year, in the month of Bul, which is the

eighth month, the house was finished in all its details according to the specification. It had taken seven years to build.

✻ This is probably the original notice of the completion of the temple. The date given above in verse I was added later. The old Canaanite names of the months are used here. *Ziv* means month of flowers, and *Bul* (October–November) month of great rain. *which is the eighth month* was added when the old names for the months had been forgotten after the exile. ✻

SOLOMON'S PALACE

7 Solomon had been engaged on his building for thirteen
2 years by the time he had finished it. He built the House of the Forest of Lebanon, a hundred cubits long, fifty broad, and thirty high, constructed of four rows of cedar
3 columns, over which were laid lengths of cedar. It had a cedar roof, extending over the beams, which rested on the columns, fifteen in each row; and the number of the
4 beams was forty-five. There were three rows of window-frames, and the windows corresponded to each other at
5 three levels. All the doorways and the windows[a] had square frames, and window corresponded to window at three levels.
6   He made also the colonnade, fifty cubits long and thirty broad,[b] with a cornice above.
7   He built the Hall of Judgement, the hall containing the throne where he was to give judgement; this was panelled in cedar from floor to rafters.[c]

[a] So Sept.; Heb. door-posts.
[b] Prob. rdg.; Heb. adds and a colonnade and pillars in front of them.
[c] rafters: so Vulg.; Heb. floor.

His own house where he was to reside, in[a] a court set 8
back from the colonnade, and the house he made for
Pharaoh's daughter whom he had married, were constructed like the hall.

All these were made of heavy blocks of stone, hewn to 9
measure and trimmed with the saw on the inner and outer
sides, from foundation to coping and from the court of
the house[b] as far as the great court. At the base were heavy 10
stones, massive blocks, some ten and some eight cubits in
size, and above were heavy stones dressed to measure, and 11
cedar. The great court had three courses of dressed stone 12
all around and a course of lengths of cedar; so had the
inner court of the house of the LORD, and so had the
vestibule of the house.

* We are told so little about the palace that we do not know
just how the buildings were related to each other. There may
well have been other buildings in the complex which are not
mentioned here.

1. *his building* was the royal palace. Such palaces were not
one building but a whole complex. The palace built at
Samaria by Omri only a century later occupied five acres.
thirteen years for the building is not excessive. The editor
understood the two notices of length of building time given
for the temple and the palace to run consecutively since in
9: 10 he has added them together. In spite of this, the temple
and palace may have been built together with the palace
taking longer to complete than the temple.

2–5. *the House of the Forest of Lebanon* took its name from its
wooden pillars. The N.E.B. translation gives a clear picture,
but at the cost of some interpretation. Four rows of *cedar*

[a] *So Arabic version; Heb. om.*
[b] *Prob. rdg., cp. verse 12; Heb. from outside.*

83

columns add up to more than forty-five. The Greek versions have three rows of columns. The N.E.B. has solved the problem by making the number forty-five refer to beams, but this is a conjecture. The meaning of the Hebrew is uncertain. Two of the rows of columns were probably placed against the stone walls with the other two running through the centre of the building so that the building had three long aisles. There may have been second and third floors in some parts of the side aisles, hence the need for windows. No clue is given as to the use to which the building was put. A judgement hall has been suggested, but a store house is more probable.

6. The measurements given suggest that *the colonnade* was built in front of the House of the Forest of Lebanon, but this is not certain. The Hebrew translated in the footnote seems to mean that there was a smaller colonnade in front of the large one, but such an arrangement seems very unlikely.

7. No dimensions are given for *the Hall of Judgement*. It may have been a part of the House of the Forest of Lebanon, or attached to the rear of that building at the opposite end to *the colonnade*. The king still at this time fulfilled his function of dispensing justice to his subjects in public.

8. *His own house* was the private part of the palace. The public part has been described already. *Pharaoh's daughter* is singled out for mention as the most distinguished of his wives (cp. 3: 1).

9. This emphasizes the quality and splendour of Solomon's building. The change from the Hebrew, which is given in the footnote, is necessary since the Hebrew is unintelligible. ✳

THE APPOINTMENTS FOR THE TEMPLE

13, 14   King Solomon fetched from Tyre Hiram, the son of a widow of the tribe of Naphtali. His father, a native of Tyre, had been a worker in bronze, and he himself was a man of great skill and ingenuity, versed in every kind of craftsmanship in bronze. Hiram came to King Solomon and executed all his works.

He cast in a mould the two bronze pillars. One stood 15[a] eighteen cubits high and it took a cord twelve cubits long to go round it; it was hollow, and the metal was four fingers thick.[b] The second pillar was the same.[c] He made 16 two capitals of solid copper to set on the tops of the pillars, each capital five cubits high. He made two[d] bands of 17 ornamental network, in festoons of chain-work, for the capitals on the tops of the pillars, a band of network[e] for each capital. Then he made pomegranates[f] in two rows 18 all round on top of the ornamental network of the one pillar;[g] he did the same with the other capital. (The 19 capitals at the tops of the pillars in the vestibule were shaped like lilies and were four cubits high.) Upon the 20 capitals at the tops of the two pillars, immediately above the cushion, which was beyond the network upwards, were two hundred pomegranates in rows all round on the two capitals.[h] Then he erected the pillars at the vestibule of 21 the sanctuary. When he had erected the pillar on the right side, he named it Jachin;[i] and when he had erected the one on the left side, he named it Boaz.[j] On the tops of the pillars 22 was lily-work. Thus the work of the pillars was finished.

He then made the Sea of cast metal; it was round in 23[k]

[a] *Verses 15–21: cp. 2 Chr. 3: 15–17.*
[b] it was...thick: *prob. rdg., cp. Jer. 52: 21; Heb. om.*
[c] the same: *so Sept.; Heb. om.*   [d] He made two: *so Sept.; Heb. om.*
[e] a band of network: *so Sept.; Heb.* seven.
[f] *So some MSS.; others* pillars.
[g] *So Sept.; Heb. adds* to cover the capitals on the top of the pomegranates.   [h] the two capitals: *prob. rdg.; Heb.* the second capital.
[i] *Or* Jachun, *meaning* It shall stand.
[j] *Or* Booz, *meaning* In strength.   [k] *Verses 23–26: cp. 2 Chr. 4: 2–5.*

shape, the diameter from rim to rim being ten cubits; it
stood five cubits high, and it took a line thirty cubits long
24 to go round it. All round the Sea on the outside under its
rim, completely surrounding the thirty[a] cubits of its
circumference, were two rows of gourds, cast in one
25 piece with the Sea itself. It was mounted on twelve oxen,
three facing north, three west, three south, and three east,
their hind quarters turned inwards; the Sea rested on top of
26 them. Its thickness was a hand-breadth; its rim was made
like that of a cup, shaped like the calyx of a lily; it held
two thousand bath of water.

27   He also made the ten trolleys of bronze; each trolley
28 was four cubits long, four wide, and three high. This was
the construction of the trolleys. They had panels set in
29 frames; on these panels were portrayed lions, oxen, and
cherubim, and similarly on the frames. Above and below
the lions, oxen, and cherubim[b] were fillets of hammered
30 work of spiral design. Each trolley had four bronze
wheels with axles of bronze; it also had four flanges and
handles beneath the laver, and these handles were of cast
31 metal with a spiral design on their sides. The opening for
the basin was set within a crown which projected one
cubit; the opening was round with a level edge,[c] and it
had decorations in relief. (The panels of the trolleys were
32 square, not round.) The four wheels were beneath the
panels, and the wheel-forks were made in one piece with the
33 trolleys; the height of each wheel was a cubit and a half. The
wheels were constructed like those of a chariot, their axles,
34 hubs, spokes, and felloes being all of cast metal. The four

[a] Prob. rdg.; Heb. ten.   [b] and cherubim: prob. rdg.; Heb. om.
[c] Prob. rdg.; Heb. adds a cubit and a half (cp. verse 32).

handles were at the four corners of each trolley, of one
piece with the trolley. At the top of the trolley there was 35
a circular band half a cubit high; the struts and panels
on*a* the trolley were of one piece with it. On the plates, 36
that is on the panels,*b* he carved cherubim, lions, and palm-
trees, wherever there was blank space, with spiral work all
round it. This is how the ten trolleys were made; all of them 37
were cast alike, having the same size and the same shape.

He then made ten bronze basins, each holding forty 38
bath and measuring four cubits; there was a basin for
each of the ten trolleys. He put five trolleys on the right 39
side of the house and five on the left side; and he put the
Sea in the south-east corner of it.

Hiram made also the pots,*c* the shovels, and the tossing- 40*d*
bowls. So he finished all the work which he had undertaken for King Solomon on the house of the LORD: the 41
two pillars; the two bowl-shaped capitals on the tops of the
pillars; the two ornamental networks to cover the two
bowl-shaped capitals on the tops of the pillars; the four 42
hundred pomegranates for the two networks, two rows of
pomegranates for each network, to cover the bowl-
shaped capitals on the two*e* pillars; the ten trolleys and the 43
ten basins on the trolleys; the one Sea and the twelve oxen 44
which supported it; the pots, the shovels, and the tossing- 45
bowls – all these objects in the house of the LORD which
Hiram made for King Solomon being of bronze, burnished
work. In the Plain of the Jordan the king cast them, in 46
the foundry between Succoth and Zarethan.

[a] *Prob. rdg.; Heb. adds* the head of.
[b] *Prob. rdg.; Heb. adds* its struts.   [c] *So many MSS.; others* basins.
[d] *Verses 40–51: cp. 2 Chr. 4: 11 – 5: 1.*
[e] two: *so Sept.; Heb.* surface of.

✳ 13–14. *Hiram* is named Huram in Chronicles (2 Chron. 2:13). There his mother is said to have been a Danite. The tribes of Dan and Naphtali both lived on the northern borders of Israel so that the confusion is natural. The Hebrew words underlying *skill, ingenuity* and *craftsmanship* would, in another context, be translated 'wisdom', 'understanding' and 'knowledge'. This is another example of the very practical way in which the Hebrews understood wisdom (cp. Exod. 31: 2–6).

15–22. *the two bronze pillars:* the description is confused. The N.E.B. has used the versions and a description of the pillars in the last chapter of Jeremiah to construct a clear picture. A second description occurs later in the chapter, verses 41–2.

20. The cushions could have been meant to catch embers from a fire burning on the top of the pillar. The literal translation of the Hebrew is 'belly', hence the R.S.V.'s 'rounded projection'.

21. The two pillars were free-standing before the doors of *the vestibule*. Their precise significance is not known, though several examples of such pillars placed before temples have been brought to light by archaeologists. Upright stone pillars, called *mazzeboth*, were used as religious objects by the Israelites from the time of the settlement in Canaan, and perhaps even before that time. These bronze pillars may be the successors of such symbols. If so, they obviously follow Canaanite patterns. In Canaan they may have been linked with fertility cults. Decoration with pomegranates is a prominent feature and that particular fruit, with its multitude of seeds, was used as a symbol of fertility. Such decoration, though, does no more than indicate cultural origins. Of much greater importance and significance was the function of the pillars. We do not know what their purpose was. Various suggestions have been made, but none is wholly convincing. A fire may have been kept burning on the tops of the pillars. An attractive suggestion is that the fire was used to link the temple more firmly with the Exodus tradition, the pillars symbolizing the 'pillars of flame by night and smoke by day'. *Jachin* and *Boaz:* these may have

been names of gods which by this time had become attached
to such pillars by tradition in Canaan. *Jachin* means 'he
establishes', and 'Baal az' means 'Baal is strong'. The second
name would have been modified into Hebrew words which
ignored the offensive Canaanite name, Baal. Thus *Boaz* means
'in him is strength'. Alternatively, the words may simply be
the names given to the pillars by the Phoenician artist who
made them, to show pride in his work; *Jachin*, 'it is solid', and
Boaz 'with strength'.

23–6. *the Sea* stood outside the temple in the court. Its
function is not given. Possibly it provided water for the ritual
washing of those who entered the temple. Such washing, real
or symbolic, is a feature of many religions. It is practised by
both Muslims and Jews. For Christians baptism has an obvious
affinity. Again it is function which determines significance
and not decoration. The decoration of the Sea was clearly
derived from Phoenicia, but that does not in itself mean that
the Sea is evidence of Canaanite religious practices being
carried on in the temple. Those who would argue so have
pointed out that the bull is the symbol of the god Baal, and
they would link the Sea with the creation myth of the defeat
of the primeval waters.

27–39. The description of *the ten trolleys of bronze* and the
ten bronze basins contains several difficult Hebrew technical
terms the precise meaning of which is not known. The
translators' task has been greatly eased by the discovery of two
such trolleys during archaeological excavations in Cyprus at
Enkomi and Larnaka. Each trolley carried one of the basins.
Their purpose was to ensure ready access to water by all
worshippers. The sacrificial rites made washing, of the
worshippers, of the instruments used during sacrifice, and of
the temple precincts, very necessary.

40. *the pots* were used to remove fat and ashes from the altar
(cp. Exod. 27: 3), as were *the shovels. the tossing-bowls* were
used for sprinkling blood on the altar and on the worshippers
(Lev. 7: 14).

89

46. The casting was done in the lower Jordan valley because of the quantities of clay there which was used as moulds. The N.E.B. has paraphrased 'clay ground' as *foundry*. Copper was mined from the escarpment on the east side of the Arabah, the continuation of the rift valley south of the Dead Sea (see map 4 on p. 119). The precise site of *Succoth and Zarethan* is not known. *Succoth* means booths or tents. It could refer to a temporary settlement set up while the foundry was being worked. ✻

THE FURNISHINGS FOR THE TEMPLE

47 Solomon put all these objects in their places; so great was the quantity of bronze used in their making that the

48 weight of it was beyond all reckoning. He made also all the furnishings for the house of the LORD: the golden altar and the golden table upon which was set the Bread of the

49 Presence; the lamp-stands of red gold, five on the right side and five on the left side of the inner shrine; the

50 flowers, lamps, and tongs, of gold; the cups, snuffers, tossing-bowls, saucers, and firepans, of red gold; and the panels for the doors of the inner sanctuary, the Most Holy Place, and for the doors of the house,[a] of gold.

51 When all the work which King Solomon did for the house of the LORD was completed, he brought in the sacred treasures of his father David, the silver, the gold, and the vessels, and deposited them in the storehouses of the house of the LORD.

✻ 48–50. The description of the golden objects is in marked contrast with what has gone before about the bronze objects. It is a bald summary only. For this reason and because the

[a] *Prob. rdg.; Heb. adds* for the temple.

golden altar and the golden table are more fully described in
the priestly account of the temple ornaments given in Exodus
(30: 1–10 and 25: 23–30 respectively), it has been suggested
that this paragraph is a later addition to the narrative added to
bring it into line with the account in Exodus. The argument is
far from decisive. This passage contains the only reference to
ten lamp-stands.

48. *the golden altar* is probably the same ornament as the
cedar altar referred to earlier. It was gold in the sense of being
overlaid with gold. This was the altar of incense which stood
within the sanctuary. *the golden table* was also made of wood
overlaid with gold. *the Bread of the Presence:* a number of
loaves of bread, in later times twelve, were always laid upon it
as an offering to God. The Priestly account is in Lev. 24: 5–9.
This custom was in origin a cereal offering. It formed a part of
the worship of Israel before the temple was built (cp. 1 Sam.
21: 4), and was brought to the temple along with the Ark to
attach the old pre-monarchical religious customs of Israel to the
temple. The custom came to be associated with the Exodus
deliverance, and so symbolized the manna with which God
fed the people in the wilderness.

49. *the lamp-stands:* in the book of Exodus only one lamp-
stand, always described as a candelabra, is mentioned. This is
the Menorah, the seven-branched candelabra, of the second
temple. *the flowers* refers to decoration on the base of the lamp-
stands. *the tongs* were probably used at the altar of incense.

50. *the cups* and *saucers* could be used for incense, or for the
oil for the lamps, which were not candles but lighted wicks in,
or connected to, bowls of oil. *the panels for the doors:* in other
translations the doors have golden hinges or sockets. This
disagreement is due to a Hebrew word of uncertain meaning.
Hinge has been accepted because the versions so interpreted
the word. But golden hinges are thoroughly unpractical because of the softness of the metal. A recent suggestion,
accepted by the N.E.B., is *panels* linking the Hebrew word with
an Accadian word meaning 'forehead'.

51. *the sacred treasures of his father David:* kings at this time frequently took gold and silver vessels and ornaments from the temples of defeated enemies, and melted them down into bullion. David had sometimes done this, and also received vessels from kings as tribute (2 Sam. 8: 9–12).

No mention has been made in the description of the temple furnishings of the altar of sacrifice. We know such an altar stood in the court outside the temple in later times (2 Kings 16: 14), and there is no reason to doubt that there was an altar of sacrifice in Solomon's day. It may be that the great rock on the top of the hill was at first used as the altar of sacrifice. If so, we do not know when a bronze altar was substituted. Perhaps a bronze altar was placed on the stone. This great stone still remained after all the destruction. It projected through the surface of the paved floor of the temple that Herod the Great built. This surface is still today the floor of the temple area, though the temple area is now a Muslim shrine, the Haram es-Sherif. The great rock is now covered by a domed building, the Dome of the Rock, and is a place of pilgrimage for Moslems. *

THE DEDICATION OF THE TEMPLE

* This account of the dedication has been put together long after the event by an editor of the deuteronomic school.

THE ARK IS BROUGHT TO THE TEMPLE

8 1[a] Then Solomon summoned the elders of Israel, all the heads of the tribes who were chiefs of families in Israel, to assemble in Jerusalem, in order to bring up the Ark of the Covenant of the LORD from the City of David, which 2 is called Zion. All the men of Israel assembled in King Solomon's presence at the pilgrim-feast in the month

[a] *Verses 1–9: cp. 2 Chr. 5: 2–10.*

Ethanim, the seventh month. When the elders of Israel 3
had all come, the priests took the Ark of the LORD and 4
carried it up with the Tent of the Presence and all the
sacred furnishings of the Tent: it was the priests and the
Levites together who carried them up. King Solomon 5
and the whole congregation of Israel, assembled with
him before the Ark, sacrificed sheep and oxen in numbers
past counting or reckoning. Then the priests brought in 6
the Ark of the Covenant of the LORD to its place, the
inner shrine of the house, the Most Holy Place, beneath
the wings of the cherubim. The cherubim spread their 7
wings over the place of the Ark; they formed a screen
above the Ark and its poles. The poles projected, and their 8
ends could be seen from the Holy Place immediately in
front of the inner shrine, but from nowhere else outside;
they are there to this day. There was nothing inside the 9
Ark but the two tablets of stone which Moses had deposited there at Horeb, the tablets of the covenant[a] which
the LORD made with the Israelites when they left Egypt.

✻ 1. *the Ark of the Covenant of the LORD* was a box made of
acacia wood. It was the old religious symbol which represented
the presence of God with the tribes. In the past it had been
carried out to war in the battles of the tribal league against the
Philistines. It was the portable religious sanctuary of a nomadic
people. It had probably always contained a sacred stone which
in the earliest times was thought to be the dwelling of God.
Jacob at Bethel set up a similar stone (Gen. 28: 18). Later the
stone in *the Ark* came to be linked with the two stone tablets
upon which the Ten Commandments were believed to have
been written at Mount Sinai. In this way the early religious

[a] the tablets of the covenant: *so Sep.; Heb. om.*

customs of the people were given new meaning, and the tribal league became the inheritor of the theological tradition of the Sinai Covenant. The bringing of the Ark to the temple was meant to add one further link to this chain. The temple and with it the house of David were now also joined to the Sinai Covenant tradition.

2. *the pilgrim-feast* was a festival during which all Israelites came to Jerusalem and lived in temporary wooden shelters, the booths as they have become known in tradition. In later times this became an annual feast. On the occasion of the dedication of the temple, the people could have come specifically for that purpose. Alternatively, a *pilgrim-feast* could have been celebrated already for some years at Jerusalem ever since the Ark had been kept there. In that case the devotion of the people was to the place where the Ark was kept, and Solomon cleverly used this to unite in their affection and loyalty the Ark, which represented the old tribal traditions of Israel, and the temple which represented the newer traditions of monarchy. *Ethanim* possibly means 'regular flowing' and was the name of the month of the autumn rains. *the seventh month* has been added to make the meaning clear at a later time when the Babylonian calendar was used. The Babylonian year began in the spring and the month of the autumn rain was then the seventh month. The Babylonians called it 'Tishri'. The dedication may have taken place in the same year that the temple was completed, or in the following year. Earlier it has been written that the temple was completed in 'the eighth month' (6: 38). Either the dedication was regarded as the act which completed the temple, or it followed eleven months after the completion. If the latter is what happened, then the dedication was postponed until the great Autumn Feast, the Feast of Succoth or Tabernacles. In Canaan the Autumn Feast marked the New Year, and it may be that the Israelites also regarded it as the beginning of the year.

4. *the Tent of the Presence* had housed the Ark. A Tent of the Presence, where Israelites could go to commune with God,

is mentioned in Exodus (cp. 33: 7-11), but not in connection with the Ark. *the Levites* were only employed in the temple after the time of Solomon. They did all the work except those duties which belonged to the priests. The deuteronomists were well disposed to the Levites, and giving them a place at the dedication of the temple was meant to support their authority.

8. This seems to mean that the doors of the *Most Holy Place* were kept open so that a worshipper looking in could see the ends of *the poles*. Were the Ark and the cherubim then hidden by a veil through which *the poles* projected? *they are there to this day* is another indication that this narrative was written long after Solomon's death. *this day* is the time of the deuter-onomists.

9. *Horeb* is the name always used by the deuteronomists for Sinai. ✻

SOLOMON'S FIRST PRAYER

Then the priests came out of the Holy Place, since the 10
cloud was filling the house of the LORD, and they could 11
not continue to minister because of it, for the glory of the
LORD filled his house. And Solomon said: 12[a]

> O LORD who hast set the sun in heaven,[b]
>   but hast chosen to dwell in thick darkness,
> here have I built thee a lofty house,   13
>   a habitation for thee to occupy for ever.

✻ 10. God showed his acceptance of Solomon's offering by taking possession of the temple. The outward sign of the divine presence was *the cloud*. In the wilderness days, when Moses entered the 'Tent of the Presence' to commune with God the pillar of cloud stood at the door of the tent (Exod. 33: 9). Later, when Moses had completed the tabernacle, the

[a] *Verses 12-50: cp. 2 Chr. 6: 1-39.*
[b] O LORD...heaven: *so Sept.; Heb. om.*

cloud covered it and the glory of God filled it (Exod. 40: 34). These descriptions from the book of Exodus may have been written later than this narrative – they belong to the priestly source – but they do witness to the consistent Israelite tradition which used the cloud symbolism. A further example is found in the passage in the book of Ezekiel which describes the prophet's vision of the new temple which would replace Solomon's temple after the return from exile (Ezek. 43). In the New Testament, at the Transfiguration, Jesus was over-shadowed by the cloud of the divine presence from which God spoke (Mark 9: 7 and cp. 2 Pet. 1: 17).

11. *the glory of the LORD:* cloud was the symbol of the divine presence. The word which was used to express that presence theologically was glory. Glory when used of a man referred to the outward signs which gave a true indication of his inner character, as the splendour and trappings which indicated the power and strength of a great king. In the same way *the glory of the LORD* was the outward indication of his presence and his nature.

12–13. The poetry is old and may well have been spoken by Solomon. The Greek version adds that it was taken from an old written source, 'The Book of the Song'. (This may be a reference to 'The Book of Jashar' (cp. Josh. 10: 13 and 2 Sam. 1: 18). The Hebrew word for 'song' has the consonants *sh.y.r.* while Jashar has *y.sh.r.* Thus the Greek translators may have misunderstood or misread Jashar as 'song'.) It appears to be a fragment of a longer poem. The first line has been added from the Greek version; it is not found in the Hebrew. The words of the poem reject the theological ideas expressed in Canaan by temple worship. Solomon's temple may have been designed and built by Phoenician craftsmen, but the religion it was meant to serve, and the theological ideas it expressed, differed sharply from those expressed in the temples of Canaan. Yahweh was not to be thought of as a fertility God, and it was not the purpose of the temple to express him as such. The first two lines of the poem imply a great contrast in nature between Yahweh and the gods of Canaan. *the sun* was one of the most important symbols of fertility. It was the warmth and light of the sun which drew life from the fields, and the dry burning heat of the sun also brought death. So *the sun* seemed to be all-powerful and in control of life and death. Yet Solomon here asserts that Yahweh *hast set the sun in heaven*. Yahweh is thus the creator of the universe, and even the sun was only one of his creatures. Nor did Yahweh have his dwelling with the sun. He has *chosen to dwell in thick darkness*. The words may refer directly to the dark inner shrine that Solomon had built at the heart of his temple, and within which the Ark rested. But it was also the thick darkness of *the cloud*. Sun and cloud are placed in the sharpest contrast with each other. The sun drives away the cloud, and the cloud in its turn obscures the light and heat of the sun. This may be the reason why cloud was used so consistently in the Israelite tradition to express the presence of God. It both linked the divine presence with the revelation at Sinai, and also contrasted it with Canaanite ideas of divinity.

The God who was taking up his residence in the temple was in full control of the forces of nature and cared for the material well-being of his people. His nature was expressed by the covenant demand he made upon his people and his dwelling with them was conditional upon their ready response to those demands. So his glory was expressed by *the cloud* reminiscent of the exodus, rather than by the brightness of the sun's light. *

THE PRAYER OF DEDICATION

* Solomon, as king, dedicated the temple. It may seem odd that the dedication was not performed by a priest. The reason is that in Solomon's day the king was a priestly figure. He was often looked upon as the nation's chief priest. He represented his people both to God and to other nations, and, through him and his rule, the blessings of God were experienced by the people. So Solomon, as king, offered the temple

97

as a dwelling place for God among his people. The various aspects of the life of a community were far less departmental-ized in those days than now, because life was much simpler and society less complex. The king was leader of the nation in every aspect of its life, and its well-being and prosperity depended directly on his energy and personal characteristics. In such circumstances, it was natural that the king should also represent the people to God and act as the national priest. All this is so whether or not the king took part in the rituals of a fertility cult as did the Canaanite kings. There is no direct evidence that such royal fertility cults were ever practised in the temple by Solomon or by any of his successors. Those who have claimed that such religious rites did take place in Israel have argued that the Jerusalem temple was meant to serve the same function as the Canaanite temples. There is no direct evidence to support such theories, only inference. On the other hand, there is much evidence to indicate that many Canaanite religious customs and ideas were always regarded as alien to Israel by the most influential civil and religious rulers. So if Solomon represented his people before God, the manner of that representation was controlled by the nature of the God he served, and those covenant demands of God which formed the spiritual ideals of the people. Yahweh was not bound to his people by the powers of nature but by the moral and spiritual force of the covenant.

The prayer of dedication can be divided into three parts: the address to the people, verses 14–21; the prayer proper, verses 22–53; the blessing, verses 54–61. The first two sections are paralleled almost exactly in Chronicles (2 Chron. 6: 3–42). The whole prayer is a production of the deutero-nomist editors, though they had some earlier pieces of writing which they incorporated into their work. The contra-diction about Solomon's standing or kneeling for prayer points to this (cp. verse 22 and verse 54). Even stronger evidence is the indication that one part of the prayer was written at a time when Israel was a self-governing monarchy,

and another part when the people were suffering in exile
(cp. verses 44–5 and verses 46–7). There is no indication anywhere that the temple had been destroyed as could be expected
in words written after the destruction of Jerusalem in 587 B.C.
So the references to exile may refer to the northern Israelites
who were taken to exile after the destruction of Samaria in
721 B.C. The prayer is filled with deuteronomic theology and
this with the references to later events makes it impossible to
believe that Solomon spoke it. Yet the content of the prayer
expresses admirably the finest spiritual aspirations of all those
in Israel who were most loyal to Yahwism. It can thus be read
as a statement of the spiritual value which the temple came to
have in the faith of Israel. ✷

THE ADDRESS TO THE PEOPLE

And as they stood waiting, the king turned round and 14
blessed all the assembly of Israel in these words: 'Blessed 15
be the LORD the God of Israel who spoke directly to my
father David and has himself fulfilled his promise. For he
said, "From the day when I brought my people Israel out 16
of Egypt, I chose no city out of all the tribes of Israel
where I should build a house for my Name to be there,
but[a] I chose David to be over my people Israel." My father 17
David had in mind to build a house in honour of the name
of the LORD the God of Israel, but the LORD said to him, 18
"You purposed to build a house in honour of my name;
and your purpose was good. Nevertheless, you shall not 19
build it; but the son who is to be born to you, he shall
build the house in honour of my name." The LORD has 20
now fulfilled his promise: I have succeeded my father

[c] *2 Chr. 6: 6 and Sept. add* I chose Jerusalem for my Name to be there,
and...

David and taken his place on the throne of Israel, as the
LORD promised; and I have built the house in honour of
21 the name of the LORD the God of Israel. I have assigned
therein a place for the Ark containing the Covenant of
the LORD, which he made with our forefathers when he
brought them out of Egypt.'

☆ 15. Solomon rehearsed once more the reasons which had
led him to build the temple. They were based upon God's
promise to David which is set out in 2 Sam. 7. God has built a
house (i.e. dynasty) for David in Solomon. Therefore Solomon was duty bound to build a house (i.e. temple) for God.

16. *a house for my Name* is typically deuteronomic language.
Names were believed both to reveal and express character, so
where God's Name was there he dwelt. For God's dwelling
with men the first essential was not a place but a person who
responded in obedient love. So God chose David (see note on
5: 3).

The Septuagint, with Chronicles, links Jerusalem with
David. For the deuteronomists the two were always closely
linked. The capture of Jerusalem, and the setting up of the
kingdom that followed, were the blessings that God conferred
on David for his obedience.

21. *a place for the Ark:* this underlines the emphasis laid upon
the covenant tradition. As the home of the Ark, the temple
was the shrine which both declared and demanded the obedience of the whole people to God's will. ☆

THE PRAYER PROPER: I. GOD'S PROMISE

22 Then Solomon, standing in front of the altar of the
LORD in the presence of the whole assembly of Israel,
23 spread out his hands towards heaven and said, 'O LORD
God of Israel, there is no god like thee in heaven above or

on earth beneath, keeping covenant with thy servants and
showing them constant love while they continue faithful
to thee in heart and soul. Thou hast kept thy promise to 24
thy servant David my father; by thy deeds this day thou
hast fulfilled what thou didst say to him in words. Now 25
therefore, O LORD God of Israel, keep this promise of
thine to thy servant David my father: "You shall never
want for a man appointed by me to sit on the throne of
Israel, if only your sons look to their ways and walk
before me as you have walked before me." And now, 26
O God of Israel, let the words which thou didst speak to
thy servant David my father be confirmed.'

☆ 22. *the altar of the LORD* is the altar of Whole-Offering
which stood in the courtyard in front of the temple. *spread out
his hands:* the normal posture for prayer.

23. The prayer rightly begins with thanksgiving. Prayer in
the Old Testament generally starts from gratitude to God for
what he has done. *there is no god like thee:* God always demanded from his people their exclusive loyalty. He would not
share their worship with other gods. To do so would have
meant a dilution of the quality of spiritual response which he
demanded. So the loyal Israelite was always in practice a
monotheist, even when he could in theory acknowledge the
existence of other gods. The prayer faithfully expresses this
attitude. Yahweh has generously supplied for his people all
that could be demanded of a god. So he was for his people the
only God. This characteristic of Israelite worship is what is
meant when Yahweh is called a 'jealous God'. It led in time
inevitably to a fully monotheistic faith. *constant love* translates
the Hebrew word *ḥesed* which describes the unique relationship established between God and his people. It is a concept
which no single word can adequately define. What it meant
can perhaps best be described as the loyal fulfilment of the

obligations of a relationship which has been freely accepted. It describes, therefore, all that keeping covenant means. God showed *constant love* as he was loyal to the covenant relationship which he had initiated with Israel. Israel showed *constant love* as the people responded to God with a loyal and willing obedience to all the requirements of the covenant pattern of life.

25. *You shall never want for a man:* the initiative in covenant always lay with God. God would constantly renew covenant by ensuring that David's house never failed for lack of an heir: David's house would respond as successive kings ruled in the manner which *constant love* demanded (cp. Ps. 89). ✳

2. SOLOMON'S PETITION

27 'But can God indeed dwell on earth? Heaven itself, the highest heaven, cannot contain thee; how much less this
28 house that I have built! Yet attend to the prayer and the supplication of thy servant, O LORD my God, listen to the
29 cry and the prayer which thy servant utters this day, that thine eyes may ever be upon this house night and day, this place of which thou didst say, "My Name shall be there"; so mayest thou hear thy servant when he prays towards
30 this place. Hear the supplication of thy servant and of thy people Israel when they pray towards this place. Hear thou in heaven thy dwelling and, when thou hearest, forgive.'

✳ 27. *But can God indeed dwell on earth?:* the prayer shows acute awareness of the problem of thinking of God dwelling permanently in any one place. God was not to be thought of as being present in the temple in any sense which implied that he was absent from the rest of the world. God cannot be circumscribed, only approached. Our relationships with him are

essentially personal. Yet God has accepted the limitation of an
earthly dwelling place because human beings need to meet
him in a particular place in order that they may become aware
of his presence in every place. Our understanding moves from
the particular to the general, and not the other way round. So
God truly dwelt in the temple. Israel, in the person of the king,
could meet him there and offer prayer. Israel would be met
there by God in all the fullness of understanding which the
need for forgiveness implies (verse 30).

Here the most important principle of the in-dwelling of God
among his people is established. It is a principle which could
be misused, as when Jeremiah had to rebuke the people of
Jerusalem of his day because of their superstitious belief that
their city could never be captured by an enemy because God
dwelt in the temple (Jer. 7: 1–15). The people had to learn in
the hard school of experience what is expressed here: that God's
presence only brings blessing to those who respond to him
with 'constant love'. For all others God's presence means
inevitable judgement. Ezekiel expressed this in his way by
describing God removing his presence from the temple before
the city of Jerusalem was destroyed (Ezek. 10: 18–19 and
11: 23–5). But the judgement of destruction was not the last
word. Ezekiel looked forward to the time when the temple
would be rebuilt and God would return to dwell there among
a consecrated people (Ezek. 43: 1–9). In the New Testament
the body of Jesus is spoken of as the temple (John 2: 19–21),
for it is there that God was believed to have come to dwell,
while in the vision of the new Jerusalem in 'The Revelation of
John' that city has no temple because God dwells in the whole
of it (Rev. 21: 22).

29. *My Name shall be there:* see comment on 5: 3 and 8: 16.

30. *when thou hearest, forgive:* the prayer continues in a litany
asking for God's help in the sufferings which will come upon
his people. These sufferings are understood as the proper
consequences of the sin of the people. Yet the presence of God
means that the sin which leads to suffering can also be followed

by repentance which leads to forgiveness and restoration. The initiative of God is not shown only in his original creation of the covenant, but also in his willingness to restore its benefits to a people who, though penitent, have in strict justice put themselves outside its scope. ✻

3. FORGIVENESS

31 'When a man wrongs his neighbour and he is adjured to take an oath, and the adjuration is made before thy altar
32 in this house, then do thou hear in heaven and act: be thou thy servants' judge, condemning the guilty man and bringing his deeds upon his own head, acquitting the innocent and rewarding him as his innocence may deserve.

33   'When thy people Israel are defeated by an enemy because they have sinned against thee, and they turn back to thee, confessing thy name and making their prayer
34 and supplication to thee in this house, do thou hear in heaven; forgive the sin of thy people Israel and restore them to the land which thou gavest to their forefathers.

35   'When the heavens are shut up and there is no rain because thy servant*a* and thy people Israel have sinned against thee, and when they pray towards this place, confessing thy name and forsaking their sin when they
36 feel thy punishment, do thou hear in heaven and forgive their sin; so mayest thou teach them the good way which they should follow; and grant rain to thy land which thou hast given to thy people as their own possession.

37   'If there is famine in the land, or pestilence, or black blight or red, or locusts new-sloughed or fully grown; or if their enemies besiege them in any*b* of their cities; or if

[a] *So Sept.; Heb.* servants.   [b] in any: *so Sept.; Heb.* in the land.

plague or sickness befall them, then hear the prayer or 38
supplication of every man among thy people Israel, as
each one, prompted by the remorse of his own heart,
spreads out his hands towards this house: hear it in heaven 39
thy dwelling and forgive, and act. And, as thou knowest a
man's heart, reward him according to his deeds, for thou
alone knowest the hearts of all men; and so they will fear 40
thee all their lives in the land thou gavest to our forefathers.

'The foreigner too, the man who does not belong to 41
thy people Israel, but has come from a distant land because of thy fame (for men shall hear of thy great fame 42
and thy strong hand and arm outstretched), when he
comes and prays towards this house, hear in heaven thy 43
dwelling and respond to the call which the foreigner
makes to thee, so that like thy people Israel all peoples of
the earth may know thy fame and fear thee, and learn
that this house which I have built bears thy name.

'When thy people go to war with an enemy, wherever 44
thou dost send them, when they pray to the LORD, turning
towards this city which thou hast chosen and towards
this house which I have built in honour of thy name, do 45
thou in heaven hear their prayer and supplication, and
grant them justice.

'Should they sin against thee (and what man is free 46
from sin?) and shouldst thou in thy anger give them over
to an enemy, who carries them captive to his own land,
far or near; if in the land of their captivity they learn their 47
lesson and make supplication again to thee in that land
and say, "We have sinned and acted perversely and
wickedly", if they turn back to thee with heart and soul 48
in the land of their captors, and pray to thee, turning

towards their land which thou gavest to their forefathers
and towards this city which thou didst choose and this
49 house which I have built in honour of thy name; then in
heaven thy dwelling do thou hear their prayer and suppli-
50 cation, and grant them justice. Forgive thy people their
sins and transgressions against thee; put pity for them in
51 their captors' hearts. For they are thy possession, thy
people whom thou didst bring out of Egypt, from the
52 smelting-furnace, and so thine eyes are ever open to the
entreaty of thy servant and of thy people Israel, and thou
53 dost hear whenever they call to thee. Thou thyself hast
singled them out from all the peoples of the earth to be
thy possession; so thou didst promise through thy servant
Moses when thou didst bring our forefathers from Egypt,
O Lord GOD.'

* 31–2. Oath-taking in a holy place was a common means of
settling disputes between individuals. The accused swore on
oath his innocence of the crime of which he stood accused and
called down a curse upon the head of the guilty offender.
The prayer asks that God should fulfil the curse, thus vindi-
cating the innocent, punishing the guilty, and establishing
justice in the life of the community.

33–4. Here again the typically deuteronomic equation of
defeat and *sin* occurs.

35. Drought was a regular and disastrous hazard of life.

36. *so mayest thou teach them the good way:* punishment for sin
is seen as not ultimately destructive. The ultimate purpose of
punishment is not to destroy but to educate the people.

37. This is a catalogue of the worst misfortunes which
could happen to a community. *famine* was an ever present
threat to communities living in Palestine because of the
uncertainty of adequate rainfall and the impossibility of

storing large quantities of water because of the porous nature
of the limestone hills. *pestilence:* all travellers to and from
Egypt and Mesopotamia passed through Palestine which was
thus particularly vulnerable to a wide range of pests and
diseases. *black blight or red* has appeared in other translations as
'blasting and mildew'. 'Blasting' was the withering of plants
brought about by cold, dry, east winds. 'Mildew' was caused
by too much rain at the growing season which led to virus
diseases. It was not only the amount of rain which was
important but also its timing. The rain came at two seasons of
the year. The Former Rains of October–November prepared
the ground for sowing. The Latter Rains of March gave the
growing grain the extra moisture which produced a good crop.
If the rains were too early or too late, wholesale crop failure
could result. *locusts* were, and are, a scourge in the lands of the
Middle East. They devour all grass and foliage leaving the
countryside desolate. The Old Testament has several names for
locusts, describing them at various stages of their growth or
their particular characteristics. Two are mentioned here.
Others are to be found in the book of Joel (Joel 1: 4).

38. *remorse of his own heart* means 'as his conscience directs
him'. For the Hebrews the heart was the seat of intelligence
and will. God is here asked to deal with men according to the
state of their consciences, i.e. the repentance must be genuine
and sincere.

40. *they will fear thee:* this does not mean the terrified submission which a human tyrant can command by a display of
ruthless power. It means the reverent submission of the will
offered by a servant to a powerful, but just and loving master.

41–3. The prayer is quite untouched by any sense of Jewish
nationalism, or any tendency to treat Gentiles as inferior
persons in the sight of God. In later times there were occasions
when, under the pressure of persecution, Jews did take up such
an attitude to Gentiles. Here all people are regarded as potential members of the covenant, though the initiative was to come
from the foreigner as he realized the superiority of Israel's

religion and became willing to respond to God with 'constant love'. There is no hint here that Israel might take the initiative in bringing the foreigner to the temple. Such an idea of active missionary vocation is extremely rare in the Old Testament.

41. *foreigner* means a member of another nation. Hebrew possesses two words for foreigners. *Nokri* is used here. The other word, *ger*, refers to a person of another nation who has made a permanent home in Israel and regards it as his community. *Ger* is usually translated 'alien'. It is important to make this point to clarify the content of the prayer. It looks forward to a time when men of goodwill from any and all nations will be drawn to the temple at Jerusalem because of what they have heard or learned of the character of the God who dwells there.

44. *go to war* refers to the Holy War, which goes back to the days of the tribal league. When the tribes were called out in the name of God to defend the league against an enemy, they regarded themselves as fighting on his behalf to defend his community. This method of fighting wars fell into abeyance after the setting up of the monarchy. War became the business of the king, and the army was recruited from professional soldiers. The people were linked to the army through the payment of taxes. In the deuteronomic code the idea of the Holy War was once more stressed (Deut. 20). Perhaps the deuteronomists, or King Josiah, were seeking to revive it as an instrument to express the desire for national independence. Certainly the deuteronomists thought of themselves, and all Israelites, as the covenant people waging war against the religion and culture of Canaan on behalf of the purity of the old religious traditions and the ideals of the tribal league.

45. With the idea of the Holy War linked to the temple, the prayer can ask God to grant to the armies of his people *justice*, clearly understanding it to mean victory.

46–53. Here the thought is widened to consider a war in which Israel was defeated and the people carried off as captives to the land of the victor. The impression given is that such an experience has already happened to at least some Hebrews, or is likely to happen in the near future. For this reason some scholars have thought that the words must have been written after the fall of Jerusalem in 587 B.C. This conclusion is doubtful. Some Judaeans were taken into exile by the Babylonians before 587 B.C., and Israelites from the northern kingdom were taken into exile by the Assyrians in 721 B.C. In fact exile was always a real possibility for some Israelites at any time after the Assyrian empire had determined to control the Fertile Crescent, i.e. from the time of the battle at Qarqar in 853 B.C.

All this supports the conclusion that the prayer of dedication was written by a deuteronomic editor and placed by him in Solomon's mouth. To us this may appear dishonest, but writers in the ancient world were given much greater latitude in their use of sources than would seem proper to us. The writer's concern was to compose a prayer which he believed best expressed what Solomon would have said on this occasion. This means, inevitably, that in writing the prayer he would be greatly influenced by his own estimate of Solomon, and might bring in references to events which happened after the death of Solomon to make his point more clearly. How closely the words approximate to what Solomon said, it is impossible to say, though the editor would not deliberately falsify what he found in the sources.

49. *justice* here means restoration to freedom.

51. The basis of the confidence with which the whole prayer is infused, both in God's willingness to act and also his capacity to fulfil his will, is stated here: the people's past experience.

53. *through thy servant Moses:* the prayer ends with a clear reference to the covenant which God established with the people through Moses at Sinai. The deuteronomists understood the covenant with the house of David as an expansion and development of the Mosaic covenant, to fulfil its purposes more effectively within the conditions of Canaan. Unfortunately,

not all Israelite kings interpreted their position in this way. So the story of the kings of Judah, and even more of Israel, contains much sadness and accounts of national defeat and humiliation. The purpose of the editors was to explain why the history of their people had worked out in this way. ✻

THE BLESSING

54 When Solomon had finished this prayer and supplication to the LORD, he rose from before the altar of the LORD, where he had been kneeling with his hands spread out to
55 heaven, stood up and in a loud voice blessed the whole
56 assembly of Israel: 'Blessed be the LORD who has given his people Israel rest, as he promised: not one of the promises he made through his servant Moses has failed.
57 The LORD our God be with us as he was with our fore-
58 fathers; may he never leave us nor forsake us. May he turn our hearts towards him, that we may conform to all his ways, observing his commandments, statutes, and
59 judgements, as he commanded our forefathers. And may the words of my supplication to the LORD be with the LORD our God day and night, that, as the need arises day by day, he may grant justice to his servant and justice to
60 his people Israel. So all the peoples of the earth will know
61 that the LORD is God, he and no other, and you will be perfect in loyalty to the LORD our God as you are this day, conforming to his statutes and observing his command-ments.'

✻ This passage is omitted in the parallel account in Chronicles, without doubt deliberately, because at the time when Chronicles was written, it was considered that the right to bless belonged exclusively to the priesthood. This view is expressed in Num. 6: 23, a passage which belongs to the priestly source.

The blessing was a prayer that the intimate relationship established between God and his people, and symbolized by the temple ceremony, should continue for ever. In this way Israel would be able to fulfil the vocation that God had laid upon her. The basis of that fulfilment, and the relationship with God which it implied, was founded completely upon a moral and spiritual affinity. Israel's loving obedience, keeping all God's commandments from the heart, was the response of gratitude by which she acknowledged that God had kept all the promises implicit in the vocation he had laid upon Israel.

54. *he rose:* this reference to Solomon's kneeling contradicts what is written above in verse 22.

56. *rest* is either the establishment of the kingdom, or the dedication of the temple as symbolizing the completion of the building. At the creation God was said to have rested when the work had been completed satisfactorily, and here, since God has fulfilled all his promises, Israel has now reached the same state of rest.

57–61. Here it is acknowledged that Israel could not fulfil the obligations she recognized unless God inspired her to do so. The initiative in all things lay with God who fulfilled his promises and who could so draw Israel to him that Israel would become capable of loving obedience and fit to be a great nation.

59. *grant justice:* it is difficult to make the meaning of the Hebrew completely clear. The petition is that God would champion the cause of his people so that then they would be victorious over every enemy. Yet, since the people whose cause God was to champion were a people living by covenant in obedient love, their cause would be just. It was an Israel of this character and quality who would provide the witness to the world that the God she served was the true God. ✻

THE SACRIFICES

62 When the king and all Israel came to offer sacrifices
63 before the LORD, Solomon offered as shared-offerings to
the LORD twenty-two thousand oxen and a hundred and
twenty thousand sheep; thus it was that the king and the
64[a] Israelites dedicated the house of the LORD. On that day
also the king consecrated the centre of the court which lay
in front[b] of the house of the LORD; there he offered the
whole-offering, the grain-offering, and the fat portions of
the shared-offerings, because the bronze altar which stood
before the LORD was too small to take them all, the whole-
offering, the grain-offering, and the fat portions of the
shared-offerings.

65 So Solomon and all Israel with him, a great assembly
from Lebo-hamath to the Torrent of Egypt, celebrated the
pilgrim-feast at that time before the LORD our God for
66 seven days.[c] On the eighth day he dismissed the people;
and they blessed the king, and went home happy and glad
at heart for all the prosperity granted by the LORD to his
servant David and to his people Israel.

* 63. It may be that the number of sacrifices as given here
has been exaggerated. On the other hand, if the whole
community had gathered for the dedication and shared in the
sacrifices, then the number could well be accurate.

64. *the whole-offering* and *shared-offerings*: see note on 3: 15.
the grain-offering was a sacrifice of corn and olive oil.

65. The congregation was made up of Israelites from the
whole of the territory over which David had established his
rule. *Lebo-hamath* marked the boundary on the north. In

[a] *Verses 64–66: cp. 2 Chr. 7: 7–10.*   [b] *Or to the east.*
[c] *So Sept.; Heb. adds* and seven days, fourteen days.

Syria the great mountain range of the Lebanon divides into
two with a wide, fertile valley between the two mountain
ranges. Damascus is situated in this valley. *Lebo-hamath* is at
the northern entry to the valley, one of the strategic points on
the great trade route through the Fertile Crescent. *the Torrent
of Egypt* marked the southernmost point where the king's
authority reached. It was the last settlement south of Gaza in
the Sinai desert. Today it is called Wadi el-Arish (for both
places see map 1 on p. 5). *for seven days:* i.e. the autumn Feast
of Tabernacles. The translation here follows the Septuagint.
The Hebrew has a feast of fourteen days. This has been copied
from the account in Chronicles (2 Chron. 7: 9), where it is
stated that a seven-day festival of dedication of the temple was
held, followed by the seven-day Feast of Tabernacles.

66. *On the eighth day* shows that the longer feast of Chronicles
was a later traditional elaboration by a pedantic expert on
liturgy. ✻

A SECOND VISION FOR SOLOMON

When Solomon had finished the house of the LORD and **9** 1[a]
the royal palace and all the plans for building on which he
had set his heart, the LORD appeared to him a second time, 2
as he had appeared to him at Gibeon. The LORD said to 3
him, 'I have heard the prayer and supplication which you
have offered me; I have consecrated this house which you
have built, to receive my Name for all time, and my eyes
and my heart shall be fixed on it for ever. And if you, on 4
your part, live in my sight as your father David lived, in
integrity and uprightness, doing all I command you and
observing my statutes and my judgements, then I will 5
establish your royal throne over Israel for ever, as I
promised your father David when I said, "You shall never

[a] Verses 1–9: cp. 2 Chr. 7: 11–22.

6 want for a man upon the throne of Israel." But if you or your sons turn back from following me and do not observe my commandments and my statutes which I have set before you, and if you go and serve other gods and prostrate 7 yourselves before them, then I will cut off Israel from the land which I gave them; I will renounce this house which I have consecrated in honour of my name, and Israel shall become a byword and an object lesson among all peoples. 8 And this house will become a ruin;[a] every passer-by will be appalled and gasp[b] at the sight of it; and they will ask, "Why has the LORD so treated this land and this house?" 9 The answer will be, "Because they forsook the LORD their God, who brought their forefathers out of Egypt, and clung to other gods, prostrating themselves before them and serving them; that is why the LORD has brought this great evil on them."'

✵ God appeared to the king not only for his own sake but also because he represented the community. The content of this second vision was a warning to the nation that the peace and blessedness which had been established at the feast of dedication would only continue if they were loyal to God and his commands. Because of the place in which the vision occurred and the terms in which it was given, it is difficult to resist the view that this passage is the work of the editors. When the final editorial work was done, some time after 587 B.C., the main problem in the readers' minds would be why God should have allowed the temple to be destroyed by a heathen nation. The answer the editors supplied here and in other places was that the fault did not lie with God. God was not so feeble that he could not have resisted the Babylonians. Nor was he so fickle that he had rejected or forgotten his

[a] become a ruin: *so Pesh.; Heb.* be high.   [b] *Lit.* hiss.

promises to the nation he had chosen. On the contrary, the destruction of the temple was God's own act for which he had used the Babylonians as his instruments. It was his just response to the repeated acts of disloyalty by almost all the successors of Solomon. To the deuteronomists loyalty in religious observance was the one single virtue most prized by God. It indicated the wholehearted commitment of Israel to their covenant obligations, and it also made possible the fulfilment of those obligations. To take part in the pagan worship of Israel's Canaanite neighbours was the greatest evil in God's eyes, not merely because God demanded exclusive loyalty, but also because such participation even to a small degree meant some acceptance of Canaanite ideals, and thus made service to God, with that loving obedience which he desired, impossible.

The destruction of the temple was Israel's responsibility, and any future rebuilding would depend upon a change of heart on the part of Israel. This was the message the deuteronomic editors wanted so passionately to convey to their contemporaries. The story of the vision was placed at this point in the narrative so that the reader, as he read the account of the division of the kingdom and the record of the successive acts of disloyalty to God by kings both of Israel and Judah, could rightly evaluate the significance of these acts and the inevitability of the disaster with which the narrative of Kings ends.

8. The N.E.B. follows the Peshitta since the Hebrew does not make sense. *gasp:* paraphrasing the literal meaning 'hiss' (cp. footnote). This was the way the Hebrews expressed astonishment and horror. ✻

A SUMMARY OF SOLOMON'S WORK AND ACHIEVEMENTS

✻ The rest of the chapter is made up of a collection of miscellaneous pieces of information about Solomon's achievements. The original facts were probably taken from state archives. Here additional legendary information has been added to those facts. ✻

SOLOMON SELLS LAND TO HIRAM

10[a] Solomon had taken twenty years to build the two
11 houses, the house of the LORD and the royal palace. Hiram
king of Tyre had supplied him with all the timber, both
cedar and pine, and all the gold, that he desired, and King
Solomon gave Hiram twenty cities in the land of Galilee.
12 But when Hiram went from Tyre to inspect the cities
which Solomon had given him, they did not satisfy him,
13 and he said, 'What kind of cities are these you have given
me, my brother?' And so he called them the Land of
14 Cabul,[b] the name they still bear. Hiram sent a hundred
and twenty talents of gold to the king.

✻ 10. *twenty years:* see comment on 7: 1.

11. *twenty cities in the land of Galilee:* the treasury was empty
so Solomon exchanged some territory in the northern part of
his kingdom for a large sum of money from King Hiram.
Because Hiram supplied much of the material for the temple,
the handing over of the territory has been linked here with
payment for temple material. This was not so. Solomon paid
for the temple material year by year (cp. 5: 11). The editors are
not willing to admit that Solomon had overstrained the
resources of his kingdom by his extravagant expenditure.

13. *he called them the Land of Cabul:* this may also be a later
addition to the record based upon a misunderstanding of the
name *Cabul*. There was, and is, a village named Cabul in
northern Galilee (see map 4 on p. 119). Whether or not this was
a part of the territory which Solomon ceded is quite uncertain. The word Cabul probably meant 'fettered', i.e.
mortgaged. The translation in the footnote, 'Sterile Land', is
taken from the suggestion of later Jewish commentators in the

[a] *Verses 10–28: cp. 2 Chr. 8: 1–18.*
[b] *That is* Sterile Land.

Mishnah. It probably represents an attempt at interpreting this passage rather than being the source of it.

14. *talents:* metals were dealt in by weight. The standard measure was a shekel, from the Hebrew verb *shaqal* which means 'to weigh'. The talent was the largest measurement. According to the Phoenician standard 3,000 shekels made a talent, while by the Babylonian standard 3,600 were needed. There was also at one time, one weight for a royal shekel and a smaller weight for an ordinary shekel. Because of such variations it is impossible to say what the value of these talents were in our money. We can only say that it was a very large sum. ✻

SOLOMON AS BUILDER

This is the record of the forced labour which King 15 Solomon conscripted to build the house of the LORD, his own palace, the Millo, the wall of Jerusalem, and Hazor, Megiddo, and Gezer. Gezer had been attacked and 16 captured by Pharaoh king of Egypt, who had burnt it to the ground, put its Canaanite inhabitants to death, and given it as a marriage gift to his daughter, Solomon's wife; and Solomon rebuilt it. He also built Lower 17 Beth-horon, Baalath, and Tamar[a] in the wilderness,[b] as 18, 19 well as all his store-cities, and the towns where he quartered his chariots and horses; and he carried out all his cherished plans for building in Jerusalem, in the Lebanon, and throughout his whole dominion. All the survivors of the 20 Amorites, Hittites, Perizzites, Hivites, and Jebusites, who did not belong to Israel – that is their descendants who 21 survived in the land, wherever the Israelites had been unable to annihilate them – were employed by Solomon

[a] Or, *as otherwise read*, Tadmor.
[b] *So Sept.; Heb. adds* in the land.

22 on perpetual forced labour, as they still are. But Solomon put none of the Israelites to forced labour; they were his fighting men,[a] his captains and lieutenants, and the com-
23 manders of his chariots and of his cavalry. The number of officers in charge of the foremen over Solomon's work was five hundred and fifty; these superintended the people engaged on the work.

✷ Most great kings left behind them a list of their achievements either in archives or inscribed on monuments. Many such lists have been brought to light by the work of archaeologists. This passage probably grew out of such a list which told how Solomon built or improved great fortresses at the strategic points which controlled access to the kingdom. The list takes the fortresses in order (see map 4 on p. 119).

15. If *the Millo* was a fortress, it would have formed an extension of the walls. It has been suggested that the Akra, the fortress built in the city in the Maccabean period, was built on the same site. But no one can be sure what *the Millo* really was. The word means 'a filling'. It may have been the name of a fortress, but it may equally well have referred to the filling in of a hollow to make an area of level ground. Such a filling might have been made to link the new buildings on the north with the rest of the city. There is one more possibility. Jerusalem was built on a steep hill and the eastern wall was quite a long way down the slope. The hillside within the city wall was terraced for rows of houses, and *the Millo* may have been the rock filling which made such terraces. *the wall of Jerusalem:* this may mean either that he strengthened the old wall, or that he rebuilt it, at least in some places, to enclose more land within the city. Presumably the building of the palace and temple on the northern side of the city made some extension of the wall

[a] *Prob. rdg.; Heb. adds* and his servants.

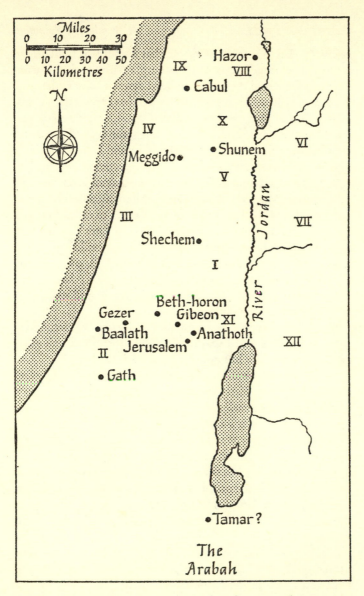

Miles

0 10 20 30

0 10 20 30 40 50
Kilometres

N

Hazor•

Cabul

Meggido•

Shunem•

Shechem•

Beth-horon
Gezer • •Gibeon
•Baalath •Anathoth
Jerusalem•

•Gath

River Jordan

Tamar?•

The
Arabah

IX VIII

IV X

V

III VII

I

XI

II XII

VI

4. The land during the reign of Solomon. The Roman
numbers mark Solomon's administrative areas.

necessary. There is some evidence that a wall was built along the top of the ridge to connect the temple with the city. *Hazor:* the great fortress in the Jordan valley between Lake Huleh and the Sea of Galilee. Archaeological work has shown that it was a large and important city, and that considerable rebuilding was done there in Solomon's time. The same type of casement wall has been found at Hazor, Megiddo and Gezer. *Megiddo:* the fortress which controlled the pass connecting the Esdraelon valley with the coastal plain. Extensive excavations have been carried out at Megiddo. A large area with many pillars has been uncovered, and has frequently been referred to as 'Solomon's Stables'. It is now known to date from a later period, and to be more probably the remains of storage buildings rather than stables. *Gezer* was situated in the foothills, overlooking the coastal plain and controlling it. Archaeology has shown that a fortress was rebuilt there in this period following the destruction of earlier buildings.

16. This explains the archaeological evidence of destruction.

17. *Lower Beth-horon* was in the Aijalon valley which gave easy access into the hill country around Jerusalem.

18. *Baalath* is less well known, and its site correspondingly less certain. It was very likely the Baalath in the old Danite territory overlooking the coastal plain, mentioned in the book of Joshua (Josh. 19: 45). It was a fortress city serving the same function as the others. *Tamar* was so little known to later generations that they had forgotten its existence, or regarded it as too unimportant to figure in this list of Solomon's fortresses. Tamar was mentioned by the prophet Ezekiel as marking the southern boundary of the kingdom (Ezek. 47: 19). It was situated in the desert in the Arabah and from its position gained its name which means 'Palm tree'. An editor or scribe, who tried to relate the places mentioned here to what he knew in his own time, thought that Tamar referred to the great city of Palmyra built at an oasis in the far north in the Syrian desert. So the Hebrew name for Palmyra, Tadmor, was substituted here for *Tamar*. When the Massoretes added vowels to the Hebrew

text, they made it clear by a note that Tadmor was to be read here. This fitted well with the prestige which had become attached by tradition to Solomon's name. 'in the land' (N.E.B. footnote): these words do not fit in easily with the rest of the verse. They were probably added by an editor who understood *Tamar* as referring to Palmyra and wished to emphasize that Solomon's territory extended as far as that city.

19. This verse is most likely an editorial addition. It is identical with a part of a verse in 2 Chron. 8: 6*b*. No names are given for any store city or the places where Solomon was supposed to have built in the Lebanon. Its purpose was to magnify Solomon's achievements.

20. When mention is made in Deuteronomy of the pre-Israelite inhabitants of the land, a stereotyped formula is used which is a list of seven peoples. Five of them are given here.

21. *annihilate:* the deuteronomists thought that all the Canaanite inhabitants of the land ought to have been killed when Israel took over their territory. They viewed the Israelite crossing of the Jordan into Palestine as a Holy War (see note on 8: 44), in which the tribal league fought with God at its head against a deadly enemy. One aspect of the Holy War was that none of those who fought should benefit materially from the victory. All that was captured – buildings, cattle and people – should be offered as a sacrifice to God who had given the victory. The Hebrew word here translated *annihilate* is the word used of offering this kind of victory sacrifice in a Holy War. It is translated as 'put under ban', i.e. dedicate, in 20: 42 and 1 Sam. 15: 3. An editor has thus reshaped archival material to portray Solomon as fulfilling God's purpose in giving Canaan to Israel by his use of the Canaanite population as slave labour.

22. *forced labour* (see note on 5: 13): this verse is the work of an editor concerned to uphold Solomon's good name. *they were his fighting men:* this statement is also unhistorical. Its purpose was to assign a function to the Israelites. David employed non-Israelites in his army, notably Uriah the

Hittite, and there is no reason to suppose that Solomon changed the practice. ✻

EXTRA INFORMATION

24 Then Solomon brought Pharaoh's daughter up[a] from the City of David to her own house which he had built for her; later on he built the Millo.

25   Three times a year Solomon used to offer whole-offerings and shared-offerings on the altar which he had built to the LORD, making smoke-offerings[b] before the LORD. So he completed the house.

✻ 24. The Hebrew word translated *Then* is thought to have been used in archival material to introduce a new topic, rather like 'item' in English. *Pharaoh's daughter* lived in the city until her house had been completed (3: 1). It was not unusual for a royal consort to have her own house, particularly such an important consort.

25. This verse is a later editorial addition. It is out of place, particularly the last sentence. Its purpose is to portray Solomon devoutly leading the worship of the people at the three great pilgrim-feasts which the whole covenant community was meant to celebrate annually at Jerusalem, as laid down in the law in Deut. 16: 16. Both the *whole-offerings* and *shared-offerings* were *smoke-offerings* in that the whole or part of the animal being sacrificed was burnt on the altar. After the exile, the verb translated as *making smoke-offerings* was used exclusively of offering incense. ✻

[a] Then...daughter up: *so Sept.; Heb.* However, Pharaoh's daughter had gone up.
[b] *So Sept.; Heb. adds* with it which.

SOLOMON AS A TRADER

King Solomon built a fleet of ships at Ezion-geber, 26
near Eloth[a] on the shore of the Red Sea,[b] in Edom. Hiram 27
sent men of his own to serve with the fleet, experienced
seamen, to work with Solomon's men; and they went to 28
Ophir and brought back four hundred and twenty
talents of gold, which they delivered to King Solomon.

✵ This trading activity witnesses both to Solomon's greatness
and also to his need of revenue to support the splendour of his
reign and his expensive building projects.

26. *Ezion-geber* was a port situated at the head of the Gulf of
Akaba which is the tongue of the Red Sea lying to the east of
the Sinai peninsula. It was well situated for trade by sea with
southern Arabia, the east coast of Africa and even India. It was
used in this way, intermittently as political conditions allowed,
until Roman times. It lay in the territory of *Edom* which David
had conquered and which Solomon and several of his successors held. It has been identified with the mound of Tell
el-Kheleifeh which is situated in the centre of the northern
shore of the Gulf of Akaba. An American archaeologist did
much work there, and at one time claimed to have found
smelters there which Solomon would have used as copper
refineries. Later more careful examination led him to withdraw the claim. The buildings were, in fact, probably stores
for grain. However, there is evidence of building on the site
dating from this period which may have been Solomon's
work. That Solomon could build and use a port so far from
Jerusalem is the measure of his power and ingenuity. That he
was concerned to open new trade routes shows how greatly
the revenues of his kingdom were being taxed by his building
policy and the general style of his reign. *Eloth* is always else-

[a] Or Elath.   [b] Or the Sea of Reeds.

where called Elath. *the Red Sea* is the usual translation of the Hebrew name which means literally 'sea of reeds'. The name originally belonged to the reed marshes separating Egypt from the Sinai peninsula in the region of the Great Bitter Lakes and Lake Timsah. Later the name came to be used in the present sense.

27. Israelites would not have had any experience of the sea.

28. *Ophir:* the site is not known. A reference in Genesis (10: 29) seems to place it in southern Arabia, and the linking of the passage with the story of the queen of Sheba, which follows, also points to the same area. According to 10: 22 the fleet went out from Ezion-geber on three-year-long voyages, and this has led to the suggestion that *Ophir* must have been more distant than southern Arabia. The coast of east Africa, and even India, have been suggested. However, southern Arabia is the most likely area. If the ships could only sail at certain seasons of the year when the winds were favourable, then a journey from Ezion-geber to southern Arabia with a fairly long stop for trading could well have taken three years. 'Apes and monkeys' mentioned in 10: 22 are certainly more likely to have come from Africa or India, but southern Arabia could have been a trading centre to which merchants from Africa and India came. *four hundred and twenty talents:* this amount of gold is very large indeed. It looks like another exaggerated figure meant to swell Solomon's importance and magnificance.

THE VISIT OF THE QUEEN OF SHEBA

10 1[a] The queen of Sheba heard of Solomon's fame[b] and came 2 to test him with hard questions. She arrived in Jerusalem with a very large retinue, camels laden with spices, gold

[a] *Verses 1–25: cp. 2 Chr. 9: 1–24.*
[b] *Prob. rdg., cp. 2 Chr. 9: 1; Heb. adds* to the name of the LORD.

in great quantity, and precious stones. When she came to
Solomon, she told him everything she had in her mind,
and Solomon answered all her questions; not one of them ₃
was too abstruse for the king to answer. When the queen ₄
of Sheba saw all the wisdom of Solomon, the house which
he had built, the food on his table, the courtiers sitting ₅
round him, and his attendants standing behind in their
livery, his cupbearers, and the whole-offerings which he
used to offer in the house of the LORD, there was no more
spirit left in her. Then she said to the king, 'The report ₆
which I heard in my own country about you*a* and your
wisdom was true, but I did not believe it until I came and ₇
saw for myself. Indeed I was not told half of it; your
wisdom and your prosperity go far beyond the report
which I had of them. Happy are your wives,*b* happy these ₈
courtiers of yours who wait on you every day and hear
your wisdom! Blessed be the LORD your God who has ₉
delighted in you and has set you on the throne of Israel;
because he loves Israel for ever, he has made you their king
to maintain law and justice.' Then she gave the king a ₁₀
hundred and twenty talents of gold, spices in great
abundance, and precious stones. Never again came such a
quantity of spices as the queen of Sheba gave to King
Solomon.

Besides all this, Hiram's fleet of ships, which had ₁₁
brought gold from Ophir, brought in also from Ophir
cargoes of almug wood and precious stones. The king ₁₂
used the wood to make stools*c* for the house of the LORD
and for the royal palace, as well as harps and lutes for the

[a] *Lit.* your affairs.
[b] *So Sept.; Heb.* men.   [c] *Mng. of Heb. word uncertain.*

singers. No such almug wood has ever been imported or even seen since that time.

13   And King Solomon gave the queen of Sheba all she desired, whatever she asked, in addition to all that he gave her of his royal bounty. So she departed and returned with her retinue to her own land.

* This story is placed here as a sequel to the reference to Solomon's trading in the Red Sea. In fact some extra information about that trading has got misplaced and is now in the middle of the story of the queen's visit, verses 11 and 12, which would read more naturally after 9: 26–8. The story of the queen's visit has frequently been dismissed as legendary. It has been interpreted as one more example of the later tendency to exalt the person of Solomon to superhuman dimensions. His wisdom was so great and well known that a queen was prepared to travel from a distant foreign land to pay homage and receive instruction. As a story it is not unlike Matthew's account of the visit of the magi to the infant Jesus. Without doubt the person of Solomon was magnified by later tradition as we have already seen in the accounts of his wisdom in earlier chapters. But there we saw that the legends of Solomon's wisdom were not simply invented, but grew out of real aspects of his work and character. The same is true of this story of the visit of the queen of Sheba. Solomon could claim to be wise in the sense that he was master of a great empire and ruled it with style. Just so, there is no reason to doubt that the queen of Sheba did visit Solomon, though it is reasonable to question whether the visit took place in the way the story tells. Legend alone would have been much more likely to create a king of Sheba.

    1. *Sheba* has usually been identified as a part of the western end of southern Arabia, approximately the same as the present state of Yemen. Some scholars have claimed that it was situated in northern Arabia, on the ground that the tribes who

later migrated to the Yemen lived in Solomon's day in
territory in northern Arabia. The point of the suggestion was
to make the queen a fairly near neighbour to Solomon, and
her journey on that ground more probable. Such a theory is
unnecessary. Archaeologists have shown that a relatively
developed and sophisticated kingdom existed in the Yemen
in Solomon's time around the city of Marib. Temples of the
moon goddess have been found, and a series of complex and
efficient dams which conserved water during the dry season
and made farming possible. This civilization continued to
exist until the Arab invasions in the time of the prophet
Mohammed. The Marib dam was broken by a great cloud-
burst in the sixth century A.D. and the prosperity of the area
declined.

Much of that prosperity was due to its monopoly of the
production of incense and spices. Incense was produced from
gum taken from trees which grew in the region. The incense
and spices were exported to many countries, and this, together
with the geographical position of *Sheba* at the south-west
point of Arabia where the Red Sea and the Indian Ocean
meet, led to it becoming a great trading centre. It linked Africa
and India with the countries around the Mediterranean basin.
Solomon's Red Sea fleet must have come into contact with
Sheba. Perhaps there was rivalry, and a conflict of interests
developed. The queen's visit was almost certainly a trade and
diplomatic visit. She had come to reach an agreement with the
new trading power which had appeared on the Red Sea. 'to
the name of the LORD' (N.E.B. footnote): 'concerning' is a
better translation than 'to'. This phrase was added by someone
who wished to confine Solomon's fame strictly to religious
matters.

2–7. Solomon would have wanted to display the might and
splendour of his kingdom, and the diplomatic discussions
would have demonstrated his wisdom in the sense of his ability
and skill as the ruler of a great empire. Here his wisdom is
understood to be knowledge, and Solomon is portrayed as an

intellectual genius who could produce at will the answer to any question. This is the Solomon of later religious tradition (see comment on pp. 47–8).

5. *spirit* in the Old Testament usually has the sense of energy. The visible signs of prosperity and even luxury were understood at this time as the outward signs of the blessedness which wisdom brought. Wisdom meant that Solomon was near to God, and, for the deuteronomists, goodness and prosperity were always equated.

6–7. The queen's mission has become the vehicle through which the deuteronomists express the gentile world's acknowledgement of the superiority of the covenant people.

8. *wives* gives the best sense. It is easy to understand how the word came to be changed to 'men'. In Hebrew the addition of one letter at the beginning of the word for *wives* turns it into the word for 'men'. So a misunderstanding could easily occur. The editors would prefer 'men' because of the disrepute of Solomon's wives. According to 11: 1–13, it was the wives who caused the downfall of his empire.

11–12. These verses have been inserted into the story. They give more information about the trading on the Red Sea.

11. *almug* is the Hebrew proper name for some kind of wood. What it was is quite unknown. Josephus, the Jewish historian who wrote in the first century A.D., suggested 'pine wood'. Another suggestion is 'sandalwood', brought from India via Sheba. We can only say with certainty that the wood was highly prized and precious, both from the distance it was brought and also the use to which it was put.

12. *stools* is just an intelligent guess. The Revised Standard Version translates 'supports'. The Hebrew noun is only used here, and the verb from which it is derived suggests no precise meaning. *harps and lutes* implies that music was used in the temple. So psalms may have been sung in the temple from Solomon's day. The worship and music of the temple may have owed just as much to Canaanite models as the architecture.

13. This means that the mission had a satisfactory outcome and, doubtless, trading agreements were concluded. Tradition continued to expand and embroider the account of the queen of Sheba's visit long after the story was written down in the book of Kings, and many legends have grown up around it. *all she desired* has been interpreted as a child who would rule her kingdom as wisely as Solomon ruled Israel. One version of this legend in Christian tradition is the basis of the claim of the royal house of Abyssinia to be descended from Solomon and the queen of Sheba. ✻

SOLOMON'S WEALTH

Now the weight of gold which Solomon received 14 yearly was six hundred and sixty-six talents, in addition to 15 the tolls levied by*[a]* the customs officers and profits on foreign trade, and the tribute of*[b]* the kings of Arabia and the regional governors.

King Solomon made two hundred shields of beaten 16 gold, and six hundred shekels of gold went to the making of each one; he also made three hundred bucklers of 17 beaten gold, and three minas of gold went to the making of each buckler. The king put these into the House of the Forest of Lebanon.

The king also made a great throne of ivory and over- 18 laid it with fine gold. Six steps led up to the throne; at the 19 back of the throne there was the head of a calf. There were arms on each side of the seat, with a lion standing beside each of them, and twelve lions stood on the six steps, one 20 at either end of each step. Nothing like it had ever been made for any monarch. All Solomon's drinking vessels 21

[a] tolls levied by: *so Sept.; Heb.* men of.
[b] and the tribute of: *prob. rdg.; Heb.* and all.

were of gold, and all the plate in the House of the Forest
of Lebanon was of red gold; no silver was used, for it was
22 reckoned of no value in the days of Solomon. The king
had a fleet of merchantmen[a] at sea with Hiram's fleet; once
every three years this fleet of merchantmen came home,
bringing gold and silver, ivory, apes and monkeys.

23   Thus King Solomon outdid all the kings of the earth in
24 wealth and wisdom, and all the world courted him, to
25 hear the wisdom which God had put in his heart. Each
brought his gift with him, vessels of silver and gold,
garments, perfumes and spices, horses and mules, so much
year by year.

✷ This passage lists a collection of items all of which illustrate
the splendour of Solomon's reign. They have been collected
together here as a supplement to the story of the visit of the
queen of Sheba, and, as in that story, details have been
exaggerated to heighten the effect.

14–15. These verses should not be regarded, as some have
suggested, as completely legendary although the yearly
weight of gold is clearly an exaggeration.

15. *tolls* from merchandize passing through Israelite
territory, and *profits on foreign trade*, are just the sources from
which Solomon would have collected taxes. *the kings of Arabia*
would be kings of northern Arabia holding territories
contiguous with those of Solomon. *the regional governors* were
those placed over the various parts of the kingdom as set out
in chapter 4. *tolls levied by* and 'men of' (N.E.B. footnote) are
translations of two Hebrew words which only vary very
slightly from each other. *tribute of* is an attempt to make sense
from Hebrew words which are not completely clear.

16–17. The *shields of beaten gold* and *bucklers of beaten gold*
were ornamental. *the House of the Forest of Lebanon* was used as

[a] *Lit.* ships of Tarshish.

a treasury. The *shields* and *bucklers* may have been carried by
Solomon's guard when they escorted him on ceremonial
visits to the temple. Rehoboam, Solomon's successor,
certainly used bronze shields in this way (cp. 14: 28). The
shields were oval in shape and were used to protect the whole
body of the bearer, whilst the *bucklers* were circular and much
smaller in size. They were carried on the arm and used to fend
off the blows of an enemy. Both *shields* and *bucklers* were made
of wood or some base metal and plated with gold, hence the
reference to their being made *of beaten gold*.

18–20. The *great throne* emphasized Solomon's splendour and
also his power. *lions* have always been a symbol of regal power,
and the *six steps* may have had a particular significance.
Babylonian ziggurats, the temple towers, had seven levels to
represent the seven levels or stages of heaven, all of which had
to be passed through to reach the highest heaven. Did Solomon
sit on his throne as king, on the seventh level, visibly declaring
himself to be God's vice-regent with access to the inner
counsels of the Almighty, and control over the human
communities of men? We have no specific evidence, but it
may have been so.

21. *gold, red gold*: these words are commonly taken to be
synonyms, as is 'fine gold' in verse 18. They may originally
have referred to differences in the origin and quality of the
gold.

22. The *fleet of merchantmen* were literally 'ships of Tarshish'.
Tarshish has generally been identified with Tartessus, a port
on the Atlantic coast of Spain at the mouth of the Guadal-
quivir river. It was a name often used to mark the farthest
boundary of the west. Jonah set out for Tarshish when he
determined to run away from God. How then could 'ships
of Tarshish' sail on the Red Sea? Two suggestions have been
offered. Tartessus was a place where metal was mined. It has
been suggested that the name was given generally to merchant
ships which carried metal. The other suggestion is not very
different. It is that only the strongest ships could make the

journey to Tartessus and so a 'ship of Tarshish' came to be a common description for what we would call an ocean-going vessel. Such ships would be needed for long trading voyages. *apes and monkeys:* earlier translations have read 'apes and peacocks'. The word translated 'peacocks' was quite unknown and the translation a guess. Egyptian texts have a similar word meaning 'monkeys', and that translation is now generally accepted. It has been claimed that the *monkeys* would have been baboons, since baboons are still found in the Yemen.

23–5. These verses are legendary. They describe the superhuman Solomon of later tradition. ✡

SOLOMON'S CHARIOTS AND HORSES

26[a] And Solomon got together many chariots and horses;
he had fourteen hundred chariots and twelve thousand
horses, and he stabled some in the chariot-towns and kept
27 others at hand in Jerusalem. The king made silver as
common in Jerusalem as stones, and cedar as plentiful as
28 sycomore-fig in the Shephelah. Horses were imported
from Egypt and Coa for Solomon; the royal merchants
29 obtained them from Coa by purchase. Chariots were
imported from Egypt for six hundred silver shekels each,
and horses for a hundred and fifty; in the same way the
merchants obtained them for export from all the kings of
the Hittites and the kings of Aram.

✡ 26. The emphasis laid upon Solomon's possession of chariots is meant to indicate the character of his rule. He was no ruler of a small, second-class power, but an emperor able to meet on equal terms with other emperors such as the pharaoh of Egypt. It is not perhaps too much to say that his possession of an army of chariots gave him much the same status in his

[a] *Verses 26–29: cp. 2 Chr. 1: 14–17; 9: 25–28.*

world as the possession of atomic weapons would give to a
ruler in our world.

In 4: 26 the numbers given were far greater than appear here,
and in the second of the two places in Chronicles where this
verse is quoted, the numbers are also far greater. The larger
numbers are exaggerated, but there is no reason to doubt the
figures given here. We know that Ahab, king of Israel less than
a century later, put 2,000 chariots into the field at the battle of
Qarqar against the Assyrians. It has been claimed that the best
evidence of a *chariot-town* so far known is found at Megiddo,
but the buildings uncovered there by archaeologists were
probably not stables but storehouses. It used to be thought
that the 'stables' were built by Solomon, but it is now thought
that they belong to the period of Ahab (869–850 B.C.).

27. This verse interrupts the thought. It is an afterthought;
the kind of description of Solomon's splendour which we have
already met more than once. The *sycomore-fig* was a type of
sycamore tree which produced poor figs. It grew in great
abundance on the foothills to the west of the Judaean hill-
country where the hill-country meets the coastal plain. This
region is called the *Shephelah* which means 'lowland', i.e. lower
hills as compared with the higher mountains of Judah.

28–9. It has been asserted frequently that Solomon was a
horse-trader, buying in Egypt and selling in Aram and Asia
Minor. There is little evidence for this, and the Hebrew of
these verses, which have been used as evidence, is far from
clear.

28. *Egypt and Coa:* Coa was a little-known area whose name
was changed in later times. It was quite unknown to the
Massoretes and Jewish commentators. They took it to be a
word for something the traders dealt in, hence the 'linen
yarn' of the Authorized Version. References have been found
to *Coa* on Assyrian inscriptions. It was a part of the area later
called Cilicia in southeast Asia Minor, situated to the south of
the Taurus mountains (see map 1 on p. 5). The city of
Tarsus, where Paul lived, later grew up in this area. The

identification of *Coa* has led to doubts about the meaning of *Egypt*. They are an odd combination of places. The Hebrew for *Egypt* is *Mitsrayim*, so the fact that another area in Asia Minor to the north of the Taurus mountains was often referred to in Assyrian texts as 'Musri' makes it probable that the Massoretes took Musri to be a corruption of *Mitsrayim* and altered the text accordingly. What happened then was that Solomon bought horses and chariots from two regions of Cilicia in Asia Minor. It is much more probable that chariots were made there than in Egypt. Cilicia had abundant supplies of wood, whilst Egypt had to import its wood from the Lebanon.

29. The last clause is ambiguous. Solomon's traders may have bought chariots and horses *for export from all the kings of the Hittites and the kings of Aram*. Equally, they may have bought them from Cilicia for export to those kings, as the Revised Standard Version understands the phrase. *the Hittites* had been the rulers of a large empire. Their homeland was in Asia Minor, and their rule, at the height of their power, spread far beyond into Syria and Palestine. Their empire came to an end about 1200 B.C., but their name continued in use for many years. Syria and Palestine are generally referred to on Assyrian inscriptions as 'the land of the Hittites'. Here *the kings of the Hittites* probably refers to small territories which had once formed part of the old Hittite empire. *Aram* was the area in which the Aramaeans lived. The most important Aramaean kingdom was Damascus. *Aram* was called Syria in the Septuagint and this has been followed in many English translations. Actually Aram was a larger area than what is now known as Syria. ✳

A CHANGE OF EMPHASIS: CHAPTER 11

✳ Much that has been written in Kings so far has emphasized the glory and splendour of Solomon's reign. This is natural because it cannot be doubted that Solomon was a great and powerful king, even though the picture that has been presented of him contains much exaggeration taken from the later, idealized portrait of him as the creator of Israel's wisdom literature and the founder of the temple. To the deuteronomic editors these aspects of Israel's life were very important, and so they were content to use that portrait. However, there was another aspect of their thought which was of equal importance to them, and which could be reconciled with the idealized picture of Solomon only with difficulty. This was the doctrine that God blessed the righteous with prosperity and punished sinners with disasters of various kinds. According to this doctrine, any king who had had such a successful and magnificent reign as Solomon was reputed to have had, was bound to leave behind for his successor a strong and powerful kingdom. In point of fact Solomon did not leave behind such a kingdom. No sooner was Solomon dead than the larger and wealthier part of the kingdom revolted, and Solomon's son, Rehoboam, was left as the ruler of a small part of his father's kingdom. Rehoboam, as ruler of Judah, was not unlike a Hapsburg emperor ruling tiny Austria after the rest of the old Austro-Hungarian empire had claimed its freedom. Such a state of affairs was far from prosperity. It was disaster and, as such, punishment for sin. How could it be explained? And just as important, how could it be reconciled with the portrait of Solomon presented so far in Kings?

Chapter 11 is the last chapter which deals with Solomon's reign. In it the editors begin to prepare the readers for the division of the kingdom which was soon to come, and with it the change in the fortunes of Solomon's line. They were not concerned with the human motivation of the events, but with tracing God's plan for his people. Here they differ sharply from modern historians, whose interests are almost entirely confined to economic and social forces, and human ambitions and follies. For the deuteronomists such matters were only of interest if they illustrated and illuminated God's dealings with Israel. That for them was the only point in writing history.

The deuteronomists found a reason why Solomon's reign should have ended disastrously in spite of all its earlier greatness. It was because Solomon had committed a great sin. They believed that the gravest sin into which any Israelite could fall was apostasy: the abandonment of the worship of Yahweh for the worship of some other god. Yahweh could not tolerate such conduct. He was a 'jealous God' who demanded exclusive obedience, not least because such sharing of worship meant also a mingling of distinctive patterns of community, and a blunting of the ethical quality of Israel's life. For the deuter-onomists, Israel could only continue to exist as the covenant community by maintaining a rigid separation from the ways of the Canaanites among whom she lived, and it was the vocation of the leaders of the nation to be for ever pointing this out to a people who were only too willing to forget it.

This deuteronomic theory was the fruit of experience. The covenant people during the time of the divided kingdom was guilty of apostasy. The people did attempt to combine the worship of Yahweh with the worship of the gods of Canaan, and their distinctive way of life suffered. At times it seemed to have disappeared entirely and for ever. The deuteronomic reform was itself an attempt to restore the covenant community to its true loyalty. Naturally, therefore, the editors saw this pattern in the history of their people, and since they were writing history as religious teachers, they emphasized it so that their readers should not miss the point. It would not be true to say that they read the pattern into history. That would mean that they had falsified history, and they had much evidence to support their theory. But they were so satisfied with the explanation their theory offered that they did not look for any other as a modern historian would do.

In this chapter and the one that follows, they record that both Solomon and his son met opposition, and they give sufficient details to show that Solomon's building programme severely strained the economy of the country, and placed such burdens on the people as would only be accepted under duress. Solomon's ambitions turned him into a totalitarian ruler and his people into potential rebels. A political crisis was

bound to come. The deuteronomists did not think in such
terms. They found evidence that Solomon was guilty of
apostasy and that for them was sufficient reason to explain all
that happened. They oversimplified, even distorted the issue,
but basically their insight was true. It was Solomon's ambition
to compete in splendour with other kings, and even outdo
them, which led to disaster; and that was a form of apostasy.
Yet his reign conveyed many benefits to Israel. It enlarged the
area of Israel's religious experience particularly by the foundation of the temple and the wisdom school, and thereby
broadened the base and the future effectiveness of the covenant
community. ✳

SOLOMON'S FOREIGN WIVES

King Solomon was a lover of women, and besides **11**
Pharaoh's daughter he married many foreign women,
Moabite, Ammonite, Edomite, Sidonian, and Hittite,
from the nations with whom the LORD had forbidden the 2
Israelites to intermarry, 'because', he said, 'they will
entice you to serve their gods.' But Solomon was devoted
to them and loved them dearly. He had seven hundred 3
wives, who were princesses, and three hundred concubines,
and they turned his heart from the truth. When he grew 4
old, his wives turned his heart to follow other gods, and he
did not remain wholly loyal to the LORD his God as his
father David had been. He followed Ashtoreth, goddess 5
of the Sidonians, and Milcom, the loathsome god of the
Ammonites. Thus Solomon did what was wrong in the 6
eyes of the LORD, and was not loyal to the LORD like his
father David. He built a hill-shrine for Kemosh, the 7
loathsome god of Moab, on the height to the east of
Jerusalem, and for Molech, the loathsome god of the
Ammonites. Thus he did for the gods to which all his 8

9 foreign wives burnt offerings and made sacrifices. The
Lord was angry with Solomon because his heart had
turned away from the Lord the God of Israel, who had
10 appeared to him twice and had strictly commanded him
not to follow other gods; but he disobeyed the Lord's
11 command. The Lord therefore said to Solomon, 'Because
you have done this and have not kept my covenant and
my statutes as I commanded you, I will tear the kingdom
12 from you and give it to your servant. Nevertheless, for
the sake of your father David I will not do this in your
13 day; I will tear it out of your son's hand. Even so not the
whole kingdom; I will leave him one tribe for the sake
of my servant David and for the sake of Jerusalem, my
chosen city.'

✻ 1–3. This account is basically historical, though the numbers have been increased by tradition. The possession of a
large harem was as much a part of Solomon's style of ruling
as were his building activities. David had kept a smaller harem
(cp. 2 Sam. 3: 2–5 and 5: 13–16). They were both essential to
the image of the powerful ruler. Naturally many of his wives
would be foreign. Such marriages were a guarantee of the
good faith of political treaties, and it was the recognized thing
that such wives should be allowed to follow their own
religious customs. The deuteronomic editor emphasizes this
so prominently at the beginning of this passage because for
him it furnished the root cause of the opposition to Solomon
which will be related later in the chapter, and the disaster of
the division of the kingdom. So the large harem which was the
pride of an eastern ruler is presented as the temptation and
source of weakness which seduced Solomon from his loyalty
to his God.

1. *and besides Pharaoh's daughter* was probably added to the

text which reads perfectly well without it. All the nations mentioned here were neighbours of Solomon with whom he shared a common frontier. *Hittite* means a former vassal of the old Hittite empire (see note on 10: 29).

2. The reference is to the law forbidding marriage with foreigners as in Deut. 7: 1-4 and Exod. 34: 11-16.

4. *When he grew old:* this is an attempt to excuse Solomon.

5-7. It was the custom of the editors to show their contempt for pagan gods by reading a term of abuse instead of the name of the god. For example, Baal was the best known Canaanite god whose name frequently occurs in the Old Testament. One of Jonathan's sons had a name which contained Baal, Meri-baal. The editors changed this to Mephibosheth. *Bosheth* is the Hebrew word for shame. It is very likely that with some of the names of the gods given here, the vowels of *bosheth* have been substituted for the original vowels of the name to indicate to the reader that he should read *bosheth*, or at least remember that word. *Molech* comes from the word for king, *melech*, as perhaps does *Milcom*. *Ashtoreth* also has the vowels of *bosheth*. This particular goddess is frequently met in Canaanite literature, and she also appears in the Greek pantheon as Astarte.

7. *a hill-shrine:* Canaanite shrines were often made on hill tops and were crowned with an artificial mound upon which an altar was set for sacrifice. Such a shrine was called a *bamah*, here translated as *hill-shrine*. Later tradition said that this particular shrine was built on the southern end of the ridge east of Jerusalem called the Mount of Olives. This particular part of the ridge is still known as the Mount of Offence.

11. *the kingdom* here seems to refer to Israel, i.e. the northern tribes who had remained loyal to Saul's family and accepted Ishbosheth as king after Saul's death. David was only accepted as king by Israel several years after he had become king of Judah (cp. 2 Sam. 2: 8-11).

13. The *one tribe* is the tribe of Benjamin. The kingdom of Judah belonged to the house of David. Of the eleven tribes of the

north only one would remain loyal. The territory of Benjamin lay immediately to the north of Jerusalem, hence *for the sake of Jerusalem*, i.e. for the security and prosperity of that city. ✳

SOLOMON'S FIRST ADVERSARY

14 Then the LORD raised up an adversary for Solomon,
15 Hadad the Edomite, of the royal house of Edom. At the time when David reduced Edom, his commander-in-chief Joab had destroyed every male in the country when he
16 went into it to bury the slain. He and the armies of Israel remained there for six months, until he had destroyed
17 every male in Edom. Then Hadad, who was still a boy, fled the country with some of his father's Edomite ser-
18 vants, intending to enter Egypt. They set out from Midian, made their way to Paran and, taking some men from there, came to Pharaoh king of Egypt, who assigned Hadad a house and maintenance and made him a grant of
19 land. Hadad found great favour with Pharaoh, who gave
20 him in marriage a sister of Queen Tahpenes his wife. She bore him his son Genubath; Tahpenes weaned the child in Pharaoh's house, and he lived there along with Pharaoh's
21 children. When Hadad heard in Egypt that David rested with his forefathers and that his commander-in-chief Joab was also dead, he said to Pharaoh, 'Let me go so that I may
22 return to my own country.' 'What is it that you find wanting in my country', said Pharaoh, 'that you want to go back to your own?' 'Nothing,' said Hadad, 'but do,
25 pray, let me go.' He remained an adversary for Israel all through Solomon's reign. This*ᵃ* is the harm that Hadad

[a] *So Sept.; Heb. obscure.*

caused: he maintained a stranglehold on[a] Israel and became king of Edom.[b]

* 14. *Hadad the Edomite:* the story may have come from the archives of the king of Edom. The editors have used it as a concrete example of the decline of Solomon's power. The earlier part of the chapter has already paved the way for an account of such decline. *Edom* lay to the south of Judah and separated it from the Red Sea. David had originally conquered Edom (cp. 2 Sam. 8: 13–14), and all later kings of Judah tried to control it because of the value of the outlet to the Red Sea. Solomon must have controlled Edom or his mining activities in the Arabah and his trading from Ezion-geber would not have been possible. The point of this story is that Solomon's hold on Edom was weaker than that of David and therefore a sign of decline.

15. *destroyed every male:* in inter-tribal warfare, the Bedouin sometimes kill all male enemies. Women and children, including boys up to a certain age, are spared.

18. Hadad fled to the wilderness in the south, *Midian,* and from there made his way to Egypt. *Paran* was a part of the Sinai desert. We do not know the name of the pharaoh who received Hadad so well. It could have been the same pharaoh whose daughter Solomon married. Both David and Solomon at the height of their powers would have been too strong and ambitious for the comfort of any pharaoh.

25. *maintained a stranglehold on:* the N.E.B. has preferred this reading of the Peshitta to the Hebrew. It is certainly stronger in meaning but unhistorical. So long as Solomon could use his Red Sea fleet there was no *stranglehold,* and we have no reason to believe that he ever lost control of the fleet. 'loathed' (N.E.B. footnote) is the better reading. This expresses the general hatred of one people for a despised rival, and all the

[a] maintained...on: *so Pesh.; Heb.* loathed.
[b] *So Sept.; Heb.* Aram.

hostility which would follow from it. This verse clearly refers to *Hadad* and not Rezon. So the N.E.B. has placed it after verse 22 to complete the account of *Hadad*. The fragment about Rezon was inserted between verses 22 and 25 because *Edom* was misread in Hebrew as 'Aram'. The mistake is easy to understand (see p. 18). Rezon became king of Damascus, the chief city of Aram. ✳

A FRAGMENT CONCERNING A SECOND
ADVERSARY

23 Then God raised up another adversary against Solomon, Rezon son of Eliada, who had fled from his master
24 Hadadezer king of Zobah. He gathered men about him and became a captain of freebooters,[a] who came to Damascus and occupied it; he[b] became king there.

✳ This fragment continues the story of David's defeat of *Hadadezer king of Zobah* (cp. 2 Sam. 8: 3). *Zobah* has not been identified, but it was a city state in Aram. Baalbek has been suggested as a possible site. David defeated the king and garrisoned the cities of the area including Damascus. When Israelite authority weakened under Solomon, *Rezon* saw his chance of greatness. He established his authority in much the same way as David himself had done at Hebron. He may have been active during the reign of David as is implied by the clause which the N.E.B. has relegated to the footnote. The difficulty of accepting it is that it would make *Rezon* a very old man when he became king. His capture of *Damascus* is a further example of Solomon's decline. It was an event which had far-reaching consequences. From that time Damascus became the capital of the state of Aram which proved to be a powerful and troublesome rival for the northern kingdom of Israel. ✳

[a] *So Sept.; Heb. adds* when David killed them.
[b] *So Sept.; Heb.* they.

JEROBOAM SON OF NEBAT

Jeroboam son of Nebat, one of Solomon's courtiers, an 26[a]
Ephrathite from Zeredah, whose widowed mother was
named Zeruah, rebelled against the king. And this is the 27
story of his rebellion. Solomon had built the Millo and
closed the breach in the wall of the city of his father David.
Now this Jeroboam was a man of great energy; and 28
Solomon, seeing how the young man worked, had put
him in charge of all the labour-gangs in the tribal
district of Joseph. On one occasion Jeroboam had left 29
Jerusalem, and the prophet Ahijah from Shiloh met him on
the road. The prophet was wrapped in a new cloak, and
the two of them were alone in the open country. Then 30
Ahijah took hold of the new cloak he was wearing, tore
it into twelve pieces and said to Jeroboam, 'Take ten 31
pieces, for this is the word of the LORD the God of Israel:
"I am going to tear the kingdom from the hand of
Solomon and give you ten tribes. But one tribe will 32
remain his, for the sake of my servant David and for the
sake of Jerusalem, the city I have chosen out of all the
tribes of Israel. I have done this because Solomon has[b] 33
forsaken me; he has[b] prostrated himself before Ashtoreth
goddess of the Sidonians, Kemosh god of Moab, and
Milcom god of the Ammonites, and has[b] not conformed
to my ways. He has not done what is right in my eyes or
observed my statutes and judgements as David his father
did. Nevertheless I will not take the whole kingdom 34
from him, but will maintain his rule as long as he lives, for

[a] *Verse 25 transposed to follow verse 22.*
[b] has: *so Sept.; Heb. has plural.*

143

the sake of my chosen servant David, who did observe my
35 commandments and statutes. But I will take the kingdom,
36 that is the ten tribes, from his son and give it to you. One
tribe I will give to his son, that my servant David may
always have a flame burning before me in Jerusalem, the
37 city which I chose to receive my Name. But I will appoint
you to rule over all that you can desire, and to be king
38 over Israel. If you pay heed to all my commands, if you
conform to my ways and do what is right in my eyes,
observing my statutes and commandments as my servant
David did, then I will be with you. I will establish your
family for ever as I did for David; I will give Israel to you,
39 and punish David's descendants as they have deserved,
but not for ever."'
40   After this Solomon sought to kill Jeroboam, but he fled
to King Shishak in Egypt and remained there till Solomon's
death.

* 26. *Jeroboam* was from Ephraim, the leading tribe of the
north. *Zeredah* was situated in what later came to be called
Samaria. *Zeruah:* the name means 'leper' which clearly is a
Judaean slander.

27. *Jeroboam* must have appeared in the later part of Solomon's reign since *the Millo* and *the wall* connecting the temple
to the city were already built.

28. *the tribal district of Joseph* was Jeroboam's own locality
since it included both the tribal groupings of Ephraim and
Manasseh. Probably the work brought to his attention the
widespread dissatisfaction with Solomon's oppressive rule. It
seems that forced labour was being demanded from Israelites
as well as Canaanite subjects (cp. 9: 20–2 and note on 5: 13).
Dissatisfaction with Solomon's rule could be most easily
exploited in the north. The house of David was southern in

origin and could claim no local tribal loyalty in the north.
There a situation developed which a brave and resourceful
adventurer could easily turn to his own advantage.

29. *the prophet Ahijah:* the fact that Jeroboam was supported,
indeed authenticated, by a prophet is of particular importance
and interest. Companies of prophets had lived for a long time
at various places in the land, often at or near old sanctuaries.
Ahijah came from *Shiloh*, the place where the Ark was kept
during the earliest days of the settlement before it fell into the
hands of the Philistines. The prophets were among the religious
leaders who were most hostile to the Canaanite way of life,
and any attempt to import it into Israel. Since in Israel prophets
could speak freely and critically even to kings (cp. 2 Sam. 12:
1–14), it was natural that some of the prophets should become
the centres of opposition to the monarchy. They believed that
the demands that it was making, as here Solomon's demand
for forced labour, were changing for the worse the character
of society. So it is quite feasible that Jeroboam's attempt to stir
the northern tribes to revolt was supported by prophets and
gained a great deal of authority from such support.

Because prophets had taken such a lead in the struggle
against the spread of Canaanite influence in both Israel and
Judah, the deuteronomists had a high regard for them, and in
the law, in the book of Deuteronomy, great authority was
given to prophets. Thus, God had given the law to Moses, and
even after his death God would ensure that in every generation
there would be a prophet who would continue Moses' work
by calling upon the people to be loyal to the law, and by
interpreting God's will to the people (Deut. 18: 15). Since
this very high office was to be given to a prophet, the people
needed to have some means of distinguishing true from false
prophets. The law gave a solution to the problem. The pre-
dictions of true prophets would all come to pass, and by that
token the people would know that they could accept their
authority (cp. Deut. 18: 21–2). This makes clear why the
greater part of this narrative is concerned with Jeroboam's

meeting with the prophet Ahijah, and the prophet's declaration
that Jeroboam would become ruler of ten of the tribes. This is
meant to tell us that Jeroboam is the instrument chosen by God
to humble Solomon's son, and that the success of the revolt
was not due to chance but a part of the divine plan.

30. The prophets taught as often by deeds as by words. They
performed some symbolic action and, if they were true
prophets, the action which they had symbolized happened.
This kind of teaching is known as prophetic symbolism. It
declared God's will and showed the inevitability of the fulfilment of that will, and also the responsibility of those who
ignored it or tried to flout it. Jesus himself was acting within
this tradition when he drove the money-changers from the
temple and when he instituted the Last Supper. Ahijah's
symbolism emphasizes something which was very important
to the deuteronomists, namely, the essential unity of the covenant people. The number twelve expressed the wholeness and
unity of the old tribal group. Now there were to be two
kingdoms, two political societies, but the idea of the one
covenant people lived on, and embraced both kingdoms in a
unity which was more important than any political division.

32. The *one tribe* is Benjamin (see note on II: 13).

39. *but not for ever:* these words probably reflect the experience of the exile. They express the faith of the deuteronomists
that God would restore the Judaeans to rebuild the temple and
give them another chance of living as his obedient servants. In
later chapters the deuteronomists will condemn Jeroboam and
his successors in very harsh words because they set out to break
the loyalty of the ten tribes to the covenant ideal and to a large
degree succeeded. The consequences of this were that God
could only look to Judah to fulfil his purposes. In this the
deuteronomists were interpreting the history in the light of
their knowledge of later events. In 721 B.C. Samaria was
destroyed by the Assyrians, and the northern kingdom came
to an end. The religious reforms which meant so much to the
deuteronomists took place in Judah, which after 721 B.C. was

in effect the one centre of the covenant people. It is, therefore, almost impossible with details such as the symbolism used by Ahijah to be sure that the deuteronomists did not create them in order to point more clearly the lessons they wished to teach.

40. *King Shishak* is the first pharaoh to be mentioned by name. He was the founder of the XXII Dynasty and reigned from 935 to 914 B.C. Since his reign began so late in the reign of Solomon, Solomon is likely to have been married to the daughter of his predecessor. *Shishak* would look upon Solomon as a rival rather than ally or friend. ✻

THE DEATH OF SOLOMON

The other acts and events of Solomon's reign, and all 41[a] his wisdom, are recorded in the annals of Solomon. The 42 reign of King Solomon in Jerusalem over the whole of Israel lasted forty years. Then he rested with his forefathers 43 and was buried in the city of David his father, and he was succeeded by his son Rehoboam.

✻ 41. *the annals of Solomon* were official records from which the editors have taken material for their history.

42. *forty years:* David is also said to have reigned for the same length of time. For both David and Solomon the number may be approximate rather than accurate. Forty was the traditional number for a generation.

43. The usual details given for a king at the beginning of his reign are not set out here for *Rehoboam*. They occur later (14: 21), after the story of the loss of the northern tribes has been told. ✻

[a] *Verses 41–43: cp. 2 Chr. 9. 29–31.*

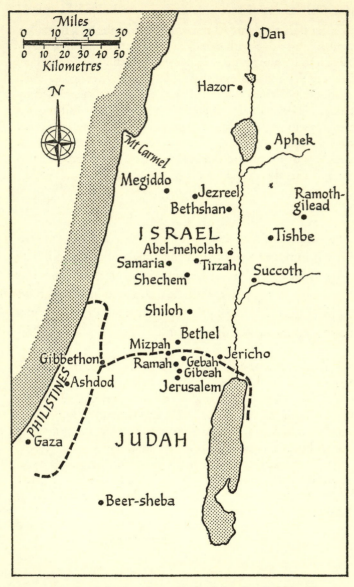

5. The land during the period of the divided kingdom.

148

The divided kingdom

⁎ We now learn that Solomon's mighty empire died with him for ever and the united kingdom of Israel and Judah which David had created came to an end. From this time the tribes of the north refused to accept the king of Judah as their ruler and formed an independent kingdom of Israel. ⁎

REHOBOAM AT SHECHEM

R EHOBOAM WENT to Shechem, for all Israel had gone **12** 1ᵃ there to make him king. When Jeroboam son of 2 Nebat, who was still in Egypt, heard of it, he remainedᵇ there, having taken refuge there to escape King Solomon. They now recalled him, and he and all the assembly of 3 Israel came to Rehoboam and said, 'Your father laid a 4 cruel yoke upon us; but if you will now lighten the cruel slavery he imposed on us and the heavy yoke he laid on 5 us, we will serve you.' 'Give me three days,' he said, 'and come back again.' So the people went away. King Reho- 6 boam then consulted the elders who had been in attendance on his father Solomon while he lived: 'What answer do you advise me to give to this people?' And they said, 7 'If today you are willing to serve this people, show yourself their servant now and speak kindly to them, and they will be your servants ever after.' But he rejected the 8 advice which the elders gave him. He next consulted those who had grown up with him, the young men in

[a] *Verses 1–19: cp. 2 Chr. 10: 1–19.*
[b] *Or, with Sept. and 2 Chr. 10: 2,* returned from.

9 attendance, and asked them, 'What answer do you advise
me to give to this people's request that I should lighten
10 the yoke which my father laid on them?' The young men
replied, 'Give this answer to the people who say that your
father made their yoke heavy and ask you to lighten it;
tell them: "My little finger is thicker than my father's
11 loins. My father laid a heavy yoke on you; I will make it
heavier. My father used the whip on you; but I will use
12 the lash."' Jeroboam and the people all came back to
13 Rehoboam on the third day, as the king had ordered. And
the king gave them a harsh answer. He rejected the advice
14 which the elders had given him and spoke to the people
as the young men had advised: 'My father made your
yoke heavy; I will make it heavier. My father used the
15 whip on you; but I will use the lash.' So the king would
not listen to the people; for the LORD had given this turn
to the affair, in order that the word he had spoken by
Ahijah of Shiloh to Jeroboam son of Nebat might be
fulfilled.

16 When all Israel saw that the king would not listen to
them, they answered:

> What share have we in David?
> We have no lot in the son of Jesse.
> Away to your homes, O Israel;
> now see to your own house, David.

17 So Israel went to their homes, and Rehoboam ruled over
those Israelites who lived in the cities of Judah.

18 Then King Rehoboam sent out Adoram, the commander of the forced levies, but the Israelites stoned him
to death; thereupon King Rehoboam mounted his chariot

in haste and fled to Jerusalem. From that day to this, the 19
whole of Israel has been in rebellion against the house of
David.

* 1. *Rehoboam* had clearly the best claim to follow his
father Solomon as king of the northern tribes as well as king
of Judah. However, no hereditary right had as yet been
established and he had to be accepted by the tribes. *Shechem*
was an old city, the principal city of the central hill-country
north of Jerusalem. It lay at the eastern end of the shoulder of
land which joined two mountains, Ebal and Gerizim, hence its
name. (Shechem means 'shoulder'.) The modern Arab city,
which is its successor, is situated in the shoulder between the
two mountains. Shechem lay farther to the east, near the site
of Jacob's well. The site, now called Tell Balatah, has been
excavated, and the excavations confirm that it was a flourish-
ing city at this time. Shechem may have been chosen to be the
site of the assembly because of its central position. It has been
suggested that it was the original meeting-place of the old
tribal league. Joshua certainly assembled the tribes there
(cp. Josh. 24: 1). If so, its choice may have been meant to
indicate that kings ought not to transgress the traditions of the
league as Solomon had done, particularly by his demand for
forced labour.

2. The part played by *Jeroboam* in the events at Shechem is
not clear. Verse 20 reads as though Jeroboam returned from
exile after he had heard of the rebellion at Shechem. This
conflicts with the reference made to him here and in verse
12. But there is no reference to Jeroboam in either verse in
the Greek text. The Greek omits verse 2 and the first clause
of verse 3. It describes 'the assembly of Israel' as negotiating with Rehoboam. This seems more likely to have been
the case. Probably verse 2 was added to the Hebrew text
together with the references to Jeroboam in verses 3 and 12
by an editor who wished to show that the prophecy of Ahijah,

recorded only a few verses earlier, was fulfilled as quickly as possible.

11. *the lash:* Rehoboam's threat, as translated by the N.E.B., is prosaic when compared with earlier translations. Rehoboam threatened them with 'scorpions'. His use of the word was idiomatic. It was the name given to a particularly unpleasant form of whip which stung the flesh of its victims.

15. The story makes plain that the division of the kingdom was unnecessary and could easily have been avoided. It was caused by the stupidity of Rehoboam, and no attempt is made to excuse him. On the other hand, the division is presented as God's will for his people. So much has already been implied in the last chapter in the account of Ahijah's prophecy, and in the same vein are the words here, *for the LORD had given this turn to the affair*. They are intended to show that the word of a true prophet was quickly fulfilled. No attempt is made to reconcile the two ways of looking at the event.

16. The reply of the assembly is a fragment of poetry. The first three lines of the poem have already appeared in 2 Sam. 20: 1. There they were spoken by Sheba when he was attempting to raise the northern tribes against David. It seems likely that they were a traditional rhyme of the north and quoted on any occasion when the longstanding suspicion between north and south was for some reason rising to the surface.

18. *Adoram* is the same person as the officer called Adoniram in the list of Solomon's officers in chapter 4. ✻

JEROBOAM BECOMES KING

20 When the men of Israel heard that Jeroboam had returned, they sent and called him to the assembly and made him king over the whole of Israel. The tribe of Judah alone followed the house of David.

21*a* When Rehoboam reached Jerusalem, he assembled all

[*a*] *Verses 21–24: cp. 2 Chr. 11: 1–4.*

the house of Judah, the tribe of Benjamin also, a hundred
and eighty thousand chosen warriors, to fight against the
house of Israel and recover his kingdom. But the word of 22
God came to Shemaiah the man of God: 'Say to Reho- 23
boam son of Solomon, king of Judah, and to the house of
Judah and to Benjamin and the rest of the people, "This 24
is the word of the LORD: You shall not go up to make war
on your kinsmen the Israelites. Return to your homes, for
this is my will."' So they listened to the word of the LORD
and returned home, as the LORD had told them.

✻ 20. *they sent and called him:* the words imply that Jeroboam
first came to Shechem after Rehoboam had returned to
Jerusalem (see note on verse 2 above). *made him king:* Jeroboam became king by the free choice of his subjects. Saul had
also been similarly elected (cp. 1 Sam. 11: 12–15). So Jeroboam's rule was potentially a very different kind of kingship
from the authoritarian rule of a Canaanite monarch such as
Solomon had imitated.

21. *the tribe of Benjamin also:* these words contradict what
was written about Judah in the previous verse. It has been
suggested that they were added by an editor, but they agree
with the references to the *one tribe* in 11: 13 and 11: 32. The
number of warriors given is an exaggeration.

22–4. A prophet again determined what was to happen.
This intervention may point to an older way of finding
leaders dating from the times of the tribal league. Leadership
was not then hereditary and new leaders may have been
designated by a prophet to show that they had been truly
chosen by God (cp. 1 Sam. 10: 17–24). At all events, this is
another example of the high status and authority given to
prophets in Kings.

22. *the man of God* is most likely a synonym for a prophet
(see comment on 13: 11).

24. *and returned home:* this contradicts the summary of Rehoboam's reign at 14: 30 which tells of continuous warfare between Jeroboam and Rehoboam. The account here of peaceful co-existence is not historical. The deuteronomists are again rewriting history to make it fit better with their theories. If Jeroboam had become king with God's approval, then Rehoboam ought to accept the situation, particularly when it had been spelled out for him by a prophet.

In the Greek Septuagint a lengthy addition to the narrative follows at this point. It collects together all the information about Jeroboam which occurs in chapters 12 to 14 and adds extra information for the most part unsympathetic to Jeroboam. It is an example of the way in which extra stories grew up in tradition around important persons in Old Testament stories. Such stories were called Midrash by the Jews. ✻

JEROBOAM'S APOSTASY

25 Then Jeroboam rebuilt Shechem in the hill-country of Ephraim and took up residence there; from there he went
26 out and built Penuel. 'As things now stand,' he said to himself, 'the kingdom will revert to the house of David.
27 If this people go up to sacrifice in the house of the LORD in Jerusalem, it will revive their allegiance to their lord Rehoboam king of Judah, and they will kill me and return
28 to King Rehoboam.' After giving thought to the matter he made two calves of gold and said to the people, 'It is too much trouble for you to go up to Jerusalem; here are
29 your gods, Israel, that brought you up from Egypt.' One
30 he set up at Bethel and the other he put at Dan, and this thing became a sin in Israel; the people went to Bethel to worship the one, and*a* all the way to Dan to worship the

[a] in Israel...one, and: *so Luc. Sept.; Heb.* the people went.

other. He set up shrines on the hill-tops also and appointed 31
priests from every class of the people, who did not belong
to the Levites.

* This passage reflects very strongly the point of view of the
deuteronomists who were totally opposed to any shrine other
than Jerusalem. There were many shrines in the territory of the
northern tribes and some of them, for example Bethel, had a
much older place in Israel's tradition than Jerusalem. Solomon's
temple had naturally become the most important shrine in the
kingdom and must have tended to overshadow the others.
Jeroboam did not set up new shrines but gave his patronage to
two of the older shrines which were in his territory and thereby made them rivals of Jerusalem. They became, as Jerusalem
was, royal shrines. There was nothing in this which was
contrary to the old tribal traditions. Indeed, it may well have
seemed to many in the north that shrines associated with the
old tradition, and untouched by the new, despotic, mon-
archical traditions of Jerusalem, were much nearer to the true
covenant traditions of Israel. The prophets who ministered
in the north, such as Elijah or Amos, never condemned those
shrines as illegitimate, much as they disliked a good deal that
went on in them. They are condemned in the narrative here
simply because they offended against the deuteronomic
doctrine that Jerusalem, and Jerusalem alone, was the legitimate shrine where God ought to be worshipped. Jeroboam
almost certainly intended his two shrines to be dedicated to
the worship of Yahweh. It was the deuteronomists who,
because of their distaste for the shrines, described them as pagan
and maintained that Canaanite gods were worshipped there.

25. *rebuilt Shechem* means that he strengthened the fortifications. *Penuel* was situated on the Jabbok river, east of Jordan
in the territory of Gilead. A strong fortress was necessary on
the other side of the Jordan if he was to hold the land there
securely. It may be that the invasion of Pharaoh Shishak

forced Jeroboam to abandon *Shechem* and make his capital east of the Jordan at *Penuel*. When he returned to the western part of his territory he may well have set up his capital at Tirzah which was more inaccessible than *Shechem*.

28. The *calves* were thrones upon which Yahweh, the invisible God, could sit. This was parallel to Solomon's setting the Ark and the cherubim in his temple as a similar throne. The deuteronomists have described the *calves* as idols of pagan deities. This is not correct but the deuteronomists may have believed it to be true. They wrote after the destruction of the northern kingdom which they believed to be God's punishment of that kingdom for the apostasy of the people and their unwillingness to repent. They believed this to be an attitude which was endemic in the northern kingdom from its beginning so they interpreted Jeroboam's actions in this way.

29. There were two shrines because of the size of the kingdom. Judah was much smaller and so Jerusalem could conveniently serve the whole kingdom. *Bethel* was in the southern part of Jeroboam's kingdom and *Dan* in the far north (see map 5 on p. 148). Both were ancient and respected shrines. The priests of *Dan* were descended from the family of Moses (cp. Judg. 18: 30), and *Bethel* had links with the patriarch Jacob.

30. The Greek text which the N.E.B. has rightly followed makes the point of the two shrines clear.

31. The hill-top *shrines* were also ancient. Most towns and villages would have possessed one. It was only after the deuteronomic reform that they were regarded as pagan. The derogatory comment on the priests also reflects the southern loyalties of the editors.

A new paragraph should begin at verse 32. Verses 32 and 33 introduce the story of Jeroboam's offering sacrifice which is the subject of the next chapter. ✳

JEROBOAM OFFERS SACRIFICE

He instituted a pilgrim-feast on the fifteenth day of the 32
eighth month like that in Judah, and he offered sacrifices
upon the altar. This he did at Bethel, sacrificing to the
calves that he had made and compelling the priests of
the hill-shrines, which he had set up, to serve at Bethel.
So he went up to the altar that he had made at Bethel on 33
the fifteenth day of the eighth month; there, in a month
of his own choosing, he instituted for the Israelites a
pilgrim-feast and himself went up to the altar to burn the
sacrifice.

As Jeroboam stood by the altar to burn the sacrifice, a **13**
man of God from Judah, moved by the word of the LORD,
appeared at Bethel. He inveighed against the altar in the 2
LORD's name, crying out, 'O altar, altar! This is the word
of the LORD: "Listen! A child shall be born to the house of
David, named Josiah. He will sacrifice upon you the
priests of the hill-shrines who make offerings upon you,
and he*a* will burn human bones upon you."' He gave a 3
sign the same day: 'This is the sign which the LORD has
ordained: This altar will be rent in pieces and the ashes
upon it will be spilt.' When King Jeroboam heard the 4
sentence which the man of God pronounced against the
altar at Bethel, he pointed to him from the altar and said,
'Seize that man!' Immediately the hand which he had
pointed at him became paralysed, so that he could not
draw it back. The altar too was rent in pieces and the 5
ashes were spilt, in fulfilment of the sign that the man of
God had given at the LORD's command. The king appealed 6

[a] *So Sept.; Heb.* they.

to the man of God to pacify the LORD his God and pray
for him that his hand might be restored. The man of God
did as he asked; his hand was restored and became as it had
7 been before. Then the king said to the man of God, 'Come
home and take refreshment at my table, and let me give
8 you a present.' But the man of God answered, 'If you
were to give me half your house, I would not enter it with
9 you: I will eat and drink nothing in this place, for the
LORD's command to me was to eat and drink nothing,
10 and not to go back by the way I came.' So he went back
another way; he did not return by the road he had taken
to Bethel.

✻ 32. Solomon offered sacrifice at the dedication of the temple
at Jerusalem. Jeroboam is shown acting in much the same way.
The editors clearly wished to compare the two to the disadvantage of Jeroboam, and to the discredit of *Bethel* as a place
of pilgrimage.

33. The *pilgrim-feast* at *Bethel* is described as an imitation of
and rival to the one already established at Jerusalem, but
celebrated a month later. This may be historically accurate.
If so, we do not know why Jeroboam altered the month.
Perhaps he hoped to draw to Bethel some of those who had
already worshipped at Jerusalem. Perhaps the two shrines had
different liturgical calendars. But the purpose of the editors in
mentioning the month was most likely to mock Jeroboam as a
liturgical ignoramus.

13: 1–10. This story is to be linked with the account of Josiah
leaving the grave of the man of God untouched when he
desecrated the Bethel sanctuary (2 Kings 23: 16–18). The
story as given here is legendary. It is an example of the kind of
literature the Jews called Midrash. There is no reason to doubt
that the editors who included the story believed it to be
historical. They would have come across it as a story attached

to the grave of a holy man at Bethel, and accepted it at its face value. It illustrated very well the point they wanted to make, that Jeroboam offended God by setting up Bethel as a royal sanctuary. The story in its present form dates from some time after Josiah's reform. It explained why a particular grave was left untouched when so many others were desecrated.

2. To *burn human bones* upon an altar was a very grave act of desecration which nothing could reverse.

5. According to the story Josiah's act would not wipe out the sanctity of Bethel. The real truth was that Bethel had never been a holy place. It was a sham from the beginning as was shown when at the first sacrifice offered there by Jeroboam, *The altar was rent in pieces* and the *ashes* on it which were impregnated with the fat of the sacrifices, the portion of the animals offered to God, were scattered. The contrast between this treatment and the signs of divine favour which marked Solomon's sacrifices at Jerusalem could not have been more marked. Perhaps the editors felt the need to denigrate Bethel specially, because of its association with the patriarch Jacob.

7. If the man of God had accepted Jeroboam's hospitality, he would have retracted by implication his condemnation of the king. This accounts for the vigour of the man of God's reply. ✳

THE DEATH OF THE MAN OF GOD

At that time there was an aged prophet living in Bethel. 11 His sons came[a] and recounted to him all that the man of God had done in Bethel that day; they also told their father what he had said to the king. Their father said to 12 them, 'Which road did he take?' They pointed out the road taken by the man of God who had come from Judah. He said to his sons, 'Saddle an ass for me.' They saddled 13 the ass, and he mounted it and went after the man of God. 14

[a] *So Sept.; Heb.* His son came.

159

He found him seated under a terebinth and said to him,
'Are you the man of God who came from Judah?' And
15 he said, 'Yes, I am.' 'Come home and eat with me', said
16 the prophet. 'I cannot go back with you or enter your
house,' said the other; 'I can neither eat nor drink with
17 you in this place, for it was told me by the word of the
LORD: "You shall eat and drink nothing there, nor shall
18 you go back the way you came."' And the old man said
to him, 'I also am a prophet, as you are; and an angel
commanded me by the word of the LORD to bring you
home with me to eat and drink with me.' He was lying;
19 but the man of Judah went back with him and ate and
20 drank in his house. While they were still seated at table
the word of the LORD came to the prophet who had
21 brought him back, and he cried out to the man of God
from Judah, 'This is the word of the LORD: "You have defied the word of the LORD your God and have not obeyed
22 his command; you have come back to eat and to drink in
the place where he forbade it; therefore your body shall
not be laid in the grave of your forefathers."'

23   After they had eaten and drunk, he saddled an ass for
24 the prophet whom he had brought back. As he went on
his way a lion met him and killed him, and his body was
left lying in the road, with the ass and the lion both
25 standing beside it. Some passers-by saw the body lying
in the road and the lion standing beside it, and they brought
26 the news to the city where the old prophet lived. When
the prophet who had caused him to break his journey
heard it, he said, 'It is the man of God who defied the
word of the LORD. The LORD has given him to the lion,
and it has broken his neck and killed him in fulfilment of

the word of the LORD.' He told his sons to saddle an ass 27
and, when they had saddled it, he set out and found the 28
body lying in the road with the ass and the lion standing
beside it; the lion had neither devoured the body nor
broken the back of the ass. Then the prophet lifted the 29
body of the man of God, laid it on the ass and brought it
back to his own city to mourn over it and bury it. He 30
laid the body in his own grave and they mourned for him,
saying, 'My brother, my brother!' After burying him, he 31
said to his sons, 'When I die, bury me in the grave where
the man of God lies buried; lay my bones beside his; for 32
the sentence which he pronounced at the LORD's command against the altar in Bethel and all the hill-shrines of
Samaria shall be carried out.'

* It was important to Hebrews at this time that after death
their bodies should lie in the family grave. For this not to
happen was looked upon as a sign of divine displeasure. So the
question arose here, how did it come about that the man of
God from Judah who had clearly proclaimed God's word, was
buried at Bethel far from his family grave? The grave at
Bethel could be interpreted as evidence that God had approved
of Jeroboam's action rather than the man of God's words. The
story told here is meant to solve the problem. Again it is
Midrash.

The prophet from Bethel may have wished to entertain the
man of God to link himself in fellowship with him as a form
of insurance. He may have thought that he could avoid future
disaster by such a claim of friendship. Whatever the motive, he
achieved his purpose by claiming to be the bearer of a
message from God which overrode that originally given to
the man of God. The man of God accepted its authority and
in so doing denied the validity of his own relationship with

God. If he were a true prophet, then God would have communicated directly with him and not through an intermediary. His paying attention to the prophet therefore called in question the validity of all that he had said and done at Bethel. In this way he was disloyal to his own prophetic vocation and dishonoured God who had sent him. The only way in which the validity of the message he had delivered to Jeroboam could be safeguarded was for him to be treated by God as a disobedient traitor. So on his way home he died and in such a manner as men could only interpret as the direct intervention of God. The meeting with the lion was no accident. If so his corpse would have been mauled and the ass killed.

The story needs a full explanation because the logic which underlies it is so foreign, and indeed repulsive, to us. But we need to understand it so that we can grasp the point it was meant to make to the readers. The understanding of the nature of God which underlies the story is crude. It shows him as applying retributive justice in a narrowly mechanical and impersonal way; the action of a harsh tyrant rather than a compassionate God who had made a covenant with his people. We must frankly say that the view of God's nature underlying this chapter is crude and insensitive, untouched by the spiritual awareness of the best of the Old Testament tradition. All this can be accounted for by understanding the origins of the narrative. It is Midrash, a story used in popular religious teaching. Like all such literature it makes a single point with clarity and force but, in so doing, oversimplifies the issues and distorts truth.

The editors accepted the story as they found it in popular tradition and used it, because, with all its limitations, it made very clearly the main point they wished to bring home to their readers. This was that coming to terms with Canaanite civilization, as they believed the northern kingdom had done, was spiritually dangerous. The one safeguard against the attractions of Canaan was rigid obedience to the old ways of Israel. The story teaches the importance of obedience, and that disobedience was so offensive to God as to call forth from him the severest punishment. The story is crude in that it shows no acquaintance with the rich, many-sided understanding of the nature of God which the deuteronomists taught. Deuteronomy has much to say of God's love for his people and his dissatisfaction with any response which fell short of heartfelt love. Nothing of that aspect of the teaching is found in this story. Yet the deuteronomists used it because they regarded its message as being important enough to excuse its limitations.

11. The two protagonists are always clearly distinguished. The man from Judah is *the man of God*. The man from Bethel is *the prophet*. What significance, if any, there is in this distinction is impossible to say. Perhaps the man from Bethel was known to belong to a prophetic guild. The antecedents of the man from Judah would have been unknown, but his word had been proved true by events. Therefore he was a *man of God* whether or not he belonged to a guild.

31. The prophet wished to be buried in the same *grave* as *the man of God* to identify himself with *the man of God* as 'kin' and, thereby, to give his own witness that the words of *the man of God* were a true prophecy.

32. *Samaria* used as the title of the northern kingdom shows that this story was written down long after the death of Jeroboam. ✳

JEROBOAM'S FALSE PRIESTS

After this Jeroboam still did not abandon his evil ways 33 but went on appointing priests for the hill-shrines from all classes of the people; any man who offered himself he would consecrate to be priest of a hill-shrine. By doing 34 this he brought guilt upon his own house and doomed it to utter destruction.

* 33. *went on appointing priests:* to the deuteronomists this was the most evil thing he could do. It cut off the people from the temple and priesthood at Jerusalem and not only physically. In creating a priesthood Jeroboam inevitably created also a teaching which was bound to be a rival to Jerusalem. In this way he was thought to have turned away the majority of Israel from their loyalty to and regard for the covenant tradition which made them the people of God. Such an act could not go unnoticed or unpunished. By this act Jeroboam had ensured that the story of the kingdom he had established must be one of disaster and ultimate extinction. *the hill-shrines:* because the religious practices of the shrines were often markedly influenced by the ideas and practices of the Canaanites, the prophets were hostile to them and Josiah tried to abolish them (see note on 12: 31). *

JEROBOAM'S SON

14 1, 2 At that time Jeroboam's son Abijah fell ill, and Jeroboam said to his wife, 'Come now, disguise yourself so that people may not be able to recognize you as my wife, and go to Shiloh. Ahijah the prophet is there, the man 3 who said I was to be king over this people. Take with you ten loaves, some raisins, and a flask of syrup, and go to him; he will tell you what will happen to the child.' 4 Jeroboam's wife did so; she set off at once for Shiloh and came to Ahijah's house. Now Ahijah could not see, for his 5 eyes were fixed in the blindness of old age, and the LORD had said to him, 'The wife of Jeroboam is on her way to consult you about her son, who is ill; you shall give her such and such an answer.' When she came in, concealing 6 who she was, and Ahijah heard her footsteps at the door, he said, 'Come in, wife of Jeroboam. Why conceal who

you are? I have heavy news for you. Go and tell Jero- 7
boam: "This is the word of the LORD the God of Israel:
I raised you out of the people and appointed you prince
over my people Israel; I tore away the kingdom from the 8
house of David and gave it to you; but you have not been
like my servant David, who kept my commands and
followed me with his whole heart, doing only what was
right in my eyes. You have outdone all your predecessors 9
in wickedness; you have provoked me to anger by making
for yourself other gods and images of cast metal; and you
have turned your back on me. For this I will bring disaster 10
on the house of Jeroboam and I will destroy them all,
every mother's son, whether still under the protection of
the family or not, and I will sweep away the house of
Jeroboam in Israel, as a man sweeps up dung until none
is left. Those of that house who die in the city shall be food 11
for the dogs, and those who die in the country shall be
food for the birds. It is the word of the LORD."

'You must go home now; the moment you set foot in 12
the city, the child will die. All Israel will mourn for him 13
and bury him; he alone of all Jeroboam's family will have
proper burial, because in him alone could the LORD the
God of Israel find anything good. Then the LORD will 14
set up a king over Israel who shall put an end to the house
of Jeroboam. This first; and what next*[a]*? The LORD will 15
strike Israel, till it trembles like a reed in the water; he will
uproot its people from this good land which he gave to
their forefathers and scatter them beyond the Euphrates,
because they have made their sacred poles*[b]* and provoked

[a] next: *so Targ.; Heb.* now.
[b] *Heb.* asherim.

16 the LORD's anger. And he will abandon Israel for the sins
that Jeroboam has committed and has led Israel to
17 commit.' Jeroboam's wife went home at once to Tirzah
and, as she crossed the threshold of the house, the boy
18 died. They buried him, and all Israel mourned over him;
and thus the word of the LORD was fulfilled which he had
spoken through his servant Ahijah the prophet.

* Here another story is told in which a prophet condemns the
family and dynasty of Jeroboam because he has seduced his
people away from their true religious allegiance. The prophet
is Ahijah who had encouraged Jeroboam's ambitions (cp. 11:
29–39). The purpose of the editors is to show how Jeroboam
was truly chosen by God to be king of Israel and then forfeited
God's approval by his apostasy. In fact Jeroboam is portrayed
as having merited God's sternest condemnation. Both Jeroboam's gaining the throne and forfeiting it for his successors
were determined by God, and were declared to be so by a true
prophet. The point is underlined by the use of the same prophet
as God's agent on both occasions. The death of a child
was understood at this time as being a punishment for a
grave sin of the parents. David's adultery with Bathsheba
was also punished by the death of their child (2 Sam.
12: 14).

The version of the story found in the Septuagint is much
simpler. It tells only of the visit of Jeroboam's wife to the
prophet at the time of her son's death without reference to any
political issues. It is likely that this version of the story is
nearer to what actually happened. The editors have used that
story as the basis for their own condemnation of the whole
dynasty of Jeroboam. The story probably began as a plain
description of a sad event in Jeroboam's life. When a child fell
seriously ill, Jeroboam sent his wife for help to the prophet
whom he had every reason to believe was well disposed
towards him. However, the child died, and the event was

regarded as a divine punishment for some sin. The editors have identified this sin as religious apostasy and made the prophet utter a sweeping condemnation of Jeroboam. In doing this they believed they were drawing out the true significance of the event which had been made clear by the later history of the kingdom. They believed wholeheartedly that Jeroboam's religious policy had led to Israel's apostasy which in its turn had led to the destruction of the kingdom. The infection of Jeroboam's ideas had spread to the south and there the whole process was repeated. So the destruction of both Samaria and Jerusalem stemmed from the action of Jeroboam. In the light of the later history, they believed that their elaboration of the story drew out its meaning and in no way falsified it. Their view of history is not ours. They felt able to deal with their sources in a way which is unacceptable to us as history-writing. Our purpose is to discover what they meant, and we shall do this best by trying to understand their methods even when we do not agree with them.

3. The prophet's acceptance of food from her would be a sure sign of his goodwill.

4. *his eyes were fixed in the blindness of old age:* this is a great contrast with chapter 11 where Ahijah was a vigorous and austere man in full possession of all his faculties. Both age and blindness are likely to be details added by the editors in the process of moulding the story to their purpose. Extreme old age signified wisdom, and the blindness indicated that the prophet's recognition of Jeroboam's wife was second sight. These details are meant to emphasize the authority from God which the prophet possessed and to underline the fact that his words were a true prophetic utterance.

11. No descendant of Jeroboam, other than the child who had just died, would be decently buried. *dogs* were the scavengers of the cities who lived on refuse as did *birds* in the open country. The prophecy indicated the complete disgrace and destruction which were to come to Jeroboam's family. Any family regarded the reverent burial of their dead as a first duty. To

be unable to carry out this duty brought a family low in the estimation of all others as cursed by God.

14. *next* makes better sense than 'now' (N.E.B. footnote). The change follows the Targum, which is a translation into Aramaic used by Jews in the synagogues from the Persian period onwards, when most of them no longer understood Hebrew (see p. xi).

15. *beyond the Euphrates:* the phrase points to the story having been written down sometime after 721 B.C. when the northern kingdom came to an end. *sacred poles* have been called *asherim* in many translations. The word is a transliteration of the plural form of a Hebrew word. This shows uncertainty as to what the word exactly meant. Clearly it was the name of some religious object closely associated with Canaanite religious practices, and held in particular horror by the deuteronomists. Asherah was the name of the mother goddess in the Canaanite pantheon. Archaeological evidence now allows us to say with a good deal of confidence that the *asherim* were wooden poles erected near the altars at the shrines. The attitude of the deuteronomists to them points to their being a prominent feature of the fertility cults of Canaan. They may have represented the tree of life in the myth of creation, or have been thought to have been symbols of the goddess Asherah. Whatever their meaning and purpose, they had come to typify for the deuteronomists all the evils of Canaanite worship, and the influence of that worship upon the life and religion of Israel which they so greatly feared and hated.

17. *Tirzah* (see map 5 on p. 148): earlier (12: 25), it was written that Jeroboam 'rebuilt Shechem' and lived there. *Tirzah* has never previously been mentioned. From references in the next two chapters it is clear that *Tirzah* became the capital of the northern kingdom and the place where the royal palace was situated, until Omri built Samaria. There is no mention anywhere of a move from Shechem to *Tirzah* (but see comment on 12: 25). The almost casual reference to the city here supports the view that the story comes from a time when *Tirzah* was

believed always to have been the capital before Samaria. *Tirzah* is probably to be identified with Tell el-Farʻah which lies a few miles north-east of Shechem. *

THE SUMMARY OF JEROBOAM'S REIGN

The other events of Jeroboam's reign, in war and peace, are recorded in the annals of the kings of Israel. He reigned twenty-two years; then he rested with his forefathers and was succeeded by his son Nadab.

₁₉ ₂₀

* With this summary the editors round off their account of Jeroboam's reign. They have only used such material as is germane to their purpose. More information was available to those who wished to consult it, and they told their readers where it was to be found. They had no fear that the picture they had drawn would not be confirmed by the rest of the information. The annals of the kings of Israel have perished and are not available to us, but we can collect some information which the editors have omitted.

The invasion of Shishak, the Egyptian pharaoh, which the editors mention only in connection with Judah and Jerusalem (14: 25), also affected the northern kingdom. He may have driven Jeroboam from Shechem to Penuel (see comment on 12: 25). An inscription of Shishak found at Karnak in Egypt claims the capture of northern cities, and at Megiddo a fragment of a monumental stele has been found which lends support to the claim that he captured that city. Then, too, the account of Rehoboam's reign over Judah speaks of continuous fighting between him and Jeroboam (14: 30). There is also an account of Jeroboam being defeated in battle by Abijah, king of Judah (2 Chron. 13). This information is fragmentary but it is sufficient to show just how selective the narrative in Kings is. And what is true of the reign of Jeroboam is true also of the treatment of all other kings both of Israel and Judah. The editors took from the annals such information about each king as they considered fitted in with the purpose of their history. ✳

THE REIGN OF REHOBOAM IN JUDAH

21 In Judah Rehoboam son of Solomon had become king. He was forty-one years old when he came to the throne, and he reigned for seventeen years in Jerusalem, the city which the LORD had chosen out of all the tribes of Israel to receive his Name. Rehoboam's mother was a woman of
22 Ammon called Naamah. Judah did what was wrong in the eyes of the LORD, rousing his jealous indignation by the sins they committed, beyond anything that their
23 forefathers had done. They erected hill-shrines, sacred pillars, and sacred poles, on every high hill and under
24 every spreading tree. Worse still, all over the country there were male prostitutes attached to the shrines, and the people adopted all the abominable practices of the nations whom the LORD had dispossessed in favour of Israel.

25*a*   In the fifth year of Rehoboam's reign Shishak king of
26 Egypt attacked Jerusalem. He removed the treasures of the house of the LORD and of the royal palace, and seized everything, including all the shields of gold that Solomon
27 had made. King Rehoboam replaced them with bronze shields and entrusted them to the officers of the escort who
28 guarded the entrance of the royal palace. Whenever the king entered the house of the LORD, the escort carried them; afterwards they returned them to the guard-room.
29*b*   The other acts and events of Rehoboam's reign are

[a] *Verses 25–28: cp. 2 Chr. 12: 9–11.*
[b] *Verses 29–31: cp. 2 Chr. 12: 13–16.*

recorded in the annals of the kings of Judah. There was 30
continual fighting between him and Jeroboam. He rested 31
with his forefathers and was buried with them in the city
of David. (His mother was a woman of Ammon, whose
name was Naamah.) He was succeeded by his son Abijam.

✻ 21. *In Judah:* the names Judah and Israel from this point
become the names of the two neighbouring kingdoms into
which the covenant people was divided. This division was to
the editors a sin which obscured the true nature and vocation of
'Israel' as the covenant people of God. *Rehoboam* had been
rejected by the northern tribes, so what is being described is
the history of Judah during part of the time that Jeroboam was
king of Israel. The account of *Rehoboam*'s reign is introduced
with a formula which will become very familiar to readers in
the succeeding chapters of Kings. It gives the name of the king,
the length of his reign, and his mother's name. This information
is given for all kings of Judah. The name of the king's mother
was important because she held an official position at court.
The names of the mothers of the kings of Israel are not given,
either because the editors did not consider them important,
or because in the northern kingdom the king's mother had no
special position at court.

22. The people of Judah are accused of apostasy which was
for the deuteronomists the greatest of all sins. This is to prepare
for and explain the invasion of Shishak.

23. *hill-shrines:* see note on 11: 7. *sacred poles:* see note on
14: 15. *sacred pillars* were large standing stones erected at
shrines to be the dwellings or symbols of gods or spirits.

24. The *male prostitutes* attached to the shrines show clearly
the character of the rites practised there. The Hebrew word
qadesh, translated *male prostitutes*, means literally 'holy men'.
The 'holy' indicates that they were carrying out their
activities at a shrine for religious purposes rather than in the
secular world. This is the clearest possible indication of just

how far the religious cults of Canaan were in thought and practice from the traditions of Israel, and just what was involved in the struggle to keep Israel free of Canaanite influence. It is easy for us to think that the deuteronomists were obsessed with an unreasoning and unreasonable hatred of Canaan. In fact, they and the prophets engaged in a life-or-death struggle for the soul of Israel. Such prostitution was forbidden in Deut. 23: 17. The N.E.B. has translated *qadesh* as *male prostitutes*. The word is a masculine noun used collectively, and probably intended to include the feminine. So the word here could well mean prostitutes of both sexes.

25. This is one of the few places where the narrative of Kings is linked with the history of other nations. *Shishak* was pharaoh between the years 935 and 914 B.C. If the dating is accurate he attacked Jerusalem in 917 B.C. Here only his attack upon Jerusalem is mentioned. No mention is made anywhere in Kings of his attacks on the cities of the northern kingdom (see comment on 12: 25 and 14: 19–20). The reason is that the editors were interested in the temple at Jerusalem more than the kingdoms either of Judah or of Israel. For them it was the temple which preserved the true religious traditions of the people and enshrined their hopes. So the great event of Rehoboam's reign to them was the pillaging of the temple and the removal of the gold shields.

27. *bronze shields:* the replacement of gold with bronze showed symbolically the decline which had taken place in the status of the temple. Such misfortune could only mean to the deuteronomists that Rehoboam was a sinner.

31. Rehoboam's mother's name is repeated in the formula which rounds off the account of his reign. It is absent from the Septuagint here. Its inclusion in the Hebrew text was probably a scribal error. *

THE REIGN OF ABIJAM IN JUDAH

In the eighteenth year of the reign of Jeroboam son of **15**
Nebat, Abijam became king of Judah. He reigned in 2
Jerusalem for three years; his mother was Maacah grand-
daughter[a] of Abishalom. All the sins that his father had 3
committed before him he committed too, nor was he
faithful to the LORD his God as his ancestor David had
been. But for David's sake the LORD his God gave him a 4
flame to burn in Jerusalem, by establishing his dynasty
and making Jerusalem secure, because David had done 5
what was right in the eyes of the LORD and had not disobeyed any of his commandments all his life, except in the
matter of Uriah the Hittite.[b] The other acts and events of 7
Abijam's reign are recorded in the annals of the kings of
Judah. There was fighting between Abijam and Jeroboam.
And Abijam rested with his forefathers and was buried in 8
the city of David; and he was succeeded by his son
Asa.

☆ 1. *In the eighteenth year of the reign of Jeroboam:* this is the
first example of the curious system of cross-referencing which
dated the beginning of the reign of a new king in either Israel
or Judah by reference to the reign of the king of the other
state. The point of this complicated method of recording may
have been to emphasize the essential unity of the covenant
people (see pp. 15–16).

2. The Hebrews were at times not as precise as we are in
their use of terms to express family relationships. Brother
could be used in a general way to mean a male relative. Here

[a] *Lit.* daughter.
[b] *Prob. rdg.; Heb. adds* (6) There was war between Rehoboam and
Jeroboam all his days (*cp. 14. 30*).

the Hebrew word for daughter has been translated *grand-daughter*. The reason is that *Abishalom* is thought to be Absalom, David's son. A daughter of Absalom would have been too old to be Abijam's mother, and Absalom is said to have had only one daughter named Tamar (2 Sam. 14: 27). Of course, Abishalom might have been quite another person, in which case daughter would be the correct translation.

3. Abijam's apostasy raises the question why God allowed such disloyalty to go on unchecked and unpunished. The answer given was that his reign was short and that God was tender-hearted to David's dynasty because of the great virtues of David.

5. The Greek version ends the sentence at *all his life*. The final clause *except in the matter of Uriah the Hittite* was probably added by a punctilious scribe. Such a comment on David's record is found nowhere else. It refers to the events recorded in 2 Sam. 11.

6. This verse has been rightly omitted from the text as a scribal error. ✳

THE REIGN OF ASA IN JUDAH

9 In the twentieth year of Jeroboam king of Israel, Asa
10 became king of Judah. He reigned in Jerusalem for forty-one years; his grandmother[a] was Maacah granddaughter[b]
11 of Abishalom. Asa did what was right in the eyes of the
12 LORD, like his ancestor David. He expelled from the land the male prostitutes attached to the shrines and did away
13[c] with all the idols which his predecessors had made. He even deprived his own grandmother[a] Maacah of her rank as queen mother because she had an obscene object made for the worship of Asherah; Asa cut it down and burnt it

[a] *Lit.* mother.   [b] *Lit.* daughter.
[c] *Verses 13-15: cp. 2 Chr. 15: 16-18.*

in the gorge of the Kidron. Although the hill-shrines 14
were allowed to remain, Asa himself remained faithful to
the LORD all his life. He brought into the house of the 15
LORD all his father's votive offerings and his own, gold and
silver and sacred vessels.

Asa was at war with Baasha king of Israel all through 16
their reigns. Baasha king of Israel invaded Judah and 17*a*
fortified Ramah to cut off all access to Asa king of Judah.
So Asa took all the gold and silver that remained in the 18
treasuries of the house of the LORD and of the royal
palace, and sent his servants with them to Ben-hadad son
of Tabrimmon, son of Hezion, king of Aram, whose
capital was Damascus, with instructions to say, 'There is 19
an alliance between us, as there was between our fathers.
I now send you this present of silver and gold; break off
your alliance with Baasha king of Israel, so that he may
abandon his campaign against me.' Ben-hadad listened 20
willingly to King Asa; he ordered the commanders of his
armies to move against the cities of Israel, and they attacked
Iyyon, Dan, Abel-beth-maacah, and that part of Kinnereth
which marches with the land of Naphtali. When Baasha 21
heard of it, he stopped fortifying Ramah and fell back on
Tirzah. Then King Asa issued a proclamation requiring 22
every man in Judah to join in removing the stones of
Ramah and the timbers with which Baasha had fortified it;
no one was exempted; and he used them to fortify Geba
of Benjamin and Mizpah.

All the other events of Asa's reign, his exploits and his 23*b*
achievements, and the cities he built, are recorded in the
annals of the kings of Judah. But in his old age his feet

[*a*] *Verses 17–22: cp. 2 Chr. 16: 1–6.*   [*b*] *Verses 23, 24: cp. 2 Chr. 16: 11–14.*

24 were crippled by disease. He rested with his forefathers and was buried with them in the city of his ancestor David; and he was succeeded by his son Jehoshaphat.

☆ 10. If *Asa* were the son of Abijam, then *Maacah* must have been his *grandmother*, hence the translation. But why was the name of the king's mother not recorded as in the case of the other kings of Judah? The omission is odd. One suggestion is that *Maacah* was Asa's mother and that Asa was the brother of Abijam and not his son. Another suggestion is that, since Abijam only reigned three years (and in the way the Hebrews reckon this could have been as little as fourteen months), Asa's mother never established her position. The old queen-mother would not be dislodged and the time was too short to compel her to give up her position. This latter suggestion would explain how the queen-mother came to be at such variance with the religious policy of the king and had to be removed.

11. In view of Asa's success against Israel we should expect the editors to look upon him with favour. The victory was God's blessing on a good king.

12. This may only be the deuteronomists' way of showing approval, and as concrete evidence of religious reform it is weak. *male prostitutes:* see comment on 14: 24.

13. The deposition of *Maacah* from being *queen mother* is factual and supports the deuteronomists' estimate of Asa. The *obscene object* was probably a wooden idol. It was *obscene* in that it offended so thoroughly against Yahwism.

16. The struggle was over the common boundary of the two countries. Baasha was trying to establish it as far south as possible, perhaps on the grounds that the old territory of Benjamin, which covered the land immediately north of Jerusalem, belonged to the northern kingdom.

17. He fortified *Ramah*, which was only four miles north of Jerusalem, to control the access to that city and the main route to the coastal plain which passed through the valley of

Beth-horon (cp. comment on 9: 17), which was near to *Ramah*. If Baasha had succeeded, then he would have had effective control of the trade routes and thus of Jerusalem itself.

18. This is the first mention of a *king of Aram*. *Aram* was the territory of the Aramaeans, and *Damascus* was its capital after it became one kingdom. In the first century B.C. the Romans created a province of Syria which included Damascus and most of Aram, but the two were not equivalent. The Romans created the province from the rump of the old Seleucid empire whose capital city was Antioch. The kings of Aram became the greatest rivals of the kingdom of Israel until 732 B.C.when *Damascus* was captured by the Assyrians. Many of the kings of Damascus were named *Ben-hadad*. Hadad was the name for the storm god, their equivalent to the Canaanite Baal. The god Hadad was also known as Rimmon (cp. 2 Kings 5: 18). Hence the name *Tabrimmon*. This name was probably Ramman. It was pronounced Rimmon – the Hebrew word for pome-granate – to show contempt for pagan gods (cp. comment on 11: 5–7).

19. *as there was between our fathers:* nothing is said in Kings of any alliance between Abijam and a king of Aram.

20. All the places mentioned were in the territories to the north of the Sea of Galilee. *Kinnereth* was an old name for the Sea of Galilee and is still in use in Israel today.

22. Asa built two fortresses of his own to secure the northern approach to Jerusalem. The sites of both *Geba* and *Mizpah* are uncertain. There is a place called *Geba* in this area but also one called Gibeah, and the Septuagint here reads Gibeah. The word *Mizpah* simply means 'an outpost' and several suitable places have been suggested. The most likely is Tell en-Nasbeh, about 8 miles north of Jerusalem.

23. *his feet were crippled by disease:* he was probably a victim of dropsy. ✳

THE REIGN OF NADAB OF ISRAEL

25 Nadab son of Jeroboam became king of Israel in the second year of Asa king of Judah, and he reigned for two
26 years. He did what was wrong in the eyes of the LORD and followed in his father's footsteps, repeating the sin which
27 he had led Israel to commit. Baasha son of Ahijah, of the house of Issachar, conspired against him and attacked him at Gibbethon, a Philistine city, which Nadab was
28 besieging with all his forces. And Baasha slew him and usurped the throne in the third year of Asa king of Judah.
29 As soon as he became king, he struck down all the family of Jeroboam, destroying every living soul and leaving not one survivor. Thus the word of the LORD was fulfilled which he spoke through his servant Ahijah the Shilonite.
30 This happened because of the sins of Jeroboam and the sins which he led Israel to commit, and because he had
31 provoked the anger of the LORD the God of Israel. The other events of Nadab's reign and all his acts are recorded
32 in the annals of the kings of Israel. Asa was at war with Baasha king of Israel all through their reigns.

* 25. *he reigned for two years:* this illustrates the problem of calculating dates on the basis of the information given in Kings. Nadab became king *in the second year of Asa*, and Baasha became king in Asa's third year. The *two years* thus means, in our reckoning, something more than twelve months.

27. *Gibbethon* is mentioned in Josh. 19: 44 as one of the cities allocated to the tribe of Dan. It must, therefore, have been in the foot-hills in the south-western part of the central hill country on the border of the coastal plain (see map 5 on p. 148). This was the territory which the tribe of Dan held originally. The Danites soon migrated to the north because of the pressure

of the Philistines upon them. The Philistines were entrenched in their cities on the coastal plain. The cities of the old Danite territory were naturally the first objective of any Philistine attempt at expansion. It may be that the Philistines had seen the opportunity for such expansion with the death of Jeroboam, and so captured *Gibbethon*. Nadab was apparently a strong king and attempted to retake it, but while he was in one corner of the kingdom, Baasha raised rebellion against him and took the throne for himself. The dynastic principle was not yet so well established in Israel that a king's son could reckon automatically on the loyalty of all his late father's subjects. Nadab probably took too much for granted and neglected to win the loyalty of his subjects.

29. *he struck down all the family of Jeroboam:* this was the usual practice in such coups. Any member of the old royal family left alive would have been extremely dangerous as a focus for malcontents, and possibly future rebellion. The prophecy of Ahijah was recorded in 14: 10–11 and this fulfilment of the prophecy provided a salutary example of the deuteronomic teaching that God quickly punishes all who are disobedient to his will. ✳

THE REIGN OF BAASHA OF ISRAEL

In the third year of Asa king of Judah, Baasha son of 33 Ahijah became king of all Israel in Tirzah and reigned twenty-four years. He did what was wrong in the eyes of 34 the LORD and followed in Jeroboam's footsteps, repeating the sin which he had led Israel to commit. Then the word **16** of the LORD came to Jehu son of Hanani concerning Baasha: 'I raised you from the dust and made you a 2 prince over my people Israel, but you have followed in the footsteps of Jeroboam and have led my people Israel into sin, and have provoked me to anger with their sins. Therefore I will sweep away Baasha and his house and will 3

deal with it as I dealt with the house of Jeroboam son of
4 Nebat. Those of Baasha's family who die in the city shall
be food for the dogs, and those who die in the country
5 shall be food for the birds.' The other events of Baasha's
reign, his achievements and his exploits, are recorded in
6 the annals of the kings of Israel. Baasha rested with his
forefathers and was buried in Tirzah; and he was succeeded
7 by his son Elah. Moreover the word of the LORD concerning Baasha and his family came through the prophet Jehu
son of Hanani, because of all the wrong that he had done
in the eyes of the LORD, thereby provoking his anger:
because he had not only sinned like the house of Jeroboam,
but had also brought destruction upon it.

✳ 33. Baasha *reigned twenty-four years* and so must have been a
strong and successful king. We are told nothing here of any of
his exploits and achievements, because none of them was of
interest to the editors. We know from the account of the reign
of Asa of Judah that Baasha tried to capture some Judaean
territory – his object may have been to control Judah as a
vassal state – but his aims were frustrated by an alliance
Judah made with the king of Aram. Nothing is recorded here
of Baasha's relations with Hadad king of Aram, and whether
or not he successfully resisted the invasion of Galilee. The city
of *Tirzah* has already been mentioned (see comment on 12:
25 and 14: 17), but here for the first time it is referred to as the
capital city of Israel.

16: 2–4. The prophecy is very similar to the prophecy
which Ahijah was said to have spoken against Jeroboam
(14: 7–11). This prophecy may well have been modelled on
the earlier one. The prophets could have developed traditional
forms of language which they used to express their messages.
This then would be the form used for cursing. But the close
similarity could equally well mean that both incidents were

editorial additions of the deuteronomists. Both Jeroboam and Baasha tried to create dynasties in Israel and in each case their sons were killed by usurpers and then the whole family annihilated. Such wholesale murders were not exceptional. They were the common practice of the time, and regarded as a necessary precaution to prevent further opposition in the state centring on some member of the former royal family. However, the deuteronomists were moralists and made these sad events the basis for moralizing. They concluded that the dynasties had been set aside because of the disloyalty of their founders to the religious traditions of Yahweh, and that this had been foretold by a prophet.

To say that the editors wrote the prophecies into the history sounds to us to be saying that they were twisting the facts, even inventing them, to make history prove their theories. This was not their purpose. For them the event itself declared the will of God. The word of the prophet clarified the issue so that no one could mistake the significance of the event. If then the editors did write in the prophecies in these two instances as a part of their editorial work, it was not to claim a significance for the events which they would not otherwise have had, but to make the real significance of the events, as they believed them to be, perfectly clear to the simplest reader. It was the prophets who were the foremost champions of the old traditions and, therefore, the leaders of the opposition to such kings. The editors believed that they were expressing the truth in showing the opposition to Jeroboam and Baasha being expressed by prophets, even if these particular incidents never in fact happened.

2. *I . . . made you a prince over my people Israel* occurs in both prophecies. (In the first instance (14: 7), the N.E.B. has used the verb 'appointed', but the underlying Hebrew is identical.) The phrase may give some clue to the reasons for the hostility which the deuteronomists expressed about both Jeroboam and Baasha. The word translated *prince* (*nagid*), has been claimed by some scholars to describe the office of a leader who worked

within the terms and respected the traditions of the old tribal league. Such a leader could never be a king in the absolute sense in which kings ruled in Canaan. The word *prince* may have been used deliberately in contrast with the word king (*melek*). The condemnation is that God has set up these leaders with the authority of a prince but that they have sought the absolute authority of a king in order to set aside the old traditions of Israel. We cannot be sure that the words prince and king are being used here in such sharp contrast to each other but that kings both in Israel and Judah did try to act despotically is beyond doubt. ✳

THE REIGN OF ELAH OF ISRAEL

8 In the twenty-sixth year of Asa king of Judah, Elah son of Baasha became king of Israel and he reigned in Tirzah 9 two years. Zimri, who was in his service commanding half the chariotry, plotted against him. The king was in Tirzah drinking himself drunk in the house of Arza, 10 comptroller of the household there, when Zimri broke in and attacked him, assassinated him and made himself king. This took place in the twenty-seventh year of Asa king of 11 Judah. As soon as he had become king and was enthroned, he struck down all the family of Baasha and left not a 12 single mother's son alive, kinsman or friend. He destroyed the whole family of Baasha, and thus fulfilled the word of the LORD concerning Baasha, spoken through the prophet 13 Jehu. This was what came of all the sins which Baasha and his son Elah had committed and the sins into which they had led Israel, provoking the anger of the LORD the God of 14 Israel with their worthless idols. The other events and acts of Elah's reign are recorded in the annals of the kings of Israel.

* 8. *two years:* clearly what is meant is something more than twelve months, but a good deal less than twenty-four (cp. verse 15).

10. Elah suffered the same fate that his father had brought upon Nadab, Jeroboam's son. The circumstances are parallel. The massacre is another example of the fact that the dynastic principle was not yet securely established in Israel. No matter how strong and powerful a king was or how long he reigned, a weak son could not hope to succeed simply on the reputation of his father. One of the marks of greatness in Omri, who was soon to become king, was that he succeeded in establishing more firmly the dynastic principle in Israel.

12. The editors once more stress the fulfilment of a true prophecy. *

THE CONSEQUENCE OF ZIMRI'S COUP

In the twenty-seventh year of Asa king of Judah, Zimri 15 reigned in Tirzah for seven days. At the time the army was investing the Philistine city of Gibbethon. When the 16 Israelite troops in the field heard of Zimri's conspiracy and the murder of the king, there and then in the camp they made their commander Omri king of Israel by common consent. Then Omri and his whole force with- 17 drew from Gibbethon and laid siege to Tirzah. Zimri, as 18 soon as he saw that the city had fallen, retreated to the keep of the royal palace, set the whole of it on fire over his head and so perished. This was what came of the sin he 19 had committed by doing what was wrong in the eyes of the LORD and following in the footsteps of Jeroboam, repeating the sin into which he had led Israel. The other 20 events of Zimri's reign, and his conspiracy, are recorded in the annals of the kings of Israel.

21 Thereafter the people of Israel were split into two factions: one supported Tibni son of Ginath, determined
22 to make him king; the other supported Omri. Omri's party proved the stronger; Tibni lost his life and Omri became king.

* 15. *seven days:* Zimri's coup misfired. He had obviously expected that the army, when it heard of Elah's death, would declare for him.

16. This is the first mention of *Omri* who was to become an important, indeed outstanding, figure in the history of Israel. No mention is made of his family so his origins must have been obscure and humble. He was a self-made man who chose soldiering as a career. This probably meant that his family possessed no land. He rose to command the army by his own ability. Clearly he was the kind of leader to whom the Israelites had looked for help in the old days when the tribal league was threatened by enemies. To call him a judge would be an anachronism, but he did possess many of the personal characteristics of a judge, and the gifts which made him a leader whom men would follow in difficult times.

21. Omri could not prevent civil war. We know no details of the war but obviously the central government had become so weak that local leaders like *Tibni* could make a bid for the kingdom itself.

22. *Omri became king* after three or four years of civil war. *

THE REIGN OF OMRI OF ISRAEL

23 It was in the thirty-first year of Asa king of Judah that Omri became king of Israel and he reigned twelve years,
24 six of them in Tirzah. He bought the hill of Samaria from Shemer for two talents of silver and built a city on it which he named Samaria after Shemer the owner of the

hill. Omri did what was wrong in the eyes of the LORD; 25
he outdid all his predecessors in wickedness. He followed 26
in the footsteps of Jeroboam son of Nebat, repeating the
sins which he had led Israel to commit, so that they provoked the anger of the LORD their God with their worthless idols. The other events of Omri's reign, and his 27
exploits, are recorded in the annals of the kings of Israel.
So Omri rested with his forefathers and was buried in 28
Samaria; and he was succeeded by his son Ahab.

✱ 23. *Omri:* the editors have dealt with his reign in the briefest
possible manner but, quite apart from what we learn of him
from extra-biblical sources, the simple contrast between the
state of the kingdom when he began to reign and the strong,
settled monarchy which he bequeathed to his son Ahab – there
was no revolt when Omri died – shows clearly the quality of
his reign. From the inscription on the Moabite stone we know
that Omri successfully invaded and controlled part of the
territory of the Moabites east of the Jordan. This in itself
shows that he was a strong and successful king. The impression
is confirmed by the fact that in Assyrian documents Israel is
always referred to as 'the land of Omri' until the destruction
of Samaria by Sargon II in 721 B.C., and on the Black Obelisk
of Shalmaneser III dated 842 B.C., which shows a later king of
Israel, Jehu, paying homage, the king is referred to as 'Jehu
son of Omri'. This description is not without its irony since it
was the same Jehu who killed Jehoram, Omri's grandson, and
thus destroyed the dynasty of Omri (cp. 2 Kings 9: 24).
    24. This verse records the only achievement in Omri's
reign which the editor deemed worthy of note. The site of
Samaria is well known. It is a hill seven miles north-west of
Nablus. Part of the site is today covered by the Arab village of
Sebastiyeh. Omri's purpose in changing the capital city is not
stated. It may have been a part of his expansionist policy.

Tirzah was on the eastern side of the hill country, at the head of a valley running down to the Jordan. Samaria is on the western side of the hill country looking out across the coastal plain and with easy communications with the Phoenician cities with which Omri made alliance. Omri would have been concerned to control as far as possible the great international trade route which passed through the Esdraelon valley, through the pass behind Megiddo and then along the coastal plain to Egypt. His choice of Samaria as his capital city may well have been his open declaration that his policy was expansionist and that he intended to control the trade route. Excavations at Samaria have shown that Omri did build the first city on that hill, though there is a little evidence of earlier building on the site. It has been suggested that his purpose in building a city on a hill which he had purchased, was to create a capital city independent of the state, belonging to himself and his family, in much the same way as Jerusalem was the capital city of Judah and yet belonged to the house of David by right of David's conquest. It may have been so, but if so, his plans were unsuccessful. His dynasty was destroyed by Jehu and lost everything, including Samaria. The wisdom of his choice of site is shown in that Samaria remained the capital city of the area for many years. Its name became the new name of the state itself, and, after the destruction of the kingdom, of the Assyrian province which replaced it.

25. *he outdid all his predecessors in wickedness:* the condemnation of Omri is typical in content but remarkable in its ferocity. He approximated in wickedness, according to the editor, to the arch-evildoer Jeroboam himself. This fierceness seems odd when otherwise the reign of Omri is not considered worthy of attention. The most probable explanation is that, like Jeroboam, he was being condemned as the founder of a dynasty which set in motion policies which the deuteronomists completely opposed. With Jeroboam it was the attempt to break up the religious unity of the people so that the two kingdoms ceased to regard themselves as the one people of God.

Omri's fault is set out at length in the narrative which follows concerned with Ahab and Elijah. He introduced a concept of monarchy which regarded itself as independent of the covenant traditions and free to change them as and when it wished to do so. The deuteronomists regarded this as the greatest threat and therefore the greatest evil which had yet confronted the covenant. If Omri and like-minded kings were successful in their intentions then the ideal of a covenant people would wither away and gradually disappear. So Omri and his dynasty were portrayed as exceptionally wicked.

The prophets who were the leaders and spokesmen of the opposition to royal power were portrayed as the heirs of the covenant tradition. Elijah is seen by the editors as a latter-day Moses who had been called by God to defend and maintain the covenant community; i.e. as the prophet promised in the deuteronomic law (Deut. 18: 15-22). The importance which the editors attached to this issue is seen in that virtually the whole of the rest of the book, six chapters, is concerned with the reign of one king, Ahab, and then mostly with his dealings with the prophet Elijah.

In this book two kings are given a prominence which far outstrips the rest. Solomon is pre-eminent as the founder of the temple at Jerusalem. After Solomon comes Ahab the opponent of Elijah. Through their treatment of the reigns of these two kings the deuteronomists intended to demonstrate the two principal lessons which their history was meant to teach: that Israel needed one sanctuary to which all the people should give their religious allegiance and through which they should express their worship; and that the covenant traditions were sacrosanct and rightly demanded obedience from all, from the king to the humblest of his subjects. The deuteronomists saw that the law which embodied the covenant tradition would need to be modified in course of time and believed that God would provide for this need by raising up prophets, men of God who were filled with the spirit. No one else, certainly no king, no matter how great his power, had authority to change, much less to set aside the law. Just as the lesson of the one sanctuary had been set out through the description of the reign of Solomon, so now the relationship of kings to the covenant traditions would be demonstrated by the conflicts of king Ahab with Elijah, the man of God. ✳

Ahab and Elijah

✳ The heading which the translators have given to the final part of the book draws our attention to the central issue of the chapters that follow, the conflict between Ahab and Elijah. The whole of the last six chapters of the book, with the exception of the concluding thirteen verses, is concerned with the reign of King Ahab. These chapters contain material from more than one source. Some of it may have come from, or at least be based on, official archives. Chapter 20 tells of some of Ahab's wars with Ben-hadad king of Aram. Other narratives, such as the story of Naboth, tell of domestic incidents within the kingdom itself, and yet others, such as chapter 17, are stories from the life of Elijah in which Ahab does not figure at all. Correspondingly, in one of the principal stories told of Ahab, the attack on Ramoth-gilead, Elijah never appears. In that story Ahab is opposed by another prophet, Micaiah, just as resolute as Elijah. What the editors have done is to draw together several narratives from the reign of King Ahab all of which are meant to illustrate his relationship with some of the religious leaders who were prominent in his reign. These leaders have popularly been called prophets, but this title needs to be used with care because they were quite distinct from the majority of those who were called prophets in Ahab's reign. Indeed, they opposed the teaching and work of the popular prophets. The most prominent of these religious leaders, in fact the only one of whom we are given any personal information, was Elijah. So these chapters can rightly be headed 'Ahab and Elijah', so long as it is understood that what is being described through the clash of these two men is a deep and bitter conflict between two opposed ideals of religion and human society, which were so basically in conflict with each other that the very existence of the one menaced the existence of the other.

Some of the information we gain from these chapters very likely came from official archives, but even that material is only used as a part of the one theme. Other archival material which did not relate to this theme has been ignored. We know from Assyrian records that the Assyrians at this time launched the first of their great military campaigns along the Fertile Crescent to conquer all the kingdoms along it and open up the way to Egypt. In 853 B.C. a coalition army from these kingdoms under Ben-hadad of Aram opposed the Assyrian advance at Qarqar and turned it back. Shalmaneser III, the Assyrian emperor, recorded that Ahab the Israelite was present at the battle with 2,000 chariots and 10,000 men. This was clearly a major enterprise in Ahab's reign but it is never mentioned in Kings. It did not fit in with the purposes of the editors, and may even have shown Ahab in too sympathetic a light. For us it is important, if only in making clear that Ahab was a strong and powerful king, a worthy successor of his father Omri. The crisis with the prophets happened during the reign of Ahab precisely because he was so strong and powerful, and therefore introducing to Israel more quickly and successfully than earlier kings the policies which the prophets hated so much. Solomon had also been a strong king and had pursued similar policies. He too had attempted to centralize all authority in the state in the hands of the crown, and had overridden the old covenant traditions in order to do so. His demands for forced labour did, as we have seen, eventually lead to rebellion. Solomon and Ahab were in this respect following very similar policies, but the editors of Kings chose to ignore this fact. Solomon founded the temple and belonged to Judah. For these reasons much was forgiven him, or over-looked, or blamed on the bad influences of foreign wives. Ahab belonged to the north and so the deuteronomists felt able to use him as their classic illustration of the dangers of over-mighty kings who regarded themselves as masters rather than servants of the covenant tradition. Ahab too had a foreign wife, Jezebel, but although she is depicted as an evil temptress, she is no excuse. Ahab is made to take the full responsibility for his policies.

Elijah had followers, pre-eminently Elisha, who continued to work after his death. We may call them prophets, as is generally done, if we remember that they repudiated much that was associated with the traditional groups of prophets and were hostile to them. Elijah opposed King Ahab and Elisha opposed Jezebel when she was queen mother after Ahab's death. So only the stories of Elijah appear in this first book of Kings. All the stories of Elisha are found in the second book of Kings together with one story of Elijah in the first chapter of that book.

The stories about Elijah and Elisha seem to have been treasured by their disciples and handed on to later generations as stories of the founders of the group. It is not surprising, therefore, that many of the stories are legendary in character and contain accounts of many miraculous occurrences. Popular stories told of leaders of a group by hero-worshipping disciples, particularly stories of saints and other religious leaders, generally contain accounts of miracles and other wonders performed by the heroes of the stories. The Elijah–Elisha stories are notable in the Old Testament as containing a great concentration of accounts of miracles. In fact only the narrative of the exodus has more. In assessing the meaning of miracle stories we must always take into account their purpose and spiritual value. God has used miracles to teach us truths about himself, his nature and purposes, which he could express in no other way. Thus the resurrection of Jesus teaches us truth about God, and brings God into relationship with us in a way that no words can. In contrast when we consider the Elijah–Elisha miracles, it is clear that many of them – some would say all of them – are simply popular stories which later generations have exaggerated or even invented to enhance the status of the founders of the group. The character of the miraculous bears all the characteristics of human folk-tale, rather than the self-revelation of God. Most of these miraculous stories are told of Elisha and so come into 2 Kings, but we need to know about them in order to be able to make a proper evaluation of the smaller number of miracle stories which appear in these chapters of 1 Kings.

Clearly the deuteronomic editors approved of Elijah. To them he was a most important figure in the history of Israel because he epitomized the rise to prominence of the kind of prophet of whom the deuteronomists approved and, indeed, looked to for spiritual guidance and leadership. Elijah was not the first prophet. Nor was he a typical prophet of his time. In the story told of Micaiah, a prophet of the same kind as Elijah, it is very clear that he stands alone and distinct from all the other prophets. There had been prophets for many years in Israel, at least since the time that the tribes had entered Canaan. Saul, after his anointing by Samuel, met a band of prophets and joined them for a time. These prophets formed communities of men who lived together near, or at, the old religious sanctuaries. The one characteristic which they all possessed, which bound them together, and which was regarded as the essential mark of the prophet, was that they were all ecstatics. This meant that they had an unusual psychological make-up and from time to time acted and spoke in a way which was abnormal. In this state they did and said things which they would never have done or said when they were themselves. If we had met them at such a time, we might have thought them to be under the influence of a drug, or even near to madness. The ancient world interpreted the same evidence in quite a different way. Their contemporaries thought that at such times the bodies and even the personalities of the prophets had been taken over by a god or a spirit, so that all that the prophet did or said at such times was thought to have the direct authority of the god or spirit. Prophecy was regarded as being the clearest and most direct way in which a god made his presence felt and his demands known to men. Such prophets were present in Israelite society from the earliest times of which we know. They were also found in all other neighbouring societies. And each society thought that their own prophets were inspired by their own particular god or gods.

The natural consequence of all this was that the groups of ecstatic prophets became closely associated with the state, and very important and influential supporters of the state and its ruler. Each ruler supported bands of prophets in the expectation that they would declare his policies to have divine approval and authority. The story of Ahab and the prophet Micaiah in chapter 22 illustrates that there were many such bands of prophets in Israel at that time who were solely concerned to give the appearance of divine approval to Ahab's policies. Such bands of prophets are often referred to as nationalistic prophets. The deuteronomists have no hesitation in condemning such prophets. They called them false prophets. The nationalistic prophets were, perhaps, the earliest examples of an established church which was more concerned to maintain its place in society than to be the mouthpiece of God to society. Elijah and Elisha and their followers were individual prophets who put their vocation from God first and were determined to fulfil it, even when such determination meant dissociating themselves from the great majority of the prophets of their time, and being so openly critical of royal policy as to lose all royal patronage and even be branded as enemies of the state. This choice was forced upon them by the fact that the policies pursued by the king were so opposed to the old traditions of Israel.

Ahab would probably have said that his aim was the simple and laudable one of modernizing the state so that it could compete on equal terms with its neighbours. In order to do this a strong centralized authority was necessary and all those with influence in society should use their influence to support the extension of royal authority. The older traditions were simply holding back the state from its proper development and ensuring that, in the end, it would be conquered by some neighbouring state such as Aram. What loyalty to the old traditions meant, he could have claimed, was shown by the Rechabites who are mentioned in 2 Kings (10: 15) and in Jeremiah (35: 1–11). This group of Israelites insisted on living in Canaan in exactly the same way as their forefathers had lived in the wilderness. They maintained a nomadic pattern of life, living on their flocks and following no agricultural pursuits. They lived in tents and refused to use any of the products of Canaanite agriculture such as wine. This was loyalty to the old traditions, but with such inflexibility that the Rechabite community was bound to die out as it fell further and further behind its neighbours. Ahab offered an alternative way of life which he believed would ensure the continued existence and prosperity of Israel in the future. It meant the abandonment of the old traditions, but that could not be helped, and those traditions as seen in the Rechabites were of no real benefit.

What Elijah and those few prophets who shared his point of view were doing was to offer a third alternative. They were just as concerned as Ahab that Israel should continue and prosper in the future, but they differed fundamentally from Ahab in that they did not look for a rejection of the old traditions but their adaptation to the conditions of life and human community in Canaan, so that Israel would be both able to hold her own alongside the neighbouring states and still be able to maintain her distinctive character as the covenant people of God. The Rechabites were content to lose the future for the sake of loyalty to the past. Ahab, and in this he was typical of all the kings, was willing to abandon the past for the sake of a future. Elijah was prepared for change but only in order to maintain the values of the past in the future. He believed that if Israel were to accept the kind of changes that Ahab wished to bring about, then Israel might have a future as one more of the several states that existed along the Fertile Crescent, but as Israel the covenant people of God who had been created by Yahweh at Mount Sinai and there linked to him for ever in a particular relationship, she would cease to exist.

This was what was at issue between Ahab and Elijah. The whole future of the covenant people hung upon the outcome of the struggle and so the deuteronomists gave it such an extended treatment. Elijah and his successors, the few prophets who maintained the fight against royal power, were the great heroes of the deuteronomists, to them the only true prophets. So in the deuteronomic law and in the history great prominence was given to prophets as the true guides of Israel and the true interpreters of the covenant tradition. This continuing need for the work of prophets and a willingness on the part of people to attend to their teaching was in the minds of the editors when they gave such prominence in their history to the struggle between Ahab and Elijah. ✳

THE CHARACTER OF AHAB'S REIGN

29 A HAB SON OF OMRI became king of Israel in the thirty-eighth year of Asa king of Judah, and he
30 reigned over Israel in Samaria for twenty-two years. He did more that was wrong in the eyes of the LORD than all
31 his predecessors. As if it were not enough for him to follow the sinful ways of Jeroboam son of Nebat, he contracted a marriage with Jezebel daughter of Ethbaal king of Sidon,
32 and went and worshipped Baal; he prostrated himself before him and erected an altar to him in the temple of
33 Baal which he built in Samaria. He also set up a sacred pole; indeed he did more to provoke the anger of the

LORD the God of Israel than all the kings of Israel before
him. In his days Hiel of Bethel rebuilt Jericho; laying its 34
foundations cost him his eldest son Abiram, and the setting
up of its gates cost him Segub his youngest son. Thus was
fulfilled what the LORD had spoken through Joshua son of
Nun.

✻ 31. No specific charge was made against Omri. Ahab is
particularly condemned because of his marriage to *Jezebel*. The
purpose of the marriage was without doubt political. Both
Omri and Ahab were brought into conflict with the neighbouring kingdom of Aram which shared a common frontier
with Israel. Both Israel and Aram wished to dominate the area
and control the great trade route which ran through both their
territories. They were inevitably jealous rivals. In this situation
Omri naturally sought allies and looked to the Phoenician
states along the sea coast. Their interests were complementary
to those of land powers such as Israel and Aram, and they
preferred an alliance with Israel in order to keep Aram, with
whom they had a common frontier, at bay. But the marriage
of Ahab to *Jezebel*, though political in purpose, also had
religious consequences. *Jezebel* was an enthusiastic exponent of
the Canaanite way of life and religion and so posed a real
threat to Yahwism. *Ethbaal king of Sidon* was king of Tyre as
Hiram had been. Since Hiram's day the kingdom had grown
and annexed other ports. *Sidon* was the name of one of these
ports but was also used as a general name for the people of the
area, equivalent to our Phoenicia. *Ethbaal* claimed to be king of
the Phoenician states.

32. *Baal* is the name most used for the Canaanite deity in the
Old Testament. It seems to have become for such devout
Yahwists as the deuteronomists the name which indicated
Canaanite worship as such, without any clear definition of its
use being needed. So in the Old Testament the name is
used in more than one way. The word *baal* means lord or

husband, and in Canaan each village had its own patron deity whom it regarded as the protector of its territory. The village baal was looked upon as the husband of the land, who fertilized it annually so that the land was fruitful and the village prosperous. On the other hand the god baal sometimes appears as a creator god, Baal the Lord of all Canaan, a great god who made claims to loyalty and obedience upon his people similar in extent to those that Yahweh was believed to make upon Israel. The village baals were probably at times regarded as manifestations of the great god, Baal. It is Baal in the second sense, the Lord and Master of Canaan, whose worship Ahab allowed to be introduced to Samaria for his political ends. This subordination of religious principle to political and dynastic ambition led to the religious crisis which called forth the protest of Elijah. Nothing that Ahab did was new in principle. Earlier kings, even Solomon, had at least tolerated Canaanite religion. What was new was the vigour and thoroughness with which Ahab pursued his policy and for which Jezebel is given so much of the blame.

34. *Hiel* is an abbreviation of Ahiel. *rebuilt Jericho:* this is also portrayed as an irreligious act which deliberately and intentionally flouted the traditions of Israel. *Jericho* was the first fortress city which God had given into the hands of the tribes after they had crossed the Jordan. Joshua laid a curse on anyone who at any future time should rebuild the city (Josh. 6: 26). The rebuilding of the city was another mark of the vigour of Ahab's reign. A fortress at the fords of the Jordan would prevent any invasion by the Moabites. Joshua's curse had said that anyone who rebuilt Jericho would do it at the cost of his eldest and youngest sons. Here once more the fulfil-ment of a prophecy is recorded. Just what happened is un-certain. The Hebrew, translated literally, means that he laid the city's foundation with his eldest son and set up the gates with his youngest son. This has been taken by some scholars to mean that *Hiel* offered his eldest son as a human sacrifice at the beginning of the rebuilding and also sacrificed his youngest

son when the gates were constructed. If this interpretation is correct, then we have here an example of the worst excesses of Canaanite religion. Archaeologists have found the bodies of infants buried in clay pots beneath the gates and houses of some cities, which seems to support this interpretation. On the other hand it has been denied that the bodies of such infants were sacrificial offerings. In some areas of the Near East the bodies of still-born children are sometimes buried immediately beneath the floor of the house where they were born. Some scholars think that the remains of the infants that the archaeologists have found were such burials. So it may have been that the two sons of *Hiel* died naturally and that their deaths were taken as the fulfilment of the prophecy. Whichever explanation is the correct one, and the N.E.B. has left it open, the incident is mentioned as a notorious example of Ahab's neglect of the religious traditions of his people. The *Jericho* mentioned here is not the present town of that name. In Ahab's time the city was situated a mile and a half north of present-day Jericho at the place now called Tell es-Sultan. The site has been excavated more than once, and most recently and thoroughly by Dr Kathleen Kenyon. Nothing remains of the city of this period. ✳

ELIJAH'S APPEARANCE

Elijah the Tishbite, of Tishbe in Gilead, said to Ahab, **17** 'I swear by the life of the LORD the God of Israel, whose servant I am, that there shall be neither dew nor rain these coming years unless I give the word.' Then the word of 2 the LORD came to him: 'Leave this place and turn east- 3 wards; and go into hiding in the ravine of Kerith east of the Jordan. You shall drink from the stream, and I have 4 commanded the ravens to feed you there.' He did as the 5 LORD had told him: he went and stayed in the ravine of

6 Kerith east of the Jordan, and the ravens brought him bread and meat morning and evening, and he drank from
7 the stream. After a while the stream dried up, for there
8 had been no rain in the land. Then the word of the LORD
9 came to him: 'Go now to Zarephath, a village of Sidon, and stay there; I have commanded a widow there to feed
10 you.' So he went off to Zarephath. When he reached the entrance to the village, he saw a widow gathering sticks, and he called to her and said, 'Please bring me a little
11 water in a pitcher to drink.' As she went to fetch it, he called after her, 'Bring me, please, a piece of bread as well.'
12 But she said, 'As the LORD your God lives, I have no food to sustain me except a handful of flour in a jar and a little oil in a flask. Here I am, gathering two or three sticks to go and cook something for my son and myself before we
13 die.' 'Never fear,' said Elijah; 'go and do as you say; but first make me a small cake from what you have and bring it out to me; and after that make something for your son
14 and yourself. For this is the word of the LORD the God of Israel: "The jar of flour shall not give out nor the flask of
15 oil fail, until the LORD sends rain on the land."' She went and did as Elijah had said, and there was food for him and
16 for her and her family for a long time. The jar of flour did not give out nor did the flask of oil fail, as the word of the LORD foretold through Elijah.

✵ 1. *Elijah* appeared on the scene with dramatic suddenness. Some scholars have thought that an introductory passage has been omitted by the editors. This seems unlikely because the abruptness of his introduction into the narrative is repeated in the lack of details given about his origins. His father's name

and family are not mentioned. It may be that we are intended
to understand by this that he came from God, and that it was
his spiritual origin which was to be taken note of rather than
his family allegiance. *Tishbe in Gilead* was east of the Jordan.
Tradition has claimed that *Tishbe* was the present El-Istib
some eight miles north of the river Jabbok, but this identification is quite uncertain. Wherever *Tishbe* was, Elijah as a
native of Gilead belonged to the group in Israel which lived
furthest from Canaan and nearest to the desert from which the
tribes had come. It is likely that the old tribal traditions were
treasured most in such an area. Elijah never specifically claimed
to be a prophet though clearly he was acting as one. The title
he used was 'servant of God'. The translation is a paraphrase.
He said that he 'stood before God'. The implication was that
the bands of prophets who were supported by Ahab, and
therefore stood before the king, could not be the servants of
God. The two offices were incompatible. *neither dew nor rain*
meant a great drought. Droughts were by no means unknown
in Canaan but this was to be one of such length and severity
that its supernatural origin would be obvious to all. The rains
fell in the winter months from October to March. Through
the summer there was no rain but the proximity of the country
to the Mediterranean sea and the hilly nature of the land meant
that there was very heavy dew for most of the year and this
added greatly to the moisture available. This drought would be
absolute and of abnormal length. The reference to 'the third
year' in 18: 1 seems to give an exact length of time but we
cannot be certain how long three years means. It might mean
thirty-six months but it could mean a good deal less. A period
of time which covered a full year and some months before
and after the year could be called three years. In the New
Testament (Jas. 5: 17), it is said that the drought lasted three
and a half years, but this number is symbolic. Three and a half
was a half of seven, the sacred number of the sabbath. In some
Jewish literature three and a half was used to symbolize
disaster. A drought of three full years duration is by no

means impossible in Palestine. Such droughts have been recorded in modern times, and Josephus quoted the historian Menander's 'Acts of Ithobalus, King of Tyre' to the effect that there was a year-long drought in Phoenicia at this time.

3. Such a drought would have been a national disaster. It would have been looked upon by the people as sent by God as punishment for some sin. The fact that it followed Elijah's words authenticated his claim to be the servant of God and, by implication, condemned the policies of Ahab which Elijah had opposed. The king both for the maintenance of his authority as well as the prosperity of the kingdom needed to bring Elijah to a better frame of mind. He sought Elijah to imprison him and force him to change his mind and his words. All this is implicit in the two brief statements *Leave this place* and *go into hiding*. The site of the ravine of Kerith is uncertain. It has been thought to be the Wadi el-Kelt a few miles north of Jericho. But the Wadi el-Kelt is on the western side of the Jordan. This both contradicts the narrative and defeats the purpose of the hideaway, which was to be outside the jurisdiction of Ahab and therefore beyond his grasp. Another suggestion is the Wadi Yabis on the east side of the Jordan.

6. This is the first example of the miraculous in the Elijah story. Some have accepted the story at its face value. Others have sought a rationalistic explanation. One suggestion is that there were living in that area a particular group of arabs who, because of their dark features and black tents, were called 'The Ravens', and that it was these arabs who fed Elijah. Whatever the origin of the story was it seems clear that the editors intended it to be understood as a miraculous feeding and an example of God's care and protection for his servant. When the Israelites were being led through the wilderness by Moses from Egypt to Canaan, God provided meat and bread for them (Exod. 16: 8 and 12). Just so here Elijah, whom God had raised up as a latter-day Moses to

re-establish the authority of the law and the covenant tradition, was fed by God when hiding in the wilderness from a tyrannical king.

9. *Zarephath* was a Phoenician village also outside the jurisdiction of Ahab. It has been identified with Sarafend which is seven miles south of Sidon.

10. *widow:* neither the woman nor her late husband seem to have had any family upon whom she could call for help. She was left alone to fend for herself and her son. Although she was a woman of some substance – she had a house and it was, or had been, prosperous enough to have a wooden room on the flat roof, the roof chamber as it is called – her plight was now desperate. She had no breadwinner and no status in the community so that she could be exploited and misused without hope of redress. Both she and her son were at the point of starvation.

13–16. Here is the second example of a miraculous event associated with Elijah. Its purpose is much the same as the story of the ravens: to demonstrate God's concern for his servant. What actually happened we cannot know. God may have continuously replenished the jar and flask by supernatural means. Equally it may have been done by some human agency, or the story may just as easily be a folk legend which has grown up around the figure of Elijah and been added to the raven story. Such stories are by no means unknown elsewhere. *

THE FATE OF THE WIDOW'S SON

Afterwards the son of this woman, the mistress of the 17 house, fell ill and grew worse and worse, until at last his breathing ceased. Then she said to Elijah, 'What made 18 you interfere, you man of God? You came here to bring my sins to light and kill my son!' 'Give me your son', he 19 said. He took the boy from her arms and carried him up to the roof-chamber where his lodging was, and laid him

20 on his own bed. Then he called out to the LORD, 'O LORD
  my God, is this thy care for the widow with whom I lodge,
21 that thou hast been so cruel to her son?' Then he breathed
  deeply[a] upon the child three times and called on the LORD,
  'O LORD my God, let the breath of life, I pray, return to
22 the body of this child.' The LORD listened to Elijah's cry,
  and the breath of life returned to the child's body, and he
23 revived; Elijah lifted him up and took him down from the
  roof into the house, gave him to his mother and said,
24 'Look, your son is alive.' Then she said to Elijah, 'Now I
  know for certain that you are a man of God and that the
  word of the LORD on your lips is truth.'

  ⁎ The authenticity of this story has been doubted on the
grounds that it is very similar to the story of Elisha's healing of
the son of the Shunammite woman (2 Kings 4: 32-7). The
reasoning behind the doubt is that since such a story was told
of Elisha, a similar story needed to be found for Elijah who was
Elisha's master. While it is true that the two stories are very
similar, a rejection of this story of Elijah on these grounds is
completely arbitrary. The real basis of the doubt is an underlying suspicion of all the miraculous narratives. If all of them
are to be dismissed as credulous folk tales or explained in
rationalistic terms, then there can be no defence for this story,
but if each story is to be examined on its own merits, then
there is more reason for accepting this story than for most of
the others.

  17-18. Hospitality to the man of God should have brought
blessing on the widow's house and the clearest form that
blessing could take was immunity from the natural disasters of
life. The opposite proved to be the case. The widow's son
fell ill and was either given up for dead, or actually seemed to
have died. It is uncertain quite what the boy's condition was.

[a] *Or* stretched himself.

It is never actually stated that he was dead. This was by far the greatest tragedy which had yet befallen the woman. Even as a widow she had a son who as he grew older could care for her, and, even more important, maintain the family name of her late husband. The death of her son meant that her marriage, indeed her life itself, had all gone for nothing. Such disaster in the presence of a man of God could only mean that God was punishing grave, but unrecognized, sin. The coming of Elijah into her life had led not to blessing but to complete and total disaster.

21. According to the Hebrew, Elijah 'stretched himself upon the child three times' (N.E.B. footnote) so that the vigour of his own health and vitality might be transferred to the boy. Elisha was later to heal in the same way (2 Kings 4: 34), as was Paul at Ephesus (Acts 20: 10). The N.E.B. has preferred the translation of the Greek Septuagint, *breathed deeply upon the child*. The preference seems to be based upon the words of Elijah's prayer that the breath of life might return to the boy's body, and the consequence that the boy began to breathe again. This rejection of a perfectly clear Hebrew verb is unnecessary. The Greek has anticipated the thinking of the N.E.B. translators in wishing to match the action of the prophet to its consequences.

In this story we get the clearest indication so far of the genuineness of Elijah's prophetic vocation, in that it expands the reader's understanding of the character of God. The Israelites believed, and none more fervently than the deutero-nomists, that God rewarded righteousness and punished sin in a quite mechanical manner. This story at least modifies that belief. It points to an insight into the nature of God as one who is loving and compassionate to his people. Can it be that the editors included this story as pointing to Elijah's vocation as God's man, to breathe new life into God's child, Israel, who was fast becoming spiritually lifeless?

All the stories told of Elijah in this chapter have been chosen to illustrate one point, that Yahweh and not Baal was the giver of life and controller of all that happened. Yahweh has been shown to control the dew and the rain. He provided food for his servants, and had absolute control over life and death. The worshippers of Baal believed that their god possessed all these powers. A conflict was bound to arise between the two. ✳

ELIJAH RETURNS TO ISRAEL

18 Time went by, and in the third year the word of the LORD came to Elijah: 'Go and show yourself to Ahab,
2 and I will send rain upon the land.' So he went to show himself to Ahab. At this time the famine in Samaria was
3 at its height, and Ahab summoned Obadiah, the comptroller of his household, a devout worshipper of the LORD.
4 When Jezebel massacred the prophets of the LORD, he had taken a hundred of them and hidden them in caves, fifty by fifty, giving them food and drink to keep them alive.
5 Ahab said to Obadiah, 'Let us go through*ᵃ* the land, both of us, to every spring and gully; if we can find enough grass we may keep the horses and mules alive and lose
6 none of our cattle.' They divided the land between them for their survey, Ahab going one way by himself and Obadiah another.

7 As Obadiah was on his way, Elijah met him. Obadiah recognized him and fell prostrate before him and said,
8 'Can it be you, my lord Elijah?' 'Yes,' he said, 'it is I; go
9 and tell your master that Elijah is here.' 'What wrong have I done?' said Obadiah. 'Why should you give me into
10 Ahab's hands? He will put me to death. As the LORD your God lives, there is no nation or kingdom to which my master has not sent in search of you. If they said, "He is

[a] Let us go through: *so Sept.; Heb.* Go into...

not here", he made that kingdom or nation swear on oath that they could not find you. Yet now you say, "Go and 11 tell your master that Elijah is here." What will happen? As 12 soon as I leave you, the spirit of the LORD will carry you away, who knows where? I shall go and tell Ahab, and when he fails to find you, he will kill me. Yet I have been a worshipper of the LORD from boyhood. Have you not 13 been told, my lord, what I did when Jezebel put the LORD's prophets to death, how I hid a hundred of them in caves, fifty by fifty, and kept them alive with food and drink? And now you say, "Go and tell your master that 14 Elijah is here"! He will kill me.' Elijah answered, 'As the 15 LORD of Hosts lives, whose servant I am, I swear that I will show myself to him this very day.' So Obadiah went 16 to find Ahab and gave him the message, and Ahab went to meet Elijah.

* 3. *a devout worshipper of the LORD:* it is surprising that he held such a prominent position at Ahab's court. The king's loyalties were probably divided between affection for the old Yahwism and attraction to the ways of Canaan.

4. *hidden them in caves:* it may be that he hid them on or near Mount Carmel. Mount Carmel is the great headland overlooking the sea south of the present-day port of Haifa (see map 5 on p. 148). A spur of the hill-country swings westward and runs right to the edge of the sea bringing the coastal plain to an end. The Carmel headland has hundreds of caves any of which could have provided perfect hiding places. This may have contributed to the reasons why Elijah chose Mount Carmel for his trial of strength with the prophets of Baal.

5. They were searching for any grass or pasture that remained by remote springs or valleys. Their object was to confiscate all

fodder for the royal horses, mules and cattle. In a time of such emergency the king could claim priority since the defence of the kingdom depended on his animals. Ahab had large numbers of cavalry and chariot teams.

12. Elijah had so frequently successfully eluded Ahab's officers that he had gained a reputation as the possessor of supernatural powers. The matter seems to have reached the stage when any report of Elijah's whereabouts that led to another fruitless search was treated as deliberate mockery by the king and punished with death. That an Israelite king could treat his subjects so, even his most senior officials, is some indication of how far the ideas of Canaan had penetrated into Ahab's mind.

15. *LORD of Hosts:* this is the first time that this title has been used in Kings. The *Hosts* may be the sun, moon and stars over whom God was thought to rule, or the heavenly beings who were present at his court. *LORD of Hosts*, Yahweh Sabaoth, was the title by which Yahweh had especially been known in the days of the old tribal league. It was then the rallying cry of the tribes for battle, and some think that it was particularly associated with the Ark, especially with the use of the Ark in battle. The *Hosts* were then the tribes who made up the league. After the settlement and the creation of the kingdom, the title was particularly associated with Yahweh as the covenant God of Israel. All that Israel had come to learn of the character of the God she served was expressed by that title. *LORD of Hosts* expressed therefore the character and demands of Yahweh the God of Israel, and embodied the emotional force of the loyalty which Israel felt to her own history, tradition and forefathers. It is in subtle touches such as this rather than in direct explanation that the narrative makes plain the full significance of the confrontation that Elijah was seeking. ✳

THE CONTEST: THE INVOCATION OF BAAL

As soon as Ahab saw Elijah, he said to him, 'Is it you, 17
you troubler of Israel?' 'It is not I who have troubled 18
Israel,' he replied, 'but you and your father's family, by
forsaking the commandments of the LORD and following
Baal. But now, send and summon all Israel to meet me on 19
Mount Carmel, and the four hundred and fifty prophets
of Baal with them and the four hundred prophets of the
goddess Asherah, who are Jezebel's pensioners.'[a] So Ahab 20
sent out to all the Israelites and assembled the prophets on
Mount Carmel. Elijah stepped forward and said to the 21
people, 'How long will you sit on the fence[b]? If the LORD
is God, follow him; but if Baal, then follow him.' Not a
word did they answer. Then Elijah said to the people, 'I 22
am the only prophet of the LORD still left, but there are
four hundred and fifty prophets of Baal. Bring two bulls; 23
let them choose one for themselves, cut it up and lay it
on the wood without setting fire to it, and I will prepare
the other and lay it on the wood without setting fire to it.
You shall invoke your god by name and I will invoke the 24
LORD by name; and the god who answers by fire, he is
God.' And all the people shouted their approval.

Then Elijah said to the prophets of Baal, 'Choose one of 25
the bulls and offer it first, for there are more of you;
invoke your god by name, but do not set fire to the wood.'
So they took the bull provided for them and offered it, 26
and they invoked Baal by name from morning until noon,
crying, 'Baal, Baal, answer us'; but there was no sound,

[a] *Lit.* who sit at Jezebel's table.
[b] sit on the fence: *lit.* bestride two branches.

no answer. They danced wildly beside the altar they had
27 set up. At midday Elijah mocked them: 'Call louder, for
he is a god; it may be he is deep in thought, or engaged, or
on a journey; or he may have gone to sleep and must be
28 woken up.' They cried still louder and, as was their custom,
gashed themselves with swords and spears until the blood
29 ran. All afternoon they raved and ranted till the hour
of the regular sacrifice, but still there was no sound, no
answer, no sign of attention.

* 17. *troubler* is used as a specific charge; that the person so
addressed had by his conduct brought the wrath of God upon
the people. After the destruction of Jericho, when the tribes
first crossed the Jordan, Achan had 'troubled' Israel by taking
for himself some of the booty of the city which had been
declared to be sacred to God. He was stoned and the place was
known as the valley of Trouble or Achor (Josh. 7: 26). Here
Ahab and Elijah each accused the other of being the cause of
the drought by giving offence to God.

19. Elijah asked for *all Israel* to be summoned to Mount
Carmel. This does not mean the whole nation but an official
assembly which represented the nation and could bind the
nation by its decisions. He was proposing that the issue should
be decided once for all, and the responsibility for the trouble
firmly and clearly allocated. *Jezebel's pensioners* is a paraphrase
of the Hebrew which may give the wrong impression.
pensioner generally means a former faithful servant, now
retired, for whom an income is provided as a recognition of
past services. This is not meant here. *pensioner* is used in the
earlier, perhaps now archaic, sense of a paid member of the
household. A better paraphrase for 'who sit at Jezebel's table'
(N.E.B. footnote) is 'the chaplains attached to the queen's
household'.

21. *sit on the fence:* the paraphrase used by the N.E.B. gets

the sense; the literal translation offered in the footnote, 'bestride two branches', is one possible interpretation of a difficult verb. In other places the verb is used to mean to limp, and some think that such is its meaning here. The Israelites are said to have been walking unsteadily and uncertainly because one leg walked for Baal and the other for Yahweh.

23. The point of the contest was that each side was to prepare and offer a sacrifice, but *without setting fire to it*. The true God would indicate his willingness to accept the sacrifice and show his power to do so by making the fire himself. *let them choose:* Elijah gave his opponents free choice of either animal to make clear that he was using no tricks. He might have produced one bull which was blemished in some way and therefore unacceptable as a sacrifice.

26–8. The actions of the prophets of Baal in calling upon their god are typical and can be paralleled by information from other sources. *danced wildly*: the verb is the same one used by Elijah when he first demanded a decision. So the prophets limped in some fashion by or around the altar which they had set up. The limping was probably a kind of ritual dance. To this day the culmination of the pilgrimage to Mecca, which it is the hope of every devout Muslim to make, is the pilgrim's perambulation of the sacred black stone there, the Ka'aba, with a peculiar limping walk, dragging one foot behind the other.

27. Elijah's mockery was subtle and effective. It underlined the fact that whatever claims the prophets made for Baal they did in fact treat him as a human being. The words may be taken in more than one sense. Some of the verbs Elijah used were probably taken from Canaanite rituals. The rites used at the sowing of the crops spoke of the waking of the god after his sleep through the summer. Baal also went on a journey to the wilderness. The charge that Baal was *deep in thought* implied that he was pre-occupied with some other matter and could not attend to more than one thing at once. *engaged, or on a journey* are clear enough in themselves. Jewish commentators

understood them as ribald mockery which meant that Baal had gone aside to relieve the wants of nature.

28. Cutting oneself *until the blood ran* was also a common practice in Canaanite worship. It was specifically forbidden in Israelite law (Deut. 14: 1). Blood was life and this release of life was a symbolic way of inducing Baal to send rain which would restore life to the soil.

29. *raved and ranted* is a paraphrase of one Hebrew verb. The verb could be translated literally, 'they acted as prophets', or even, 'they prophesied'. It means, of course, that they were in an ecstatic state. It is an indication of just how widespread was the practice of ecstasy, and just how much a part of the regular activity of a prophet, that the word can be used so and must be paraphrased to make its meaning clear. Our total dissociation of prophecy from conduct of this kind is the true measure of the victory of Elijah and the other prophets who followed him, in maintaining the traditions of Israel and adapting them to life in the conditions of Canaan. ✱

THE CONTEST: ELIJAH'S OFFERING

30 Then Elijah said to all the people, 'Come here to me.' They all came, and he repaired the altar of the LORD which
31 had been torn down. He took twelve stones, one for each tribe of the sons of Jacob, the man named Israel by the
32 word of the LORD. With these stones he built an altar in the name of the LORD; he dug a trench round it big
33 enough to hold two measures*a* of seed; he arranged the
34 wood, cut up the bull and laid it on the wood. Then he said, 'Fill four jars with water and pour it on the whole-offering and on the wood.' They did so,*b* and he said, 'Do it again.' They did it again, and he said, 'Do it a third

[a] *The Heb. measure called* seah.   [b] They did so: *so Sept.; Heb. om.*

time.' They did it a third time, and the water ran all 35
round the altar and even filled the trench. At the hour of 36
the regular sacrifice the prophet Elijah came forward and
said, 'LORD God of Abraham, of Isaac, and of Israel, let it
be known today that thou art God in Israel and that I am
thy servant and have done all these things at thy command.
Answer me, O LORD, answer me and let this people know 37
that thou, LORD, art God and that it is thou that hast
caused them to be backsliders.'[a] Then the fire of the LORD 38
fell. It consumed the whole-offering, the wood, the
stones, and the earth, and licked up the water in the
trench. When all the people saw it, they fell prostrate and 39
cried, 'The LORD is God, the LORD is God.' Then Elijah 40
said to them, 'Seize the prophets of Baal; let not one of
them escape.' They seized them, and Elijah took them down
to the Kishon and slaughtered them there in the valley.

✻ 30–2. Did Elijah repair an old altar or build a new one? The
text is ambiguous: verse 30 'he repaired the altar of the LORD',
but verse 32 'he built an altar in the name of the LORD'. For
this reason, and because of the reference to Jacob as Israel in
verse 31, a reference which has been taken from Gen. 35: 10,
a part of the priestly tradition, some have thought that verse 31
and the first part of verse 32 are a late addition to the text. If
these words are omitted, then Elijah repaired an old altar. It is
more likely that the words are original and that the ambiguity
was deliberately created by the editors. Elijah's repairing an
old altar on Mount Carmel must have embarrassed them. It
was an open contradiction by one of their heroes of their
strongly held view that the only legitimate place for the
offering of sacrifice was the temple at Jerusalem. It would be
much less offensive to them for Elijah to build a new altar on

[a] *Or* thou that dost bring them back to their allegiance.

the mountain and sacrifice upon it in these unique circumstances. That created no precedent. The altar was destroyed
with the sacrifice. They have also emphasized that the altar
represented Israel as the whole covenant people, which is
underlined by the reference to Jacob as Israel.

32. The *trench* served to define the altar area.

35. Elijah commanded water to be poured over the altar to
make plain to all that there was to be no trick. Some scholars
have suggested that the pouring of water was a piece of
sympathetic magic, i.e. water was poured to encourage rain.
The contest had two interdependent aims: to demonstrate the
supremacy of Yahweh, and to show that he, and not Baal, gave
rain. In view of the drought, the water may have been
intended as a most costly offering along with the bull. It has
been suggested that Elijah substituted naphtha for water and
thus ensured a highly combustible sacrifice. The suggestion is
ridiculous. The prophets of Baal would have known the
properties of naphtha just as well as Elijah, and such a deception
would have made Elijah no more than a wonder-working
charlatan. The prophets of Baal, whatever their errors, were
sincere. They looked for a sign from their god. Would
Elijah have looked for less?

36. By *the hour of the regular sacrifice* the time at which the
second daily sacrifice, the evening sacrifice, was offered is
meant. In the post-exilic temple this was the ninth hour of the
day, i.e. 15.00 hours. The words may have been added by an
editor to harmonize with the practice of the temple. In his
prayer Elijah linked himself and what he was doing with the
tradition of the tribal league by referring to the patriarchs.

37. *thou that hast caused them to be backsliders:* the Hebrew of
this clause is very difficult to understand. The N.E.B. has
given an accurate rendering of the words, but the sense of the
clause is so contrary to what we would have expected Elijah to
say that it is possible that the words were used in a rare, idiomatic sense which is otherwise quite unknown. Hence the
quite different translation which is offered in the footnote.

Our knowledge of the Hebrew of the Old Testament period is confined solely to the Old Testament. All other Hebrew literature of the period, with the exception of a few inscriptions, has been lost. Some Hebrew words might well have had a far wider range of meaning than we know of from their usage in the Old Testament, and to limit all occurrences of a word to the generally established meaning could well lead to a distortion of meaning in some places. Here the problem is an adverb whose usual meaning is 'backwards'. To turn backwards is generally taken to mean to turn away from, hence *backsliders*. It might possibly also have meant backwards in the sense of a return from apostasy, which is the sense which underlies the translation offered in the footnote.

38. What was *the fire of the LORD*? Most of those who have offered an explanation have suggested lightning. But *the fire* here is not thought to be a part of the order of nature. God was using the forces of nature for his own purposes (cp. Job 1: 16 and 2 Kings 1: 10–12).

39. The fire decided the issue. The people declared their allegiance to Yahweh and, by implication, their rejection of Baal. The contest had demonstrated to them that Yahweh was no mere wilderness God whose writ did not run in the settled, agricultural land of Palestine. On the contrary, Yahweh was in control of the whole land. He gave rain and so was lord of agriculture and all its operations. The Israelites had no need to seek the help of any foreign god for any purpose. *The LORD is God* conveys the same meaning as Elijah's name. Elijah means, 'My God is Yah', Yah being an abbreviated form of Yahweh, and *LORD* is the translation of Yahweh. Can it be that the name Elijah was given to the prophet by tradition to associate him with this contest? This would explain why nothing was said about his family when he first appeared at the beginning of chapter 17.

40. The prophets of Baal were taken away from the mountain so that their slaughter should not defile a holy place. They were slaughtered by a stream so that the water would wash

away the blood. Elijah thought that by this slaughter he was removing a dangerous corruption from the life of Israel. The editors also took the same view. Deuteronomic literature always speaks of Canaanites as an evil influence of such malignity that it could only be destroyed ruthlessly. It is in the way the prophets of Baal were treated much more than in the details of the contest that we see just how primitive at times were the religious and ethical responses of even the greatest of the early Israelites.

Each reader will at some stage ask, 'What actually happened on Mount Carmel?' The answer is that we can never know with absolute certainty. We have only this narrative to tell us and it can be interpreted in more than one way. The story may have exaggerated or distorted what happened, or be legendary (see p. 191). All we can do is to interpret the evidence available in what seems to us to be the most satisfactory way. In making our interpretation the larger meaning and consequences of the contest are more important than the mechanics of the operation. The contest is presented as a victory for Yahweh and as one which convinced the witnesses that Yahweh had declared his presence and shown his superiority to Baal. What was done conveyed conviction to the witnesses. That is the first point which must be taken into consideration in making our judgement. The second point is that it was Yahweh who acted and his action must have been consistent with his own nature which has now been revealed much more fully to us. So we can only accept an interpretation which convinced the eyewitnesses and is consistent with the God we know. Miracle implies the use of the power of nature to achieve spiritual ends and demonstrate in the action something new of the character of God. ✳

THE END OF THE DROUGHT

41 Elijah said to Ahab, 'Go back now, eat and drink, for
42 I hear the sound of coming rain.' He did so, while Elijah himself climbed to the crest of Carmel. There he crouched

on the ground with his face between his knees. He said to 43
his servant, 'Go and look out to the west.' He went and
looked; 'There is nothing to see', he said. Seven times
Elijah ordered him back, and seven times he went.[a] The 44
seventh time he said, 'I see a cloud no bigger than a man's
hand, coming up from the west.' 'Now go', said Elijah,
'and tell Ahab to harness his chariot and be off, or the rain
will stop him.' Meanwhile the sky had grown black with 45
clouds, the wind rose, and heavy rain began to fall. Ahab
mounted his chariot and set off for Jezreel; but the power 46
of the LORD had come upon Elijah: he tucked up his robe
and ran before Ahab all the way to Jezreel.

✻ 41. The acceptance of the sacrifice was the sign that God
would end the drought. *eat and drink* may mean that the king
had fasted before and during the contest. It may also mean that
friendship had been restored between the king and the prophet.

42. *he crouched on the ground with his face between his knees:* the
posture was probably that of ecstatic absorption.

43. *Seven times:* this may have been a part of a ritual.

44. *be off:* to return to the palace. That was the appropriate
place for the king to be at the time when the evidence of God's
power and concern for his people was visibly demonstrated
through the land.

45. *Jezreel:* the present Zerin, is 17 miles inland in the
Esdraelon valley (see map 5 on p. 148).

46. *ran before Ahab all the way to Jezreel:* a further example of
the abnormal powers of a man in ecstasy. The point of the
running was to show to all whom he met on the way, and to
those at the royal palace, that he was the agent who had
secured the blessing of rain, and that the king and his subjects
were now committed to exclusive loyalty to Yahweh. ✻

[a] and seven times he went: *so Sept.; Heb. om.*

JEZEBEL'S VICTORY

19 Ahab told Jezebel all that Elijah had done and how he
2 had put all the prophets to death with the sword. Jezebel
then sent a messenger to Elijah to say, 'The gods do the
same to me and more, unless by this time tomorrow I have
3 taken your life as you took theirs.' He was afraid and fled
for his life. When he reached Beersheba in Judah, he left
4 his servant there and himself went a day's journey into
the wilderness. He came upon a broom-bush, and sat
down under it and prayed for death: 'It is enough,' he
said; 'now, LORD, take my life, for I am no better than
5 my fathers before me.' He lay down under the bush and,
while he slept, an angel touched him and said, 'Rise and
6 eat.' He looked, and there at his head was a cake baked on
hot stones, and a pitcher of water. He ate and drank and
7 lay down again. The angel of the LORD came again and
touched him a second time, saying, 'Rise and eat; the
8 journey is too much for you.' He rose and ate and drank
and, sustained by this food, he went on for forty days and
9*a* forty nights to Horeb, the mount of God. He entered a
cave and there he spent the night.

* Immediately the narrative moves to Jezreel, and Queen
Jezebel appears on the scene, all the triumph of the contest on
Mount Carmel disappears. That contest had seemed to be the
decisive moment in which Israel had reaffirmed loyalty to
Yahweh. It now appears as a temporary setback for the
supporters of Baal. Some scholars have felt this point so
strongly that they have questioned whether the contest on
Mount Carmel really had the national significance which the
editors believed it to have had. A national defeat for Baal

could not have been reversed so easily, they believe. They have interpreted the contest, therefore, as a minor incident, a trial of strength between Elijah and the local baal of the land which the editors had magnified into an event of national importance. Others have questioned whether the chapters are arranged in the correct chronological sequence. Clearly, they are meant to appear to follow each other in order, but the sequence may be an artificial arrangement of the editors. If the events of chapter 19 really preceded those of chapter 18, then the sudden inexplicable reversal in Elijah's status and fortunes was created by the editors rather than by events. Neither of these solutions is necessary. The problem has been created through lack of understanding of the methods of the editors. Throughout the book they have been highly selective in their choice of narratives, and have omitted much material which they did not consider useful for their purposes. Here the introductory verses of the chapter cover quite a considerable period of time. The reversal of Elijah's fortunes was not so abrupt as it is made to appear.

2. *The gods do the same to me and more:* this is a well-known formula for swearing a solemn oath. It is more likely that she swore by 'god', meaning Baal Shemayim whose worship she wished to see replace that of Yahweh in Israel. Either the singular or the plural is a possible translation of the Hebrew. The Hebrew word most frequently used for god (God) is always used in the plural form. The particular meaning must be understood from the context. When the word is used of Yahweh, it is obvious that the singular is meant. When used of pagan deities, it is most often plural in meaning, but here the singular would seem to be the better translation. What becomes clear for the first time in these opening verses is that Jezebel was the great protagonist of Baal and the most determined opponent of Elijah. The struggle between Baal and Yahweh now continues in the struggle between Jezebel and Elijah.

3. *Beersheba* was the last settlement in Judah on the edge of

the desert (see map 5 on p. 148). Elijah realized there just how poor his prospects were and so went on alone.

4. *I am no better than my fathers before me:* he was starving and as good as dead. He appeals to God to end his misery by sending a quick death.

8. There is a clear parallel between the way Elijah was cared for and the way the Israelites were cared for when they passed through this same area on their way from Egypt to Canaan. The *forty days and forty nights* is doubtless symbolic – Moses stayed on the mount for the same period of time when receiving the law – and so it is pointless to attempt to locate Horeb on the basis of this statement as being a particular distance from Beersheba. *Horeb* was the name by which the sacred mountain of Israelite tradition was known in Deuteronomy. In other traditions it was called Sinai. Elijah thus returned to the original place where God revealed himself to the tribes and in so doing created the people of Israel. The prophet had fled from Ahab's power but he had also gone on pilgrimage to the place where Israel's existence began. He had a problem on his mind, a question to put to God which he believed would be most clearly answered at Horeb. Why had God allowed the protagonists of Baal to triumph? Even more, why had God allowed Elijah to appear to triumph and then suffer even greater humiliation and defeat? The end result of Elijah's work seemed to be that the cause of God was at a lower ebb than before his ministry began.

9 *a. He entered a cave* again points the parallel between Elijah and Moses who also encountered God in a cave (Exod. 33: 21). ✳

GOD'S WORD TO ELIJAH

9*b* Suddenly the word of the LORD came to him: 'Why
10 are you here, Elijah?' 'Because of my great zeal for the LORD the God of Hosts', he said. 'The people of Israel have forsaken thy covenant, torn down thy altars and put

thy prophets to death with the sword. I alone am left, and
they seek to take my life.' The answer came: 'Go and 11
stand on the mount before the LORD.' For the LORD was
passing by: a great and strong wind came rending mountains and shattering rocks before him, but the LORD was
not in the wind; and after the wind there was an earthquake, but the LORD was not in the earthquake; and after 12
the earthquake fire, but the LORD was not in the fire; and
after the fire a low murmuring sound. When Elijah 13
heard it, he muffled his face in his cloak and went out and
stood at the entrance of the cave. Then there came a voice:
'Why are you here, Elijah?' 'Because of my great zeal for 14
the LORD the God of Hosts', he said. 'The people of Israel
have forsaken thy covenant, torn down thy altars and put
thy prophets to death with the sword. I alone am left, and
they seek to take my life.'

The LORD said to him, 'Go back by way of the wilder- 15
ness of Damascus, enter the city and anoint Hazael to be
king of Aram; anoint Jehu son*a* of Nimshi to be king of 16
Israel, and Elisha son of Shaphat of Abel-meholah to be
prophet in your place. Anyone who escapes the sword of 17
Hazael Jehu will slay, and anyone who escapes the sword
of Jehu Elisha will slay. But I will leave seven thousand in 18
Israel, all who have not bent the knee to Baal, all whose
lips have not kissed him.'

* Elijah was a true prophet, a successor of Moses, through
whom God would give the people instructions for the new
situation that faced them. Some have thought that the contest
on Mount Carmel had not proved successful because of the

[*a*] *Or* grandson (*cp. 2 Kgs. 9: 2*).

savage bloodshed with which Elijah had concluded it. As though God refused to be served by such means. This is an attractive thought for us but it can hardly be true. The message which God gave to Elijah at Horeb about Hazael, Jehu and Elisha was no less bloodthirsty. What was wrong about the contest on Mount Carmel was that in it Elijah was too much concerned with the past. He had learned from the tradition that God had created and sustained his people in the wilderness by miraculous acts. He saw his task as freeing Israel from Baal worship by claiming from God another series of miracles. What he had not yet understood, and what God had now to teach him, was that miracles could not do the work that he had to do. A miracle could prove that Yahweh was a mightier God than Baal. It could not show that the real point why Yahweh demanded exclusive worship was because Yahweh was a God of a totally different character than Baal, and looked for a people and a community exhibiting different values from those of the people who worshipped Baal. Yahweh was the God who revealed himself as being essentially personal; who laid obligations on his people in his law which they could only properly fulfil by creating a society which placed the highest value upon human personality and human values. God used miracles, but only when they fulfilled and in no sense obscured his purposes. The contest on Mount Carmel had been a failure because it did just that. Its result had been to stimulate Jezebel to seek another trial of strength with Elijah.

9*b*-11. At Horeb God declared his will to Elijah much as he had declared it years before to Moses. Moses had stood before God on the sacred mountain when the law was given to him, and on another occasion was hidden by God in a cleft of the rock when God passed by him. The editors here have presented Elijah as meeting God in both these ways, and in so doing have given a confused picture. The passage begins with Elijah in the cave, and the revelation from God came to him in the cave. In between God is said to have spoken to him and commanded him to stand on the mountain. It looks as though a few sentences have been inserted into the passage to make the parallel between Elijah's receiving his message and Moses' receiving the law closer and therefore more pointed. Elijah has then been made to give his explanation of his reason for being at Horeb twice. The latter part of verse 9 together with verse 10 and the first part of verse 11 are best regarded as an addition to the main narrative. If they are omitted, the sense becomes much clearer. The passage then reads: *Suddenly. . .the LORD came to him* (verse 9). *For the LORD was passing by: a great and strong wind came* etc. (verse 11). The significance of the addition is that it shows just now important it was to the editors that readers should not miss the parallel between Moses and Elijah.

11–12. In the cave at Horeb all the great natural forces which were associated with the exodus tradition passed by Elijah, but the Lord was not in them. They were instruments that God had used in the past, but not essential elements in his character. After the symbols of power came *a low murmuring sound*. The Revised Standard Version has kept the well-known translation, 'a still, small voice'. *Sound* has a wider range of meaning than 'voice'. We are not told whether or not the *sound* conveyed meaning, but the general point is clear. The God who had revealed himself in the past in wonders and displays of power sought also to reveal himself and his purposes through the minds and personalities of men who were willing to be his servants.

15–16. It was Elisha not Elijah who had contact with Hazael and Jehu, and the account of Elijah's call of Elisha to be his successor has nothing to say of anointing. In fact there is no evidence that prophets ever were anointed to confer office upon them or to recognize their vocation. So the command of God was not obeyed. Was it ever given? The traditions about Elijah and Elisha may well have grown up independently. If so, an editor has bound them together by making Elisha Elijah's chosen successor, and written this story to link them together. 2 Kings 2: 1–18 seems to be a parallel narrative with the same purpose.

16. *Jehu son of Nimshi:* in 2 Kings 9: 2 Jehu is said to have been the grandson of Nimshi. The Hebrew word *ben* usually means son but it can have a wider meaning (see note on 15: 2). *Abel-meholah* was mentioned at 4: 12. According to the Christian historian Eusebius who lived about A.D. 260–340, it was situated in the Jordan valley some 10 miles south of Beth Shan. Others place it east of the Jordan (cp. Judg. 7: 22).

18. The number *seven thousand* is not to be taken literally. It is symbolic, made up of the combination of seven, the number which expresses completion – the sabbath is the seventh day – and thousand, the number which expresses magnitude. The point being made was that many struggles lay ahead but that God would ensure the survival of his faithful people. Bending the knee and kissing Baal may be metaphorical, but could be meant literally. Worshippers kissed images of the gods to show their devotion. ✳

THE CALL OF ELISHA

19 Elijah departed and found Elisha son of Shaphat plough-ing; there were twelve pair of oxen ahead of him, and he himself was with the last of them. As Elijah passed, he
20 threw his cloak over him, and Elisha, leaving his oxen, ran after Elijah and said, 'Let me kiss my father and mother goodbye, and then I will follow you.' 'Go back,' he
21 replied; 'what have I done to prevent you?' He followed him no further but went home, took his pair of oxen, slaughtered them and burnt the wooden gear to cook the flesh, which he gave to the people to eat. Then he follow-ed Elijah and became his disciple.

✳ 19. *Elisha son of Shaphat*, other than in this passage, first appears in 2 Kings where the aged Elijah designates him his successor before he dies. This short passage has been inserted here because of the reference to Elisha in God's word to Elijah. *Elisha* was the son of a wealthy family since they could plough with twelve pair of oxen. The *cloak*, elsewhere said to have been made of hair (2 Kings 1: 8), was the distinguishing mark of Elijah, and is used here as the outward mark of a prophet. Elijah's gesture was the equivalent of ordination which Elisha recognized and accepted.

20. *what have I done to prevent you?:* the translation is an interpretation. Another suggestion is that a verb has been omitted. If this is restored, or added, we read, 'but remember what I have done to you'.

21. The killing of the oxen was a symbolic way of showing that Elisha's old way of life had come to an end and that he had completely committed himself to the life of a prophet.

THE MEANING OF CHAPTER 20

✻ This chapter is odd in that it seems to have no connection either with what has gone before or with what follows. Elijah is never mentioned and the interest in Ahab is more sympathetic than the earlier chapters would have led one to expect (20: 13–21, contrast 22: 1–28). Chapter 20 tells of some of Ahab's wars with one of his neighbours, the king of Aram. Possibly the writer has had access to the royal archives, though it is not a direct transcription of the archives. It contains some material which is more like folk-tale than archive material. The verses which tell of the involvement of prophets in the story are particular examples of such material. The question has been asked why the editor used this material in Kings. It does not seem to contribute anything to the great theme of the struggle between Ahab and Elijah.

One answer which has been offered is that the whole purpose of the chapter is to lead up to the prophecy of Ahab's coming death. If this is so, then it would have had more dramatic point if it had been followed immediately by the story of Ahab's death, which in point of fact is told in chapter 22. Since Elijah figures in the story of Naboth in chapter 21, it has been suggested that chapters 20 and 21 ought to be transposed. Then chapters 17, 18, 19 and 21 which all deal with Elijah would come together, and chapters 20 and 22 follow. Elijah does not appear in either of those two chapters. But Elijah does appear in the first chapter of 2 Kings which destroys the principle upon which the transfer has been made.

In fact no change of order of chapters is necessary. This chapter is in its right place and plays its part in the overall purpose of the editors in the account of the Ahab–Elijah struggle. The particular purpose of chapter 20 is to serve as a concrete example of the lesson that God taught Elijah in the cave at Horeb, namely that God did not choose to influence and control men and societies by demonstrations of superior power, as in the contest on Mount Carmel, but through his influence on men. If this was so then the story of Ahab's actions as king ought to illustrate it.

In this chapter, and the two which follow it, we are shown God working and fulfilling his purposes through men. God used kings as his servants and, when they were unwilling, he used prophets to recall them to their true allegiance. In this story Ahab was in conflict with Ben-hadad king of Aram, and the conflict was so unequal, and its outcome seemed so sure, that Ben-hadad thought he could demand the most ignominious terms for surrender from Ahab. Ahab, supported by a prophet, determined to fight and won a remarkable and unexpected victory. So unexpected was it that an explanation needed to be found. It was that Yahweh was the God of the hill-country. The Aramaeans should choose the site of their next battle on the plains where Yahweh's writ did not run. A second battle was fought on the plain and again, against all natural expectation, Ahab won. Yahweh controlled events on the plains as much as in the hill-country. In the battles the same lesson was being demonstrated as on Mount Carmel: Yahweh was God

of all lands and territories. His people could in all places claim
his protection and he their allegiance.

In the days of the old tribal league the tribes could be called
together in the name of God to fight for the existence of the
league against foreign invaders. Such wars were conducted
under strict rules as holy wars. The deuteronomists were
interested in the idea of the Holy War (see note on 8: 44), as
in all else that belonged to the time of the tribal league. They
looked upon that period as the time in Israel's history when the
people were loyal to God before they had been seduced by the
temptations of Canaan. In this chapter Ahab's victories over
the Aramaeans are portrayed as battles in a holy war. He was
victorious against vastly superior forces, we are told, because
God was fighting for him. He ought, therefore, to show exemplary loyalty to the traditions of the tribal league. When
Ben-hadad was taken prisoner he should have been sacrificed,
'annihilated' (see note on 9: 21), unless God through one of
his prophets had decreed otherwise. Ahab freed Ben-hadad
without any consultation with a prophet. This was an arrogant
and irreligious act which demonstrated clearly his contempt
for the religious traditions of Israel, and, by implication, his
contempt for God. Israel could never serve God wholeheartedly under such a king and since, in the conditions of those
days, abdication or deposition was impossible, Ahab had to die.

The issue here is the same as on Mount Carmel – the people
must decide for Baal or Yahweh – but here it is worked out in
terms of God working through human society rather than his
imposing his will by a demonstration of supernatural power. ✳

BEN-HADAD'S THREAT

Ben-hadad king of Aram, having mustered all his forces, **20**
and taking with him thirty-two kings with their horses
and chariots, marched against Samaria to take it by siege
or assault. He sent envoys into the city to Ahab king of 2

3 Israel to say, 'Hear what Ben-hadad says: Your silver and
gold are mine, your wives and your splendid sons are
4 mine.'*a* The king of Israel answered, 'As you say, my lord
5 king, I am yours and all that I have.' The envoys came
again and said, 'Hear what Ben-hadad says: I demand that
you hand over your silver and gold, your wives and your
6 sons. This time tomorrow I will send my servants to
search your house and your subjects' houses and to take
7 possession of everything you prize, and remove it.' The
king of Israel then summoned all the elders of the land
and said, 'You see this? The man is plainly picking a
quarrel; for I did not demur when he sent to claim my
8 wives and my sons, my silver and gold.'*b* All the elders and
all the people answered, 'Do not listen to him; you must
9 not consent.' So he gave this reply to Ben-hadad's
envoys: 'Say to my lord the king: I accepted your
majesty's demands on the first occasion; but what you
now ask I cannot do.' The envoys went away and reported
10 to their master, and Ben-hadad sent back word: 'The
gods do the same to me and more, if there is enough dust
11 in Samaria to provide a handful for each of my men.' The
king of Israel made reply, 'Remind him of the saying:
"The lame must not think himself a match for the
12 nimble."' This message reached Ben-hadad while he and
the kings were drinking in their quarters.*c* At once he
ordered his men to attack the city, and they did so.

[a] *Or* are your wives and your sons any good to me?
[b] for I did not...gold: *or, with Sept.*, for he sent to demand my wives
and children; my silver and gold I did not refuse.
[c] in their quarters: *or* at Succoth.

✻ 1. No indication is given of just when Ben-hadad made his threat. We know that Ahab fought alongside Ben-hadad against the Assyrians at Qarqar in 853 B.C., but did he fight as an ally or as a vassal? If as an ally, then after the victory Ben-hadad must have determined to make Ahab a vassal and this chapter describes an attempt to do so. But Ahab is thought to have died shortly after the battle of Qarqar, and in 22: 1 we are told that there had been three years peace between Israel and the Aramaeans before Ahab's death. If we accept that statement then the events described here must have happened before 853 B.C. and in that case Ahab very likely fought at Qarqar as a vassal of Ben-hadad. *thirty-two kings:* Ben-hadad attacked at the head of a large coalition. His success must have seemed inevitable and he was probably in control of most of the territory of Israel when he sent his message to Ahab.

3–6. This was a demand for a most humiliating kind of unconditional surrender. Quite what the terms were is not altogether clear as the alternative translations offered in footnotes *a* and *b* show. According to the text Ben-hadad demanded the handing over to him of the royal treasury together with the royal harem and the king's children, doubtless as hostages. All this Ahab agreed to. Then Ben-hadad added a further demand that his soldiers should pillage freely the city of Samaria. To this Ahab objected. According to the alternative translation offered in the footnotes, Ahab agreed to hand over the contents of the treasury but resisted a further demand for his wives and children. The issue is clear whatever the particular demand was that caused Ahab to resist.

10. *The gods do the same to me and more:* the well-known formula for swearing a solemn oath (see note on 19: 2).

11. Ahab quoted a proverb which the N.E.B. has loosely paraphrased. The proverb warned a soldier strapping on his armour not to boast like a successful warrior unstrapping it.

12. *their quarters:* the Hebrew word *succoth* is both the name of a place and also the name given to temporary wooden shelters, booths or bivouacs. This accounts for the alternative

translation. *quarters* is to be preferred here since the place Succoth was too far away from Samaria to allow an immediate attack. *

AHAB'S VICTORY

13 Meanwhile a prophet had come to Ahab king of Israel and said to him, 'This is the word of the LORD: "You see this great rabble? Today I will give it into your hands and 14 you shall know that I am the LORD."' 'Whom will you use for that?' asked Ahab. 'The young men who serve the district officers', was the answer. 'Who will draw up the line of battle?' asked the king. 'You', said the prophet. 15 Then Ahab called up these young men, two hundred and thirty-two all told, and behind them the people of Israel, 16 seven thousand in all. They went out at midday, while Ben-hadad and his allies, those thirty-two kings, were 17 drinking themselves drunk in their quarters.[a] The young men sallied out first, and word was sent to Ben-hadad 18 that a party had come out of Samaria. 'If they have come out for peace,' he said, 'take them alive; if for battle, take them alive.'

19 So out of the city the young men went, and the army 20 behind them; each struck down his man, and the Aramaeans fled. The Israelites pursued them, but Ben-hadad king of Aram escaped on horseback with some of the 21 cavalry. Then the king of Israel advanced and captured[b] the horses and chariots, inflicting a heavy defeat on the Aramaeans.

[a] in their quarters: *or* at Succoth.
[b] *So Sept.; Heb.* destroyed.

✻ 13. At the moment when Ahab's situation seemed hopeless, God spoke to him through a prophet and assured him of victory. So the victory was shown to be God's, even before it happened.

14. The prophet suggested a stratagem to outwit the enemy. A group of young military officers were collected to act as commandos and attack the enemy camp. *the district officers* were military officials responsible for producing the required number of fighting men from their districts.

15. Supporting the commandos was an army gathered from the whole people. It was called *the people of Israel* to show that it was the successor of the army of the old tribal league by means of which God had won many victories. The number *seven thousand* may be symbolic. At Horeb Elijah had been told that God had left the same number of faithful in Israel (see note on 19:18).

16. *their quarters:* see note on verse 12 above.

18-19. The over-confident Ben-hadad showed his contempt for the enemy by commanding them to be taken alive. It would be a walk-over, he implied. In point of fact it was a rout, and Ben-hadad was defeated. God had once again come to the rescue of his people. In just such a victory Gideon had routed the Midianites in the days of the league (cp. Judg. 7).

21. *captured* from the Septuagint has been preferred to the Hebrew 'destroyed' (N.E.B. footnote). It is much more in line with the general charge against Ahab that he did not obey the law of the holy war. ✻

BEN-HADAD RETURNS TO BATTLE

Then the prophet came to the king of Israel and said to 22 him, 'Build up your forces; you know what you must do. At the turn of the year the king of Aram will renew the attack.' But the king of Aram's ministers gave him this 23 advice: 'Their gods are gods of the hills; that is why they

defeated us. Let us fight them in the plain; and then we
24 shall have the upper hand. What you must do is to relieve
the kings of their command and appoint other officers in
25 their place. Raise another army like the one you have lost.
Bring your cavalry and chariots up to their former
strength, and then let us fight them in the plain, and we
shall have the upper hand.' He listened to their advice and
acted on it.

26   At the turn of the year Ben-hadad mustered the Aram-
27 aeans and advanced to Aphek to attack Israel. The
Israelites too were mustered and formed into companies, and then went out to meet them and encamped
opposite them. They seemed no better than a pair of
new-born kids, while the Aramaeans covered the
28 country-side. The man of God came to the king of Israel
and said, 'This is the word of the LORD: The Aramaeans
may think that the LORD is a god of the hills and not a god
of the valleys; but I will give all this great rabble into your
hands and you shall know that I am the LORD.'

29   They lay in camp opposite one another for seven days;
on the seventh day battle was joined and the Israelites
destroyed a hundred thousand of the Aramaean infantry
30 in one day. The survivors fled to Aphek, into the citadel,
and the city wall fell upon the twenty-seven thousand men
who were left. Ben-hadad took refuge in the citadel,
31 retreating into an inner room; and his attendants said to
him, 'Listen; we have heard that the kings of Israel are
men to be trusted. Let us therefore put sackcloth round
our waists and wind rough cord round our heads and go
out to the king of Israel. It may be that he will spare your
32 life.' So they fastened on the sackcloth and the cord, and

went to the king of Israel and said, 'Your servant Ben-hadad pleads for his life.' 'My royal cousin,' he said, 'is he still alive?' The men, taking the word for a favourable 33 omen, caught it up at once and said, 'Your cousin, yes, Ben-hadad.' 'Go and fetch him', he said. Then Ben-hadad came out and Ahab invited him into his chariot. And Ben-hadad said to him, 'I will restore the cities which 34 my father took from your father, and you may establish for yourself a trading quarter in Damascus, as my father did in Samaria.' 'On these terms', said Ahab, 'I will let you go.' So he granted him a treaty and let him go.

* 22. *At the turn of the year:* there was a regular time during the year when wars were conducted. It was the late spring and early summer. At that time the harvest had been gathered in so that men were free to fight, and the enemy had stores of grain which were worth looting.

24. Ben-hadad replaced the tribal chiefs with professional officers to make his army more efficient.

26. The site of *Aphek* is uncertain. Several places of that name are known. The most likely to be meant here is either the *Aphek* in the Esdraelon valley near Mount Gilboa, or the *Aphek* east of the Jordan, lying east of the lake of Galilee.

29–30. The narrative emphasizes even more than in the account of the first battle that this was to be God's victory. The Aramaeans had chosen Aphek to neutralize the influence of Yahweh. The disparity between the numbers of the two forces is even greater than before, and nature itself fought for Israel in that the city wall destroyed great numbers of the enemy. This calls to mind the victory of the tribes at Jericho (cp. Josh. 6). What we have here is no prosaic description of an actual battle. The conflict between Ahab and Ben-hadad was real enough but had been described in such a manner that the editors must have been evoking quite deliberately the old memories of the tribal league and the belief that God fought with and for his people and ensured victory. For the editors the battle against Aram was a part of such a war because Israel was now facing an enemy as destructive of her distinctive life and loyalty to God as any of the enemies of old, and far stronger and more subtle.

32-4. Using the same conventional picture of the holy war, the editors have shown here what they considered to be Ahab's disloyalty to the religious traditions of his people. Ben-hadad when taken prisoner was treated as a friend. The N.E.B. has paraphrased the Hebrew in calling him *cousin*. Ahab actually called him 'brother'. Ahab treated the victory as though it were entirely his own by using it as a basis for commercial and boundary negotiations (cp. 1 Sam. 15: 1-23). The cities restored were probably those lost by Baasha, an earlier king of Israel (cp. 15: 20). Ahab showed no gratitude to God or to the prophet who was God's instrument, nor any sensitivity to the traditions of his people. This is a further example of Ahab being depicted as a king who set himself above law and custom. Could any man be at one and the same time a faithful brother to Ben-hadad and a loyal son to Yahweh? ✳

A PROPHECY OF AHAB'S DEATH

35 One of a company of prophets, at the command of the LORD, ordered a certain man to strike him, but the
36 man refused. 'Because you have not obeyed the LORD,' said the prophet, 'when you leave me, a lion will attack you.' When the man left, a lion did meet him and attacked
37 him. The prophet fell in with another man and ordered
38 him to strike him. He struck and wounded him. Then the prophet went off, with a bandage over his eyes, and thus
39 disguised waited by the wayside for the king. As the king was passing, he called out to him, 'Sir, I went into the

thick of the battle, and a soldier came over to me with a
prisoner and said, "Take charge of this fellow. If by any
chance he gets away, your life shall be forfeit, or you shall
pay a talent of silver." As I was busy with one thing and 40
another, sir, he disappeared.' The king of Israel said to
him, 'You deserve to die.' And he said to the king of
Israel,*a* 'You have passed sentence on yourself.' Then he 41
tore the bandage from his eyes, and the king of Israel saw
that he was one of the prophets. And he said to the king, 42
'This is the word of the LORD: "Because you let that man
go when I had put him under a ban, your life shall be
forfeit for his life, your people for his people."' The king 43
of Israel went home sullen and angry and entered Samaria.

* Ahab by his treatment of Ben-hadad had shown where his
loyalty lay. A prophet now declared God's response, and by
the manner in which he did it, ensured that Ahab acknowledged
the justice of God's response. The story is reminiscent of the
way in which the prophet Nathan declared God's verdict on
David for his adultery with Bathsheba. The whole narrative
has the character of folk tale.

35–6. Prophets, as God's men, claimed instant and un-
questioning obedience. The story about the fate of the man who
would not strike the prophet taught the lesson very effectively.
This is another example of the kind of literature which the Jews
call Midrash.

38. *and thus disguised:* it seems that the prophets wore some
visible mark on their foreheads by which they could be
recognized.

40. '*You deserve to die.*' *And he said to the king of Israel:* these
words have been added by the N.E.B. to clarify the sense. The
translators think that they were at some time accidentally

[a] You deserve...Israel: *prob. rdg.; Heb. om.*

omitted from the text. The words '*You have passed sentence on yourself*' are then understood as the response of the prophet to the king. In the Hebrew they are the king's reply to the prophet and do read strangely.

41–3. The fact that Ahab accepted meekly the rebuke of the prophet shows that he accepted his authority. Ben-hadad's life, as a prisoner taken in battle, was forfeit to God. Since Ahab had intervened, his own life must take the place of Ben-hadad's. So the king's rejection of Israel's tradition in favour of the ways of Canaan would not lead to glory but to his own death.

42. *put him under a ban:* this is the phrase used to describe those spoils of war which must be sacrificed according to the law of the holy war (see note on 9: 21). ✷

NABOTH'S VINEYARD

21 Naboth of Jezreel had a vineyard*[a]* near the palace of
2 Ahab king of Samaria. One day Ahab made a proposal to Naboth: 'Your vineyard is close to my palace; let me have it for a garden; I will give you a better vineyard in
3 exchange for it or, if you prefer, its value in silver.' But Naboth answered, 'The LORD forbid that I should let you
4 have land which has always been in my family.' So Ahab went home sullen and angry because Naboth would not let him have his ancestral land. He lay down on his bed,
5 covered his face and refused to eat. His wife Jezebel came in to him and said, 'What makes you so sullen and why do
6 you refuse to eat?' He told her, 'I proposed to Naboth of Jezreel that he should let me have his vineyard at its value or, if he liked, in exchange for another; but he would not
7 let me have the vineyard.' 'Are you or are you not king in

[a] So Sept.; Heb. adds which was in Jezreel.

Israel?' said Jezebel. 'Come, eat and take heart; I will
make you a gift of the vineyard of Naboth of Jezreel.' So 8
she wrote a letter in Ahab's name, sealed it with his seal
and sent it to the elders and notables of Naboth's city,
who sat in council with him. She wrote: 'Proclaim a fast 9
and give Naboth the seat of honour among the people.
And see that two scoundrels are seated opposite him to 10
charge him with cursing*a* God and the king, then take him
out and stone him to death.' So the elders and notables of 11
Naboth's city, who sat with him in council, carried out the
instructions Jezebel had sent them in her letter: they 12
proclaimed a fast and gave Naboth the seat of honour, and 13
these two scoundrels came in, sat opposite him and
charged him publicly with cursing*a* God and the king.
Then they took him outside the city and stoned him, and 14
sent word to Jezebel that Naboth had been stoned to death.

✻ Ahab's style of ruling raised the fundamental issue of the
relationship of the king to the law. The whole pattern of
Israel's life as the covenant people was directed by laws and
customs which declared how God would have the people live.
Ahab determined to change this. For him the king was the sole
instrument of the divine will. What the king willed was what
God willed and the people should obey. The story of Naboth
is a clear illustration of the working out of the principle and of
the changes its acceptance would make in the life of the community. Even when the old forms were kept as they were in
Naboth's case, the law was corrupted and the spirit of the
nation changed. If Ahab's ideal of kingship had triumphed,
Israel would have ceased to be a society capable of moral and
spiritual growth.

2. Ahab acted reasonably and justly according to his lights.

[a] cursing: *lit.* bidding farewell to.

He did not seek to confiscate the land. He offered Naboth other land or its value in money. In the light of this offer he regarded Naboth's refusal as totally unreasonable.

4. *ancestral land:* Naboth was being asked to give up his patrimony by right of which he had a status in the society of Jezreel. Other land could not give him that status nor money compensate him for its loss. In addition it is quite possible that the tombs of his ancestors were situated on the ancestral family land. To sell such land would have been a shameful act of impiety and betrayal. In the impasse which had been reached, what was at stake was Ahab's respect and acceptance, or disrespect and rejection, of the reason which had led Naboth to refuse the offer. How much did Ahab respect and value the law and custom by which Israel lived?

7. Ahab, when urged on by Jezebel, had no respect for the spirit of the law, though he maintained its forms. It could well have been that he was not sufficiently strong to oppose openly the old traditions, but was astute enough to realize that he could gain his end and destroy the law by a clever manipulation of its processes. The story claims that Jezebel took the initiative in subverting the law, and Jezebel has come down to us as the epitome of such unscrupulous double-dealing, but she could have done nothing without Ahab's acquiescence, and he was not a weak king.

8. *sealed it with his seal:* i.e. sent it with the authority of the king.

9. *Proclaim a fast:* this meant that the elders were to declare that some misfortune which had happened to their city was a punishment from God for some corporate sin. The city needed to make atonement by a fast. On such an occasion the people would have been particularly conscious of God having been offended, and fearful lest such offences should continue. This was exactly the right atmosphere in which their emotions could be aroused and they could be convinced easily that some particular person was the author of their misfortunes.

10. *two scoundrels:* two witnesses were essential since the law

required that number for such a serious charge. With the evidence of the witnesses and in the emotionally charged atmosphere of the fast, it was easy for the elders to make sure that Naboth was tried and condemned with full observance of all the due processes of the law. *cursing God:* the Hebrew reads that Naboth was accused of 'blessing' God. The usual explanation of this has been that the editors were so outraged and horrified by the blasphemy of cursing God that they could not even bring themselves to write the words. Instead they wrote the opposite, feeling that the reader would rightly understand the true nature of the charge made against Naboth, and their own pious scruples. The N.E.B. footnote offers a rather different meaning. Since 'Be blessed' or a similar phrase was a common formula used when friends parted, they suggest that Naboth was accused of bidding farewell to God. In either case a euphemism has been used to mask a blasphemous expression.

13. Naboth with his sons (cp. 2 Kings 9: 26) was executed and his land was forfeit to the crown. The law had been observed in the letter and destroyed in the spirit, and more than the law, since all those who had played any part in the legal farce in deference to or fear of the king had been corrupted. God's purpose for the law was to ensure that society was righteous, but used thus as an instrument of royal power, it destroyed the moral basis of society.

This story perhaps more than any other makes clear what the deuteronomists believed to be at stake in the fight to prevent Israel from becoming one more Canaanite community. It also demonstrates why the deuteronomists were always highly suspicious of kings. For them the office was such that even the best of men could hardly resist corruption. ✳

AHAB'S REWARD

As soon as Jezebel heard that Naboth had been stoned 15 and was dead, she said to Ahab, 'Get up and take possession of the vineyard which Naboth refused to sell you, for he

16 is no longer alive; Naboth of Jezreel is dead.' When
Ahab heard that Naboth was dead, he got up and went to
17 the vineyard to take possession. Then the word of the
18 LORD came to Elijah the Tishbite: 'Go down at once to
Ahab king of Israel, who is in Samaria; you will find him
in Naboth's vineyard, where he has gone to take possession.
19 Say to him, "This is the word of the LORD: Have you
killed your man, and taken his land as well?" Say to him,
"This is the word of the LORD: Where dogs licked the
blood of Naboth, there dogs shall lick your blood."'
20 Ahab said to Elijah, 'Have you found me, my enemy?'
'I have found you', he said, 'because you have sold your-
21 self to do what is wrong in the eyes of the LORD. I will
bring*a* disaster upon you; I will sweep you away and
destroy every mother's son of the house of Ahab in
22 Israel, whether under protection of the family or not. And
I will deal with your house as I did with the house of
Jeroboam son of Nebat and of Baasha son of Ahijah,
because you have provoked my anger and led Israel into
23 sin.' And the LORD went on to say of Jezebel, 'Jezebel shall
24 be eaten by dogs by the rampart of*b* Jezreel. Of the house
of Ahab, those who die in the city shall be food for the
dogs, and those who die in the country shall be food for
25 the birds.' (Never was a man who sold himself to do what
is wrong in the LORD's eyes as Ahab did, and all at the
26 prompting of Jezebel his wife. He committed gross
abominations in going after false gods, doing everything
that the Amorites did, whom the LORD had dispossessed

[a] he said,...bring: *or* he said. 'Because you...LORD, I am bringing...
[b] by the rampart of: *or, with some MSS.,* in the plot of ground at (*cp. 2
Kgs. 9: 36*).

in favour of Israel.) When Ahab heard this, he rent his 27
clothes, put on sackcloth and fasted; he lay down in his
sackcloth and went about muttering to himself. Then the 28
word of the LORD came to Elijah the Tishbite: 'Have you 29
seen how Ahab has humbled himself before me? Because
he has thus humbled himself, I will not bring disaster
upon his house in his own lifetime, but in his son's.'

＊ 15. In the eyes of the people Naboth had been rightly
executed for blasphemy. In reality he had been murdered to
fulfil the ambitions of the king. Murder always left the society
in which it had been committed defiled until the criminal had
been brought to justice.

17. *the word of the LORD came to Elijah the Tishbite:* Israelite
society, even though unconscious of the fact, was defiled with
injustice. God could not tolerate this, and so himself through
the person of his prophet became the vindicator of Naboth,
both to clear the dead man's name and also to free the community from guilt.

19. Since Ahab had shed innocent blood, his own blood must
be shed. Justice would be done in that Ahab would suffer the
same ignominious end as Naboth has suffered. *dogs* were the
scavengers of any eastern community, living on the refuse of
society. That they had *licked the blood of Naboth* was the visible
sign that he had died as one cast out by both God and men.
Ahab must suffer the same fate. It was he who truly had
offended God and this needed to be declared publicly.

20. The meeting of Elijah with Ahab was brief and dramatic.
The account of its ends here. Verses 21-6 have been added to
the narrative by an editor who used this incident as the basis
for a judgement upon the whole family of Ahab. It is so
severe that verses 27-9 which follow read strangely after it.
Those verses originally followed verse 20 and the repentance
of Ahab which they describe meant that he acknowledged the
justice of Elijah's words and accepted the verdict.

21–6. These verses express the attitude of the deuteronomic editors to the kings of Israel. This point of view has already been expressed more than once; the kings have become an infection in the body politic which must be eradicated before the body itself is destroyed. What proved true of Jeroboam and Baasha and their dynasties has also proved true of Omri and his dynasty. The editor here has in mind the revolt which Jehu was to lead successfully. It is described in 2 Kings.

21. *I will bring disaster:* the N.E.B. makes the opening words of the verse the beginning of a new sentence with its verb in the future tense. In the footnote an alternative translation is offered which makes this verse an extension of verse 20 and uses the present tense. The Hebrew has a present participle which is usually used with the future sense but when used by a prophet can refer to the present. What was prophesied was regarded as so certain and so imminent that though technically in the future it could be spoken of as present. A future action that God wills is as sure and certain as a present action.

23. *Jezebel* is singled out for special mention. This was not only for her vigour and influence over Ahab, but also because the editors have more than once been at pains to make the point that marriage to a foreign wife was a source of corruption to a king. *by the rampart of Jezreel:* there is a divided witness both in the Hebrew manuscripts and in the Versions as to the place where Jezebel would die. The difference depends upon one Hebrew letter. Some manuscripts read the consonants *ḥl*, which gives the translation *ramparts*, and others *ḥlq*, which means 'plot of ground'. The latter word is found in 2 Kings where the fulfilment of the prophecy is described.

24. The threat to Ahab's family is of total annihilation. The name and memory of Ahab was to be removed root and branch from Israel, and all his family were to die in such a way that it would be clear to the nation that the whole family had been rejected by God. Their bodies would be treated as refuse.

The scene is now set for the final act in the story of Ahab and Elijah. Ahab has shown himself in his true colours and

Elijah, as God's prophet, has declared him to be fit only for death. The last chapter of the book will show how Elijah's prophecy was fulfilled, thus showing Elijah to be a true prophet and Ahab as no true king in God's eyes. ✳

AHAB PLANS TO ATTACK RAMOTH-GILEAD

For three years there was no war between the Aramaeans **22** and the Israelites, but in the third year Jehoshaphat king 2*a* of Judah went down to visit the king of Israel. The latter 3 said to his courtiers, 'You know that Ramoth-gilead belongs to us, and yet we do nothing to recover it from the king of Aram.' He said to Jehoshaphat, 'Will you join 4 me in attacking Ramoth-gilead?' Jehoshaphat said to the king of Israel, 'What is mine is yours: myself, my people, and my horses.' Then Jehoshaphat said to the king of 5 Israel, 'First let us seek counsel from the LORD.' The king 6 of Israel assembled the prophets, some four hundred of them, and asked them, 'Shall I attack Ramoth-gilead or shall I refrain?' 'Attack,' they answered; 'the Lord will deliver it into your hands.' Jehoshaphat asked, 'Is there no 7 other prophet of the LORD here through whom we may seek guidance?' 'There is one more', the king of Israel 8 answered, 'through whom we may seek guidance of the LORD, but I hate the man, because he prophesies no good for me; never anything but evil. His name is Micaiah son of Imlah.' Jehoshaphat exclaimed, 'My lord king, let no such word pass your lips!' So the king of Israel called one 9 of his eunuchs and told him to fetch Micaiah son of Imlah with all speed.

[*a*] *Verses 2–35: cp. 2 Chr. 18: 2–34.*

10   The king of Israel and Jehoshaphat king of Judah were seated on their thrones, in shining armour,[a] at the entrance to the gate of Samaria, and all the prophets were prophesy-
11 ing before them. One of them, Zedekiah son of Kenaanah, made himself horns of iron and said, 'This is the word of the LORD: "With horns like these you shall gore the
12 Aramaeans and make an end of them."' In the same vein all the prophets prophesied, 'Attack Ramoth-gilead and win the day; the LORD will deliver it into your hands.'
13 The messenger sent to fetch Micaiah told him that the prophets had with one voice given the king a favourable answer. 'And mind you agree with them', he added.
14 'As the LORD lives,' said Micaiah, 'I will say only what the LORD tells me to say.'

    ✷ 1. The opening reference to *three years* of peace reads as though the peace had followed the events of chapter 20 and perhaps were the consequence of Ahab's generous treatment of Ben-hadad. There can be no certainty of this. The years of peace may have been due to the alliance of Aram and Israel and other kingdoms against the common enemy Assyria. Once the threat of Assyrian invasion had been removed by the victory at Qarqar, then the old rivalries and jealousies came to the fore once again.

    2. *Jehoshaphat king of Judah:* this is the first mention of a king of Judah since chapter 15. Asa was the last king of Judah to be mentioned and it was said of him that there was hostility between him and Israel (cp. 15: 16). In fact Asa was an ally of the king of Aram against Israel. Here *Jehoshaphat* appears as an ally of Ahab against Aram, though in reality *Jehoshaphat* was much more a vassal than an ally. No account is given of how this new relationship between Israel and Judah had come into

[a] *So Sept.; Heb. adds* robes.

being, but it is not difficult to see it as a consequence of the resurgence of Israelite power which had begun under the powerful King Omri and continued under Ahab. This view is supported by the further fact which we learn from 2 Kings 8: 18 that *Jehoshaphat*'s son, Joram, had married Athaliah, Ahab's daughter, and so became his son-in-law.

3. *Ramoth-gilead* was an important Israelite town. It lay in the region east of the Jordan (see map 5 on p. 148). Its site has not been identified with certainty, but it was likely to have been near the modern city of Irbid which is now the centre of the region in much the same way as *Ramoth-gilead* was then. It was important enough to be mentioned in Solomon's list of his twelve regions. In view of this it is odd that Ramoth-gilead should not have been demanded back from Ben-hadad as a part of the bargain for his life, if the narratives in chapters 20 and 22 are linked together.

6. The prophets had a prominent place in political life. Here they were consulted on a matter of utmost importance for the life of the state. The band of prophets first consulted clearly belong to those that have been called nationalistic (cp. comment on p. 192). They saw their function as being to support the king and the state with an uncritical loyalty.

8. *Micaiah son of Imlah* was the same kind of prophet as Elijah. He would be as resolute for God as Elijah had been. The question has been asked why Elijah does not appear in this chapter. It was Elijah who prophesied the coming death of Ahab, and *Micaiah* is an otherwise unknown prophet who appears here and then never again. This story was originally independent of the Elijah stories. The editors have used it here since it fulfils their purpose so admirably.

10. *in shining armour:* the N.E.B. has omitted the word 'robes' as being a dittography of the following word. The consonants of the Hebrew words for 'robes', and *entrance* which immediately follows, are almost identical. The Hebrew actually reads 'clothed in robes', and with the omission of

'robes' the N.E.B. has understood 'clothed,' as the Septuagint has done, as meaning *in shining armour*. The word translated *entrance* usually means 'threshing floor' and has been so translated here in the Revised Standard Version. Clearly the word has a wider meaning to indicate a large open space such as a threshing floor was. A threshing floor, besides being large and open, needed to be on an exposed position to catch the wind. The open space here was not appropriate for that function. It was the space just outside the gate of the city where public meetings took place, the equivalent of the forum of a Roman city.

11. The skills and techniques of prophecy, ecstatic speech and symbolic actions, were used by the nationalistic prophets to commend the wishes of the king to God and to persuade God to intervene in the struggle on behalf of the king. The symbolic action of Zedekiah who *made himself horns of iron* was believed to commit God to similar support of Ahab's enterprise.

14. *I will say only what the LORD tells me to say:* Micaiah's sole concern was to be the mouthpiece and instrument of God through whom the divine will could be made clear. ✳

MICAIAH PROPHESIES

15 When Micaiah came into the king's presence, the king said to him, 'Micaiah, shall we attack Ramoth-gilead or shall we refrain?' 'Attack and win the day,' he said; 'the
16 LORD will deliver it into your hands.' 'How often must I adjure you', said the king, 'to tell me nothing but the
17 truth in the name of the LORD?' Then Micaiah said, 'I saw all Israel scattered on the mountains, like sheep without a shepherd; and I heard the LORD say, "They have no
18 master, let them go home in peace."' The king of Israel said to Jehoshaphat, 'Did I not tell you that he never

prophesies good for me, nothing but evil?' Micaiah went 19
on, 'Listen now to the word of the LORD. I saw the LORD
seated on his throne, with all the host of heaven in
attendance on his right and on his left. The LORD said, 20
"Who will entice Ahab to attack and fall on*a* Ramoth-
gilead?" One said one thing and one said another; then a 21
spirit came forward and stood before the LORD and said,
"I will entice him." "How?" said the LORD. "I will go 22
out", he said, "and be a lying spirit in the mouth of all his
prophets." "You shall entice him," said the LORD, "and
you shall succeed; go and do it." You see, then, how the 23
LORD has put a lying spirit in the mouth of all these
prophets of yours, because he has decreed disaster for you.'
Then Zedekiah son of Kenaanah came up to Micaiah and 24
struck him in the face: 'And how did the spirit of the
LORD pass from me to speak to you?' he said. Micaiah 25
answered, 'That you will find out on the day when you
run into an inner room to hide yourself.' Then the king of 26
Israel ordered Micaiah to be arrested and committed to
the custody of Amon the governor of the city and Joash
the king's son.*b* 'Lock this fellow up', he said, 'and give 27
him prison diet of bread and water until I come home in
safety.' Micaiah retorted, 'If you do return in safety, 28
the LORD has not spoken by me.'*c*

☆ 15. *Attack and win the day:* these words openly obeyed the
king but were in reality mockery, and Ahab was perceptive
enough to know it.

17. *shepherd* was a common metaphor for king.

19. *I saw the LORD seated on his throne:* this picture of God

[a] Or *at*.   [b] son: *or* deputy.
[c] *So Sept.; Heb. adds* and he said, 'Listen, peoples, all together.'

reigning in heaven and sending agents to do his work on earth is found in other places in the Old Testament (cp. Isa. 6: 1–8 and Job 1: 6–12).

20. *Who will entice Ahab to attack and fall on Ramoth-gilead?*: there is a deliberate ambiguity in the words of the question. The same preposition in Hebrew can mean 'at' or 'on'. So Ahab was to be enticed to fall on Ramoth-gilead, i.e. attack it, in order that he might fall at Ramoth-gilead, i.e. die there. Even the nationalistic prophets were used by God, though it was far from their intention.

22. The phrase *a lying spirit* has troubled many people as being contrary to the moral nature of God. Yet what the spirit was to do was to assist in bringing about an event which had already been prophesied to be of God in the plainest possible terms. In chapter 21 Elijah prophesied a violent and shameful death for Ahab. There is no doubt, much less lie, there. The nationalistic prophets were to have a part in bringing about that prophecy of Elijah by what they themselves prophesied. They prophesied in good faith but the prophecy was ambiguous. They were so certain that they could rightly interpret the prophecy that they discounted the ambiguity. Their arrogance caused them to lie. Of course, there is also an element of determinism running through the story. It was told by the deuteronomists to show how Elijah's prophecy came true, and in the light of that conviction Ahab and all the other actors in the story were shown as moving to a pre-ordained destiny. The purpose of the deuteronomic history was to teach moral lessons and the deuteronomists, as all Israelites at that time, accepted without demur that God was responsible for all that happened, whether prophecies which enticed Ahab to Ramoth-gilead or the death of the king. The question whether certain things such as lies and murder were so evil in themselves, that the moral nature of God was compromised by any involvement with them, did not trouble them. Their moral and spiritual insight was strong, but simple and lacking in refinement. Refinement did come later through

the probing and questionings of later Jewish thinkers, and most of all through the life and teaching of Jesus.

24. It was the slur upon the intelligence of the prophets, that they did not understand what they were saying, which caused Zedekiah to strike Micaiah. *And how did the spirit of theLORD pass from me to speak to you?*: neither the integrity nor the genuineness of the prophetic inspiration of Zedekiah was in question. Micaiah's answer was clear and straightforward. Events would tell. That was the test accepted by the deuteronomic law; a true prophet was one whose prophecy came to pass.

26. A son of Ahab named *Joash* is otherwise unknown. This does not mean that Ahab could not have had a son of that name, but some archaeological evidence has come to light which points to one of the king's officials having the title *the king's son*. This explains the alternative translation 'deputy' (N.E.B. footnote).

28. The last words of the Hebrew have been omitted from the text. They are a quotation from the prophet Micah (Mic. 1 : 2) and were added to the verse by some editor who thought that Micah and Micaiah were the same person. ✽

AHAB'S DEATH

So the king of Israel and Jehoshaphat king of Judah 29 marched on Ramoth-gilead, and the king of Israel said to 30 Jehoshaphat, 'I will disguise myself to go into battle, but you shall wear your royal robes.' So he went into battle in disguise. Now the king of Aram had commanded the 31 thirty-two captains of his chariots not to engage all and sundry but the king of Israel alone. When the captains saw 32 Jehoshaphat, they thought he was the king of Israel and turned to attack him. But Jehoshaphat cried out and, when 33 the captains saw that he was not the king of Israel, they

34 broke off the attack on him. But one man drew his bow at random and hit the king of Israel where the breastplate joins the plates of the armour. So he said to his driver, 'Wheel round and take me out of the line; I am wounded.'

35 When the day's fighting reached its height, the king was facing the Aramaeans propped up in his chariot, and the blood from his wound flowed down upon the floor of the

36 chariot; and in the evening he died. At sunset the herald went through the ranks, crying, 'Every man to his city,

37 every man to his country.' Thus died the king. He was

38 brought to Samaria and they buried him there. The chariot was swilled out at the pool of Samaria, and the dogs licked up the blood, and the prostitutes washed themselves in it, in fulfilment of the word the LORD had spoken.

39   Now the other acts and events of Ahab's reign, the ivory house and all the cities he built, are recorded in the

40 annals of the kings of Israel. So Ahab rested with his forefathers and was succeeded by his son Ahaziah.

    ✻ 32. *Jehoshaphat cried out* his battle cry, and thus revealed his identity to his attackers.

    34. The story emphasizes that Ahab's death was God's doing. Ahab was no coward as the manner of his death shows. He disguised himself not out of fear but in order to outwit his fate. Thirty-two enemy captains specifically sought him in the battle to kill him but without success. Ahab, though wearing heavy armour, died as the result of a random arrow which by an unlucky chance found a chink in his armour. Such a combination of elaborate precautions, phenomenal luck in escaping determined enemies, and cruel mischance is meant to teach the inevitability of the judgement and the will of God. Elijah had prophesied Ahab's death and die he must. Jehoshaphat

though visibly royal was not killed, and not because he ran away.

38. This verse was added by an over-zealous editor. It is meant to show how the prophecy of Ahab's death was ful-filled in detail, but is self-defeating since it records events in Samaria and not in Jezreel. The real fulfilment of the prophecy is related in 2 Kings 9: 25-6, where Jehu is said to have killed Ahab's son Jehoram at Jezreel and left the body on the ground that had formerly belonged to Naboth. The reference to *the prostitutes*, which corresponds to no part of the original pro-phecy, is a further cause of suspicion. Some scholars have tried to eliminate them. The Hebrew word used here is very similar to a word meaning 'armour', and on that basis it has been suggested that the original reference was to Ahab's armour being washed in the pool. If so, the reference to *the prostitutes* came about through a scribal error. Another suggestion is that the reference to dogs was a veiled reference to male sexual perverts. They are referred to as 'dogs' in Deut. 23: 18 (translated 'male prostitute' in the N.E.B.). Then to add to the ignominy the reference to prostitutes was added. Another explanation which has been offered is that to wash with the blood of a king was regarded as a particularly potent fertility rite, though it is difficult to see what advantage such a rite would have been to such women! The verse is best regarded as a clumsy attempt of a pious editor to ensure that no detail of the original prophecy went unfulfilled.

39. *the ivory house:* archaeological work has shown that it was the custom in many places to decorate the finest buildings with inlays of carved ivory. Examples of such work were found during the excavations of the site of Samaria. Ahab's *ivory house* was a building decorated in this way. It was an indication of his wealth and the power of a kingdom which could produce such wealth. *all the cities he built:* as a strong king he would have been a builder of cities and fortresses. The archaeologists have found examples of large and elaborate building complexes which they have dated in this period.

Because of their affinity in style with the finds at Samaria, it is a reasonable assumption to hold that they were built by Ahab. Such work has been found at Hazor and most dramatically at Megiddo. The great store houses there, which used to be attributed to Solomon, and have often been called 'Solomon's stables', are now thought to have been the work of Ahab. *

THE REIGN OF JEHOSHAPHAT IN JUDAH

41[a] Jehoshaphat son of Asa had become king of Judah in the
42 fourth year of Ahab king of Israel. He was thirty-five years old when he came to the throne, and he reigned in Jerusalem for twenty-five years; his mother was Azubah
43 daughter of Shilhi. He followed in the footsteps of Asa his father and did not swerve from them; he did what was right in the eyes of the LORD. [b]But the hill-shrines were allowed to remain; the people continued to slaughter and
44 burn sacrifices there. Jehoshaphat remained at peace with
45 the king of Israel. The other events of Jehoshaphat's reign, his exploits and his wars, are recorded in the annals of the
46 kings of Judah. But he did away with such of the male prostitutes attached to the shrines as were still left over from the days of Asa his father.

47 There was no king in Edom, only[c] a viceroy of Jehosha-
48 phat; he built merchantmen[d] to sail to Ophir for gold, but they never made the journey because they were wrecked
49 at Ezion-geber. Ahaziah son of Ahab proposed to Jehoshaphat that his own men should go to sea with his; but Jehoshaphat would not consent.

[a] *Verses 41–43: cp. 2 Chr. 20: 31–33.*
[b] But...there: *verse 44 in Heb.*
[c] only: *prob. rdg.; Heb. om.*   [d] *Lit.* ships of Tarshish.

Jehoshaphat rested with his forefathers and was buried 50
with them in the city of David his father, and was
succeeded by his son Joram.

✵ The narrative returns to the short summaries which were
given for almost all the earlier kings.

41. *Jehoshaphat,* whose reign is recorded here, has already
appeared in the narrative as an ally or vassal of Ahab. The
editors speak well of him because of his reform in driving out
'male prostitutes' from the shrines. The approval was not
whole-hearted since he tolerated the shrines themselves.

46. *male prostitutes:* see the note on 14: 24.

44. *remained at peace:* see the note on 22: 2.

47. *Edom* has not been mentioned since 11: 14–25, where
Solomon's loss of control of that kingdom was narrated. One
of the kings of Judah who reigned after Solomon must have
regained control of *Edom* and thus control of Ezion-geber, the
Red Sea port. This naturally led to an attempt to restart the
lucrative trade with Ophir.

48. The enterprise was unsuccessful because Jehoshaphat's
men were inexperienced sailors. *merchantmen:* see note on
10: 22.

49. Ahaziah with his Phoenician connections could have
provided experienced sailors.

THE INTRODUCTION TO THE
REIGN OF AHAZIAH

Ahaziah son of Ahab became king of Israel in Samaria in 51
the seventeenth year of Jehoshaphat king of Judah, and
reigned over Israel for two years. He did what was wrong 52
in the eyes of the LORD, following in the footsteps of his
father and mother and in those of Jeroboam son of Nebat,
who had led Israel into sin. He served Baal and worshipped 53

him, and provoked the anger of the LORD the God of Israel, as his father had done.

This is no more than the formal introductory formula to the reign of Ahaziah. The account of the reign is found in 2 Kings 1. This is the clearest possible indication of the artificiality of the present division of the two books of Kings. They were written as one volume and were meant to be read as such.

✳   ✳   ✳   ✳   ✳   ✳   ✳   ✳   ✳   ✳   ✳   ✳   ✳

A NOTE ON FURTHER READING

Fuller commentaries on 1 Kings are to be found in J. A. Montgomery, *The Book of Kings* in the *International Critical Commentary* series (1951), and John Gray, *I and II Kings* in the *S.C.M. Old Testament Library* (2nd ed., 1970).

Readers will find background material in B. W. Anderson, *The Living World of The Old Testament* (Longmans, 1959), and in E. W. Heaton, *The Hebrew Kingdoms* in the New Clarendon Bible (Oxford University Press, 1968).

Maps and illustrations will be found in C. M. Jones, *Old Testament Illustrations* in this series (1971). Those who wish to learn more about the archaeology of Palestine should consult K. M. Kenyon, *Archaeology in the Holy Land* (Benn, 1969), and those who are interested in the institutions of Israel will find a vast amount of information in R. de Vaux, *Ancient Israel: its Life and Institutions* (Darton, Longman and Todd, 1965). Fuller information about the struggle with Canaanite religion will be found in Th. C. Vriezen, *The Religion of Ancient Israel* (Lutterworth Press, 1967) and in Helmer Ringgren, *Israelite Religion* (S.P.C.K., 1966). Information on all these and many other subjects will be found in the articles of the Bible Dictionaries, such as *Peake's Commentary on the Bible* (Nelson, revised 1962), and the four volumes of *The Interpreter's Dictionary of the Bible* (Abingdon, 1962).

A TIME CHART OF THE PERIOD

THE UNITED KINGDOM Solomon c. 961–922		OTHER POWERS
THE DIVIDED KINGDOM		*Egypt*
Judah	*Israel*	XXII Dynasty 935–725
Rehoboam 922–915	Jeroboam I 922–901	Shishak 935–914
Abijam 915–913	Nadab 901–900	
Asa 913–873	Baasha 900–877	*Assyria*
Jehoshaphat 873–849	Elah 877–876	Shalmaneser III 859–824
	Zimri 876	Battle of Qarqar 853
	Omri 876–869	
	Ahab 869–850	*Damascus*
	Ahaziah 850–849	Ben-hadad I ?900–860
		Ben-hadad II 860–843

APPENDIX

MEASURES OF LENGTH
AND EXTENT

	span	cubit	rod[a]
span	1	...	...
cubit	2	1	...
rod[a]	12	6	1

The 'short cubit' (Judg. 3: 16) was traditionally the measure from the elbow to the knuckles of the closed fist; and what seems to be intended as a 'long cubit' measured a 'cubit and a hand-breadth', i.e. 7 instead of 6 hand-breadths (Ezek. 40: 5). What is meant by cubits 'according to the old standard of measurement' (2 Chr. 3: 3) is presumably this pre-exilic cubit of 7 hand-breadths. Modern estimates of the Hebrew cubit range from 12 to 25·2 inches, without allowing for varying local standards.

Area was measured by the 'yoke' (Isa. 5: 10), i.e. that ploughed by a pair of oxen in one day, said to be half an acre now in Palestine, though varying in different places with the nature of the land.

MEASURES OF CAPACITY

liquid measures	equivalences	dry measures
'log'	1 'log'	...
...	4 'log'	'kab'
...	$7\frac{1}{5}$ 'log'	'omer'
'hin'	12 'log'	...
...	24 'log'	'seah'
'bath'	72 'log'	'ephah'
'kor'	720 'log'	'homer' or 'kor'

[a] Hebrew literally 'reed', the length of Ezekiel's measuring-rod.

According to ancient authorities the Hebrew 'log' was of the same capacity as the Roman *sextarius*; this according to the best available evidence was equivalent to 0·99 pint of the English standard.

WEIGHTS AND COINS

	heavy (Phoenician) standard			light (Babylonian) standard		
	shekel	mina	talent	shekel	mina	talent
shekel	1	...	...	1	...	...
mina	50	1	...	60	1	...
talent	3,000	60	1	3,600	60	1

The 'gerah' was $\frac{1}{20}$ of the sacred or heavy shekel and probably $\frac{1}{42}$ of the light shekel.

The 'sacred shekel' according to tradition was identical with the heavy shekel; while the 'shekel of the standard recognized by merchants' (Gen. 23:16) was perhaps a weight stamped with its value as distinct from one not so stamped and requiring to be weighed on the spot.

Recent discoveries of hoards of objects stamped with their weights suggest that the shekel may have weighed approximately 11·5 grammes towards the end of the Hebrew monarchy, but nothing shows whether this is the light or the heavy shekel; and much variety, due partly to the worn or damaged state of the objects and partly to variations in local standards, increases the difficulty of giving a definite figure.

Coins are not mentioned before the Exile. Only the 'daric' (1 Chr. 29. 7) and the 'drachma' (Ezra 2:69; Neh. 7:70–72), if this is a distinct coin, are found in the Old Testament; the former is said to have been a month's pay for a soldier in the Persian army, while the latter will have been the Greek silver drachma, estimated at approximately 4·4 grammes. The 'shekel' of this period (Neh. 5:15) as a coin was probably the Graeco-Persian *siglos* weighing 5·6 grammes.

INDEX

257

Index

new**providence**
MEMORIAL LIBRARY

3/07

377 Elkwood Avenue
New Providence, NJ 07974

BIO
Richard
Flo

377 Elkwood Avenue
New Providence, NJ 07974

Richard the Lionheart

Richard the Lionheart

King and Knight

---

by

Jean Flori

translated by

Jean Birrell

PRAEGER

Westport, Connecticut
London

NEW PROVIDENCE
MEMORIAL LIBRARY

Published in the United States and Canada by
Praeger Publishers, 88 Post Road West, Westport, CT 06881
An imprint of Greenwood Publishing Group, Inc.
www.praeger.com

English language edition first published outside of the United States and Canada by Edinburgh
University Press Ltd © 2006.

First published 1999, Editions Payor et Rivage
106 boulevard Saint-Germain
75006 Paris
France

B↓T 49.95   8/07

Library of Congress Cataloging in Publication Data

Flori, Jean.
   [Richard Cœur de Lion. English]
   Richard the Lionheart : King and Knight / Jean Flori ; translated by Jean Birrell.
     p.   cm.
   Originally published: Edinburgh : Edinburgh University Press, 2006. First published: Paris :
Payot & Rivages, c1999.
   Includes bibliographical references and index.
   ISBN-13: 978-0-275-99397-9 (alk. paper)
   ISBN-10: 0-275-99397-3 (alk. paper)
   1. Richard I, King of England, 1157–1199. 2. Great Britain—History—Richard I, 1189–
1199. 3. Great Britain—Kings and rulers—Biography. 4. Crusades—Third, 1189–
1192. I. Title.
DA207.F57 2007
942.0392092—dc22
[B]   2007001870

Library of Congress Catalog Card Number: 2007001870

ISBN-10 0-275-99397-3
ISBN-13 978-0-275-99397-9

Printed in Great Britain

10 9 8 7 6 5 4 3 2 1

Contents

Map 1. Capetian and Plantagenet Lands in the 12th Century

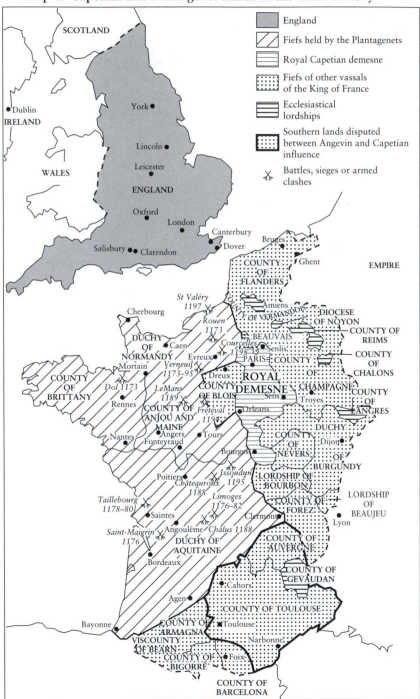

Legend:

- England
- Fiefs held by the Plantagenets
- Royal Capetian demesne
- Fiefs of other vassals of the King of France
- Ecclesiastical lordships
- Southern lands disputed between Angevin and Capetian influence
- ✕ Battles, sieges or armed clashes

SCOTLAND

Dublin
IRELAND

WALES

York

Lincoln

Leicester

ENGLAND

Oxford

London

Salisbury Clarendon

Canterbury
Dover

Bruges
Ghent

EMPIRE

COUNTY OF FLANDERS

St Valéry 1197

Cherbourg

Rouen 1173

Amiens

COUNTY OF VERMANDOIS

DIOCESE OF NOYON

COUNTY OF REIMS

DUCHY OF NORMANDY

Caen

Courcelles 1198

BEAUVAIS

Mortain

Evreux

Senlis

PARIS

Verneuil 1173–95

Dreux

COUNTY OF CHALONS

COUNTY OF BRITTANY

Dol 1173

LeMans 1189

COUNTY OF BLOIS

ROYAL DEMESNE

COUNTY OF CHAMPAGNE

COUNTY OF LANGRES

Rennes

COUNTY OF ANJOU AND MAINE

Fretéval 1194

Sens

Troyes

Nantes

Angers
Fonteyraud

Tours

Orleans

DUCHY

Dijon

COUNTY OF NEVERS

OF BURGUNDY

Bourges

Poitiers

Issoudun 1195

LORDSHIP OF BOURBON

Châteauroux 1188

Taillebourg 1178–80

Saintes

Limoges 1176–82

COUNTY OF FOREZ

LORDSHIP OF BEAUJEU

Saint-Maigrin 1176

Angoulême Châlus 1188

Clermont

Lyon

DUCHY OF AQUITAINE

COUNTY OF AUVERGNE

Bordeaux

COUNTY OF GEVAUDAN

Agen

Cahors

COUNTY OF TOULOUSE

Bayonne

COUNTY OF ARMAGNAC

Toulouse

VISCOUNTY OF BEARN

COUNTY OF BIGORRE

Foix

Narbonne

COUNTY OF BARCELONA

Map 2. The Third Crusade, 1191–7

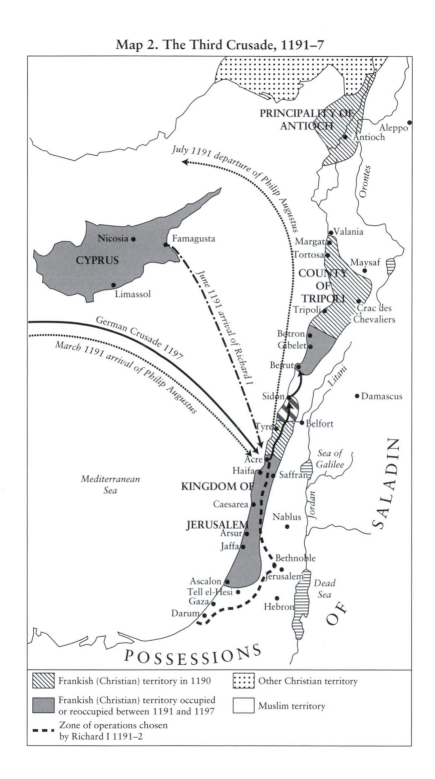

PRINCIPALITY OF ANTIOCH

Aleppo

Antioch

Orontes

July 1191 departure of Philip Augustus

Valania

Margat

Tortosa

Maysaf

Nicosia   Famagusta

CYPRUS

COUNTY OF TRIPOLI

Tripoli

Crac des Chevaliers

Limassol

June 1191 arrival of Richard I

Botron

Gibelet

Berut

German Crusade 1197

Litani

March 1191 arrival of Philip Augustus

Sidon

Damascus

Tyre   Belfort

Acre

Haifa   Saffran

Sea of Galilee

Mediterranean Sea

KINGDOM OF JERUSALEM

Caesarea

Nablus

Jordan

SALADIN

Arsur

Jaffa

Bethnoble

Ascalon

Jerusalem

Dead Sea

Tell el-Hesi

Gaza

Hebron

Darum

OF

POSSESSIONS

	Frankish (Christian) territory in 1190		Other Christian territory
	Frankish (Christian) territory occupied or reoccupied between 1191 and 1197		Muslim territory
	Zone of operations chosen by Richard I 1191–2		

Chart 1. The Plantagenets

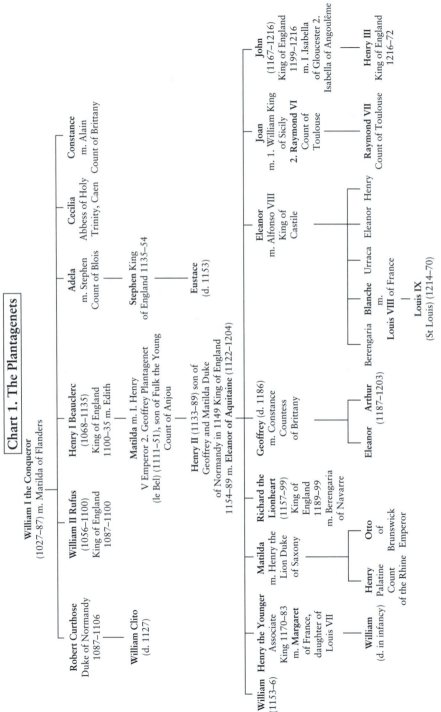

Chart 2. The Capetians

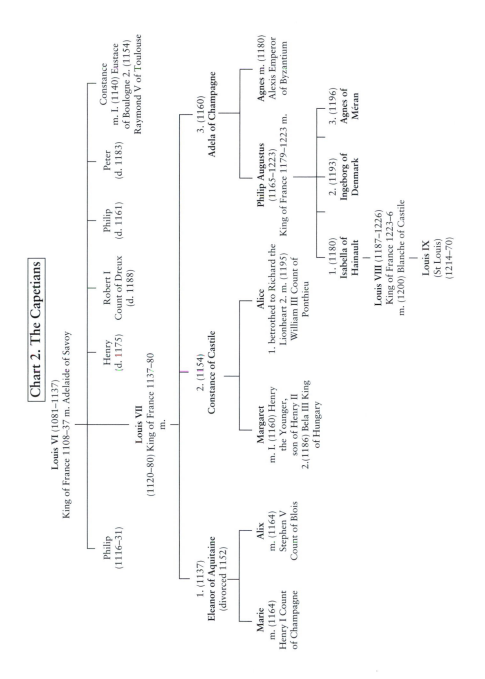

Louis VI (1081–1137)
King of France 1108–37 m. Adelaide of Savoy

Philip
(1116–31)

Louis VII
(1120–80) King of France 1137–80
m.

Henry
(d. 1175)

Robert I
Count of Dreux
(d. 1188)

Philip
(d. 1161)

Peter
(d. 1183)

Constance
m. I. (1140) Eustace
of Boulogne 2. (1154)
Raymond V of Toulouse

1. (1137)
Eleanor of Aquitaine
(divorced 1152)

2. (1154)
Constance of Castile

3. (1160)
Adela of Champagne

Marie
m. (1164)
Henry I Count
of Champagne

Alix
m. (1164)
Stephen V
Count of Blois

Margaret
m. I. (1160) Henry
the Younger,
son of Henry II
2.(1186) Bela III King
of Hungary

Alice
1. betrothed to Richard the
Lionheart 2. m. (1195)
William III Count of
Ponthieu

Philip Augustus
(1165–1223)
King of France 1179–1223 m.

Agnes m. (1180)
Alexis Emperor
of Byzantium

1. (1180)
**Isabella of
Hainault**

2. (1193)
**Ingeborg of
Denmark**

3. (1196)
**Agnes of
Méran**

Louis VIII (1187–1226)
King of France 1223–6
m. (1200) Blanche of Castile

Louis IX
(St Louis)
(1214–70)

Introduction
Richard: a 'Roi-Chevalier'?

What could be more normal than for a future king of England to be born in Oxford? Yet the birth on 8 September 1157 of the child who would soon be known to history as 'Richard the Lionheart' is paradoxical in a number of ways. The familiar epithet conveys all the principal features of his indomitable character: courage, valour, prowess, the pursuit of glory, the thirst for fame, generosity in war and peace, a sense of honour combined with a sort of haughty dignity made up of both arrogance and pride. In fact, it is an epithet which both suggests and summarises the virtues of the chivalry which Richard will forever embody for the late twelfth century, while perhaps also concealing its vices. William Marshal, his contemporary, had fulfilled the same role for the preceding generation, or so his panegyrist claimed.[1] But there is one difference, and an important one: William Marshal was a knight in the true sense of the term, living off his sword and his lance; Richard was King of England, the perfect, indeed first, example of the 'roi-chevalier'.

RICHARD, THE PRINCE WHO BECAME KING

Richard was not meant to be king. By the time of his birth, his father, Henry II, had already fathered three children by Eleanor of Aquitaine, the queen 'divorced' by Louis VII, King of France. Henry had married her immediately after the divorce, in 1152; their first-born son, William, died in 1156, at the age of three. Then, before Richard, Eleanor had given birth to a second son, the future 'Young Henry', King of England in his father's lifetime, and to a daughter, Matilda, who was to marry Henry the Lion, Duke of Saxony. Louis VII had feared that Eleanor was infertile, but she had eight children by her second husband, seven of whom reached adulthood and played important roles on the European political stage. After Richard came Geoffrey, future husband of the Countess of Brittany; Eleanor, who was to marry King Alfonso VIII of Castile and

whose children included Blanche of Castile, mother of St Louis IX of France; Joan, future wife of King William of Sicily and, after his death, of Count Raymond VI of Toulouse; and lastly John, known to history as John Lackland, who would become King of England in his turn after Richard's death in 1199. Richard was not the eldest child. It was the Young Henry who would normally have succeeded his father and it was only his death that made Richard heir apparent. Even then, as we will see, his father would have preferred his younger brothers, Geoffrey, or even John, in this role after the Young King's death in 1183.

RICHARD THE ANGEVIN

The second paradox is that this future king of England was not English at all; he spent scarcely a year in his kingdom in the ten years of his reign. English historians until recently portrayed him as a bad king with little interest in the government of his kingdom, primarily concerned with chivalric adventures.[2] It was purely by chance that he was born in Oxford; Henry II himself spent less than a third of his reign in England and behaved more like a French than an English king. Since its conquest by Duke William of Normandy, in 1066, England had been ruled by its conquerors and one can quite properly speak of an Anglo-Norman kingdom. With the death of William the Conqueror, a dynastic quarrel between his sons led to a fratricidal war. After defeating his brothers at Tinchebrai in 1106, Henry I Beauclerc again united England and Normandy under one rule. Only his wife, Edith, introduced a little English blood into the veins of his heirs. But Henry Beauclerc had no son and it was his daughter Matilda who became the logical, but not unchallenged, heiress to the throne.[3]

Matilda was the widow of the Emperor Henry V, and so prestigious was this marriage that she continued to be called 'the Empress'. In 1128 she married Geoffrey Plantagenet, also called Geoffrey the Fair, heir to Fulk V, Count of Anjou.[4] Until then, the future count of Anjou had been curtailed in his ambitions for territorial aggrandisement by the princes of Brittany to the west, Normandy to the north, Poitou to the south and Blois to the east, though he had managed to seize Touraine from the latter. Thanks to this marriage he could aspire to a more brilliant future by becoming King of England. This hope was at first dashed by a pre-emptive strike. Adela, Henry I's sister, had been married to the Count of Blois, by whom she had a son, Stephen. On Henry's death in 1135, Stephen of Blois, too, claimed the throne of England, where he established and consolidated his power, despite rebellions and civil wars. Geoffrey Plantagenet[5] managed nevertheless to seize Normandy in the name of his wife, Matilda, and transmit

it to his son, Henry, who was installed as duke in 1149; he had been knighted a few days earlier by David, King of Scots.[6] Geoffrey died two years later, when he was scarcely forty years old. His son, Henry, was not yet twenty when he succeeded him as Count of Anjou.

It was at this point that the dramatic event referred to above occurred, making the Count of Anjou, future father of Richard the Lionheart, one of the most powerful princes in the West: his marriage to Eleanor, heiress to the duchy of Aquitaine. Eleanor herself was no ordinary person. She was the granddaughter of the troubadour prince, William IX of Aquitaine, who sang of *fin'amor*, that new form of expression of an emotional love, both carnal and sensual, that would later be called courtly, and that defied social conventions, even marriage.[7] His tumultuous and public love affair with Dangereuse, the aptly-named wife of the Vicomte of Châtellerault, scandalised the Church. William was by no means the only prince to keep one or more concubines, but he was the first to act so openly and so shame-lessly. He installed his official mistress in his palace at Poitiers, in the new Maubergeon tower (hence her nickname 'la Maubergeonne') and appea-red with her at his side at public ceremonies. Such moral laxity occasioned both surprise and shock, to William IX's amusement. He had been so brazen as to have la Maubergeonne painted nude on his shield, enthusias-tically proclaiming that it was his wish 'to bear her in battle, as she had borne him in bed'.[8] This total and exclusive love for his mistress also led him, in 1121, to marry her daughter to his legitimate son. A daughter, Eleanor, was born of this marriage a year later. She undoubtedly inherited her fiery temperament from this exceptional grandfather and also her taste for poetry and literature, which she passed on to Richard, who could also turn his hand to poetry.

In July 1137, soon after the sudden death of her father, William X, while on a pilgrimage to St James of Compostella, Eleanor, his heiress, was married to the son of Louis VI, King of France. He was then seven-teen years old, Eleanor barely sixteen. A few days later, with the death of Louis VI, the young couple became King and Queen of France. Though marriage was at this period an essentially social and political transaction, so that the courtly literature of the period sometimes reckoned love and marriage to be incompatible, the spouses seem at first to have been strongly attracted to each other.[9] But they were very different people. Louis VII was certainly in love, but he was introverted, austere, strictly educated and deeply pious, even devout. His manner, we are told, was more that of a monk than a king. Eleanor, in contrast, was high-spirited, lively and, according to some, of easy morals; rumour was not slow to accuse her, rightly or wrongly, of having affairs. Their cultural

environment divided the young couple even more, accentuating this disparity of character. Occitanian civilisation delighted in and glorified love, pleasure, songs and laughter, poetry, colour, fashion, music and the 'joy of the court'. These 'courtly' morals seemed lax, profane and even impious to the moralists of the austere court of the King of France. The style of dress favoured by the people from the Midi, who spoke the *langue d'oc*, astonished and shocked the unimaginative Northerners, speaking their *langue d'oïl* in a court that preferred theology to poetry.

Much has been written about these cultural divergences, which go some way to explain the breakdown of the marriage and the couple's eventual separation.[10] There was also the fear of the Capetian kings of not having a male heir, and after several years of marriage, Eleanor had given birth only to a daughter, Marie, future Countess of Champagne. The couple were further alienated during the Second Crusade, in 1147, which Louis undertook as a penitent. Eleanor accompanied him. At Antioch she met her uncle, Raymond, brother of William X and son of the troubadour prince, William IX of Aquitaine; this encounter plunged her once again into the Occitanian courtly culture of which she had been deprived at the French court, and which she rediscovered with pleasure and nostalgia. It was even said that Eleanor was not indifferent to the charms of her uncle.[11] The Minstrel of Reims, who, a century later, repeated the many stories hostile to Eleanor, goes so far as to claim that the queen fell in love with Saladin, seduced by his warlike prowess. She was prepared, he says, to abandon her Christian faith and join him when Louis, warned by a chambermaid, stopped her in the nick of time. Eleanor made no secret of her contempt for him; he was not worth 'a rotten apple', which convinced Louis he should repudiate her, on the advice of his barons.[12] John of Salisbury gives a more sober account, but he still notes in passing that it was Eleanor who first raised the matter of the consanguinity of the two spouses, because she wanted to remain in Antioch with her uncle.[13]

Louis, at all events, was jealous. Further, Eleanor was actively supporting the military and political schemes of Raymond, who was trying to persuade the crusaders to reconquer Edessa, which had fallen into Turkish hands. It was, in fact, the loss of this city that had led to the Second Crusade. But Louis VII, crusader, pilgrim and penitent, was racked by remorse at the fate of those who had recently perished in the burning of the church of Vitry, a military operation gone badly wrong for which he blamed himself; all he wanted was to go to Jerusalem, to atone and pray at the Sepulchre.[14] The idea of a separation had already been mooted and it now took firm hold; the efforts of Pope Eugenius III to reconcile the couple on their return from the crusade succeeded only in postponing the

event by a few months.[15] The end came after the birth in 1150 of a second child, another girl, Alice. Louis VII probably concluded that he was never going to have a son by his wife.[16] It is also possible that his deep piety, in accord with a doctrine sometimes then professed, made him regard relations between spouses in the absence of sincere love as adulterous.[17]

Their separation, or rather the annulment of their marriage, was decreed by a council assembled at Beaugency in March 1152, at Louis VII's request. The stated reason was traditional, and in this case irrefutable: consanguinity. It was a useful pretext for breaking the marriage ties of princes, almost all of whom had ancestors in common.

So Eleanor was free. Barely two months after the annulment, to general surprise, and without seeking, as custom required, the permission of Louis VII, still her suzerain for Aquitaine, she married again. Still beautiful at the age of twenty-nine, she took as her husband Henry Plantagenet, Count of Anjou and Duke of Normandy, ten years her junior. Was this marriage premeditated? Some historians believe it was, on the basis of rumours reported by Gerald of Wales.[18] Yves Sassier relates these to the negotiations, in August 1151, which ended the dispute between Henry and Louis VII over Normandy; Louis had conceded the Norman Vexin in return for recognition of the homage owed by Henry to the king of France for Normandy, no longer to be sworn 'in the marches' (that is, on the borders of the two territories), as in the past, but in Paris itself. During these negotiations, it was said, Henry had had 'the audacity to dishonour Queen Eleanor of France by an adulterous union'; his father, Geoffrey the Fair, had tried to dissuade him from marrying such a woman, first because she was the wife of his lord, and second because he had slept with her himself when he was seneschal of France. Geoffrey died in September 1151, two weeks after the conclusion of the negotiations, which can be seen as lending credibility to such a 'confession' by a father to his son; it would also strengthen the argument for premeditation, given concrete form in this premature affair between Henry and Eleanor in the summer of 1151. But it is also possible that it was all a piece of Capetian anti-Angevin propaganda, devised in 1216, when Gerald of Wales was writing.[19]

However that may be, the marriage took place, and quickly. If we are to believe Gervase of Canterbury, it was Eleanor who took the initiative, secretly sending messengers to Henry to tell him that she was now free and urging him to marry her. The duke moved quickly to clinch a marriage that he had long wanted, seduced by Eleanor's nobility and even more, adds Gervase, by his desire to possess the honour, that is, the territories and lordships, that was hers.[20] Henry was not her only suitor; while

Eleanor was making her way to Aquitaine, she repulsed the advances of the young Count Theobald of Blois-Champagne at Blois, and then, soon after, those of Henry's own brother, Geoffrey, who even tried to abduct her. There can be no doubt that she was seen as a desirable catch. The motives for these attempts on her, however, including the one that succeeded, were, as always at this period, primarily political.[21]

Like Eleanor, Henry II was a vassal of Louis VII, and one who had already proved troublesome and, on occasion, a rival in the political sphere. With the 'divorce', Eleanor had recovered possession of her dower, the duchy of Aquitaine. As a result of this new marriage, the Plantagenet couple became rulers of a huge ensemble of territories, the biggest in the kingdom, far surpassing in size that of their common suzerain, the King of France, Eleanor's former husband. To ensure a male successor, Louis married again, in 1154; by his second wife, Constance of Castile, he had two more daughters, Margaret, later married to Henry the Young King, elder brother of Richard the Lionheart, and Alice (sometimes called Alix, Aelis or Adelaide in the texts), who was to be betrothed, unsuccessfully as we will see, to Richard himself. In 1160, still in search of a legitimate male heir, Louis VII married a third time, and at last, by his new wife, Adela of Champagne, he had a son, in August 1165. This was the future Philip Augustus, principal enemy of Richard the Lionheart, a long-awaited son whose birth seemed so miraculous that he should really, said one French chronicler, have been called 'Dieudonné'.[22] The marriage alliances proposed between the two families, to which we will return, testify both to the strange love–hate relationship existing between them, and to their desire to use this eminently diplomatic mechanism in a vain attempt to settle their political differences. The interlocking relationships between the two families that had begun with Eleanor were thus to be continued into the next generation. They further intensified the bitterness of the conflict that set Plantagenet against Capetian throughout the twelfth century and beyond, up to Bouvines (1214).

For the moment, at the time of Eleanor's second marriage, in 1152, it was the Plantagenet who seemed to be in the ascendant. Through his wife, Henry II ruled Aquitaine, a vast, rich and populous territory, nearly a third of France at that time;[23] it was also, admittedly, a region frequently disrupted by the internecine quarrels and revolts of turbulent barons, who were scarcely controlled by the feudo-vassalic bonds that were still largely alien to the mentality of the local aristocracies.[24] Henry had inherited Anjou and Maine from his father and Normandy from his mother. His lands therefore stretched unbroken from the Pyrenees to the English Channel. In the name of his mother, the Empress Matilda, he also claimed

England, still in the hands of Stephen of Blois, in spite of the efforts of her supporters. But here too, fate was to prove kind to the Plantagenet. In 1153, a few months after his marriage to Eleanor, Henry learned of the death of his rival, Eustace of Blois, Stephen's son. Deprived of an heir, the old man was ready to make an agreement that would end the conflicts that had continued to disrupt England. He agreed to remain king only in his own lifetime and to bequeath his kingdom to Henry II on his death. To avoid creating too large a state, Henry, on receiving the throne, was to grant his county of Anjou to his brother Geoffrey. Stephen died the following year and Henry II was crowned King of England on 19 December 1154, in Westminster Abbey.[25] He took care not to keep his promise, made when Eleanor was still the wife of Louis VII. Thanks to this omission, the Plantagenet empire (to use the accepted but questionable expression) now extended from the frontiers of Spain to the borders of Scotland. It was a disparate empire, certainly, without ethnic unity, but rich in its varied products, its maritime trade and its diverse resources.[26] It was also rich in men, in particular fighting men; it was in his lands, Anjou, Poitou, the Loire valley and Normandy, that the largest number of fortified castles were found and also the most battle-hardened warriors.[27] It was here, too, that chivalry was born and the tournament invented.[28] The vassal, as historians have repeatedly said, perhaps with some exaggeration, became more powerful than his suzerain. A confrontation between them was inevitable. The political situation alone guaranteed it. The dissensions and personal grudges of these two interconnected families only made a bad situation worse.

In spite of the valuable addition of England, a prosperous and prestigious kingdom, the heart of the Angevin empire, to use the accepted expression, lay in France, principally in Anjou and the Loire valley, but also in Poitou and Normandy.[29] Henry II, the new King of England, as has recently been emphasised, was above all a man of the Loire valley; he was 'born at Le Mans, died at Chinon and was buried at Fontevraud – all places which lay within the borders of his patrimony, the lands he inherited from his father'.[30] Henry spent at most thirteen years in England in a reign that lasted over thirty-four years, and Richard made only occasional visits to his English subjects.[31] Though born in Oxford during one of Henry and Eleanor's usually brief visits to the country, Richard, son of a count of Anjou and a duchess of Aquitaine, was a prince of France through and through. His father Henry was reputed to speak French and English, and to have some grasp of several 'European' languages, whereas Eleanor knew no English at all.[32] As for Richard, in daily life he spoke the northern French of his father, and read and wrote the *langue d'oc* of his

mother, but his Latin seems to have been limited[33] and his English non-existent; at this period the elites of Great Britain spoke Latin and Anglo-Norman, a form of old French. King of England and emblematic image in his country, Richard was in no way an English king.

KINGSHIP AND CHIVALRY

A third paradox is that this prince who became a king was not destined to be a knight or, to be more precise, to be primarily known and celebrated as a knight. After all, in his day as in our own, kings and princes were expected to behave as such; their role was to rule, not to enforce rule, to be generals rather than soldiers. Dukes and counts, and even more so kings, were often criticised, if usually by men of the Church, for allowing themselves to be carried away by the excitement of battle and the desire for prowess, forgetting their role as princes, of whom other qualities were expected. Of course, a ruler had to set an example, leading his troops into battle, exhorting them by word and deed, even participating in the fighting, as a true army general. The panegyrist of Duke William the Conqueror, Richard's ancestor, compared his hero to Julius Caesar after his victory over the Saxons at Hastings in 1066. He possessed, he says, the talents of a strategist and of an army general. But William was superior to Caesar, who had been content to direct his contingents from a distance, whereas William took an active part in battles. At Hastings he had stopped those who had turned to flee with his lance, so repudiating the rumour that he was dead; he had removed his helmet so that he could be recognised, rallying those whose courage had failed. Later, charging with his men, the Duke broke his lance, but he was still, said the chronicler, 'more fearsome with the stump of his lance than those brandishing long javelins'.[34] Confident of his own valour, he had even proposed to Harold that, to avoid unnecessary deaths, they should decide the fate of England by a judicial duel. We may well question his sincerity,[35] but it remains evidence of a cast of mind which gradually penetrated aristocratic milieus: the adoption of the warrior values which in this way became chivalric.

In the age of William the Conqueror, these values were still in gestation. They became predominant a century later, in the age of Richard the Lionheart, who himself made a major contribution to the process. It is probably the most profound socio-cultural development differentiating the two periods. Under William, in spite of what has just been said, chivalry had not yet been born. William himself, on his deathbed, is supposed to have confessed the sin of which he felt guilty as he prepared to

appear before his Judge: 'I was brought up in arms from childhood, and am deeply stained with all the blood I have shed.'[36] In the eleventh century, knights had no defined social role or specific ethic, even less an ideology. They were mounted warriors, professional soldiers. The Latin word that would later be used exclusively for knights, *milites*, was then used indifferently for all warriors, whether they fought on horseback (*equites*) or on foot (*pedites*). For the most part, these *milites* were of inferior social rank, in the service of the princes (*principes*) who recruited, directed, commanded and paid them; they also sometimes fed and armed them. The aristocracy, or, if preferred, the nobility, were quite distinct from the mass of these *mediocres* who formed the *militia*, a word which then meant the army, the men of war as a whole. It was only at the end of the twelfth century that the word came to be reserved for the knights as a body.[37] It then becomes clear why moralists, before 1100 and sometimes long after, disapproved of those princes who abandoned a part of their dignity by mixing with the common soldiers, not only to lead them, but to live in their midst and fight alongside them, imbued with the same values, once seen as inferior, seeking glory in feats of arms, the skilful blows with the lance and the sword that were celebrated from the end of the eleventh century in the *chansons de geste* which delighted princes and knights alike. Indeed, the epics themselves helped to disseminate these values and the adoption of these forms of behaviour, erasing social differences to glorify the warrior virtues of men, whatever their social rank.

At the beginning of the twelfth century this glorification of the turbulent and intoxicating values of 'youth', of which Roland is the archetype, was still met with hostility by the churchmen who had so far been the sole repositories of culture and sole diffusers of ideological models. The chroniclers of the First Crusade, an edifying epic if ever there was one, while emphasising the valour of the princes and crediting them (as is always the way) with the victories won by their men, nevertheless expressed some reservations about their warlike frenzies, which led to a fatal confusion of functions. Raoul of Caen in the case of Tancred, and Fulcher of Chartres in the case of Baldwin of Boulogne and Robert of Normandy openly deplored the way their heroes behaved like knights, however valiant, to the detriment of their role as leaders, princes or kings.[38] The social distance between nobility and knighthood was still too great at this period for it to be wholly acceptable for a king to turn himself into a knight in this way.

In Richard's day, some of these reservations persisted, as we will see, but such was the social and above all the ideological rise of chivalry in the second half of the twelfth century that its models of behaviour came

to be universally accepted.[39] By the end of the century, chivalry already had an ethical code, the product of a fusion of the purely professional values of its distant lowly origins and the aristocratic virtues of its leaders, princes and kings. Nobles now saw knighthood as an honour and, by gradually denying access to it to non-nobles, further strengthened its elitist character. The *chansons de geste*, as we have seen, were partly responsible for this fusion. Romances played an even greater role, particularly those concerned with the 'matter of Britain'; they lauded the ideal aristocratic government of King Arthur, surrounded by his Knights of the Round Table, but above all they glorified chivalry for its own sake, to the extent of conferring on it an ethical and religious dimension bordering on myth.[40]

Richard the Lionheart was born at precisely the time when chivalry was coming to prevail at all levels: militarily, with the general adoption of a new method of fighting, the compact charge with couched lance and the decisive advances in defensive armour that accompanied it, assuring the knights absolute supremacy on the battlefield; socially, with the gradual closing-off of knighthood to non-nobles and its transformation into an elite body with an increasingly aristocratic bias; ideologically, with the adoption by the nobility of chivalric values, on which they in their turn exerted influence; and culturally, with the diffusion of the chivalric ethic through the medium of romance and courtly literature.[41]

It was into this world that Richard was born and in which he grew up. Nothing is known about his education or about the influence of his parents or his entourage.[42] We can only speculate. It is difficult to believe, however, that this influence was non-existent or even negligible. His ancestors on both sides were endowed with strong personalities, inclining him towards the various aspects of chivalry discussed above. Reference has already been made to his maternal great-grandfather, Duke William of Aquitaine, regarded today as the first troubadour, and to his mother, Eleanor, a lively, vivacious woman, unpredictable but cultivated, a friend of literature and a patron of poets. It was to Eleanor, for example, that Wace, in 1155, dedicated his *Roman de Brut*; he had been inspired by the *History of the Kings of Britain* of Geoffrey of Monmouth, source of the Arthurian legend so quickly taken up by romance writers, beginning with Chrétien de Troyes, in order to glorify chivalry.[43] Wace was not alone; from 1154, many writers flourished under the patronage of the English court, on Eleanor's initiative. Benoît de Sainte-Maure followed Wace's example in dedicating his *Roman de Troie* to Eleanor. Literary scholars are today agreed that she, and in due course her two daughters, Marie of Champagne and Alice of Blois, played an important

role in the dissemination of the Tristan legend and the growth of the chivalric romance in general, even though we should not allow the greater visibility of their role to obscure that of other patrons.[44] Thanks to Eleanor and her entourage, it is likely that the young Richard grew up in a strongly chivalric atmosphere.

His identification with chivalry might just as well have been suggested by his maternal great-grandfather William IX, the troubadour, as by his paternal Angevin ancestors. Had William not claimed in one of his songs that it was only knights who deserved the love of ladies, and consigned to fiery tortures any who preferred monks or priests?[45] This was the beginning of the famous dialogue between the clerk and the knight which was to feature so prominently in the literary debates of the day and which led on to those 'courts of love' which are now seen as a purely literary fiction, but in which Eleanor and her daughters played an important role.[46] In fact, allusions to Eleanor's own marital situation are not hard to find in many of the judgements in the courts of love that are attributed to her, and it is quite possible that they were satirical in origin and intended to discredit her.[47] However that may be, it remains the case that these debates preoccupied contemporaries and contributed to the development of the chivalric mentality.[48]

In spite of the relative indifference shown towards chivalry by Richard's father, Henry II,[49] there is no shortage of examples of men imbued with it well in advance of their time. I will mention only three, in connection with Geoffrey Plantagenet, Richard's grandfather. The chronicler of Marmoutier, admittedly writing about 1180, describes Geoffrey's knighting, at Whitsun 1128, in words very similar to those used by *chansons de geste* and romances:

> They dressed him in a suit of incomparable armour of double-linked mail, which no thrust with lance or javelin could pierce. Chausses of double mail were put on his legs. Spurs of gold were fixed to his feet; a shield painted with two golden lion cubs was hung round his neck; on his head was placed a helmet sparkling with many precious stones, so well tempered that no sword could bite into or dint it. He was given a lance of ash, with a point of Poitevin iron. Lastly, he was handed a sword taken from the royal treasury, bearing the ancient mark of the famous smith Wayland, who had long ago forged it with great difficulty and great care. Thus armed, our new knight, who was soon to become the flower of chivalry, leaped onto his horse with the greatest agility.[50]

Already visible in this text is a veneration of chivalry linked to the mythical character of arms, and in particular the sword, whether called Joyous, Durendal or even Excalibur, that was solemnly presented when the young

prince became a knight. At this time, Geoffrey was still a prince without power, a *bacheler*, one of the 'young';[51] but once he became count, he still felt himself to be a knight, as can be seen at Le Mans in the magnificent funerary plaque he chose to ornament his tomb. Geoffrey expressed his sympathy, one day, for some captive knights, his enemies but also his companions in arms, a sign that the concept of chivalry was emerging and creating solidarities that transcended differences of social rank. This was in 1150, only seven years before the birth of Richard the Lionheart. During a conflict with the Poitevins, Geoffrey had taken four prisoners, *milites*, who were incarcerated by Josselin on his orders in his castle of Fontaine-Milon. The count then forgot all about them. Josselin managed one day to bring the sorry state of these captives to the count's attention. Geoffrey, a great lord, instructed that they be washed, clothed, fed and allowed to leave as free men, even providing them with horses. He spoke these words with a chivalric ring, in which the incipient notion of solidarity, both magnanimous and self-interested, can be seen:

> He who does not sympathise with his own profession is truly inhumane of heart. If we are knights (*milites*) we ought to have compassion for knights, especially for those reduced to impotence. So bring these knights out, free them from their bonds, have them eat and wash, and provide them with new clothes so that they sit this very day at my own table.[52]

With ancestors such as these, was Richard not, so to speak, 'predestined' to become what he was in his lifetime and what he remains for all eternity, a 'roi-chevalier'? This is the question I will try to answer in this biography; in Part One I will examine his role as prince and king in history and in Part Two I will analyse the different and sometimes controversial elements which, for the chroniclers of his day, helped to make Richard a true model of chivalry.

A few crucial questions will then need to be addressed. What influences formed his character and determined his behaviour, real or assumed? Why did the image of Richard as a king who was also a knight so quickly and so soon supplant all others, creating a quasi-definitive point of reference? Why did Richard deliberately, it would appear, choose to present himself in this chivalric guise and disseminate this image of himself by what we would today call a 'media campaign', using all the methods then at his disposal, limited perhaps but by no means ineffective? Last but not least, what is the historical and ideological significance of the choice and, even more, success of this image, which has been adopted by history and disseminated by legend, an image based on historical accounts and documents in which history and legend are sometimes inextricably interwoven?

NOTES

1. For William the Marshal, paragon of chivalric values, see Painter, *William Marshal*; Crosland, J., *William Marshal* (London, 1962); Crouch, *William the Marshal*; and especially Duby, *William Marshal* (in spite of the sometimes justified but more often excessive or misplaced criticisms of John Gillingham, 'War and Chivalry in the *History of William the Marshal*', in Coss P., and S. Lloyd (eds), *Thirteenth-Century England II* (Woodbridge, 1988), pp. 1–13, repr. in Gillingham, *Richard Cœur de Lion*, pp. 227–41).
2. See, for example, the revealing title of J. T. Appleby's *England Without Richard, 1189–1199*. This traditional image is criticised by John Gillingham in most of the works mentioned later in this book and in the bibliography.
3. For these points see Zumthor, P., *Guillaume le Conquérant* (Paris, 1978); Boüard, M. De, *Guillaume le Conquérant* (Paris, 1984).
4. For the county of Anjou and its development before this date, see Halphen, L., *Le Comté d'Anjou au XIe Siècle* (Paris, 1906); Guillot, O., *Le Comte d'Anjou et son Entourage au XIe Siècle* (Paris, 1972).
5. The name should really be spelled Plantegenêt; Wace, in *Le Roman de Rou* (lines 10269ff.), says that this byname was applied to Geoffrey 'Plante Genest qui moult amout bois e forest'. Henry II was never given this surname. See on this point the observation of J.-M. Bienvenu, 'Henri II Plantagenêt et Fontevraud', *Cahiers de Civilisation Médiévale*, 113–14, pp. 25–32, especially p. 25, note 1.
6. For these events and the political significance of the dubbing, see Chibnall, M., 'L'Avènement au Pouvoir d'Henri II', ibid., pp. 41–8, especially pp. 44–45.
7. For the role of William IX of Aquitaine in the formation of 'courtesy' and courtly literature, see Bezzola, 'Guillaume IX'; Lejeune, R., 'L'Extraordinaire Insolence du Troubadour Guillaume IX d'Aquitaine', in *Mélanges Pierre Le Gentil*, pp. 485–503; and especially Payen, *Prince d'Aquitaine*; see also Martindale, J., ' "Cavalaria" et "Orgueill", Duke William IX of Aquitaine and the Historians', in Harper-Bill and Harvey, *Ideals and Practice of Medieval Knighthood*, II, pp. 87–116. For courtly love and literature, see Bezzola, *Littérature Courtoise*, especially vols 2, 3, 1 and 3, 2. Much ink has been spilled on the subject of courtly love and its interpretation is still controversial today. See, for example, the contrary views of Rougemont, *L'Amour et l'Occident*; Lazar, *Amour Courtois et Fin Amors*; Newman, *Meaning of Courtly Love*; Frappier, *Amour Courtois*; and Rey-Flaud, *Névrose Courtoise*. The best summary of the subject today is that of R. Schnell, *Causa Amoris*, summarised in his 'Amour Courtois'.
8. William of Malmesbury, *Gesta Regum Anglorum*, V, 6, §439, vol. 2, p. 510.
9. William of Newburgh says that Louis was 'strongly attached' to his spirited wife: I, p. 92.
10. See on these points, and in particular on Eleanor of Aquitaine: Kelly, *Eleanor of Aquitaine*; Labande, 'Une Image Véridique'; Pernoud, *Aliénor d'Aquitaine*;

Markale, *Aliénor d'Aquitaine*; Brown, E. A. R., 'Eleanor of Aquitaine: Parent, Queen and Duchess', in Kibler, *Eleanor of Aquitaine*, pp. 9–34; and, more recently, Owen, *Eleanor of Aquitaine*. See also Sassier, *Louis VII*.

11. See William of Tyre, *Historia Rerum in Partibus Transmarinis Gestarum*, XVI, 27, RHC Hist. Occ. I, p. 752; the best edition is that of R. B. C. Huygens (Turnhout, 1986).

12. *Ménestrel de Reims*, §10, p. 7.

13. John of Salisbury, *Historia Pontificalis*, ed. M. Chibnall (London, 1965), pp. 42–53.

14. See on this point Graboïs, 'The Crusade of Louis VII'.

15. According to John of Salisbury, *Memoirs of the Papal Court*, ed. M. Chibnall (London, 1956), pp. 61–2, the pope made them sleep together in the same bed at Tusculum but, on leaving them, had few illusions as to the solidity of the relationship. See also on this point Labande, 'Une Image Véridique', pp. 189ff. Brooke, C., *The Medieval Idea of Marriage* (Oxford, 1991), pp. 123ff.

16. I cannot agree with John Gillingham ('Love, Marriage and Politics in the Twelfth Century', *Forum for Modern Language Studies*, 25 (1989), pp. 292–303, repr. in Gillingham, *Richard Cœur de Lion*, pp. 243–55, especially p. 251) that Louis was afraid he would have no more children by Eleanor not because she was infertile (her two daughters proved that) but because she no longer loved her husband and no longer felt with him the pleasure that was then believed necessary to procreation. It was the absence of sons that really worried Louis, not that of daughters, irrespective of number.

17. See Brundage, J. A., 'Carnal Delight: Canonistic Theories of Sexuality', in S. Kuttner and K. Pennington (eds), *Proceedings of the Fifth International Congress of Medieval Canon Law* (Vatican, 1980), pp. 365ff., especially p. 383; Brundage, ' "Allas! That evere love was synne" '; Brundage, *Law, Sex and Christian Society*. There is no shortage of contrary opinions; see on this point the enriching approach, including literature, of Baldwin, 'Five Discourses'; even more Baldwin, *Language of Sex*.

18. Gerald of Wales, *De Principis Instructione*, III, 27, pp. 299–300; *Concerning . . .*, p. 14.

19. See on this point Bartlett, R., *Gerald of Wales: 1145–1223* (Oxford, 1982), pp. 91ff.

20. Gervase of Canterbury, I, anno 1152, p. 149.

21. For a recent re-examination of the motives for this marriage and Eleanor's 'temperament', see the fine study of J. Martindale, 'Eleanor of Aquitaine'.

22. 'Iste antonomastice debet vocari a deo datus [Godgiven], quia . . .': Rigord, c. 1, p. 7. For Philip Augustus, see Cartellieri, *Philipp II*; Baldwin, *Philip Augustus*.

23. Favreau, R., 'Les Débuts de la Ville de La Rochelle', *Cahiers de Civilisation Médiévale*, 30 (1987), pp. 3–32.

24. For the 'anarchic' state of Aquitaine at this period, see the suggestive but exaggerated picture painted by Powicke, *Loss of Normandy*, pp. 29ff.
25. Ralph of Coggeshall, pp. 14ff.; Ralph of Diceto, II, pp. 16ff.
26. For the Angevin empire, its resources and its strategic and commercial importance, see in particular Gillingham, J., *The Angevin Empire* (London, 1984), repr. in Gillingham, *Richard Cœur de Lion*, pp. 7–91. For the commercial importance of the region as a source of conflict between the Plantagenets and the counts of Toulouse, see Benjamin, R., 'A Forty Years War: Toulouse and the Plantagenets, 1156–1196', *Historical Research*, 61 (1988), pp. 270–85; Martindale, J., 'Succession and Politics in the Romance-speaking World, c. 1000–1400', in M. Jones and M. Vale (eds), *England and her Neighbours: Essays in Honour of Pierre Chaplais* (London, 1989), pp. 19–41, especially pp. 34ff.
27. For the role of castles in Angevin policy at the time of Fulk Nerra, see Bachrach, B. S., 'Fortifications and military tactics: Fulk Nerra's strongholds circa 1000', *Technology and Culture*, 20 (1979), pp. 531–49; Bachrach, B. S., 'The Angevin strategy of castle-building in the reign of Fulk Nerra 987–1040', *American Historical Review*, 88 (1983), pp. 533–49; for his use of the vassalic tie, see Bachrach, B. S., 'Enforcement of the Forma fidelitas: the techniques used by Fulk Nerra, Count of the Angevins (987–1040)', *Speculum*, 59 (1984), pp. 796–819. For the links between castles and chivalry, see Settia, A. A., 'La fortezza e il cavaliere: techniche militari in Occidente', in *Morfologie Sociali e Culturali in Europa fra Tarda Antichità e Alto Medioevo, 3–9 aprile 1997* (Spoleto, 1998), pp. 555–84.
28. According to a tradition well-established in the thirteenth century, the tournament was invented by Geoffrey de Preuilly, who died in 1066. This is challenged by Barber, *The Knight and Chivalry*, p. 156. It remains highly plausible; see the discussion in Flori, *Chevaliers et Chevalerie*, pp. 132ff.
29. The expression 'Angevin empire' has been standard since Gillingham's *The Angevin Empire*; it had earlier been used by nineteenth-century historians, for example Kate Norgate, *England under the Angevin Kings* (New York, 1887), vol. 1, pp. 169ff. Numerous recent works have emphasised the inadequacy of this expression, which suggests a political, linguistic and cultural unity that was largely lacking. In fact, only Eleanor and, up to a point, Richard assured the existence of what would more appropriately be called the 'Plantagenet zone'. See on this point the numerous related works collected in *Y a-t-il une Civilisation du Monde Plantagenêt?* (Actes du Colloque d'Histoire Médiévale, Fontevraud, 26–8 avril 1984), CCM, 113–14 (1986), in particular the synthesis of R.-H. Bautier, 'Empire Plantagenêt ou espace Plantagenêt', ibid., pp. 139–47.
30. Gillingham, *Richard the Lionheart*, p. 27.
31. Petit-Dutaillis, *Feudal Monarchy*, p. 157.
32. Dor, J., 'Langues Française et Anglaise, et Multilinguisme à l'Epoque d'Henri II Plantagenêt', *Cahiers de Civilisation Médiévale*, 28, pp. 61–72.

33. Gerald of Wales, *Invectiores*, 3; in his dedicatory letter to the King (1189) accompanying his gift of his *Topographia Hibernica*, Gerald deplored the fact that Richard could not manage without an interpreter, which suggests that he had difficulty in understanding Latin. Elsewhere Gerald notes that the King was once reprimanded by the Archbishop of Canterbury for having said *coram nobis* instead of *coram nos*. Hugh of Coventry, 'who knew Latin very well', stood up for the King, saying: 'Stick to your grammar, sire, because it is better', causing general laughter among those present. Was this the reply of a courtier, or a reference to the classical usage preferring the ablative to the accusative? Whatever the case, this remark by Hugh (not the King) does not justify Gillingham's claim that the King 'was sufficiently well educated in Latin to be able to crack a Latin joke at the expense of a less learned Archbishop of Canterbury': *Richard the Lionheart*, p. 33. If indeed there was a joke, it was made by Hugh, not Richard.

34. William of Poitiers, *Gesta Guillelmi Ducis*, 22–4, 40, pp. 198, 202, 250. The phrase implies the existence of several techniques for the use of the lance at the time of Hastings, as we also see from the Bayeux Tapestry. See Flori, *Croisade et Chevalerie*, pp. 348ff.

35. According to Strickland (*War and Chivalry*, p. 44), it was primarily an attempt on William's part to gain time.

36. *Orderic Vitalis*, ed. Chibnall, vol. 4, p. 80.

37. Flori, '*Principes* et *milites*'.

38. Raoul of Caen, *Gesta Tancredi*, c. 29, RHC Hist. Occ. III, p. 630; Foucher of Chartres, *Historia Hierosolymitana*, I, 14, p. 347.

39. For this social and ideological rise, see Flori, *Essor de la Chevalerie*.

40. It is impossible to refer here to the very large number of works dealing with these themes. Their main conclusions as relevant to us here are summarised in Flori, *Chevaliers et Chevalerie*, especially pp. 235ff.

41. See Flori, 'Noblesse, Chevalerie et Idéologie Aristocratique'.

42. It is significant that there is almost nothing about the chivalric education, or indeed any education, of the young Richard in Orme, *From Childhood to Chivalry*.

43. See on this point the introduction by Wace's best editor, I. Arnold in *Le Roman de Brut*, I, pp. LXXVIIIff.

44. For the literary influence of Eleanor, direct or indirect, see in particular Lejeune, R., 'Rôle Littéraire d'Aliénor d'Aquitaine et de sa Famille', *Cultura Neolatina*, 14 (1954), pp. 5–57; Lejeune, 'Rôle Littéraire de la Famille d'Aliénor d'Aquitaine'; Benton, J. F., 'The Court of Champagne as a Literary Center', *Speculum*, 36 (1961), pp. 551–91; Kibler, *Eleanor of Aquitaine*; Owen, *Eleanor of Aquitaine*. See also Broadhurst, K. M., 'Henri II of England and Eleanor of Aquitaine: Patrons of Literature in French', *Viator*, 27 (1996), pp. 53–84, who considerably plays down the role as direct patron of Henry II, and even more of Eleanor.

45. 'A lady who loves a loyal knight does not commit a mortal sin; but if she loves a monk or a clerk she is out of her mind; she should by right be burned with a brand'; Farai un vers pos mi sonelh, Payen, *Prince d'Aquitaine*, p. 94; on William's role in this sphere, see Bezzola, 'Guillaume IX'.

46. For the debate between the clerk and the knight, see in particular Oulmont, *Débats du Clerc et du Chevalier*; Gouiran, G., ' "Car tu es cavalliers e clercs" (Flamenca, line 1899): Guilhem ou le Chevalier Parfait', in *Clerc au Moyen Age*, pp. 198–214; Grossel, M.-G., ' "Savoir Aimer, Savoir le Dire", notes on the debate between the clerk and chevalier', ibid., pp. 279–93.

47. This is argued by John Gillingham in *Richard the Lionheart*, pp. 61–2.

48. See on this point Flori, 'Le Chevalier, la Femme at l'Amour'; Flori, 'Mariage, Amour et Courtoisie'; Flori, 'Amour et Chevalerie dans le Tristan de Béroul'.

49. Richardson, H. G., and G. O. Sayles, *The Governance of Medieval England from the Conquest to Magna Carta* (Edinburgh, 1964), pp. 267ff.

50. Jean de Marmoutier, *Historia Gaufredi Ducis*, in *Chroniques des Comtes d'Anjou*, pp. 180ff.

51. For the meaning of these terms and their social and even more their ideological connotations, see Duby, 'Les "Jeunes" '; Köhler, 'Sens et Fonction du Terme "Jeunesse" ', to be read in conjunction with Flori, 'Qu'est-ce qu'un Bacheler?'.

52. Jean de Marmoutier, *Historia Gaufredi Ducis*, p. 196.

PART I

Prince, King and Crusader

1

The Early Years

∽

FROM THE MARRIAGE OF ELEANOR AND HENRY II TO RICHARD'S BIRTH (1152–7)

Louis VII responded angrily to Eleanor's remarriage to Henry II, all the more so as it had taken place without his agreement as suzerain. The King of France prepared an attack on Normandy, which was to be supported by the counts of Boulogne, Champagne and Perche and also by Geoffrey of Anjou, Henry II's younger brother, supplanted by Henry, spurned by Eleanor and recently knighted by Theobald of Blois.[1] The plan was for Geoffrey to raise Anjou against his brother while the coalition invaded Normandy and Aquitaine. But Henry returned from the Cotentin, ravaged the Norman Vexin and restored order in Anjou, making such an impression on Louis VII that he abandoned his enterprise; he may in any case have been uneasy about the legitimacy of a military operation undertaken for what was only a relatively minor violation of a feudal law that was still in its infancy. Henry was able to embark without too much difficulty for England, where the death of Eustace of Blois had made his elderly father Stephen a temporary king and Henry the immediate heir.

As early as 1153, the birth of William, the new couple's first child, seemed both to demonstrate heavenly favour and to assure their future. The King of France, in comparison, appeared bereft, lacking a male heir and deprived both of the valuable counsel of Abbot Suger of Saint-Denis, who had died in 1151, and the fulminations of Bernard of Clairvaux, who died in 1153. Louis took note of the success of his rival; he had pacified Normandy and Anjou and, with the birth of his son, deprived the King of France's two daughters by his marriage to Eleanor of all rights to Aquitaine. He resigned himself to accepting the peace offered by Henry in 1154 and returned Vernon and Neufmarché in the Norman Vexin. He then applied himself, more modestly but to better effect, to his role as defender of the peace and protector of churches, a role already adopted by his father, on Suger's advice. By establishing himself as guarantor of order and justice in his kingdom, he gradually strengthened his

authority; he also cleverly exploited his royal prerogatives, presenting himself as arbiter between the princes of the kingdom and dispenser of justice in the name of a feudal law still in formation, turning respect for the peace of God into a royal mission.[2]

He continued, however, to strengthen his ties with the neighbouring princes. He made Theobald of Blois-Champagne his direct vassal and his seneschal. He was reconciled with Raymond V of Toulouse, who was already in conflict with the counts of Barcelona and Provence, and who had everything to fear from the claims to his lands of the Plantagenets as princes of Aquitaine; in 1154, Louis married his sister Constance, widow of Eustace of Boulogne, to the count of Toulouse. He himself, that same year, married another Constance, the daughter of King Alfonso of Castile. It looked for a while as if an alliance between the Capetians and the houses of Toulouse and Castile might emerge, in opposition to the Plantagenet alliance with the counts of Barcelona and Aragon. Louis VII felt sufficiently confident to go as a penitent on a pilgrimage to St James of Compostella; this enabled him to put the 'Eleanor' episode behind him, embark on a new life with Constance, consolidate in passing his Iberian alliances and affirm his authority and protection over the bishoprics of Languedoc, in the name of the 'King's peace'.[3] He was not yet ready to embark on military operations against the Plantagenet, whose outcome he had every reason to fear. It was a time for negotiated settlements and an attempt at peaceful coexistence.

Henry II went along with this, at least for the time being. Now King of England, he needed to pacify his kingdom after the long years of conflict between the supporters of Matilda and those of Stephen. The barons had taken advantage of the disorder and anarchy resulting from this civil war to emancipate themselves from a failing royal authority, building castles and assembling armed bands composed both of native Englishmen and of numerous foreigners hoping to profit from the pillaging of these 'war-lords'. So Henry devoted himself to the restoration of order and peace in England, with considerable success. He expelled the foreign mercenaries or took them into his own service; he destroyed the rebel castles or installed royal garrisons; he subjugated the aristocracy; and, with the assis-tance of his chancellor, Thomas Becket, he took a firm hold on the admin-istration of his kingdom. He even managed to obtain the submission and homage of the King of Scotland, who had taken advantage of the civil war to rid himself of English tutelage and lay hands on Northumberland.

A policy of peace with France was therefore opportune. It was con-ducted jointly by Henry II and Thomas Becket. In 1156 Henry met Louis VII on the borders of Normandy and the Capetian domain and did

homage for all his 'French' lands, including Anjou, Maine and Aquitaine. This brought to an end the half-hearted Capetian attempts to support his brother Geoffrey against Henry II. Geoffrey was abandoned to his sad fate. Henry compensated him by payment of an annual rent and Geoffrey soon succeeded in getting himself recognised as lord of Brittany, which then passed, as we will see, into the Plantagenet sphere of influence. Henry II's homage to Louis for Aquitaine gave him legitimacy in the eyes of the still turbulent barons of that region.

PEACEFUL COEXISTENCE (1157–64)

The birth of Richard, in 1157, came during this period of what can almost be called 'entente cordiale' between the kings of France and England. In June 1158, Thomas Becket went with great pomp to Paris to present Louis VII with a proposal from Henry II which was intended to unite the two houses: a marriage between Margaret, the daughter born a few months earlier to the second wife of the King of France, and Henry, then aged three, heir to the throne of England since the recent death of his elder brother William. The plan became a reality in August of that year. Margaret's dowry was to consist of the Norman Vexin, with its castles, in particular those of Gisors, Vaudreuil, Neauphle and Danglu, which controlled communications between Paris and Rouen. The dowry was to remain in the hands of the King of France until the actual cere-mony, which would take place when the children reached marriageable age. Margaret, however, was to be handed over into Henry's custody immediately. The King went to Paris in September to collect her, where the enthusiastic population joyfully celebrated the prospect of peace between the two dynasties.[4] The desire for a union of the two houses was so strong that it was even stipulated that if the Young Henry were to die, Margaret would marry another of Henry II's sons, which at this date meant Richard or a child as yet unborn.

There was another dimension to this alliance. By agreeing to grant Henry II the honorific but hollow title of seneschal of France, for which he had asked, Louis VII was effectively allowing the armies of the King of England to intervene in Brittany, to which Henry claimed rights through his recently-deceased brother Geoffrey. As seneschal, Henry could inter-vene militarily and judicially in Brittany under the cloak of 'standing orders' from the King of France, which he soon did, forcing Conan IV of Brittany to surrender the city of Nantes.[5]

Overall, it was the Plantagenet who benefited most from this peaceful coexistence, especially as Henry was seeking to extend his

Iberian alliances. In March 1159, in Aquitaine, he received Raymond Berenger IV, Count of Barcelona and also, in his wife's name, effective ruler of the kingdom of Aragon. A new projected marriage alliance was agreed, for political reasons as always. This time it concerned Richard, who was betrothed to one of the daughters of the Catalan prince. On the day of their marriage, the spouses were to receive the Duchy of Aquitaine, promised to Richard as his inheritance from Eleanor. This project, like many others involving Richard, came to nothing. It is an illustration, however, of the important diplomatic role then played by the children of princely houses.

For the moment, it sealed a very promising political alliance. It would permit Henry II, with the assistance of Berenger and of allies that he had acquired among the great lords of the region, to conduct a military campaign against Raymond of Toulouse. Henry was taking up on his own account the old claims of the dukes of Aquitaine to the county of Toulouse, in the name of Philippa, only daughter of the Count of Toulouse and wife of William IX of Aquitaine, who had been supplanted by her uncle on her father's death. The county of Toulouse offered many advantages, especially strategic and commercial, as it assured access from the Atlantic to the Mediterranean.

Before embarking on hostilities, Henry II tried vainly to obtain from Louis VII, in the name of their friendship, a promise not to intervene in the conflict. But Raymond of Toulouse was not only the vassal of the King of France; he was also his brother-in-law, as husband of Louis' sister Constance. On both counts, therefore, Louis warned Henry that, if he went ahead with the attack, he, Louis, would side with his threatened vassal, in accord with feudal law. Henry pressed on regardless. He assembled his host and levied a tax enabling him to recruit troops of archers and foreign mercenaries, the 'routiers'; then, in June, he marched from Poitiers towards Toulouse, seizing Cahors and many fortified places in Quercy and Rouergue on the way. But when he arrived before the walls of Toulouse, he learned that Louis VII had joined his vassal in the town, which precluded an attack as contrary to the law; it would be a deliberate assault on the person of the suzerain king and the royal dignity. Henry hesitated, then gave in and withdrew.[6] However, he harboured a grudge against Louis for this setback, which he saw as something of a humiliation. He made preparations for other battles and fortified Normandy, even making several incursions into Capetian territory and installing his garrisons in several fortresses.

The threatened conflict was nevertheless averted by a treaty signed at Chinon at Whitsun 1160. This restored the status quo, and made

provision for the marriage between Henry and Margaret to be celebrated well before they reached marriageable age, perhaps in three years if the Church would allow. The castles of the Norman Vexin comprising the dowry were to be handed over at once to three knights of the Order of the Temple, all of whom were Normans. Henry's claims to the county of Toulouse were unaffected and he held on to Cahors and the fortresses he had captured in Quercy. In fact, it was a treaty not short of potential sources of future conflict, in both Normandy and the Toulousain. Louis VII and Henry were well aware of this; from now on their rivalry was to be unceasing.

For the moment, however, it remained fairly muted, confined to the diplomatic sphere. On 4 October 1160 the Queen of France, Constance of Castile, died giving birth to a daughter, Alice. As Louis VII had no son, it was Margaret, promised to Henry the Young King, who became heiress to the throne. But to general surprise, five weeks later, Louis married Adela of Champagne, thus bringing back into his camp the related houses of Blois-Champagne and Burgundy. He could also hope for the early birth of the longed-for heir. Henry II responded by obtaining from Pope Alexander, in return for supporting his cause, an age dispensation permitting the official marriage between Henry and Margaret, which was celebrated on 2 November 1160 at Neubourg. The King of England immediately seized the dowry, that is, the Vexin and Gisors. The chronicler William of Newburgh is quite specific on this point: Henry II brought forward the date of the wedding so as to get possession of the dowry, currently in the safekeeping of the Templars.[7] Louis was displeased and some skirmishes followed, in Touraine and on the borders of the Vexin. A truce concluded in the spring of 1161 brought these limited military operations to a halt. There was even talk of a marriage between Richard, then aged four, and Alice, the second daughter of Louis VII and Constance of Castile, who was still a baby.

During this period Henry II consolidated his power in England and set out to subjugate the Welsh princes, though at first with little success. The Welsh were a fierce people, who practised guerrilla warfare and ambushes, used the bow and the javelin, fought on foot and waged a merciless war in mountainous territory. The cavalry military tactics imported from Normandy and France were ill-suited to this type of terrain and conflict, as would be noted a few years later by Gerald of Wales, well-informed about Celtic customs and regions.[8] Henry had more success in another Celtic region, Brittany, to which he made claims; in 1166, having defeated the Bretons, he deposed Duke Conan at Rennes. Conan's only heiress was his very young daughter, Constance. Resorting to his usual strategy of

marriage alliances, Henry earmarked her for Geoffrey, his third surviving son, so putting down a marker in Brittany.

BETWEEN PEACE AND CONFLICT (1165–70)

The Plantagenet–Capetian conflict flared up once again, however, as early as 1164, for a number of reasons. The first, the quarrel between the King and his chancellor, Thomas Becket, who took refuge in France, has often been greatly exaggerated. It is sometimes argued that this quarrel absorbed all of Henry II's energies, but this is almost certainly incorrect. The second had more substance: Louis VII took advantage of the fact that Henry was occupied on the Welsh border to intervene in Auvergne, whose territories depended both on Aquitaine and France. This conflict, which began in 1164, was marked by changes of fortune and shifting alliances that are of no direct concern to us here; what is relevant is the undoubted desire of both kings to assert their authority and extend their influence in both Auvergne and the Vexin at the cost of minor military operations, but without getting caught up in a general confrontation. Though his situation was at first uncertain, Louis VII managed to strengthen his influence over the princes of the kingdom of France in Burgundy, Auvergne and Bas-Languedoc. He was reassured and emboldened by the birth of his son Philip, 'Dieudonné', on 21 August 1165. If the child survived, the Plantagenet claims based on marriages made or projected would be weakened or nullified.

The Becket affair was another bone of contention between the two sovereigns. It is so well known that it is hardly necessary to dwell on it here. The chancellor had been Henry's friend and firm supporter in the project to strengthen royal power; once appointed Archbishop of Canterbury, he transmuted into a stubborn defender of the ecclesiastical liberties he now saw as threatened by the very royal absolutism he had hitherto enthusiastically promoted. On 30 January 1164 he refused to sanction the Constitutions of Clarendon, by which Henry II abolished several ecclesiastical privileges and made the clergy and the churches subject to taxation. Thomas was declared a rebel to his king and fled to France, where he was welcomed and protected, in spite of all Henry's requests to Louis not to do so. Relations between the two kings deteriorated and numerous meetings proved fruitless.

The conflict was exacerbated in 1167 when Raymond V of Toulouse, who had recently repudiated Constance, Louis VII's sister, distanced himself from the Capetian and, seeking friends in new quarters, turned to Henry II. By the spring of 1167, in spite of a last attempt at peace talks

in the Vexin, the two kings were preparing for war. Louis VII even considered an invasion of England with the assistance of Matthew of Boulogne.[9] He invaded the Vexin, burned Les Andelys and incited the Bretons into rebellion against Henry, while the latter's troops ravaged Perche. Pope Alexander III, himself threatened by the imperial troops of Frederick II, appealed to the two belligerents to make peace. A truce was concluded on 7 April 1168. Henry soon took advantage of it to crush the Bretons of the district of Vannes, who had refused homage. He won a double concession from the pope: Alexander III suspended Thomas Becket and recognised the validity of the marriage concluded between the heiress of Brittany and Geoffrey, which strengthened the legitimacy of Plantagenet claims to the county.

At this point, Henry seemed to be winning on all fronts. He was considering a settlement by which he would pass on to his sons not the reality of power, which he was determined to retain, but the territories over which they would one day exercise power; it was to be both gift and partition. The Young Henry was to have the title of king and inherit his father's lands: England, Normandy, Anjou and Maine; Richard would inherit Aquitaine from his mother, with the title of Count of Poitiers; Geoffrey would get Brittany through his wife Constance. Before this could take effect, it was necessary to pacify these lands. But early in 1168 a new revolt broke out in Aquitaine, provoked by the counts of Lusignan and Angoulême.[10] They were rapidly crushed by the army of Henry II, which laid waste their domains and destroyed the castle of Lusignan, storm centre of the revolt.

Louis VII took note of all these successes on the part of his rival. He decided to negotiate and sent word to Henry, who left Queen Eleanor at Poitiers in the care of a trusted warrior, Patrick of Salisbury, and set off for a conference with the King of France. The rebellious Poitevins took advantage of his absence to refortify their castles and hatch various plots. Henry therefore postponed his meeting with Louis, much to the latter's irritation, causing him to make contact with the rebels and give them increasingly open support in their battle against the Plantagenet. The rebels even dared to mount an attack on Eleanor herself, while she was on a journey. The Earl of Salisbury lost his life in the skirmish, but only after succeeding in getting the Queen to safety. He was killed 'shamefully', stabbed in the back by the count of Lusignan, 'à la poitevine' said those hostile to the rebels. This episode provided William Marshal with the opportunity to make his name; to avenge his master (he was then in the service of Earl Patrick, who was his uncle), he threw himself into the fray, confronting many enemy knights, six of whom he killed. But he himself received a wound in his

thigh which brought him down. He was taken back to the rebel camp as a prisoner and dragged round with them on their travels. But a grateful Eleanor secured his release by paying a ransom and took him into her own service. This was the beginning of a brilliant career which made William the 'best knight in the world', mentor and guide of Henry the Young King in all matters of chivalry; he was a valiant foe and recognised as such by Richard before he rallied to the legitimate king.[11]

This episode further heightened the tension between the two rulers. For a while, the king of France obstructed the proposed marriage between his daughter Alice and Richard. Peace seemed remote, all the more so as the revolt within the Plantagenet empire spread, not only within Aquitaine and Brittany but also in the Celtic lands of the British Isles, Wales and Scotland. Nevertheless, the endeavours of Louis VII and his ally Philip of Flanders came to nothing in the Vexin and Louis requested a truce. Henry II agreed, a peace being to his own advantage at the time.

Peace was concluded in January 1169 at Montmirail, both sides making concessions.[12] Louis recognised the Plantagenet gains in Brittany and agreed not to support the Poitevin and Breton barons against Henry; they laid down their arms and threw themselves on his mercy, which he had promised the King of France he would grant. In return, Henry solemnly renewed his homage to Louis for the lands he held in his kingdom. His sons similarly did homage for the lands that would one day be theirs according to the terms of the settlement described above. The Young Henry, promised the kingdom of England, did homage for Normandy, Maine and Anjou, to which was attached the title of seneschal of France. Richard, then a boy of twelve, knelt in his turn before the King of France, who took his hands in his own, raised him up and kissed him. This established publicly, in the eyes of all present, the ties of vassalage that would in future bind these men. Richard did homage for Aquitaine, the patrimony of his mother Eleanor, whose favourite son he seems to have been, and who was anxious to hand the government of her duchy over to him as soon as possible.

This official ceremony is the first time we see the young Richard take part in an important public event. His future marriage to Alice was once again reaffirmed. The little girl, then aged nine, was handed over into the care of Henry II, who seems to have taken advantage of her himself. The meeting at Montmirail also attempted to achieve a reconciliation between Thomas Becket and Henry, but in vain. The prelate remained intransigent, refusing any concessions.

Henry II had no intention of keeping his promise to the rebellious barons, whom he was determined to subdue. A few weeks after the truce

of Montmirail, he went to Aquitaine and defeated many of the rebels, including the Count of Angoulême, William Taillefer, and Robert de Seilhac; according to the chronicler Geoffrey of Vigeois, Robert was put in chains and left without food or water to die.[13] It was clear from Henry's campaign of repression in Aquitaine that he had no intention of allowing Richard, still, admittedly, very young, to act on his own account in the duchy for which he had done homage to the King of France.

AUTONOMY WITHOUT A RUPTURE? (1170–4)

Everything changed a year later, when Henry II fell seriously ill. He decided to implement the settlement already planned for Richard and for his brothers, Henry and Geoffrey. Henry was to have Normandy and all the continental lands he held from his parents; Geoffrey would have Brittany and at a later stage the county of Mortain would go to John.[14]

The Young Henry was duly crowned King of England on 14 June 1170, at Westminster, by the Archbishop of York, against the advice of both the pope and Thomas Becket, who was still out of favour. Henry II profited from the occasion to have King William of Scotland and David his brother do homage and swear loyalty to his son.[15] But he omitted to have Henry's wife, Margaret of France, crowned Queen, much to the annoyance of her father, the King of France, who retaliated by invading Normandy. Henry made peace at Vendôme on 22 July, promising a future coronation for Margaret, who was eventually crowned Queen of England, though not until September 1172, at Winchester, by the Archbishop of Rouen.[16] The Young Henry, meanwhile, in spite of his coronation, remained firmly under his father's thumb; Henry II remained the only true king of England and allowed his son no initiative.

Richard soon went with his mother to the lands allocated to him. Geoffrey of Vigeois says that in 1170, at Eleanor's request, Henry handed the duchy of Aquitaine to his son Richard. This decision only took concrete form some months later. In the meantime, Henry had recovered his health and had gone to Rocamadour to offer up thanks. Further, Thomas Becket had been murdered, in his own cathedral, by knights who believed their actions would be pleasing to the king. The responsibility for this murder weighed heavily on Henry, who would later do penance for it.

It is only in 1171 that Richard emerges from obscurity and enters history, at his mother's side. He laid the foundation stones for the monastery of Saint-Augustin in Limoges. After a tour of reconciliation through

Aquitaine, during which they cancelled the confiscations and sanc-
tions recently imposed by Henry II, Richard and Eleanor summoned
their southern vassals to their Christmas court for 1171. Richard was
then proclaimed Duke of Aquitaine in the abbey of Sainte-Hilaire in
Poitiers, where, in June 1172, he received the lance and banner, insignia
of his investiture, from the hands of the bishops of Bordeaux and
Poitiers. Soon after, at Limoges, he was given the ring of St Valérie,
patron saint of Aquitaine; this added to the earlier investiture the seal of
the mystic union binding the Prince of Aquitaine to this saint, whose cult
was then being promoted by the monks of Saint-Martial of Limoges.[17]
Richard was fifteen years old and, with the support of Eleanor, whose
heir he was, he could now see himself as the legitimate Count of Poitiers;
this may have provoked the jealousy of his elder brother Henry, who
was never allowed such a free rein by his father.

   But this was not what Henry II had in mind for Richard. He persisted
in his determination to rule all his lands, on both sides of the Channel. He
had made a public confession for the murder of Thomas Becket and had
been exonerated, even accepting a public penance at Avranches in May
1172.[18] Restored to health and to the good graces of the Church, he held
his Christmas court at Chinon in 1172, in the company of Eleanor and
his children.[19] This was the last public show of a family unity that was
already shattered.

   Nevertheless, Henry II tried to gain new allies for himself and for his
family. In February 1173, the Count of Toulouse came to Limoges and,
in the presence of the king, Eleanor, Richard and numerous princes, did
homage for his county to Henry II and to his son Richard, Duke of
Aquitaine; he promised to provide Henry with forty horses annually and,
in case of need, with the military service (*servitium*) of a hundred knights
(*milites*) for a period of forty days.[20] Henry also tried to extend his influence by political and matrimonial alliances, for example with Count
Humbert of Maurienne, whose lands were of great strategic importance
as they controlled the Alpine passes. His heiress was a seven-year-old
daughter, and Henry wanted to marry her to his last available son, John,
then aged five. The official betrothal took place in 1173 and the little girl
was handed over in customary fashion to the custody of the King of
England,[21] but for the moment John really did 'lack land'. His father
offered, therefore, to grant him three castles with their territories, Chinon,
Loudun and Mirebeau, a promise that enraged his eldest son. Henry was
now eighteen; he had been crowned King of England and invested by
public and solemn homage with the duchy of Normandy and the counties of Anjou and Maine, but he was still king, duke and count only in

name. He was entirely without personal power, land and consequently income, totally dependent on the goodwill of his father, who firmly retained all power and all land in his own hands. The endowment proposed by his father for John came from the Young King's portion and was a source of deep resentment; he asked his father to hand over to him at least a part of the inheritance with which he had been invested, that is, to implement in his lifetime the settlement and partition agreed two years earlier. Henry II categorically refused.

This was the end of the family unity that the previous year's Christmas court at Chinon had been intended to demonstrate. From then on, conflicts that had so far been latent erupted openly between father and son;[22] or perhaps, at least at first, between Henry II and Eleanor, since it seems clear that it was the quarrelling spouses who were the real enemies.[23] The dissension between them had become obvious, and Eleanor's decision to hand over the government of her inheritance to Richard at an early date, so removing it from her husband, seems to have been inspired by their deteriorating relationship. As we have seen, Henry had viewed his marriage primarily as a means to increasing his power. Had he ever loved Eleanor? It is hardly possible to know. What is clear is that he was passionately and openly in love with one of his mistresses, Rosamund Clifford. Henry was then aged forty; his deserted wife, still handsome for her age, was over fifty. We should not give too much credence to the later legends to the effect that Eleanor was prey to such deep jealousy and mad rage that she murdered her rival. It is not difficult, however, to believe that a woman who had once been flattered and courted felt frustrated and humiliated by the repeated adulteries of her husband, and even more so by her exclusion from government.[24] The majority of contemporary chroniclers, in the traditional manner, attributed the quarrels and the wars that tore this royal family apart to a divine punishment resulting from the murder of Thomas Becket or the earlier moral excesses of their ancestors, but they still emphasised the fact that Eleanor urged her sons to rebel.[25]

It seems likely that this resentment constituted the psychological backdrop to Eleanor's decision to act openly against Henry II, though this does not preclude, obviously, as John Gillingham has shown, more purely political motives or, if preferred, principles and opportunities. Henry II had made it clear by his attitude to the Young King that he had no intention of relinquishing in his favour *de facto* power in the lands he had granted him *de jure*. Eleanor, on the other hand, clearly had every intention of surrendering real power to Richard in Aquitaine. At Limoges, Raymond of Toulouse had done homage for his county not only to

Richard, the new Count of Poitiers, but also to Henry II, and perhaps even to Henry the Young King, in Eleanor's presence.[26] Yet the old claims to the county of Toulouse derived from her lineage alone; Eleanor was determined to retain real power over 'her' Aquitaine and transmit it to Richard directly, not through the intermediary of Henry, whose authority was not accepted by many of the local barons. She may have seen these multiple homages from which she was excluded as a real threat, foreshadowing her own exclusion not only as wife but as Duchess of Aquitaine, and threatening also the future of Richard, her favourite son. According to Ralph of Coggeshall, the initiative (and blame) for the revolt lay with the Young Henry, who was in too much of a hurry to 'reign in his father's lifetime'.[27]

The rather muted political personality of the Young King makes this doubtful; it was surely Eleanor who was pulling the strings. And it was this revolt, with its political and military dimensions, led by a wife against her husband, which surprised and shocked many contemporaries. History provided no precedent and some of the moralists of the day assumed that the driving force behind the revolt must be a man and tried to establish his identity; they thought they had found him in the person of Ralph de Faye, Eleanor's uncle and counsellor, and seneschal of Poitou, who had frequently rebelled against Henry II. This was wholly in accord with the conservative thinking of many men of the age, especially ecclesiastics, for whom a woman was supposed to play the role of helpmeet, subject to her husband, and hidden away behind the scenes. The second half of the twelfth century, however, saw women emerge from the shadows and gradually assume a position centre stage; in literary works and tournaments alike, their role became public and their personalities show through. Eleanor, more than any other woman, embodies this trend, of which she is the singularly precocious and assertive emblem. She had no need of any male prompting to take such action. There is no cause for doubt: only Eleanor could have fomented such an insurrection.[28]

She was acting against her husband but on behalf of her sons, and probably especially Richard. Yet it was the Young Henry who was the first to defect, on the pretext advanced by Eleanor and her circle: 'It is not right,' they said, 'that you should be king only in name, and that you should not have the power in the kingdom that is your due.'[29] Henry emphasised the humiliation inflicted on him by his father and suddenly abandoned him, at Chinon, to take refuge with the King of France, his father-in-law, who joyfully received him. His two brothers, Geoffrey and Richard, also abandoned Henry II, egged on by Eleanor, and joined him

at the French court. Only the youngest, John, remained with his father, willingly or not.[30] A veritable conspiracy was hatched at the court of Louis VII, who promised the rebellious sons military assistance against his long-time rival. He listed his grievances for the benefit of the King of England's ambassadors: Henry had kept Margaret's dowry for himself instead of handing it over to his eldest son; he had received the liege homage of the Count of Toulouse, luring him away from his allegiance to Louis; he had attempted to raise the people of Auvergne against the King of France. Louis promised, therefore, to support the cause of Eleanor and her sons. To bind Richard to him, Louis VII even made him a knight and made profuse protestations of friendship.[31] Richard, Henry and Geoffrey swore an oath at the French court not to conclude a separate peace with their father without the agreement of the barons of France. By his lavish generosity and sweeping promises, Henry the Young King rallied many knights and great men of the kingdom of France to his cause. The Count of Flanders did homage in return for the promise of several castles and £1,000; the Count of Boulogne did the same in return for a few castles; the Count of Champagne was promised the castle of Amboise and 500 *livres angevines*.

The conspirators formed an alliance and determined to act quickly; they invaded Normandy, which they pillaged and burned. The insurrection spread even in England itself; the Earl of Leicester, leader of the revolt, was joined by William, King of Scots, the Earl of Chester and several other lords. Hugh Bigod joined them with many warriors. The King of Scots invaded the north of England. It looked as if Henry II was done for, abandoned by all, which many saw as divine vengeance for the murder of Thomas Becket.

In Normandy, in June 1173, the coalition was at first successful. Philip of Flanders, an ally of the Young King, besieged Aumale and Neuf-Marché; Louis VII laid siege to Verneuil and, in July, the Earl of Chester seized Dol in Brittany. Richard joined the insurgents in Normandy. Everything seemed to be going their way. But at the siege of Driencourt, Matthew of Boulogne, brother of Philip of Flanders, was killed by a crossbow bolt, which so cooled the latter's military ardour that he abandoned the attack. While Louis VII was failing to take Verneuil, Henry assembled more than 20,000 mercenaries, at enormous cost, and marched on the town; Louis refused to meet him in battle and made an inglorious retreat, after pillaging and burning the suburbs, in spite of the truce that had been agreed with the townspeople.[32] Henry maintained the impetus, recovered Dol and ravaged Brittany. An offer of peace on the part of the Old King was nevertheless rejected by his sons; they were

badly advised by the King of France, who was hoping to resume the offensive by marching on Rouen, while Philip of Flanders and the Young King planned a landing in England with Flemish troops to support the insurgents. But Henry II had realised the danger. He returned to England with his prisoners of note and an army of 500 Brabançons, only to hear almost at once that his supporters had been wholly successful: the King of Scots was captured on 13 July and Hugh Bigod submitted on 25 July.[33] When he heard that the Old King had left for England, Philip of Flanders and the Young King abandoned their plans for a landing and instead joined Louis VII, who was now besieging Rouen. But Henry II, victorious in England, had returned with his mercenaries and he succeeded in routing the allied armies, who raised the siege. The defeated coalition broke up. Peace was signed at Montlouis at the end of September 1174. Louis VII had lost the contest with his powerful vassal, who was a far better strategist. He was obliged to restore to Henry the fortresses occupied in Normandy, while the sons of the Old King humbly submitted to their father.[34] Order had apparently been restored to the benefit of the Plantagenet, who seemed to be the most powerful monarch in Christendom, whereas the King of France had suffered a serious blow to his prestige.

What role had Richard played in this conflict? In the spring of 1173 he had withdrawn to Poitou to organise the revolt there. A very large number of barons had rallied to his cause, the lords of Angoulême, Lusignan, Taillebourg and Parthenay amongst many others; they were loyal to Eleanor and her son but probably even more anxious to free themselves from all tutelage.[35] But the revolt was not unanimously supported in Aquitaine, in particular among the lords of Gascony and a large part of the Limousin. Further north, the Viscount of Thouars was almost alone in remaining loyal to Henry II. The insurgents at first enjoyed some success, but here too, Henry II, at the head of an army consisting of both his household knights and a large number of mercenaries, knights and infantry (routiers, Brabançons, *cotereaux* and Flemings),[36] eventually got the better of them, thanks to forced marches, at which Wace marvelled,[37] and his undoubted skills as a strategist. By November 1173, from his base at Chinon, he took the castles of Preuilly and Champigny and subdued the region.

Richard, still an adolescent, seems not yet to have been as skilful a war leader as his father; nor had he shown much initiative. He was in difficulties, and Eleanor was anxious to join him to bolster his position with her moral and political support among the barons of Aquitaine. She disguised herself as a man, but was recognised, arrested and handed

over to Henry II, who kept her a prisoner, initially at Chinon. For the first time, Richard had to exercise his responsibilities as war leader alone. For a while, he tried to continue the fight, seeking to establish himself in La Rochelle, a fortress that was reckoned to be impregnable; but its inhabitants were loyal to the Old King and rejected him. He then tried to withdraw to Saintes, which took his side, but he was surprised by a rapid movement of his father's troops, who seized the town and its garrison. Richard managed to escape, taking refuge in the castle of Geoffrey de Rancon at Taillebourg; by this time he had very few soldiers left. The fighting dragged on until July 1174, by which date the total victory of the Old King was no longer in doubt. The order of events makes this plain: on 8 July, as we have seen, Henry II was not afraid to leave Chinon for England with his wife Eleanor among his captives of note, accompanied by the ladies who had made up her court in Poitiers, that is, the wives and fiancées of his rebellious sons: Margaret, wife of the Young Henry; Alice, betrothed to his second son; Constance of Brittany, betrothed to the third; and Alice of Maurienne, promised to the fourth. Henry II had them all in his power. He first confined Eleanor at Winchester, then in a tower at Salisbury, under the vigilant eye of lords who were fiercely loyal to him.[38] Did he really, at this point, offer Eleanor her freedom on condition she took the veil at Fontevraud? It seems unlikely, in spite of the bonds that had developed between Eleanor and the abbey by 1172 (though probably not before).[39] In any case, Eleanor remained a prisoner. To be sure of enjoying both heavenly favour and popular support in England, Henry made a pilgrimage to Canterbury, to the tomb of Thomas Becket, now a saint, to seek his posthumous assistance. His prayers were answered the very next-day, 13 July 1174, when, on his return to London, he learned of the capture of William the Lion, King of Scots. He was now able to concentrate on reducing Aquitaine, where Richard, abandoned by Louis VII, was still supporting a revolt that was doomed, not daring to face his father's troops head on. Besides which, on 8 September, Henry II and Louis VII made a truce that ignored him. Richard finally realised that all was lost; at Poitiers, on 23 September, he went to his father's court and threw himself at his feet, weeping and begging for forgiveness. His brothers followed his example a few days later, in accord with the treaty of Montlouis.

The revolt of Eleanor and her sons had been a total failure. Henry II had restored the status quo; he retained real power, while generously granting his repentant sons a degree of autonomy, though less than he had himself proposed before the revolt, when they had haughtily

rejected it. Henry the Young King received two castles in Normandy, Geoffrey half of his inheritance of Brittany, Richard two castles (unfortified) in Poitou and half the revenues of Aquitaine. The sons did homage to their father, with exception of the Young Henry, because he remained king.[40]

The two Henrys were reconciled; they now ate at the same table and shared the same bed.[41] Richard seems to have been content with the title of Duke of Aquitaine and to have acted in his lands simply as his father's representative. In January 1175 he was despatched to subdue a new revolt of the barons, many of whom were his former allies. Richard acted as his father's proxy in his own duchy. In fact Henry ordered the loyal Poitevins to be obedient to Richard.[42]

Eleanor, who remained a prisoner of Henry II until his death, seemed at this point to have failed in her struggle. For her, 1174 was an *annus horribilis*. It is possible that we have pictorial evidence of her anxieties and her hopes, although the interpretation has proved extremely difficult and controversial.[43] After her liberation, perhaps in 1193, the year of Richard's capture, she had this dramatic moment in her life painted on the walls of a chapel dedicated to St Radegund, at Chinon, in a richly symbolic scene; it may immortalise the moment when Eleanor was taken to England as a prisoner. As she rides behind her victorious husband, she looks back one last time at her sons, Henry and, above all, Richard, to whom she has just handed the falcon, mark of his princely power. By this gesture, the defeated queen seems to be entrusting her own future and the fate of her duchy of Aquitaine to Richard, her much-loved son and her last hope.[44]

NOTES

1. Robert of Torigny, pp. 499ff.
2. For this transformation see Graboïs, 'La Trêve de Dieu'.
3. Robert of Torigny, p. 504. For the penitential aspect of this pilgrimage, see Graboïs, 'Louis VII, Pèlerin', especially p. 16.
4. Robert of Torigny, anno 1158, p. 507.
5. Sassier, *Louis VII*, p. 282.
6. Gillingham, *Richard the Lionheart*, pp. 39–40; Sassier, *Louis VII*, pp. 285ff. According to Ralph of Coggeshall (p. 15), it was Louis VII's army, coming to the assistance of Raymond de Saint-Gilles, that forced Henry to raise the siege.
7. William of Newburgh, p. 159. See also Roger of Howden, I, p. 218.
8. Gerald of Wales, *Expugnatio Hibernica*, cap. 38, *Giraldi Cambrensis Opera*, ed. Dimock. pp. 395ff.

9. Gervase of Canterbury, I, p. 203.

10. For the origins of these revolts, see Norgate, *England under the Angevin Kings*, pp. 120ff.; Gillingham, *Richard the Lionheart*, pp. 53–4; Sassier, *Louis VII*, p. 470; Kessler, *Richard I*, pp. 13ff.

11. Robert of Torigny, anno 1168, p. 517; Roger of Howden, I, p. 273; Gervase of Canterbury, p. 205. See also *Guillaume le Maréchal*, lines 1624–1904; and the discussion in Duby, *William Marshal*, which remains valuable despite the criticisms of John Gillingham (see note 1 to Introduction); see also Crouch, *William Marshal*.

12. Robert of Torigny (anno 1169, p. 518) puts this meeting on 6 January 1169, as does Gervase of Canterbury (I, p. 207), followed by Régine Pernoud (*Aliénor d'Aquitaine*, p. 13). John Gillingham puts it in January 1169 (*Richard the Lionheart*, p. 57), Yves Sassier on 6–7 February of the same year in *Louis VII*, p. 392.

13. Geoffrey of Vigeois, *Chronicon, Recueil des Historiens*, 12, p. 442.

14. Roger of Howden, II, pp. 5–6, gives the date of 1170 for the grant of the county of Mortain to John, then one year old, but it must surely have been later. The *Gesta Henrici* (I, p. 7) make no reference to it.

15. Roger of Howden, II, p. 5; Gervase of Canterbury, II, p. 209; William of Newburgh, p. 160; Ralph of Coggeshall, p. 16.

16. Matthew Paris, *Chronica Majora*, II, p. 286.

17. Geoffrey of Vigeois, *Chronicon, Recueil des Historiens*, 12, pp. 442–3.

18. Matthew Paris, *Chronica Majora*, II, p. 282. See also Petit-Dutaillis, *Feudal Monarchy*, p. 150.

19. The Young Henry and his wife Margaret celebrated Christmas at Bonneville: Robert of Torigny, p. 521.

20. Geoffrey of Vigeois, *Chronicon, Recueil des Historiens*, 12, p. 443; Robert of Torigny, p. 521; Roger of Howden, II, p. 45.

21. *Gesta Henrici*, I, p. 36; Matthew Paris, *Chronica Majora*, II, p. 286.

22. There is a good discussion of the origins and progress of this family conflict in Kessler, *Richard I*, pp. 13ff.

23. Labande, 'Une Image Véridique'.

24. In the words of E.-R. Labande ('Une Image Véridique', p. 209), 'Eleanor did not take her revenge by assassinating Rosamund; she did better. She stirred up Poitou.'

25. Matthew Paris, *Chronica Majora*, II, p. 286; William of Newburgh, pp. 170–1; Gerald of Wales, *De Principis Instructione*, II, 4; Gervase of Canterbury, I, p. 80; Richard of Poitiers, addenda, pp. 418–21.

26. Gillingham, *Richard the Lionheart*, pp. 63–6.

27. Ralph of Coggeshall, pp. 17–18.

28. I take this phrase from E.-R. Labande ('Une Image Véridique', p. 200).

29. Matthew Paris, *Chronica Majora*, II, p. 285.

30. Gervase of Canterbury, I, p. 80; see also, in *Recueil des Historiens des Gaules et de la France*, 16, pp. 629–30, the Archbishop of Rouen's letter to

Eleanor, written by Peter of Blois, urging her to be once again obedient to her husband: after citing the biblical references advocating the submission of a wife to her husband, he concluded: 'We know well that if you do not return to your husband, you will be the cause of a general ruin', so emphasising the dominant part played by Eleanor in the revolt.

31. Roger of Howden, II, p. 55.
32. Robert of Torigny, p. 522; Roger of Howden, II, pp. 49–50; Ralph of Diceto, I, p. 374; *Gesta Henrici*, I, pp. 50–4; William of Newburgh, I, pp. 174–5. For the much-debated interpretation of these military operations, see Strickland, *War and Chivalry*, pp. 126, 211.
33. Matthew Paris (*Chronica Majora*, II, pp. 293–4) applies to the capture of William of Scotland a prophesy of Merlin that he later applied to the defeat of Henry II himself; see also Matthew Paris, *Chronica Majora*, II, pp. 342–3.
34. Robert of Torigny, p. 523.
35. Robert of Torigny, p. 522; *Gesta Henrici*, I, p. 42.
36. For the role of mercenaries in the armies of Henry II, see Chibnall, M., 'Mercenaries and the Familia Regis under Henry I', *History*, 62 (1977), repr. in Strickland, *Anglo-Norman Warfare*, pp. 84–92; Prestwich, J. O., 'The Military Household of the Norman Kings', *English Historical Review*, 96 (1981), repr. in Strickland, *Anglo-Norman Warfare*, pp. 93–127; and, more generally, Brown, 'Military Service and Monetary Reward'.
37. Wace, *Le Roman de Rou*, lines 70ff., I, p. 5.
38. *Gesta Henrici*, I, p. 72; Ralph of Coggeshall, p. 18.
39. For this offer, see Kelly, *Eleanor of Aquitaine*, p. 190; for the development of links between Eleanor and Fontevraud, see Bienvenu, J.-M., 'Aliénor d'Aquitaine et Fontevraud', *Cahiers de Civilisation Médiévale*, 113–14 (1986), pp. 15–27.
40. *Gesta Henrici*, I, pp. 78–9; Roger of Howden, II, pp. 67–8; Ralph of Diceto, pp. 394–5; Matthew Paris, *Chronica Majora*, II, p. 295.
41. Matthew Paris, *Chronica Majora*, II, p. 297.
42. *Gesta Henrici*, I, p. 81; Roger of Howden, II, p. 83.
43. This scene was first interpreted as showing a departure for the hunt. In a recent article, U. Nilgen has challenged the very existence of women in the scene, arguing that it shows Henry II followed by his two sons, reconciled in 1174: 'Les Plantagenêt à Chinon. A Propos d'une Peinture Murale dans la Chapelle de Sainte Radegonde', in *Iconographia* (*Mélanges Piotr Skubiszevski*) (Poitiers, 1999).
44. For the interpretation of these wall paintings, see Kenaan-Kedar, 'Aliénor d'Aquitaine Conduite en Captivité'. In spite of the often pertinent remarks of U. Nilgen in the article cited in note 43, I accept almost in its entirety the interpretation of Kenaan-Kedar, but with two qualifications: first, I am not convinced that the person behind Eleanor represents Joan, then aged only nine; second, it seems to me that it is not Richard who is holding the

falcon out to Eleanor, but the other way round: Eleanor, defeated and a prisoner, turns back towards Richard after handing him the falcon, her emblem, sign of seigneurial power and symbol of her confidence that he will guarantee the continuity of a political policy she can no longer herself pursue. The gesture of Eleanor, with her open hand, seems to me to support this interpretation; it remains, of course, as hypothetical as all previous interpretations.

2

Richard the Younger Son, Count of Poitou (1174–83)

∽

SUBMISSION OR A CHANGE OF HEART?

In the dying days of 1174, Richard learned the lessons of defeat: he was not yet ready to take on his father. He submitted, therefore, like his brothers; by doing so, he retained at least some power in Aquitaine, if under the iron hand of Henry II, to whom he had done homage. Father and sons, apparently united, celebrated Christmas together at Argentan; Richard's newfound support for his father and his loyalty seemed sufficiently sincere for him to be entrusted with the pacification of his former Poitevin allies in Aquitaine.[1]

Historians have reacted very differently to this dramatic turnaround. Some have seen it as evidence of a degree of psychological instability on Richard's part, of his indecisiveness, of the ease with which he could change his mind;[2] they have quoted the nickname given him by one of his allies among the rebels, now his adversary, the troubadour knight Bertran de Born: 'Yea and Nay' ('Oc e No').[3] Bertran himself was a man who changed his mind frequently, whenever it suited his interests; what he loved most was war, and he had tried force of arms to gain the castle of Hautefort, which was also claimed by his brother Constantine. Other scholars have taken the nickname 'Yea and Nay' as evidence of the very opposite, that is, of the decisiveness and lack of hesitation with which Richard threw himself so wholeheartedly into his enterprises.[4] This is the preferred interpretation of John Gillingham, for whom his hero can do no wrong, and who believes that Bertran de Born gave this name to Richard 'not because he was of a fickle, changeable disposition, but because his words were few and to the point'.[5] Yet others believe it may refer to a lack of scruple about breaking his word, in which he would resemble his brother Henry in the unflattering portrait painted by Walter Map, who saw Henry as a prime example of untrustworthiness.[6] In fact, it is by no means easy to interpret the nicknames given by Bertran de Born to the

sons of Henry II; it is far from clear why he called Henry the Young King 'Mariner' and we can only guess at the reasons for the nickname 'Rassa' given to his brother Geoffrey.[7] In these circumstances, it would be wise not to give too much credence to these speculations. Bertran de Born's nickname for Richard may very well be highly subjective and lacking in any real basis.

We are left with the undeniable fact that, at this point, Richard gave every appearance of total voluntary submission to his father. Henry II, for his part, was careful to spare the susceptibilities of his defeated sons, and in particular Richard. He himself took on the pacification of Anjou, his paternal inheritance, despatching Geoffrey to perform the same function in Brittany, admittedly under the supervision of Roland de Dinan,[8] and instructing Richard – Duke of Aquitaine but usually designated Count of Poitou in the texts – to restore order in his own region.

The campaign of pacification in Aquitaine was far from easy. In the first place, it involved punishing the rebels, Richard's former allies, and above all reducing their influence and capacity for trouble-making by dismantling their castles. These were numerous and solidly built of good stone, as had now been the practice for almost a century in this area. Some had recently been restored, their defences improved and their walls strengthened and flanked by towers from which archers and crossbowmen could attack assailants attempting to undermine the walls or put ladders up against them for an assault. No new means were available, in contrast, to the attackers attempting to take castles. The most effective method, if it was possible to get close to the walls, was sapping; this involved digging a gallery under the foundations and immediately shoring it up with wooden pit props, which were then set on fire, causing the part of the wall immediately above to collapse, creating a breach through which the assailants could enter. But such operations were time-consuming, risky and, where moats kept the attackers at a distance, impossible. Another method was to launch an assault from movable wooden towers that were taller than the castle walls. Or the walls could be attacked with a variety of devices: catapults, ballistae, mangonels or battering rams. All these methods were dangerous and expensive in manpower. The only other method was the siege, which deprived the garrison of assistance and provisions. But this, too, was a lengthy process: castles were equipped with cisterns and reserves of food and forage for the animals which were herded into them in case of need, when, that is, there were no fields enclosed within the walls, as was often the case with fortified towns. In fact, apart from the assault, sometimes tried as a last resort, attackers mostly tried to take castles by trickery, either entering through secret passages or luring some

or all of the garrison outside the walls by a ruse; or they persuaded it to surrender by promising to spare lives or, on the contrary, by terror, laying waste to the surrounding countryside, burning the neighbouring villages and massacring or mutilating the hostile population.

Richard achieved some spectacular results in this campaign, quickly establishing a solid reputation as a valiant warrior. It was here that he earned the nickname 'Lionheart'. His first success, which attracted considerable attention, was the capture of Castillon-sur-Agen, in August 1175, which he took after a siege lasting two months, forcing the garrison into surrender by the effectiveness of his siege engines. He captured thirty knights and numerous men-at-arms and had the walls of the castle razed.[9] In the spring of 1176, he turned his attention to other barons, including Vulgrin of Angoulême, who had just invaded Poitou,[10] and Aimar of Limoges, who had just changed sides and joined the rebels, having previously been loyal to Henry II.[11] Before taking on these men, Richard visited his father to seek advice and assistance; he got enough to enable him to recruit a mercenary army with which, in May, near Saint-Maigrin, he defeated the barons of the Limousin and Angoulême; the rebel army was itself largely made up of Brabançons. This was the only real pitched battle Richard fought on this expedition or, indeed, before his departure on crusade.[12] He then marched on Limoges, which capitulated in June.

Before turning his attention to the castles of the count of Angoulême, Richard went back to Poitiers, where he received assistance from his brother Henry. The Young King had asked permission from his father to go on a pilgrimage to St James of Compostella, but Henry II had dissuaded him, preferring to send him to Richard's aid.[13] The two brothers together laid siege to Châteauneuf, which they took in a fortnight. They soon separated, however, perhaps not on the best of terms. Henry might well have found it something of a humiliation to be forced to serve on these terms, on his father's instructions and as no more than an assistant to his younger brother in the pacification of a land in which he had no personal interest. Perhaps also, if we are to believe Geoffrey of Vigeois, Henry (who loved to 'appear prodigal rather than generous', and was therefore constantly having to ask his father for funds) was jealous when he saw his younger brother, with his ample revenues, surpass him in largesse and pomp.[14] Already visible here are the first seeds of the dissension that would eventually pit brother against brother. In August 1176, however, they were both instructed to escort their young sister Joan, aged eleven, to Saint-Gilles-du-Gard, where she was to be handed over to the envoys of her future husband, William,

King of Sicily. Henry escorted her from Normandy to Poitou; Richard
saw her safely through Aquitaine. The marriage was celebrated in
Palermo on 9 November.

Richard then continued his campaign against the rebel castles alone.
He besieged Limoges, where most of the rebels had gathered. Against all
expectations, they surrendered after a siege of only six days. William of
Angoulême surrendered his town and most of his castles to Richard, who
sent the defeated count and a few other hostages and prisoners to his
father, as proof of his submission; his father cleverly sent them back,
placing them at Richard's disposal.[15]

At the end of 1176, while Henry II was celebrating Christmas in
Nottingham, surrounded by his other sons, Richard held his first
Christmas court in Bordeaux. Soon after, he embarked on a new campaign of pacification, intended to ensure the safety of the pilgrim routes
to St James of Compostella, along which his brother Henry and perhaps
also his father wanted to travel. It was rumoured that many pilgrims had
been robbed by brigand lords and by the headmen of the Basque and
Navarrese villages. Early in January 1177, Richard marched on Dax,
held by Centule, Count of Bigorre, quickly taking it. Then he took
Bayonne, captured the castle of Saint-Pierre and finally destroyed a
fortress built by the Basques and Navarrese near the pass of Cize, from
which they had been robbing and holding pilgrims for ransom. He forced
these communities to allow free passage to pilgrims, without exactions,
pillage or taxes. Then, under the impression he had pacified the region
once and for all, he returned to Poitiers on 2 February and dismissed his
mercenaries. This proved a major error, as these men of war, now
without pay, turned to plunder; they lived off the countryside, wreaking
havoc throughout the Limousin, before being defeated and exterminated
at Malemort, on 21 April, by the outraged local populations, who had
raised an 'army of peace'.[16] Bernard Itier called it 'the butchery of
Malemort', a phrase that captures the fury of the massacre, a consequence of the fear and hatred the mercenaries had aroused.[17]

Henry the Young King, meanwhile, again intervened, at his father's
request, in the lordship of Châteauroux, whose lord, Ralph of Déols, had
died, leaving a three-year-old daughter as his sole heiress. Henry II had
demanded custody of the little girl in his capacity as suzerain, but her
family refused and prepared to resist. The Old King decided to punish
them. He instructed Henry – not Richard, on whom, as Duke of
Aquitaine, the lordship of Châteauroux depended – to raise an army in
Normandy and Anjou and take possession of the lordship. He himself
then crossed to the Continent with the intention of settling matters in

person. He seized the heiress of Déols and sent her, in semi-captivity, to Chinon. She was eventually married to one of his barons.

Reassured that order had been restored in his 'empire', Henry II took advantage of his presence at the head of a large army to present Louis VII with a series of demands that had little legal justification: the surrender of the French Vexin, which the King of England regarded as part of Margaret's dowry; also that of Bourges and the whole of Berry, as the dowry of Alice, betrothed to Richard; and the renunciation of all Capetian claims to the Auvergne.[18] It was tantamount to an ultimatum, which Louis realised. He offered a legalistic reply: Alice had now been in Henry's custody for seven years and the expected marriage had still not been celebrated; the situation was beginning to look suspicious and it was being said that Henry had made the little girl his concubine. Louis made his fears known to Cardinal Peter of Saint-Chrysogone, legate of Pope Alexander III in France. The cardinal advised him to urge the King of England, under pain of interdict, either to celebrate the marriage in the very near future or return the princess and her dowry to the King of France. On this basis, Louis VII accused Henry II of mistreating Alice and demanded that the marriage take place. Henry had no desire to relinquish either the dowry or the girl, so was forced to compromise; on 21 September 1177, near Nonancourt, he promised that the marriage between Alice and Richard would take place.[19] To seal their agreement, the two kings made professions of friendship in the treaty and promised to take the cross together. This was an ad hoc agreement, accepted by Henry because he could not go against papal decisions without seriously alienating both public opinion and the Church. In fact he had been bluffing and his bluff had been called. He resolved to take his revenge on the rebels of Aquitaine, beginning with the lords of Déols, the original reason for his journey to the Continent.

Richard was directly affected by these decisions. They brought to the forefront the question of his marriage to Alice, which he seems not to have wanted for reasons that will become apparent. They also raised the question of his suzerainty over Berry and the Auvergne, which belonged in part to Aquitaine.

This time, Richard was involved in the operations. He was obliged to accompany his father on a campaign of reprisals in the Limousin, where he punished Aimar of Limoges and Raymond of Turenne, who were ordered to surrender their fortresses. The pacification seemed complete by the end of 1177, which also saw a major acquisition. In December the count of La Marche, more or less subject to the Duke of Aquitaine, and whose only son had died, decided to sell his lands and depart for the Holy

Land; he may also have wished to atone for the repudiation of his wife and murder of her presumed lover. Henry bought his county for 6,000 silver marks and added it to his own lands. By Henry's own estimate, it was worth over 20,000 marks.[20] When he held his Christmas court at Angers in 1177 the Old King had every reason to feel satisfied. The festivities were particularly sumptuous and he was surrounded by his sons, Henry, Richard and Geoffrey, and a very large number of knights.[21]

The barons of Aquitaine were not, however, all subdued, particularly in the Limousin. The canons of Limoges proceeded to elect as their bishop Sebrand Chabot, scion of a family that had rebelled in 1173. Richard may have expelled the canons by force, but the pope confirmed the election and Henry II had to accept it.[22] During the course of the same year, 1178, Richard's younger brother Geoffrey was knighted by his father in August and went to the marches of Normandy and France in search of fighting and opportunities to demonstrate his prowess;[23] the Young Henry, meanwhile, was beginning to win fame in tournaments. In the words of one chronicler, under the protection of his mentor, William Marshall, he 'spent huge sums of money on them, putting his royal majesty aside, and from being a king turned himself into a knight'.[24] Richard, meanwhile, busied himself with ruling and led his armies into the Basque country in order to frustrate the ambitions of Alfonso II, King of Aragon.

After holding his Christmas court at Saintes, Richard had to face new problems in Aquitaine. Vulgrin of Angoulême, the son of William Taillefer, who was involved in preparations for his departure for Jerusalem, failed to do homage to Richard; so did Geoffrey of Rancon, the perpetual rebel, whose castles, Pons, Richemont and Taillebourg in particular, commanded important routes between Bordeaux, Saintes and La Rochelle. Richard, after failing to make headway at Pons, turned to Richemont, which capitulated after three days and was razed to the ground. He then dared to attack the most formidable castle of the three, Taillebourg, reputedly impregnable. In fact no-one had ever put this to the test, so much did the castle, perched on a steep rock and protected by impressive walls, seem to defy all assault. Richard laid siege to it, pitching his camp very close to the ramparts, bringing up his siege engines and systematically laying waste to the surrounding countryside, cutting down vines and burning villages. These depredations enraged the garrison and provoked a sortie, enabling Richard to penetrate the fortifications. The garrison, which had taken refuge in the citadel, capitulated soon after.

By capturing such an impregnable fortress in the space of three days, Richard quickly acquired a reputation as an invincible warrior. He had

himself taken part in the fighting and stormed into the town alongside his men.[25] On hearing the news, Geoffrey of Rancon surrendered his castle of Pons without a fight, as did Vulgrin his fortified towns of Montignac and Angoulême. Richard had the fortifications of all these places dismantled and once again dismissed his bands of mercenaries, who pillaged Bordeaux and its surroundings to survive. The crimes of these routiers throughout the Midi were such that the Lateran Council was roused to action and issued a decree against them; it compared them to heretics, granted those who took up arms against them the same privileges as pilgrims and crusaders, and excommunicated those who hired them. They did this in vain; all the warring parties needed their effective contribution and could not afford to dispense with their services.[26]

Basking in the glow of success, Richard returned to England, where his father was ready to entrust him with the effective government of Aquitaine, under the double title of Count of Poitou and Duke of Aquitaine. This is how he was styled on 1 November 1179 at the coronation in Reims of the young King Philip 'Dieudonné', later 'Augustus', son of Louis VII. Relations between Henry II and Louis seem to have improved since the King of France had ceased to support the rebels within the Angevin empire. One indication of this is provided by a curious episode relating to the coronation, which had occurred earlier that year, on 15 August, when the court was staying at Compiègne. During the course of a hunting expedition, the young Philip, not yet fifteen years old, got lost in the dense forest, where he wandered about for a long time, terrified, before being brought back to the court by a charcoal burner; this man was described by the French chronicler Rigord, in the clichés of the time, as black, enormous, deformed, horrible to look at and altogether terrifying. Even though this peasant was Philip's rescuer, his appearance managed to unsettle the young boy so badly that he lay for many days hovering between life and death.[27] All over the kingdom, prayers were offered up for the recovery of the sole heir to the throne. Rigord, who recounts this episode, 'forgets' to report that Louis VII had requested and been permitted by Henry II to make a pilgrimage to the tomb of St Thomas Becket to pray and seek the intercession of the new saint; Henry had received the King of France with great ceremony and accompanied him amidst signs of friendship to Canterbury.[28] The prayers of King Louis were answered and Philip recovered his health. It had been necessary only to postpone the date of the coronation until All Saints' Day.

On 1 November 1179, however, Louis VII was not present at the long-awaited coronation of his son. These events had so undermined his strength that, on his return from his pilgrimage, he had suffered an attack

of paralysis; he died a few months later, on 18 September 1180. Henry II was not at the coronation either, perhaps to avoid having to appear, at highly ritualised ceremonies ruled by strict etiquette, in an inferior position to that of the King of France. His children, however, were present. Though King of England, the Young Henry did homage as Duke of Normandy and Count of Anjou, by virtue of which title he was also seneschal of France, giving him the honour of leading the procession bearing the crown which the Archbishop of Reims would place on Philip's head. Geoffrey also did homage to the king for Brittany, and Richard for Aquitaine.[29] The feudal order was thus respected, and harmony seemed to prevail. Eleanor, from her prison, did not appreciate this submission on Richard's part, if we are to believe a remark of Geoffrey of Vigeois.[30] In order to ensure the military service of his vassals and of his lay subjects in general, Henry II proclaimed the Assize of Arms in all his domains, on both sides of the Channel. The Assize fixed the military obligations of each individual, that is, of knights in possession of a fee (they had to serve with hauberk, helmet, sword and lance) and of free men (who had to serve with hauberk, helmet, sword and lance if they had an annual income of more than sixteen marks, with haubergeon, iron headpiece and lance if only ten marks).[31] The measure emphasised the importance Henry attached to the military service of his men, in addition to the recruitment of mercenary soldiers. He was preparing himself for a likely conflict.

A NEW FRENCH ADVERSARY

In spite of his youth, the new King of France very quickly proved a more formidable and cunning adversary than his father. He was resolved to resume the struggle against the Plantagenets at the earliest opportunity and exploit the fault lines already visible by encouraging the divisions between father and sons. On 29 May, at Saint-Denis, he took the crown and also crowned his young wife, Isabella, niece of the Count of Flanders and daughter of Margaret and Baldwin of Hainault. Philip of Flanders gave his niece as dowry the region that would later be known as Artois, retaining its revenues for himself in his own lifetime. The family of the Count, who had accompanied Louis VII on his pilgrimage to Canterbury, were now playing an increasingly prominent role at the French court. It was Count Philip of Flanders who carried the sword during the coronation procession. The house of Champagne and its supporters, so influential at the French court during the reign of Louis VII, were very visibly absent.[32] Adela of Champagne, Louis VII's widow, reacted to the ousting of her family by seeking the assistance and protection of the King of

England. Henry made haste to Normandy and, amidst general surprise, acted as mediator and conciliator: he proposed a peace treaty to his young overlord, which was signed at Gisors in June 1180. Thanks to Henry, King Philip agreed to a reconciliation with his mother Adela. The conciliatory attitude of Henry II in this affair may be explained in diplomatic terms; he was hoping that Philip, in return for his services, would support the candidacy as emperor of his son-in-law, Henry the Lion.[33]

After the coronation, Richard returned to Aquitaine, which was once again disturbed by revolts, occasioned by the inheritance of Vulgrin of Angoulême. As his suzerain, Richard claimed custody of his heiress, his daughter Matilda. But the traditional customs regarding succession in these regions gave the brothers of the deceased father rights that Richard was not prepared to recognise; the brothers refused to surrender the county and went to join their dissident half-brother, Aimar of Limoges, who was impatient to avenge the affront of the defeat he had suffered earlier. A new coalition was put together, directed by the Limousin barons and joined by the Count of Perigord, the viscounts of Ventadour and Turenne and Bertran de Born, who was hoping to attract the support of Henry the Young King.[34] Richard moved quickly and even before the arrival of the military assistance he had requested from his father, on 11 April 1182, he seized the castle of Périgueux, entered the Limousin and devastated the region. Henry II came to the rescue and ordered the Young Henry to join him. Richard and his father then embarked together on a new pacification of the Limousin, seizing, one after the other, fortresses belonging to Aimar of Limoges and Count Elie of Perigord. They were joined by the Young Henry at Périgueux, at the siege of the castle of Puy-Saint-Front. Faced with a deployment of military force on this scale, the conspirators surrendered and sued for peace. Richard razed the walls of the castle and Elie had to hand over his two sons as hostages.

THE REVOLT AND DEATH OF THE YOUNG KING

Richard's victory seemed total, but it had once again been achieved only with the assistance of his father and his brother Henry. This harmony risked being short-lived. The Young King seems to have harboured fresh resentment against his younger brother, whose reputation, brilliance, affluence, splendour and independent life, far from heavy parental supervision, aroused his envy. Also, like his father, he had been able to observe the extent to which the lords of Aquitaine were angered by the rather dictatorial and brutal, even cruel, manner in which Richard ruled the region; they had complained of this to Henry II when he had summoned

them to Grandmont.[35] Passing through Limoges on his way to Périgueux, the Young Henry had ceremoniously offered the monks of Saint-Martial a cloak on which was embroidered his title *Henricus Rex*. His eagerness to rule as befitted his title was palpable.[36] A few Limousin barons, including Bertran de Born, had hoped to win the Young King's support for their cause; always on the lookout for battles to fight, Bertran also deplored the fact that the Young King had participated with his father in the conference at Senlis which had ended the war that had broken out between Philip Augustus and Philip of Flanders, who had fallen out of favour; the count had renewed his promise to deliver Artois to the King of France as Isabella's dowry.[37] Bertran, a troubadour, had been hoping there would be a war and he castigated the pusillanimity of the Young King in song:

> Papiol, leave promptly: say to the Young King that I do not like it when people sleep too much. The Lord Yea and Nay likes peace, I sincerely believe, even more than his brother John the Disinherited.[38]

The Young Henry, already jealous of his brother, was also tormented by rumours to the effect that his mentor, William Marshall, had become the lover of his wife, Margaret; he showed signs of extreme irritability during this period.[39] He wanted to be recognised for what he was: the eldest son, the king, the legitimate heir. He told his father how he felt at the Christmas court of 1182, held by Henry with his sons at Caen. Bertran de Born was present, perhaps summoned by Henry II. After all, he had recently risen against Richard and written some bitter verses against the Young Henry. In fact Henry had disappointed his admirers by submitting to his father and being reconciled with Richard before the walls of Périgueux.[40] The troubadour knight expressed his disillusionment and that of the barons of Aquitaine in two songs. One of them openly stirred the wounded pride of the Young King by referring to his dependence on his father:

> Because he behaves like a good-for-nothing by living as he does on what is handed out to him, counted and measured. A crowned king who is dependent on another for his living bears little resemblance to Hernaut, the Marquis of Beaulande, or to the glorious William who conquered the Tour Mirande, how glorious that was! Because in Poitou he lies and deceives people, he will no longer be so loved as before.[41]

Cracks had already appeared in the family unity that had been on show at the court at Caen when Henry II, at a gathering in Le Mans, asked his sons to do homage to their elder brother, the designated heir; this suggested that the Young King was to be regarded as his successor and suzerain of his younger brothers, who would in future hold their 'fiefs'

from him. Geoffrey made no objection, but Richard refused: he held Aquitaine from his mother, Eleanor, and had every intention of remaining independent of his brother. According to one chronicler, he responded angrily in no uncertain terms:

> Are we not born of the same father and the same mother? Is it not improper that in the lifetime of our father we should be forced to submit to our elder brother and recognise him as our superior? Anyhow, if our father's property passes to the eldest son, I claim in full legitimacy the property of my mother.[42]

Later, under pressure from his father, Richard agreed to do homage, but this time it was Henry who refused to receive it. Richard hurled insults, uttered threats and prepared for war. He withdrew to Poitou where he fortified new castles and repaired others.[43]

The rift seemed definitive; Bertran de Born rejoiced and fanned the flames. The Young Henry might find allies in Aquitaine even against Richard. In fact a new revolt had broken out there in the autumn of 1182, provoked once more by Aimar of Limoges and the counts of Angoulême, who recruited many mercenaries. Bertran de Born joined them and hoped to rally the Young Henry to his cause, expecting to obtain his assistance against his brother Constantine. He emphasised in a song the ready-made cause or, rather, pretext, for the breach: Richard had recently fortified a castle, Clairvaux, beyond his own domains, in Anjou.[44] This time, thought Bertran, the Young King could hardly allow the insult to go unavenged:

> Between Poitou and L'Ile-Bouchard, and Mirebeau and Loudun and Chinon, at Clairvaux, a fine castle has fearlessly been built on a plain. But I would not wish the Young King to know about or see it, because it would not be to his liking. But I am very afraid, it is such a dazzling white, that he can see it quite clearly from Mateflon.[45]

The conflict between the two brothers was unmistakably getting worse. Henry the Young King and Geoffrey sided with the rebel barons against Richard, who bowed to his father's advice and surrendered Clairvaux. The Old King then tried to reconcile his sons and pacify the barons. A peace was to be signed at Mirebeau and Henry II sent Geoffrey to summon the rebel lords. This was a mistake. Geoffrey joined the rebel barons, soon followed by the Young King, who invaded Poitou together with his brother. After recruiting Brabançons and other mercenaries, they devastated Poitou, Richard's territory, killing, burning and mutilating. Once again, Richard sought his father's help. Henry II, fearing for his son's life, came to the rescue at Limoges, then held by the Young Henry; by mistake, he was met by a volley of arrows, one of which only just missed his chest.[46] In turn, the Young King appealed to the King of France, which brought

the Capetian and Henry II face to face once again, further dividing the Plantagenet family. Philip Augustus sent his own Brabançon mercenaries to the Young Henry, who, with their help, took Saint-Léonard-de-Noblat, then Brantôme, and pillaged the surrounding area. The rebel barons, meanwhile, devastated the Limousin while Bertran de Born managed to drive his brother out of the castle of Hautefort. The Young King, however, soon found himself short of money; he was forced to plunder and pillage to procure it.

The military operations, which were confused and characterised by numerous exactions, burnings, massacres, mutilations, depredations, thefts of relics and forced 'loans' from church treasuries, are of limited relevance to my argument here, so I will pass over them without further comment; I will, however, return to some of these episodes in Part Two, because they serve as a good illustration both of the nature of war in the twelfth century and of the way it was perceived by the knights.

The outcome of the conflict is, however, directly relevant. Henry the Young King, pressed by his father's troops and by Richard's, had several times expressed a desire to take the cross to expiate his sin in rebelling against his father. Henry II was touched by this and seems twice to have believed in his sincerity and agreed to pay for his pilgrimage. Each time it had been a trick and the Young Henry had promptly rejoined the rebels. When he fell seriously ill at Martel, in June 1183, after plundering the treasury of Rocamadour, the Young King once again appealed to his father, employing the familiar arguments. Henry II took no notice, fearing a new deception. This time, however, it was not a trick, and the Young King died, at the age of twenty-seven, after confessing his sins and promising to reimburse all the victims of his pillaging. He passed on his vow of pilgrimage to Jerusalem to his faithful William Marshal, who was to perform the pilgrimage in his place. He died at Martel, alone 'in the midst of those barbarians', in the words of Ralph of Diceto, on 11 June 1183.[47] His father was devastated when, too late, he realised the truth. He had his son's body carried first to Le Mans and then to Rouen, where it was buried.

With the death of the Young King, the rebellion quickly petered out. The princes returned home and Geoffrey fled, then obtained a pardon from his father. The barons of Aquitaine were left to bear the king's anger alone. Aimar of Limoges surrendered his castle, but Henry II had it razed by his seneschal.[48] Richard, with his ally, Alfonso II of Aragon, an enemy of the Count of Toulouse, laid waste the lands of the Count of Périgord, meeting little opposition. Soon after, Philip Augustus managed to restore peace between Raymond of Toulouse and Alfonso,[49] and the quarrel briefly died down.

The Young King was lamented long and loud by all those who saw
him as the perfect expression of knighthood.[50] All the chroniclers sang
his praises in sometimes exaggerated terms.[51] William Marshal, his tutor
in chivalry, his mentor and friend, wrote his funeral elegy in a few verses:

> In Martel died, it seems to me,
> The one who embodied within himself
> All courtesy and prowess
> Breeding and largesse.[52]

Bertran de Born, too, mourned his hero in a famous lament:

> You would have been the king of the noble and emperor of the brave, lord, if
> you had lived longer, for you had gained the name *Young King*; you were
> indeed the guide and father of youth.[53]

In the same song, Bertran compared Henry to Roland, because no-one
before him had loved war so much. It was by this yardstick that the troubadour knight measured the merits of princes, as is emphasised by the
author of his *Vida I*:

> Bertran always wanted war to prevail between the father and the son, and
> between the brothers, one against the other; and he always wanted the King
> of France and the King of England to be at war with each other.[54]

The author of the *Vida II* has an anecdote which is no doubt fictitious
but which nicely expresses the feelings of its protagonists. He imagines a
dialogue between Henry II and Bertran de Born: Bertran had once
boasted that he was so brave that he didn't think he had ever needed to
summon up all his courage (*son esprit*); so the King, when he had taken
him prisoner, said: 'Bertran, you are now going to need all your wits
about you (*votre esprit*).' The troubadour replied that he had lost
courage and wits alike with the death of the Young King. At these words,
the Old King wept, thinking of his son; he pardoned Bertran and gave
him clothes, lands and honours.[55]

Walter Map, who had known the Young King well and called himself
his friend, painted a more nuanced portrait of him soon after his death,
in which admiration is tinged with criticism, and which throws much
light on the turbulent relations between Henry II, Henry the Young King
and Richard:

> As a man of war he had great vision, raising this calling from the lethargy into
> which it had fallen and bringing it to perfection. As his intimate friend, we
> can describe his virtues and his graces. He was the handsomest of men in both
> build and looks, the most gifted in eloquence and affability, the most blessed
> in love, grace and favour; he was so potently persuasive that he tricked almost

all his father's trusted followers into rising against their liege lord . . . in all things he was rich, noble, lovable, eloquent, beautiful, valiant and charming, a 'little lower than the angels'; he applied all his virtues to evil ends and, perverting all his gifts, this man who was brave among the brave became a parricide in his indomitable heart, so that he placed his father's death among his highest desires. It is said that Merlin had prophesied of him: 'The lynx, getting to the heart of all things, will threaten his own people with ruin' . . . he was a prodigious traitor, prodigal in misdeeds, a clear spring of crimes, a pleasing source of mischief, a magnificent palace of sin and the fairest kingdom thereof . . . I frequently saw him break his word to his father. He frequently put a spoke in his father's wheel; but came back to him every time he was worried; he was always ready to commit new crimes, because forgiveness increased his self-confidence . . . War was a fixture in his heart. Knowing his death made Richard, whom he loathed, his father's heir, he died raging mad, but the lord was not angry to see his end.[56]

The death of the Young King restored friendly relations for a while between the sons and their father. Before dying, Henry is said to have asked his father to pardon Eleanor and restore her freedom.[57] The request was granted only in part, but family relations significantly improved. One can almost speak of a reconciliation. The Young Henry's death also put an end, temporarily, to the clashes between the kings of France and England. But Richard, now the eldest son, would quickly take up the torch of rebellion and revive the discord between them. The problem of who was to succeed his father was far from settled and the Old King seemed disinclined to appoint him his successor.

NOTES

1. Robert of Torigny, p. 524; *Gesta Henrici*, I, p. 81; Roger of Howden, II, p. 83. For the events described in this chapter, see Norgate, *England under the Angevin Kings*, pp. 169ff.
2. This is argued most strongly by Régine Pernoud: *Richard Cœur de Lion*, pp. 41ff.
3. For the conflicts between Richard and the Limousin barons, and in particular the role played by Bertran de Born, see the old but still useful study of P. Boissonnade, 'Les Comtes d'Angoulême, les Ligues Féodales Contre Richard Cœur de Lion et les Poésies de Bertran de Born (1176–1194)', *Annales du Midi*, 7 (1895), pp. 275–99, to be read with and sometimes corrected by the introductory notes of G. Gouiran (*Bertran de Born*).
4. This is the opinion of Kurt Lewent, 'Old Provençal Miscellany, 4: The Pseudonym "Oc-e-no"', *Modern Language Review*, 38 (1943), pp.

113–14, which seems to have been adopted by J. Choffel: *Richard Cœur de Lion*, pp. 78ff.

5. Gillingham, *Richard the Lionheart*, p. 243.
6. Walter Map, dist. IV, c. I; Gouiran seems here to be confusing the Young Henry with Richard: *L'Amour et la Guerre*, p. LXVIII.
7. 'Is it an allusion to the fact that the prince came from Outremer?' asks the editor of Bertran de Born, G. Gouiran (*Bertran de Born*, p. LXVII). The choice of 'Rassa' seems rather less obscure; it is an allusion to discord, division and factions, and could equally well be applied to any of the brothers, even to their father.
8. Robert of Torigny, p. 524.
9. *Gesta Henrici*, I, p. 82; Roger of Howden, II, p. 83.
10. Ralph of Diceto, pp. 406ff.
11. According to John Gillingham (*Richard the Lionheart*, pp. 72–3) this revolt was not a continuation of that of 1173, and Aimar switched allegiance because he was disappointed in his hopes of an inheritance in England, through his wife Sarah, eldest daughter of Reginald Earl of Cornwall (an illegitimate son of Henry I), who had died just before Christmas 1174. On his death, Henry II seized his lands in England and Normandy to give them to his son John.
12. *Gesta Henrici*, I, p. 120.
13. *Gesta Henrici*, I, p. 115.
14. Geoffrey of Vigeois, *Chronicon*, ed. Labbe, p. 335.
15. Roger of Howden, II, p. 93; *Gesta Henrici*, I, p. 121. For the meaning of these surrenders of prisoners, see Strickland, *War and Chivalry*, pp. 188–9.
16. *Gesta Henrici*, I, pp. 131–2; Geoffrey of Vigeois, *Recueil des Historiens*, 11, p. 446.
17. Bernard Itier, *Chronique*, p. 25.
18. *Gesta Henrici*, I, p. 168; for the issue of the Vexin and the dowry, see Kessler, *Richard I*, pp. 29ff.
19. Roger of Howden (II, p. 143) says that the marriage was conditional and dependent on the handing over of the dowry. See also Matthew Paris, *Chronica Majora*, II, p. 300.
20. Robert of Torigny, p. 525.
21. Robert of Torigny, p. 526.
22. Geoffrey of Vigeois, *Recueil des Historiens*, 12, pp. 446–7.
23. Roger of Howden, II, p. 166; Matthew Paris, *Chronica Majora*, II, p. 301.
24. Matthew Paris, *Chronica Majora*, II, p. 308. These exploits of the Young Henry in tournaments lasted three years. We should note in passing that tournaments had been forbidden by the Church since the Lateran Council of 1179, as the same chronicler recalls a little further on (p. 310).
25. Ralph of Diceto, I, p. 431; Matthew Paris, *Chronica Majora*, II, p. 315: 'The intrepid Richard threw himself into the town, pell-mell with the enemies who could find nowhere to take refuge.' Robert of Torigny (p. 527) describes the

events in words that evoke Caesar and his Gallic Wars: 'Ricardus dux Aquitaniae . . . castrum Talleborc, quod videbatur inexpugnabile, munitum arte et natura, obsedit, cepit, diruit.'

26. Third Lateran Council, canon 27: *Conciles Œcuméniques*, p. 482; see also Matthew Paris, *Chronica Majora*, II, p. 310; *Gesta Henrici*, I, p. 228.
27. Rigord, §3, p. 11.
28. Robert of Torigny, p. 527; *Gesta Henrici*, I, p. 241; Roger of Howden, II, p. 192; Ralph of Diceto, I, p. 432; Gervase of Canterbury, I, p. 293; Matthew Paris, *Chronica Majora*, II, p. 309.
29. Rigord, 4, p. 12; Ralph of Diceto, I, p. 438; Roger of Howden, II, p. 194; Matthew Paris, *Chronica Majora*, II, p. 314.
30. Geoffrey of Vigeois, *Recueil des Historiens*, 13, p. 449.
31. *Gesta Henrici*, I, p. 169, and *Select Charters and Other Illustrations of English Constitutional History*, ed. W. Stubbs (Oxford, 1913), 9th edn, pp. 181–4.
32. Gerald of Wales, *De Principis Instructione*, p. 229.
33. *Recueil des Historiens des Gaules et de la France*, XVIII, p. 33; for these episodes see Cartellieri, *Philipp II*, vol. 1, pp. 88–90.
34. Geoffrey of Vigeois, *Recueil des Historiens*, 18, pp. 213–14; Bertran de Born, ed. Gouiran, nos 10, 11.
35. See, for example, *Gesta Henrici*, I, pp. 291–3; Gervase of Canterbury, I, pp. 82ff.
36. See Gillingham, *Richard the Lionheart*, p. 89.
37. Ralph of Diceto, II, p. 10; Ralph of Coggeshall, p. 20; Boussard, *Gouvernement d'Henri II*, p. 450.
38. Bertran de Born, ed. Gouiran, no. 15: 'Corz e gestas e joi d'amour', p. 281.
39. *Guillaume le Maréchal*, lines 5128ff.; Duby, *William Marshal*, pp. 46ff.
40. *Chronique des Evêques de Périgueux*, *Recueil des Historiens des Gaules et de la France*, XII, p. 392.
41. Bertran de Born, ed. Gouiran, no. 11, p. 203: 'D'un sirventes no-m cal far loignor ganda'; text p. 209: stanza 2.
42. Matthew Paris, *Chronica Majora*, II, pp. 317–18.
43. Roger of Howden, II, p. 274.
44. The interpretation of these events is difficult because the chroniclers give different versions. See for example, *Gesta Henrici*, pp. 291ff.; Roger of Howden, pp. 274ff.; Ralph of Diceto, II, pp. 18–19; Geoffrey of Vigeois, ed. Labbe, p. 337. According to Gillingham, Richard's intention was to protect himself not against the Young Henry but against the Viscount of Châtellerault: *Richard the Lionheart*, pp. 90–2.
45. Bertran de Born, ed. Gouiran, no. 10, p. 190.
46. Roger of Howden, II, pp. 274–6; *Gesta Henrici*, I, pp. 292–3.
47. Ralph of Diceto, II, p. 19. See also *Gesta Henrici*, I, pp. 300–4; Roger of Howden, II, pp. 278–9; Geoffrey of Vigeois, *Recueil des Historiens*, 18, p. 218.

48. Geoffrey of Vigeois, ed. Labbe, pp. 337ff. and *Recueil des Historiens*, 18, pp. 220ff.
49. Rigord, §25, p. 37.
50. Norgate, *England under the Angevin Kings*, vol. 2, p. 229.
51. Robert of Torigny, p. 533; Gerald of Wales, *De Principis Instructione*, pp. 172–3; William of Newburgh, p. 233; Matthew Paris, *Chronica Majora*, II, pp. 317–18; Ralph of Coggeshall, p. 20.
52. *Guillaume le Maréchal*, lines 6985–8.
53. Bertran de Born, ed. Gouiran, no. 13: 'Mon chan fenis ab dol et ab maltraire', p. 241 (p. 218 of Paden translation); see also song no. 14, pp. 260ff., less surely attributed to Bertran.
54. Life of Bertran de Born according to the *Vida I*, trans. Gouiran, *Bertran de Born*, pp. 1–2.
55. *Vida II*, trans. Gouiran, *Bertran de Born*, pp. 3–4.
56. Walter Map, IV, 1.
57. Geoffrey of Vigeois, *Recueil des Historiens*, 18, p. 220.

3

Richard the Eldest Son, Duke of Aquitaine (1184–9)

∾

CONFLICTS AND THE DEATH OF GEOFFREY

The death of his brother made Richard the legitimate heir to the Plantagenet empire. He had no intention of replacing Henry in his role of king-in-waiting, lacking all power, even less of relinquishing the government of Aquitaine, whose prince he meant to be, as successor to his mother, still a prisoner or at least under house arrest.

But this was the offer, not to say order, he received from his father, at Angers, in September 1183. Two factors persuaded the Old King to adopt these new arrangements. The first was unchanged since the time of the Montmirail settlement: Henry had no wish to divide his empire between his sons or even to share real power with them. The most he would accept was a sort of confederation of fiefs which they would hold, under his authority, and which he would transmit on his death – but only then – to his designated successor. Richard was now the eldest son, but Henry II distrusted him for his quick temper, his fits of rage and his independent temperament. He perhaps preferred, at least on occasion, his brother Geoffrey and even more, since Geoffrey's recent treachery, his hitherto neglected youngest son, John. The conquest of Ireland provided an opportunity to repair in part this neglect: Henry II meant John to inherit the crown and, in 1185, after knighting him at the age of eighteen, to all intents and purposes made him King of Ireland.[1]

The second reason is closely linked to his growing interest in John. Henry wanted to amend the earlier settlement to the latter's advantage. Richard was to take the place of his deceased brother and become King of England, leaving Aquitaine to John.

Richard controlled his anger, asked for a few days to think things over, then let his actions speak for themselves: he leapt on his horse, rode posthaste to Poitou and sent a messenger to inform his father that he would allow no-one to lay hands on Aquitaine. The dissension had

resurfaced and a furious Henry made an extremely unwise statement to the effect that Aquitaine would belong to whoever could take it. John and Geoffrey quickly joined forces; they hired mercenaries and began to lay waste to Poitou. Richard did the same, taking on a large number of routiers, including a leader who was to become his faithful right arm and one of the most famous warriors of his day, Mercadier. Bertran de Born, too, now changed sides to join Richard, whom he had previously opposed. With Richard's assent, he had obtained from Henry II sole possession of his castle, and his loyalty to the Count of Poitou would in future be total. He helped Richard against Aimar of Limoges, the perennial rebel and once his ally.[2]

Henry II soon realised the disastrous consequences of his angry outburst and tried in vain to restore harmony with placatory speeches. But only military action could achieve his purpose. Fearing the two brothers would go too far against Richard, he helped the latter to carry out several raids in Brittany, which had the immediate effect of causing Geoffrey to return to his duchy and separating him from John. And so, but not without difficulty, Henry II was able to reconcile the three brothers in time for the Christmas court of 1184, which was held at Westminster.

He also needed to reach a settlement with Philip Augustus. With the death of the Young Henry, the King of France had demanded the return of Margaret's dowry and he was also pressing Henry to marry Alice to Richard at long last. The two kings met in December 1183, between Gisors and Trie, and a compromise was agreed. Henry did homage to Philip for his continental lands, something he had always previously refused to do; Philip Augustus agreed to relinquish Gisors to Henry, in return for an annual payment of £1,700 and on condition it was given to whichever of Henry's sons married Alice, who had now been in Henry's custody for a very long time.[3]

Why this new and vague reference to a husband for Alice? Many explanations are possible: Henry II, who had probably made Alice his concubine while she was still a child, was reluctant to separate from her and wanted to play for time; Richard, for his part, had little desire to marry Alice and, in any case, a more prestigious match, with one of the daughters of the Emperor Frederick Barbarossa, was on the horizon, though her death soon scotched these hopes. These seem to me the most probable reasons. It is not impossible, as argued by Gillingham, that Richard and his father were at one in wanting to keep Alice perpetually in their custody and unmarried, thereby keeping all options open, while simultaneously preventing the King of France from marrying her to a rival.[4] The disadvantages of such a scheme, however, seem to me to

make it highly improbable, unless we assume a truly Machiavellian plot on the part of Henry II. In fact, by constantly postponing the celebration of the marriage, Henry was providing the King of France with a permanent lever and pretext for hostilities.[5] Can this really have been what he wanted? And is it plausible to suppose a sustained agreement between Henry and Richard, on such a delicate matter, when father and son were so frequently at odds? In some ways, the marriage would be advantageous to Richard since, if he rebelled against his father, he would be able to call with some confidence on the support of the King of France. Both diplomacy and political advantage seem to me to argue in favour of a celebration of the marriage. The obstacles preventing it, consequently, must have been of a different nature, and were probably personal and private.[6]

After the Trie agreement, Henry II tried to settle the problem of his succession by more devious means. John, who was to get Ireland, seemed for the moment content, though his army was to be decisively routed soon after his arrival in the country.[7] Geoffrey, however, asked for Anjou to be added to his duchy of Brittany. Richard was enraged and prepared to confront his brother once again. He returned to Poitiers soon after the 1184 Christmas court. In the following April, Henry thought he had found a solution that would satisfy both parties while forcing Richard to give way, though without losing face. Eleanor, as we have seen, had enjoyed relative freedom since the summer of 1183. She had been allowed, for example, to leave England and travel to Rouen to visit her son's tomb. Henry now decided it would be expedient to restore her political rights, at least temporarily.[8] Richard could hardly refuse to do homage to his mother, legitimate 'lord' of Aquitaine, and this he did, before returning to his father's court, where the atmosphere now seemed more relaxed. E.-R. Labande has pointed out that the grant of temporary liberty of Eleanor was a political manoeuvre on the part of her husband. He wanted

> to use her simply as a means of blackmailing Richard to make him give way . . . as soon as Richard showed signs of submitting again, Eleanor was brought back to England and a blanket of silence descends, as far as she is concerned.[9]

In fact, by this agreement, Henry retained real power in Aquitaine as elsewhere; Eleanor was temporarily restored as Duchess of Aquitaine, but only in name, and Richard was once again no more than the heir to his mother's lands.

The Christmas court of 1185, held by Henry II at Domfront, reveals a relative harmony. Henry seemed to have recovered a degree of serenity

tinged with realism. He refused the crown of Jerusalem, for example, which was offered to him on the death of his cousin, Baldwin IV, aged only twenty-four. He wanted to devote himself to the government of his Angevin empire.

But Geoffrey had not spoken his last word; he persisted in claiming at least part of Anjou, cradle of his father's power, which would put him almost on a par with Richard. He was probably egged on by the French court, which renewed its pressure. Henry and Philip Augustus met once again, at Gisors, on 10 March 1186. The matter of the dowry of Margaret, the Young King's widow, was settled to general satisfaction: in return for payment of an annual indemnity of 2,700 *livres angevines* to Margaret (who was shortly to marry Bela II of Hungary), Henry could keep her dowry, together with Gisors. Philip Augustus promised not to raise the issue again. Philip and Henry also agreed on a husband for Alice: it was to be Richard.[10]

This agreement between the two kings encouraged Henry II to support Richard in the conflict that arose, in April 1186, between his son and Raymond of Toulouse. During the earlier confrontation, Raymond had supported the Young Henry against Richard. His mercenaries had ravaged part of Limousin and may have reconquered some of the lands lost long ago in Quercy. Determined to take his revenge and recover them, Henry II granted a large sum of money to Richard to enable him to recruit an army. Richard invaded Raymond's lands with his soldiers and subdued them. Raymond appealed in vain for the assistance of the King of France. Philip had no wish to annoy Henry and took no action, so attracting the derision of Bertran de Born, always in favour of war.[11] In any case, the King of France had other schemes in mind. Geoffrey, still in revolt against both his father and Richard, took refuge at his court, where he won the friendship, affection and, some said, even the love of Philip Augustus; they were seen together everywhere, in public and in private, and scarcely left each other's side. Philip made Geoffrey seneschal of France, a title reserved, as we have seen, for the Count of Anjou, and so seemingly accepting him as such. This risked increasing the tension between the two monarchs. But then, during a tournament, Geoffrey fell awkwardly from his mount and was badly trampled by other horses. He died soon after, aged twenty-eight, on 21 August 1186, in spite of the attentions lavished on him by the many doctors summoned by Philip Augustus. His embalmed body was solemnly buried in Paris, in the choir of the cathedral of Notre Dame, then still unfinished.[12] The King of France showed such despair on this occasion that contemporaries were deeply impressed. This is how Gerald of Wales describes the scene:

King Philip was afflicted with such deep sorrow and despair at his death, that, in proof both of his love for him and of the honour in which he was held, the count was ordered by him to be buried before the high altar in the cathedral church of Paris, which is dedicated to the blessed Virgin; and at the end of the funeral service, when the body was being lowered into the grave, he would have thrown himself into the gaping tomb with the body, if he had not been forcibly restrained by those who were around him. However, the grief of his father was beyond all grief that had ever been.[13]

NEW DISAGREEMENTS

The grief of the two kings did not, however, bring them any closer together. Philip Augustus demanded custody of Brittany and also of Geoffrey's two daughters, until the elder, Eleanor, reached marriageable age. He received Geoffrey's pregnant widow, Constance, at his court where, on 29 March, she gave birth to a son, posthumously named Arthur; his name is clear evidence of the influence of chivalric romances on this family and of the political advantage they hoped to gain from them among the people and especially the Celtic people, among whom the Arthurian legends were especially popular. Philip threatened, should he refuse, to invade Normandy, and even began to do so. The risk of war was very great and Henry tried to calm things down by sending Ranulf Glanville to negotiate a truce, which was to last until 13 January 1187.[14] Philip agreed to cease his attacks on Normandy provided that Richard stopped attacking Count Raymond of Toulouse.[15] The King of France also once again raised the matter of Alice's dowry. Numerous meetings were held to discuss this, but to no avail. At one of them, on 25 March 1187 at Nonancourt, the truce was renewed, but Richard did not consider himself bound by these agreements and continued his war. This gave Philip Augustus the pretext to intervene in Berry, in June, and lay siege to Châteauroux. Richard, assisted by his brother John, stood firm and refused to surrender the town, waiting for the large army assembled by his father to come to his aid.

With its arrival, a pitched battle between the two royal armies seemed inevitable. On 23 June, however, the two kings drew back. Such battles were extremely risky and assumed the character of a judgement of God. Kings generally avoided them. Before Bouvines, the Capetian kings had fought only one, at Brémules in 1119. Even here, the battle was not all-out, as Orderic Vitalis observed.[16] Henry II, though engaged in conflicts all his life, never fought a pitched battle; nor, as has been said, did Richard, before his departure on crusade.[17] At Châteauroux, the two

kings were apparently as one in wishing to avoid such a risky venture, in which death, mutilation or – a king or a prince's worst fear – capture, were at stake. In any case, the Church intervened in an attempt to end this major conflict between two Christian kings at a time when the situation in the Holy Land desperately required unity behind the Cross and the despatch of reinforcements to save the kingdom of Jerusalem, threatened by the Muslim armies which, united under Saladin's command, were reviving the recently dormant notion of the jihad. The papal legates entrusted with this message did their best to reconcile the kings, both of whom were willing, as long as they did not lose face.[18] It was also said that a celestial sign had warned Richard's pillaging mercenaries, in Châteauroux itself, to stop this impious war: one of his routiers had lost at dice in the square in front of the church; in his disappointment, blaspheming horribly, he had thrown a stone at a statue of the Virgin holding the Infant Jesus; the child's arm had been broken and it had proceeded to bleed profusely, to the amazement of the assembled routiers.[19] This was interpreted as clear proof of divine disapproval.

On top of this, the vassals of the crown of France were increasingly reluctant to participate in Philip's military campaigns and offered to mediate. Henry requested a truce, on the pretext of his need to prepare for his departure for Jerusalem. Philip did not believe him, but engaged in talks all the same. Richard, at the instigation of the Count of Flanders and the Archbishop of Reims, had a change of heart and took on the role of intermediary, shuttling back and forth between the camps of his father and the King of France. His role as mediator won him Philip's goodwill. Yet another truce was agreed, to last for two years, which settled nothing in the long term.[20] For the moment, however, Philip Augustus retained his recent conquests, in particular Issoudun and Fréteval.

This was not all; Richard, following in the footsteps of his brother Geoffrey, accompanied the King of France to his court in Paris, and the two men were soon on equally affectionate terms. This new-found intimacy was a cause of serious concern to Henry II; they were constantly seen together, they ate at the same table and, said several chroniclers, they were inseparable even at night.[21] Henry had good reason for his anxiety, because such a relationship would inevitably give rise to new political and family problems. Philip had told Richard that his father had planned to marry Alice to his brother John, who would then receive Anjou and possibly Poitou.[22] In other words, Richard was to be supplanted in favour of his younger brother. Henry tried to calm Richard down and woo him back by soft words and promises. It looked as if he had succeeded when

his son left Philip's court, but not so. Richard rode posthaste to Chinon, seized his father's treasure chest and returned to Poitou, where he forti-fied his castles. Relations deteriorated, but, in the end, Henry managed to convince Richard of his good intentions and he eventually did homage to his father at Angers.[23]

TOWARDS THE CRUSADE?

This may still only have been a truce, but a new turn of events was to reconcile the two protagonists in the longer term. On 4 July 1187, in the Holy Land, Guy of Lusignan, King of Jerusalem in right of his wife Sibylla, heiress to the kingdom, foolishly agreed to the pitched battle proposed by Saladin on terrain highly unfavourable to the Christians. This was ill-conceived strategically: after an exhausting march in the heat of the day, followed by a sleepless night, with the troops weary, without water and poorly commanded, the battle ended in a total rout at the Horns of Hattin.[24] The Christian army was annihilated; the captive Templars and Hospitallers were put to death on the spot, in the presence of Saladin, who executed Raymond of Châtillon with his own hands. Even worse, the relic of the Holy Cross, regarded as a talismanic protec-tor, passed into Saladin's hands;[25] Jerusalem fell soon after. All that remained to the Christians was a narrow coastal strip, with the fort-resses of Antioch, Tripoli and Tyre and a few isolated castles in Muslim territory.

The news caused immense dismay in the West. Pope Urban III died on hearing it; his successor, Gregory VIII, died in his turn, in December 1187, after urging the emperor, and then the whole of Christendom, to take the cross.[26] Outremer appealed for help and messengers were sent to the West in an attempt to rekindle enthusiasm for the crusade; they sometimes made use of mimed scenes designed to move their audiences.[27] These envoys included Jocelyn, Archbishop of Tyre, who made moving speeches to the kings, but was slow to persuade them as they were reluc-tant to leave.[28] The crusading message was powerfully put across, mean-while, in France, England and Wales by such eloquent preachers as Peter of Blois and Archbishop Baldwin of Canterbury.[29] It was now some years since Henry II had taken a crusading vow but he still postponed his departure. He had insufficient confidence in his family to be able to leave without fear of what they would do in his absence. Nor was Philip Augustus without his anxieties. Apart from the risk of the conflict flaring up again in his absence, he was concerned about his succession. His wife Isabella had so far failed to provide him with an heir. The birth of a son,

the future Louis VIII, in September 1187, hardly encouraged him to abandon his family. In any case, the two kings could only depart simultaneously, so deep was their mutual distrust.

Richard beat them to it; he was the first to answer the call, in November 1187, as all the chroniclers observed. Immediately he heard news of the capture of Jerusalem, even before hearing the Archbishop of Tyre preach, he took the cross at Tours, from the hands of its archbishop, and promised to avenge the insult to Christ. The chroniclers all also emphasise, which is significant, that he took this decision without seeking the advice of his father or regard for his wishes.[30] But it was still some time, as we will see, before he was to fulfil his promise.

Richard's decision led Philip Augustus to revive his demands; he could hardly allow Richard to depart for an indefinite period without his marriage to Alice being finally celebrated. When Henry II returned to England after holding his Christmas court at Caen, Philip seized his opportunity; early in January 1188, he threatened to invade Normandy and lay it waste unless the King of England returned Gisors and its territory or married Alice to Richard.[31] Henry immediately returned to Normandy and requested a meeting, which took place on 21 January, between Gisors and Trie.[32] The Archbishop of Tyre took advantage of this meeting between the kings to preach an impassioned appeal on behalf of the crusade; its impact on his audience was much enhanced, we are told, by the appearance in the sky of a cross signifying heavenly approval of his cause. The kings, persuaded by the intervention of the Holy Spirit, agreed to be reconciled and to take the cross; many of their vassals followed suit, notably Count Philip of Flanders. To distinguish the various contingents, it was decided that they would wear crosses of different colours, red for the French, white for the English and green for the Flemings. While Richard prepared for his voyage, Henry II sent letters to the Emperor Frederick, who promised Richard free passage through his lands, and to the new King of Hungary, Bela, who made a similar commitment. Richard was clearly planning an overland journey.[33] The Emperor Frederick also took the cross and made his preparations to depart. He left two months later, only to be drowned on the way, on 10 June 1190, attempting to swim across a river in Asia Minor.[34]

The two kings each took immediate advantage of their decision: they proclaimed a moratorium on the debts of crusaders (their own included) and imposed new and heavy taxes on both the laity and the clergy, amounting to approximately ten per cent of annual income and consequently known as the Saladin Tithe. The crusaders, of course, were exempt, perhaps causing some of them finally to make up their minds.[35]

But the princes and kings did not depart. Worse, war flared up between them yet again. The Poitevin barons, embroiled in their own quarrels, actually rebelled once more, incited by Aimar of Angoulême, brother and successor of William Taillefer, and by Geoffrey de Rancon and Raymond of Toulouse. It was Geoffrey of Lusignan, however, even though he was the King of Jerusalem's brother, who fanned the flames by treacherously killing one of Richard's close advisers. To avenge his death, Richard took up arms and defeated Geoffrey's troops, sparing his men if they would take the cross; he put the rest to the sword and seized a number of castles. But the other barons resisted, with the support, or so it was said, of Henry II's money, which obviously roused Richard's wrath against his father.[36] He eventually succeeded in crushing Geoffrey and then, with his army of Brabançons, attacked the lands of Toulouse. He rapidly seized many castles in Quercy, in violation of the earlier agreement specifying the maintenance of the status quo.[37] It was probably Richard's success in the Toulousain that brought him into a close alliance with Sancho VI of Navarre, and it may well be that it was now that agreement was reached on the marriage between Richard and Sancho's daughter, Berengaria, which was 'officially' celebrated at Limassol three years later.[38]

Raymond of Toulouse asked for Philip's assistance, and this attempted annexation finally roused him to anger. The King of France invaded Berry, after receiving assurances from Henry II that this time he would not come to Richard's aid. Philip took Châteauroux with great ease on 16 June 1188 and he appeared to have the support of many lords, who abandoned Richard and went over to his side. Yet again, Richard was in serious difficulties. He informed his father of the secret accord between Philip and Raymond of Toulouse.[39] Yet again, Henry came to his aid; he assembled an 'immense army', largely consisting of foot soldiers and Welsh archers, invaded the kingdom of France and devastated the countryside between Verneuil and La Mayenne.[40] Philip felt he had to abandon Berry in order to protect the heartland of his kingdom, facing Normandy. Richard's hands were thus freed, and he tried vainly to recapture Châteauroux, held by a close ally of the King of France, William des Barres, of whom more later. During the siege, Richard was attacked by a group of French warriors, put to flight, thrown from his horse and saved in the nick of time by a butcher.[41]

Further north, there were more clashes after the failure of talks held in the traditional meeting place, under an elm tree, between Gisors and Trie. The only outcome was the destruction of the elm, felled by the French, enraged at having been kept waiting in the full glare of the sun, throughout the deliberations, while the English delegation strutted about in the

shade of this ancient tree.[42] The Bishop of Beauvais, decidedly more of a warrior than an ecclesiastic, invaded Normandy, burned several towns and devastated the region; the King of France did the same. He formally renounced all ties with Henry II and went so far as to announce his intention of seizing Berry and the Norman Vexin. In the face of this threat, on 30 August, Henry roused himself from his torpor; he led his army into France, burning a number of towns and villages in his turn and, with Richard, rode on Mantes, where he had been told he would find the King of France. During the skirmishes, Richard captured William des Barres, who was paroled, but who fled, it was said, on his servant's rouncey. This may have been the reason for the animosity Richard showed towards him in future. The victory of the Plantagenets was stunning and the booty abundant. Reassured about his father's intentions, Richard returned to wage war in Berry, burning Vendôme on the way, its lord having sided with Philip.[43] Bertran de Born applauded the resumption of hostilities, always the cause of princely generosity towards the knights:

> I cannot help but spread my song around, since the lord Yea and Nay has been burning and shedding blood, because a great war makes the miserly lord generous.[44]

The conflict seemed to be getting bogged down, but really it was running out of steam, the French barons being reluctant to fight against other princes who had taken the cross, risking excommunication. The counts of Flanders and Blois refused to bear arms until they had returned from crusade. Their defection led to another set of talks, at Châtillon, on 7 October 1188, which proved abortive.[45]

There was a further consideration: these campaigns were expensive and a heavy drain on the money set aside for the crusade. Public opinion, encouraged by the Church, was turning against the war. These circumstances combined to favour a negotiated agreement and preparations were made for a meeting to be held at Bonsmoulins. The parties started from widely divergent positions. The King of France proposed that the respective conquests be nullified by a return to the status quo, which meant that Richard would have to return Quercy to the Count of Toulouse, in return for which Philip would surrender Berry. Hoping that by negotiating directly with Philip he would get a better deal, Richard soon announced that he would accept the judgement of the King of France, much to the annoyance of his father.[46] Philip Augustus saw his opportunity and set out to widen the rift between father and son: he made it known to Richard, through the intermediary of several princes, that his father was preparing to disinherit him in favour of his younger brother, John.[47]

It was in this unsettled atmosphere that the talks at Bonsmoulins took place, starting on 18 November 1188. Before they ended, Richard laid down his conditions: first, he refused to surrender his conquests in Quercy and second, he asked his father to designate him unequivocally his heir. As usual, Henry prevaricated and gave an evasive answer, thereby reinforcing Richard's fears and causing him to move closer to Philip Augustus.

During the talks, Philip and Richard spelled out once again their common demands: Richard was to be designated heir; he should be given assurances that he would soon be made King of England; homage should be done to him in this capacity; and he would at last marry Alice. Henry refused these demands and took no action. Richard got the message and his earlier suspicions appeared justified. He proclaimed: 'Things are now made plain that I had thought incredible'; then, in theatrical fashion, he turned his back on his father and did homage to the King of France for his continental possessions.[48] The rupture was complete, in spite of the conclusion of a truce until mid January 1189. The French chronicler Rigord is probably mistaken in putting the emphasis on the question of the marriage of Alice:

> At the same period, Richard Count of Poitiers asked his father for the wife he was rightfully owed, that is, the sister of King Philip of France, who had been handed over to his custody by Louis, of blessed memory; and with her, he asked also for the kingdom, because the pact said that whichever of the sons of the king of England had her for wife, would also have the king-dom on the death of the present king. Richard said that this was his by right because, after the death of his brother Henry, he was the eldest. The King of England, irritated on hearing this, declared that he would do no such thing. On account of which Richard was deeply troubled, separated pub-licly from his father, went over to the Most Christian King of the French and, in his father's presence, did homage to King Philip and signed a treaty under oath.[49]

Roger of Howden's account is probably more reliable. He emphasises the advantages to Richard in doing homage to Philip:

> During this meeting, Richard Count of Poitou, without either the counsel or approval of his father the King of England, became the man of King Philip of France for Normandy, Poitou and Anjou, Maine, Berry and the Toul-ousain, and for all his other continental fiefs; and he swore loyalty to him against all, except for the loyalty he owed his father. For this oath and homage, King Philip of France promised to restore to him Châteauroux and all the castles and lands he had occupied in Berry; and he returned Issoudun to him . . .[50]

Gerald of Wales interprets this same episode slightly differently, emphasising the duplicity of Henry II and the alliance of Richard and Philip against him:

> The Count of Poitou, seeing at last that he could in no way obtain from his father, by his entreaties, the oath of loyalty of the barons, and who suspected his father, from wickedness and jealousy of his successor, unjustly to prefer his younger brothers, at once, and in the presence of his father, went over to the French king. He immediately did homage to him for all the Continental lands which would be his by hereditary right. And for this reason, they bound themselves by oath in a mutual alliance, and the king promised the count his aid to conquer, against his father, these continental lands. This was the cause of the discord and the implacable dissension which never ceased, in his father, to the last day of his life.[51]

At all events, Richard had performed an act of defiance and nobody was in any doubt about this at the time. When King Henry held his Christmas court in 1188 at Saumur, in the company of John alone, he had to face the sad truth that his policy had failed; his sons had rebelled against him one after the other and his barons were beginning to abandon him and make overtures to Richard, while Philip and his allies were invading his lands.[52] Illness, furthermore, was taking its toll; he informed Richard and warned him that it would prevent him from attending the peace talks arranged for the middle of January. He summoned him to his bedside. Richard's distrust of his father was so great that he did not believe a word of it, assuming it was just another trick. The tension continued, therefore, as did the skirmishes, without any serious attempts to make peace. It took the intervention of the papal legate John of Anagni to make the two kings agree to meet and submit their differences to arbitration, under the direction of several prelates.

The meeting was held at Whitsun 1189, at La Ferté-Bernard. Once again it was a failure, and once again Philip spoke for Richard, now his ally: his demands, recorded by several chroniclers, are clearly summarised by Matthew Paris:

> The King of France requested that his sister, Alice, long ago handed over to the custody of the King of England, should be given as wife to Richard, Count of Poitou, and that the latter be given assurances that he would receive the kingdom of England on his father's death. He also requested that John, son of Henry, take the cross and leave for Jerusalem, stating that Richard would certainly not leave without his brother. But the King of England would not agree to any of these demands, and they separated on bad terms.[53]

In fact, in response to this proposal from Philip and Richard, Henry made one of his own. It, too, was hardly new. He suggested that John, and not Richard, should marry Alice, which Philip refused, as did Richard; this would have been to agree to being set aside in favour of his younger brother.[54] Fearing that the talks would collapse, Cardinal Anagni tried to put pressure on Richard by threatening his lands with an interdict if he refused to submit to his father. A furious Richard accused the cardinal of colluding with Henry, who, he said, must have bought him with his gold; he rushed at him, his sword drawn, and only the intervention of several barons was able to calm him down; they assured him that the legate had resorted to this threat only in the interests of the success of the crusade.[55]

THE DEATH OF THE OLD KING

The failure of the talks, in any case, was complete. Henry withdrew to Le Mans and hostilities resumed. Philip and Richard seized La Ferté-Bernard, Montfort, Beaumont, Ballon and a few other castles in the neighbourhood of Le Mans belonging to the King of England. Then, after feinting a march on Tours, they laid siege to Le Mans, where Henry II had thought he was safe. He had been despaired of and confessed his sins (though not all of them, observed a hostile chronicler),[56] but then taken a turn for the better and he was now ready to confront his enemies.

Philip was preparing to mount an assault on Le Mans when Henry's seneschal set fire to the suburbs, to make it easier to defend the town and to hamper the attackers; but the flames spread over the walls and burned down the town. The French took advantage of this to enter the citadel behind the men of the King of England, who fled in great haste towards Normandy with seven hundred knights, pursued by Richard.[57] The latter reached Henry's rearguard, which was commanded by William Marshal, who had remained faithful to the Old King. Here, according to one chronicler, Richard had his horse killed under him by a thrust from the lance of an enemy knight,[58] which prevented him from continuing his pursuit. Henry was able to escape and take refuge in Tours. The *History of William the Marshal* tells us that this knight was William himself and that he decided to spare Richard, at Richard's request, because he was without his hauberk; William confined himself to killing his horse to make it impossible for him to proceed.[59]

While Henry II, who was again sick, took refuge in Chinon, Philip and Richard ravaged the Touraine. Philip, who was familiar with the fords, showed his army a way across the Loire, near Tours. Rigord emphasises this exploit, hitherto unheard of in history, embellishing it with a sign

from heaven of biblical inspiration: the King of France entered the river, sounded its depth with his lance, placed markers to indicate the ford and had his army make the crossing; miraculously, the water level dropped as the French crossed. This event struck fear into the inhabitants of Tours and the combined forces of Philip and Richard soon took the town in a furious and victorious assault.[60] Henry's defeat became inevitable and he was abandoned by nearly all his supporters, with the notable exception of the faithful William Marshal. The Old King's son John had also gone over to the enemy, at a very late stage, apparently without his father's knowledge.[61]

Henry was defeated and forced to submit. Worn out, it was all he could do to ride to Ballon, between Tours and Azay-le-Rideau, to meet his victors, who dictated their terms. Henry had to accept this 'shameful peace', from which he never recovered.

Its terms can be summarised as follows: territorially, it amounted, by and large, to a return to the status quo. Everything that had been taken from the King of England was to be restored, including Châteauroux and the region of Bourges, but the King of France was to have peaceful ownership of everything that his ancestors had possessed in Auvergne. Bertran de Born was up in arms and accused Philip of going soft; he composed a song praising the valour of Richard, compared to a lion, and condemning the pusillanimity of Philip: 'Papiol, make haste, tell Richard from me that he is a lion. And King Philip seems to me a lamb, letting himself be stripped of his possessions in this way'.[62] Some of the chroniclers saw the clause dealing with Auvergne as the fulfilment of a prophesy of Merlin reported by Geoffrey of Monmouth.[63] The King of France was also to receive an indemnity of 20,000 marks for the expenses incurred in the siege of Châteauroux and his assistance to Richard. Henry was to do homage in person to Philip, which he had previously refused. Richard was to receive the homage of the lords of lands in all his father's continental possessions. Lastly, Alice, the sister of the King of France, was to be handed over into the custody of Richard, who would marry her on his return from the Holy Land.

Was the Old King, vanquished and humiliated, still dreaming of taking his revenge? Gerald of Wales, though admittedly only he, suggests that he was; he tells a strange story to this effect:

> It had been concluded in the agreement that [King Henry] should give his son, the Count of Poitiers, the kiss of peace, and should banish from his heart all anger and indignation; and when this was done, and the kiss given, although it was really a charade, as he left, the Count heard his father mutter, 'May the Lord grant me not to die until I have taken due vengeance upon you.'[64]

Richard, adds Gerald, went straight to tell the King of France and his court, where everyone laughed heartily, so futile seemed the Old King's wish.

And futile it was. Henry was carried to Chinon, where he died not long after, defeated by illness and exhaustion, and perhaps even more by despair. He was only fifty-six years old, but he surrendered to death on learning that the list of barons who had betrayed him was headed by his son John, on whose behalf he had undertaken his last battles. Devastated, lying on his couch, he turned his face to the wall and lay prostrate for several hours. He died on 6 July, after reigning for thirty-four years and seven months. The rapacious courtiers wasted no time; they seized his belongings, even stripping him of his rich robe, leaving him almost naked on the ground.[65] Many chroniclers attributed the rebellion of his sons and his death to divine punishment.[66]

Henry II had often expressed a wish to be buried at Grandmont and had made the appropriate arrangements. But it was the middle of summer, the weather was hot and transporting his body posed many problems. William Marshal chose Fontevraud for his burial, the great nearby abbey in which Henry, even before Eleanor, had long shown interest.[67] So his body was carried from Chinon to Fontevraud and into the abbey church, where his beautiful effigy can still be seen. Richard went very briefly, in the evening, to contemplate the corpse, without apparently showing the slightest emotion. If we are to believe some chroniclers, his father, though dead, showed rather more: on Richard's arrival, blood began to flow from his nostrils and only stopped when he left.[68] One chronicler alone, writing much later and more conciliatorily, completes this episode with a scene that may have been inspired by Peter's repentance after his denial of Christ:

> His son Richard, learning of the death of his father, went in great haste to see him, his heart overflowing with remorse. As soon as he arrived, blood began to flow from the nostrils of the corpse, as if the soul of the deceased was indignant at the arrival of he who had been the cause of his death, and as if the blood was crying out to God. At this sight, the Count was filled with self-loathing and began to weep bitterly.[69]

Richard now became the rightful king of England.[70]

NOTES

1. *Gesta Henrici*, I, p. 336; Ralph of Diceto, p. 34; Matthew Paris, *Chronica Majora*, II, p. 322.
2. Bertran de Born, ed. Gouiran, no. 18, p. 306.

3. *Gesta Henrici*, I, p. 306.

4. Gillingham, *Richard Cœur de Lion*, p. 105.

5. Admittedly, one could just as well put forward the contrary argument, that is, if Richard had married Alice, he would have had even more reasons for rebelling against his father, confident of the King of France's support.

6. In spite of the reluctance of most (good) historians to admit that considerations of this sort play a part in the conduct of political affairs, it remains the case that personal preferences often play a significant role in the decisions of those in power. This is particularly true of the Plantagenet family.

7. In April 1185, according to the *Gesta Henrici*, I, p. 339.

8. *Gesta Henrici*, I, p. 337.

9. Labande, 'Une Image Véridique', p. 215.

10. Roger of Howden, II, p. 308; *Gesta Henrici*, I, p. 344.

11. *Gesta Henrici*, I, p. 345; Bertran de Born, ed. Gouiran, no. 26, pp. 531ff.

12. *Gesta Henrici*, I, pp. 350, 361; Roger of Howden, II, p. 309; Ralph of Diceto, II, p. 41; Ralph of Coggeshall, p. 20 (1186); Matthew Paris, *Chronica Majora*, II, p. 324; Rigord, 44, p. 68 (with a date in need of correction).

13. Gerald of Wales, *De Principis Instructione*, pp. 175–6.

14. *Gesta Henrici*, I, pp. 353–5, 358; Ralph of Coggeshall, p. 20; Ralph of Diceto, II, p. 48.

15. 'Summa petitionis Francorum haec fuit ut, si Ricardus comes Pictavensis ab infestatione comitis Sancti Egidii temperaret, ab infestationibus essent immunes Normanni', wrote Ralph Diceto (II, pp. 43–4), which does not stop John Gillingham from wondering whether the agreement extended to the war in Toulouse: *Richard Cœur de Lion*, p. 104.

16. *Orderic Vitalis*, ed. Chibnall, vol. 6, p. 238. For the rarity of pitched battles in the twelfth century, see Duby, *Dimanche de Bouvines*, p. 148; Flori, *Chevaliers et Chevalerie*, pp. 114ff.

17. If we exclude his battle against Aimar of Limoges near Saint-Maigrin in 1176. See, on this point, Gillingham, J., 'Richard I and the Science of War in the Middle Ages', in Gillingham and Holt, *War and Government*, pp. 78–91.

18. For the ambivalent attitude of Henry II towards the crusade, see Mayer, H. E., 'Henry II and the Holy Land', *English Historical Review*, 97 (1982), pp. 721–39.

19. Rigord, §51, p. 78; Gervase of Canterbury, I, p. 369; Gerald of Wales, *De Principis Instructione*, III, 20, pp. 248ff.

20. *Gesta Henrici*, II, p. 5; unsurprisingly, Rigord (§51, p. 78) attributes this retreat to English fear in the face of the courage of the French armies. Gervase of Canterbury also emphasises the anxieties of Henry II and Richard's role as mediator between his father and Philip: I, pp. 370–3.

21. *Gesta Henrici*, II, p. 7. Gillingham (*Richard Cœur de Lion*, p. 107) is quite right to say that such behaviour between men emphasises only friendship

and affection, without any suggestion of a homosexual relationship. But neither, for that matter, is such a relationship ruled out.

22. Gerald of Wales, *De Principis Instructione*, III, 2.
23. *Gesta Henrici*, II, p. 9.
24. See Housley, N., 'Saladin's Triumph over the Crusader State: the Battle of Hattin, 1187', *History Today*, 37 (1987), pp. 17–23; Kedar, B. Z., 'The Battle of Hattin Revisited', in Kedar, *The Horns of Hattin*, pp. 190–207. Gervase of Canterbury (I, p. 375) reproduces a letter from Terric, a Templar, describing Saladin's victory. See also Ralph of Coggeshall, p. 21.
25. For the protective function of the Holy Cross, see Murray, A. V., ' "Mighty against the ennemies of Christ": the Relic of the True Cross in the Armies of the Kingdom of Jerusalem', in J. France and W. G. Zajac (eds), *The Crusades and their Sources. Essays Presented to Bernard Hamilton* (Aldershot, 1998), pp. 217–38.
26. Roger of Howden, II, p. 322; Bull 'Audita tremendi', 20 October 1187, text in Mansi, 21, p. 531; see also Richard, J., 'L'Indulgence de Croisade et le Pèlerinage en Terre Sainte', in *Il Concilio di Piacenza e le Crociate* (Plaisance, 1996), pp. 213–23.
27. These propaganda efforts using visual aids are remarked on in particular, oddly enough, by a Muslim historian, Ibn al Athir; see the text trans. Jean Richard in *L'Esprit de la Croisade* (Paris, 1969), pp. 112ff., repr. in Gillingham, *Richard Cœur de Lion*, p. 111.
28. See on this point Painter, S., 'The Third Crusade: Richard the Lionhearted and Philip Augustus', in Setton, *History of the Crusades*, vol. 2: *The Later Crusades*, pp. 45–8; Richard, *Crusades*, pp. 217–18.
29. Roger of Howden, II, p. 338; Gerald of Wales, *Itinerarium Kambriae* and *Descriptio Kambriae*, vol. 4, pp. 14ff., 75ff., 151ff.; for the preaching of the Third Crusade, see Cole, P. J., *The Preaching of the Crusades to the Holy Land, 1095–1270* (Cambridge, Mass., 1991), pp. 63–79.
30. Gerald of Wales, *De Principis Instructione*, p. 239; Ralph of Diceto, II, p. 50; William of Newburgh, p. 271; Matthew Paris, *Chronica Majora*, II, p. 329; Ambroise, lines 63ff.; *Itinerarium*, lib. II, c. 3; Roger of Howden, III, p. 175, and so on.
31. Roger of Howden, II, p. 334.
32. *Gesta Henrici*, II, p. 59; Roger of Howden, II, p. 335; Ralph of Diceto, II, p. 51; Matthew Paris, *Chronica Majora*, II, p. 330; Rigord, 56, p. 83; Ambroise, lines 130–6; *Itinerarium*, lib. II, c. 3.
33. Ralph of Diceto, II, pp. 52–4.
34. *Gesta Henrici*, II, p. 89. The German expedition continued under the command of his son, Frederick V of Swabia; the body of Frederick Barbarossa was taken by the crusaders to be buried at Tyre. See also William of Newburgh, p. 329; Ralph of Diceto, II, p. 84.
35. William of Newburgh, p. 272; Ralph of Coggeshall, pp. 24–5; Rigord, §58, p. 85.

36. Gerald of Wales, *De Principis Instructione*, p. 144.

37. Rigord, §60, p. 90.

38. Bertran de Born accused Philip Augustus, on this date, of failing to react to Richard's conquests in the Toulousain and urged him, at the very least, to respond to Richard's perjury in rejecting his sister and concluding a marriage with the daughter of Sancho VI: Bertran de Born, ed. Gouiran, pp. 553–4, and song no. 27: 'S'ieu fos aissi senher e poderos', p. 557. This theory is also confirmed by the assertion of Ambroise (lines 1135ff.) that Richard had loved Berengaria when he was still only Count of Poitou.

39. *Gesta Henrici*, II, pp. 39–40.

40. Matthew Paris, *Chronica Majora*, II, p. 331; William of Newburgh, p. 276.

41. Gervase of Canterbury, I, p. 434.

42. *Gesta Henrici*, II, p. 47; Roger of Howden, II, p. 345; Ralph of Diceto, II, p. 55; Matthew Paris, *Chronica Majora*, II, p. 336.

43. *Gesta Henrici*, II, p. 46; Roger of Howden, II, p. 344. For Richard's animosity towards William des Barres, see below, pp. 104–5, 305–6.

44. Bertran de Born, ed. Gouiran, p. 569, song no. 28: 'Non puosc mudar mon chantar non esparga'.

45. Roger of Howden, II, p. 345.

46. Roger of Howden, II, p. 346; *Gesta Henrici*, II, p. 49.

47. Gervase of Canterbury, I, p. 435.

48. Gervase of Canterbury, I, p. 435; Ralph of Diceto, II, pp. 57–8.

49. Rigord, §63, p. 92.

50. *Gesta Henrici*, II, p. 50; a little further on (p. 60), the chronicler notes that 'the King of France restored Châteauroux to him, but in word only, not in fact'.

51. Gerald of Wales, *De Principis Instructione*, pp. 153–4.

52. William of Newburgh, p. 277.

53. Matthew Paris, *Chronica Majora*, II, pp. 336–40; see also Roger of Howden, II, p. 363; *Gesta Henrici*, II, p. 66; Gerald of Wales, *De Principis Instructione*, p. 282.

54. Roger of Howden, II, p. 363.

55. Matthew Paris, *Chronica Majora*, II, p. 339.

56. Gerald of Wales, *De Principis Instructione*, pp. 259ff.

57. Matthew Paris, *Chronica Majora*, II, p. 340.

58. 'Militari lancea perfosso': Gerald of Wales, *De Principis Instructione*, p. 283.

59. *Guillaume le Maréchal*, lines 8836ff.

60. Rigord, §66, pp. 95–6.

61. William of Newburgh, p. 277.

62. Bertran de Born, ed. Gouiran, song no. 28, pp. 615ff.

63. Ralph of Diceto, II, pp. 63–4; Matthew Paris, *Chronica Majora*, II, pp. 342–3.

64. Gerald of Wales, *De Principis Instructione*, p. 296.

65. Roger of Howden, II, p. 366; *Guillaume le Maréchal*, lines 9079ff.; Gerald of Wales, *De Principis Instructione*, p. 305.
66. Gerald of Wales, *De Principis Instructione*, p. 302; see also William of Newburgh, pp. 278ff.; Ralph of Coggeshall (p. 25) judges the Old King more favourably, finding him a better sovereign than his son Richard.
67. See on this point Bienvenu, J.-M., 'Henri II Plantagenêt et Fontevraud', in *Henri II Plantagenêt et son Temps*, pp. 25–32.
68. *Gesta Henrici*, II, p. 71; Roger of Howden, II, pp. 366–7; Gerald of Wales, *De Principis Instructione*, p. 305; William of Newburgh (pp. 278ff.) fails to mention the episode of the bleeding nostrils.
69. Matthew Paris, *Chronica Majora*, II, p. 344.
70. C. T. Wood has convincingly shown that Henry intended to be buried at Grandmont and that the choice of Fontevraud was fortuitous: 'La Mort et les Funerailles d'Henri II', *Cahiers de Civilisation Médiévale*, 28 (1994), pp. 119–23. I am not convinced, however, by his interpretation of either the *Gesta Henrici* (II, pp. 71–9) or the *Histoire de Guillaume le Maréchal* (pp. 335ff.), which, he claims, 'both stubbornly insist on calling Richard "Count of Poitiers" and not "King of England"' (p. 123), thus showing that, in their eyes, Henry remained without a successor. There is a much simpler explanation: before his coronation, Richard remained Count of Poitiers; he was soon after to become Duke of Normandy and then King of England.

4

King Richard

⁓

Richard's first political act seems to have been to order his mother's release,[1] which Matthew Paris saw as yet another fulfilment of a prophecy of Merlin.[2] The task was entrusted to Richard's old enemy, William Marshal, who hastened to England only to find that Eleanor was already free. Once at liberty, she quickly emptied the prisons, so as to free all the political prisoners who had been enemies of her husband and imprisoned like her, and for the same reasons.[3] Matthew Paris says that Richard gave Eleanor carte blanche to do as she wished, and adds:

> The great men of the kingdom were also instructed to obey the wishes of the queen in everything. As soon as this power had been granted, she released from their captivity all the prisoners detained in England; she had learned from experience how painful it is to human beings to bear the torments of captivity.[4]

Next, Eleanor repossessed her dowry, which Richard increased with a number of gifts. Very quickly, in spite of her age (she was sixty-seven), she became extremely active and behaved as if she was Queen of England, or at least its regent, with the unanimous approval of the baronage,[5] or at least of those who had remained faithful to her; but what was to be done about the others?

This was a real problem: how to treat barons who had stayed loyal to the Old King, and so were enemies of the new king and his mother? They had every reason to fear the wrath of the son. First to feel its effects was the seneschal of Anjou, Stephen de Marçai, a man described as 'savage and domineering', who was summarily instructed by Richard to surrender all his father's treasure. Made a prisoner, he was led in chains to Winchester where he was forced to hand over 30,000 *livres angevines* and to promise 15,000 more in the hope of being restored to favour.[6] But Richard seems to have avoided gratuitous acts of revenge in the case of the barons and servants who had remained sincerely faithful to Henry II; some were even rewarded for their loyalty.[7] He treated with contempt and without pity, however, those who had betrayed the

Old King and rallied to his own cause out of what he judged to be self-interest.

Richard's benevolent behaviour towards some of the men who had been most faithful to the Old King, such as Maurice of Craon, Baldwin of Béthune and William Marshal, reveals something of his character and of an attitude dictated by a combination of chivalric and political motives: it was, after all, prudent not to discourage loyalty to kings, past or present, and to demonstrate that faithful service to legitimate authority would receive its just reward. In his memoirs, William Marshal admirably sums up Richard's attitude and also that of those who had stayed loyal servants of Henry out of respect for the monarchy.

Richard's accession was potentially very dangerous for William. Henry II had promised him the hand of a rich heiress but the succession of the rebel son might mean the end not only of William's hopes in this direction but of his office as marshal, his freedom and even his life, given recent events. His fears increased when the king alluded to the incident, only a few days earlier, in which William had killed Richard's horse under him, during Henry's flight to Chinon. Richard claimed that William had wanted to kill him but failed in his attempt. The marshal dared to correct him, in spite of the risks of contradicting the future King of England. This is how he describes his first interview with the new king:

'So, Marshal, the other day you wanted to kill me and I would be dead, without any doubt, if I had not turned your lance aside with my arm; that was a very bad day for you'. William replied to the Count: 'I never intended to kill you, and made no attempt to do so; I am still strong enough to direct a lance. If I had wanted to, I would have struck you full in the body as I did that horse. In killing it, I believe I did nothing wrong and I have no regrets.' With a great sense of justice, the Count replied: 'Marshal, you are pardoned, I will never bear you any malice.'[8]

The significance of the episode was clear: the King of England had wiped the slate clean of the insults to and forgotten the grievances of the Count of Poitou. William must have been hugely relieved; he could continue to serve and to hope. In fact Richard retained this model knight, former tutor in chivalry of his brother Henry, in his personal service and gave him, though he was nearly fifty, the hand of one of the richest heiresses in the country, Isabel de Clare, Countess of Striguil and Pembroke, then aged seventeen; it was a marriage that made William one of the richest barons in the kingdom. Richard could not resist, however, slipping in one barbed remark: his father Henry, he reminded him, had only promised her to him; it was he, Richard, who had actually given her to him.[9]

DUKE OF NORMANDY AND KING OF ENGLAND

With these reassurances, the loyal servants of Henry II rallied to
Richard's support, mainly with enthusiasm. They continued in the immediate entourage of the new king.

For the moment, Richard was still only Count of Poitou. He became
Duke of Normandy on 20 July 1189,[10] when the Archbishop of Rouen
girded him with the ducal sword and handed him the banner, the *vexillum*, in a ritual ceremony comparable in its form and in the vocabulary
employed to describe it to the dubbing of a knight. It was, however,
a princely investiture, modelled on the coronation ceremonies of the
Western Frankish kings and further proof, if such be needed, that the
dubbing of knights derived from the handing of arms to kings, and then
princes, and disseminated within chivalry the old royal ideology associated with it.[11]

On the occasion of these ceremonies, Richard performed acts of generosity that served the political purpose of strengthening his power. For
example, he married his niece Matilda, daughter of his sister Matilda and
Henry the Lion, Duke of Saxony, to Rotrou, heir to the county of Perche;
this procured him a valuable ally who would help to protect a sensitive
area of his empire, on the borders of Maine, which had proved a serious
weakness during the recent conflicts. Before returning to England to
receive the crown, Richard took similar measures in Aquitaine, Maine
and Anjou, for the peace and security of his empire, as Ralph of Diceto
observed.[12] He was also concerned for the safety of Tours, the strategic
importance of which he had recently had cause to appreciate, and long
a bone of contention between Philip Augustus and the Plantagenets.

Richard met the King of France to discuss this matter on 22 July,
between Chaumont and Trie. He had not yet been crowned King of
England but was already seeing old problems from a new perspective.
This caused him to adopt positions closer to those taken in the past by
his father, distancing himself from those he had defended when merely
Count of Poitou. Philip had revived his old claims for the return of the
Norman Vexin, together with Gisors. Richard managed to persuade him
to withdraw this demand in return for the promise of payment of 4,000
marks as war reparations; this was in addition to the 20,000 marks
already promised by Henry II at the meeting at Ballon, after his defeat at
Le Mans. Richard also promised that he would at last marry Alice; he
could no longer invoke some external impediment to his own wishes.
Philip, for his part, agreed to return to his former ally all the lands
recently conquered, with his help, from his father, in particular Tours,

Le Mans and Châteauroux, but excepting Graçay and Issoudun, which remained in the hands of the King of France. Overall, the agreement was not unfavourable to Richard, who got more than he promised, in particular Gisors and the Vexin. Here, the French chronicler Rigord seems to express the general feeling among the French: Gisors should be returned to the King of France. What is more, there had been an omen foreshadowing this: only the day after the conclusion of this accord (and Rigord is careful to include the two events in the same sentence), when the Count of Poitou was riding with his men across the wooden bridge leading to Gisors, it collapsed; Richard was thrown into the waters of the moat, along with his horse.[13]

Reassured as to the state of his continental possessions, Richard embarked for England at Barfleur. Like his father before him, he was resolved to keep all power in his own hands, both on the Continent and in Great Britain. First, however, he had to decide the fate of his younger brother John, who had switched to Richard's camp so late in the day as to leave doubts as to his trustworthiness. Admittedly, he had come to Richard to seek a reconciliation and Richard had treated him 'honourably';[14] but what lay ahead? There could be no question of Richard granting his brother a major appanage, in particular in some strategically important continental land, well provided with castles.

He behaved towards John, nevertheless, with great generosity. This, at least, is what most of the chroniclers, self-seekingly or insincerely, proclaimed. Before his departure on crusade, to which no obstacle now remained, Richard confirmed to John everything his father had promised. Then, on 20 August, he married him to the heiress of the Earl of Gloucester, in spite of the opposition of Archbishop Baldwin of Canterbury, who had prohibited the marriage because the pair were related in the third degree.[15] To these lands, Richard later added four English counties (Cornwall, Devon, Dorset and Somerset) and land in Ireland, which matched his father's promise to grant John an estate worth £4,000 a year. According to some writers, Richard's generosity was ill-judged, even excessive, and helped to turn his younger brother's head. Many people had warned him against John; he was only waiting, they said, for Richard to depart on crusade and would conspire against him the minute his back was turned.[16] Some said that the very scale of these grants to a young man as unstable as John was proof that Richard did not intend to return from the Holy Land, leaving the kingdom to his brother.[17] At least, this was whispered by John's supporters. They began to fortify their castles, while a number of nobles took the younger brother's side and would line up against Richard soon after his departure, as foreseen by

William Longchamp, who had warned about it when appointed chancellor of the kingdom.[18]

In fact it is clear that Richard himself did not trust his brother and the lands he gave him, however extensive, did not amount to a serious threat, as they did not constitute a viable entity and lacked strategic or military value; furthermore, they did not eat into what counted most in Richard's eyes, that is, the Angevin empire, the heart of which lay in France. His distrust of John was real, in spite of this endowment. He was also mistrustful of one of his illegitimate half-brothers, Geoffrey, who had initially been made Bishop of Lincoln by his father, but never consecrated, as he was reluctant to enter orders; Henry had then made him chancellor. The Old King had been very fond of Geoffrey and frequently stated his preference for him, as opposed to either John or Richard. He had promised to make him Archbishop of York, one of the highest ecclesiastical offices in the land, but this had not been to Geoffrey's liking; he preferred the knightly lifestyle, hunting and mixing in elegant society rather than in clerical circles. He may not have abandoned all hope of playing an important political role and no doubt remembered that William the Conqueror, too, had been a bastard and that this had not stopped him becoming King of England. For reasons of personal preference and ambition he had so far refused any form of ordination. But as soon as Richard became king, he had Geoffrey elected Archbishop of York and ordained, like it or not, on 23 September. Once holding high ecclesiastical office, he had lost all opportunity of carving out a role in secular politics. As for John, before Richard left for the Holy Land, he made him swear on oath not to set foot in England in his absence. In fact, he was later released from this oath by Eleanor, on condition he had the agreement of the Chancellor.[19]

When Richard had arrived in Portsmouth from Barfleur and set out for London, on 13 September 1189, he had been welcomed enthusiastically by the people. For a variety of reasons, they had had enough of his father's reign and his excesses, and even more of the recent financial measures which were generally held to be oppressive, particularly by the clergy; the latter had also criticised Henry for his adulteries, his excessively cruel laws, in particular mutilation for hunting offences,[20] and the murder of Thomas Becket. A month later, Richard was anointed and crowned in Westminster Abbey by Archbishop Baldwin of Canterbury, in a solemn ceremony described in great detail by Roger of Howden.[21] Behind the clerical dignitaries who headed the procession came four barons bearing candles in candelabra, followed by John Marshal with the two gold spurs from the royal treasury; then came two earls, William Marshal, now Earl of Pembroke and Striguil, with the royal sceptre,[22] and William of Salisbury,

with the rod of command. They were followed by David, brother of the King of Scots, and Robert, Earl of Leicester, flanking John, the King's brother and Earl of Mortain and Gloucester, holding three swords from the royal treasury; lastly, after six earls carrying a table on which various royal insignia lay, came William de Mandeville, carrying the royal crown, followed by the future king, Richard, Count of Poitou and Duke of Normandy. Having taken his place, the future king swore the three traditional oaths of the kings of England: to bring peace and honour to God and the Holy Church as long as he lived, to guarantee justice for his people and lastly to suppress bad laws and perverse customs but observe and enforce good ones. Richard was then undressed and anointed with the holy oil on the head, chest and hands, before being dressed in the royal robes; next the Archbishop handed him the sword for the pursuit of heretics and all enemies of Holy Church, after which two earls attached the gold spurs to his feet; lastly, wearing the royal mantle, Richard was crowned. He took his place on his throne and heard mass. The ceremony was followed by the royal banquet, attended by a great number of people, all seated according to their rank, in a display of splendour and largesse that made a deep impression on all present.[23]

Richard had given orders that neither women nor Jews were to be admitted to these festivities. Matthew Paris gives reasons for this edict, promulgated a few days in advance: 'The spells and magic charms indulged in during coronations by Jews and witches of ill repute really were feared.'[24] John Gillingham is dismissive of the argument of those historians, such as James Brundage, who see the exclusion of women as evidence of misogyny, a natural repulsion on Richard's part for the female sex, and who go on to postulate his homosexuality;[25] according to them, he wished to make this banquet a bachelor occasion, a sort of 'gay party'.[26] According to Gillingham, it was customary for women to be excluded from English coronation festivals, in which case, in strict logic, every early medieval King of England must have been homosexual. I will return to this rather extreme view later.[27] It seems unlikely, however, that the exclusion of women really was traditional; had this been the case, Matthew Paris would hardly have felt the need to report that it was the subject of an edict or have invoked an explanation that is notably obscure. Nor is it known whether the prohibition was applied or if it gave rise to protests or disturbances.

This is not the case with the exclusion of the Jews. In spite of the prohibition, some Jews were anxious to take part in the festivities, hoping to offer the new King their best wishes for a joyous reign and present him with gifts as a sign of their affection; it was a time when a latent

anti-Semitism was beginning to come out into the open, as always when there was talk of a new crusade. Many Christians, as had been made clear in 1096, at the time of the First Crusade, tended to lump together as enemies of the faith and of Christ, along with Muslims, from whom they were about to try to recover the Holy Places, the heretics and Jews who were resident in the West.[28] The King's sergeants, under orders to keep the peace and supported by the large crowd that had assembled at the entrance, unceremoniously expelled those Jews who tried to enter, beating and even robbing them; they were set upon and beaten up, many being injured and some killed.

As news of these events spread, the inhabitants of London decided to join in; the mob took advantage of the disturbances to roam the city hunting down Jews, unleashing pogroms, burning and looting their houses and, in some cases, forcing them to choose between conversion and death. Many Jews had themselves baptised to escape the massacre.[29] It was also an opportunity for many Christians who had taken a crusading vow to rob Jews of their possessions and so provide themselves, at the expense of these 'enemies of Christ', with the means to finance their expedition against the Muslims. They entered Jewish houses, searching out and destroying records of debts. They were encouraged by a rumour to the effect that King Richard himself had given orders for their persecution.[30]

The Jewish community was then fairly numerous in England, and relatively prosperous, as it had been protected by Henry II. In France, in contrast, as soon as he had acceded to the throne, Philip Augustus had expelled the Jews from the kingdom, to widespread acclaim. Rigord congratulates him, even suggesting that the new King was only doing his duty according to his coronation oath.[31] Many of these Jews had fled to England, where they had been made welcome by Henry II. This had caused some unfavourable comment among the nobility and the ecclesiastics, proof of the latent anti-Semitism referred to above. Richard of Devizes puts into the mouth of an old Jew a speech full of cutting irony in which he tells a young co-religionist how his people were treated in England: you need to avoid London, he said, which is a veritable haunt of brigands, delinquents, bandits, madmen, sodomites, paedophiles, prostitutes and beggars, and a few other towns such as Canterbury, Rochester, Oxford and Exeter; instead, you should try to settle in Winchester, a veritable 'Jerusalem of the Jews', where the inhabitants and even the churchmen and the monks would make him welcome.[32]

Was a connection made in England as well as France between the threefold oath of the King and these violent attacks on the Jews? Settled in Christian territory, the Jews formed an 'alien' community, regarded as

far too wealthy at a time when many crusaders, about to go and fight for Christ in the Holy Land, were having difficulty finding the funds they needed, and when others, including some of the clergy, were crushed by the Saladin Tithe. All these factors, psychological, religious and economic, combined to intensify the hostility, even though Richard declared that the Jews were under his protection and ordered that the culprits be found, if perhaps without high hopes or great determination.[33] The wave of pogroms quickly spread, therefore, to other towns, including Lincoln and Norwich, reaching a peak of intensity a few months later in York. Here, a large number of Jews who had taken refuge in the castle were besieged by a mob inflamed by the preaching of a fanatical hermit. As in 1096 in the Rhineland, the Jews who were hunted down usually preferred suicide to conversion. Some, however, accepted the baptism that was 'offered' to them, to save their lives; in vain, however, as they, too, were massacred. Given the scale of the disturbances, Richard sent a force commanded by William Longchamp to York, on 3 May 1190, but those who had fomented the riots had already escaped to Scotland. The citizens of York were only obliged to pay a fine and William Longchamp replaced the sheriff, who had colluded in the disorder.[34]

PREPARING FOR THE CRUSADE

Well before this, in December 1189, Richard himself left England to prepare for his departure for the Holy Land. To this end, he summoned his barons, from England and from the rest of the Angevin empire, and tried to persuade them to follow him. To win their agreement, he had to meet the major part (more than two-thirds) of the costs associated with such a major expedition; in particular, to pay for the ships necessary to transport the host of knights, foot soldiers, archers and war and siege technicians. All these 'pilgrims' were volunteers, even if sometimes under pressure, but paid for by their lords, who subsidised their expenses, upkeep, food and wages. The Saladin Tithe, as we have seen, made a major contribution, nearly £60,000, but even that was not enough, partly because much of it had been frittered away in various ways, in particular on the war between Henry II and Philip, and other activities unconnected with the crusade. This had led to much criticism, especially from the clergy.[35] Matthew Paris clearly expresses the general feeling on the subject:

> At this time there was levied throughout England a tax equalling a tenth of movable goods, on the pretext of using this money for the needs of the Holy Land. This forcible exaction angered clergy and people alike; because although called a charitable donation, it was pure and simply robbery.[36]

Further, before leaving for the East, Richard had to pay to the King of France the indemnities specified in their earlier treaty. Richard may have found a very large sum of money, estimated at more than 100,000 silver marks, in his father's treasury,[37] but this was not enough for the expenses he was about to incur. So he embarked on the systematic sale of offices. He began by demanding that all those who had served his father, more or less obsequiously or self-interestedly, should pay a substantial sum to retain their posts. The case of Stephen de Marçai, the former seneschal of Anjou under Henry II, has already been mentioned. Seized and clapped in irons, he had been taken to Winchester as a captive before the coronation. To obtain his freedom, he had been forced to pay Richard 30,000 *livres angevines* and promise 15,000 more to remain in office, but in vain.[38] Ranulf Glanville, Eleanor's former gaoler, was also fined £15,000. The same principle was soon universally applied: William Longchamp, to become Bishop of Ely, is supposed to have paid more than 3,000 silver marks, hardly exorbitant. Other less prestigious offices, such as that of sheriff, were also 'sold', and so were counties, castles, lordships and lands, not to speak of the many more or less forced loans taken from churches. William of Scotland bought his 'liberty' at a cost of 10,000 silver marks; he did homage to Richard, along with his brother David, and soon afterwards Richard proclaimed William quit of all the obligations imposed by Henry II, which won him the deep gratitude of the Scots. Overall, by means of these various procedures, or rather, expedients, the new King of England managed to amass immense riches, greater than any of his predecessors, according to the chroniclers.[39] He himself is supposed to have joked that, to raise money, he would have sold London itself if he could have found a buyer.[40] This orgy of selling was all grist to the mill of those in John's entourage who wanted to create the impression that the King cared little for his kingdom and did not intend to return.

The new King had other preoccupations than his finances: he had to arrange for the administration of his empire in his absence, beginning with the kingdom of England. As we have seen, he did not trust his brother John. He had once declared that he would not leave for the Holy Land without him and this may still have been his intention. But apart from the risk of disputes all along the way, such a solution would have the serious disadvantage of leaving the kingdom without a direct heir were the two brothers to die simultaneously during the expedition; in that case the kingdom would revert to Arthur, Geoffrey's son, then aged two, raising the prospect of new dynastic conflicts.

There remained Eleanor. By now she was already advanced in years, but still fit, lively, authoritarian and keen to resume her place on the political

stage. She was well able to take on the job of 'queen mother' and be the true administrator and ruler of the kingdom. The perfect solution would be to assure the dynastic succession, but this was a thorny problem given that Richard, as we have seen, was deeply averse to marrying Alice; this was in spite of his repeated promises to the King of France, which prevented him from making another marriage alliance for political advantage, in the usual way. He was contemplating doing so, nevertheless, as we have seen, probably encouraged by Eleanor, who had little confidence in her son John and would countenance no talk of Arthur, the other legitimate claimant. But for the moment, all discussion of this subject was bedevilled by Richard's recently renewed promise to Philip. The King of France would hardly fail to make capital from so blatant a violation of Richard's word. It was a situation that required careful handling.

To guarantee Eleanor's income and independence, Richard enlarged her dower lands. He gave her, the chroniclers point out with some emphasis, the dowers of three queens: that given by Henry I to his wife Edith, that granted by King Stephen to his wife Matilda and that left to Eleanor by Henry II. In future, recognised on oath by all the barons, Eleanor was able, as Richard of Devizes emphasises, to 'live off her own', no longer dependent on the Exchequer or, as we would put it, on 'the public purse'.[41] Richard associated with her in a sort of regency council two royal officers he felt he could trust, Hugh du Puiset, from an old aristocratic family, and William Longchamp, Bishop of Ely. The two men did not get on, and Richard later ruled in favour of the latter. William was a highly cultured man endowed with natural authority, appointed chancellor then justiciar of the kingdom, as well as papal legate, which made him the most powerful man in England. But the native population, like most of the chroniclers, criticised him for his humble origins, his arrogance, his extravagance and his 'contempt for the English'.[42]

Satisfied as to the future of England, Richard could embark at Dover for Calais, on 11 December, to organise the administration of his continental lands in his absence. At this point he learned of the death of William of Sicily, husband of his sister Joan. The couple had no children and Tancred of Sicily had seized the island to the detriment of the designated heiress, Constance, the wife of the Emperor Henry VI and daughter of Roger of Sicily. This had led to a conflict between Tancred and Henry VI, Richard's ally and relative. Richard intended travelling via Sicily to settle this dispute, and in particular to recover his sister and her dowry, both still in Tancred's hands.[43]

On arrival in Calais, Richard was received by Philip of Flanders, who had also taken the cross and who accompanied him to his Norman lands,

where the king celebrated his Christmas court, near Caen. The chronicler Ambroise, who was present, noted with regret that almost no *chansons de geste* were performed; jongleurs were excluded, a moral austerity required by the crusading vow.[44] Richard confirmed or appointed seneschals to rule Normandy, Anjou, Maine and Aquitaine in his absence; in the event, they proved worthy of the confidence he placed in them and maintained the provinces in peace and free from major disturbances throughout his long years away.

Richard's main concern was to ensure the defence of his territories against a possible attack by supporters of Philip Augustus, even in the absence of the two kings. He met the King of France to discuss this issue on 30 December, and again on 13 January 1190, at Gué-Saint-Rémy, near Nonancourt.[45] The two kings concluded what amounted to a non-aggression pact, whose clauses can be summarised as follows: the King of England promised assistance to defend the King of France if anyone attacked Paris; the King of France to assist the King of England if there was an attack on Rouen. The counts and barons of the two sides swore not to make war amongst themselves while their kings were on crusade. The two kings decided that if one of them died or returned from the crusade before the other, he would leave those of his troops and his possessions in the service of God, at the disposal of whichever of them remained.[46] They agreed to leave together, from Vézelay.

The date of their departure was frequently put back. This was first because the preparations took longer than expected, then because of the tension persisting between the two kings and lastly because Queen Isabella of France died on 15 March 1190 giving birth to stillborn twins. Some princes, consequently, departed on crusade before the kings. Frederick Barbarossa, as we have seen, left well before them, even though he had taken the cross later than them.

Another concern of Richard was to assure peace and order in Aquitaine, his favourite province. The barons of Aquitaine, supported by Raymond of Toulouse, might at any moment foment revolts and disturbances.[47] Richard therefore summoned most of the lords of the region to the court he held at La Réole at Candlemas 1190. It was probably then that he revived the negotiations for his marriage with Berengaria, which obviously had to be kept secret so as not to provoke Philip's wrath until such time as Richard had his agreement to release him from his engagement to Alice. John Gillingham rightly compares this assembly and the family council held in Normandy the following March to the very similar court held twenty years earlier to arrange the marriage of Richard's sister Eleanor to Alfonso VIII of Castile.[48]

Before leaving Aquitaine, Richard set out to pacify it, making a show of force by leading a punitive expedition against some robber barons of Gascony during May and June. He compelled the brigands by force of arms to demolish the fortifications they occupied.[49] The Basque lords and communities, as we have seen, had long had a reputation for looting and kidnap, to which the *Guide for Pilgrims to St James of Compostella*, written a few years earlier, frequently refers. This *Guide* indicated to pilgrims the routes they should follow to join the 'French way' leading across Spain to Compostella; it listed the secondary sanctuaries of pilgrimage to be visited on the way and noted the best places for breaking the journey. It is a mine of information about the way in which the various peoples encountered on the way were then regarded. Few deserved praise in the eyes of its author, least of all the Basques and the Navarrese. The Gascons, whose country had to be crossed, were, he said, 'loudmouthed, talkative, given to mockery, libidinous, drunken, greedy eaters, clad in rags and poverty-stricken', but they were also 'skilled fighters and notable for their hospitality to the poor'. The Basques, in contrast, who spoke a barbarous and incomprehensible language, were very hostile; they 'come out to meet pilgrims with . . . cudgels', and threaten and beat them, and extort by force an unjust tribute that only merchants should pay, not travellers or pilgrims. The author of the *Guide* demands that the Church excommunicate without further ado those lords who protected them and profited by their exactions, of which they shamefully took a share. He went so far as to name some of them, including the King of Aragon. The overall picture he paints of these peoples reveals the fear in which they were held:

> This is a barbarous people, different from all other peoples in customs and in race, malignant, dark in colour, ugly of face, debauched, perverse, faithless, dishonourable, corrupt, lustful, drunken, skilled in all forms of violence, fierce and savage, dishonest and false, impious and coarse, cruel and quarrelsome, incapable of any good impulses, past masters of all vices and iniquities. They resemble . . . the Saracens in their malignance, and are in every way hostile to our people of France. A Navarrese or a Basque will kill a Frenchman for a penny if he can.[50]

This highly unfavourable judgement probably had some basis in reality, that is, in the robberies so common on the routes by way of the Pyrenean passes, and perhaps also in the personal experiences of the author or his friends; it was certainly also influenced by the still-vivid memories of the disaster of Roncevaux, perpetuated by the *Chanson de Roland*, which featured Saracens rather than Basques, so contributing to the widespread confusion between them. It may also reveal a latent hostility on the part

of the author, who supported the King of France against the English, allies of the King of Aragon and hostile to the Count of Toulouse.

As he was preparing to leave the West, Richard tried to strengthen this alliance against Raymond of Toulouse by forging even closer ties with King Sancho VI of Navarre, who was himself on the point of allying with Alfonso II of Aragon with a view to fighting against the King of Castile. It is highly plausible, therefore, that it was at this point that Richard revived his project for a marriage with Berengaria, temporarily stalled on account of his recent treaty with Philip of France. As it happened, there had been several new cases of exactions by the lords of the region. Richard had to demonstrate that he would not tolerate these outbreaks of brigandage which amounted to defiance of his authority. He therefore launched a punitive operation all along the Pyrenean passes and laid siege to the castle of Chis, which he took, hanging its castellan, who was guilty of having preyed on pilgrims.[51] His intervention had the twofold effect of making the region safe for pilgrims and asserting his authority in these borderlands, perpetually disrupted by the temptation to seek independence.

Having arranged for the maintenance of order in Aquitaine during his absence and laid the foundations for the alliances that would contribute to it, Richard returned to Chinon. Here he proclaimed the crusading ordinances, which listed the various prohibitions that would be operative during the course of the crusade and the punishments laid down for those contravening them, in some cases extremely harsh, in others relatively light; those guilty of murder, violence, insults, abuse, blasphemy or theft were severely punished, by death or mutilation.[52] He then proceeded to Tours, where, in June 1190, he gave orders to the leaders of his fleet to sail round Spain with provisions, weapons and general supplies, and also a part of his army, which he would join in Marseille. In Tours, he received from the hands of the archbishop the traditional insignia of the pilgrim, the staff and the scrip, which he carried at Vézelay, on 2 July, where he met King Philip Augustus, as agreed. Was it an ill omen that, when Richard leaned on his pilgrim's staff, it broke?[53]

Before setting out together, on 4 July, the two kings reached a final agreement which was later to assume great importance thanks to the differing interpretations put on it: they agreed to share evenly the costs and the difficulties of the expedition, and also the glory, the conquests and the booty that would result. They also agreed to join up at Messina, as they were proposing to leave by different routes.[54]

How readily had Philip accepted Richard's failure to marry his sister before his departure, as laid down in the treaty? According to the

Continuation of William of Tyre, Richard had succeeded in making a deal with Philip:

> He . . . came to King Philip in France. He brought a request to the king, saying, 'Sire, I must tell you that I am a young man,[55] and newly crowned king, and as you know I have undertaken the same road as you to go overseas. If it is your pleasure, I would ask that you should put off the marriage until I come back. I shall be bound to you by oath to marry your sister within 40 days of my return.' The king decided that he ought to agree, and so he received the request favourably and allowed the postponement.[56]

The text is late and we have no other source for this request for a postponement. Yet it is not implausible, and Philip Augustus could easily have been taken in by it despite the Plantagenets' previous record of procrastination where this marriage was concerned. Previously, Henry II could always be blamed; now, relations between Philip and Richard were much improved. Further, the two kings were about to depart on crusade, from which women were excluded on papal orders. Philip Augustus, who had himself just lost his wife, might understand Richard's reluctance to marry his perpetual betrothed only to leave her alone at such a dangerous juncture.

It was therefore as bachelors that Richard and Philip set off together for the Holy Land, leaving from Vézelay, the sacred and already mythical site where St Bernard had preached the Second Crusade. From Vézelay, they travelled towards Lyon, which they reached on 14 July 1190. Here, once again, the chroniclers recorded an evil omen: a wooden bridge collapsed as the pilgrims crossed over, precipitating them into the waters of the River Rhône. Ambroise, whose use of figures is less rigorous than that of his predecessors of the First Crusade,[57] grandiloquently reports that the crusader army was then reckoned at 100,000 men, that a hundred of them were thrown into the river, but that, by a miracle, only two were drowned; this was hugely comforting and negated the baleful significance of the incident. Pure in the eyes of God, they would obtain this 'mercy' and access to Paradise.

At Lyon, the two kings separated, on the pretext of the greater ease of provisioning the two armies. Philip went towards Genoa, where he intended to embark, as the Genoese were his allies, while Richard headed for Marseille, where he hoped to find his fleet. The two kings had agreed to meet up in Sicily, as we have seen, at Messina. Whoever arrived first would wait for the other.

In spite of some evil omens, the crusade seemed, at last, to have got off to a good start.

NOTES

1. For the events described in this chapter, see Kessler, *Richard I*, pp. 76ff.; Gillingham, *Richard the Lionheart*, pp. 125ff.; Pernoud, *Richard Cœur de Lion*, pp. 75ff.; Norgate, *England under the Angevin Kings*, pp. 273ff.; Brundage, *Richard Lionheart*, pp. 250ff.
2. Matthew Paris, *Chronica Majora*, II, p. 346.
3. *Gesta Henrici*, II, p. 74; Roger of Howden, III, p. 4; however, William of Newburgh (p. 293) disapprovingly reports that too many prisoners were released, gallows birds who were a baneful presence throughout the country.
4. Matthew Paris, *Chronica Majora*, II, p. 346.
5. Ralph of Diceto, II, pp. 67–8; Richard of Devizes, p. 14.
6. Richard of Devizes, p. 4.
7. Roger of Howden, III, p. 5.
8. *Guillaume le Maréchal*, lines 9320ff.
9. *Gesta Henrici*, II, p. 73; Roger of Howden, III, p. 7. See also on this last point the useful remarks of Georges Duby (*William Marshal*, p. 123) and John Gillingham (*Richard the Lionheart*, pp. 125ff.).
10. Roger of Howden, III, p. 3: 'Ricardus . . . accinctus est gladio ducatus Normanniae'; *Gesta Henrici*, II, pp. 72–3; Ralph of Diceto (II, pp. 66–7) notes that Richard received 'tam ensem quam vexillum de ducatu Normanniae'.
11. See on this point Flori, 'Chevalerie et Liturgie'; Flori, *Essor de la Chevalerie*, pp. 43–116.
12. Ralph of Diceto, II, pp. 66–7.
13. Rigord, §67, p. 97.
14. *Gesta Henrici*, II, p. 72.
15. *Gesta Henrici*, II, p. 78; Roger of Howden, III, p. 6; Matthew Paris, *Chronica Majora*, II, p. 347.
16. William of Newburgh, pp. 301–2.
17. Richard of Devizes, p. 6.
18. Richard of Devizes, pp. 29–30; he also shows that Eleanor, who anticipated a revolt by John, was attempting to persuade the barons to remain loyal to Richard: pp. 60–1.
19. *Gesta Henrici*, II, p. 106; Richard of Devizes, pp. 13–14.
20. Matthew Paris, *Chronica Majora*, II, pp. 213–14; William of Newburgh, pp. 280ff.
21. *Gesta Henrici*, II, pp. 79–82; Roger of Howden, III, pp. 8–10; Richard of Devizes, p. 3; Ralph of Coggeshall, pp. 26ff.
22. In the *Histoire de Guillaume le Maréchal*, William is surprisingly discreet about his own role and does not describe the coronation, which he refers to in only a few lines: lines 9567–9.
23. Ambroise, lines 175–200, 206ff.; *Itinerarium*, III, c. 5.
24. Matthew Paris, *Chronica Majora*, II, pp. 349ff.

25. Brundage, *Richard Lionheart*, pp. 257ff.
26. Gillingham, *Richard the Lionheart*, p. 130; Gillingham, J., 'Some Legends of Richard the Lionheart: their Development and their Influence', in Nelson, *Richard Cœur de Lion*, p. 63.
27. See below, pp. 384–5.
28. Riley-Smith, J., 'The First Crusade and the Persecution of the Jews', *Studies in Church History*, 21, *Persecution and Toleration* (1984), pp. 51–72; Chazan, R., *European Jewry and the First Crusade* (London, 1987); Flori, J., 'Une ou Plusieurs "Première Croisade"? Le Message d'Urbain II et les Plus Anciens Pogroms d'Occident', *Revue Historique*, 285 (1991), 1, pp. 3–27; Flori, J., *Pierre l'Ermite et la Première Croisade* (Paris, 1999), pp. 221ff., 251ff.
29. *Gesta Henrici*, II, pp. 88ff.; Roger of Howden, III, p. 12; William of Newburgh, pp. 295ff.; Ralph of Coggeshall, pp. 26–8.
30. William of Newburgh, pp. 295ff. We will return to Richard's attitude to these displays of anti-Semitism: see pp. 268ff.
31. Rigord, §8, p. 18; §12, p. 25; §14, p. 26; §16, p. 28, etc.
32. Richard of Devizes (pp. 64–8) emphasises their wealth, due, he believed, to excessive royal favour. His open anti-Semitism makes it clear that he disapproved of what he regarded as Henry's indulgence.
33. Roger of Howden, III, p. 12; Ralph of Diceto, II, p. 75. I will return to the interpretation of these events.
34. William of Newburgh, p. 323; Matthew Paris, *Chronica Majora*, II, pp. 349–50ff.
35. Ralph of Coggeshall (pp. 24–5) is highly critical of these acts: 'Justo Dei judicio (qui odio habet rapinam in holocaustum), orta est magna dissensio inter praedictos reges et principes, unde tota illa pecunia violenter collecta, in donativis militum et stipendiis exercituum penitus consumpta est.'
36. Matthew Paris, *Chronica Majora*, II, p. 356.
37. Roger of Howden, III, p. 8.
38. Richard of Devizes, p. 4.
39. See *Gesta Henrici*, II, pp. 90–1; Roger of Howden, III, pp. 13, 25; Richard of Devizes, pp. 7ff.; Ralph of Diceto, II, p. 72.
40. Richard of Devizes, p. 9; William of Newburgh, p. 306: 'Cumque ab amicis propter hoc familiari ausu increparetur, respondisse fertur, Lundonias quoque venderem, si emptorem idoneum invenirem.'
41. *Gesta Henrici*, II, p. 99; Roger of Howden, III, p. 27; Richard of Devizes, p. 14: 'Ut que prius de fisco vixerat deinceps viveret de proprio.'
42. Roger of Howden, III, pp. 33, 72, 143.
43. *Gesta Henrici*, II, p. 102; Roger of Howden, III, p. 29.
44. Ambroise (line 250) says the King spent Christmas at Lion-sur-Mer (according to Gaston Paris; the *Itinerary of Richard I* (p. 23), followed by Ailes (p. 33), prefers Lyons-la-Forêt).
45. Roger of Howden, III, p. 30.

46. *Gesta Henrici*, II, p. 105; see also Roger of Howden, III, p. 30.
47. For the perennial conflict between the counts of Toulouse and the Plantagenets, see in particular Benjamin, R., 'A Forty Years War: Toulouse and the Plantagenets. 1156–1196', *Historical Research*, 61 (1988), pp. 270–85.
48. Gillingham, *Richard the Lionheart*, p. 140. For the diplomatic importance of this marriage, see Powicke, *Loss of Normandy*, pp. 85–98. For a more detailed discussion, see Gillingham, J., 'Richard I and Berengaria of Navarre', in Gillingham, *Richard Cœur de Lion*, pp. 119–39.
49. Richard of Devizes, p. 11.
50. *The Pilgrims Guide. A 12th Century Guide for the Pilgrim to St James of Compostella*, trans. J. Hogarth (Confraternity of St James: London, 1992, repr. 1996), pp. 19, 20, 23–4.
51. Roger of Howden, III, p. 35; Richard of Devizes, p. 11.
52. Roger of Howden, III, p. 59; *Gesta Henrici*, II, pp. 110, 130.
53. Roger of Howden (III, pp. 36–7) seems to be the only chronicler to report this detail. It may have been a later invention, foreshadowing the fatal turn of events.
54. Ambroise, lines 370ff.; *Itinerarium*, II, p. 8.
55. Richard was then nearly thirty-three, but the term 'young' had a less precise meaning in this period than today.
56. *Continuation de Guillaume de Tyr*, p. 102 (p. 92 of Edbury translation).
57. For the chroniclers' use of numbers in the First Crusade, see Flori, J., 'L'Usage "Epique" des Nombres, des Chroniques aux Chansons de Geste; Eléments de Typologie', *Pris-Ma*, 8 (1992), pp. 47–58; Flori, J., 'Un Problème de Méthodologie: la Valeur des Nombres chez les Chroniqueurs du Moyen Age (à Propos des Effectifs de la Première Croisade)', *Le Moyen Age*, 3/4 (1993), pp. 399–422; and more recently, Flori, *Pierre l'Ermite*, pp. 425–7.

5

Richard in Sicily (1190–1)

⟨⟩

FROM MARSEILLE TO MESSINA

The Third Crusade aroused great enthusiasm among Christians from the beginning. Both Richard and Philip assembled large armies and Richard's fleet made a deep impression on contemporaries. Philip, for his part, negotiated with his Genoese allies for the transport of a total of 650 knights, 1,300 squires and 1,300 horses, together with provisions for 8 months, wine for 4 and also fodder; a payment of 5,850 silver marks was agreed.[1] Richard's fleet, meanwhile, consisting of 107 ships, headed for the Straits of Gibraltar.[2] Richard waited for it in Marseille from 31 July until 7 August, but in vain, as it was delayed for a variety of reasons. A storm in the Bay of Biscay had battered the ships and so terrified the sailors that many of them thought their end had come. On 6 May, however, they had been reassured by a vision of St Thomas Becket himself, a sure sign of divine protection. Having reached the Portuguese coast, they went to the assistance of the Christians then besieging Silves, which they attacked on 12 July and recovered from the Muslims; the town surrendered on 6 September and, two days later, the church, which had been turned into a mosque, was restored to its original purpose.[3] In Lisbon, they delivered the town to the King of Portugal but, in the grip of religious fanaticism, behaved with great brutality towards the Jewish and Muslim populations resident in the town and in the service of King Sancho; they raped women and looted and burned houses, until the King eventually barred them from entering the citadel and clapped some of them in gaol.[4] The fleet left Lisbon on 24 July, passed through the Pillars of Hercules on 29 September and sailed along the coast towards Marseille, by way of Almería, Cartagena, Demia, Valencia, Tarragona, Barcelona, Empurias, Collioure, Narbonne, Agde and Montpellier; it reached Marseille on 22 August.[5]

Richard had been too impatient to wait for it. According to Gervase of Canterbury, he had heard worrying rumours to the effect that his fleet had been dispersed by the storm, that a hundred of his ships had sunk with all their provisions and that his companions had been massacred in Spain.[6]

On 7 August, either running out of patience or putting a brave face on adversity, Richard hired ships to carry him to Messina in small stages, sailing along the coast by way of the Islands of the Lérins, Nice, Savona and Genoa. In Genoa they found Philip Augustus, who was ill, perhaps prostrated by seasickness. The two kings held several meetings at Portofino, during which strains in the relationship emerged. Philip asked Richard to lend him five galleys; the King of England offered only three, which the King of France refused.

After a few days' rest, the fleet resumed its progress along the Italian coast. When it reached the mouth of the Tiber, a few kilometres from Rome, Richard did not deign to visit the pope, Clement III, whom he held in low regard. The meetings held soon after with the Calabrian monk Joachim of Fiore explain why: discussing the Antichrist, who, according to the visionary monk, would soon appear and seize the apostolic throne, Richard unhesitatingly identified this Antichrist with Pope Clement III, a clear indication of the poor state of relations between the sovereign and the pontiff.[7] Richard found time, on the other hand, to spend five days in Salerno, famous for its school of medicine, though whether he consulted any of its famous doctors is not known. While in Salerno, he received the reassuring news that his fleet had set sail for Messina. Before crossing the straits to meet up with it, he decided to go with a small party to Mileto, at the extreme tip of Calabria, where the Norman Robert Guiscard had distinguished himself more than a century before. He may have heard of the warlike exploits of this famous knight in France, Normandy or, more recently, Salerno, where Robert's memory remained very much alive. Returning from this expedition, Richard only just managed to escape from some peasants he had unwisely provoked by trying to steal a falcon belonging to one of them.[8] Anxious to put this incident behind him, he crossed the straits later that same day, on the evening of 22 September.

ARRIVAL IN MESSINA

Richard's arrival in the Sicilian port was more glorious, indeed even triumphal, which he had done everything in his power to ensure. He had joined up with his fleet and he entered the port at its head, in a carefully staged spectacle designed to impress the crowds assembled on the quays. Eyewitnesses all report the unanimous admiration of all who watched this grandiose scene and emphasise Richard's success with the people:

> The populace rushed out eagerly to behold him, crowding along the shore. And lo, on the horizon they saw a fleet of innumerable galleys, filling the

Straits, and then, still far off, they could hear the shrill sound of trumpets. As the galleys came nearer they could see that they were painted in different colours and hung with shields glittering in the sun. They could make out standards and pennons fixed to spearheads and fluttering in the breeze. Around the ships the sea boiled as the oarsmen drove them onwards. Then, with trumpet peals ringing in their ears, the onlookers beheld what they had been waiting for: the King of England, magnificently dressed and standing on a raised platform, so that he could see and be seen.[9]

Such a display was not to everyone's liking and the King of France was distinctly put out. He himself had arrived much more discreetly, with his troops, on 16 September. He had been lodged in the royal palace and his warriors in the city. Richard and his men had to camp outside the town. The King of England claimed not to be offended. The first meetings between Richard and Philip were cordial; from the beginning, the two armies fraternised and the two kings made a show of friendship, even affection, which was much remarked on and unanimously praised; it seemed to bode well for the success of the venture.[10]

Events, however, soon put this cordiality to the test and revealed the discord between the two kings. They were obliged to stay longer in Sicily than Philip had wanted. Almost immediately after Richard's arrival, the King of France had signalled his desire to set sail for the Holy Land at once, but adverse winds forced him to return to port. The two armies, therefore, had to continue to coexist, which provided plenty of opportunities for disagreements.

They very quickly emerged in connection with the disturbances provoked by the somewhat blustering arrival of Richard's soldiers. According to Ambroise, the native inhabitants of the town, descendants of the ancient rulers of the island, both Greeks (called Griffons by the Westerners), Muslims or Lombards (Longobards), had been irritated by the triumphalist and even arrogant entry of Richard's ships. They had booed his men; they saw them, says Ambroise, a good Norman, as the descendants of those Normans who had conquered their island a century earlier, under the leadership of Robert Guiscard and his brother Roger. Clashes very quickly followed, particularly between the crusaders and the Longobards. In spite of his fairly obvious prejudices and his emphasis on the (less than convincing) causes of the local antipathy towards Richard's crusaders, Ambroise concedes that the latter did not always treat native populations with the dignity expected of 'pilgrims', but behaved more like thuggish mercenaries in a conquered country; they had earlier, as we have seen, run riot in Portugal. Their reputation as 'skirt-chasers' was well established and feared by the local inhabitants, especially men of Muslim origin,

unlikely to take lightly what they saw as lax morals in dealings with their womenfolk.[11] The shopkeepers, furthermore, inevitably cashed in on this sudden influx of people, which increased demand and led to shortages and price rises. All three elements emerge clearly in this vivid account:

> . . . the burgesses, the Grifon rabble of the town and the louts, descendants of Saracens, insulted our pilgrims, putting their fingers to their eyes and calling us stinking dogs. Each day they ill-treated us, murdering our pilgrims and throwing them into the latrines. Their activities were well attested . . . When the two kings had arrived the Grifons then kept the peace, but the Lombards would quarrel and threaten our pilgrims with the destruction of their tents and the taking of their goods, for they feared for their wives, to whom the pilgrims spoke, but they did this to annoy those who would not have thought of doing anything. The Lombards and the townsfolk always had bitterness against us, for their fathers said to them that our ancestors conquered them. So they could not love us but rather they tried to starve us.[12]

The disorders had many causes. They provided several of the chroniclers with another opportunity to emphasise the moral superiority of the King of England over the King of France: the latter chose to ignore these frictions and kept a low profile, whereas Richard set himself up as legislator and judge in a foreign country. He acted quickly to put a stop to the misdeeds on both sides by severely punishing the wrongdoers, whether crusaders or Sicilians. Those guilty of robbery or rape were dealt with according to the harsh legislation governing crimes and offences committed during a 'pilgrimage'. Richard, as a result, was feared and respected by the inhabitants. According to Richard of Devizes, the Griffons called one king 'the Lion', the other 'the Lamb'.[13]

RICHARD AND TANCRED

Politics and family relationships aggravated the tensions. Richard's sister Joan was the involuntary cause. She had been married, as we have seen, to the King of Sicily, William the Good, but he had died without children, leaving the succession to Sicily open. It was disputed between two claimants, a bastard cousin of William, Tancred of Sicily, and Constance, William's aunt, wife of Henry of Hohenstaufen, soon to become the Emperor Henry VI. Constance had been designated by William as heiress to Sicily, which was then a rich kingdom, a model of multicultural society and of great strategic importance.[14] But a majority of the Sicilian nobility disliked the idea of a German king and had opted for Tancred; they were supported by the barons of Calabria and Apulia, and also by Clement III, alarmed at the prospect of a German monarch taking power

in southern Italy, leaving him under threat on all sides. These combined forces had recently succeeded in quelling a revolt by a few Sicilian barons, assisted by German warriors, who had taken Constance's side. The crusaders arrived on the island at a turbulent period, just when the conflicts had temporarily died down.

For the time being, Tancred had the upper hand. He was keeping Joan, the dead king's widow, in close confinement, almost a prisoner, for purely material reasons: he had no wish to surrender the dower which should revert to her on her husband's death or to hand over to Richard the donation that William had promised to his father, Henry II. The grandiose arrival of Richard's fleet may at least in part have been intended to intimidate Tancred, who quickly released Joan, in Palermo, but empty-handed; she arrived in Messina on 28 September.[15]

Joan's release might have brought the kings of France and England closer, but in the event it widened the rift between them. When they visited her together at Michaelmas, on the day after her arrival, the twenty-seven-year-old Philip Augustus, a widower for three months, was much impressed by the beauty of Joan, now herself a twenty-five-year-old widow. Did he fall in love with her at first sight? Some of the army certainly thought so, and the chroniclers emphasise the great change in his mood; it was obvious that Philip had recovered his zest for life. According to Roger of Howden, 'the King of France looked so joyful that people said he was going to marry her'.[16] It is not clear why Richard took such exception to this nascent idyll. Régine Pernoud thinks that he was unable to countenance a new matrimonial tie between the crowns of France and England at a time when he was planning to break his own longstanding commitment to Alice.[17] But here, surely, on the contrary, was a potential solution to his problem. He could have suggested a sort of swap, substituting for one alliance, already endlessly protracted and frequently postponed, another, based on both political interest and personal attraction. William of Newburgh tells us that Philip Augustus was genuinely anxious to contract this union and still trying to achieve it five years later, in spite of the poor relations then existing between the two sovereigns.[18] Did Richard want to save his sister for an even more advantageous marriage? We know that, at one point, there was a project to marry her to a brother of Saladin and that eventually, in 1196, she was married to Raymond of Saint-Gilles, ending nearly forty years of conflict between the houses of Aquitaine and Toulouse.[19] But there was no thought of marrying her to a Muslim prince in September 1190, and Richard's policy was then to isolate the Count of Toulouse rather than make alliances with him, as his preparations to marry Berengaria of Navarre reveal. Before he could

make this marriage, Richard had to persuade Philip Augustus to release him from his betrothal to his sister Alice. There could hardly have been a better opportunity to do so. Nevertheless, the day after their meeting, Richard removed Joan from any possible approaches by Philip; he took her to the other side of the straits and arranged for her to be lodged in a fortified Calabrian convent, after expelling the Griffons.[20]

Another potential source of conflict was Richard's attitude to Tancred, who had behaved very deferentially towards Philip and, as we have seen, lodged him in his palace. It is possible that Tancred, aware of their earlier strained relations, might have been hoping to set the two kings against each other. He came very close to doing so, as was revealed when Richard embarked on a policy of intimidating Tancred, hoping to force him to hand over Joan's dower. On 2 October he occupied the monastery of St Saviour and used it to store the provisions for his ships, which made the inhabitants fear he was planning to conquer the whole of Sicily.[21] As a result, fights broke out between Richard's men and the inhabitants of Messina, who shut the gates of their town against them; Richard's efforts to stop these fights were in vain. The French soldiers, meanwhile, were able to circulate freely within the town. Richard's men concluded that the French were in collusion with Tancred's Sicilians.[22] To restore order, Richard proposed a conference between the two kings and the leading men of Messina, which took place on 4 October. But during the negotiations there was a fresh outbreak of rioting, and one of the sections of Richard's encampment, that of the Aquitainians, was attacked. Richard asked the King of France to help him restore order. Philip refused to get involved and tried unavailingly to reconcile the two parties. This time, Richard could not contain his anger. He returned to his camp, called his men to arms, exhorted them to fight as if they were attacking enemies of the faith in a holy war and gave the order to seize the town.[23] He himself led the assault, which gave the chroniclers an opportunity to laud his knightly valour.[24] The town was taken fairly rapidly, though not without a few losses, and part of it was looted by Richard's men. Ambroise makes no effort to conceal this, and sees the episode as the cause of the future conflicts between the two kings:

> . . . for the town was soon pillaged and the galleys, which were neither mean nor poor, were burned. They acquired women, fair, noble and wise women. I do not know the whole story, but whether it was wisdom or folly, before it was well known through the army, the French could see our pennoncels and our banners of many kinds on the walls. The king of France was jealous of this, a jealousy that was to last all his life and there was the war conceived which led to the devastation of Normandy.[25]

In fact Philip refused to accept the presence on the walls of the banners of his vassal, Richard; they amounted to a public proclamation of a right of conquest. Following earlier agreements stipulating that their conquests would be shared, Philip demanded that his own banners should be displayed (perhaps as well as Richard's). To avoid a further deterioration in their relations, Richard agreed to the town being put into 'neutral' hands, that is, held by the military orders, the Templars and Hospitallers, until a diplomatic solution could be found for the problems with Tancred and until Richard got what he wanted, that is, Joan's dower.[26] To maintain his dominance, Richard built a castle on the heights above the town, its name in itself enough to reveal his intentions: he called it 'Mate-Grifons' (or 'Subdue the Griffons'), which, hardly surprisingly, 'infuriated the Greeks'.[27]

Faced with this show of force, Tancred gave in. On 6 October an agreement was reached, ratified in November. Tancred was to retain Joan's dower but pay 20,000 ounces of gold in compensation; to this he added a further 20,000 ounces, to be handed over to Richard until the celebration of a marriage that would seal the agreement between the two princes: one of Tancred's daughters, 'a beautiful and intelligent young lady', was promised to Arthur of Brittany, Richard's nephew, whom he was to designate his heir if he were to die childless.[28] According to Ambroise, Richard promised to return this sum if Arthur did not marry Tancred's daughter. The sums paid as compensation were carefully counted out and shared between the two kings in accordance with the initial agreements; Rigord says that Philip Augustus got only a third when he should have had half, a claim which seems a trifle excessive in the circumstances, given the grounds for the compensation and the minimal role Philip had played in the operation.[29]

Both parties could feel satisfied with this settlement: Tancred now had Richard as an ally in his conflict with the Emperor Henry VI; Richard was now in possession of a considerable sum of money, which he intended to use to ensure the success of his expedition. Joan put no objections in his way. Furthermore, he could also draw on the sum deposited with him until the celebration of the highly hypothetical marriage between Tancred's daughter and Arthur, then two years old.

Two days later, on 8 October, Philip and Richard, now reconciled, together took steps to fix an acceptable price for the provisions supplied by Sicilian merchants and to establish regulations applicable to all the crusaders. Of particular concern were games of chance, above all dice, always a potential source of trouble when the losers refused, or were unable, to pay up; such games were forbidden to the ordinary soldiers

and restricted to twenty *sous* a day in the case of the clergy and knights, but no such restrictions were placed on the grandees and even less so on the kings, who could 'play as they wished'.[30] All these arrangements testify to one overriding concern, keeping order within the crusader army and preserving harmony between it and the inhabitants of Messina during what promised to be a lengthy stay. Winter was approaching and it was too late to think of braving the storms that were common in the Mediterranean at that season. Preparations were therefore made to spend Christmas in Sicily.

RICHARD'S PENANCE

It was probably in the lead-up to Christmas that a strange ceremony took place that amazed contemporaries and has much exercised recent historians. Roger of Howden, who describes it, unfortunately fails to provide a date. Richard, for reasons unknown,[31] was stricken with remorse for his previous moral conduct. 'Under divine inspiration', he remembered 'his shameful life': the prickings of lust had until now pervaded his whole being; God, however, who wanted not that the sinner should die but that he be converted and live, 'opened the king's eyes to His Mercy and gave him a penitent heart'. The King summoned all his bishops and archbishops, made a public confession and submitted to a penance:

> Naked, holding in his hands three bundles of peeled rods, he threw himself at their feet and was not ashamed to confess before them the ignominy of his sins, with humility and such contrition of heart that no-one could harbour the slightest doubt that it really was the work of He who, by his glance alone, makes the earth tremble. Then he abjured his sin and accepted the appropriate penance from the bishops. From that hour, he was transformed into a man who feared God and did Good, and did not fall back into his iniquity.[32]

For many years, historians have seen this 'iniquity confessed' as the 'sin of sodomy', that is, an avowal by the King of England of his homosexuality. We will return to this hotly contested issue later.[33] At all events, the words employed can leave us in no doubt it was a sexual sin which Richard felt guilty about and wanted to expiate, so as not to incur divine punishment, whether because of the approaching Nativity, the risk of death as a crusader–pilgrim in the service of God, the end of the world – which he believed might be imminent – or the arrival of his future wife, Berengaria of Navarre. Whatever the reason, Richard had decided to turn over a new leaf and start a new life.

RICHARD AND THE END OF THE WORLD

It is in this context that we should see the visit of the Calabrian monk Joachim of Fiore, abbot of Corazzo. This aged monk, now nearly eighty, was famous for enjoying the gift of prophesy and, even more, for having been able to decipher the book of prophesy *par excellence*, the Apocalypse of John, which then fascinated Christians; it announced the unfolding of history as it had been foretold, even programmed, by God. Richard was no exception; he too believed that the events of history, past, present and future, were inscribed in this book which, if correctly interpreted, would make it possible to situate oneself in relation to these events, in particular in relation to the Last Days, those of the 'end of time' preceding the Last Judgement and marked by the appearance of the Antichrist, who would come on earth to gather the impious behind him and fight against Christ and his faithful, before being crushed by the glorious return of the Messiah. These conceptions, at once historical, prophetic and mystical, and which surfaced at various moments in medieval history, are no longer of great concern to the majority of people today, secular in outlook and largely ignorant of biblical culture.[34] This is why so many historians, who share this common mindset, tend to assume that only learned monks, noses deep in their arcane texts, paid any attention to such erudite speculations.[35] This is very far from the case. In the Middle Ages, culture was essentially clerical and Christian in tone, inspired by the Bible, even through the distorting mirror of patristic tradition. Pious people, laity and clergy alike, believed that history was linear and that it would ineluctably come to an end, what we today call the 'end of the world', and which might better be called the 'Last Age'.

Richard, therefore, had the elderly scholar brought to Messina to explain the main points of his prophetic interpretation of history. Roger of Howden describes the meeting in detail.[36] The discussion that took place between the hermit and the 'roi-chevalier' deserves our attention, because it illustrates so well the sort of issues that were of concern to both clergy and laity in this area.

The debate turned on the interpretation that should be given to Chapter 12 of the Apocalypse, in which the apostle John describes the tribulations of a woman crowned with stars and threatened by a dragon. This allegorical vision has always been considered as symbolising the battle between good and evil throughout the ages and in particular the tribulations of the Church persecuted by the devil right to the end of time. The chronicler is careful to transcribe the biblical text

on which the debate was based. It describes the vision of John in these words:

> It was a Woman enveloped in sun. Under her feet, the moon; on her head, a crown of twelve stars. She was pregnant and cried out, suffering the pains of childbirth. And lo, there was a great red dragon with seven heads and ten horns, and on its heads seven diadems. Its tail swept a third of the stars out of heaven, and threw them down to earth. The dragon stood before the Woman about to give birth, in order to devour her child the moment it was born. And the Woman brought forth a male child, a son, he who ought to lead all the nations with a sceptre of iron. And this son was raised up towards God and towards his throne. The Woman fled into the desert where God had prepared a refuge for her to nourish her there for one thousand two hundred and sixty years.[37]

Like the majority of commentators in all periods, Joachim saw this woman as representing the Church and the dragon as the devil who persecuted it.[38] The seven heads symbolised seven powers persecuting the true faith. Here Joachim was innovating, and his new interpretation was of particular interest to Richard. The old monk believed he could put a name to these seven heads; they were the rulers who were enemies of the faith, the pagan princes of Antiquity, succeeded in this role by the Muslim princes: Herod, Nero, Constantius, then Mahomet, Melsemut,[39] Saladin and, lastly, the Antichrist in person. Richard was living, therefore, in the last but one age of the world, and it was his duty to fight Saladin, whose end was near. Joachim was emphatic on this point:

> One of these heads is certainly Saladin, who today oppresses the Church of God, and reduces it to slavery, along with the Sepulchre of Our Lord and the Holy City of Jerusalem, and with the land once trodden by the feet of Christ. And this Saladin will very soon lose his kingdom of Jerusalem, and he will be killed; and there will be an end to the rapacity of the vultures, and there will be a great massacre of them, like there has never been since the beginning of the world. And their houses will be deserted, and their cities will be desolated; and the Christians will return to these lost pastures, and they will settle there.[40]

A prediction as precise as this with regard to the imminent end of Saladin could hardly fail to be of the greatest interest to the crusader king. It helps to clarify the motives that led Richard to summon the Calabrian hermit so that he could question him on these matters and learn what role God had laid down for him in the fulfilment of the prophesy. Joachim lived up to all his expectations when he gave details of what God expected of him, as Roger of Howden makes clear:

> Then, turning towards the King of England, [Joachim] said: 'It is you who are destined by Our Lord to fulfil all these prophesies, and he will enable you to

accomplish them. He will grant you victory over all your enemies, and He will glorify your name for eternity.'[41]

In a second version, though still written before 1194, Roger adds an important detail. Richard had wanted to know more and had asked Joachim to say exactly when this event would come about. The hermit's reply was reasonably encouraging, because it fixed the date for Saladin's end in four years' time, that is, in 1194:

> Then the King of England asked him: 'When will this be?' Joachim replied: 'When seven years have passed since Jerusalem was lost.' The king then said: 'Might we, then, have come here too soon?' To which Joachim replied: 'Your coming is, on the contrary, an absolute necessity, because it is to you that God will give the victory over His enemies, and he will exalt your name above all the princes of the earth.'[42]

Richard's mission was therefore clear: he was mandated by God to destroy the power of Saladin, the sixth head of the dragon that persecuted the Church. This would be the beginning of the Last Age, marked by the coming of the Antichrist. The question then was how long the interval would be between the disappearance of Saladin and the coming of the Antichrist, marking the beginning of the Last Age. Joachim believed it would be short; for him, the Antichrist had already been born in Rome, and he would soon seize the apostolic throne and exalt himself 'above all that is called God', before being destroyed by the Lord Jesus with his coming, according to the prophesy of the apostle Paul.[43] This only increased Richard's animosity towards Clement III; in these circumstances, he said, the prophesy might already have been fulfilled, and Pope Clement would then be the Antichrist!

Nevertheless, though a lay prince, Richard had a different interpretation of this point; it derived from a tradition well established since the tenth century by the monk Adso of Montier-en-Der in his treatise on the Antichrist, which had already inspired the First Crusaders.[44] On this basis, Richard expounded his views, connecting the Antichrist with Jerusalem, where he was headed, rather than Rome, which he had bypassed:

> I thought for my part that the Antichrist would be born in Antioch or Babylon, in the line of Dan, to reign in the Temple of Our Lord in Jerusalem, and to walk on the soil on which Christ had walked. That he would reign there for three and a half years, dispute against Eli and Enoch, and kill them before dying himself. And that after his death, God would allow sixty days for repentance, during which those who had strayed from the path of truth and been seduced by the preaching of the Antichrist and his false prophets, might repent.[45]

The bishops present were fully in agreement with Richard and the trad-itional exegesis, which is recounted at great length in its various versions by Roger of Howden, in nearly ten extremely dense pages; he gives a full description of this Antichrist to come, who would be born in Babylon in the tribe of Dan (hence among the Jews) and who would win the Jews over to his cause by passing himself off as the Messiah, before being destroyed by Christ on his glorious return. The age of repentance would then follow, preceding the Day of Judgement. We can see here where the two interpretations overlap and where they diverge: the traditional inter-pretation, accepted by Richard, emphasised the close links between the Antichrist, Jerusalem and the Jews; that of Joachim linked the Antichrist to Rome, the papacy and the Muslims. The two interpretations were agreed, however, on one crucial point: the appearance of this Antichrist was certainly imminent, and would precede by only a short time the return of Christ to Jerusalem and Judgement Day.

Even if he preferred to keep to the traditional interpretation of the origin of the Antichrist, there was nothing to prevent Richard from adopting the interpretation of Joachim with regard to the Woman of Chapter 12 of the Apocalypse, or from seeing his own expedition against Saladin as a fulfilment of the prophesy in accord with the theories of the Calabrian monk. Richard could then see himself as the strong right arm of God destroying the sixth head of the dragon, thereby hastening the dramatic appearance of the kingdom of God. It is easy to understand the interest of the King of England in the speculations of Joachim, and also the reasons for his preoccupation with repentance during this period, explaining the penitential ceremony described above.

THE TWO KINGS DISAGREE

How long this preoccupation with repentance, which we might call an attack of mysticism, persisted, we do not know. The stay in Sicily, however, dragged on and the army grew restless. To dispel the boredom, Richard gave feasts and distributed generous gifts. Games and jousts were organised. In one of them, on 2 February 1191, just outside Messina, Richard's immediate entourage was to take on that of Philip Augustus, in the latter's absence. They encountered a peasant on the road, carrying a huge load of sturdy canes. For fun, they seized them and began, there and then, to employ them as lances in an impromptu joust. Richard confronted a close friend of Philip Augustus, with whom he had already clashed, William des Barres, a 'valiant knight of the household of the king of France'. William's rod tore the king's surcoat, much to

Richard's annoyance; he tried to unseat him, but without success, as William clung on to his horse's neck. The encounter was threatening to turn nasty, and some of those closest to Richard, Robert of Breteuil and Robert of Leicester, tried to intervene on the King's behalf to save him from losing face. Richard sent them packing, insisting he would finish the matter on his own. Unable to get the better of his opponent, however, he lost his temper; in a rage, he ordered William never to show his face in his presence again, declaring that he would from this day on regard him as an enemy; he even demanded that the King of France remove William from his inner circle. Nor had his anger abated next day; he refused to accept the apologies that Philip Augustus came in person to offer on William's behalf and, two days later, even rejected an attempt at mediation on the part of several princes of the kingdom of France.[46] In spite of the bad feeling already existing between Richard and William, and of the King's known irascibility, the incident seems to suggest a deeper malaise between the two kings. At all events, Philip gave in this time and banished William from his presence, with instructions to leave Messina. Perhaps in a show of contrition, Richard then behaved with particular generosity towards the army and the King of France. During the month of February, says Roger of Howden, he showered more money on the earls, barons, knights and men-at-arms of the host than any of his predecessors had ever done in a whole year, and he gave several ships to the King of France.

Whether this was enough to end the discord between them is doubtful. Yet Richard needed a reconciliation with the King of France at this juncture. Towards the end of the month, news came that Queen Eleanor, accompanied by Berengaria of Navarre and Philip of Flanders, had arrived in Naples with a large escort. Richard sent ships to bring them to Messina. But Tancred refused to let them embark, on the flimsy pretext that the town was already overcrowded so could not support the Queen's escort. However, their ships had already left Naples and were forced to divert to Brindisi. To sort out this odd affair, Richard went to Catania to meet Tancred. The chroniclers describe the cordial and relaxed atmosphere of their encounters, which continued for five days, from 3 to 8 March, and were marked by many feasts and displays of generosity: Tancred gave Richard four large naves and several galleys; Richard presented Tancred, as a sign of friendship, with Excalibur, the mythical sword of King Arthur, which had recently been discovered.[47]

These festivities could not conceal the atmosphere of distrust prevailing between the two men. During his stay, in the course of numerous discussions, Richard learned why Tancred had been so suspicious of

Eleanor. It was all down to Philip Augustus, who had attempted a risky diplomatic manoeuvre. It was known that Eleanor was approaching; in Lodi, on 20 January, she had met the Emperor Henry VI, who was also said to be marching on Sicily. Tancred obviously feared collusion between Richard and Henry. Philip Augustus, angry that his sister Alice had been supplanted, decided to stir things up. According to Tancred, Philip told him that Richard was intending to deceive him by ignoring the terms of the treaty they had concluded and suggested they form an alliance against Richard. While speaking to him, Tancred became convinced of Richard's good faith, so revealed all and openly accused Philip in these words:

> I am now convinced and have proof: what the king of France made me believe about you through the agency of the duke of Burgundy and by his own letter derived from his jealousy and in no way from his love for me. In fact he informed me that you were not going to respect the peace and loyalty promised, that you had already transgressed against the agreements made between us and that you had entered this kingdom solely to get rid of me; but that if I wanted to march against you with my army, he would come to my aid as far as he was able, to defeat you, you and your army.[48]

Richard professed astonishment and claimed he could not believe it. So Tancred gave him Philip's letters, clear proof of the King of France's treachery, and insisted that it was Philip of Flanders who had delivered them, bearing the seal of the King of France. Richard left with this evidence, just when it became known that Philip, in his turn, had arrived to visit Tancred; his stay was short and he was back in Messina the next day.

FROM ALICE TO BERENGARIA

A showdown between the two kings was now inevitable. Philip quickly registered Richard's frosty demeanour and enquired as to the cause. Richard showed him the letters. Philip was discomfited and at first unsure how to reply, but then improvised a defence that only made things worse; the letters, he claimed, were forgeries produced by Richard:

> 'These writings are recent forgeries. I am certain of it now: he is trying to fabricate reasons to quarrel with me. Does he think, by such lies, he can reject my sister whom he has sworn to marry?' The king of England then replied: 'I do not reject your sister; but it is impossible for me to marry her, because my father slept with her and had a son by her.'[49]

This grave and public accusation was by no means implausible. There had long been rumours to this effect, and Richard had no difficulty in finding

credible witnesses to back him up. Philip Augustus, now doubly wrong-footed, opted for a low-key response that would allow his possible dealings with Tancred to be glossed over. He agreed to release Richard from his oath to marry Alice so freeing him to marry Berengaria. Against all the odds, thanks to Philip's faux pas, Richard had found the solution to a hitherto insoluble problem.

The agreement was concluded soon after, in March. In return for a payment of 10,000 silver marks, Richard was formally released from his betrothal to Alice and was free to marry as he wished. Philip could recover his sister, who was to be handed over to him on his return from the crusade. The agreement was less clear with regard to the dowry, that is, Gisors and the Vexin; they were to be returned to Philip, according to some, to remain with Richard, according to others.[50] The duchy of Brittany was to be dependent in future on the Duke of Normandy, who would answer for it as vassal of the King of France. According to the English chroniclers, with this treaty, guaranteed by oath and bearing their seal, the two kings became friends again.[51]

This is by no means sure. If we are to believe Rigord (who unsurprisingly omits all reference to the affair of the letters or the ensuing treaty), Philip Augustus called on Richard to set sail for the Holy Land before the middle of March. Richard apparently replied that he was unable to do so until August. Philip then proposed a deal: if he sailed with him, Richard could marry Berengaria in Acre. If not, he would have to marry Alice. Richard had no wish to do either, but many of his barons, including William of Châteaudun and Geoffrey de Rancon, had sworn that they would leave with Philip, which had angered Richard. According to Rigord, this was the cause of the jealousy and discord between the two kings.[52] It is clear that Philip resented the way in which Richard had been able to exploit his error of diplomacy. In fact he and his men set sail on 30 March, a few hours before the arrival of Eleanor and Berengaria, making it obvious that he did not wish to meet them. It took him only twenty days' sailing to reach Acre, on 20 April.

As soon as Philip's ships had left, Eleanor and Berengaria made their entry to Messina. The old queen had not been afraid to undertake such a long journey to provide her son with a wife, which has led some historians to conclude that this marriage was desired, conceived and arranged by her, and perhaps even imposed on Richard.[53] However that may be, Eleanor seems to have survived the rigours of the journey without any problems; she remained in Messina only four days before setting off back for England, on 2 April; on the way, she stopped in Rome to deliver to the pope a message from Richard seeking confirmation of

the appointment as Archbishop of York of his illegitimate half-brother Geoffrey. By the time she arrived, Clement III, who had died on 10 April, may already have been replaced by Celestine III, who was consecrated on 14 April.

That same day, Richard, too, left Messina, dismantling and taking away with him the wooden castle of Mate-Grifons. His imposing fleet, now even larger, left port on 10 April. It had not yet been possible for him to marry Berengaria, as it was still Lent, so the marriage had to be postponed. But Richard had joyfully and eagerly welcomed his future wife. William of Newburgh remarks in passing how well Queen Eleanor had done in bringing him this young girl: it was the best way of stopping Richard from indulging in his customary sexual excesses:

> [Queen Eleanor] in spite of her great age, the length and difficulty of the journey and also the rigours of winter, led or rather driven and drawn by maternal affection, came to join her son in Sicily. From the ends of the earth, she brought him, for him to marry her, the daughter of the king of Navarre, a young woman renowned for her beauty and good sense. It may seem strange, even unsuitable, that he was thinking of pleasure when he was preparing for war, and that he intended at once to take his wife with him to the combat. Yet this decision was not only useful but salutary to the young king: useful, because he had no son to succeed him and needed to seek an heir; salutary, because at his age, inclined to the pleasures of the flesh by long indulgence in them, he protected himself by this salutary decision, by providing himself with a remedy against the very grave danger of fornication just when he was about to face danger for Christ.[54]

NOTES

1. Cartellieri, A., *Philipp II*, pp. 99f., 125ff.; Gillingham, *Richard the Lionheart*, pp. 143–7; Kessler, U., *Richard I*, pp. 105ff.; Richard, *The Crusades*, p. 220.
2. Ambroise, lines 305ff.; *Itinerarium*, II, p. 7.
3. Ralph of Diceto, II, p. 65.
4. Roger of Howden, III, p. 18; *Gesta Henrici*, II, p. 119.
5. Roger of Howden, III, p. 54.
6. Gervase of Canterbury, II, p. 87.
7. *Gesta Henrici*, II, pp. 151ff. This is confirmation of Richard's eschatological preoccupations and of the close link between the crusade and expectations of the end of time. It also illustrates the readiness with which people compared the pope to the Antichrist in person at this period.
8. Roger of Howden, III, pp. 54–5; *Gesta Henrici*, II, p. 125. For Robert Guiscard and how he was remembered in southern Italy, see Taviani-Carozzi,

H., *La Terreur du Monde. Robert Guiscard et la Conquête Normande en Italie* (Paris, 1996); Taviani-Carozzi, H., *La Principauté Lombarde de Salerne (IXe–XIe Siècle). Pouvoir et Société en Italie Lombarde Méridionale* (Rome, 1991); Bünemann, R., *Robert Guiskard (1015–1085). Eine Normanne erobert Süditalien* (Cologne–Weimar– Vienna, 1997). For the incident involving the falcon and its significance, see pp. 266–7 below.

9. The translation is that of John Gillingham (*Richard the Lionheart*, p. 149). For Richard's arrival in Messina, see *Itinerarium*, II, pp. 13–14; Ambroise, line 587; *Gesta Henrici*, II, pp. 125–6ff.; Roger of Howden, III, pp. 55–8; Richard of Devizes, p. 15.

10. Richard of Devizes, p. 10.

11. For another example, a few years earlier and in Syria, of criticism of the Western morality that permitted women to speak freely in the streets to men other than their husbands, see Ousama Ibn Munqidh, *Enseignements de la Vie*; see also Miquel, A., *Ousama, un Prince Syrien face aux Croisés* (Paris, 1986), p. 94.

12. Ambroise, lines 549–58, 605–20 (pp. 38, 39 of Ailes translation).

13. 'Unde et unus dictus est agnus a Grifonibus, alter leonis nomen accepit': Richard of Devizes, p. 17.

14. See the useful synthesis of H. Bresc and G. Bresc-Bautier, *Palerme, 1070–1492* (Paris, 1995).

15. Richard of Devizes (p. 17) notes that Tancred had given Joan a mere million *terrini* for her ordinary expenses ('mille milibus terrinorum ad expensas'). This enormous sum, corresponding, according to an editorial note, to a ton of gold, cannot be correct; it is much larger than the sum paid when an agreement had been reached; see also p. 25.

16. 'Et rex Franciae adeo faciem hilarem exhibebat, quod populus dicebat quod rex Franciae duceret eam in uxorem': *Gesta Henrici*, II, p. 126; see also Roger of Howden, III, p. 56: 'The king saw her and was delighted'.

17. Pernoud, *Richard Cœur de Lion*, p. 113.

18. William of Newburgh, p. 458.

19. Roger of Howden, IV, p. 13. For the conflict between the two houses, see Benjamin, R., 'A Forty Years War: Toulouse and the Plantagenets, 1156–1196', *Historical Research*, 61 (1988), pp. 270–85.

20. Richard of Devizes, p. 17.

21. *Gesta Henrici*, II, p. 127; Roger of Howden, III, p. 56.

22. Collusion is clearly suggested by both Roger of Howden (III, p. 57) and Richard of Devizes (p. 18); see also Ambroise, line 865, and *Itinerarium*, II, p. 18, which even speaks of a secret treaty between Philip and Tancred.

23. *Gesta Henrici*, II, pp. 127–8; Roger of Howden, III, p. 58; William of Newburgh, p. 324.

24. For this theme and this episode, see below, pp. 301ff.

25. Ambroise, lines 816–30 (p. 42 of Ailes translation).

26. Roger of Howden, III, p. 58; see also William of Newburgh, p. 325.
27. Ambroise, lines 940ff.; *Gesta Henrici*, II, p. 138. Roger of Howden (III, pp. 67–8) sees this as the fulfilment of an ancient prophesy, whose text he gives in Anglo-Saxon.
28. *Gesta Henrici*, II, pp. 133, 136; Roger of Howden (III, pp. 61–3) gives the text of this agreement, about which Philip informed the pope by letter.
29. Ambroise, lines 976ff.; *Itinerarium*, II, p. 21; Rigord, §72, p. 106. He also emphasises that Tancred had first offered considerable sums to Philip Augustus if he himself, or his son Louis (still a baby), would marry one of his daughters. Philip refused out of respect for the Emperor Henry VI.
30. Roger of Howden, III, p. 59; *Gesta Henrici*, II, pp. 110, 130.
31. It may have been after his visit to the hermit Joachim of Fiore, but we cannot be certain, because Roger of Howden puts this visit after the penance. The two events must, however, be related, and both testify to a very strong religious preoccupation at this time. It seems likely that eschatological tensions (or fears? or hopes?) have some bearing on this crisis of conscience.
32. *Gesta Henrici*, II, p. 147; there is a briefer version in Roger of Howden (III, p. 56), who also says that the ceremony was held in the chapel of Walter de Moyac, admiral of Richard's fleet.
33. See below, pp. 380ff.
34. For these periods of intense eschatological anticipation, see in particular Landes, R., 'Lest the Millennium be Fulfilled: Apocalyptic Expectations and the Pattern of Western Chronography, 100–800 CE', in W. Verbeke et al. (eds), *The Use and Abuse of Eschatology in the Middle Ages* (Louvain, 1988), pp. 137–211; Landes, R., 'Sur les Traces du Millennium: la "Via Negativa"', *Le Moyen Age*, 98 (1992), pp. 356–77 and 99 (1993), pp. 5–26; Landes, R., 'Radulphus Glaber and the Dawn of the New Millennium: Eschatology, History and the Year 1000', *Revue Mabillon*, 7 (1996), pp. 137–211.
35. It is traditional to cite in this context Norman Cohn's *The Pursuit of the Millennium. Revolutionary Millenarians and Mystical Anarchists of the Middle Ages*, revised edn (London, 1970), though it is far from satisfactory. Preferable, in spite of their many prejudices, are McGinn, B., *Visions of the End. Apocalyptic Traditions of the Middle Ages* (New York, 1979); Verbeke et al., *Use and Abuse of Eschatology*; McGinn, B., *Apocalypticism in the Western Tradition* (London:Variorum, 1994), to be corrected and qualified by the works of R. Landes cited in note 34. For the role of Islam in prophetic interpretation in the Middle Ages, see Alphandéry, P., 'Mahomet. Antichrist dans le Moyen Age Latin', in *Mélanges H. Dérembourg* (Paris, 1909), pp. 261–77, where it is played down, and, more recently, Tolan, J. V., (ed.), *Medieval Christian Perception of Islam; a Book of Essays* (New York–London, 1996).
36. *Gesta Henrici*, II, pp. 151ff.; Roger of Howden, III, pp. 75ff.
37. Apocalypse 12: 1–6.
38. For the interpretation of this passage before Joachim, see, for example,

Lobrichon, G., 'La Femme d'Apocalypse 12 dans l'Exégèse du Haut Moyen Age Latin (760–1200)', in Iogna-Prat D., et al., *Marie, le Culte de la Vierge dans la Société Médiévale* (Paris, 1995), pp. 407–39. For the influence of Joachim, see Reeves, M. and B. Hirsch-Reich, *The Figurae of Joachim de Fiore* (Oxford, 1972), especially pp. 512ff. For the distant origins of this interpretation in its prophetic context, see Bodenmann, R., *Naissance d'une Exégèse* (Tübingen, 1986).

39. This was probably Abd'el Moumen or the Almohads in general.
40. *Gesta Henrici*, II, p. 152.
41. *Gesta Henrici*, II, p. 153.
42. Roger of Howden, III, pp. 77–8.
43. Second Epistle of Paul to the Thessalonians, 2: 4.
44. Adso of Montier-en-Der, ed. D. Verhelst, *Adso Dervensis. De Ortu et Tempore Antichristi* (Turnhout, 1976), trans. in part in Carozzi C., and H. Carozzi-Taviani, *La Fin des Temps* (Paris, 1982), pp. 20–34; for the importance of eschatology to the First Crusaders, see Alphandéry P., and A. Dupront, *La Chrétienté et l'Idée de Croisade*, vol. 1, 2nd edn (Paris, 1995); and, more recently, Flori, J., *Pierre l'Ermite et la Première Croisade* (Paris, 1999), pp. 276ff., and *passim*.
45. Roger of Howden, III, p. 78; *Gesta Henrici*, II, p. 154.
46. Roger of Howden, III, pp. 93ff.; *Gesta Henrici*, II, pp. 155ff.
47. *Gesta Henrici*, II, pp. 158–9; for the discovery of Arthur's tomb at Glastonbury, see Gransden, A., 'The Growth of the Glastonbury Traditions and Legends', *Journal of English History*, 27 (1976), pp. 337–58; Keen, *Chivalry*, pp. 113ff. Matthew Paris (*Chronica Majora*, II, p. 379) and Ralph of Coggeshall (p. 36) both date the discovery of the Arthurian tombs to after Richard's departure. According to Gerald of Wales (*De Principis Instructione*, VIII, pp. 127–8), the search for Arthurian tombs was instigated by Henry II. According to Emma Mason ('The Hero's Invincible Weapon. An Aspect of Angevin Propaganda', in Harper-Bill and Harvey, *Ideals and Practice of Medieval Knighthood*, III, pp. 121–37), the sword Excalibur should be identified with the sword 'forged by the smith Wayland' and given to Geoffrey the Fair at his knighting in 1127, a sword taken from the royal treasury. It had no connection with Glastonbury. According to H. Bresc ('Excalibur en Sicile', *Medievalia*, 7 (1987), pp. 7–21), the sword given by Richard to Tancred was the one received by Richard at his investiture as Duke of Normandy. This seems unlikely given the political significance of the latter. All in all, neither of these possible identifications is preferable to the one suggested by the sources.
48. *Gesta Henrici*, II, p. 159; Roger of Howden (III, pp. 97ff.) adds one detail: Tancred and Philip were to attack Richard's army at night.
49. Roger of Howden, III, p. 99; *Gesta Henrici*, II, p. 160.
50. According to Roger of Howden (III, p. 100) and *Gesta Henrici* (II, p. 161), Gisors and its territory was to be returned to Philip at the same time as his

sister. According to Ralph of Diceto (II, p. 86), Richard was to keep the dowry, Gisors and the Vexin, in return for a payment of £10,000; this is also the view of Richard of Devizes (p. 26) and Matthew Paris (*Chronica Majora*, II, p. 364). For the clauses of the treaty and their application, see Gillingham, *Richard the Lionheart*, p. 160.

51. Roger of Howden, III, p. 100; *Gesta Henrici*, II, p. 161.
52. Rigord, §73, p. 108.
53. This interpretation, which is primarily based on a remark by William of Newburgh (p. 346) emphasising the length and problems of the journey, is supported by Richard, *Histoire des Comtes de Poitou*, vol. 2, p. 272; Kelly, *Eleanor of Aquitaine*, p. 332; Richardson, 'Letters and Charters of Eleanor of Aquitaine'; Brown, E. A. R., 'Eleanor of Aquitaine: Parent, Queen and Duchess', in Kibler, *Eleanor of Aquitaine*, pp. 9–34, especially pp. 20ff., 32; Labande, E.-R., 'Les Filles d'Aliénor d'Aquitaine: Etude Comparative', *Cahiers de Civilisation Médiévale*, 113–14 (1986), pp. 109ff. and others. It is fairly convincingly challenged by John Gillingham, 'Richard I and Berengaria of Navarre', in Gillingham, *Richard Cœur de Lion*, pp. 119–39.
54. William of Newburgh, pp. 346–7. Not all the chroniclers shared William's opinion of Berengaria's beauty; Richard of Devizes said she was 'more good than beautiful'.

6

Cyprus and Acre

⌒

THE CYPRIOT INTERLUDE

The imposing fleet of the King of England left Messina on 10 April 1191 and should have reached Acre by the middle of May. It took a month longer thanks to a sudden storm which had huge political consequences: the conquest of the island of Cyprus by Richard's crusaders and the creation of a Latin kingdom of Cyprus which lasted for a century. This relatively easy victory won Richard fame and riches; it was lavishly praised, as a result, by the chroniclers, who liked to extol the courage of the King of England during this conquest.[1] But it led to a further deterioration in relations between the kings of England and France, when Richard gave the throne of Cyprus to Guy of Lusignan, the disputed king of Jerusalem, supported by Richard against his rival, Conrad of Montferrat, the preferred candidate of Philip Augustus.

There was seemingly nothing to suggest such an outcome when, on 10 April, the King of England's ships, over 200 in all,[2] peacefully set sail, in perfect order, for Crete, their first port of call on the voyage to the Holy Land. So as to prevent his ships getting separated during the hours of darkness, Richard's flagship carried a lighted torch by way of a lantern at the masthead, for the rest of the fleet to follow. Ambroise, presumably not a seaman, marvelled at this idea of the King's; his ship, he said, 'led the proud fleet, as the mother hen leads her chicks to food'.[3] But things went badly wrong two days later when, on Good Friday, 12 April, a storm scattered the ships. Most of them reached the appointed rendezvous in Crete, but twenty-five were missing, including two of particular importance, one containing Richard's treasure chest and one carrying Berengaria and Joan, who were accompanying Richard on crusade. On 18 April, Richard sent his other ships to look for them, while he himself went on to Rhodes to organise operations. He remained there for ten days before learning, on 1 May, that the ship carrying Berengaria and Joan had been found and was anchored off Limassol, on the south coast of Cyprus. The other vessels had been shipwrecked and run aground on the coast. Many of his

men had drowned, among them his vice-chancellor, Roger Mauchat, whose body was recovered, still bearing the royal seal around his neck. The wrecks had been pillaged by the Cypriots and the sailors who had survived had been captured and held prisoner. Berengaria and Joan had been invited by Isaac Comnenus to disembark, which boded ill; they had so far politely declined so as to gain time.

Richard joined them with his fleet on 1 May. He called on Isaac to release his prisoners and restore the booty that had been seized. Isaac's refusal came as no surprise and Richard prepared to use force.

Isaac Comnenus, inappropriately known as 'Angelus', had made Cyprus an independent kingdom after having himself appointed its governor in the name of the Byzantine emperor. He then assumed the title of emperor and held on to his position by means of dubious alliances with, among others, the Muslim Saladin. He was accused of doing everything to assist the latter and to prevent provisions from reaching the crusaders. It was said by some that he and Saladin had even sealed their friendship by drinking each other's blood.[4] He was detested by the crusaders and Richard can have had few illusions as to the outcome of his diplomatic move. If we are to believe Ambroise, Isaac simply gave the messenger a reply that was discourteous in the extreme and is untranslatable if highly expressive, much angering the King of England and spurring him into immediate action:

> The king took a messenger and had him rowed to the shore; he was sent to the emperor, to ask him courteously to restore their goods to the prisoners and to redress the wrongs he had done to the pilgrims . . . the emperor . . . said to the messenger, 'Pah sir!', nor would he ever give a more courteous reply, but rather began to growl mockingly. The messenger retired promptly and took the reply back to the king faithfully. The king heard the dishonourable reply and said to his men, 'Arm yourselves!'[5]

In the face of such provocation, if indeed it really happened, Richard could not but resort to violence. On the other hand, with or without the insulting response, he had an opportunity to punish Isaac and force him into line politically. He therefore ordered his army to land on a beach defended by Isaac's Cypriots, who had hastily erected barricades. After a volley from his archers, Richard, at the head of his men (and the chroniclers emphasise, with minor differences of detail, that the King himself was the first to disembark), jumped out of the boats and attacked the makeshift defences set up by the Greeks, who soon fled before this furious onslaught. The crusaders, following close on their heels, entered the town where they gorged themselves. At one point Richard thought

he might be able to confront the emperor in person and challenge him to a duel, but Isaac slipped away and fled on a fast horse which so much impressed the chroniclers that they recorded its name, Fauvel. Isaac withdrew with his army to a place a few kilometres from the town and prepared to offer battle next day, 8 May.[6]

Richard pre-empted him. During the night, he unloaded the horses, weapons and warriors from his ships, advanced on Isaac's camp and prepared to attack. Ambroise seizes this opportunity to laud the King's courage. He records the magnificent reply he made to a clerk who came to warn him of the dangers of such an attack, against enemies who were so numerous, begging him to desist. The King's reply, true or not, was bound to be a huge success with his knights: 'Sir clerk, concern yourself with your writing and come out of the fighting; leave chivalry to us, by God and Saint Mary!'[7]

The victory was complete. Richard's men surprised the Greeks as they slept and the battle quickly degenerated into a rout. The emperor managed yet again to escape on his wonderful horse, Fauvel, which the tired mounts of Richard's army had no hope of catching. But his camp fell into the crusaders' hands, with its treasury and large quantities of booty: vessels of gold, the royal tent, fabrics and victuals of every type and the imperial standard, embroidered with gold, which Richard destined for the monastery dedicated to St Edmund, warrior king and martyr to the faith.[8] The lords of the island began to go over to Richard from 11 May and Isaac considered suing for peace.

That same day, a ship arrived in Limassol from the Holy Land. It carried a delegation of the princes of Outremer led by the King of Jerusalem, Guy of Lusignan, his brother Geoffrey (who had often rebelled against Richard in Aquitaine), Raymond of Antioch, Bohemond of Tripoli and Humphrey of Toron. They declared themselves ready to give Richard their assistance if he would side with them in the dynastic quarrel which had for some time now pitted Guy of Lusignan against his rival, Conrad of Monferrat, called the Marquis.[9] It will be helpful here to give a brief summary of the main lines of this highly complicated affair.

Guy of Lusignan had become King of Jerusalem through his wife Sibylla. He had been defeated by Saladin, taken prisoner and then, in May 1188, released. This had seriously damaged his prestige and powerful hostile elements were seeking to discredit him, along with his supporters, in particular Bohemond of Tripoli, who was accused of treason. Guy was no great warrior, admittedly, and no rival for Conrad in this sphere, but he seems to have been the victim of a major propaganda campaign on Conrad's behalf designed to emphasise this failing.[10] His reputation for

military incapacity, too readily accepted by historians, is in need of qualification. But Conrad of Monferrat had successfully defended the town of
Tyre and he became for many a symbol of Christian resistance to the
Muslims. On the strength of this, he dared to refuse Guy of Lusignan and
his brother Geoffrey entry to Tyre. Relations between the two factions
further deteriorated in October 1190, when Queen Sibylla and her two
daughters died in an epidemic then raging throughout the region. The
dynastic issue then became urgent, since Guy was king only through his
late wife. At this point it was remembered that Sibylla had a half-sister,
Isabella, then married to Humphrey of Toron. The Conrad faction, supported not only by the powerful local family of Ibelin but also by many
French, German and Pisan crusaders, persuaded a few churchmen,
including the Archbishop of Pisa and Bishop Philip of Beauvais, to declare
the marriage between Isabella and Humphrey void; this was in spite of
the protests of Archbishop Baldwin of Canterbury, who opposed the
annulment, which he believed to be contrary to canon law. But Baldwin
soon died, and the annulment was proclaimed with the aid of Isabella's
mother, who declared that her daughter had been married against her
will, which was manifestly untrue. In spite of the fierce protests of Isabella
and Humphrey, who appear to have married for love, political expediency
prevailed; Humphrey was invited to make himself scarce and the unfortunate Isabella was married against her wishes to Conrad on 24
November 1190. After which, Conrad, like Guy before him, laid claim to
the throne of Jerusalem through his wife. But Guy continued to fight for
his title; he withdrew to Tyre, where he quickly realised that his best hope
lay in obtaining the assistance of Richard against Conrad, who was supported by Philip Augustus on the prompting of the French barons.

When he received this delegation, Richard was well aware of the
issues. Geoffrey of Lusignan was an old adversary with a strong rebellious streak, admittedly, but he had taken the cross as a penance for his
revolt. In any case, Aquitaine was now far away and, in a foreign land,
'local' solidarities acquired new strength. The Lusignan were an old
Poitevin family, distantly related to Richard's own ancestors. Guy's
nephew, Hugh of Lusignan, was already in Richard's army. Everything
combined to make the King look favourably on the offers of allegiance
made by the barons. Added to which, it provided him with an opportunity to oppose Philip Augustus, against whom he harboured deep resentment and who also, already ensconced in Acre, risked robbing Richard
of the position he so badly wanted, that of top dog. He therefore
accepted their plea and their homage. To bind them to him more closely,
he opened his treasury to Guy of Lusignan, to whom he made a gift of

2,000 marks and also twenty goblets, two of pure gold.[11] This alliance marked a new rift between the two kings, which could now only widen.[12]

Next day, Sunday 12 May, in Limassol, Richard married Berengaria of Navarre, who was immediately crowned Queen of England by the bishop of Evreux.[13] Richard then hoped to reach a rapid agreement with Isaac, who had in the meantime come up with a tempting proposition: he sued for peace, offering a sum of 20,000 gold marks as compensation for the booty stolen from the shipwrecked sailors, whom he promised to liberate; he also agreed to take the cross and accompany Richard to the Holy Land with 100 knights, 400 Turcopoles (lightly armed cavalry, Easterners or converted Muslims)[14] and 500 sergeants on foot. He declared himself ready to do homage to Richard, swear an oath of loyalty and surrender several castles as security. To confirm this alliance, he proposed the customary marriage: his only daughter would marry whoever Richard nominated.[15] Isaac came in person to Richard's camp to finalise the treaty. But when, in the heat of the afternoon, the princes withdrew to their tents for the siesta, Isaac changed his mind; badly advised, it was said, he fled and prepared to resist, in a sort of blind rage; in a fit of anger, he was even supposed to have cut off the nose of a lord more level-headed than he who had advised him to submit to the King of England.[16] Richard seems not to have been unduly upset and we may wonder whether the general siesta which had made possible Isaac's flight had not been, as it were, an invitation to do exactly that. In fact his 'treachery' allowed the King of England to embark on the conquest of the whole island. He entrusted the command of his land army to Guy of Lusignan and himself assumed leadership of other sea-borne troops, landing at will to seize towns and castles, and attacking Isaac from the rear. They failed to capture Isaac himself, but the lords of the island rallied to Richard, one after the other. Isaac's daughter, who was 'most beautiful and a very young girl' according to Ambroise, had taken refuge in one of these coastal castles; preferring not to resist, she surrendered to Richard who, out of pity, took her hostage and sent her to his young queen, Berengaria, as had been stipulated in the earlier, broken agreement.[17]

Isaac eventually realised that further resistance was futile and agreed to surrender. Mockingly, and so as not to break his word, Richard had chains of silver forged to hold him captive.[18] It was now 1 June; Richard had made himself master of the island of Cyprus in the space of a few days. He entrusted its government to Richard of Canville and Robert of Thornham, who had served him well during its conquest. Not long after, the island was sold to the Templars.[19] It was bought back by Guy of Lusignan in May 1192, for 100,000 besants, the Byzantine

currency in use at the time of the crusades; Guy's brother Amaury turned it into a solid feudal kingdom.

This rapid conquest by Richard was more significant than might at first appear. The island occupied a strategic position of the highest importance on the route for ships sailing for the Latin kingdoms of Outremer, which were able to survive only thanks to the constant stream of troops arriving by sea from the West, usually in Italian ships. In future Cyprus provided them with a safe port of call, an entrepot and a base they could fall back on or use for conquest and reconquest; it would remain a Christian bastion until the battle of Lepanto in 1571. It was a major gain for Christendom in general and for the crusaders in particular. For Richard, the venture was personally extremely profitable; he gained a glory that was all the greater because his chroniclers, in particular Ambroise, were so skilful in publicising it and in lauding his exploits.[20] The rapidity of the conquest impressed contemporaries and still testifies to Richard's abilities as a strategist. He also acquired financial resources that were of immense value to such an extravagant and ostentatious prince. In addition to the booty resulting from the various victories won on the island and to the indemnities 'offered' by Isaac, the King levied on all the island's inhabitants a tax which had all the appearance of a tribute imposed by the victor on the vanquished: to preserve their liberties and their customs in relative autonomy, the islanders had to pay into his treasury half of their movable goods. This wealth, gained at little cost, made the King of England the richest prince on the expedition. He was able to draw on it in ways that gave him huge advantages: he could recruit knights and warriors, he could behave generously and splendidly and he could dazzle his companions and, at the same time, by comparison, take some of the sheen off the reputation of his rival, Philip Augustus; he might be his vassal, but he now surpassed him in every sphere.

THE CAPTURE OF ACRE (12 JULY 1191)

Richard embarked for Acre on 5 June, with the 'King of Jerusalem' and his allies on board. His wife, Berengaria, his sister, Joan, and the young daughter of Isaac Comnenus were once again in another ship. He had every reason to feel pleased with himself. He soon landed on the Syrian coast and proceeded to the strongly fortified castle of Margat, built and held by the Hospitallers. There he left Isaac a prisoner. Then, again by sea, he went to Tyre, where he had his first taste of the consequences of his alliances, when the garrison refused him entry to the town on the orders of Conrad, supported by the King of France. He set sail again on

7 June and continued to Acre, which was in a peculiar situation: the fortified town was in the hands of the Saracens, but it had been kept under close observation by the Christians since the spring of 1189, when Guy of Lusignan had boldly established himself on the heights above the town, in a fortified place known as the Hill of Toron. Guy had subsequently been joined by contingents of crusaders from all over the West, in particular Flemings, Danes and Germans, and then by Philip Augustus and his men. But the besiegers had themselves been under siege for several months by the armies of Saladin. It was during this double siege, so favourable to epidemics given the lack of hygiene, close conditions and poor nourishment, that Sibylla and her two daughters had died.

The Christian siege of the town had been ineffective because the Saracens in the garrison were occasionally able to receive fresh provisions by sea, when Muslim ships succeeded in forcing the blockade. It would have to be stormed. With this in mind, soon after his arrival on 20 April, Philip Augustus had begun to construct siege engines, in particular wooden towers to dominate the ramparts, from which various projectiles could be launched into the town. But his fleet was not big enough to ensure a total maritime blockade and he could not steel himself to attempt a direct assault. His chronicler, Rigord, disingenuously claims that he deliberately postponed this assault, which would probably have succeeded, as a courtesy to Richard, so that they could share the glory, but this version of events seems highly implausible.[21]

As he approached Acre, on 7 June 1191, Richard's fleet encountered a large merchant ship, which the texts call a dromon, and which the chroniclers bombastically describe as the biggest ship built since Noah's ark.[22] It flew a French flag, but his seasoned sailors were not convinced; some sources with a particularly pro-Richard bias say it was the King himself who was suspicious. On his orders, his fleet sailed towards the dromon to investigate and launched a small boat which, by way of salute, received a salvo of arrows and Greek fire. This was a weapon invented by the Byzantine fleet, hence its name, but perfected by the Muslims. It consisted of a blend of naphtha, petrol and bitumen, which occurs naturally in this part of the Near East; it was put in pottery containers, set alight with a wick and then hurled at enemy ships or at their houses, wooden fortifications, assault towers and other war engines. It was a weapon particularly feared by the Westerners; they had no experience of it and were badly frightened when they saw that water could not douse the flames, which burned even on the sea. Such a reception was enough to convince them that this was indeed an enemy ship. In fact it belonged to Saladin; it was loaded with provisions, weapons of various sorts and

reinforcements, and it was trying to force the blockade and bring help to the besieged fortress of Acre. Richard at once gave orders for his galleys to attack the heavy Saracen vessel which was becalmed and unable to escape. Divers immobilised it by destroying its steering oar, then sank it, though there is some doubt as to whether it was Richard's sailors who were responsible or whether the Muslims, realising that all was lost, had preferred to scupper it. The assault was launched and it was victorious; the vessel carried 1,500 men, of whom many were killed in the fighting, others were taken prisoner and yet others were drowned on Richard's orders. A large stock of arms was found on board, containers of Greek fire and even, it was said, containers full of venomous snakes, which the Acre garrison had intended to throw from the town into the Christian camp. This capture caused a great sensation and the chroniclers dwell on it at length, including Rigord, usually reluctant to write in praise of Richard.[23] Of course, he relied on the accounts of the King of England's men for his information.

Nothing could have suited Richard's purpose more than for him to be seen as a saviour from the moment of his arrival. He was greeted almost like the Messiah, first because of this victory, second because the crusaders had been awaiting the arrival of his large army for such a long time and third because they hoped that the combined crusader armies would now attack and take Acre, where the siege had dragged on endlessly and unavailingly.[24] Surely Richard's first victory was a good omen? This, at least, is how the crusaders saw it and the new arrivals were fêted.

Right from the start, Richard had an eye to his publicity. His fleet had made a big impression; he entered the camp with great pomp and soon assumed his role as war leader.[25] On 10 June, he loudly proclaimed that he was ready to hire men of war, as Philip Augustus had done before him. But Richard went one better: where Philip had offered three gold besants a month to knights who entered his service, Richard offered four. His men-at-arms, too, were better paid, and recruits flocked to join him. Perhaps Richard's initiative should simply be seen as an example of his superior qualities as a commander and of the negligence of Philip, who had 'laid off' his sergeants. The result, in any case, was that the Saracens succeeded in destroying Philip's machines, but not those of Richard, which were better guarded.[26] This higher pay much pleased the soldiers but was far from popular with the King of France and his allies.

Another incident was equally displeasing to them. On 8 June, when he received the Italian delegations, Richard declared himself ready to hire the Pisans, but categorically rejected the Genoese, whom he saw as

too closely bound up with Philip and Conrad. Harmony decidedly did not prevail in the Christian camp. In these circumstances, was a joint attack a realistic possibility? According to Rigord, Philip had proposed this immediately after Richard's arrival and Richard had at first agreed. However,

> when King Philip wanted to mount the assault next morning with his troops, the king of England would not allow his own men to join in and he forbade the Pisans, with whom he had made a sworn treaty, to take part in it.[27]

The siege, therefore, was resumed, and it was to drag on for a long time yet. Richard re-erected before the port of Acre the castle of Mate-Grifons, originally built in Messina, then dismantled and transported in pieces. He also unloaded from his ships enormous round stones that had also been brought from Messina and were intended for use as projectiles in the perrieres and mangonels which were the artillery of the period.[28] Other perrieres, more powerful than those of Philip, were built on the spot, and given evocative names: the Malecosine ('Bad Cousin') of the Muslims in the town was now opposed by Richard's Maleveisine ('Bad Neighbour'); there was a third such machine in the camp of the Hospitallers, also famous because it had been paid for by money donated by the army in response to the eloquent preaching of a priest, and which was called, in consequence, Periere Deu ('God's Catapult').[29] Richard also built many battering rams intended to weaken the walls in an attempt to create breaches. One such attempt almost succeeded, but it took place when most of the soldiers were in their camp, eating; the assault was undertaken only by a small band of undisciplined squires and Pisans, who broke in the face of the concentrated Saracen attack.[30]

Attempts were also made to create wider breaches by bringing the walls down using the complicated sapping technique already described, digging tunnels beneath the foundations and shoring them up with wooden props which were then fired. To combat these operations, all the besiegers could do was dig their own tunnels into those of the attackers and drive them back, or hurl a variety of objects or Greek fire at the sappers before they could start digging. It was thus all-important to get close to the ramparts. To protect themselves against these various projectiles, the crusaders dug tunnels or, more often, if the soil was rocky, constructed covered wooden corridors protected with earth or fresh animal hides that were not readily combustible. All these approach works were carried out amid the salvoes of the archers and crossbowmen of both armies. The account given by Ambroise, who was actually present and who was also knowledgeable about military matters, is full of detail and

a veritable mine of information for the historian on the art of warfare and the siege and battle techniques of the period.[31]

These military operations were carried out for the most part in the absence of the two kings, both of whom were laid low by illness, first Richard, then Philip. It was probably a form of scurvy called 'Léonardie', which caused bouts of fever and other problems, including loss of hair and even nails; this is possible in Richard's case, though he may have been suffering from malaria, and it is likely, indeed almost certain, in the case of Philip. Others were affected, including the Count of Flanders, who died from it. Ambroise paints a vivid picture of the distress of the army, which had already experienced its terrible effects:

> So the armies were in this state, sad and melancholy, sorrowful and cast down, because the two kings who should have taken the city were ill. On top of this, the Count of Flanders had died, to the great sorrow of the army. What more can I say? The illness of the kings, the death of the count, put the armies into such distress that there was no joy or happiness.[32]

Between bouts of fever, the two kings often had themselves carried to positions close to the walls and even sometimes took part in operations. Rigord, on behalf of Philip Augustus, and Ambroise and the many English chroniclers, on behalf of Richard, praised their courage and their decisive action, as leaders and sometimes also as archers.[33] We will return to this point in Part Two.

Many assaults were attempted in the second half of June, following more or less effective operations, mostly conducted by King Philip's sappers. But the element of surprise was usually lacking, on one side or the other. On the Muslim side, lookouts situated on the ramparts warned the garrison of any imminent assault; by one means or another (drums, signals or carrier pigeons[34]), the news was passed to Saladin's troops, who then engaged in diversionary tactics to prevent the assault or even took advantage of a concentration of troops elsewhere to launch an attack on the Christian camp. Meanwhile, the Christians sometimes got information in messages which, say several chroniclers, reached them attached to arrows shot from the walls by a mysterious contact. He let them know, for example, that Saladin was planning to evacuate the entire garrison of Acre by night, and they were consequently able to frustrate his plans. The Muslims, too, got information from spies who, under cover of night, slipped out of the garrison, across the Christian lines, into Saladin's camp, or vice-versa.

Nevertheless, the Muslim garrison began to despair; food was running short and weariness had set in. The leaders of the garrison made

proposals of surrender; they offered, if allowed to leave the town freely, safe and sound and with their weapons and baggage, to surrender the citadel intact, with all the wealth it still contained, to the Christians who had now been besieging it for two years. But the kings of France and England rejected this proposal; they wanted an unconditional surrender and to take full advantage of a victory they were confident they could win; in particular, they wanted to recover the lost territories, Jerusalem and the Holy Cross.[35] A last attempt by Saladin to break the siege and liberate the garrison failed on 4 July. The Christians prepared for a general assault, intensifying their sapping activities and beginning to fill in the moats which prevented them from reaching the walls to destroy them. Many sections of the wall were on the point of collapse.

Faced with this threat, and after many Christian attacks, the garrison had no alternative but to agree, on 12 July 1191, to surrender the town on harsh conditions: the Muslims were to hand it over in its present state with everything it contained, including arms, wealth and ships. In exchange for their lives, they would liberate 1,000 Christian prisoners of modest rank and 200 knights to be chosen by the two kings; the Muslims of the garrison would be spared, in return for payment of a sort of ransom of 200,000 gold besants (or dinars); some of their leaders would be handed over as hostages to guarantee the treaty was observed. Those Muslims who wanted to convert would be set free; at least this was originally agreed. But it was soon noticed, say the chroniclers, that many Muslims who had 'converted' rejoined Saladin's army and it was then forbidden to baptise them. Lastly, Saladin was to restore to the Christians the relic of the Holy Cross which had come into his hands in 1187 at the Battle of Hattin.[36] Saladin was horrified by these demands, but had no opportunity to object; the garrison had surrendered and the Christians had already entered the town. A Muslim chronicler describes the surrender from Saladin's point of view:

When the Sultan learned the content of their letters he was extremely upset and disapproved strongly. He called his counsellors, informed them of developments, and asked their advice on what should be done. He was given conflicting advice and remained uncertain and troubled. He decided to write that very night . . . disapproving of the terms of the treaty, and was still in this state of mind when suddenly the Muslims saw standards and crosses and signs and beacons raised by the enemy on the city walls. It was midday on Friday 17 jumada II 587 [12 July 1191]. The Franks altogether gave a mighty shout, and struck a heavy blow into Muslim hearts. Great was our affliction; our whole camp resounded with cries and lamentations, sighs and sobs. The Marquis [Conrad of Montferrat] took the King's standards into the city and planted

one on the citadel, one on the minaret of the Great Mosque – on a Friday! –
one on the Templars' tower and one on the Battle tower, each one in place of
a Muslim standard. The Muslims were all confined to one quarter of the city.[37]

The Christian armies made their triumphal entry into Acre on Friday 12
July. They raised their standards as a sign of possession. This led on an
apparently trivial incident which was to have far-reaching consequences.
One of the leaders of the German crusaders, Duke Leopold of Austria,
raised his standard next to those of the three kings – of England, France
and Jerusalem – as several other princes had done. Richard's men, probably on his orders, unceremoniously tore it down and tossed it over the
walls. Leopold was angry and, failing to get any redress, soon left for
home. He harboured a grudge against Richard and this episode may be
seen as one (though not the only) cause of Richard's capture on his return
from the crusade. We will return to the matter of the significance of this
deliberate humiliation, which John Gillingham takes pains to justify.

At this point, admittedly, Leopold carried little political clout. He had
arrived in Acre before the two kings and participated in the siege since
the spring of 1191. There, he had found the remnants of the German
army, scattered after the unfortunate drowning of the Emperor Frederick
Barbarossa, but rallied under his own banner the previous October by
Frederick of Swabia, the dead emperor's son. But Frederick himself had
soon died of sickness, like so many others, during the terrible siege and
Leopold found himself leader of a much-reduced German army, with
little power and without adequate financial resources. One English
chronicler says that he had even taken service with the King of England,
along with many other princes and nobles, obtaining from him the sub-
sidies that made it possible to maintain his army.[38] If this was the case,
he had no right to raise his own banner on the walls, which suggested he
was making a claim to a share in the spoils reserved for the victors. Only
the two kings were justified in such a claim (and perhaps also their
respective candidates for the throne of Jerusalem). Richard and Philip, as
we have seen, had agreed to divide all their conquests between them. In
these circumstances, concludes Gillingham, 'for [Leopold] to raise his
standard in Acre was totally unrealistic.'[39] This is undeniable at the level
merely of realpolitik, if, that is, it really is the case that Leopold had
entered fully into Richard's service, which is by no means certain. But
Richard's attitude was, in any case, neither adroit nor prudent. It was a
gratuitous personal humiliation and it made it blindingly obvious that,
in the eyes of the two kings (and above all, in this instance, in those of
Richard), all those crusaders who had spent long months pursuing the

terrible siege of Acre were now expected quietly to fall into line behind the two sovereigns. Many crusader princes, nobles, knights and lesser men, who had suffered for so long, felt frustrated and humiliated. Their sense of being seen as of little or no importance may have encouraged many more of them to consider returning home.

The two kings proceeded to share the booty and the prisoners. The friction between them had not decreased. Soon after Richard's arrival, citing earlier agreements, Philip Augustus had not hesitated to claim half the riches Richard had acquired in Cyprus. This surprising claim had both outraged and amused the King of England. He had pointed out, not unreasonably, that it was his army alone that had conquered Cyprus and that it had, in any case, no direct connection with the crusade, whereas the agreement applied to conquests made in common by the armies of the two Kings during the expedition. In these circumstances, Richard joked, the King of France ought to give him his share of Flanders, which Philip was on the point of acquiring following the death of Count Philip.[40] The division of Acre presented fewer difficulties but was still not completed without incident; the Marquis of Montferrat, for example, balked at surrendering his Saracen prisoners, who were supposed to be returned to Saladin in exchange for Christians. Further, the handover of the town to the crusaders posed some problems. The former Christian inhabitants, who had been expelled, obviously wanted to recover their possessions. Philip Augustus came to their defence and Richard eventually came round to this commonsense solution.

The town of Acre was thus back in Christian hands and the religious buildings restored to their original purpose; the churches that the Muslims had turned into mosques were reconsecrated, as was only right, said Ambroise, with a certain vindictive glee:

> You should have seen the churches as they left them in Acre, with their statues broken and defaced, the altars destroyed, crosses and crucifixes knocked down, to spite our faith and satisfy their wrong beliefs, and carry out their idolatries! But they later paid for this.[41]

It had been rumoured for some time that Philip Augustus was once again sick and thinking of returning to France. Others, as we have seen, were ready to follow him. Richard tried to persuade them to stay. On 20 July he promised to swear an oath to remain in the service of God in the Holy Land for three years, or at least until the crusaders managed to make Jerusalem Christian again, and he asked the King of France to do the same. Philip refused.[42] Worse, he asked the King of England to agree to his return to France.

Many reasons have been put forward to explain this decision. The first is his state of health; there is no doubt that Philip had been seriously ill. So had Richard, probably, but Philip had been slower to recover. The chroniclers as a whole are in no doubt as to the reality of his sickness. Even Ambroise admits it, though not regarding it as a sufficient cause:

> He was going back because of his illness, so the king said, whatever is said about him, but there is no witness that illness gives a dispensation from going with the army of the Almighty King, who directs the paths of all kings.[43]

Another reason suggested is Philip's mistrust of Richard, who, it was said in the French camp, had wanted to poison him. Philip may have feared for his life and even more (because he was not a coward) for the fate of his dynasty, as his son was only four years old. There were also accusations that Richard was colluding with Saladin, because he had been seen to be vying with him in courtesies and exchanges of gifts. These were malicious rumours, circulated long after the event, to which we will return, and which are best ignored for the moment.[44] More plausible and realistic seems to be the jealousy felt by the King of France for a rival who surpassed him in everything: in physical presence, in wealth and consequently largesse, in prowess, in diplomacy and in the art of self-promotion. Richard was certainly able to win wars and battles, but he was even better at taking the credit for his successes and playing the victor. His volubility and his extrovert temperament only made the King of France retreat further into his shell; he was an introvert, vindictive, even given to black moods, aggravated by illness and the suspicions sowed by his ally, Conrad of Montferrat.

There was another, more political, reason for Philip's decision to return home. Count Philip of Flanders, as we have seen, had died on 1 June. The time had come to enforce in Artois the rights that had been ceded long ago. This prospect, for a sovereign as prudent and realistic as Philip Augustus, was as important a reason as all the others combined, and he decided to leave to Richard the glory of the hypothetical reconquest of Jerusalem, since he would get it in any case, and himself settle for more down-to-earth conquests that would increase the power of his kingdom.[45] Neither the supplications of the barons of France nor the exhortations of Richard could persuade Philip Augustus to remain. His departure was a serious blow to his reputation and, by the same token, helped to enhance even further the prestige of his rival, who stayed behind 'in the service of the King of Heaven'.

On 28 July the two kings met once again to try to resolve the dispute over the succession to the throne of Jerusalem. They managed to arrange

a compromise acceptable to both parties, at the price of concessions on both sides. Guy of Lusignan would continue to be regarded as King of Jerusalem in his own lifetime, sharing the revenues of his kingdom with Conrad, who would also receive the lands of Tyre (of which he was already master), Sidon and Beirut (which he had still to subject). Geoffrey of Lusignan would receive the lordships of Jaffa and Ascalon, also largely in enemy hands. On Guy's death, even if he were to have an heir in the meantime, the crown would pass to Isabella, hence to Conrad, and their heirs.

Next day, 29 July, Philip went formally to the King of England to ask him to authorise his return to his kingdom. Richard agreed to his request, which he could hardly refuse, but had his suspicions: was Philip, he wondered, planning to take advantage of his absence to mount assaults on his continental lands, on Normandy, perhaps, or Poitou? Might he be going to join up with his brother John who, he had learned at Messina, had made another attempt to seize control of the government of the kingdom of England? He therefore asked Philip to conclude a sort of non-aggression pact for as long as he, Richard, remained in the Holy Land. Most of the chroniclers report this pact in various but basically similar forms.[46] William of Newburgh, for example, emphasises Richard's suspicions:

> The king of England, however, on account of their recent disagreement, distrusting his good intentions, demanded and received from him a security on oath, in the presence of persons of honour, as it is said, to the effect that he would abstain from injuring his territories or subjects until his return.[47]

Ambroise, who may have been present, is even more precise:

> King Richard wished that Philip would . . . swear on the relics of saints that he would do no harm to his land, nor harm him at all while he was on God's journey and on his pilgrimage, and that when he had returned to his land, that he would cause no disturbance or war nor do him any harm, without warning him by his French [messengers] forty days before. The king made this oath, giving as pledges great men, of whom we still remember the duke of Burgundy and Count Henry, and other pledges five or more in number, but I cannot name the others.[48]

Philip swore on the Gospels. Then, in line with the earlier agreement, he left a large part of his army behind, under the command of Duke Hugh of Burgundy. On 31 July he left Acre, accompanied as far as Tyre by Conrad of Montferrat, his candidate, from where he set sail for France (3 August). He stopped over in Antiochetta, where he knighted the son of its lord, finally reaching Rhodes and then Rome, where he tried in vain

to get the pope to release him from his oath on the grounds of Richard's 'treachery'. The pope was not taken in and, according to several chroniclers, instead laid him under tighter bonds:

> From the oath which you swore to the king of England for the preservation of peace until his return, which, as a Christian prince, you ought to maintain without an oath, we by no means grant you absolution; but approving its rectitude and utility, we confirm it by our apostolic authority.[49]

The English chroniclers point out forcefully that it was now that Philip decided to conspire with the Emperor Henry VI against Richard.[50]

Richard, too, was probably not fooled by the King of France's oath, however great the binding moral force of such a solemn religious act during this period. If he remained behind, it was primarily because he was still greedy for prowess in the name of God and determined to achieve the goal the crusaders had set themselves, the recovery of Jerusalem and the Holy Places from Saladin. He may still have been influenced by the prophecies of Joachim of Fiore, but we cannot be sure. The desire for personal glory was enough on its own to make this roi-chevalier wish to perform exploits more glorious than a mere siege, even a successful one; a siege in which, moreover, often sick, he had played only what he saw as a subordinate role, that of war leader, strategist or archer. Richard aspired to different exploits, those of a true knight, with the lance or the sword. Where better than the Holy Land to win these spiritual rewards and this renown among men? And among ladies, too, as the trouvère Conon of Béthune sang, at this same period and of this same occasion, as he departed for Syria:

> For her I go sighing to Asia,
> Since I must not fail my Creator.
> . . .
> And great and small should surely know
> That that is where knightly deeds are done
> Where Paradise and honour are won,
> And reputation, renown and the love of one's lady. [51]

NOTES

1. We will return to some of the details in these accounts which, though not of any great historical interest, are significant with regard to the way in which the conquest was perceived and described by the chroniclers; they reflect with some accuracy the picture deliberately projected and widely accepted at the time, which is consequently still influential.

2. Exactly 219, according to Richard of Devizes (p. 28). We cannot be certain, for that matter, that the conquest of Cyprus had not been premeditated by Richard.
3. Ambroise, lines 1185ff. (p. 48 of Ailes translation).
4. William of Newburgh, p. 350; Ambroise, lines 1385ff.
5. Ambroise, line 1455 (p. 52 of Ailes translation); for what Isaac actually said, according to Ambroise, see ibid., note 121. See also *Itinerarium*, II, 32.
6. *Gesta Henrici*, II, p. 164; Roger of Howden, III, pp. 105ff.
7. Ambroise, lines 1611–16 (p. 53 of Ailes translation).
8. *Gesta Henrici*, II, p. 164. For the role of St Edmund as prototype of the warrior martyr, see Cowdrey, H. E. J., 'Martyrdom and the First Crusade', in P. W. Edbury (ed.), *Crusade and Settlement* (Cardiff, 1985), pp. 47–56.
9. *Gesta Henrici*, I, p. 165; Roger of Howden, III, p. 108.
10. See the opinion of Ambroise, lines 2420ff.; Roger of Howden, III, pp. 20ff., 70.
11. Ambroise, lines 1701ff.
12. For these events, see the histories of the Third Crusade, in particular Painter, 'The Third Crusade', pp. 45–86; Runciman, *The Crusades*, vol. 3, pp. 34–75; Mayer, H. E., *Geschichte der Kreuzzüge* (Stuttgart, 1965), trans. J. Gillingham, *The Crusades* (Oxford, 1972), pp. 134–48; Riley-Smith, *The Crusades*; Richard, *The Crusades*, pp. 216ff.
13. Roger of Howden, III, pp. 110–11.
14. For the Turcopoles, see Richard, J., 'Les Turcopoles au Service des Royaumes de Jérusalem et de Chypre: Musulmans Convertis ou Chrétiens orientaux?', in *Croisades et Etats Latins d'Orient* (Variorum, 1992), pp. 259–70.
15. For the political impact of this agreement, see, with some caution, Collenberg, W. H. Rüdt de, 'L'Empereur Isaac de Chypre et sa Fille, 1155–1207', in *Byzantion*, 38 (1968), pp. 123–79.
16. Ambroise, lines 1833ff.; for these events, see *Gesta Henrici*, II, p. 165; Roger of Howden, III, p. 109; *Itinerarium*, II, p. 38; Richard of Devizes, p. 37.
17. Ambroise, lines 2065ff. (p. 61 of Ailes translation); Roger of Howden, III, pp. 110–11.
18. For this episode, see below, p. 364.
19. Rigord, §82, p. 118.
20. For the historical value of the evidence of Ambroise, sometimes disputed but recently reasserted, see Colaker, M. L., 'A Newly Discovered Manuscript Leaf of Ambroise's "L'Estoire de la Guerre Sainte" ', *Revue d'Histoire des Textes*, 22 (1992), pp. 159–68.
21. Rigord, §74, p. 108; there is the same formulation, but for very different reasons, in Ambroise (lines 1833ff.), who says, 'they put great pressure on him to move at once against Acre, for the king of France would not on any account make an assault . . . before his arrival' (p. 58 of Ailes translation).

22. For a fuller account of this episode and its significance, see below, pp. 315ff.
23. Rigord, §75, p. 110.
24. Ambroise dwells at length on the sufferings endured by the Christians before Richard's arrival: lines 2385–4565.
25. For what follows, see Kessler, *Richard I*, pp. 151ff.
26. Roger of Howden, III, p. 113; see also Ambroise, lines 4810ff. and *Itinerarium*, III, 8.
27. Rigord, §74, p. 109.
28. Ambroise, lines 4795ff.
29. Ambroise, lines 4745–6, 4760.
30. Ambroise, line 4945.
31. For these methods, see, with some caution, Lot, F., *L'Art Militaire et les Armées au Moyen Age en Europe et dans le Proche-Orient* (Paris, 1946); corrected by Smail, *Crusading Warfare*, with the addition of Marshall, *Warfare in the Latin East*; for sieges in general, see Bradbury, *The Medieval Siege*; Rogers, R., *Latin Siege Warfare in the Twelfth Century* (Oxford, 1992); for the castles of Outremer, see Kennedy, H., *Crusader Castles* (Cambridge, 1994).
32. Ambroise, lines 4693–701 (p. 96 of Ailes translation).
33. See, for example, Ambroise, lines 4927ff. (on Richard), also lines 4819ff. on Philip Augustus.
34. For the use of carrier pigeons by the Muslims in the First Crusade, see Edgington, S. B., 'The Doves of War; the Part Played by Carrier Pigeons in the Crusades', in Balard, *Autour de la Première Croisade*, pp. 167–75.
35. Roger of Howden, III, p. 114; *Gesta Henrici*, II, p. 174.
36. For the conditions of the surrender of Acre, see Roger of Howden, III, pp. 120–1; *Gesta Henrici*, II, p. 178; and with very little variation in Imad ad-Din, *Conquête de la Syrie*, p. 312.
37. Baha ad-Din, RHC Hist. Or. III, pp. 238–9 (Gabrieli, *Arab Historians*, pp. 222–3).
38. William of Newburgh, pp. 360, 382–3.
39. Gillingham, *Richard the Lionheart*, p. 177, probably relying largely on Richard of Devizes.
40. *Gesta Henrici*, II, p. 171; Roger of Howden, III, p. 114; William of Newburgh, pp. 353–4.
41. Ambroise, lines 5245ff., French translation p. 390 (p. 104 of Ailes translation).
42. Roger of Howden, III, p. 123; William of Newburgh, p. 357.
43. Ambroise, lines 5257ff. (p. 105 of Ailes translation).
44. See below, pp. 276ff.
45. This was clearly understood by William of Newburgh (p. 357): 'Et quoniam idem rex vacanti Flandriae obtinendae inhiare videbatur, ut honestam discessionis causam pretexteret, peregrini aeris mendaciter causari molestiam credebatur'.

46. *Gesta Henrici*, II, p. 184; Ralph of Coggeshall, p. 34; Richard of Devizes, p. 48.
47. William of Newburgh, p. 357 (p. 592 of Stevenson translation).
48. Ambroise, line 5305 (p. 105 of Ailes translation); *Itinerarium*, III, c. 22.
49. William of Newburgh, p. 358 (p. 593 of Stevenson translation).
50. Roger of Howden, III, pp. 123, 167; William of Newburgh, p. 357.
51. Conon of Bethune, 'Ahi! Amors com dure departie', in A. Wallensköld (ed.), *Les Chansons de Conon de Béthune* (Paris, 1921), pp. 6–7.

7

Richard versus Saladin (1191–2)

∽

With the departure of Philip Augustus, Richard was left to face Saladin alone. The Muslim prince had been held in check, for the first time, by the two sovereigns at Acre. Whatever the merits, and they were undeniable, of the armies under Philip's command, the prestige of a victory would now redound on the King of England alone. For contemporaries, and to a considerable extent for the historians who have relied on them, the inglorious defection of the King of France effaced the feats of arms and the stubborn action of the French crusaders. In other words, Richard's reputation rests not only on his own exploits, real or magnified, but also on what is widely regarded as the shameful behaviour of his French rival. The inevitable comparison between the behaviour of the two rulers is overwhelmingly favourable to the King of England: he came, he saw and he conquered. Not for him a retreat from the field of battle at the first opportunity; Richard made himself the champion of Christendom.

A BITTER VICTORY

For his part, Philip returned home, if not as a coward, at least damned as too blatant a political realist who had apparently put his own interests before those of the service of God. The efforts to justify his behaviour, in an attempt to dissipate the shame widely felt at his premature return, can scarcely conceal the embarrassment of his most faithful partisans at what is widely seen as his flight. They are reduced, on uncertain grounds (to which we will return), to invoking his ill-health or accusing Richard of treachery, complicity with the enemy, collusion with Saladin and even attempting to assassinate Philip Augustus or, more likely, his candidate, Conrad of Montferrat; they also emphasise, not without exaggeration, the generosity of the King of France, who left behind enough money to support 500 knights and 1,000 foot soldiers for three years, figures which are debatable.[1]

His enemies, we can be sure, did not fail to hammer the point home; they emphasised the great disparity between the conduct of the two kings,

contrasting the pusillanimity and mean-mindedness of Philip with the magnanimity, courage and disinterestedness of Richard, wholly devoted to God's cause. We cannot but wonder, as we read some of these texts, whether Philip's departure, though it certainly weakened the crusading army, did not, in the end, do more for Richard's reputation than his continued presence would have done. Perhaps the King of England was not too upset by this defection, which left him a clear field and allowed him to appear as the undisputed leader of the crusader armies. At least this is hinted at by a curious passage in a Muslim chronicler: during the first negotiations between the crusaders and Saladin, he says, Richard had been seen by the Saracens as dominated by the French; he had vehemently objected to this interpretation, loudly proclaiming that he was in no way under the King of France's thumb but was, on the contrary, the real leader, prevented only by illness from implementing the proposed agreements.[2] Now, relieved of his rival and suzerain, Richard had a free hand to perform the chivalric exploits in the Holy Land to which he aspired.

For the moment, his first priority was to persuade both his allies and his enemies to respect the clauses of the truce concluded with Saladin. There was foot-dragging on both sides. Conrad the Marquis, a supporter of Philip, was hardly disposed to make Richard's task any easier and he refused point blank to hand over the Muslim prisoners in his hands. It needed all the best efforts of the Duke of Burgundy to calm the fury of Richard, who was all for embarking on an immediate siege of Tyre to force Conrad to hand his prisoners over. For his part, Saladin seems to have had great difficulty in amassing the considerable sums of money demanded by the clauses of the treaty. Saladin and Richard therefore agreed without much difficulty to put back the date of the exchange, originally fixed for 9 August, then postponed to 20 August. It was in any case an opportunistic agreement, as neither camp trusted the other and rumours of duplicity circulated freely. Saladin was even accused of wanting to kill the prisoners, as he had done after the Battle of Hattin, when he had watched the beheading of the Templars, sometimes personally lending a hand. Conversely, the Muslims were convinced that Richard had no intention of surrendering his prisoners. It was in this climate of mutual suspicion that a misunderstanding arose, to which we will return.[3] What is indisputable is that, on 20 August, the Christians waited in vain for Saladin's emissaries. According to Muslim sources, Saladin, perhaps deceived by a movement by some of Richard's troops, suspected a trap and expected a sudden attack by the Christian armies advancing towards him. He decided, therefore, to wait on events. Richard, believing he had been or was about to be tricked, gave orders for the Muslim captives to be beheaded. Ambroise,

who was on the spot, was unmoved and seems even to justify this act of revenge:

> But [in order to] bring down the pride of the Turks, disgrace their religion and avenge Christianity, he brought out of the town, in bonds, two thousand and seven hundred people who were all slaughtered. Thus was vengeance taken for the blows and the crossbow bolts. Thanks be to God the Creator.[4]

Other chroniclers attempt to justify this act of 'gratuitous' cruelty on grounds that are plausible but unproven. Richard, they say, had succumbed to an uncontrollable fury at Saladin's procrastination; he was being unconscionably slow in implementing the clauses of the treaty, in particular with regard to the surrender of the Holy Cross, but also with regard to the exchange of prisoners and the payment of the ransom.[5] The Muslim chroniclers, without denying that Richard had grounds for dissatisfaction, emphasise the baleful consequences of his action: the conflict between Christians and Muslims was in future much more bitter and massacres more enthusiastic. This point emerges clearly from a very detailed passage in the Arab chronicler Baha ad-Din:

> Then they brought up the Muslim prisoners whose martyrdom God had ordained, more than three thousand men in chains. They fell on them as one man and slaughtered them in cold blood, with sword and lance. Our scouts had informed Saladin of the enemy's manoeuvres and he sent reinforcements to the advance guard, but by then the slaughter had already occurred. As soon as the Muslims realised what had happened they attacked the enemy and battle raged, with casualties on both sides, until night fell. The next morning the Muslims wanted to see who had fallen, and found their martyred companions lying where they fell, and some they recognised. Great grief seized them, and from then on the only prisoners they spared were people of rank and men strong enough to work. Many reasons were given to explain the massacre. One was that they had killed them in reprisal for their own prisoners whom Muslims had previously killed. Another was that the king of England had decided to march to Ascalon and did not want to leave so many prisoners behind in Acre. God alone knows what his reason really was![6]

Needless to say, as the two adversaries had promised, though in a form they had hoped would serve as a deterrent, the massacre of the captive Muslims was quickly followed by the reciprocal extermination of Christian prisoners. The Holy Cross was not, of course, surrendered, much to the annoyance of the Christians, as another Muslim chronicler emphasises:

> The cross of the Crucifixion was returned to the Treasury – not to be respected, but to be humiliated: the Franks were very angry because we

kept this cross, and this renewed their misfortune both day and night. The Greeks, then the Georgians, had offered large sums for it and sent messenger after messenger to recover it; but they had no success and did not get what they wanted.[7]

Was the order to execute the captives a consequence of Richard's anger at Saladin's refusal, or at least at his reluctance to keep his promise to return the True Cross? It is not impossible, given the importance the King of England, and even more perhaps the Christians of Outremer, attached to the relics Saladin had seized and which Richard had staked his reputation on recovering.[8] The text quoted above is the only one to explain Richard's decision on strategic grounds. It deserves, nevertheless, to be taken seriously. After the victory at Acre, Richard had effectively to choose between two options. The first was to march immediately on Jerusalem to take possession of it, which was what the mass of crusaders wanted; it was, after all, why they had left their homelands. But the town was strongly fortified, manned by a large garrison and, most of all, a long way from the sea, sole source of provisions and reinforcements. Richard quickly realised that such an expedition was hazardous in the extreme. As a result, to the disappointment of the majority of his men and especially the French, he opted instead to secure possession of the coast and its towns, in particular Ascalon and Jaffa; these two were crucial to the present, and even more the future, success of military operations in Outremer. It was only with difficulty that he managed to persuade the crusaders to leave Acre, where they had been enjoying all the varied pleasures of the warrior's repose, as is made plain by both Christian and Arab sources, though with differing emphases. Ambroise, for example, deplored the promiscuous conduct of the crusaders while confessing how difficult it was for them to be deprived of female company; they had to leave all women behind in the town except for the very oldest, 'the good old women pilgrims, the workers, the laundresses who washed their linen or their heads, and were as clever as monkeys at getting rid of fleas'.[9] An Arab chronicler, Saladin's personal secretary, is even more specific; in a style polished to extreme preciosity, he describes Christian women in a way that would not have been found surprising in a Western writer describing Oriental women, proof that the exotic imagination was operative on both sides and producing similar effects: they were, he says, seductive and immodest, supple and lascivious, charming, perverse, beguiling, shamelessly offering themselves to the warriors for their comfort, persuaded they were performing a meritorious sacrifice in surrendering their charms to God's pilgrims.[10]

ARSUF AND THE CONQUEST OF THE COAST

Regretfully, the crusading army left Acre and set off for Jaffa to conquer the coast, before, or so at least the army hoped, marching on Jerusalem, the avowed goal of their expedition. Ambroise, in the manner of jongleurs, delights in describing for his audience, in words he knew would please them, the marvellous army of these valiant Christian knights marching out, armour sparkling, coloured banners flapping in the wind, painted shields clattering. This is all in the best tradition of the *chansons de geste*, which painstakingly describe what would be most pleasing to the public of their day: the departure of a large troop of valiant warriors, clad in glittering armour, in good order, grouped into 'battles' (battalions) under the command of leaders of the 'host' (army) who marshalled them at will into an impressive parade:

> There you would have seen chivalry, the finest of young men, the most worthy and most elite that were ever seen, before then or since. There you would have seen so many confident men, with such fine armour, such valiant and daring men-at-arms, renowned for their prowess. There you would have seen so many pennoncels on shining, fine lances; there you would have seen so many banners, worked in many designs, fine hauberks and good helmets; there are not so many of such quality in five kingdoms.[11]

During the march on Jaffa, Richard demonstrated real qualities as a strategist, to which we will return; his army followed a route close to the sea, which the accompanying fleet now controlled. He was thus at no risk of an attack on his right flank. His left flank was protected by the infantry, who had to bear the shock of the incessant swirling attacks of the Turks, who remained faithful to the already tried and tested tactics which had so surprised and disoriented the Christians on the First Crusade.[12] They kept swooping down on them, avoiding close contact, content to harry the Frankish columns with their hurled javelins and the arrows shot by their mounted archers. This was a technique that had once been unknown to Westerners. By now, however, they had had time to learn not only how effective it was but also how to protect themselves against it. Basically, the Christian knights had to ignore the provocation and instead patiently bear the hail of arrows and darts without succumbing to the temptation to pursue these wheeling and charging horsemen, whose main aim was to get the usually compact and serried Frankish armies to break ranks, separate and scatter. When discipline was maintained, they were almost invincible and, under Richard's command, it was; this amazed the Muslim chroniclers, who both praised and bemoaned the strict order maintained

by the armies of the King of England, whose mounted warriors stayed in formation, stoical under the hail of arrows which hit without killing them, thanks to the quality of their coats of mail; so numerous were the arrows stuck fast in their hauberks that they looked, it was said, like hedgehogs.[13] Saladin's army was content to keep company with Richard's troops, but at a distance, occasionally harassing his columns in the hope of getting them to split up, concentrating their efforts on the rearguard, commanded by Hugh of Burgundy. At one point it was in serious danger and ready to break formation and make a charge that would be hazardous but might rid them of their attackers. But Richard managed to get the Duke to see reason, then put his rearguard under his own orders, relying on the Templars and Hospitallers, who had more experience of this difficult role of guard dog. The march south was still fraught with difficulty; Saladin's men, who kept a close watch on the Christian army, went ahead of it, razing villages and destroying orchards and crops along its route, practicing a scorched earth policy, in an attempt to starve them. Once again, Richard's strategy frustrated their plans, because the fleet, which kept close to the shore, was able to keep the crusaders supplied with the necessary minimum of provisions.

A few battles were fought, in which Richard distinguished himself, as we will see in Part Two. He was even wounded by a javelin, though not seriously, on 3 September, when coming to the assistance of the Templars, temporarily in difficulties.[14] The march itself was exhausting and oppressive in the muggy heat of summer. The crusaders were obliged always to wear their coats of mail for protection against the incessant flights of enemy arrows. South of Caesarea, which the Turks had devastated before their arrival, their sufferings were doubled when, near Arsuf, in a stifling forest parched by the sun, they feared it might at any moment be set alight by Saladin's Turks and turned into an inferno.

Saladin, meanwhile, had assembled all the troops at his disposal. He had decided to give battle and was waiting for the crusaders on the plain of Arsuf, on the edge of the forest from which the Christians were emerging. The decisive encounter took place on 7 September. It was fought on Richard's terms; he had already drawn up his army in battle order while it was on the march, placing on the two most exposed flanks his most reliable and seasoned warriors, those of the military orders: in the vanguard were the Templars, then the mass of the army, consisting of contingents of various origins, Bretons and Angevins, then Poitevins, followed by the Normans and the English, with the dragon standard, and lastly, protecting the rear, the Hospitallers. All rode in serried ranks in two columns commanded one side by Richard and the other by Hugh of Burgundy.[15]

In the middle of the day, the Turks unleashed their first attack, to the sound of war cries, horns and trumpets blaring and drums beating; a hail of arrows rained down on the Christians, killing many men and even more horses, especially among the Hospitallers of the rearguard. The master of the order, Garnier of Nablus, lost so many mounts that he repeatedly asked Richard for permission to charge to relieve the pressure. Richard refused, waiting for the right moment to unleash a general attack. Tired of mounting losses while unable to respond, and impatient to prove their courage, the marshal of the order and an English knight, Baldwin Carew, could no longer bear to remain inactive, which they found humiliating and irksome; they charged the Turks with the cry of 'St George', in spite of Richard's orders; they were followed by part of the army, scattered the protective cordon of foot soldiers as they went.

Such an improvised attack by proud and undisciplined knights was by no means uncommon and frequently ended in a rout for the Christians. In this case, however, it was turned into a victory. Richard quickly realised that he had to abandon his previous plan of a delayed attack and immediately support the impromptu charge. He gave the order to attack and charged headlong at the enemy with his troops, forcing the Turks into flight. Better still, he managed to prevent the victorious crusader knights from pursuing the fleeing Turks; they therefore avoided the traditional trap of Turkish tactics, a simulated flight followed by rapidly wheeling round to ambush the crusaders just as, in the pursuit, they lost the cohesion that was their strong point. Saladin actually managed to regroup his soldiers and prepare a second assault, which broke in its turn on the defences reordered by Richard and William des Barres, whose courage in charging so impressed Richard that he was reconciled with this old and hated enemy. Many famous crusaders met their deaths in this second attack, including James of Avesnes, regarded as a model of chivalry, who found a 'glorious martyrdom'.[16]

So, unlike at Hattin in 1187, though in not dissimilar circumstances, Saladin was well and truly beaten on the battlefield, in spite of (or perhaps because of) the indiscipline of a couple of quick-tempered knights. Credit for the victory belonged to the crusaders as a whole, but it was mainly attributed to Richard, whose skill in the 'science of war' had enabled him to adapt to an unexpected situation and turn a rash charge that might easily have led to the loss of the Christian army into a victory. His fame as a strategist and as a knight acquired a whole new dimension, all the greater in that his personal deeds were subsequently lauded to the skies by the chroniclers, and in that the victory of Arsuf seemed like revenge for the defeat by the magnificent Saladin at Hattin.

The prestige of Saladin, in contrast, suffered a serious blow, especially with his allies, who lost some of their confidence in him and resolved never again to confront the Franks in open country. Saladin and his men resorted even more systematically than before to a scorched earth policy, destroying the fortresses they feared they would be unable to hold against the Franks. Consequently, they began to dismantle the fortress of Ascalon, choosing not to defend it, in spite of its vital importance, so as to be free to concentrate all their efforts on the defence of Jerusalem, which Saladin believed would be Richard's next objective.

JERUSALEM FORGOTTEN

Yet Richard was in no hurry to march on either Ascalon or Jerusalem. He chose instead to fortify Jaffa, which he reached on 10 September. Historians, like the King's contemporaries, have debated at length the reasons for this decision. The chroniclers emphasise the divisions emerging at this point within the crusader armies. Some wanted to proceed to Ascalon with all speed in order to take it before it was dismantled, a process that had only just begun. This was urged primarily by Guy of Lusignan, who had a direct interest in the matter, since Richard had invested him with the lordship of Ascalon. Others, mostly among the ordinary soldiers, wanted at long last to launch an attack on Jerusalem, the Holy City, to fulfil their pilgrims' vows. Yet others, in particular among the Christians of Outremer and the French, emphasised the risks of such an expedition into the interior, far from the coast and the support of the fleet; a safe port should first be established, they argued, as close to Jerusalem as possible, which could be used by future reinforcements from the West. In the end, Richard decided in their favour; he took his army to Jaffa, where they once again tasted the delights of the warrior's repose for the two months of their stay. This again shocked the moralists, for whom the crusade was a holy and pious war, its success far more dependent on the moral purity of the crusaders than on strategic considerations. Ambroise does not hesitate to repeat their criticisms.[17]

This decision was not illogical. The army needed to rest after the hard fighting of Arsuf; the reconstruction and fortification of a port close to Jerusalem might prove extremely useful in future; nor was it by any means certain that the Christians could have saved Ascalon from the destruction that had already begun; it was even less certain that they could easily capture a Jerusalem defended by the Muslim forces of Saladin. But it was a surprising choice, nevertheless, because the liberation of Jerusalem was the ultimate objective of the crusade. Richard himself seems to have

believed it was possible; in a letter dated 1 October, he expressed high
hopes of being able to retake Jerusalem and the Sepulchre of Christ in the
near future, before returning home.[18] The retreat to Jaffa was unpopular
with the majority of crusaders, including Ambroise, generally so
favourable to Richard; he emphasises the disappointment of the majority
of the army, and their unhappiness at a decision which took them further
away from Jerusalem, when they had got so close. The Continuator of
William of Tyre even tried to attribute this decision, as shocking as it was
contrary to all expectations, to a traitorous defection. Probably confusing this episode with another approach to Jerusalem, to which we will
return, he presents Richard as coming close enough to the city to glimpse
the Temple and the Holy Sepulchre, but forced to abandon his advance
on hearing news of the retreat of Hugh of Burgundy's men, making him
responsible for his retreat:

> The king proceeded . . . to . . . Montjoie [which] is two leagues distant from
> Jerusalem. The king dismounted to say his prayers for he had seen the holy
> city. It is the custom for all pilgrims who are going to Jerusalem to worship
> there, since the Templum Domini and the Holy Sepulchre now come into
> view. After the king had said his prayers, lo and behold a messenger came to
> him from one of his friends in the army telling him that the duke of Burgundy
> and the greater part of the French were returning to Acre. When the king
> learned that the duke had gone back, he was extremely angry and upset. He
> immediately turned round and came to Jaffa.[19]

After travelling to Acre to collect Berengaria and Joan, Richard returned
to Jaffa, where he embarked on the rebuilding of the town's fortifications. There were several skirmishes in the vicinity, in which the King
himself took part, regardless of the danger and much to the anxiety of
his friends, who were uneasy at seeing him exposing himself in this way
in minor operations. Indeed, one of these clashes could easily have turned
out disastrously but for the devotion of one of his knights, William de
Préaux, who acted as a decoy, allowing himself to be taken prisoner by
the Saracens, so allowing Richard to escape.[20]

In addition to the rebuilding of Jaffa, Richard engaged in various diplomatic manoeuvres during the months of October and November 1191.
The first involved the Genoese, whom he had previously shunned on
account of their alliance with his rival Philip Augustus. Now that he was
sole leader of the army, his policy became one of evenhandedness between
the Genoese and the Pisans he had previously favoured. In fact he seems
to have been considering, in the medium or long term, a land and sea
expedition to Egypt, which was regarded as the key to possession of

Jerusalem. Fifty years later, similar geopolitical conceptions led St Louis to make his first attack on Damietta, Mansourah and Cairo, and he, too, after his defeat, fell back on fortifying this same port of Jaffa. Richard was well aware that, for such an expedition to stand any chance of success, he would need the combined fleets of all the Italian cities, which ruled the seas, especially that of Genoa, which had been particularly active in the region since the time of the First Crusade.

He also made an approach to Saladin, through the intermediary of his brother, al-Adil Saif al-Din, called Saphadin by the Western chroniclers. Through his mediation, Richard tried to obtain a satisfactory agreement following his two victories. To do this, he had to find a solution to the thorniest issues dividing the two parties, namely the return of the True Cross, of Jerusalem and of the coastal strip, ideally as far as the River Jordan. The arguments of the two princes, as reported by the Arab chronicler Baha ad-Din, illustrate the diplomatic methods that made possible the tricky business of negotiating agreements in the middle of a war between Christians and Muslims. They also shed light on the aims of the war, on the respective religious outlooks of the two camps, who invoked different traditions and prophecies, and even more on the importance attached by both to Jerusalem, eternal bone of contention between Christians and Muslims.

> On 26 ramadan [17 October 1191] al Malik al-Adil was on duty with the outposts when the King of England asked him to send over a messenger . . . he also sent a letter to the Sultan which said in effect that 'I am to salute you and tell you that the Muslims and the Franks are bleeding to death, the country is utterly ruined and goods and lives have been sacrificed on both sides. The time has come to stop this. The points at issue are Jerusalem, the Cross, and land. Jerusalem is for us an object of worship that we could not give up even if there were only one of us left. The land from here to the other side of the Jordan must be consigned to us. The Cross, which for you is simply a piece of wood with no value, is for us of enormous importance. If you will return it to us, we shall be able to make peace and rest from this endless labour.' When the Sultan read this message he called his councillors of state and consulted them about his reply. Then he wrote: 'Jerusalem is as much ours as yours. Indeed it is even more sacred to us than it is to you, for it is the place from which our Prophet made his ascent into heaven and the place where our community will gather on the day of judgement. Do not imagine that we can renounce it. The land also was originally ours whereas you are recent arrivals and were able to take it over only as a result of the weakness of the Muslims living there at the time. As for the Cross, its possession is a good card in our hand and could not be surrendered except in exchange for something of outstanding benefit to Islam.'[21]

On these fundamental issues, then, the disagreement between the two camps was too deep. For two months, throughout October and November, negotiations continued between Richard (with the assistance of Humphrey of Toron, who spoke Arabic) and Malik al-Adil, a peerless diplomat, extremely skilled in creating a climate of confidence and mutual esteem. This was later held against Richard, who was accused of being far too friendly with these infidels. The chroniclers on both sides even report a proposed marriage alliance intended to bring the conflict to an end: on 20 October Richard offered his sister Joan in marriage to al-Adil, if Saladin would agree to hand over to the couple the lands in Palestine coveted by both sides. According to John Gillingham, this was a sort of diplomatic game, initiated by Richard to sow discord in the enemy camp, in which an amused Saladin then joined.[22] This may not be the correct interpretation as the Muslims seem to have taken the offer seriously and seen the marriage as a convenient way of procuring peace. At least this is the firm opinion of one of their chroniclers, who attributes the failure of the scheme to the pressure put on Joan by some Christian leaders – in his opinion too 'intolerant' – not to 'deliver her body to a Muslim'.[23] The Christian chroniclers would seem to support this by emphasising Joan's categorical refusal to marry an 'infidel'. At all events, the proposal came to nothing and Richard, while preserving his courteous relations with the two Muslim princes, began to prepare for an expedition against Jerusalem.

His intention was to depart on 31 October 1191, leaving a few of his companions to carry on the task of completing the rebuilding of the walls of Jaffa. His march on the Holy City was delayed by skirmishes and clashes, some of them serious. One took place on 6 November: some Templars, who had gone foraging accompanied by their squires, were surprised by Bedouins who were on the point of killing them when a small party of Frankish knights came to the rescue, led by Andrew of Chauvigny. But they, in their turn, were then attacked by a larger Muslim band. One thing led to another, and the skirmish turned into a fierce battle involving, according to Ambroise, who is probably exaggerating, nearly 4,000 men. The battle was going badly for the crusaders when Richard in person came to their assistance, ignoring the advice of his men. If we are to believe Ambroise, Richard was shocked by the over-cautious tenor of this advice and gave a lofty response, which nicely conveys the feeling of solidarity which contributed so much to his reputation as a 'roi-chevalier': 'When I sent them here and asked them to go, if they die there without me then would I never again bear the title of king.'[24]

On 22 November Richard's army reached Ramlah, which had also been destroyed by Saladin's troops. They camped there as best they could

for six long weeks, in constant heavy rain, while Saladin, in Jerusalem, continued to fortify the town and prepare for the siege that seemed imminent. Ambroise vividly describes the terrible consequences of this bad weather and the sufferings bravely endured in the expectation of an early arrival in Jerusalem.

> There it was cold and overcast, with heavy rain and great storms that took many of our animals, for it rained there so excessively that it could not be measured in any way. Rain and hail battered us, bringing down our pavilions. We lost so many horses at Christmas and both before and after, so many biscuits were wasted, soggy with water, so much salt pork went bad in the storms; hauberks rusted so that they could hardly be cleaned; clothes rotted; people suffered from malnourishment . . . but their hearts were comforted by the hope that was in them that they would go to the [Holy] Sepulchre . . . in the army now was their joy complete, both deeply felt and fully expressed. There you would have seen hauberks being burnished, men nodding and saying, 'God, we call on Your help! Virgin Lady, Holy Mary! God, we worship You and praise and thank You. Now we will see Your Sepulchre!'[25]

Enthusiasm at the prospect of an imminent assault on the Holy City was not, however, universal. The Templars, Hospitallers and many of the *poulains*, Latin Christians who had been born or lived for a long time in Outremer, feared that the siege of Jerusalem would be long and dangerous and its outcome unpredictable; the Christians, far from their bases and the sea, would be perpetually at risk of being trapped between the ramparts and a relieving Muslim army, like the First Crusaders at Antioch in 1098. The council met on 13 January 1192 and decided to accept the arguments of these 'wise men'; the idea of besieging Jerusalem was abandoned once again and it was decided to set off back towards the coast to fortify Ascalon and ensure a safe point of entry for future crusaders.

This was an admission of failure, or at least of impotence. The abandonment of their goal, the longed-for Jerusalem, when they were only a few kilometres away, was demoralising for many of the 'pilgrims', who immediately decided to return home. The French, noted Ambroise, took advantage of the new situation to defect, retreating to Jaffa, Acre or Tyre. Richard's prestige, great though it had been, suffered an irreversible blow, for which the English chroniclers tried hard to compensate by emphasising his earlier successes and prowess.

Richard and the remnants of his army returned to Ascalon on 20 January 1192. For nearly four months they laboured to rebuild the devastated town and turn it into a true fortress. They got little help from the French, who joined them only late in the day, at the beginning of February, and stayed only a short time, preferring the more agreeable life

of Acre. This did not mean, however, that it was more peaceful; in fact
dissension was rife. The French, with the aid of their Genoese allies, tried
to take advantage of a fight between the Pisans and the Genoese, a new
expression of the hostility which persisted between the two 'kings', Guy
of Lusignan and Conrad of Montferrat, to seize the town. The Marquis
plotted more than ever and apparently even tried to win favour with
Saladin. Richard was honour bound to intervene. He set off for Acre, but
arrived too late; Conrad and Hugh of Burgundy had already retreated to
Tyre, where they were living it up and preparing to return home, while
Conrad refused point blank to put himself under Richard's orders in
Ascalon. The rivalry between Conrad and Guy turned into an open confrontation in which the former, supported by the French and most of the
barons of Palestine, once again opposed the latter, supported by Richard.
The King of England, meanwhile, had received unwelcome news; his
brother John was conspiring to depose him and Richard in his turn considered leaving the Holy Land and returning to England. He decided to
leave part of his army behind, but under whose command? However
reluctantly, he had to face the fact that only Conrad could now unite
behind him the whole body of barons and crusaders. Guy was totally isolated and would be unable, in Richard's absence, to make good his
claims. He would have to give his support to Conrad, which he recognised with a heavy heart. He offered his unfortunate candidate the
kingdom of Cyprus in compensation; it was bought back from the
Templars for the sum they had already handed over, the first instalment
of the staggered payment agreed for the island.

The coast was now clear for Conrad, and Richard made his agreement
known through his nephew, Count Henry of Champagne. Preparations
were made for the coronation of the new King of Jerusalem. Then, on
28 April, a dramatic event intervened: Conrad was murdered by
two 'Assassins', fanatical supporters of a Shi'ite Muslim sect led by
Rashid ed-Din el Sinan, known as 'The Old Man of the Mountain';
opposed to Sunnite orthodoxy, and drugged with hashish according to
their enemies (hence the term *hachichiya* from which comes our 'assas-
sin'), these fanatics were in a sense 'programmed' by their master to kill
whoever he indicated. The two men in question, disguised as monks, had
won the confidence of the Christians and they accosted Conrad as he was
on his way to dine with the Bishop of Beauvais, his friend. They stabbed
him as he was reading a letter they had handed to him. Rumour, started
or kept going by the French, at one point accused Richard of having
armed these fanatics. The idea was given credibility by the degree of animosity Richard had shown towards Conrad and by the haste with which

his nephew married Conrad's widow, and so acceded to the throne of Jerusalem.[26]

With Conrad dead, a new king had to be appointed, since no-one at this stage seriously considered Guy of Lusignan. It was once again Isabella who transmitted the right to the throne. This was not without its problems: Isabella had been married to the Marquis against her will, although already the wife of Humphrey of Toron; it could now be argued that Humphrey had once again become her legitimate husband. To settle the matter quickly, and in spite of the fact that the young widow, then aged only twenty-one, was pregnant with Conrad's child, she was married to Henry of Champagne on 5 May 1192. The count enjoyed widespread support as the nephew both of the King of France, through his father, and of the King of England, through his mother, Marie of Champagne, Richard's half-sister. The speed of this marriage, contracted only a week after the death of Isabella's previous husband, is clear proof that trouble was expected. Ambroise attributes the haste to the febrile atmosphere in the French camp and jokes that he, too, would have been in a hurry to marry this young woman, 'for she was very beautiful and noble'.[27] However, the new king of Jerusalem by virtue of his wife, the unfortunate Isabella, never bore the title although he reigned until he died in an accident in 1197. Isabella then made a third 'political' marriage, this time to Amaury of Lusignan, Guy's brother, who died in his turn in 1205. This young woman, still under thirty, had transmitted the crown to four kings in succession by the time of her own death, not long after. Her life offers a perfect example of how the Western aristocracy saw marriage at this period, that is, simply as a means of settling – or creating – political problems.

This solution, which had the approval of most of the barons, made Richard the true master of the crusader armies, now reunited under his command. He was now in a position to attempt to reconquer the principal fortified places along the coast and in the immediate hinterland, with the aim of facilitating a future reconquest of Jerusalem. On 22 May, he seized the fortress of Darum, dominating the route between Sinai and Egypt; he celebrated Whitsun there in the company of the armies of Hugh of Burgundy and of his nephew Henry of Champagne, the new lord of Jerusalem, to whom he entrusted the fortress. Reassured by the unwonted harmony prevailing amongst previously hostile factions, the crusaders had no doubt that it was Richard's intention to reconquer Jerusalem at last. But the King of England was extremely hesitant. It was true that the armies were now reunited, but the objections put forward before by those with local knowledge remained valid in his eyes. He was

not at that stage aware that the Saracens, shut up in Jerusalem, were deeply disheartened and probably incapable of putting up an effective resistance. Further, on 29 May, Richard received more bad news from England, through the vice-chancellor, John of Alençon: his brother John had won the support of many English barons and was conspiring against him, in spite of Eleanor, but with the tacit support of Philip Augustus. Richard was in a quandary; he was afraid that if he did not return urgently to England, it would be the end of his kingdom and his empire, so he informed his entourage of his intention to leave the Holy Land.[28]

RICHARD'S RENUNCIATION

Within the army, consternation reigned. There were some who could not believe that a hero as glorious as Richard could abandon the Holy Land without having attempted to recover the Holy Sepulchre from the Muslims. The barons of France, Normandy, Poitou, England, Maine and Anjou met in council and decided to launch an attack on Jerusalem, with or without Richard. This resolution was a snub for the king but was greeted with enthusiasm by the ordinary crusaders, who, says Ambroise, danced with joy till after midnight. An angry Richard withdrew, alone, to lie down in his tent, visibly depressed, vexed and discouraged.[29] He remained in this state of brooding semi-prostration for several days, while the armies set off, at the beginning of June, for Ibelin. At last, one day, near Ascalon, one of his chaplains, William of Poitiers, in tears, and not without some apprehension, agreed to the King's request to tell him what the army thought of him: they were critical of his frequent indecisiveness, he said; they accused him of forgetting all that God had already done for his faithful, forgetting his own past feats, at Messina, Cyprus and Acre, and forgetting the dangers and the sickness that he, with God's grace, had survived. William ended his harangue with a well-chosen exhortation, likely to produce in Richard the proud reaction for which he was hoping:

> King, remember and take good care of the land of which God has made you guardian, for he entrusted everything to you when the other king left . . . now are we all given up to death. Now everyone, great and small, everyone who wished to honour you, says that you are father and brother of Christianity and if you leave her without help now, then she is dead and betrayed.[30]

Moved by this speech, Richard was silent, but the next day he announced his decision: he would remain in the Holy Land until the following Easter and he would lead the armies to Jerusalem to besiege it.

His announcement was greeted by an explosion of joy in the crusader army. The ordinary soldiers, said Ambroise, carried a bag of provisions slung round their necks and declared this was all they needed to see them to their goal. The march on Jerusalem began, on 6 June, in joyful mood. It was marked by several minor clashes. During one of them, Richard and a small band of knights pursued the Saracens as far as Emmaus, then followed them through the hills, arriving quite close to the town, probably at the spot known as Montjoie, from which Jerusalem was visible. Never had Richard been so close to the Holy City. Ambroise makes a point of this and emphasises that the garrison in the town was panic-stricken; if Richard had been accompanied by his army, Jerusalem would have been theirs:

> The noble king mounted, before day, and taking with him the man who had told him, sought out the Turks, to their harm, as far as the spring at Emmaus. At dawn he surprised them and succeeded in killing twenty and took Saladin's crier, his announcer, sparing him alone . . . he pursued the Saracens into the mountains catching one up in a valley, knocking him from his horse, dead. When he had killed the villain he could see Jerusalem clearly. In Jerusalem, so I have been told, they were so afraid that if the king had had the army with him, when it was seen, Jerusalem would have been set free and taken over by the Christians, for all the Saracens came out of the city fleeing, because they thought the army was coming . . .[31]

Was this one last lost opportunity? Perhaps, because Henry of Champagne, who had gone to Acre in search of reinforcements, was slow to return, and the army stayed put, idle, awaiting his arrival. It was heartened, as in the First Crusade, by the discovery of a new fragment of the True Cross, which a holy hermit (according to an Anglo-Norman text) or a holy abbot (according to Ambroise) had managed to hide during the Muslim occupation and which he now presented to Richard.[32] Even more heartening, perhaps, was a bold stroke by the King which turned out well. Learning from his spies that a large caravan had left Egypt and was heading for Jerusalem, loaded with foodstuffs, fabrics and a wide range of other goods for its garrison, Richard ambushed and seized it, after a battle that was brief, but made much of by the chroniclers, as we will see.[33] The large quantity of booty was at once shared out among the men, which gave a great boost to their morale. Conversely, the incident had a demoralising effect on the Saracens in Jerusalem, noted by the Muslim chroniclers and echoed by Ambroise. Nevertheless, as John Gillingham rightly observes, far from being in a better position than six months earlier, the crusaders were actually worse off: Saladin had a larger army at his disposal, and he was better placed than before to cut

off the crusader army's supplies by intercepting provisions arriving from the coast, thanks to the troops he had stationed in the region. Richard was only too aware of this, according to Ambroise. Once again, a council was called and the French urged the King of England to lay siege to Jerusalem. Once again, Richard refused:

> The king replied: 'That cannot be. You will never see me lead a people [in an undertaking] for which I can be criticised and I do not care if I am disliked for it. Know for certain that wherever our army may go Saladin knows what we are about and what our strength is. We are a long way from the sea and if he and his Saracens were to come down on the plains of Ramla and intercept our provisions . . . this would not be wise for those who would be besieging . . . and if I were to lead the army and besiege Jerusalem and such a thing were to happen . . . then I would be forever blamed, shamed and less loved. I know in truth and without doubt that there are those here and in France who would have wanted and who want and greatly desire that I should do such a thing, which would everywhere be told to my shame.'[34]

So, if we are to believe him, it was to avoid the dishonour of a defeat for the whole army that Richard refused to lead the crusader army to the walls of Jerusalem. Instead, he proposed an expedition against Egypt, which might appear equally risky to a modern observer. Once again, the matter was put before the council of barons, which consisted of twenty men: five Templars, five Hospitallers, five barons of Outremer and five barons of France. To the immense despair of the majority of crusaders, the council opted for the overland expedition to Egypt, supported by a fleet stationed off the coast. The advice of the local lords had prevailed, which confirmed the strategic soundness of Richard's choice in their eyes. But it was profoundly shocking to many of the crusaders and, once again, the French went their own way. Hugh of Burgundy seized the opportunity to spread defamatory stories about the King of England and songs accusing him of cowardice. This was too much for Richard, who replied in the same kind and declared himself ready to besiege Jerusalem, but refused to take responsibility for an expedition made against his wishes. The army was deeply divided and, in these circumstances, all idea of taking Jerusalem had to be abandoned. On 4 July the army retreated. Jerusalem was never to be recovered. It was a failure both for the crusaders and for Richard, whose prestige was badly damaged. Worse, he must have wondered whether he had lost out on both fronts: by agreeing to remain in the Holy Land until the following Easter, he had seriously jeopardised the future of his empire in the West, leaving the field clear for his brother John, without the compensation of the successes he had counted on in the East.

He was forced to negotiate with Saladin, though without having suffered a defeat. The first contacts seemed promising, as it was in Saladin's interests to secure the departure of this valiant opponent. He offered to grant the Christians full sovereignty over the coastal territories, including Ascalon, on condition its fortifications were destroyed, and he guaranteed free access to the Holy Places to unarmed pilgrims. The agreement foundered over the question of Ascalon, as Richard was extremely reluctant to dismantle its defences. On the other hand, he demolished on his own initiative the defences of Darum, which he no longer needed now the expedition to Egypt had been abandoned. Having returned to Acre on 26 July, he was planning to besiege Beirut when, on 28 July, he was told that Saladin had attacked Jaffa the day before; the inhabitants had been forced to abandon the town, which was promptly looted, and take refuge in the citadel. They had concluded a truce with Saladin for an 'honourable surrender': if they were not rescued by 1 August, they would hand over the town. Richard at once set out by sea, accompanied by the Pisans and Genoese, while an army commanded by Hugh of Burgundy and the military orders tried to reach Jaffa by land; it was held up by a Saracen army which barred the route. Richard, too, was delayed, by unfavourable winds, and only reached Jaffa on the night of 31 July, without any clear idea of where to land; the shore was occupied by the Muslim soldiers and he was afraid of arriving too late and of falling into a trap. He gave the order to remain offshore, to the despair of the besieged, many of whom now surrendered. It was then that one of them, a priest, dived into the water and went to beg Richard to intervene before the entire garrison was captured and executed; the massacre, he said, might already have begun. Richard hesitated no longer; his ships approached the shore and he himself leapt into the water, forcing his men to follow. Under a hail of enemy arrows, they established a beachhead on the shore while the King, with a small band of warriors, stormed into the town, which the Saracens were busy looting. The confusion was total; the Saracens fled and many were massacred. Richard recovered his prestige, at least according to Ambroise: he had surpassed Roland, Oliver and all the epic heroes; no one, Christian or 'pagan', even at Roncevaux, had ever done as he did.[35]

Saladin had prudently withdrawn. He believed he would soon be able to take his revenge, because Richard's weakened armies had few horses at their disposal. So he prepared an attack on the Christian camp pitched outside the town. During the night of 4 August, his troops made their move, hoping to surprise the crusaders in their sleep. The manoeuvre was on the point of succeeding when, in the first light of dawn, a Genoese

spotted the sparkle of their arms and armour. He gave the alert and Richard, rudely awoken, quickly organised the defence of the camp. He arranged his men in two lines. The first, composed of infantry carrying shields and pointing their lances outwards, formed a sort of bristling defensive hedge. Behind them, archers and crossbowmen shot arrows and darts as fast as they could; each crossbowman was assisted by a man-at-arms who prepared one bow, because they were slow to load, while the crossbowman fired another. In the face of this efficiently and rapidly organised defence, the Saracen charge failed, and Richard then counter-attacked with only a handful of knights, since they had so few horses. The king's bravery on this occasion was so outstanding that al-Adil, Saladin's brother, was amazed and sent him two new horses in the press, to replace those killed under him; this was an eminently chivalric act to which we will return.[36] The chroniclers enthused over the exceptional courage shown by Richard, who, they said, had won the victory single-handed; they compared him once again to the greatest warrior heroes of history and legend.

So Richard had once again defeated Saladin. Discouraged and humiliated by seeing his large army sent packing by a handful of Christian warriors, Saladin agreed to negotiate; in any case, his allies, exhausted and depressed by the ruin of the country, were reluctant to pursue the war as long as Richard and his armies remained on Palestinian soil. Better, they reasoned, to secure his departure. Nor was Richard sorry to talk. He too wanted an agreement that would allow him to return home, head held high after these last exploits. He again fell ill, and only recovered, some chroniclers caustically remarked, when he heard of the death of his perennial enemy, Hugh of Burgundy.[37] All he wanted was to return to England and restore order to his kingdom. He knew, in any case, that he was unlikely to achieve more decisive successes by force of arms. It was better to negotiate, in spite of the hostile comment provoked by any hint of doing business with the 'infidel'.

The English chroniclers, however, went out of their way to stress everything justifying this decision. Richard had spent generously and exhausted his treasury; he was beginning to run short of money and, consequently, soldiers. His physical strength was impaired by the sickness that laid him low. The plague was beginning to take a terrible toll on his army. Grim rumours had reached him from England, where John was conspiring with the barons and the King of France and had already occupied several royal castles; his chancellor had been expelled; even the Templars and the Hospitallers advised him to return home, raise a new army and return with fresh troops to reconquer Jerusalem.[38] That is why

he eventually gave way over Ascalon, after talks which went on for nearly a month.

TREATING WITH THE INFIDEL?

The treaty that resulted was in reality a truce for three years and eight months, in accordance with the Muslim doctrine that does not permit a definitive treaty to be concluded with the infidel.[39] The clauses of the agreement, drawn up on 9 August and ratified on 2 September, were to come into force at Easter the following year. The terms are well known from many sources: a truce was concluded between the Christians and the Muslims for 'three years, three months, three days and three hours'; all the coastal territories, from north of Tyre to south of Jaffa, with the castles of Tyre, Acre, Haifa, Caesarea, Jaffa and a few others, were guaranteed to the Christians, who could fortify the towns; Jerusalem and its lands remained in Saladin's hands; Christian pilgrims, including the crusaders then in the Holy Land, were to have free access to the Holy Sepulchre, without any taxes or impediments, in their capacity as pilgrims, that is unarmed;[40] to provide religious services, the Latin Christians were allowed to maintain two priests and two deacons in the principal Christian Holy Places, that is, Jerusalem, Nazareth and Bethlehem. Curiously, there was no reference to the return of the Holy Cross, once a main plank in the crusaders' demands. William of Newburgh was expressing the popular sentiment when he wrote that the truce 'was not altogether honourable if you think of the destruction of the town [of Ascalon], but, from a more general viewpoint, on the whole it was useful'.[41] The judgement of Jacques de Vitry, Bishop of Acre, a few years later, was less favourable; summarising the crusade's achievements, he denounced the quarrels between the two kings and their vain search for personal glory, and he emphasised Richard's responsibility in accepting this treaty, an unsatisfactory outcome for this enterprise:

> The enemy of the human race sent discord and rivalry between the two kings . . . they each sought their own glory and laboured for their personal cause, and not for that of Jesus, detesting each other and tearing each other apart, to the very great joy of their enemies and the confusion of the Christian people . . . the Christians, covered with confusion and prostrated by grief, abandoned all hope of recovering the Holy City; they groaned and felt the deepest distress at losing the fruit of all their sacrifices, at seeing their efforts reduced to nothing, because they were not pursued to the end. If the king of England had concealed his plans to withdraw, or at least had postponed for a while their implementation, we would have been able to obtain better

conditions from the Saracens, a truce that would have been useful and honourable. But he was too impetuous, in too much of a rush to depart, and he
agreed, against the interests of the Christians, without discussion or objection, to all Saladin's proposals relating to the clauses of the truce.[42]

The judgement is harsh, but it is a fair expression of the feelings and resentment of the local Christians faced with the disappointing results of an
enterprise that had promised so much and which, through the faults of
its leaders, had failed to achieve the concrete results they had counted on.

The majority of the crusaders, relieved or disappointed, were quick to
take advantage of the permission granted by Saladin and went to the Holy
Sepulchre to perform their devotions and so obtain the palms and indulgences granted to pilgrims. They might not have reconquered the
Holy Places as soldiers of God, but at least they had visited them as pilgrims. Richard was not among them. The chroniclers who were
favourable to him quickly came up with a reason that was likely to
increase his renown: to those who urged him to go, he replied that he
refused to receive from the pagans as a favour what he had been unable
to obtain as a gift from God.[43]

Even in semi-failure, the king of legend retained his grandeur and
dignity.

NOTES

1. Rigord, §81, pp. 116ff.; William the Breton, *Gesta Philippi Augusti*,
   pp. 118ff. See on this point Gillingham, *Richard the Lionheart*, p. 181.
   See also the reason incorrectly invoked by the Continuator of William of
   Tyre: Philip, who was sick, could not leave the kingdom without an heir,
   Richard having maliciously conveyed the (false) news of the death of his
   son, Louis: *Continuation de Guillaume de Tyr*, pp. 128–31 (p. 109 of
   Edbury translation).
2. Imad ad-Din, *Conquête de la Syrie*, p. 309.
3. See below, pp. 356ff.
4. Ambroise, lines 5507ff. (p. 108 of Ailes translation); *Itinerarium*, IV, c. 4.
5. Ambroise, lines 5409ff.; Matthew Paris, *Chronica Majora*, II, p. 374;
   Richard of Devizes, p. 47; Roger of Howden, III, p. 127; *Gesta Henrici*, II,
   p. 188; Ralph of Diceto, p. 94.
6. Baha ad-Din (Gabrieli, *Arab Historians*, p. 224).
7. Imad ad-Din, *Conquête de la Syrie*, pp. 330–1.
8. See on this point Matthew Paris, *Chronica Majora*, II, p. 378; also Baha
   ad-Din in Gabrieli, *Arab Historians*, pp. 226–7.
9. Ambroise, line 4678.
10. Imad ad-Din, *Conquête de la Syrie*, pp. 202ff.

11. Ambroise, lines 5733–48 (p. 111 of Ailes translation).
12. See on this point Flori, 'Encore l'Usage de la Lance'; Flori, J., 'Chevalerie Chrétienne et Cavalerie Musulmane; Deux Conceptions du Combat Chevaleresque vers 1100', in Buschinger, *Monde des Héros dans la Culture Médiévale*, pp. 99–113, repr. in Flori, *Croisade et Chevalerie*, pp. 389–405.
13. Imad ad-Din, *Conquête de la Syrie*, pp. 336–7. See also the texts of Baha ad-Din quoted in Gillingham (*Richard the Lionheart*, p. 187) and Pernoud (*Richard Cœur de Lion*, p. 164).
14. Ambroise, line 6059; *Itinerarium*, IV, c. 15; for Richard's exploits, see below, pp. 351ff.
15. Ambroise, lines 6137ff.; *Itinerarium*, IV, c. 17.
16. Ambroise, lines 6647ff.; *Itinerarium*, IV, c. 20; for this battle, see Smail, *Crusading Warfare*, pp. 161ff.
17. Ambroise, lines 6989ff.
18. The letter is translated by Gillingham in *Richard the Lionheart*, p. 192.
19. *Continuation de Guillaume de Tyr*, p. 134 (p. 111 of Edbury translation); the author seems to place the death of Hugh of Burgundy soon after this episode, which suggests he is thinking of an incident which took place some months later.
20. Roger of Howden, III, p. 133; *Gesta Henrici*, II, p. 192; Ambroise, lines 7090ff.; *Itinerarium*, IV, c. 28.
21. Baha ad-Din (Gabrieli, *Arab Historians*, pp. 225–6).
22. Gillingham, *Richard the Lionheart*, pp. 196–7; see also on this point Brundage, *Richard Lionheart*, pp. 149ff.; Labande, E.-R., 'Les Filles d'Aliénor d'Aquitaine: Etude Comparative', *Cahiers de Civilisation Médiévale*, 113–14 (1986), pp. 109–10.
23. Imad ad-Din, *Conquête de la Syrie*, pp. 349–51; see also Baha ad-Din (Gabrieli, *Arab Historians*, pp. 226–7), recording Richard's proposal to substitute his niece for his sister, which suggests the marriage proposal was serious.
24. Ambroise, lines 7344ff. (p. 131 of Ailes translation).
25. Ambroise, lines 7680ff. (p. 135 of Ailes translation).
26. For the sect of the Assassins and their role in this affair, see Lewis, *Les Assassins*, especially pp. 36ff., 160ff.
27. Ambroise, lines 9040ff. (p. 154 of Ailes translation).
28. Ambroise (lines 9433ff.) gives a good description of Richard's perplexity and of the various reactions to his decision.
29. Ambroise, lines 9480–509.
30. Ambroise, lines 9675ff., French translation p. 436 (p. 162 of Ailes translation).
31. Ambroise, lines 9843ff. (p. 164 of Ailes translation).
32. See the differing texts in Pernoud, *Richard Cœur de Lion*, p. 187, quoting from Johnston, R. C., *The Crusade and Death of Richard I* (Oxford, 1961), and Ambroise, lines 10089ff.

33. See pp. 377ff.

34. Ambroise, lines 10152ff. (p. 168 of Ailes translation).

35. Ambroise, lines 11205ff.

36. See p. 366ff.

37. 'The pleasure this news gave him caused the fever to abate', wrote Richard of Devizes (pp. 75ff.).

38. Roger of Howden, III, pp. 184–5; see also Ralph of Coggeshall, pp. 51–2; Matthew Paris, *Chronica Majora*, II, pp. 391–2.

39. See on this point Morabia, A., *Le Gihad dans l'Islam Médiéval* (Paris, 1993), pp. 204ff.

40. For the clauses of this truce, see Ralph of Diceto, II, p. 105; William of Newburgh, pp. 377–8; Roger of Howden, III, pp. 184–5; Ambroise, lines 11708ff.

41. William of Newburgh, pp. 377–8.

42. Jacques de Vitry, *Historia Orientalis*, end of Book 1, ed. J. Bongars (Paris, 1611), 1, pp. 122ff.

43. 'Sed adquiescare non potuit digna magni cordis indignatio, ut [quod] de Dei dono non poterat, de gratia gentilium consequerentur': Richard of Devizes, p. 84. The Arab chroniclers gave a different explanation, to which we will return: see pp. 408ff.

8

The Lion Caged (1192–4)

⌀

RICHARD'S ODYSSEY

Richard left Acre for England on 9 October 1192, well before the date set for his return, Easter 1193.

His crusade had hardly been a military success, since Jerusalem and the larger part of the Holy Land remained in Muslim hands and since he had been obliged to negotiate with the infidel to obtain at least some territorial gains. Only a few decades later, in February 1229, at Jaffa, the Emperor Frederick II was notably more successful without fighting or shedding a drop of blood, thanks to a simple show of force followed by a treaty. The Saracens returned all the conquests made by Saladin after his victory at Hattin in 1187, including Jerusalem, except for the terrace of the Temple. This victorious emperor, cultured and tolerant, was nevertheless reviled, booed by the Templars and Hospitallers as he entered Jerusalem, rejected by the local barons and execrated by the pope and the churchmen of the day precisely because he had chosen to negotiate with the infidel rather than exterminate or even fight them. Richard's warlike and sometimes bloodthirsty exploits, which achieved so little, won much wider acclaim than the diplomatic and peaceful successes of the Emperor Frederick. This strange paradox speaks volumes about contemporary attitudes and also about the popularity of holy war, a notion then becoming widely accepted and which has sadly persisted.

It is one of the ironies of history that, had Richard kept his word and remained in Palestine until Easter 1193, he might well have won a decisive victory over the Muslims and made territorial gains as considerable as those of Frederick II. Had this been the case, we can be sure that his chroniclers would have trumpeted them to the skies. If he had been killed during one of these battles, he might well have become 'St Richard', just as Louis IX became St Louis by dying before the walls of Carthage in 1270, during the 'Last Crusade'. This is mere speculation, of course, and as such futile, but it is by no means an improbable scenario. From the day of the King of England's premature departure, fierce dynastic rivalries

erupted within Saladin's own family, and when he died, on 4 March 1193, confusion reigned. The Muslim unity which this Kurdish prince – who was neither Arab nor Turk – had with difficulty constructed round the notion of jihad, and which was already showing signs of strain, definitively collapsed.[1] The Ayyubid empire broke up and Saladin's heirs partitioned it and fought over it. A victory on Richard's part would have been made much easier. By this time, however, the King of England had already spent several weeks in the prisons of the Emperor Henry VI. Rewriting history is a fruitless intellectual game, it is true, but the temptation to indulge in it, even briefly, is sometimes irresistible.

Nevertheless, Richard's acquisitions, though limited, were not wholly negligible. The reconquest of the coast and the fortification of Jaffa and Acre created bases that were indispensable to any future conquest. A century later, Acre was to be the last bastion of the Christian East. Successfully stormed by the Muslims on 18 May 1291, its fall marked the end of the Latin states of Outremer. It led also, not long afterwards, both to the dramatic end of the Order of the Temple, which had lost its purpose and whose wealth was coveted by the King of France, and to the transformation of the Order of the Hospital, which proved more astute; they withdrew first to Rhodes and then to Malta, where they devoted themselves once again to their role of providing hospitality and assistance, to the detriment of the military role they had adopted in imitation of the Templars.[2] Without the effort put by Richard (and later, of course, by Frederick II and St Louis) into preserving and fortifying these bases, any idea of reconquest would have been wholly illusory.

When he left for England, was Richard intending to return to the Holy Land, at the head of an even more powerful fleet and army, once he had restored order in his own lands? According to some English chroniclers, he had sworn to do exactly this.[3] The Continuator of William of Tyre describes him consoling Henry of Champagne for having to slight the walls of Ascalon as he left:

> He told the count not to be dismayed that Ascalon was to be razed because he was having to go. 'If God grants me life, I shall come and bring so many men that I shall recover Ascalon and your whole realm, and you will be crowned in Jerusalem.'[4]

In the event, it was impossible for Richard to carry out this project, even if it really had been his intention; he was captured on his return from the crusade and held prisoner for many long months. When he was freed, in February 1194, he renewed his oath, but accompanied it with a condition which would never be fulfilled: if God helped him to avenge himself

on his enemies and allowed him to recover and pacify his lands, he would return to assist the Christians of Outremer and fight against the pagans.[5]

Richard set sail, as we have seen, on 9 October 1192, in a boat that was described by William of Newburgh as 'more rapid but less safe' than that of Berengaria and Joan, whom he had sent on ahead. He was anxious, we are told, 'not to have to suffer boredom at sea for too long'.[6] The remark is meant to explain Richard's choice of a swift ship that would shorten the crossing, but one cannot but observe that yet again the King preferred to be separated from his wife for what was likely to be a lengthy journey. Was he really as much in love with her as was claimed?

The date was already on the late side for a crossing that might prove protracted and even dangerous, depending on the weather. Autumn storms are often severe in the Mediterranean and the prevailing winds adverse, slowing the progress of sailing vessels. Richard's ship put in at Cyprus; he may have been planning to travel overland to Marseille and from there to Aquitaine, which would save him a long and dangerous voyage along the Spanish coast, followed by a risky passage through the Straits of Gibraltar, then in Muslim hands, before facing the still more formidable perils of the Atlantic. But a storm disrupted his plans and he found himself on an unknown coast, which several chroniclers locate 'in Barbary', three days' sail from Marseille.[7] He abandoned the idea of a landing on the coasts of Languedoc-Provence because of rumours, this time well-founded, that Philip Augustus had once again incited the barons of Aquitaine into revolt, with the assistance of the Count of Toulouse. Berengaria's brother, Sancho of Navarre, had led a military incursion into the lands of Raymond of Toulouse, thus proving the solidity of the alliance concluded by Richard's marriage to Berengaria, but the region remained hostile; it was closed to any passage by the King of England from the coast of Languedoc towards Aquitaine. A southern passage, from beyond the Pyrenees, via Barcelona and across Aragon, was no easier, and here Richard also ran the risk of being captured beforehand by the fleets of Genoa or Toulouse, masters of the seas in those parts. The declared hostility of the King of France (who had joined up with John to take advantage of Richard's absence to try and recover the Vexin) ruled out a passage east of Marseille. In any case, the Emperor Henry VI, Richard's enemy since the Sicilian affair and now, to make matters worse, allied to Philip Augustus, would not grant him a safe conduct for the Rhône-Rhine route through his empire.

So Richard had to find another route.[8] The accounts of the events that followed vary and often verge on the fantastic. The sources do not agree on a number of details and it is possible that certain chroniclers

embroidered their accounts in such a way as to play up the legendary dimension of his wanderings, the sober reality of which was already the stuff of romance. Sadly, it is sometimes now impossible to distinguish fact from fiction. Some sources speak of a shipwreck which threw the King's ship onto the coast of Istria, between Aquileia and Venice.[9] Others suggest that this was a deliberate choice on the part of the King. Ralph of Coggeshall claims to have spoken to an eyewitness, Anselm, Richard's chaplain, who 'told me everything he had seen and heard';[10] according to him, Richard was thrown onto the Barbary coast 'by a just judgement of God obscured from our eyes', and there learned of his enemies' dark plots; it was then, apparently, that he decided on a change of plan, setting sail for Corfu, perhaps intending to land in Venice to cross the empire incognito:

> Then, learning that the count of Saint-Gilles and other lords of the lands through which he would have to pass were all in league against him, and had prepared ambushes for him all along his route, he decided to return to his lands by crossing German territory incognito and he set sail in this direction.[11]

It was at this point that two pirate ships decided to attack his galley. Happily, one of the sailors recognised Richard, whose imposing presence and fame overawed them. For his part, the King was so impressed by their courage and audacity that he asked for their help, in return for money, and boarded their ship with a small group of companions, including Anselm and some Templars; their intention was to land by design on the Dalmatian coast.

From then on, accounts differ in detail but are agreed on essentials. Richard tried, without making himself known, to return home from the Adriatic coast by way of Venetia, Austria, Bohemia and Moravia, from where he may have hoped to reach Saxony, ruled by Henry the Lion, husband of his sister Matilda, and before reaching a North Sea port and a ship bound for England. He set out with only a handful of companions, more or less well disguised; they included, in addition to Anselm, two of his faithful friends, the knight Baldwin of Béthune and a clerk called William de l'Etang, a few Templars and some squires, at least one of whom fortunately spoke German.

Put ashore by the pirates near Zadar (Gorizia), Richard quickly sent a message to the local lord through one of his men, asking for a safe conduct for himself and his companions to travel through his lands. He claimed to be Hugh, a merchant returning from Jerusalem, with one of his friends, the knight, Baldwin of Béthune. He accompanied his request with the gift of a ring set with a ruby, hoping this would increase the

chances of a favourable reception. Unfortunately, Richard was unaware of the identity of this lord, who turned out to be Count Meinhard of Görtz, a vassal of Duke Leopold of Austria, the prince who had been humiliated by Richard at Acre and had sworn to take revenge. To make matters worse, Meinhard was also the nephew of Conrad of Montferrat, Richard's 'enemy' in the Holy Land. According to Matthew Paris, Meinhard apparently recognised the ruby as a stone that Richard had bought some time before from a Pisan merchant.[12] In any case, by one means or another, Meinhard realised that this merchant was none other than the King of England. Things could have turned out very badly indeed but he behaved magnanimously, in spite of his hostility:

> Then the lord of those parts examined the ring and said: 'No, he is not called Hugh, it is King Richard.' And he added: 'I have sworn to arrest all the travellers who belong to his retinue and to accept no gift from them. However, given the nobility of this gift, and of him who sends it and has so honoured me, without knowing me, I return the gift and I grant free right of passage'.[13]

This was by any standards a chivalric attitude but it was not maintained for long. The messenger reported these words to Richard and the little group dispersed without further ado, at night, travelling for a while without encountering any obstacles. This was a wise move, as Meinhard proceeded to warn his brother of Richard's imminent arrival in his lands, so that he could arrest him. The brother, Frederick, ordered one of his men, a Norman from Argentan who, said Matthew Paris, had married his niece and was devoted to him, to find Richard, promising him a rich reward (half the town!) if he was able to identify him. After combing the region, the Norman managed to locate him. Once again, Richard was in danger, but once again he was protected by his lucky star. This Norman, say the chroniclers, had been searching for Richard not so as to harm but to protect him. Having at last obtained, by tearful pleading, confirmation of Richard's identity, this providential ally exhorted the King to flee secretly; he even generously provided Richard with a horse before returning to inform his master it had all been a mistake. The angry lord gave orders for the arrest of this sham merchant, but Richard had had the time to take advantage of the friendly Norman's wise advice.[14] He escaped this second danger and left the town secretly with an even smaller company, consisting of William de l'Etang and the young servant who spoke German.

So once again they were wanderers. Driven by hunger, they entered the suburbs of Vienna, on the banks of the Danube, where, by a stroke of extreme ill luck, Duke Leopold of Austria was then in residence. They were only about a hundred kilometres from Moravia, whose prince was

friendly towards Richard, and must have hoped soon to reach it and at last be free. But Richard was again unlucky, or unwise. It seems likely that neither he nor his companions made as much effort as necessary to be discreet and pass unrecognised, even though, according to Roger of Howden, they wore their beards and hair long in the local style.[15] Perhaps it was impossible for a man like Richard to behave with discretion. It certainly proved too difficult for his companion. The King's young servant (*puer*) went into the town to change some money to buy food. But, used to a princely lifestyle, he flashed his money about and behaved sufficiently arrogantly and pretentiously to attract the attention of the locals, who seized him and demanded to know who he was. He claimed to be the servant of a rich merchant returning from pilgrimage. When they let him go, he went back to Richard to tell him what had happened and exhorted him to flee. But Richard was weary, perhaps even still unwell after his sickness in Acre; this time he did not intend to run away and wanted to rest for a few days in the town, and so the servant continued to visit the local market to buy food.

A day came (21 December 1192) when, inadvertently (perhaps), he tucked his master's gloves under his belt. This time, the gloves, which were probably costly and possibly emblazoned, attracted the attention of the town guard, who had been ordered to be on the lookout for Richard. They seized the servant, beat him up and inflicted 'many tortures' on him, threatening to tear out his tongue if he did not tell them the truth. He told all. The magistrates informed the Duke, who had the house watched. Richard, always the great lord in spite of his disguise, would surrender only to the Duke in person.[16] When informed of this, Leopold went immediately to the house and the King surrendered his sword and his person into Leopold's hands. 'The duke was overjoyed and led the king away with him with great honour. Then he entrusted him to the care of worthy knights who guarded him closely, night and day, their swords drawn.'[17]

Ralph of Coggeshall attributes this misfortune to divine judgement, though admitting that he did not understand its real significance. Could it have been a punishment by God for Richard's past debauchery?[18]

THE CAPTIVE KING

Richard was now in the hands of his enemy who, in defiance of ecclesiastical law, kept him prisoner in his castle of Dürnstein, overlooking the Danube. The chroniclers note that Leopold treated him well and did not put him in chains, but nevertheless kept him under such close surveillance

that his life was intolerable.[19] Ralph of Diceto seized the opportunity to point out that the inhabitants of these parts were still savages, sunk deep in barbarism.

Revenge was probably not Leopold's only motive for taking Richard prisoner. He knew that many great princes had an interest in his capture and were ready to pay dearly for his person. Alternatively, he might hope for a heavy ransom to be paid by the English court. It was certainly an act of great perfidy and contrary to the law which, as is well known, prohibited the ill-treatment of pilgrims and placed them, like crusaders, under the direct protection of the Church.

The chroniclers were at pains to emphasise that Leopold's offence was harshly punished by the Church, and then by God, even in this world, not to speak of the next. Roger of Howden listed all the various ills with which God punished this sin: Leopold was first excommunicated by the Church; then his towns burned down without any obvious cause; the Danube burst its banks and more than 10,000 people perished in the floods; his lands were devastated by exceptionally fierce storms; the soil lost its fertility and no corn would grow; the nobles, lastly, were afflicted by an unknown sickness. But, like Pharaoh before him, Leopold stubbornly persisted in his fateful course, refusing to repent until, at point of death, he was forced to make amends so that the bishops would at least grant him a Christian burial.[20]

Other chroniclers emphasise the terrible circumstances of his death. William of Newburgh, Ralph of Coggeshall and Ralph of Diceto all make a point of his reprehensible failure to repent almost until his last breath and dwell at length on the horrible details of his end, which assumed in their eyes the status of a judgement of God. It happened on 26 December 1194. Leopold was taking part in a sort of tournament, with contests in which, 'according to the custom of the region', the warriors sought to demonstrate their prowess. He fell from his horse and suffered an injury to his foot. Gangrene set in, the foot had to be amputated and he died soon after 'as a punishment for having betrayed King Richard'.[21] His body lay unburied for a very long time because his heirs refused to free the English emissaries Leopold had kept as hostages. Matthew Paris fills out his account with details designed to demonstrate the workings of an immanent justice. Out riding with friends, Leopold's horse stumbled; the Duke was thrown and broke his leg. The injury very quickly went black and the limb swelled, causing the Duke terrible agonies. He begged for it to be amputated, but no-one would take on the task. He was obliged to wield the knife himself, everyone else having refused, paralysed by horror. But even this was not enough to save Leopold or lessen his agony. At last,

defeated and repentant, he recognised the injustice of his treatment of
Richard and his men and, on the advice of the bishops, swore to return
the part of the ransom still in his possession and to free his hostages. He
died after suffering appallingly, but his body remained unburied long
afterwards because his son, persisting in his father's iniquity, refused to
keep the promises Leopold had made on his deathbed.[22]

The chroniclers' insistence reveals the extent of the resentment, certainly in England and probably elsewhere, felt at the capture of Richard,
who was both a king and a crusader, in time of peace, and in spite of all
the laws and customs then in force. William of Newburgh adds, for good
measure, that the arrest of Richard was also marked by heavenly signs
and prodigies in many places.[23] It is easy to see how all these stories contributed to the growth of his legend, placing him in the category of
Persecuted Innocence.

Such infringements of morality or law were not, of course, uncommon.
Never before, however, had anyone at this social level, a prince and then
an emperor, openly perpetrated a deed of such baseness against a victim
of such high rank.[24] It has to be said, however, that the offenders made no
secret of their activities, contrary to the later legend to the effect that
Richard was held captive in a secret prison, its whereabouts unknown. The
earliest traces of this story are to be found in the middle of the thirteenth
century, in the account of the Minstrel of Reims. He tells how Richard was
imprisoned in a castle in an unknown location in Austria. A minstrel called
Blondel de Nesle, whom Richard had brought up from boyhood, was
greatly distressed and vowed to find him; he travelled the length and
breadth of the country in search of some sign of his presence. Then, one
day, he heard from an old widow who had given him lodgings that a
captive of high rank had been held in a nearby castle for four years (!). The
minstrel made his way to the castle where he made out he was a jongleur
and delighted its sire with his songs and stories. He was invited to stay on,
and was seeking a way of discovering the identity of the captive when
providence once again intervened. While Blondel was resting in an orchard
at the foot of a tower, Richard saw him through a loophole in his prison
tower, and made himself known to him by singing a song they had long
ago composed together and that was known only to them:

> And while he was thinking about this, the king looked out through a loop-
> hole and saw Blondel. And he wondered how he could make himself known
> to him. And he remembered a song that the two of them had composed and
> that none but the two of them knew. So began he to sing the first words loud
> and clear, because he sang well; and when Blondel heard him, then he knew
> for a certainty that this was his lord. His heart was more joyful than it had

ever been. He at once left the orchard, and went to his chamber where he slept; and he took his viol and he began to play a strain, and as he played he rejoiced that he had found his lord.[25]

Now convinced that Richard was the captive prince, Blondel asked leave of the sire to return to England, where he told his story to the King's friends. They all rejoiced, 'for the king was the most bountiful man that ever buckled spur'.[26]

Whatever the arguments of R. R. Bezzola and Régine Pernoud, we should perhaps not assume the authenticity of this attractive legend, which attempted to deflect a little of Richard's reflected glory onto jongleurs and minstrels.[27] Indeed, the men responsible for Richard's capture made no secret of their activities. On the contrary, they gave them maximum publicity, so that everyone was aware of them, further proof that they intended a sort of auction, especially when Richard was 'bought' from Leopold by the Emperor Henry VI.

On 28 December 1192, according to Roger of Howden, the Emperor Henry VI sent King Philip Augustus of France a letter informing him of the good news of the capture, by his kinsman Leopold, of 'the enemy of our empire, the sower of discord in your kingdom'. After summarising the rather inglorious circumstances of the arrest, in a house below the walls of Vienna, the emperor added that Richard was now in his custody and ended with these very explicit words:

> As he is now in my power, and as he has always endeavoured to cause you trouble and difficulties, we have thought it right to make the above facts known to Your Majesty, aware that this news would be pleasing to you and bring you great joy.[28]

Philip Augustus was, indeed, delighted. He at once asked Leopold to keep the King of England in his custody, conferred with John and prepared to take maximum advantage of Richard's absence. In January, John went immediately to Paris, where he replaced his brother Richard in all his functions, as noted by Roger of Howden:

> Then John, the brother of the king of England, went to the king of France and became his man for Normandy and the other continental lands of his brother, and also for England, or so it was said; and he swore that he would marry Alice, his sister; and he returned Gisors and the whole of the Norman Vexin to the king of France; with his sister, the king of France granted him part of Flanders and promised to help him to take possession of England and the other lands of his brother.[29]

Now assured of French help, John returned to England to incite a massive uprising destined to win him the throne; he sought allies on

all sides, spread rumours that Richard was dead and proclaimed himself king. But Eleanor, the majority of the English barons and the justiciars appointed by Richard were not persuaded by the rumour and prepared to resist this new rebellion.

News of Richard's capture reached England in late January or early February 1193, as we see from a letter of the Archbishop of Rouen, Walter of Coutances, who at once informed the council. It was decided to send an embassy to Richard to procure his freedom. By the time it arrived, he was in the hands of the Emperor Henry VI who, after several weeks of haggling, had bought him from Leopold for the sum of 75,000 silver marks and the promise that, as the price of his freedom, Richard would release the prisoners he had taken in Cyprus, in particular Isaac Comnenus and his daughter.

The first English ambassadors, two Cistercian monks, met Richard for the first time at Ochsenfurt, on the river Main, when Leopold was escorting him to Henry VI, at Speyer. On learning of his brother's treachery, Richard showed no surprise, but rather scornfully doubted his ability to seize by force the kingdom he so desired.[30] And John's plan for a landing in England did indeed come to nothing. Faced with the defences set up along the English coast by Eleanor and her loyal supporters, John and his Flemish allies abandoned their attempt.[31] Philip Augustus had more success and invaded Normandy; this was in contravention of the oath he had first sworn in Messina and then renewed in Acre that he would not attack Richard's lands as long as he had not returned from the Holy Land.

At Speyer, Henry VI initially treated Richard very harshly, having him kept under close guard by a brutish soldiery. Even at night, notes a chronicler, they surrounded the King's bed, their swords at their sides, and 'would permit none of his men to spend the night with him'.[32] Once again, we are told, Richard showed himself to advantage. The chroniclers – though they were not there at the time and so were effectively repeating Richard's own stories about his captivity – assure us that even in these trying circumstances the King remained courteous, cheerful and good-humoured. To pass the time, he humiliated his guards by making jokes and sarcastic remarks at their expense; he ridiculed them, took a malign pleasure in getting them drunk and challenged them to trials of strength and games of skill which he invariably won.[33]

Throughout this long period, Henry VI refused to allow Richard into his presence. At last, as a result of the mediation of the Abbot of Cluny and William Longchamp, Richard's chancellor in England, Henry summoned his bishops and counts to hold a sort of public trial before them,

intended to justify the King of England's incarceration. To explain his ire, he enumerated a long list of grievances which are set out in detail by the chroniclers. Many were based on rumours which, according to Richard of Devizes in particular, had deliberately been spread in Germany by the Bishop of Beauvais on his return from the Holy Land:

> When he landed in Germany, at every stage of his journey, he spread the word amongst the people that that traitor, the king of England, from the very day of his arrival in Judea, had plotted to betray his lord, the king of the French, to Saladin; that he had had the Marquis [Conrad of Montferrat] assassinated so that he might seize Tyre; that he had done away with the duke of Burgundy by poison; that at the end he had sold the whole Christian army to the enemy because it was not loyal to him; that he was an extremely savage man, iron-hearted and unlovable in his ways, skilful in wiles and most skilful in dissimulation; that the king of France had come back home so quickly because of all these things; and that because of these things the French who remained behind retreated without conquering Jerusalem. The rumour gained in strength as it was spread, and it stirred up all men's anger against this one man.[34]

The emperor seems to have adopted many of these accusations on his own account. He alleged that Richard had lost Sicily by colluding with Tancred, so consolidating this usurper on the throne; he had seized Cyprus, imprisoning Isaac Comnenus, one of his kinsmen, and had gone on to sell the island to a stranger; he had treacherously had Conrad of Montferrat, his friend and vassal, assassinated; he had even attempted to have other 'Assassins' kill the King of France, Philip Augustus, after opposing him all the time they had been together in the Holy Land, betraying his mission as a crusader; he had insulted Leopold of Austria, his (Henry's) vassal; lastly, he had constantly derided and insulted the Teutons (that is, the Germans) throughout the expedition. Faced with so many accusations, Richard became livid and then, with passion and skill, he victoriously vindicated himself of these calumnies, turning the situation to his own advantage:

> The emperor made these and many other accusations against him; and at once the king, standing in their midst, beside the duke of Austria who wept copiously at his lot, began to respond to each of the accusations in a speech of such brilliance and clarity that it inspired admiration and respect in every hearer; there no longer remained in their hearts the least suspicion regarding the accusations made against him. In fact, he used indisputable assertions and convincing arguments to throw light on the truth of the deeds criticised and to show how they had come about. In this way he demolished all the baseless suspicions that hung over him, without hushing up the truth regarding his actions. In particular, he firmly denied having betrayed anyone or engineered the death

of a prince, swearing that on such a matter he would always be ready to prove his innocence in whatever form was pleasing to the court of the emperor. He spoke at length in the presence of the emperor and his princes with the greatest eloquence, because he was very articulate. Then the emperor rose and summoning the king to approach him he embraced him; then he conversed with him and made many professions of friendship. From that day on, the emperor showed him the highest honour and treated him as if he was his brother.[35]

So, to his virtues as king and warrior, Richard added those of the good advocate, capable of transforming, in an instant, the fierce hostility of the emperor into fraternal affection. Even William the Breton, who can hardly be accused of prejudice in Richard's favour, says that the envoys of Philip Augustus who were present at the assembly were impressed by Richard's bearing and his eloquence during this trial, which probably took place at the beginning of March. In fact, only a few days later, Henry VI attempted to mediate between Richard and Philip Augustus, but in vain.

This touching brotherly reconciliation was not enough, however, to persuade the emperor to give Richard his liberty. After the trial, Henry kept him prisoner in the fortress of Trifels. At least here he was able to establish better relations with his gaoler and receive the English envoys who were trying to secure his freedom in return for a ransom, the details of which were now under discussion. Ralph of Coggeshall says that the first negotiations, conducted before the end of March, resulted in an agreement, the details of which vary according to the chronicler.[36] Richard was to be freed once the ransom was paid. The terms of this proposition were reported in England, in March, by the Bishop of Salisbury, Hubert Walter; negotiations continued and, on 19 April 1193, the royal chancellor returned to England bearing a letter from Richard and another from the emperor, adorned with his gold seal.[37] The ransom proposed was huge and Henry added a further obligation: the provision, as a feudal vassalic service, of military assistance in the form of fifty ships and two hundred knights.

Richard's letter contained his instructions for raising this enormous sum of money by the imposition of extremely heavy taxes and contributions, to which we will return, on all the inhabitants of the kingdom, including churchmen, much to their displeasure. But the tax raised less than expected and to procure the required sum it was necessary to sell, borrow and sometimes demand the requisition of the wealth accumulated in church treasuries, causing further recriminations on the part of the clergy.[38] Richard's liberation was therefore delayed because the emperor refused to let him go as long as most of the ransom remained

unpaid. On 24 June, at Worms, after a meeting between Richard and Henry VI, in the presence of several bishops, the dukes of Louvain and Limbourg and the English ambassadors, a new agreement was reached: Richard would be freed in exchange for 100,000 silver marks of Cologne as ransom, with a further 50,000 marks indemnity to help Henry to conquer Sicily and Apulia; Richard would give his niece Eleanor, daughter of Geoffrey of Brittany, in marriage to the son of Duke Leopold of Austria; and he would surrender to the Duke the prisoners he had taken in Cyprus, Isaac Comnenus and his daughter. This treaty, sanctioned by a deed and an oath, was quickly made known to Philip Augustus and John, who strengthened their alliance in order to act before Richard was set free.[39]

Roger of Howden says that Henry VI had promised the King of England that he would effect a reconciliation between him and Philip Augustus; if this proved impossible, he would free Richard without demanding any money. Henry did indeed fail in this endeavour, but it seems highly unlikely that he had ever intended to release the King for nothing. On the contrary, everything suggests that he had cleverly raised the stakes by showing he was open to overtures from Richard's enemies, the King of France and John. In 1193 Philip Augustus made a number of diplomatic and political moves that were resolutely hostile to Richard. The English chroniclers primarily emphasise the first, already mentioned, that is, the attempted invasion of England by a fleet of John's French and Flemish allies. This initiative was linked, they suggest, to the negotiations going on at the same time between the courts of France and Denmark with a view to arranging a marriage between the King of France and the eighteen-year-old sister of King Knud VI, Princess Ingeborg of Denmark. Philip hoped by this marriage to make himself heir to Danish claims to England and have the use of the formidable fleet of this northern kingdom to enforce them.[40] But Knud VI remained notably unenthusiastic and refused to allow his fleet to be involved in this speculative enterprise which, as we have seen, came to nothing. The marriage with Ingeborg, celebrated on 14 August, brought Philip only a dowry of 10,000 silver marks, and it too was short-lived. On his wedding night, as is well known, the King conceived for this very beautiful princess an unconquerable physical aversion, unexplained to this day, and decided there and then to separate from her; thereafter he did everything in his power to have the marriage that had become intolerable to him annulled.[41]

His second initiative was to put financial proposals to Henry VI intended to counterbalance the ransom offers already made by the English. The Bishop of Dreux and the Archbishop of Reims were sent in

turn to the emperor's court with instructions to ask Henry to hand Richard over to the King of France, or at the very least to keep him in captivity so that Philip would have a free hand to attack Richard's continental possessions, in particular Normandy. This meant that the emperor was now in a position to hedge his bets and raise the stakes. Even more serious for Richard, during the summer of 1193 an alliance between Henry and Philip Augustus seemed a distinct possibility. The King of England was desperate to prevent this and he turned to his allies, the German princes, often in revolt against the emperor, but reconciled with him by Richard's efforts. Thanks to this swift diplomatic action, the Franco–German alliance aborted and Richard managed to avoid falling into the hands of his worst enemy.

The negotiations resumed on a different basis. At Worms, on 29 June, Henry VI agreed to free Richard as soon as he received the sum of 100,000 marks, to be deducted from the total sum of 150,000 marks. To ensure payment of the balance, Richard was to provide hostages. He would be excused further payment if he was able to persuade his brother-in-law, Henry the Lion, to switch his support to the emperor. At the end of the summer of 1193, Richard had managed to regain the advantage in the game of diplomatic chess being played out in Germany between the King of England and the King of France. He was not yet, however, in the clear. It was probably during this difficult period that Richard composed a lament (called a *rotrouenges*). Dedicated to his 'sister the countess', Marie of Champagne, it forcefully expresses his sense of abandonment at a time when his liberation was constantly being delayed, because of the slowness of his vassals and subjects in paying his ransom, as feudal law required; it is song that gives posterity a new image of this man of many talents.[42]

ELEANOR INTERVENES

Richard, while deploring the behaviour which had kept him a prisoner for two winters, was well aware of the real reason for his prolonged incarceration, that is, the delay in paying his enormous ransom. It was slow to arrive. Eleanor, meanwhile, acted with all her customary energy to procure her son's freedom. Not only did she press the governors and justiciars to assemble the necessary sums, but she also engaged in intense diplomatic activity, persuading various powers to intervene on his behalf. The pope, as we have said, had already excommunicated Leopold; he threatened to impose the same penalty on Philip Augustus if he was too open in his attacks on the lands of Richard, still regarded as a crusader, but this threat

remained purely verbal. Nor was any action threatened against Henry VI, the ruler who held Richard captive. In three letters, whose authenticity has sometimes been questioned,[43] probably drawn up for her by her chancellor, Peter of Blois, Eleanor sharply criticised Celestine III for his inactivity and for the half-heartedness of the efforts made by the papacy to end this blatant injustice:

> Often, for matters of small importance, you have sent your cardinals to the ends of the earth with sovereign powers; but in a matter so heartbreaking and deplorable, you have despatched not a single sub-deacon, not even an acolyte. The kings and princes of the earth have conspired against my son; far from Our Lord, he is kept in chains, while others ravage his lands; he is held by the heels, while others scourge him. And all this time, the sword of St Peter remains in its scabbard. Three times you have promised to send legates, and you have not done so . . . alas, I now know that the promises of a cardinal are mere words.[44]

These strong words had little effect. Eleanor had to rely on her own efforts to pursue her goal. She renewed her pressure on those ruling England and the rest of the Angevin empire to assemble the money for the ransom. The feudal duty of aid which required vassals to help pay their lord's ransom became, in this case, a crushing burden, which the barons passed on to their own men. To free their king, it has frequently been said, his subjects had to pay a quarter of their moveable goods.[45] In fact this is an average overall estimate. The novel element on this occasion was the extension of this obligation to all the estates, clergy as well as laity. According to Ralph of Diceto and Roger of Howden, in order to fulfil their obligations, parishes had to surrender the treasure they had accumulated over the ages. Archbishops, bishops, abbots, priors, earls and barons all had to pay a quarter of their annual revenues and twenty shillings per knight's fee; the Cistercian monks and Praemonstratensian canons, who specialised in sheep farming, surrendered a whole year's crop of wool; the clergy living off the tithe gave a tenth.[46] In fact, as Ralph of Coggeshall observed, no church, order, rank or sex escaped the obligation to contribute towards the King's ransom.[47]

These new and unpopular taxes came at a bad time, when England was suffering from unaccustomed storms, floods and a harsh winter followed by widespread soil infertility, phenomena which were quickly seen as evil omens associated with the King's arrest. William of Newburgh notes that this universal tax, the first of its kind, was badly received in all senses of the word: the money was slow to come in and, worse, led to widespread malpractice; his assertion that it was often embezzled by dishonest royal agents, which meant yet more collections and impositions,

ruinous to the clergy and the baronage and stripping the churches bare, is hardly objective. Richard, meanwhile, despatched message after message from his prison, urging his mother and his officials to hasten payment of his ransom.[48]

Having at last assembled most, though not all, of the necessary money, Eleanor could leave for Germany, in late December 1193, in search of her son. She was in Cologne shortly before Christmas where she made it known that she was in possession of the agreed sum.[49] Henry VI decided to set Richard free on 17 January 1194, and simultaneously revealed one of his projects: to make Richard his vassal by conferring on him the title of King of Provence, which would automatically make him suzerain of Raymond of Saint-Gilles.[50] This would be to the advantage of both kings: Richard might hope by this means to exercise pressure on his new vassal, the Count of Toulouse; Henry would find his prestige as emperor enhanced by becoming the overlord of one of the most powerful kings in the West.

It was at this point that Philip Augustus, sensing that the tide was turning in Richard's favour, tried one last manoeuvre with his ally John. They put a counter-proposal to the emperor, a veritable last-minute bid, which could torpedo the agreement just when it was about to be signed. They made Henry VI a very tempting offer to keep Richard in captivity:

> While negotiations for the release of the king of England were continuing, envoys from the king of France and Count John, brother of the king of England, came to the emperor; they offered him 50,000 silver marks on the part of king of France and 30,000 silver marks on the part of Count John on condition that he kept the king of England captive until Michaelmas. Or, if the emperor preferred, they would give him 1,000 silver marks at the end of every month, as long as he kept the king of England in captivity; or, if the emperor preferred, the king of France would give him 100,000 silver marks and Count John 50,000 silver marks on condition that he delivered the king of England to them or at least kept him in captivity for one year from that date. See how much they loved him![51]

It was an attractive offer and Henry hesitated. He delayed the date of Richard's release yet again. While Eleanor, then aged seventy-two, waited anxiously, Philip Augustus seized his opportunity and invaded Normandy, taking Evreux. One chronicler says that Henry VI himself informed Richard of these counter-proposals from his enemies, causing the king to fear that all was lost and despair of ever emerging from his prison.[52]

Before making his final decision, the emperor summoned the princes of the empire, who debated the fate of the King of England. The council

met at Mainz on 2 February 1194. The majority of the German princes, some favourable towards Richard because of marriage or kinship ties, some won over by his diplomatic activities, others disgusted by the whole affair, voted to release the prisoner, in line with the commitments already entered into by Henry VI.

Two days later, on 4 February, Richard was free, on specific conditions. Henry VI would receive as ransom the sum of 150,000 silver marks of Cologne. Eleanor paid two-thirds of this sum, 100,000 marks, immediately; the rest would follow. Until the full payment was made, hostages were surrendered to the emperor, among them men of high rank close to Richard: two sons of his brother-in-law, Henry the Lion, Duke of Saxony, and one son of his father-in-law, the King of Navarre. In addition, Richard had to agree to become the emperor's vassal, not only for the kingdom of Provence but for England itself, which he surrendered to the emperor to receive back as a fief. According to the chroniclers, this was a last-minute demand of Henry's; it had no real political consequences subsequently, but it was of great symbolic value and was felt by Richard as a form of humiliation he found extremely hard to accept. He agreed to it nevertheless, on the advice of his mother, anxious to get the matter settled once and for all and probably also fearing yet another volte-face on the part of the emperor:

> To escape from captivity, Richard, King of England, on the advice of his mother Eleanor, resigned the kingdom of England, handed it to the emperor as to the lord of the universe and invested him with it; but, in the presence of the lords of Germany and England, the emperor, as agreed, at once returned to him the kingdom of England, which he would hold from him in return for an annual tribute of 5,000 pounds sterling; the emperor invested him with a double cross of gold. However, on his deathbed the emperor released Richard, King of England and his future heirs from all that and the other clauses of the agreement.[53]

Richard was free at last. Together with Eleanor and Archbishop Walter of Rouen, he quickly left Mainz and travelled to Cologne and then Antwerp, from where he set sail for England, landing at Sandwich on Sunday 13 March 1194. William of Newburgh, no doubt unduly influenced by his biblical studies, said that Eleanor had been prudent to hasten at all costs the conclusion of the agreement to free Richard; because, like Pharaoh after his decree liberating the Jewish people, the perfidious emperor had 'repented' of having let the King of England go, so releasing 'a tyrant of such singular cruelty and such formidable force that he presented a danger to the whole world', and had wanted to send his armies in pursuit to recapture him.[54]

It was too late, as Philip Augustus noted, not without some unease. What he had feared in July 1193, and warned his ally John to beware of, had now come to pass: 'The devil had been let loose.'[55]

NOTES

1. The death of Saladin can be firmly established from Baha ad-Din, a close associate (Gabrieli, *Arab Historians*, pp. 246–51), who says he died on Wednesday 27 safar (4 March 1193), the twelfth day of an illness that had begun on Saturday 16 safar (21 February 1193). It would seem, therefore, that the dates of 28 February, given by Pernoud (*Richard Cœur de Lion*, p. 279), and 3 September, given by Balard (*Les Croisades* (Paris, 1988), p. 175), are incorrect.

2. For the changes in the military religious orders after the loss of the Holy Land, the defence of which was their raison d'être, see in particular Riley-Smith, J., *The Knights of St John in Jerusalem and Cyprus (c. 1050–1310)* (London, 1967); Luttrell, A., *The Hospitallers in Cyprus, Rhodes, Greece and the West, 1291–1440* (London, 1978); Luttrell, A., *Latin Greece, the Hospitallers and the Crusades, 1291–1440* (London, 1982); Demurger, A., *Vie et Mort de l'Ordre du Temple* (Paris, 1985) 2nd edn (1989), pp. 213ff.; Forey, *Military Orders*, pp. 204ff.; Barber, *The New Knighthood*.

3. Ralph of Coggeshall, pp. 51–2; Matthew Paris, *Chronica Majora*, II, pp. 391–2.

4. *Continuation de Guillaume de Tyr*, p. 152 (p. 121 of Edbury translation).

5. Roger of Howden, III, p. 233.

6. William of Newburgh, pp. 382ff.

7. Ralph of Coggeshall, pp. 52ff.; Matthew Paris, *Chronica Majora*, II, pp. 392–5; William of Newburgh, pp. 382ff.

8. For these events and their interpretation, see Kessler, *Richard I*, pp. 256ff.; Gillingham, *Richard the Lionheart*, pp. 221ff.; Pernoud, *Richard Cœur de Lion*, pp. 213ff.

9. Roger of Howden, III, p. 195; Rigord, 88, pp. 121ff.; William of Newburgh, pp. 382ff.

10. Ralph of Coggeshall, p. 52.

11. Matthew Paris, *Chronica Majora*, II, p. 393.

12. Matthew Paris, *Chronica Majora*, II, pp. 392–5. One wonders how Meinhard could possible have known this. It is probably a fabrication.

13. Ralph of Coggeshall, p. 54.

14. Matthew Paris, *Chronica Majora*, II, pp. 392–5; Ralph of Coggeshall, p. 55.

15. Roger of Howden, III, pp. 186ff.

16. 'Jubet ducem adesse praesentem, ipsi soli de redditurum promittens': Ralph of Coggeshall, p. 56.

17. Ibid.; see also the rather fanciful version of the episode in William of Newburgh, pp. 382ff.

18. Ralph of Coggeshall, p. 57.
19. According to Diceto (pp. 106ff.): 'by giving him such odious custodians, he made his captivity more painful than if he had been closely chained'. See also Matthew Paris, *Chronica Majora*, II, p. 394; Ralph of Coggeshall, pp. 56–7; Roger of Howden, III, pp. 194ff.
20. Roger of Howden, III, pp. 276–7.
21. William of Newburgh, p. 431; Ralph of Coggeshall, p. 65; Ralph of Diceto, II, p. 124.
22. Matthew Paris, *Chronica Majora*, II, pp. 409ff.
23. William of Newburgh, p. 401.
24. Even Rigord is critical of this capture, which he considered to be immoral and contrary to all custom.
25. *Ménestrel de Reims*, §80–1, p. 43. John Gillingham further embroiders on the legend by reversing the roles and presenting Blondel as wandering from castle to castle singing this same song to make himself known, and Richard responding by singing the chorus: 'Some Legends of *Richard the Lionheart*; their Development and their Influence', in Nelson, *Richard Cœur de Lion*, pp. 51–69; *Richard the Lionheart*, p. 224. The first version of the legend, in the Minstrel of Reims, may be less appealing but is more sober.
26. *Ménestrel de Reims*, §82, p. 44 (p. 276 of Stone translation). The desire to enhance the status of minstrels and jongleurs and encourage their masters to treat them generously is obvious.
27. Pernoud, *Richard Cœur de Lion*, pp. 220ff.; Broughton, *Legends of Richard Cœur de Lion*.
28. Roger of Howden, III, p. 195.
29. Ibid., p. 204.
30. Ibid., p. 196.
31. Matthew Paris, *Chronica Majora*, II, p. 401; for these plans, see Cartellieri, *Philipp II*, pp. 45ff.
32. 'Neminem suorum cum eo pernoctare permittens': Ralph of Coggeshall, p. 58.
33. Ralph of Coggeshall, pp. 57ff.; Matthew Paris, *Chronica Majora*, II, p. 396.
34. Richard of Devizes, p. 80.
35. Ralph of Coggeshall, p. 58 (based on the French translation in *Richard Cœur de Lion*, ed. Brossard-Dandré and Besson, p. 236).
36. Matthew Paris, *Chronica Majora*, II, p. 398; Ralph of Coggeshall, p. 60; Ralph of Diceto, p. 110.
37. Ralph of Coggeshall, p. 60; William of Newburgh, p. 398; Roger of Howden, III, p. 209.
38. For the popular reaction to these levies, see below, pp. 266ff.
39. Roger of Howden, III, pp. 214–15.
40. Ibid., p. 224; William of Newburgh, pp. 367ff.; Matthew Paris, *Chronica Majora*, II, p. 46; Gervase of Canterbury, I, p. 529; see on this point Powicke, *Loss of Normandy*, pp. 91ff.

41. See on this point Baldwin, *Philip Augustus*, pp. 82–7, 210; Baldwin, *Language of Sex*, pp. 6, 74, 226.
42. *Rotrouenge* attributed to Richard the Lionheart; the text is in Bec, P., *La Lyrique Française au Moyen Age, XIIe–XIIIe Siècle* (Paris, 1978), vol. 2, pp. 124–5; also, with a modern French translation, in *Chansons des Trouvères* (Paris, 1995), p. 380. There is an English translation in John Gillingham's *Richard the Lionheart* (pp. 236–7, 303) based on that of Kate Norgate (*Richard the Lion Heart*).
43. Labande, 'Une Image Véridique', pp. 221ff.
44. *Recueil des Historiens des Gaules et de la France*, 19, p. 277. This translation is based on the modern French of Régine Pernoud in *Aliénor d'Aquitaine* (p. 310); see also her slightly amended translation in her *Richard Cœur de Lion* (p. 224) and the partial translation in Labande, 'Une Image Véridique' (p. 222).
45. Petit-Dutaillis, *Feudal Monarchy*, p. 142.
46. Ralph of Diceto, II, p. 110.
47. Ralph of Coggeshall, p. 60.
48. William of Newburgh, pp. 390ff.
49. Roger of Howden, III, pp. 226ff.
50. Ibid., p. 225.
51. Ibid., p. 229.
52. Ibid., pp. 231–2.
53. Ibid., p. 202.
54. William of Newburgh, pp. 404–5.
55. Roger of Howden, III, pp. 216–17.

9

Richard versus Philip Augustus (1194–8)

$\backsim$

Early in February 1194, Richard, free at last, left Mainz and headed for a North Sea port, accompanied by his indefatigable and admirable mother; Philip Augustus, meanwhile, hastily took possession of the lands and fortresses he had been granted by John as the price of his support.

These concessions were far from negligible, consisting of the whole of Normandy east of the river Seine, with the exception of Rouen and its territory, and also several places on the left bank of the Seine, in particular Vaudreuil, a potential base for an attack on Rouen. In his desperate search for allies and support, John had also conceded Bonsmoulins to the Count of Perche and Vendôme to the Count of Blois and granted many fortresses, in particular those commanding the main routes into Touraine, including Tours, Amboise, Montbazon, Montrichard, Loches and several others of lesser importance. In Aquitaine, he had accepted the claims to autonomy of that perpetual rebel, Ademar of Angoulême. Emboldened by these successes, Philip Augustus was anxious to make the most of his opportunities with the least possible delay; having seized important Channel ports (Wissant, Saint-Valéry, Le Tréport and Dieppe) for the first time in the history of the Capetian monarchy, he moved to take possession of other Norman fortresses promised by John, before Richard could resume power. He had occupied Gisors and the Norman Vexin in April 1193. In February 1194, he seized Evreux, Vaudreuil and Neubourg, from which he launched an attack on Rouen which failed because the town was stoutly defended by Robert of Leicester. Then, at Sens, he received the homage of Geoffrey de Rancon and Bernard de Brosse, two of Richard's Aquitainian vassals who had gone over to the King of France. Philip was under no illusions. He knew only too well that he would soon have to do battle with Richard, now more than ever his implacable enemy, as John would be unable to resist him for long. On 10 February, not before time, John was dispossessed of his lands and excommunicated.[1] The tide was turning.

While making his way from Mainz to Antwerp, Richard was not content simply to put as much distance as possible between himself and

the scenes of his captivity. As soon as he felt out of danger, he took the time to strengthen his relations with the princes and prelates of the Rhineland, or at least with those who had pronounced in his favour.[2] Drawing once again on his much diminished treasure chest, he rewarded them generously for their past support and made agreements that were to prove useful at the time of the imperial election following the death of Henry VI. He also established a network of alliances with an eye to his future battle against his hereditary enemy, the King of France, on whom he was determined to have his revenge. He thus received the homage of the archbishops of Mainz and Cologne, the Bishop of Liège, the Count of Holland, the Duke of Brabant and several other Rhineland lords.[3] On both sides, then, preparations were under way for a conflict made inevitable by the interplay of political interests and rivalries, but which would assuredly be further envenomed by accumulated personal resentments and enmities.

RESTORED TO POWER

In the short run, Richard had to resume possession of his kingdom and restore it to order. He set about his task as soon as he arrived, having landed at Sandwich on 13 March at seven o'clock in the morning, where he was joyfully acclaimed though by only a sparse crowd. There were several reasons for this low-key reception. Many people had lost hope of seeing Richard return alive and had eventually been persuaded by the rumours spread by John's supporters that he was dead or would be a prisoner for ever. The romance writers would be inspired by the popular theme of the good king who had disappeared; by the fourteenth century, there were ballads and romances which had as their hero the historical but idealised figure of Robin Hood and later, in the nineteenth century, Walter Scott would create his fictitious character, Ivanhoe. Another reason for the semi-clandestine nature of Richard's arrival was fear of the French fleet and of his English and Flemish enemies; the time and place of his landing was kept secret, and it was effected secretly and in an unannounced location. Nevertheless, several chroniclers, admittedly writing after the event and anxious to emphasise God's intervention in man's affairs, report that Richard's return to his kingdom was marked by celestial signs. Not all of them were favourable, some presaging famines and catastrophes attributable to inclement weather.[4]

Richard went first to the tomb of St Thomas Becket at Canterbury to give thanks, then to Bury St Edmunds to venerate the warrior king and

saint, martyred by the pagans. Next, in London, he was welcomed with much rejoicing by clergy and people and given a triumphal reception in St Paul's Cathedral.[5]

The chroniclers say nothing of the reaction of the barons. Some, as we have seen, had sided with John. With the announcement of Richard's release, most of them submitted to the king, but a few recalcitrants held out. They included the castellans of Tickhill and Nottingham, who were besieged by the faithful Hubert Walter, newly appointed Archbishop of Canterbury and chief justiciar. Walter had been Richard's companion in the Holy Land and he was a man in whom the King, rightly, had complete confidence; he now became his right-hand man. This close and total involvement of a man of the Church in secular, profane and even military affairs provoked some unease and criticism on the part of some ecclesiastics. Such an involvement was hardly new, of course. Thomas Becket was a case in point, under Henry II, with consequences that are well known. Another more recent instance was that of William Longchamp, who had acted in Richard's absence. But never before had the participation of an ecclesiastic in the conduct of government been so total or so fruitful. Hubert Walter, according to John Gillingham, was not only 'unquestionably the king's man' but 'one of the most outstanding government ministers in English history'.[6]

For the moment, Hubert Walter proved his loyalty to the King by besieging the castles of the supporters of his rebellious brother. The garrison of Tickhill quickly surrendered without a fight, once it had been ascertained that Richard really had returned safe and sound to England. The defenders of Nottingham, however, sure of the strength of their walls, held out. Richard made a sudden appearance there, on 25 March, with an army loudly blowing its horns and trumpets, but this failed to intimidate the garrison; deadly arrows were shot at them from the battlements. This angered the King, who gave orders for an assault. According to the custom that would later prove his downfall, Richard personally took part, protected only by a light coat of mail and a large shield borne before him by a sergeant. The attack had to be called off when night fell.

Next day, Richard tried to dishearten the resistance by having some captured soldiers hanged under the walls.[7] The besieged garrison knew only too well what this signified: as was normal at the time, similar treatment awaited them if the fortress was taken by assault.[8] Next day, 27 March, two knights from the garrison obtained permission to visit their assailants' camp to establish if the King really had returned to his kingdom. Once this was confirmed, all resistance was in vain and the

garrison surrendered on 28 March, after a siege of three days. Richard behaved with relative magnanimity; he kept the leader, Robert the Breton, in prison (where he was put to death not long after, on his orders)[9] but agreed to free most of the captives in return for large ransoms.[10] He was encouraged in this decision by his urgent need for money, which had other consequences to which we will return. Then, in the recaptured town, he began to organise a second coronation, designed to reaffirm, solemnly and definitively, that the interlude was over and a new reign had begun.

On 10 April, Richard held his first court, at Northampton; next day, he received the allegiance of the King of Scots; on 15 April he was at Winchester, where he took possession of the castle. He then announced the date of his new coronation (or, if preferred, crown-wearing), which was to be on Sunday 17 April, at Winchester, in the presence of William of Scotland and Eleanor of Aquitaine, the queen mother, or rather the *de facto* queen. Richard seems to have paid little attention to Berengaria, who was never crowned in England. Where, one wonders, was she at this period? Roger of Howden says that, having reached Rome on her return journey from the Holy Land, she stayed there for some six months, in the company of Joan and the daughter of Isaac Comnenus; she then travelled via Pisa and Genoa to Marseille, where she was received with great honour by the king of Aragon, who conducted her to the borders of his territory. The little party was then taken into the care of Count Raymond V, whose son, Raymond VI, was later to marry Joan, whom he presumably first met on this occasion. The Count of Toulouse escorted his guests across his lands to the borders of Aquitaine, from where Berengaria travelled to Poitiers, her husband's capital, which she was seeing for the first time.[11] She was presumably in Poitiers at the time of the second coronation, but at that solemn ceremony, as at the true coronation in 1189, Richard appeared alone, without a queen at his side.

After this symbolic reaffirmation of kingship, Richard remained only a short time in his kingdom, which had quickly rallied to his cause. He was first and foremost an Angevin and anxious to reassert his authority as quickly as possible in his continental empire, where his enemies had done him much harm. He also wanted revenge.

OPENING BATTLES AND VICTORY AT FRETEVAL

Richard's first task was to assemble an army, which was expensive. His treasure chest was empty, exhausted by the payment of his ransom, his diplomatic largesse, his extravagance and the civil wars. It would have

to be replenished. This was done in part by resorting to some of the measures he had employed on his first accession to power. He instituted a new land tax, the carucage; he granted a few privileges to the Jewish communities and the towns in return for cash; and he demanded fresh payments from those appointed to office in 1189, who had believed they were becoming office-holders for life, but who now made the disagreeable discovery that they were only leaseholders. In most cases, however, the offices had proved so lucrative that they were able to pay up once again without too much pain, thereby publicly and officially registering their 'joy' at the return of their king.

It was not long before Richard had recruited an army, composed principally of mercenaries, Welsh archers and Brabançon pike men. They assembled at Portsmouth, where he planned to embark in the first days of May. A storm forced him to return to port and postpone his departure till 12 May, when he eventually left England, never to return.

Landing at Barfleur, he received a tumultuous welcome as a saviour. William Marshal, who was at his side, remembered it long afterwards. The crowd that flocked to see Richard was so dense that an apple tossed into the air would have found nowhere to land; people presented him with gifts, and there was singing and dancing and general rejoicing. Everyone sang the same refrain: 'God has arrived in strength. It is time for the French king to go.'[12] The Normans were then apprehensive about the activities of Philip Augustus, who had that very day embarked on the siege of Verneuil, which he had tried in vain to take the previous year. Once again, the garrison resisted courageously, even going so far as to taunt the King of France, confident that Richard would soon arrive to liberate them.

But Richard was not yet in a position to do so. Delayed by the storm, he arrived at Verneuil ten days too late. From Barfleur he went first to Lisieux, where he spent the night with one of his loyal supporters, the archdeacon John of Alençon. This was the scene of a strange episode described by William Marshal. Richard was resting after a meal, unable to sleep because of his worries about the siege of Verneuil. His host, John of Alençon, approached him, his face drawn, on the verge of tears. Richard asked what was wrong:

> John, why are you looking like that? You have seen my brother John, no use lying! He has nothing to fear! Let him come, he has no reason to be afraid! He is my brother, by my faith! He will never have any cause to be frightened of me. If he has been foolish, I will not blame him, but those who have led him astray have already had what they were looking for, and will have even more in future. But I will say no more at this time.

John of Alençon then went to tell John of his brother's goodwill towards him. The treacherous younger brother entered 'fearfully', and threw himself at his brother's feet. Richard raised him up and kissed him, saying: 'Do not be afraid, John. You are a child; you have got into bad company; they are of evil disposition, those who have given you such bad advice. Get up, go and eat.'[13]

According to Roger of Howden and William of Newburgh, this touching reconciliation between the two brothers took place on the initiative of Eleanor, their mother.[14] Observing that Richard was still without an heir, she was no doubt concerned for the future of the Plantagenet empire, should her elder son die. She certainly had no confidence in John, who had already given many examples of his ineptitude as a ruler. But she still preferred him to Arthur, the only other possible heir, son of a daughter-in-law she detested, a feeling that was doubtless reciprocated. The chronicler adds that from this moment Richard and John were friends again, but that the King still did not wish to grant his brother a single castle or any lands.[15] This was a minimal sensible precaution and John soon gave proof both of his change of heart and of his volatility and perfidy. Returning to Evreux, which Philip Augustus had placed in his custody, John betrayed his former ally and had the French garrison massacred before surrendering the town to his brother.

Richard, meanwhile, was hastening to the rescue of Verneuil. He reached Tubœuf on 21 May, where a knight from the besieged garrison warned him that the town was about to fall; speed was of the essence. Without waiting for the main body of his army, Richard despatched a few groups of knights and foot soldiers, who crossed the enemy lines and reinforced the garrison, boosting its morale. According to the French chronicler Rigord, the siege engines of the King of France has already succeeded in battering down a section of the walls when news arrived from Evreux that the French warriors had been captured and many of them beheaded. Philip Augustus, 'dismayed and furious', abandoned the siege on 28 May and rode to Evreux. He expelled John and sacked the town, not even sparing the church of St Taurin,[16] while his army, left behind at Verneuil, raised the siege next day, abandoning part of their camp and their provisions, which were immediately taken over by the besieged inhabitants. According to Matthew Paris, it was the imminent arrival of Richard that caused them to flee:

The great feast of Whitsun was approaching; but so that on that holy day the French would not be able to boast of having won a victory, they learned at

nightfall that the king of England was preparing to do battle, and that he would arrive next morning. This news caused terror among the French, who had often experienced the valour of Richard, and they judged it preferable to flee rather than to fight; and indeed they abandoned their camp, to their great loss and shame.[17]

Richard entered Verneuil in triumph on 30 May.[18] While Philip Augustus, in mid June, besieged, took and destroyed the castle of Fontaine, near Rouen (where there were only four knights and twenty men-at-arms), then Châteaudun, Richard's troops surrounded Loches; this was with the assistance of Navarrese contingents brought by Sancho of Navarre, brother of Berengaria, who had devastated the lands of the rebel barons of Aquitaine, Aimar of Limoges and Geoffrey de Rancon, on the way. Sancho had then been recalled to Navarre by the death of his father, but his army remained and besieged the castle, though with little success. Richard was then in Tours, where, on 11 June, he levied 2,000 marks in various fines and confiscations at the expense of the city's burgesses and canons, who had, in his opinion, been too quick to give their support to Philip Augustus.[19] On 13 June, he joined his troops at Loches, which he successfully stormed next day. This was an important victory, as the fortress commanded the principal routes of Touraine. It enabled Richard quickly to pacify the region and rally it to his cause.

After a vain attempt to agree a truce, which failed because of Philip's desire to include the Poitevin barons, which Richard refused, the King of France established his camp near Vendôme, where the King of England was then staying. On 3 July, the two kings challenged each other and Philip appears to have announced his intention of attacking next day, at Fréteval. In fact, he did the very opposite, and retreated. Richard caught up with him, attacked his rearguard and followed it as it fled, leaving the rest of his army under the command of William Marshal. In total disarray, the French army scattered. Philip Augustus himself only just escaped capture; pursued by his enemy, he entered a church to pray, while Richard, believing he was still ahead, galloped past, assisted by the mercenary leader Mercadier, who provided him with a fresh horse so he could continue the chase. It is clear that Richard had intended to kill Philip or at least take him prisoner. Returning empty-handed, he went back to Vendôme, where his army had seized the King of France's camp and all the rich booty it contained.[20]

Rigord deliberately glosses over the battle of Fréteval, which he presents very briefly as an trivial affair of little importance.[21] It is of considerable interest to historians, however, for two reasons. The first is historical

and military: it gave Richard's armies total ascendancy. The second is practical and documentary: at this period the chancery and the archives, even
the royal treasury, were still largely nomadic and itinerant, following the
King on his travels, even to the battlefield. It is one of the reasons why
monarchs were reluctant to engage in pitched battles. At Fréteval, Philip
had unsuccessfully attempted a bluff, as a result of which he lost his camp
and a large number of documents, which then had to be reconstituted; this
massive task led to the creation of the *archives royales*.[22] Régine Pernoud
has justly observed that 'on that day many records of royal decrees that
would in other circumstances have been kept in the *Trésor des chartes*
in the French *archives nationales* were instead removed to the English
archives'.[23]

On his return to Vendôme, the King of England observed with satisfaction that the seizure of the camp had been carried out without the uncon-
trolled pillage that so plagued medieval armies. In this case, William
Marshal had maintained discipline and his rearguard had remained vigilant, taking no part in the fighting or in the collection of booty in the
French camp. While the victors boasted of their success, Richard made a
point of publicly and loudly praising the conduct of the Marshal, in words
that reveal his sure strategic sense:

> The Marshal did far better than any of you. I tell you, if you do not already
> know: for he would have come to our aid, if we had needed it. And for this
> reason, I put a higher price on his actions than on all that the rest of us have
> achieved. When you have a good rearguard, you have nothing to fear from
> your enemies.[24]

TRUCES AND HOSTILITIES (1194–6)

Immediately after Fréteval, Richard set about the task of pacifying
Aquitaine and restoring order there. Assisted by the armies of Sancho of
Navarre, he took the castle of Taillebourg and seized lands held by
Geoffrey de Rancon, then Angoulême and the lands of Count Ademar,
who was defeated on 22 July. He then returned to the north, where he
prepared once again to challenge his rival for mastery of the borders of
Normandy, that eternal source of contention between the kings of France
and England. With this in mind, he summoned his barons to Le Mans.[25]

During Richard's campaign in Aquitaine, Philip Augustus had not
remained idle in Normandy while John Lackland and the Earl of
Arundel had besieged Vaudreuil. This castle, a few kilometres from Pont-
de-l'Arche, was of considerable strategic importance as it controlled

access to a bridge over the Seine that was essential to any defence of or assault on Rouen. Philip was at Châteaudun but by dint of forced marches he rapidly arrived at the besieged castle; then, with a small company of crossbowmen, he fell unexpectedly on the besieging troops, who panicked and fled into the surrounding forests, leaving their war machines behind.[26] A truce followed, signed somewhere between Verneuil and Tillières on 23 July. It ratified the status quo, which was to be maintained. In Normandy, this was favourable to the King of France, as Philip retained not only Vaudreuil but Gisors and the Vexin, with the fortresses of Vernon, Gaillon, Tillières and Nonancourt, as well as many castles in Upper Normandy, including Arques, Aumale, Mortemer and Beauvoir, previously ceded by John and which Richard had been unable to recover. Richard was authorised only to repair the fortifications of four castles, at Drincourt (Neufchâtel-en-Bray), Le Neubourg, Conches and Breteuil.[27] This truce was to last until November 1195, but it was in practice frequently violated by small-scale and poorly documented military operations, aimed at gaining possession of a few fortresses here and there.[28]

The chroniclers, temporarily abandoning the rather confused military engagements characterising this truce of over a year, break off from their narratives of the war to give accounts of several important events which also deserve our attention.

The first was the death of Raymond V of Toulouse, who was succeeded by his son Raymond VI. In 1196, he married Richard's sister Joan, widow of the King of Sicily, thus effectively ending the disputes which had previously set the Plantagenets and the house of Saint-Gilles at odds. This tolerant prince allowed the most diverse religious movements to flourish in his lands, including the Cathars, the Albigensians and the Waldensians, to the great displeasure of the ecclesiastical authorities, with the tragic and disastrous consequences that are well known: the preaching of the Albigensian Crusade by Pope Innocent III, the sack of Occitania by the northern French barons, the subjugation of the county of Toulouse and the violent eradication of these 'heresies' by the Inquisition and the burning of many 'heretics' at the stake. They record in passing another marriage, that of Alice, for so long betrothed to Richard; at last, in August 1195, Richard returned her to her brother, who promptly married her to the Count of Ponthieu, who set out to enforce his rights to Eu and Arques, so re-igniting the war in Normandy.[29]

The second event to impress the chroniclers was the defeat in Spain of King Alfonso VIII of Castile at Alarcos, in 1195, at the hands of the Almohads. William of Newburgh made this an excuse to repeat the (fictitious) version of the origins of Islam and its prophet, Mahomet, and

to tell the story of Muslim expansion up to his time, emphasising like Ralph of Coggeshall the traditional view that defeats suffered by the Christians at the hands of these infidel precursors of the Antichrist should be imputed to their sins.[30] Rigord and William the Breton also record this Christian defeat, but offer a more social interpretation to which we will return; for them, it was a consequence of a mistaken decision on the part of the King of Castile, who, neglecting or despising the nobility and the knights, had wrongly placed his confidence in the common people, in the armies of peasants (*rustici*), unsuited to battle and ignorant of the customs and values of chivalry.[31] The defeat of Alfonso's armies caused great unease in Western Christendom, and in particular worried Richard. Matthew Paris says that when the Muslims (whose armies he estimated at the huge figure of 1,600,000 warriors!) heard that the pope had summoned a council to preach a crusade against them, and that the leader of this expedition was to be Richard, the illustrious king of the English, now free again, they were so terror-struck that they went back home.[32]

In Sicily, too, the situation had changed: Tancred had died; on hearing this news, the emperor Henry VI marched on Apulia, seized Salerno and avenged himself on its inhabitants, who had sided with Tancred by handing over to him Constance, Henry's wife. He had the chief men of the town killed and their wives and daughters were handed over to his soldiers. Henry then took Melfi, destroyed various Apulian fortresses and seized Sicily.[33] The success of his former gaoler over his ally Tancred can hardly have pleased Richard, though he no doubt derived some consolation from the terrible death in that same year of the man who had captured him, Leopold of Austria.

The chroniclers record many other events from this time of truce, including the measures taken in both France and England for the better government of the country, to increase control over the population and to organise for an imminent war. Both sides prepared their armies. In France this was through the institution of the *prise des sergens*, specifying the number of men-at-arms to be provided by the abbeys, towns and communes, the duration of their service and the compensatory financial contributions to be paid by those who were exempted.[34] In England rules for the appointment of judges were instituted, and various regulations introduced dealing, for example, with the Jews and with John Lackland's former supporters. John himself had his county of Mortain restored to him, together with his rights over Eu and the county of Gloucester, with all its dependencies except castles, and an annual revenue of 8,000 *livres angevines*.[35]

In August 1194, Richard also issued a decree authorising the holding of tournaments in England, in spite of the renewed prohibition of these warlike exercises by the pope. This measure had many advantages in the King's eyes. It made it possible for English knights to be trained for the impending war, and it meant they no longer needed to go abroad to fight in tournaments, with the risks of collusion this entailed; it was popular with the barons, many of whom were keen tourneyers, while also allowing tournaments to be supervised, as they were permitted only in certain places and under royal control; lastly it replenished the royal treasury through the payment of entry fees, the sums calculated according to the rank of the competitors, ranging from one mark for a simple knight to ten marks for a baron and twenty for an earl.[36]

Hostilities resumed in July 1195, well before the date set for the end of the truce. According to Roger of Howden, the cause may have been a surprising offer of an alliance made in June by the emperor Henry VI to Richard, who hesitated to agree to such a strange proposition. But Philip Augustus may have learned of it and he destroyed several castles in Normandy, so breaking the truce.[37] Yet another truce was concluded in August, and a peace proposed on the following terms: Louis, Philip's son, would marry Eleanor, Richard's niece, who would receive Gisors, Neauphle and the Norman Vexin, and also 20,000 silver marks from Richard; Philip would return his Norman conquests to Richard. As security for this agreement, Alice was returned to her brother, who, as we have seen, soon married her to John, Count of Ponthieu.[38]

In spite of these peace proposals, hostilities resumed. In an attempt to end them, the two kings met once again near Vaudreuil. However, as they were actually meeting, the walls of the castle collapsed, 'undermined by the French'. Philip's strange behaviour in having his own engineers destroy a fortress then in his possession has much puzzled historians. But John Gillingham has convincingly argued that the King of France must have realised that he could no longer hold onto the castle; it was better to destroy it, therefore, than let it fall into enemy hands.[39] Richard was furious and at once launched an attack on Philip, who hastily retreated across a bridge over the Seine, destroying it after him, so putting himself safely out of reach. Richard then entered the territory of the King of France, destroying crops and fruit trees. Further south, his troops took Issoudun and other places in the vicinity of Bourges, which compensated for the losses suffered in Normandy. Soon after, news arrived that the emperor of Morocco had been victorious in Spain and was besieging Toledo, whereupon the two kings agreed on a truce to last until 8 November.[40]

This truce was no better respected than its predecessors and fighting resumed in Normandy, where Richard laid siege to the castle of Arques. But his troops were put to flight by the arrival of those of Philip, who destroyed Dieppe and the ships he found there, before being himself surprised and driven out by Richard. Fighting also resumed in Berry. Here, Philip Augustus was in difficulties in Issoudun, which he had entered in order to defend it, but whose suburbs were destroyed by Mercadier.[41] Richard's troops, however, suddenly raised the siege, 'by the miraculous action of Our Lord', said Rigord. Richard, he goes on, agreed to do homage to Philip for Normandy, Poitou and Anjou. A new truce followed in December 1195, ratified by a peace conference held in January 1196 at Louviers.[42]

The clauses of the peace of Louviers were more favourable to Richard, suggesting that his armies had by this time got the upper hand. The King of France surrendered Issoudun and its territory and everything he had taken in Berry, Auvergne and Gascony; he also returned Arques, Eu and Aumale and all the castles seized by force. This was to recognise Richard's lordship over the whole of Normandy, with the exception of the Vexin and a few castles like Vernon, Gaillon, Pacy, Ivry and Nonancourt. In Aquitaine, the King of France acknowledged that his former allies, the counts of Angoulême and Périgueux, and also the Viscount of Brosse, were the vassals of Richard and owed him homage and military service. If the agreement was violated, the guilty party was to hand over 15,000 marks.[43]

Once again, the accord was a dead letter. The peace of Louviers was very quickly broken by Philip Augustus, who demanded in vain that the Archbishop of Rouen do homage to him. Hostilities resumed. Philip assembled an army, besieged Aumale, which he took in April, then Nonancourt, while Richard seized the securities for the treaty and took Jumièges. In England, meanwhile, William FitzOsbert, nicknamed 'Longbeard', made himself the champion of the poor and the people, provoked disturbances in London and was finally captured by treachery and summarily executed.[44]

The war was to be merciless, particularly in Normandy. We see this in the diplomatic negotiations which took place in the spring of 1196. Richard was trying to win over Brittany, which was clearly aspiring to independence. He tried, therefore, to put pressure on its princes: he summoned to his court Geoffrey's widow, Constance of Brittany, who had since been remarried to Ranulf, Earl of Chester, who had been appointed governor of Brittany; he also tried to secure custody of Arthur, her son. But his efforts came to nothing: Constance was abducted by her husband and her son Arthur was unable to free her; with the support of the Breton lords, he took refuge at Philip's court and came down firmly against

Richard, whose lands were devastated by his men. In reprisal, Richard conducted some harsh military campaigns in Brittany and forced the Bretons to submit.[45] This affair made the King of France even more determined to resume the war.

WAR WITHOUT MERCY (1196–7)

Hostilities resumed with renewed vigour in the spring and summer of 1196, with their dreary succession of castles destroyed, taken and retaken, of villages burned, of massacres of garrisons considered disloyal, of prisoners blinded and sent back to the enemy to discourage him, all to no avail. War was not 'chivalric' for everybody, a point to which we will return.[46] Overall, things went well for Philip, who managed to secure the alliance of several princes, in particular Renaud of Boulogne and Baldwin of Hainault. With the latter's help, Philip broke the truce, seized Vierzon and besieged Aumale, which Richard tried in vain to relieve, having taken Nonancourt thanks to the treachery of its castellan. This time, in contrast to Fréteval, it is the English chroniclers who fail to record the setback, while Rigord emphasises the scale of the defeat. Richard's armies withdrew, abandoning Aumale to the King of France, who destroyed its fortifications, already badly damaged by his own siege machines. He followed up this victory by taking the castle of Nonancourt.[47]

These successes worried Richard, who feared an attack on Normandy. To prepare for it, he decided to build a massive fortress, Château-Gaillard, at Les Andelys, in spite of the opposition of the Archbishop of Rouen, the local lord. Expropriated by Richard, the Archbishop laid an interdict on the duchy of Normandy; for many months, no religious services were held and the dead went without Christian burials. Eventually, an agreement was negotiated, through the intermediary of Pope Celestine III, by which Richard ceded Dieppe to the Archbishop in compensation.[48] When he held his Christmas court at Bur in 1196, Normandy was still under the interdict and the duchy was suffering.

For many months, Richard was preoccupied by the building of Château-Gaillard, where he personally supervised the works from July 1196. The ruins of the castle are still deeply impressive today. The site itself, a rocky spur dominating the Seine, with a vertical drop of nearly a hundred metres, made it an impregnable fortress. The double circuit of high, thick walls laid out in an ellipse and their formidable round donjon made it all the more daunting. Château-Gaillard, designed and built by the King of England, epitomises the military architecture of the day and testifies to Richard's strategic genius in such matters. All the resources of

military technology are effectively deployed, in particular the intensive use of arrow slits and the avoidance of 'dead angles', but also the many only slightly jutting towers that enabled archers and crossbowmen to shoot at almost any point close to the wall where assailants might hide or regroup for another doomed assault.

From the beginning, Château-Gaillard impressed the French, in spite of the prophetic boasts, real or imagined, of Philip Augustus. Gerald of Wales says that the King of France declared that he wished the walls were made of iron, so great was his confidence that the castle would one day be his, along with the rest of Normandy.[49] It was, of course, taken by Philip Augustus during the summer of 1203.[50] For the moment, however, it barred access to Normandy and even constituted a threat to the Vexin, which Richard hoped to reconquer.

But first it was necessary for Richard to offset Philip's diplomatic successes and find new allies. This he did by means of the marriage to which we have already referred, that of his sister Joan to Count Raymond VI of Toulouse.[51] William of Newburgh may be wrong in his date for this marriage (which took place in October 1196, not 1197), but he alone makes these pertinent observations on the subject:

> There also ended at this time, with God's aid, the war in the Toulousain which had been one of the chief concerns of the illustrious King Henry and his son Richard and which, in forty years, had caused a large number of deaths. For the count of Toulouse, having concluded an agreement with the King of England, married, with great pomp, his sister, who had previously been married to the king of Sicily and who, on the latter's premature death, had returned to her brother; this ended their inveterate hatred, which subsided. So the king of England, who had till then had to divide his attentions and fight on three fronts . . . in Brittany and in the Toulousain, could in future turn all his attention to the third, that is, the war against the king of France; he at once became a more powerful and terrible threat to his enemies; on both sides the war was fought all out.[52]

To secure this agreement, Richard had to make several sacrifices. He renounced his ancestral claims to Toulouse, recognised full possession of Quercy to his new brother-in-law and even gave Joan the county of Agen as a dowry, though it remained a fief of the Duke of Aquitaine. But these concessions freed him from a heavy burden and constant threat on his southern flank. This meant that the troops of mercenaries which had ravaged the Breton and Toulousain countryside under the leadership of Mercadier and his terrible routiers headed back to Anjou.

War resumed in the spring of 1197, and was marked by numerous crimes. On 15 April, Richard attacked the port of Saint-Valéry, which

belonged to the Count of Ponthieu, an ally of the King of France, burned the town, seized the relics of its patron saint and carried them off to Normandy. Having earlier decreed a commercial blockade of his enemies in England, to make an example of them, he burned the ships loaded with provisions which he found in the port, seized their cargo, distributed it among his soldiers and had the ships' crews hanged.[53] This vigorous enforcement of the embargo gave food for thought to the counts of Hainault and Flanders, regions whose wealth was largely dependent on the traditional trade with England. Striking while the iron was hot, in the summer of 1196, Richard sent an embassy to Baldwin of Flanders and Renaud of Boulogne led by William Marshal; the result was a treaty marking a complete reversal of alliances: the two princes deserted Philip Augustus and joined Richard, greatly weakening Philip's cause. With their mercenary armies (of *cotereaux*), they began to ravage his lands.[54]

Meanwhile, Richard resumed his offensive in eastern Normandy. In May 1197 his troops, led by William Marshal, seized the castle of Milly. The Marshal himself joined in the assault, taking several prisoners, whom he handed over to the King of England. He was criticised by Richard for having thrown himself into such an enterprise, given his age (he was fifty-two) and his rank, and when he no longer needed to demonstrate his prowess; he should have directed the assault, not led it, and given the young knights, the *bachelers*,[55] a chance to distinguish themselves. 'Sir Marshal,' said the King, 'a man of your station ought not to risk his life in adventures of that kind. Leave them to the young knights who still have a reputation to win.'[56]

Not long after, during the same campaign, the routiers of Mercadier made an important capture, that of Philip of Dreux, Bishop of Beauvais and cousin of the King of France; he was also the sworn enemy of Richard, about whom, as we have seen, he had spread many damaging rumours, and whose liberation he had done everything to delay. Hearing that his castle of Milly was under attack, the Bishop had dared to put himself at the head not of a spiritual army but of a secular one, for which he is severely criticised by the chroniclers. Taken prisoner by Mercadier, he was handed over to Richard, who was delighted, and who had him imprisoned in Rouen, stubbornly refusing all offers of ransom. The Bishop then appealed to the pope about the cruel treatment being meted out in this way to a man of the Church. The pontiff intervened without success, the King of England sending him, by way of a reply, his prisoner's hauberk, with the words: 'Is this your son's tunic?' The pope took the hint and gave his verdict: this bishop had been captured under arms, as a warrior; he could therefore be ransomed, having behaved like a soldier of

Mars, not of Christ.[57] The bishop made numerous approaches to his captor, offering a huge ransom. According to William of Newburgh, when his chaplains came to beg Richard to spare him, the King made the following reply:

> I appoint you judge between me and your lord. All the wrong he has been able to do me, all the damage he has done me, I am ready to forget, with one exception: when, on my return from the East, I was a prisoner of the Roman emperor, I was treated with respect for my royal person, and served with all due honour. But one evening, your lord came and, the very next morning, I was made aware of his purpose in coming and of the business he had plotted with the emperor that night. For, from that moment, the emperor's hand laid more heavily upon me, to the point where I was put in irons, loaded with so many chains that a horse or an ass could scarcely have borne their weight. Decide for yourself, therefore, what sort of imprisonment your lord should receive at my hands, he who made sure I suffered like that at the hands of my gaoler?[58]

Soon after, Baldwin of Flanders, now an ally of Richard in return for 5,000 silver marks, took Douai and besieged Arras. The two kings waged war by proxy of their allies but avoided direct confrontation. Philip took Dangu, near Gisors, and then tried to relieve Arras. But by destroying the bridges and opening the sluices, the Count of Flanders isolated the armies of the King of France who, caught in a trap, had to sue for peace, having vainly tried to lure Baldwin back into his own camp. In September 1197 Richard authorised the Count of Flanders to agree a truce of one year and four months.[59] During this period, with his hands free in the south, the King of England invaded Auvergne and seized a handful of castles belonging to Philip.[60] The new truce was no more respected than its predecessors; preparations for war, the fortification of castles, the rebuilding of defences and diplomatic manoeuvres continued apace.

One event deserves special mention, the election to the imperial throne following the death of Henry VI, in Messina, on 28 September 1197, when his son, the future Frederick II, was only two years old. As the imperial crown was elective, not hereditary, a fierce competition followed. The brother of the late emperor, Philip of Swabia, made himself the candidate of the party in power, the Hohenstaufen, supported by Philip Augustus. Opposing him, the Guelf party, allied to Richard and tired of the constant descents on Italy in defence of Sicily, opposed his candidature. Supported by the Rhineland princes, they offered the crown to Richard the Lionheart. This offer undoubtedly delighted the King of England, who must have savoured his revenge. However, being a realist and caring more for the interests of his own empire than the pursuit of a title without territorial basis, Richard wisely declined the offer. He proposed in his stead his

nephew, Otto of Brunswick, son of his sister Matilda and Henry the Lion, Duke of Saxony, dead two years before. The two candidates, elected by their respective supporters, disputed the throne until July 1198, when Otto was eventually elected, not without controversy.[61]

During the summer of 1197, Richard enjoyed some new diplomatic successes. Not only did he strengthen the links already established with the princes of the Rhineland and the Low Countries, but he won over to his side many other lords who had formerly been allies of the King of France, among them the counts of Saint-Pol and Guisnes, Counts Geoffrey of Perche and Louis of Blois, who joined the counts of Flanders and Hainault, and also the Bretons loyal to Arthur, already won over. Philip, too, tried to seduce the vassals of his enemy, but managed only to recruit two turbulent barons of Aquitaine already well known to us: Aimar of Limoges and Ademar of Angoulême. We will observe in due course the fateful consequences of this unfortunate alliance which, at the time, seemed to cause Richard little anxiety.

THE YEAR 1198

Military operations resumed at the end of the summer of 1198. Once again, Baldwin of Flanders invaded Artois, seizing Aire and, on 6 September, laid siege to Saint Omer. The inhabitants sent an embassy to Philip Augustus urging him to come to their aid; otherwise they would have to surrender. All Philip would promise was to come to their rescue by the end of September, until when they should hold the town if they could; if this was impossible, the castellan must act as he thought fit. In the event, the town soon surrendered to the Count of Flanders, who took possession on 4 October.[62]

Philip, meanwhile, was suffering other setbacks at Richard's hands in Normandy. The King of England entered French territory and laid it waste together with Mercadier; near Vernon, Philip was put to flight and lost twenty of his knights and more than sixty mounted men-at-arms, as well as many foot soldiers. Richard pursued Philip, who fled and shut himself in the castle, with Richard in pursuit. Crossing the Epte at Dangu, Richard established himself in the French Vexin and in a single day seized Courcelles and Boury, while one of his contingents took Sérifontaine. Philip's army, coming to the assistance of Courcelles, was intercepted by Richard's troops, who defeated it. Once again, Philip Augustus had to flee for his life, galloping to Gisors, where he took refuge.

The chroniclers made much of a detail which seemed to them deeply significant. While he was crossing the bridge (over the Epte) at Gisors,

it collapsed and the King of France was thrown into the river; he swallowed some water and would have drowned if he had not been quickly rescued. But many of his men were lost, including the Count of Bar and John, brother of William des Barres. The battle was a disaster for the French. Roger of Howden gives the names of the vassals and allies of the King of France who were captured (a long list of forty-three names), to whom must be added a hundred knights and a hundred and forty horses 'clad in iron', many mounted sergeants and an even larger number of infantry. The Normans suffered few losses: three or four knights taken and one man-at-arms. Richard himself described this campaign, in which Mercadier also took part, in a letter to the bishop of Durham.[63]

Even Rigord recognised the scale of the defeat, but he attributed it to divine punishment, because the King of France had allowed the Jews to return to Paris, against all advice and in contravention of his own earlier edict. It was inevitable, said the chronicler, that disappointments and God's punishment would follow. In any case, only a little earlier, nature, too, had provided some baleful omens. In Brie, during the consecration of the species, the wine really had changed into blood and the bread into flesh; in the Vermandois, a dead knight had been resuscitated and foretold the future; in Paris a man had been killed by lightning and the storm had done great damage to the vines and the harvest; more or less everywhere, stones as big as nuts, sometimes as big as eggs, even bigger said some, had fallen from the sky. In the face of such evident signs, major upheavals, or worse, were only to be expected. Rigord adds: 'It was rumoured that the Antichrist had been born in Babylon and that the end of the world was nigh.'[64]

As we see, popular belief in the imminence of the end of the world had not disappeared in the seven years since Richard had debated the subject with Joachim of Fiore. It was a good time for the priest Fulk of Neuilly and his assistants to preach a new crusade, which was well-supplied with celestial signs and a variety of miracles, in an atmosphere of marvels comparable to the preaching of the First Crusade.[65]

In an effort to recover lost ground, the King of France gathered his armies and proceeded to attack Normandy, taking and burning Evreux. Richard retaliated by sending Mercadier, who, with his routiers, plundered Abbeville and robbed the merchants there, killing some and capturing others, who were carried off as booty to be ransomed. The two kings then sought a truce. Philip needed time to rebuild his army and replenish his treasury. He offered to return to Richard all his conquests except Gisors. But Richard was not interested in peace and would agree only to a truce, in November 1198, with a further meeting fixed for

January 1199. Taking advantage of this period of calm, the two kings each proceeded to fortify their castles. On 25 December Richard held his Christmas court at Domfront, while Philip was at Vernon. It was to be the King of England's last Christmas.

At the end of December, new peace initiatives were actively promoted by Pope Innocent III, who wanted to end the discord between the two kings for the sake of the new crusade being preached by Fulk of Neuilly. Innocent sent his legate Peter of Capua to Richard, and he tried in vain to persuade him to agree to negotiate with Philip Augustus. The legate emphasised the damage done to Christendom by this quarrel, which prevented the faithful from going to the assistance of the Christians of Outremer and recovering Jerusalem, but Richard stood firm and gave vent to his grievances: not so very long ago, when he himself had been a crusader and under the protection of the Church, had his lands not been attacked by this same King of France? How could he agree to a peace? At the very most, he would accept a truce for five years. Peter of Capua was delighted and, emboldened, went on to plead for the liberation of the warrior bishop of Beauvais. This was too much for Richard, who exploded, launching into a long diatribe against the 'Apostle' (the pope) who, he reminded the legate, had not lifted a finger to protect him and who now had the gall to send his legate to persuade him to free a tyrannical robber who pillaged and burned. This is how William Marshal, who seems to have been present at this meeting, recorded his violent speech, which brought the meeting to an abrupt end, with the pontifical legate sent packing and reviled as a lying traitor, a cheat and a simoniac:

> The Pope takes me for a fool.
> I know very well that he turned his back on me
> When I sent word to him from afar
> And besought him in my need.
> For I was taken prisoner while in God's service.
> And I begged him earnestly and asked him
> That he should help me in my need
> Or that he should do what he ought.
> He never wished to intervene,
> Nor did he ever deign to take any trouble for me.
> Now he petitions me on behalf of a robber,
> A tyrant, an arsonist,
> Who so delighted in war
> That he laid waste my land
> And fought day and night!

Get out of here, sir traitor,
You lying, cheating, faithless knave,
Purchaser of churches!
Take care that I never, in the field or on the highway,
Set eyes on you again.[66]

So the year 1198 ended badly for peace, for the legate, and also, to some extent, for Richard. But for him, the year 1199 was to be even worse.

NOTES

1. Roger of Howden, III, pp. 235–7.
2. See Poole, 'Richard the First's Alliances with the German Princes'.
3. For these events, see Gillingham, *Richard Cœur de Lion*, p. 238; Kessler, *Richard I*, pp. 307ff.
4. Ralph of Coggeshall, pp. 62–5.
5. Ralph of Diceto, p. 114.
6. Gillingham, *Richard Cœur de Lion*, p. 244.
7. Roger of Howden, III, pp. 239–40; Ralph of Coggeshall, p. 63.
8. For the meaning of these executions and the fate of rebels in similar circumstances, see also Strickland, *War and Chivalry*, pp. 204ff., 231ff.
9. Ralph of Coggeshall, p. 63; Roger of Howden, III, p. 240; see also Strickland, *War and Chivalry*, p. 256.
10. Roger of Howden, III, pp. 249ff.
11. Ibid., p. 228.
12. *Guillaume le Maréchal*, lines 10429–52.
13. Ibid., lines 10380–92, 10409–13.
14. Roger of Howden, III, p. 252; William of Newburgh, p. 424: 'Mediante matre . . .'
15. Roger of Howden, III, p. 252.
16. William of Newburgh, pp. 418–19.
17. Matthew Paris, *Chronica Majora*, II, p. 405.
18. Rigord, §96, p. 127. See also William of Newburgh, p. 418; Roger of Howden, III, p. 252; Ralph of Diceto, II, p. 115.
19. Roger of Howden, III, pp. 252–3; William of Newburgh, p. 419; Ralph of Diceto, II, p. 114.
20. Roger of Howden, III, pp. 255–6; Ralph of Diceto, II, pp. 117–19.
21. Rigord, §100, p. 129.
22. Ralph of Diceto, II, p. 117; William the Breton (*Gesta Philippi*, pp. 196ff.; *Philippidos*, pp. 118–21) mentions the loss of the royal seal and of many charters and fiscal documents. William the Breton adds that this loss led to the reconstitution of the lost documents under the direction of the chamberlain, Walter the Younger. Fréteval was thus the impetus to the creation of the *archives royales*. See also on this point Baldwin, *Philip Augustus*, pp. 407ff.

23. Pernoud, *Richard Cœur de Lion*, p. 238. For the loss of domanial documents at Fréteval, see Bisson, T. N., 'Les Comptes des Domaines au Temps de Philippe Auguste, Essai Comparatif', in Bautier, *La France de Philippe Auguste*, pp. 525ff.
24. *Guillaume le Maréchal*, lines 10668–76.
25. Ralph of Diceto, II, p. 117; Roger of Howden, III, p. 257.
26. Rigord, §104, p. 130.
27. Roger of Howden, III, pp. 257–9.
28. Ibid., p. 276.
29. Ibid., p. 301; Rigord, §102, pp. 130–1.
30. William of Newburgh, pp. 445–55; Ralph of Coggeshall, p. 70.
31. Rigord, §103, p. 131; William the Breton, §78, p. 198.
32. Matthew Paris, *Chronica Majora*, II, p. 410.
33. Roger of Howden, III, pp. 269ff.; Ralph of Diceto, II, pp. 123ff.; Matthew Paris, *Chronica Majora*, II, p. 410.
34. See on this point Contamine, *War in the Middle Ages*, pp. 83–4; for the military measures taken in France, see Audouin, 'L'Armée Royale', complemented and corrected by P. Contamine, 'L'Armée de Philippe Auguste', in Bautier, *La France de Philippe Auguste*, pp. 577–94.
35. Roger of Howden, II, pp. 262ff.; III, p. 287.
36. Roger of Howden, III, p. 268; Ralph of Diceto, p. 121.
37. Roger of Howden, III, p. 300.
38. Ibid., p. 302.
39. Gillingham, *Richard the Lionheart*, pp. 254–5.
40. Roger of Howden, III, p. 300; William of Newburgh, pp. 455–6; Rigord, §104, p. 133.
41. Rigord, §104, p. 133.
42. Ibid., §107, p. 132; William of Newburgh, pp. 460ff.
43. Roger of Howden, IV, p. 3; Rigord, §108, p. 132; William of Newburgh, p. 462; Matthew Paris, *Chronica Majora*, II, pp. 416ff.
44. Roger of Howden, IV, pp. 5ff.
45. Ibid., pp. 7ff.
46. For contemporary methods of warfare, see below, pp. 230ff.
47. Rigord, §§113, 115, pp. 136–7; William of Newburgh, p. 483. Roger of Howden (IV, pp. 4–5) does not mention the capture of Vierzon and blames Philip Augustus for the collapse of the truce.
48. Roger of Howden, IV, p. 14; William of Newburgh, pp. 487ff., 500.
49. Gerald of Wales, *De Principis Instructione*, III, 25, pp. 289–90. For the huge cost of Château-Gaillard, see Gillingham, *Richard the Lionheart*, pp. 264–5.
50. Rigord, §141, p. 158.
51. Roger of Howden, IV, p. 13. See also above, p. 183ff.
52. William of Newburgh, p. 491.
53. Roger of Howden, IV, p. 19; Matthew Paris, *Chronica Majora*, II, p. 440; William of Newburgh, p. 491; Roger de Wendover, p. 268. For the political

meaning of this transfer of relics, see Bozoky, E., 'Le culte des saints et des reliques dans la politique des premiers rois Plantagenêt', in *La Cour Plantagenêt (1154–1204)* (Poitiers, 2000), pp. 283ff.

54. *Guillaume le Maréchal*, lines 10688–810; Rigord, §115, pp. 139ff.
55. For the ambiguity of the word *bacheler*, see Flori, 'Qu'est-ce qu'un *Bacheler?*'
56. *Guillaume le Maréchal* (the translation comes from Gillingham, *Richard I*, p. 308).
57. Roger of Howden, IV, pp. 16, 21–3; Ralph of Diceto, II, p. 152; *Guillaume le Maréchal*, lines 11265ff. Philip of Beauvais was finally freed in return for a ransom of 10,000 silver marks: Roger of Howden, IV, p. 78. See on this point the judicious remarks of Strickland, *War and Chivalry*, p. 47. The affair did nothing to dampen Philip's passion for war and he also fought at Bouvines in 1214.
58. William of Newburgh, pp. 493–4.
59. William of Newburgh, p. 491; Matthew Paris, *Chronica Majora*, II, p. 441.
60. Roger of Howden, IV, p. 20.
61. Ibid., p. 39.
62. Ralph of Coggeshall, pp. 83ff.; Ralph of Diceto, II, pp. 163–4; Roger of Howden, IV, p. 54.
63. Roger of Howden, IV, p. 55.
64. Rigord, §122, p. 140; §121, p. 140.
65. Ibid., §120, p. 139. For the marvels recorded during the preaching of the First Crusade, see Flori, J., *Pierre l'Ermite et la Première Croisade* (Paris, 1999), pp. 227ff.
66. *Guillaume le Maréchal*, lines 11603ff.

10

The Death of the Lion (1199)

⌒

LAST BATTLES

Richard's anger at the legate's request was not feigned. The King was genuinely shocked that the pope should express such deep concern at the fate of Philip of Dreux, his irrevocable and traitorous enemy, when, not so very long ago, this same pope had done nothing to help Richard emerge from the emperor's gaols. Peter of Capua realised this; he fled from the royal court, fearing, at least according to William Marshal, that he might lose his masculinity if he stayed.[1] Queen Eleanor had also intervened personally on Philip's behalf, at Rouen. And while his guards had been escorting him to a meeting with her, the Bishop had attempted to escape, rushing into a church and claiming right of sanctuary. He had been dragged out by force and Richard had given orders for him to be taken to Chinon and kept under closer guard.[2] Peter of Capua's efforts in this matter were doomed from the start.

Hastily leaving Richard's quarters, the legate made his way to those of the King of France, where his encounter was the subject of much laughter and where it was agreed that this king was certainly 'not a lamb, but a lion'. Peter was then asked to return to try at least to procure the five years' truce that Richard had been ready to accept before the ill-fated request on behalf of Philip of Dreux. But the legate was sufficiently scared to refuse point blank and this delicate diplomatic mission had to be entrusted to the Archbishop of Reims. Meanwhile, William Marshal had managed with some difficulty to calm the King down, pointing out that it was very much in his own interests to agree to a truce confirming the status quo. Richard, he said, had made many gains. The King of France must be in dire straits if he was reduced to suing for peace or for a truce, proof, surely, that he had had enough. What did it matter if the terms of the truce meant that Richard had to cede a few isolated castles in the middle of Normandy? How were their garrisons to survive if they were unable to depend for their provisions on the surrounding countryside? To hold onto them, the King of France would himself have to keep them supplied with men, arms and

victuals, which would be as costly as a war.[3] Richard was persuaded and, on 13 January, accepted the truce. He at once instructed William le Queu to make sure that the garrisons of the castles surrendered to Philip Augustus were unable to procure any supplies or levies from the neighbouring lands. The truce freed Richard's hands in Normandy, enabling him to devote himself to other matters.

He decided to go to Aquitaine to deal with the rebels in Limoges and Angoulême. First, he despatched his faithful Mercadier, at the head of his formidable routiers. On the way, they escaped an ambush laid by other mercenaries, in the pay of the King of France, which meant Richard could accuse Philip of having broken the truce. Once he had assembled an army, Richard joined Mercadier, who was already fighting in Aquitaine.

For a long time now Bertran de Born, ever the warmonger, had been urging Richard to come and take his revenge on the treacherous Poitevins and Limousins, and rekindle the fires of war in the region. During the King's captivity, he had written several songs denouncing the shameful behaviour of the emperor; on Richard's return to England in 1194, he composed songs denouncing the barons of the Limousin – though they are not named, it was clear who was meant – who had betrayed the King:

> I wish the king could read hearts, and would pass among us here and learn which of the barons is false to him and which is true, and would recognise the disease that is laming Limousin, which was his and could be worth having, but a horse canker is spoiling it.[4]

In 1199, Richard was fighting once again. In March he was present at the siege of the castle of Châlus-Chabrol, near Limoges, which was held by Aimar of Limoges. The siege, conducted by Mercadier's men, dragged on, even though the garrison was small, consisting of only about forty men. The sappers laboured to undermine the walls, the crossbowmen and archers showered projectiles of every sort on the defenders and Richard, as usual, took an active part in operations. On the evening of 26 March, having dined, he rode up to the ramparts to inspect the progress of the sappers and perhaps to loose off a few arrows at the men defending the walls. On this particular evening, there was only one; protected by a comical apology for shield (a frying pan), he was boldly letting fly a few bolts from the battlements. Richard, a keen amateur of prowess, went closer to appreciate, admire and applaud the audacity, or rashness, of this solitary archer, who bent his crossbow and fired. Richard was not wearing armour, as he had not been expecting to fight. He was protected only by his helmet and by a shield which, as usual, was carried before him by a sergeant. The bolt hit the King in the left shoulder. Whether from defiance,

courage, arrogance or pride, Richard saluted and congratulated the archer, affecting to regard his wound as negligible. He had received so many, back in the Holy Land! He returned to the camp, urging his men to continue the siege.

Back in his tent, he tried to remove the bolt, but in vain; the wooden shaft broke off, leaving the iron barb in the wound. A surgeon tried to do better and managed, with great difficulty, to extract the bolt. Surgical techniques in the West were still very rudimentary; Muslim doctors, far ahead in this field, derided, amongst other things, their poor hygiene, neglect of disinfection and ignorance of antisepsis.[5] In spite of this, there were a surprising number of recoveries in the twelfth century, following serious wounds inflicted in battle, cures owed in equal measure, perhaps, to the skill of certain *mires* (physicians) and the extraordinary vitality of some of their patients.[6]

Richard had his fair share of the latter, but by this date he was worn down by age, by fighting and perhaps by excesses of every sort, those of the table, at the very least, as is suggested by the fact that he had put on weight, not to say become fat. This royal patient, furthermore, was famously short of patience and he refused to comply with his doctors' orders. He was not prepared to alter his habits, though whether this made any difference is impossible to say.[7] In the event, the wound went septic, gangrene set in and Richard realised he was doomed. He sent news to his mother, who had retired to Fontevraud; she hurried to his side, despite her great age, arriving in time to receive his last words and his last breath. Peter Milo, Abbot of Le Pin, received Richard's confession and administered extreme unction. One of the most powerful kings in Europe prepared to die, wounded by an arrow shot from the battlements of a minor castle in the Aquitaine he had loved so dearly.

The castle, meanwhile, had surrendered. Richard wanted to know who had fired the fatal shot, not to abuse but to pardon him. The man was summoned. On his deathbed, the Lionheart, chivalric to the last, questioned him, pardoned him and gave orders that he should be spared. Then, as the morality and religion of the day demanded,[8] he divested himself of his earthly possessions; naked he had come into the world, he was now going to a place where earthly riches had no currency. He relinquished his kingdom, dividing it as he thought best. He handed his power and his lands to his brother John (to whom, nevertheless, the name 'Lackland' stuck), bequeathed three-quarters of his fortune and his jewels to his nephew, the Emperor Otto, and asked for the remaining quarter to be sold and the proceeds distributed among his servants and the poor. Lastly, he gave instructions for the disposal of his body. A charter dated

21 April at Fontevraud reveals that Eleanor was present at Richard's bedside in his dying moments.[9] Eleanor, *mater dolorosa*, was to see that his body was carried to the royal abbey of Fontevraud, where she would retire to spend her remaining days, close to the tombs of her husband and her much-loved son. But here, also, there was to be a division: Richard's body was to go to Fontevraud, but his heart was to go to Rouen, capital of Normandy, the duchy for which he had fought so hard, but which his brother would lose within a few months. His entrails were to remain where he died, in the ungrateful land of Aquitaine, on which he had expended so much sweat and blood.

He died on the evening of 6 April 1199.

THE KING'S DEATH: HISTORY AND LEGEND

Was this the death of a knight? Of a king? Of a saint? Or of an adventurer? The sources which describe his end differ and sometimes contradict each other. It was seized on by legend, sometimes to be sublimated, often to be tarnished, at all events to be shrouded in obscurity. In the simplified version I have given, I keep to the main facts, of which we can be fairly confident. For the rest, legend was so quickly and so closely intertwined with history that until modern times even serious historians (not to mention the rest) have often found it difficult to separate the wheat from the chaff. Doubts persist on a number of points, for example the actual place where Richard died, the real reasons for his presence beneath the walls of a castle often claimed to be of no strategic importance and even the identity and personal motives of the man who loosed the fatal bolt.

These and many other points were still unclear only a few years ago in France, England, Germany and the United States, which is strange given that a French scholar had long ago shed light on almost all of them. His work appeared exactly a century before that of the English historian John Gillingham, who rehabilitated him in a book published in 1978, and then more fully in an article that appeared in 1979.[10] This French scholar, who was for so long ignored (one wonders why!), was the abbé Arbellot, who, beginning in 1878 with his meticulously documented article, 'La Vérité sur la Mort de Richard Cœur de Lion' (*'The Truth about the Death of Richard the Lionheart'*), repeatedly tried to draw the attention of historians to the points in question.[11] Most of the texts I quote in the following pages were first cited by François Arbellot and then by John Gillingham. All I have tried to do here is use and translate, wherever possible, better and more recent editions than those available to the learned abbé.

WHERE AND BY WHOM WAS RICHARD KILLED?

In 1958 it was still felt necessary to debate these questions and refute a later legend in which Richard was carried to Chinon, where he died.[12] This story has no basis in fact beyond a confusion which scarcely merits attention. It is, however, necessary to examine more closely the evidence suggesting that Richard died during the siege of Nontron, on the Limousin–Angoumois border, a castle that belonged to the Bishop of Angoulême though it was then in the hands of Aimar of Limoges. The earliest reference to this tradition is found in Gervase of Canterbury, who also attributes the King's death to a certain John Sabraz. According to Gervase, Richard was besieging this castle because it belonged to the Count of Angoulême (though it was actually, as we have said, then held by Aimar of Limoges). The besieged garrison, running short of provisions, proposed an honourable surrender to Richard that would have spared their lives, but he refused, so driving the defenders into a desperate resistance:

> [The king of England] besieged a castle of the count of Angoulême, which was called Nontron, and compelled it to surrender. In fact, because provisions in this castle had run out, the defenders sent messengers to the king to ask him to show pity on them and spare their lives. The king remained obdurate and refused to grant them any mercy, wishing to obtain by might alone what the besieged offered him freely, if under some compulsion; he had perhaps forgotten that in such cases despair can engender peril. A young man called Johannes Sabraz, who was on the walls of the castle, haphazardly shot a bolt from his crossbow, and beseeching God that He would Himself direct the blow and so deliver from oppression the innocent besieged, let fly his arrow. The king, who had emerged from his tent, heard the fatal sound of the crossbow. To avoid the blow, he ducked his head and leaned forward, and so was mortally wounded in the left shoulder . . . those who were with him before his death tell that he insistently asked for the man who had struck him with this bolt. The man was brought before him, trembling; he fell at his feet and, in tears, begged for mercy; the king willingly granted him his peace, pardoned him his wound and his death, and forbade any of his men to injure him on account of this misfortune.[13]

Gervase is one of the few chroniclers who puts Richard's death at the castle of Nontron and who names the man who killed him as Johannes Sabraz. For William the Breton, who romanticises Richard's death in his *Philippidos*, truly an epic tale, the archer who entrusted his avenging bolt to Destiny is called only Guy.[14] For Roger of Howden, it was Bertrand de Gourdon who shot an arrow from the top of the ramparts of the castle of Châlus, and hit the King in the arm, inflicting an incurable wound. After

the castle had been taken, Richard had all the prisoners hanged with the exception of the man who had wounded him, doubtless intending, says the chronicler, to inflict on him later a more painful and dishonourable death. Then, having abandoned all hope of a cure, he had the offender brought into his presence, and it was then that he proudly revealed the motives behind his purely personal animosity:

> Then he summoned Bertrand de Gourdon, the man who had wounded him, and said: 'What wrong have I done you, that you should kill me like this?' The man replied: 'With your own hands, you killed my father and my two brothers, and now, you tried to kill me too. Take your revenge however you wish. Whatever the terrible tortures you devise, I will suffer them willingly, so long as I know that you are dying too, you who have inflicted so many great ills on the world.'[15]

The King then ordered that Bertrand be freed from his chains and pardoned him for his death. He even gave instructions that he be allowed to leave and given a hundred English shillings. Unbeknown to the King, however, Mercadier kept him in prison and, once Richard was dead, had him flayed alive.

The abbé Arbellot clearly demonstrated that the murderer flayed by Mercadier could not have been Bertrand de Gourdon, who was still alive in 1209, when he took part in the Albigensian Crusade.[16] He is also to be found at the siege of Toulouse in 1218 and doing homage to Louis VIII in 1226 and to St Louis in 1227; he was still alive in 1231. There can be no doubt that this is a literary fiction. In fact, as we will see below, the crossbowman was called Peter Basil, and he probably had no particular reasons for taking any revenge on Richard. The dramatic dialogue reported by Roger of Howden has to be attributed to a desire to romanticise the King's death.

Roger of Howden is right, however, to place the tragic event at the siege of Châlus. The two erroneous references to Nontron and to Bertrand de Gourdon noted above nevertheless transmit a half-truth in that they bring out the reasons which brought Richard to the area: his desire to fight and reduce the fortresses of the Count of Angoulême and Aimar of Limoges. In this, Richard was acting as a feudal prince, a suzerain seeking to inflict a harsh punishment on treacherous vassals, according to the law.

This simple fact has long been obscured by the fanciful story of a treasure that had been found by one of the peasants of Aimar of Limoges and then hidden by the latter in his castle of Châlus. In this version, Richard was conducting the siege so he could lay hands on this treasure. We need to examine this theory, always bearing in mind that the majority of

sources, with the exceptions noted above, agree on one fundamental point, namely that it was at Châlus that Richard died. They differ, on the other hand, on the subject of the reasons for Richard's presence beneath the walls of this particular castle.

RICHARD AND THE TREASURE HUNT

As Gillingham has shown, the majority of historians who had previously written about Richard the Lionheart enthusiastically adopted the story of the hidden treasure.[17] They included, in England, at the turn of the nineteenth and twentieth centuries, Kate Norgate, author of one of the most detailed biographies written about Richard;[18] in Germany, the best biographer of Philip Augustus, A. Cartellieri;[19] and in France, Alfred Richard. This reliable historian of the county of Poitou was in no doubt as to the motives that had led Richard to embark on the siege of Châlus; it was, he said 'pure greed. It had been rumoured for some time that a treasure of incalculable value had been discovered on the lands of the Viscount of Limoges.'[20] In a book published in 1973, Gillingham, too, accepted this thesis;[21] it was still being supported a year later by the American historian James Brundage[22] and, more recently still, by J. Choffel[23] and Régine Pernoud in France.[24] Most of these authors see Richard as meeting a senseless death at Châlus during an unnecessary siege, devoid of political significance and conducted for base and sordid motives of self-interest, in the course of an absurd treasure hunt.

This thesis fits in very neatly with the traditional view, held by the majority of historians for more than a century, of the personality and conduct of Richard the Lionheart: a frivolous man and a mediocre king, a sort of Don Quixote who neglected the realities of government, preferring to engage in chivalric adventures and pointless or irrelevant quests. John Gillingham has refuted this erroneous and excessively one-sided view of the man and this mistaken or at least exaggerated judgement, showing that Richard was a wiser ruler than has generally been thought, in particular with regard to his continental lands.[25] The sources that describe the cause of his death should be examined without prior moral assumptions, and the ideology which may have led the authors of some of these sources to nudge their readers in the desired direction should be closely scrutinised.

The oldest medieval sources are fairly evenly split on the matter of the treasure. Of the eleven that describe the episode at Châlus, five refer to the treasure and six do not. In general, moreover, those that mention it

are older and more trustworthy than those that do not. This is the case, in particular, with two French chroniclers, Rigord and William the Breton, and two English chroniclers, Roger of Howden and Ralph of Coggeshall, often quoted in the preceding pages.

Rigord, a monk at the royal abbey of St Denis, finished his chronicle about 1206; he is clearly pro-Capetian and intensely hostile to the King of England, which must always be kept in mind. His description of Richard's motives for going to Châlus is therefore worthy of our consideration; in any case, his is one of the best versions of the story:

> In the year of Our Lord 1199, on 6 April, Richard, King of England, died, seriously wounded near the town of Limoges. He had been engaged in the siege of a castle which the inhabitants of Limoges call Châlus-Chabrol, during Holy Week, on account of a treasure that had been found by a knight in this place. Impelled by his extreme ambition, the king demanded that this treasure be handed over to him. The knight who had found this treasure had fled to the Viscount of Limoges. Now, while the king was besieging this castle, which he vigorously attacked every day, a crossbowman unexpectedly shot a crossbow bolt and mortally wounded the King of England, who, a few days later, went the way of all flesh. He lies at Fontevraud, in an abbey of nuns, alongside his father. It is said that the treasure in question consisted of statues of pure gold representing an emperor seated at table with his wife, his sons and his daughters, testifying for posterity to the period in which they lived.[26]

Were these Roman statues? No-one knows. Rigord, it should be noted, is a little hesitant regarding the nature of this discovery; he tells us only what was said (*ut ferebatur*) about it. Nor does he know the name of the crossbowman. The soberly factual nature of his account, nevertheless, lends it credibility, despite his strange precision on the subject of the treasure and his failure to say anything about its fate.

William the Breton, chaplain to Philip Augustus, is even more prejudiced in favour of the King of France and more hostile to Richard. He knew and used Rigord's account. In his first work, the *Gesta Philippi Augusti*, he largely reproduces it, but seems to have had some doubts about the nature of the treasure, the description of which he omits. He employs the expression 'so it is said' (*ut dicebatur*) with regard to the discovery itself.[27] His second work, written after the victory of Philip Augustus at Bouvines (that is, between 1214 and 1220), is of a very different type. It is a dithyrambic eulogy of the King of France, composed in bombastic epic style. In it, he devotes several lines to the discovery but still says nothing of its nature; there are no gold statues here. Nor does he mention the Viscount of Limoges.

William does, however, tell us how the treasure was found: a peasant from the Limoges area, ploughing his fields, came across it and took it to his lord, a man by the name of Achard of Châlus (otherwise unknown to history). Richard heard rumours of this discovery and laid siege to Châlus, refusing the castellan's request for a truce, even during Lent, and rejecting all offers of conciliation or arbitration. William then introduces into his story the Fates, the three sisters who, in ancient Roman religion, control human destiny. One of them, Atropos, decides to punish Richard, who is guilty of numerous sins, which she spells out: he is greedy and impious, he respects neither God nor His laws, he had rebelled against his own father and violated feudal laws, treaties and his own word, not to speak of the laws of nature; he was guilty, furthermore, of introducing into France that deadly weapon, the crossbow. He was doomed therefore to suffer the very fate dealt out to so many others by this baleful import. At Châlus, Atropos arranges for Achard to find a crossbow and instructs him to give it to a certain Dudo, who will become the messenger of fate by firing the fatal arrow.[28]

Clearly, this account is closer to myth than history. It was intended to exalt and glorify Philip Augustus while, in contrast, blackening Richard's memory. William still omits all reference to the statues, but introduces characters unknown elsewhere, Dudo, the executioner, and Achard of Châlus. The story of Richard's death told at the court of Philip Augustus some fifteen years after the event seems not altogether reliable.

We are back with history when we turn to the English chronicler, Roger of Howden, generally regarded as one of the most reliable sources of the period for the history of the kings of England. It is on his account that most modern historians have based their own version of the events of 1199; it is therefore worth quoting at length:

> Meanwhile, Guidomar, Viscount of Angoulême, having found a large treasure of gold and silver on his lands, sent a goodly part of to Richard, his lord, King of England; but the king rejected it, saying that, by right of suzerainty, the treasure ought to revert to him in its entirety. The Viscount categorically refused to agree to this. The King of England therefore came to the region with a large army to make war on the Viscount; he besieged his castle, called Châlus, in which he hoped the treasure had been hidden; and when the knights and the sergeants of the garrison came out to offer to surrender this castle on condition that their lives, their limbs and their arms were spared, the king refused to receive them, but swore that he would take them by force of arms and hang them. So the knights and the sergeants returned to their castle, distressed and troubled, and prepared to defend it.[29]

There follows the account already given above: the King is wounded by a crossbow bolt and summons the archer, who reveals the reasons for his animosity. The King then insists on pardoning him in a scene which Roger put into verse:

> Erect before the king, his eyes full of menace, he asked for death. The king recognised his desire to go to his execution and understood that he was afraid of receiving his pardon. 'You will live in spite of yourself! Live, because I pardon you, be the hope of the vanquished in these conquered lands! You will be an example of the generosity of my heart!'[30]

Roger of Howden is in general a credible historian. He died in 1201, so he was writing not long after the events he describes. Nevertheless, as regards the death of Richard and his activities in Aquitaine, he was not necessarily well-informed, or at least much less so than when dealing with the government of England or the crusade, in which he himself partici-pated. Having retired to his vicarage of Howden in Yorkshire, he devoted himself from 1192 to describing affairs in England in particular, and more precisely those affecting the regions close to his parish, in the north of the country. He knew about distant events such as those in Aquitaine only from very indirect and sometimes inaccurate reports. A number of errors can be identified in his account of the events surrounding Richard's death. For example, the name he gives to the Viscount of Limoges (Widomarus) is probably a conflation of the real name of the then viscount (Ademarus, or Aimar) and that of his eldest son, Guy (Wido). Roger was mis-taken, too, as we have seen, about the name of the archer, which allowed him to introduce the theme of chivalric vengeance, turning this mortal injury into the culmination of a medieval feud. He also romanti-cised the King's last moments by introducing the episode of the pardon, and even more its rejection by the young man; he even composed a poem describing Richard's decision to spare the man's life against his wishes, so that he would remain for ever a committed witness, 'the hope of the van-quished';[31] Roger was not at this point particularly favourably inclined towards Richard. Also, after describing the King's death, he incorporated into his story many poems and epitaphs composed about him, which will be discussed later in this book. One of them was very much along the same lines and presents the crossbow bolt as a providential punishment for Richard's many crimes.

> Poison, greed, murder and monstrous sexual urge,
> Shameful appetite, exaggerated pride, blind cupidity
> Reigned twice times five years. A crossbowman,
> By his skill, his arm, his bolt and his strength, laid it all low.[32]

It is not unreasonable to conclude, therefore, that Roger of Howden was relying for these facts on rumours that had reached him second hand and that he selected the elements that made it possible for him to interpret Richard's death as a judgement of God, punishment for the most notorious of his faults, to which we will return in the second part of this book. The story of the treasure served the same purpose.

The treasure is also mentioned by another, better-informed chronicler, the Cistercian monk Ralph of Coggeshall, in Essex, who based his account on the report of an eyewitness to the siege, probably Milo, Abbot of Le Pin, another Cistercian monastery situated a dozen kilometres from Poitiers. Milo, Richard's almoner, was present during the King's last moments.[33] His account of Richard's death is by far the most reliable and detailed we have. He too saw it as a punishment of God, and he preceded his account with a long reminder of Richard's moral failings, the faults he did nothing to correct, and the greed which had led him to overburden the English with taxes, levies and exactions. For him, Richard had reached 'the pinnacle of his evil' at the end of his life, amassing wealth to conciliate vassals in what he referred to as 'Gaul'. He goes on to describe his death:

> During Lent in the year 1199, the two kings [of France and England], after holding a peace conference, at length arranged a truce for an agreed period of time. Then, during Lent, King Richard took advantage of this opportunity to lead an army of his own against the Viscount of Limoges, who had rebelled against his lord and made a treaty of friendship with Philip while the two kings were at war. Some say that a treasure of incalculable value was found on the Viscount's lands; that the king summoned him and ordered him to hand over the treasure; and that when the Viscount refused the king's anger was even fiercer.[34]
>
> Then he laid waste the Viscount's lands with fire and the sword, as though incapable of refraining from warfare even in this holy season [Lent], until at last he came to Châlus-Chabrol, besieged a keep and attacked it furiously for three days, ordering his sappers to undermine the keep to cause it to collapse, which eventually it did. In this tower were neither knights nor warriors fit to defend it, only a few of the viscount's servants who waited in vain for their lord to come to their aid. They did not think it was the king in person who was besieging them, but perhaps someone from his household. Then the king himself attacked them, with crossbowmen, while the others were mining the walls, and hardly anyone dared to show themselves on the ramparts of the keep, or defend it in any way. Only, from time to time, they threw down from the top of the walls huge stones which, landing with a crash, terrified the besiegers, though without killing the miners or preventing them from continuing their work, because they were protected on all sides by their engines.

On the evening of the third day, that is the day after the Annunciation, the king, having dined, approached the keep with his men, with total confidence, not wearing armour, except for his iron headpiece; and he attacked the defenders, as was his custom, shooting arrows at them. However, there was an armed man who, all day until dinner, had remained on the battlements of this tower, receiving, without being wounded, all the darts, from which he protected himself by turning them aside with a frying pan. This man, who had carefully observed the assailants, suddenly reappeared. He bent his crossbow and fiercely loosed his arrow in the direction of the king, who was watching him and applauded him. He hit the king in the left shoulder, near the neck vertebrae, in such a way that the bolt was deflected in a backwards direction and embedded itself in his left side just as the king was ducking, but not enough, to gain the protection of the rectangular shield that was carried in front of him.

After receiving this wound, the king, always admirably brave, uttered no sigh, let no groan be heard, and allowed nothing to show in his face or manner that might, at the time, have saddened or frightened those around him, or, conversely, have provided his enemies, by this wound, with encouragement to behave with greater boldness. Then, as he felt no pain (to the point that most of his men remained unaware of the calamity that had struck him), he returned to his lodgings, which were close by. There, while pulling the arrow from his body, he broke the wooden shaft; but the point, a hand's breadth long, remained in his body. While the king lay in his chamber, a surgeon from the infamous household of the most impious Mercadier, cutting into the king's body by the light of flaming torches, inflicted serious and even fatal injuries on him. He could not easily find the iron buried on this too obese body; and even when he had found it, he could extract it only with great violence.

Balms and plasters were applied [to the wounds] with care; but the wounds that had been inflicted on him subsequently began to get worse and to turn black, and to swell up from day to day, so much so as to lead to his death, the king behaving incontinently and taking no notice of the advice of his doctors. Entry to the room where he lay was refused to everyone, except for four persons from among the most noble, who freely went in to see him, for fear that news of his illness would quickly become public. However, doubting that he would be cured, the king wrote asking his mother to come, she then being at Fontevraud. He prepared for his death by the salutary sacrament of the body of Our Lord, after confessing to his chaplain, who administered to him that sacrament from which he had abstained for nearly seven years, out of respect, as people say, for so great a mystery, because of the mortal hatred which he bore in his heart for the king of France. He freely pardoned his murderer the death that he had inflicted on him; and so, on 6 April,[35] that is to say, the eleventh day after being wounded, he died at the close of the day, after being anointed with sacred oil. His body, after the entrails had been removed, was carried to the nuns of Fontevraud and buried

there with royal honours, near to his father, by the bishop of Lincoln, on Palm Sunday [11 April 1199].[36]

In spite of the extremely detailed nature of his account, which plainly relies on an eyewitness, Ralph of Coggeshall twice feels the need to emphasise that he is not certain of his facts. This is the case, in particular, with the discovery of the famous treasure, which he is careful not to make the main reason for the siege. 'Some people report' (*Nonnulli . . . referent*), he says, that the Viscount had discovered a treasure, and that the King had summoned the Viscount into his presence and that he had refused to hand it over (or possibly denied the fact). On the other hand, he is emphatic on one key point: Richard had arrived in the region well before this in order to punish the Viscount of Limoges, who was guilty of felony and treason, as a vassal who had abandoned his lord, Richard, Duke of Aquitaine, and given his support to his worst enemy, the King of France, all this in the middle of a war, before 13 January 1199. This was in itself a sufficient reason for Richard to come and lay siege to one of his castles, after devastating and burning his lands and, as the chronicler points out, well before the discovery of the treasure. The treasure was an additional reason, coming on top of an earlier military and political decision, based on feudal law. Ralph goes on to give a very detailed account of all the circumstances surrounding the King's death, the result of a crossbow bolt fired by a warrior from the little garrison, whom Richard pardoned before his death. Either he did not know the name of this archer or he saw no need to spell it out.

We are led to the conclusion that the real motive for the siege of Châlus may simply have been the desire to put down, yet again, a rebellious vassal, not least because, as we have seen, the Viscount of Limoges was one of Richard's most persistent enemies in Aquitaine. Many chroniclers point us in this direction. One of them, Gervase of Canterbury, has already been mentioned; he is mistaken in locating the King's death at Nontron, but correct in seeing Richard's struggle with the Viscount of Limoges, who held the castle of Châlus, as the real reason for the siege and subsequent death of the King. Another writer, Adam of Eynsham, recounts how, when he had accompanied his master and friend, Bishop Hugh of Lincoln, who had left Normandy to protest to Richard about the seizure of his lands by Richard's agents, they had been forced to end their journey at Angers; this was in the spring of 1199. At this date, he says, Richard was engaged in a military campaign against the Count of Angoulême, whom he was determined to bring down once and for all; it was said that he was conducting this expedition

with such great ferocity that the people of the surrounding regions were in a state of terror.[37] For news of this to have reached Angers, and persuaded the bishop of Lincoln to abandon his journey, this military operation must have been more than simply an improvised expedition intended to lay hands on some treasure.

There is a very similar account in the *Histoire de Guillaume le Maréchal*, which, though not written until around 1220, was based on the very detailed memories reported to the author by the knight himself. Richard, he says, had gone to the Limousin to punish the Viscount and seize his castles; he was besieging one of them (which he calls Lautron) when he received, from a 'minister of the devil' whom he does not name, a poisoned crossbow bolt which caused the death of 'the best prince in the world'.[38] He, too, makes no mention of the treasure, but emphasises that Richard was engaged in a true military campaign against his faithless vassals.

Ralph of Diceto is another chronicler who does not mention the treasure. His account, written before 1202, is of great interest despite its brevity:

> Richard, King of England, after reigning for nine years, six months and nineteen days, was hit by an arrow by Peter Basil on 26 March, at the castle of Châlus, in the region of Limoges, in the duchy of Aquitaine. Afterwards, on Tuesday 6 April, this man devoted to the service of Mars ended his days near this same castle. He was buried at Fontevraud, at the feet of his father, Henry II.[39]

There is no reference here to the treasure or, admittedly, to the reasons for Richard's presence in Châlus, but he is very specific about the place, the dates of the injury and subsequent death, and about the name of the man who fired the fatal bolt, Peter Basil. This name is also given by Roger of Wendover and by a note attributable to a chronicler of the greatest importance, Bernard Itier.

Roger of Wendover was writing about 1230, and relied on earlier chronicles. For the death of Richard, he drew principally on Ralph of Diceto, but added details gleaned elsewhere. He tells us, for example, like Roger of Howden, that Richard pardoned his murderer, called Peter Basil. Above all, and unlike his model, he describes Richard's motives for going to Châlus, namely a war against his rebellious Poitevin barons. A few years later Matthew Paris repeats much the same information:

> At this same time, a truce having been concluded, as we have said, between Philip, King of France, and Richard, King of England, the latter turned his

standards and his arms against some barons of Poitou who had rebelled against him. He set fire to their cities and their towns; he laid waste their vines and their orchards, and even massacred without pity some of his adversaries. Then, having entered the duchy of Aquitaine and the Limousin, he laid siege to the castle of Châlus where, on 26 March, he was wounded, by Peter Basil, with a dart which was, it was said, poisoned; at first he had attached no importance to this wound. During the twelve days that he survived, he vigorously pursued the siege of this castle, seized it and kept in close captivity the knights and sergeants who had defended it. Then, having placed his own garrison in the castle, he fortified it.

But the injury which he had received, poorly cared for at the beginning, began to swell; black spots appeared on the wound, spreading everywhere, and causing the king unbearable pain. At last this very valiant prince, sensing the end was near, prepared for death with a true and heartfelt contrition and a sincere spoken confession; he fortified himself with communion in the body and blood of Our Lord, and he pardoned the man responsible for his death, that is, Peter Basil, who had wounded him; having delivered him from his chains, he allowed him to leave freely. He wished that his body be buried at Fontevraud, at the feet of his father, whom he had betrayed; he bequeathed his indomitable heart to the church of Rouen; then, ordering that his entrails should be buried in the church of the castle already mentioned, he bequeathed them, as a gift, to the Poitevins. And he revealed to some of those close to him, under the seal of secrecy, the reason why he had divided his mortal remains in this way. To his father he had bequeathed his body for the reason indicated; to the inhabitants of Rouen, on account of the incomparable loyalty of which they had given proof, he sent his heart as a gift; as for the Poitevins, because of their malevolence, he assigned them . . . the receptacle of his excrements, not judging them worthy of any other part of his body.

After these bequests, the swelling having suddenly spread to the region of his heart, this prince devoted to the service of Mars, breathed his last on a day of Mars [that is, *dies martis*, or Tuesday], 6 April, in the aforementioned castle. He was buried at Fontevraud, as he had ordained in his lifetime; and with him, many believed, were buried at the same time the glory and honour of chivalry.[40]

We will return in Part Two to the question of Richard and chivalry. What is of interest to us here is the emphasis put by both Roger of Wendover and Matthew Paris on what took Richard to Châlus, that is, his determination to punish his rebellious barons. There is, furthermore, independent corroboration of this: several documents refer to the revolt of the Count of Angoulême and Aimar of Limoges and to the campaign Richard launched against them in the spring of 1199.[41] It is quite unnecessary to invoke a ridiculously paltry quest for a hypothetical treasure to explain it.

There is another piece of evidence confirming this. It is of particular importance because it is the work of a contemporary chronicler from Limoges, Bernard Itier, sub-librarian of the abbey of St Martial of Limoges since 1189 (where he became librarian in 1204), and exceptionally well placed to know all the details of the events unfolding at Châlus, only thirty-five kilometres away. His chronicle consists of notes written in his hand in two manuscripts (now bound together as a single document in one manuscript in the French Bibliothèque nationale), constituting a sort of autograph notepad. In both editions of this chronicle, that of H. Duplès-Agier (1874) and the more recent one of J.-L. Lemaître (1998), there are only these few lines for the year 1199: 'In the year of grace 1199, there died King Richard, Hugh of Clermont, abbot of Cluny, Elias, priest in charge at Tarn, Viscount Ademar the Older and Henry, Archbishop of Bourges.'[42] That is all, and it is not much for the death of a king such as Richard. Under the same year, however, Bernard adds important details: 'Many towns were besieged, that is, the Citadel of Limoges, Sainte-Gemme, Nontron, Noailles, Châlus-Chabrol, Hautefort, Saint-Maigrin, Aubusson, Salagnac, Cluis, Brive, Augurande, Sainte-Livrade, Piégut.' This sentence is confirmation that the region was under attack and that many strongholds were under siege, including Châlus. The current binding of the chronicle makes it impossible to establish a formal link between these sieges and Richard's presence at Châlus, though it seems more than probable on the basis of the other sources.

There exists elsewhere, however, a marginal note unknown to the first editor of the chronicle in 1874, which also seems to be in the hand of Bernard Itier. The more recent editor mentions it but does not include it in his edition, as it does not appear in the manuscripts used as the sole basis of his edition. It was discovered in a manuscript of the Chronicle of Geoffrey of Vigeois and published by P. Labbe in 1657, on the basis of a Lastours manuscript.[43] However, thanks to a faulty transcription, the preamble to this note was garbled and omitted by Labbé. It is found in a more complete form in two other manuscripts of the Chronicle of Geoffrey of Vigeois, as has been shown by several scholars, beginning with the abbé Arbellot.[44] The introductory lines seem to establish that the note is all in the hand of Bernard Itier, which is wholly in keeping with his habit of jotting marginal notes in manuscripts. It is found in connection with the passage in which Geoffrey mentions Richard Duke of Aquitaine and Gascony.

In the text edited by Labbe, the note appears without preamble; in one of the other manuscripts, it is preceded by the sentence: 'Haec

scripsit Bernardus Iterii' (Bernard Itier wrote this); the other has a fuller version:

> B. Itier wrote this on the Friday before the feast of St John the Baptist in the year that King Richard, known as the Lionheart, died and was buried with his father in the abbey of Fontevraud, to the joy of many and the sorrow of others.

The text of the note attributed to Bernard appears in all three manuscripts, with very slight variations, and reads as follows:

> In the year of Our Lord 1199 ['one thousand two hundred less one'] Richard, the most warlike King of the English, was struck in the shoulder by an arrow while besieging the keep of a castle in the Limousin, called Châlus-Chabrol. In this tower were two knights, with about thirty-eight others, both men and women. One of the knights was called Peter Bru, the other Peter Basil. It was the latter, it is said, who fired with his crossbow an arrow which struck the king who died on the twelfth day, that is to say, the Tuesday before Palm Sunday, 6 April, in the first hour of the night. Meanwhile, while on his sickbed, he had ordered his forces to besiege a stronghold called Nontron belonging to Viscount Ademar and another town called Montagut [Piégut?], which they did. But, when they heard of the king's death, they withdrew in confusion. The king had conceived the plan to destroy all the Viscount's castles and fortified towns.[45]

This last statement, coming from a man living locally and familiar with the events unfolding in 1199, confirms what is suggested by the sources of so many others: Richard's main purpose in coming to the region was the subjugation of his rebellious vassals by a large-scale military operation, made possible by the truce concluded with the King of France. His troops besieged many towns, castles and strongholds (mentioned by Bernard Itier in his chronicle), including Châlus, belonging to Aimar of Limoges, and Nontron, also held by Aimar from the Bishop of Angoulême. His aim, as has been said, was to destroy their power once and for all, by ravaging their lands, vines and orchards and by destroying their castles. There is no need of a treasure refused (or denied) by Viscount Aimar to explain Richard's hostility towards him.

How, then, are we to explain the frequent references to this treasure? In the case of the French chroniclers, the explanation is easy: it was, as we have said, a good way of blackening Richard's reputation. The English chroniclers also had plenty to reproach him with, on account of his morals but even more so because of the heavy taxes with which, for the first time, he had burdened the clergy; whereas to talk of treasure confirmed their views of Richard's insatiable greed. It was a good way of making the point,

as they had done in his father's case too, that no-one on this earth escapes God's punishment.

Is this to say that it was no more than a malicious fabrication? That would be going too far. The rumour may well have had some basis in fact. Gillingham has tried to explain it as a possible verbal confusion, based on the name 'Châlus-Chabrol'. According to Rigord, the local people called this place *Castrum Lucii de Capreolo*, which became, in the local dialect, Châlus-Chabrol. In the seventeenth century, the discovery of the treasure was linked to a certain Lucius, a legendary proconsul of Aquitaine living at the time of the emperor Augustus, who was immensely wealthy; he was nicknamed Capreolus (the goat) because of his skill in military operations conducted in mountainous country. It is possible, he says, that these legends were already in circulation in Richard's time, in which case the confusion becomes explicable.[46]

But one can argue just as convincingly, it seems to me, that these legends known in the seventeenth century derived from references to the treasure found in Richard's own day, particularly the story of the statues of gold representing members of the imperial Roman court, as told by Rigord. The most trustworthy account of a treasure of Roman origin is certainly his. The question remains open as to whether the rumours he reports were based on real facts, more or less amplified and romanticised, or whether they were purely imaginary. It is impossible to know.

The hypothesis of a treasure discovered at this particular time is by no means improbable; in troubled times it was common for lords or rich individuals to hide their riches to prevent them falling into the hands of their enemies. This was a region, as we have seen, that had long been disrupted by almost continuous local wars. One of these hoards might well have been discovered, therefore, before Richard's arrival in the region, and rumours surrounding it have reached him. This would hardly be surprising. In 1892, for example, as Gillingham has noted, a hoard of almost a thousand silver coins struck in the reign of Richard I was found precisely at Nontron. It could easily have been hidden to keep it from Richard, whose troops were attacking the castle, in 1199, while he lay dying at Châlus.

True or false, the discovery of a treasure of this type played only a subsidiary role; it may, as one of the chroniclers claimed, have increased the belligerent ardour of the King of England and Duke of Aquitaine against two of his vassals perpetually in revolt, and especially against Aimar of Limoges, lord of the castle of Châlus-Chabrol, whose fortresses, like those of the Count of Angoulême, controlled the routes linking Poitou and Bordeaux, two capitals of Richard's Angevin empire.

Richard died, then, not as a treasure hunter but as a prince seeking to enforce feudal order in his lands; he was acting as Duke of Aquitaine more than as King of England, but above all as a warrior and a 'roi-chevalier', which is how he was seen by contemporaries.

NOTES

1. *Guillaume le Maréchal*, lines 11625–6: 'Il ne retornast por sa croiz, Qu'il i cuidast perdre les coiz.'
2. Roger of Howden, IV, pp. 40–1.
3. *Guillaume le Maréchal*, lines 11671–88.
4. Bertran de Born, ed. Gouiran, no. 35, p. 703: 'Be-m platz car trega ni fis' (p. 438 of Paden translation).
5. See Miquel, A., *Ousama, un Prince Syrien face aux Croisés* (Paris, 1986), pp. 135ff.
6. For surgery in war, see Paterson, L., 'Military Surgery: Knights, Sergeants and Raimon of Avignon's Version of the Chirurgia of Roger of Salerno (1180–1209)', in Harper-Bill and Harvey, *Ideals and Practice of Medieval Knighthood*, III, pp. 117–146.
7. Some sources, especially later, claim or suggest that he might have survived if he had obeyed his doctors, in particular if he had refrained from sexual relations: Ralph of Coggeshall, p. 96 (the editor notes that the passage in question is a marginal addition in one manuscript, MS C, but appears in the text of the other, MS V); William the Breton, *Philippidos*, V, 5, lines 600–5; *Ménestrel de Reims*, pp. 69–70; *Chronicle of Walter of Guisborough*, ed. H. G. Rothwell (London, 1957), p. 142.
8. William Marshall, later, conforms to this ideological schema in a ceremony magisterially described by Georges Duby: *William Marshal*, pp. 17ff.
9. This charter, co-signed by Eleanor, Peter of Capua, Maurice of Poitiers, Berengaria and Guy of Thouars, has been edited and translated by A. Perrier, 'De Nouvelles Précisions sur la Mort de Richard Cœur de Lion', *Bulletin de la Société Archéologique et Historique du Limousin*, 87 (1958), p. 50.
10. Gillingham, *Richard the Lionheart*; J. Gillingham, 'The Unromantic Death of Richard I', *Speculum*, 54 (1979), pp. 18–41, reprinted in Gillingham, *Richard Cœur de Lion*, pp. 155–80.
11. Arbellot, F., 'La Vérité sur la Mort de Richard Cœur de Lion', *Bulletin de la Société Archéologique et Historique du Limousin*, 26 (1878); reprinted as 'Mort de Richard Cœur de Lion', in *Récits de l'Histoire du Limousin* (1885).
12. Perrier, 'Mort de Richard Cœur de Lion', pp. 38–50.
13. Gervase of Canterbury, pp. 592–3.
14. William the Breton, *Philippidos*, V, 5, 520ff.
15. Roger of Howden, IV, pp. 82–4.

16. Tudèle, Guillaume de, *Chanson de la Croisade Albigeoise*, ed. and trans. E. Martin-Chabot, vol. 1 (Paris, 1960), p. 40; he must be distinguished from another Bertrand de Gourdon, a *faidit* from Pennautier, who also took part in this crusade, but a little later: see Anonyme, *Chanson de la Croisade Albigeoise*, vol. 3 (Paris, 1961), p. 263.
17. Gillingham, 'Unromantic Death'.
18. Norgate, *England under the Angevin Kings*, vol. 2, pp. 381ff.; Norgate, *Richard the Lion Heart*, pp. 324ff.
19. Cartellieri, *Philipp II*, vol. 3, pp. 207ff.
20. Richard, *Histoire des Comtes de Poitou*, vol. 2, p. 321.
21. Gillingham, *Life and Times of Richard I*, pp. 212ff.
22. Brundage, *Richard Lionheart*, pp. 237ff.
23. Choffel, *Richard Cœur de Lion*, pp. 255ff.
24. Pernoud, *Richard Cœur de Lion*, pp. 249ff.
25. See in particular on this point, Gillingham, J., 'The Art of Kingship: Richard I, 1189–99', *History Today* (April, 1985), repr. in Gillingham, *Richard Cœur de Lion*, pp. 95–103.
26. Rigord, §126, p. 144.
27. William the Breton, *Gesta Philippi Augusti*, p. 204.
28. William the Breton, *Philippidos*, vol. 5, lines 491ff.
29. Roger of Howden, IV, pp. 82–3.
30. Ibid., p. 83. The abbé Arbellot gives a 'poetic' and not wholly accurate French version: 'Mort de Richard Cœur de Lion', p. 3.
31. 'Cerne diem, victis jactis spes bona partibus esto, exemplumque mei': Roger of Howden, IV, p. 83.
32. Ibid., p. 84.
33. For the value of this evidence, see M. Powicke, 'Roger of Wendover and Coggeshall Chronicles', *English Historical Review*, 21 (1906), pp. 286–96; Gillingham, 'Unromantic Death', pp. 163–6.
34. Or 'denied' (*quo a vicecomite negato*). This English translation is taken in part from Gillingham, *Richard Cœur de Lion*, p. 15.
35. In error, it seems, the author says 'the seventh of the ides of April'; all the other chroniclers say 'the eighth', that is, 6 April. Ralph of Coggeshall himself confirms this date when he says that Richard died on the eleventh day after his injury, which he had received on 26 March.
36. Ralph of Coggeshall, pp. 94–6.
37. Adam of Eynsham, *Magna Vita Sancti Hugonis*, ed. D. L. Douie and H. Farmer (Edinburgh, 1962), vol. 2, pp. 130ff.
38. *Guillaume le Maréchal*, lines 11751–68.
39. Ralph of Diceto, II, p. 166.
40. Matthew Paris, *Chronica Majora*, II, pp. 451ff.
41. Gillingham, 'Unromantic Death', pp. 174–8.
42. *Chroniques de Saint-Martial de Limoges*, ed. H. Duplès-Agier (Paris, 1874), p. 66; Bernard Itier, *Chronique*, p. 30.

43. Geoffrey of Vigeois, ed. Labbe, vol. 2, p. 317.
44. Arbellot, 'Mort de Richard Cœur de Lion', pp. 7–8, 61–4; see also Gillingham, 'Unromantic Death', p. 168.
45. The Latin text is in Geoffrey of Vigeois, ed. Labbe vol. 2, p. 342, Gillingham, 'Unromantic Death', pp. 167–8, and Bernard Itier, *Chronique*, p. 161; it is found in the three known forms in Arbellot, 'Mort de Richard Cœur de Lion', pp. 61–3; there is an earlier French translation ibid., p. 8.
46. Gillingham, 'Unromantic Death', p. 178; Gillingham, *Richard Cœur de Lion*, p. 21.

PART II

A King as Mirror of Chivalry

11

Richard's Image and Chivalry

The affair of the treasure of Châlus should certainly be kept in proportion, but the death of the king, beneath the walls of this modest fortress
in the Limousin, remains a romantic and in some ways a paradoxical
event. The Lionheart died as a warrior, but not as a knight; he was killed
by an arrow shot by a crossbowman in a minor incident during a routine
siege, not by a blow from a lance or a sword received during a heroic
charge. But his disregard for the suffering caused by his wound, his lofty
disdain and insouciance in the face of death, his instructions for the
burial of his body, heart and entrails, and the at once condescending and
generous words he addressed to his killer all combine to make his last
hours the stuff of legend, in spite of the banality of the actual cause.

The story of his death gave chroniclers an opportunity to pass judgement, consciously or unconsciously, on Richard as a king and as a man;
in this way they reveal, sometimes in spite of themselves, how they saw
him and what sort of values, positive or negative, he incarnated in their
eyes. We have already noted this in the way that chroniclers favourable
to the Capetian kings, like Rigord and William the Breton, made use of
the affair of the treasure. We need to look more closely at the mental attitudes of those who transmitted these stories and, as they did so, intentionally or not, shed light on Richard together with a judgement
expressed according to their own value systems. We need to ask what it
was in Richard's character that they found fascinating and admirable or
what, on the contrary, alienated, irritated or angered them, provoking
criticism and even condemnation. Their choice of aspects of his character and behaviour to record and the way in which these aspects were
emphasised, exaggerated or even caricatured tell us not so much about
the personality of Richard himself as about they way in which he was
perceived by his contemporaries.

In spite of their differences and their sometimes diametrically opposed
prejudices, these judgements are surprisingly similar in painting a portrait of Richard which reflects the contemporary image of the knight. The
King emerges as the embodiment of chivalry at the period of its growth,

when it was becoming aware of itself, at once triumphant, seductive and annoying.

JUDGEMENTS AND ASSESSMENTS OF RICHARD

The majority of chroniclers pass judgement on Richard, particularly when relating the circumstances of his death, in a way that reflects their own origins. They express the values and interests of the social groups to which they belonged. Most of them were English churchmen, so it is hardly surprising to find that their praise or blame of princes and kings depends on the extent to which their behaviour conformed to the norms of established morality, but also (and perhaps even more) on the degree to which they favoured the interests of the English clergy, that is, their own.

We see this, for example, with William of Newburgh when he compares the successive reigns of Henry II and his son, Richard I, noting similarities and differences, largely of degree, in their dispositions and behaviour. With regard to Henry II, he notes first his conjugal infidelities (something he does not do, it should be noted, in the case of Richard), his immoderate liking for the 'delights of Venus' and the 'shameful' circumstances of his marriage to Eleanor, herself guilty of impropriety when Queen of France. He also criticises the excessive favour Henry showed to the Jews and his role in the murder of Thomas Becket, for which the King repented, but not deeply enough to William's mind. His attitude had thus brought down on himself the punishment of God, in the form of all the misfortunes resulting from the rebellion of his sons.

The picture is not, however, wholly negative. Henry loved justice, says William, and defended the poor and the weak; for example, he abolished the cruel law that made the shipwrecked fair game. He loved peace and always tried to find a peaceful resolution of conflicts, turning to war only as a last resort. Finally, and this was William's parting shot, until he instituted the Saladin tithe, Henry had never overburdened the people with taxes or dared to impose taxes on the clergy. He had been the guarantor of public order, the guardian of the property and liberties of the Church, the defender of orphans, widows and the poor and generous in almsgiving; and he had honoured ecclesiastics; in all this, he had conformed to the model the Church held up before kings and, later, knights, so that it has come to be thought of as the chivalric ideal! His conduct had displeased some, certainly, but compared with his son Richard, he had been a good ruler. On this point, the chronicler is emphatic: observing the evils afflicting the country today, he said, one could only conclude that 'this man hated by nearly everyone during his lifetime had been an exceptional

and beneficent prince'. The difference between the government of the father and the son was now clear for all to see, as in those biblical times which set standards for comparison, when Rehoboam had surpassed his father Solomon in iniquity and oppression.[1]

When Ralph of Coggeshall came to describe Richard's death, he presented it primarily as an act of divine punishment, but also of divine grace, since God, by ending his evil activities, prevented him from adding to his past crimes even greater ones yet. In fact, in his warlike fury, the King threatened those who rebelled and those who were subject alike. Ralph is here alluding to Richard's immoderate appetite for war in general, and more particularly to his contempt for the ecclesiastical precepts of the Truce of God, which prohibited the use of arms during important periods of the religious calendar; it was during Lent, after all, that the King had besieged Châlus. Ralph notes in passing that Richard had died ingloriously in an unremarkable place, not in battle, as would have been more appropriate for such a bellicose monarch.[2]

The majority of the ecclesiastical chroniclers emphasise rather the oppression with which Richard, in their view, had burdened the Church, and the taxes he had levied on the people and, most of all, on the clergy; they fail to point out that he had been in desperate need of money, on the one hand to finance his crusade and on the other to procure his freedom by payment of a huge and shameful ransom, when, as a crusader, he should have enjoyed ecclesiastical protection. Overall, if we put aside for the moment the moral judgements passed on the 'private person' on account of his sexual conduct and, to some extent, his rebellion against his father,[3] it is by the yardstick of his financial policy, made burdensome for these two reasons, that churchmen judge the reign of Richard the Lionheart unfavourably.

Some chroniclers simply liken Richard to his predecessors, condemned for the same misdeeds. Gerald of Wales, in his *De Principis Instructione*, records the prophesy of a hermit called Godric who had died in 1170. In a vision, this holy man had seen Henry II and his four sons prostrate before an altar; but then, to his horror, he had seen them get up, climb onto the altar, scale the crucifix, sit on it and even dare to defile it; then he had seen Henry and his two sons, John and Richard, fall headlong from the altar with a great crash. The hermit offered his own interpretation of his vision: it foretold the fall of the King, and of his two sons when they became kings in their turn, in accord with the judgement of God directed against them because of their oppression of the Church.[4]

Elsewhere, Gerald returns to this theme when describing Richard's death. He compares it to that of William Rufus a century earlier, killed

accidentally by an arrow, directed, as it were, by the hand of God. Richard, too, had encountered the avenging hand of the Lord in the form of a bolt from a crossbow, a weapon he himself had often exploited with cruelty, as the chronicler reminds us. The real reason, however, was not his immoderate use of this weapon, but his despoliation of the Church. Gerald expressed this by reproducing lines composed on the subject:

> Christ, he who made your chalice his prey became the prey at Chalus,
> You laid low with a short bronze bolt him who stripped the silver from the Cross.[5]

This was clearly a vindictive allusion to what was seen as the King's excessively onerous financial policy towards the Church, on the pretext of crusading.

Matthew Paris, too, interprets the King's death harshly and records several epitaphs written for the occasion. Like Ralph of Coggeshall he emphasises above all the King's sins and the way that God, through his death, had spared him from committing even worse. Nor did he forget his depredations at the expense of the Church:

> This epitaph was written on his death and on his funeral: 'The land of Poitou and the soil of Châlus cover the duke's entrails. He wanted his body to be enclosed beneath the marble of Fontevraud. Neustria, it is you who have the invincible heart of the king. This vast ruin is itself divided into three different parts; and this illustrious man, though dead, is not of those that a single place can contain.' Another versifier composed these elegant lines on the occasion of this tragic and irreparable passing: 'King Richard, the linchpin of the kingdom, is buried at Châlus; for some he was terrible, for others he was gentle; for the latter he was a lamb, for the former a leopard. The name Châlus means the "fall of light." This name had not been understood in past centuries; what it presaged was unknown and it was a closed book to the vulgar. But when the light fell, light fell on this secret, as if to compensate for the light that had gone out'. Yet another composed on the subject this satirical distich: 'O Christ, he who made your chalices his prey has become a prey to death at Châlus, You have ejected from this world with a little bronze him who pillaged the bronze from your Crosses'[6]

It is on the basis of criticisms such as these that historians have sometimes accused Richard of financial oppression serious enough to have ruined his empire. This is to exaggerate, as John Gillingham has shown: the English taxpayer had not been 'bled dry' by 1199; Richard's taxations were no more oppressive than those of Philip Augustus during the same period; the King of France probably had access to greater resources than his

English counterpart.[7] In evaluating such criticism we have to allow for the prejudices of the chroniclers, due to their 'class' background, or rather to their 'order'. What they really held against the King was his failure to maintain the privileges of the clergy in their totality. For this reason, they claimed, God had punished Richard as a 'bad king'.

They concur, as we have said, in their emphasis on his warlike behaviour, whether criticising it or, on the contrary, praising it when directed against the enemies of the Church or of Christendom in the Third Crusade. For them, Richard was above all a valiant warrior and an indomitable fighter, with a 'lion's heart'.

THE ORIGINS OF THE NAME 'LIONHEART'

Why Lionheart? For its warlike implications, obviously; the epithet was commonly used for men whose ferocious ardour in battle was their most striking characteristic, like Henry the Lion, Duke of Saxony, Richard's brother-in-law. In heraldry – its origins datable to the second half of the twelfth century – the lion symbolises the indomitable valour and dignity of the king of beasts.[8] The symbol is found in the *Roman de Renart*, written during this period, in which the king, Noble, is a lion. Chrétien de Troyes, a contemporary of Richard, popularised this symbol by associating it with one of the heroes of the Arthurian court in his romance *Yvain, the Knight with the Lion*. The epitaphs recorded by Matthew Paris and quoted previously refer to Richard's 'invincible heart' and recall that he had been gentle as a lamb to his friends, but terrible as a lion (or a leopard) to his enemies. This was intended as praise. It is akin to the judgements passed on good knights by the authors of the *chansons de geste*, in which it is the warlike virtues rather than the Christian meekness of their heroes that are praised.[9]

Further, this animal had been adopted as an emblem by the Plantagenet family. It often appeared on their clothing, as we see from a chronicler's description of the dubbing of Geoffrey, Richard's grandfather, in 1127.[10] The image of a lion had also been evoked in connection with Henry II; a prophesy had foretold that 'the lion's whelps', his children, would be terrible and bloodthirsty and would rise up against and fight their father.[11] Describing the incident on 5 August 1192 when the King of England had come to the rescue of the Earl of Leicester, in grave danger after being unhorsed, Ambroise says that the Turks, as soon as they saw Richard arrive, rushed as one against him and his banner, on which lions appeared: 'Then you would have seen so many Turks rush towards the Lion Banner!'[12]

The sobriquet 'Lionheart' appears, as we have seen, in an obituary that can probably be attributed to Bernard Itier.[13] The King had already acquired the nickname by the time of the Third Crusade according to Ambroise, who describes the feats performed at Acre by 'the valiant king, the lionheart'.[14] He refers quite naturally to the valour of his hero and to his indomitable, even vindictive, character, which was often contrasted with the excessive pusillanimity of his opponents, compared, by contrast, to lambs. This opposition occurs in a number of texts comparing Richard and Philip Augustus. In Sicily, for example, Philip bore patiently, some said allowed or even incited, the offences of the inhabitants of Messina, whereas the King of England, for whom every person was a subject who should obey his laws, would not permit the outrages of these 'Griffons' to go unpunished; so they called Philip 'the Lamb' and Richard 'the Lion'.[15]

Matthew Paris records another episode, which took place in 1192. He describes the king at Jaffa, launching himself into the midst of the Turks, slaughtering them right, left and centre, 'like a lion' putting all other animals to flight.[16] Later on, however, he feels the need to attribute to Richard alone both of the two opposed positive virtues symbolised by the lion and the lamb. First he recalls, rather contradicting himself, how the King, from the day of his coronation, had refused to sell bishoprics and 'melted down his treasures' for the Third Crusade and the liberation of the Holy Land; he goes on to emphasise the patience with which Richard had borne being handed over by the devil to the Duke of Austria, who had sold him to the emperor like a beast of burden, and how he had pardoned the treachery of his brother John, who had so often conspired against him. Thus, although a lion in his ferocity in battle against rebels, he showed himself to have the meekness of a lamb. But, he adds, the lamb in him prevailed over the lion, which was why he could at last emerge from purgatory and receive the crown of life.[17]

Nevertheless, legend found it necessary to elaborate on the name Lionheart, and explain it in more romantic fashion by introducing an element of the marvellous. An English romance of the early fourteenth century drew on this nickname and the legend of the 'eaten heart', already popular a century earlier, to associate Richard's surname with a romantic escapade during his captivity in Germany. The daughter of the king of the Germans, it said, had fallen in love with the royal prisoner, and the couple had enjoyed several nights of passion in his prison cell. When her father learned of this, he decided to get rid of Richard by introducing a starving lion into his cell. But heroically protecting himself against the wild beast's teeth with forty silken kerchiefs belonging to his lady, Richard managed to kill the lion and tear out its heart, which he

then triumphantly consumed before the astonished eyes of the princes of the German court.[18]

The byname Lionheart seemed straightforward enough at the end of the twelfth century: it referred logically to Richard's royal dignity, but perhaps even more to his courage, likened to the indomitable valour of the king of beasts. This is how it was understood by Ralph of Coggeshall when he described Richard putting numerous Saracens to flight, with a handful of knights, all, like him, disdainful of death: brandishing the royal banner, Richard threw himself on the enemy, felling, unseating and slaying them 'like a ferocious lion'.[19]

Bertran de Born uses the same image of the Plantagenet king, contrasting it to that of his French rival. This was in connection with the Franco–English agreement of 22 July 1189, by which King Philip received the Auvergne in exchange for his conquests in Berry, which were returned to the King of England. The troubadour knight deplored this agreement because it marked the end of the war by which he lived, and he tried, in a sirventes, to provoke a resumption of hostilities by comparing the King of France to a lamb and the King of England to a lion.[20] In this same connection, Richard himself, soon after, composed a sirventes, in a dialect mixing French and Provençal, in which he emphasised with a certain irony the qualities and the failings that were attributed to him, and even more those of his enemies; we should note that all concern so-called 'chivalric' virtues. The sirventes is addressed to the Dauphin of Auvergne and his cousin Guy who, at the instigation of the King of England and the Duke of Aquitaine, had rebelled against Philip Augustus after the French king had taken Issoire; but they had not yet received the support they had been promised (through lack of money, pleaded Richard); having learned from experience, they did not come to the aid of the King of England when he resumed his war against Philip.[21] This is how Richard reproached them:

I. Dauphin, I demand an explanation, from you and Count Guy: recently, you behaved like a bloody warrior and you swore and promised me your loyalty, like Isengrin to Renart, that same Isengrin you resemble with your grizzled hair.

II. You have denied me your aid for the sake of cash, because you know the treasury of Chinon is bare. You seek the alliance of a rich king, valiant and true to his word; since I am tight-fisted and craven, you switch to the other camp.

III. Let me ask you also how you enjoyed losing Issoire. Are you taking your revenge by raising an army of mercenaries? I can promise you one thing, at least, despite your broken word: in King Richard you will find a doughty warrior, standard in hand.

IV. I have seen you prodigal and open-handed, but since then, in order to build strong castles, you have abandoned generosity and love affairs and stopped going to court and ceased to frequent tournaments; but there is no need to be afraid because the French are [as lily-livered as] Lombards.

V. Go, sirventes, wing your way to Auvergne: tell the two counts from me that if they now make peace, God will help them.

VI. What does it matter if some base churl breaks his word; a squire knows no law! But let him beware in future lest his affairs take a turn for the worse![22]

Richard describes himself as a knight and praises the values of chivalry, to which I will return, which consisted not only of valour in battle but also of largesse, gallantry and courtesy, a liking for celebration and tournaments, and a respect for one's pledged word, all values which frequently conflicted with the harsh realities that were beginning to influence behaviour: the need for money and the bourgeois 'realism' that was gradually penetrating aristocratic circles, and against which they defended themselves more successfully in ideology and literature than in real life.[23]

A KNIGHTLY PHYSIQUE

While we can at least attempt to sketch a portrait of Richard's character, even the haziest of physical portraits is impossible. A few rare representations of Richard survive, for example the funerary statue at Fontevraud and his seals, but they can hardly be regarded as realistic. They conform to the rules of their genre and make no pretence of accuracy. Nor is there much written evidence for his physical appearance, apart from a few scattered references that are equally suspect: Matthew Paris, for example, describing in conventional language an episode (quite possibly invented) in Richard's life, tells of a knight who did not dare to appear before the King, because 'although physically comparable to the most handsome of men, [he] sometimes presented a terrifying appearance'.[24]

Here and there, however, we can glean a few scraps of information by reference to what we know about his father, Henry II, to whom he was often compared. By combining three probably authentic accounts written by a contemporary, Peter of Blois,[25] the French historian Charles Petit-Dutaillis has painted this picture of Henry II:

He is . . . a reddish headed man of medium height; he has a square, leonine face and goggle eyes which are soft and gentle when he is good humoured but flash lightning when he is annoyed. His horseman's legs, broad chest, and athletic arms reveal him as a man who is strong, active, and daring. He takes no care of his hands and only wears gloves when hawking. His clothes and head-dress are becoming but never extravagant. He fights the obesity which

threatens by sobriety and exercise and, thanks to walking and horsemanship, he preserves his youthful vigour and tires out his strongest companions. From morning to night he is engaged unceasingly on affairs of state. He never sits down except when he mounts his horse or takes a meal and he frequently rides in one day a journey four or five times the length of a normal day's ride. It is very difficult to find out where he is or what he will do during the day for he frequently changes his plans.[26]

We may note in this description several traits which were probably also found in his son, such as the comparison with a lion, the tendency to obesity (though Richard seems not to have fought against it by sobriety), the hyperactivity, the passion for riding and hunting, and the unpredictability, or at least extreme changeability, of his moods and ideas. Petit-Dutaillis adds (not something said by Peter of Blois) that he was 'libidinous', which might equally well be said of his son, as we will see.

Gerald of Wales compares Richard to his brother Henry the Young King. Both, he says, were tall, or at least of 'more than of middle height' (still vague, but suggestive), and both had the presence of men used to command; but he emphasises, like many others, that Henry loved tournaments while his brother preferred war.[27] Richard seems in his youth to have been slimmer than his father, but threatened by obesity even before his departure on crusade, in spite of the endless hours spent on horseback and the intense and frequent bouts of warfare. William of Newburgh describes him even then as

broken and exhausted by the precocious and excessive practice of the profession of war, to which he had been unreasonably devoted since he had been a young boy, so that it seemed likely he must rapidly succumb to the trials of an expedition to the East.

He also noted that the pallor of his face then contrasted with his corpulence.[28] Some chroniclers describing the king's wound at Châlus also refer to his obesity.[29]

In spite of this relative vagueness on the subject of his physical appearance, it is possible to see Richard as a solidly built man, an expert huntsman and warrior, a man of action, finding his greatest enjoyment in battle and confrontation in games and combat. In this he resembled the knights of his day, and they could recognise themselves in him. A poem attributed to the tutor of the young Richard, Geoffrey of Vinsauf, who died in 1210 – though the attribution is disputed – laments the death of the King, 'lord of arms, glory of kings', and inveighs against the man who had dared to kill him, calling him 'unworthy knight, perfidious knight, treacherous knight, knight who shames earth'.[30] This formulation, with its insistent

repetition of the word 'knight' (*miles*), testifies to the notion, widespread at an early date, that, being both king and knight, Richard could only have been killed by a member of the knightly class, but by a member both unworthy and traitorous.

Richard himself identified with chivalry in all its aspects. We remarked on this earlier in his sharp rejoinder in Cyprus to a cleric who advised him to abandon the idea of attacking the Greek troops who were too numerous for his liking: 'Sir clerk, concern yourself with your writing and come out of the fighting; leave chivalry to us, By God and Saint Mary!'[31]

WHAT IS CHIVALRY?

What do we mean by the word 'chivalry'?

In contemporary writings, the *chansons de geste* and romances of the second half of the twelfth century, the French word *chevalerie* had already so influenced its old Latin equivalent *militia* as to have profoundly modified its original meaning. The word *militia* had once meant the army as a whole and the *milites* had simply been soldiers, whether on foot or on horseback.[32] During the eleventh century, the word *miles*, first in the singular (as a personal denomination, with qualitative connotations) and then in the plural (to indicate a whole group, with purely professional connotations), came within the ideology to indicate a professional class and greater worth. Whereas it had once been the norm to contrast, within the *militia* (that is, within the whole group of *milites*, or soldiers), the cavalry (*equites*) and the foot soldiers (*pedites*), towards the end of the eleventh century, and to an even greater extent subsequently, *milites* came to mean warriors on horseback, unless indicated to the contrary, or by a slip of the pen. *Milites* were then opposed to *pedites*. Beginning with the texts contemporary with Richard I, it is possible to translate *milites* systematically as knights (*chevaliers*). This semantic shift was not neutral; it reveals a change in perception. From then on, in the minds of contemporaries, the real fighting men, those 'who counted', were the knights.[33]

This shift of meaning undoubtedly resulted from the influence on Latin of the vernacular languages, which were closer to the military realities of the day than Latin, the language of the Church and the educated. In fact, the vast majority of the terms relating to weapons and to warriors are of Germanic rather than Latin origin. The terms *miles*, *milites* and *militia* thus underwent a shift of meaning made necessary as, in the minds of the writers, the old realities evoked by these Latin terms came to be identified with the newer realities evoked by other words in current usage in the vernacular.

Originally, the terms which came to designate knights in the majority of the 'vulgar' languages, such as Old German (Ritter) and Old English (*cniht*), referred to the humble social origins of the common soldiery and the stable hand; in the Old French of the twelfth century *chevalier* and *chevalerie* put the emphasis firmly on the mount and on the way in which service was performed: this was military service with full equipment. *Chevalier* designated from the beginning the elite warrior on horseback (and not only the horseman)[34] and *chevalerie* was applied to these men as a group – broadly speaking, the heavy cavalry – but also to their actions: *faire chevalerie* was to engage in military action as a knight, and the word then came to refer principally to spectacular feats of arms, glorious and heroic charges; subsequently, the term would evoke any behaviour deemed worthy and true to the ethic of chivalry at the period when, at the end of the twelfth century and perhaps even more in the thirteenth, it acquired institutional value; from then until the end of the Middle Ages, it would impose a cultural model, the chivalric ideal, which prefigured in some of its aspects that of the 'gentleman', which would succeed it.

We should not, however, as is too often done, attach to the words *chevalier* and *chevalerie*, from their initial appearance (in the first half of the twelfth century) the ethical, social and ideological connotations which are undeniably present in these words at the end of that century, in the time of Richard the Lionheart; even less so in the case of the corresponding earlier Latin vocabulary. A statistical study of the Latin words *miles*, *milites* and *militia*, and of their French equivalents, *chevalier* and *chevalerie*, during this period, from the eleventh to the thirteenth century, clearly reveals the gradual fusion of the original diverse connotations of these words.[35] It is in the age of Richard I that this fusion took place. The terms relating to chivalry had not yet wholly lost their old overtones, connected with the purely professional, even subordinate, origin of the military service evoked; yet they had already acquired numerous nobler connotations, on the professional, but also and even more so on the social, ethical and ideological planes. The study of this precise vocabulary in the romances of Chrétien de Troyes, Richard's contemporary, brings out the crucial importance of this period, and particularly that of romances, in the formation of chivalry and the 'chivalric mentality'.[36]

The new image of chivalry, still blurred, had begun to emerge, however, a century earlier, in the second half of the eleventh century. It was linked to the appearance of a new fighting technique that probably originated in the border regions of Normandy, Anjou and Touraine; this innovation helped to widen the split within armies that had already long

differentiated mounted soldiers from foot soldiers. The Bayeux Tapestry probably provides the oldest iconographical evidence of this, but its development can be traced during the twelfth century in many other pictorial sources: manuscript illuminations, frescoes and paintings, historiated capitals and various sculptural motifs, in wood, stone or bronze, from bas-reliefs to sculpture in the round, even chessmen, add images to the descriptions found in Latin chronicles, *chansons de geste* and romances of the same period.[37]

This technique probably spread through the intermediary of the Normans, who employed it in their many, diverse and strikingly successful military campaigns in late eleventh-century Europe, and even more during the crusades, where warriors from all over Europe fought alongside each other and which therefore constituted a formidable cultural melting pot and an incomparable means of spreading customs and techniques, especially in the sphere of war. The technique in question is the compact charge with lance 'couched' in a rigid horizontal position. Universally adopted in Western Europe in the first third of the twelfth century, it became the only fighting method of the elite mounted warriors, the knights, and it characterised chivalry, which became, in parallel, more aristocratic, turning itself into an elitist guild and then a closed caste. It developed its special methods of training (the quintain, the tournament and later the joust), an ethic, a professional code and an ideal which was celebrated by poets and by the authors of the epics and chivalric romances which became fashionable in this period and went on to enjoy unflagging success, in various forms, until the end of the Middle Ages. The new method of fighting is frequently described in all the literary works of the period, proof, if such be needed, of the almost exultant interest it aroused in the contemporary public.

This new technique was made possible by a number of earlier developments: the adoption of the stirrup, probably Chinese in origin, which reached Eastern Europe in the seventh or eighth century, before spreading to the West; the rearing of new breeds of horse, both stronger and faster, able to bear the weight of armed warriors for longer periods; and improvements in horse harness, encouraging the development and spread of deeper saddles with pommels front and rear, giving the warrior a better seat and incomparably greater stability than in the past.[38] The various phases in the development of horse harness and weaponry of knights can be traced in the iconography.[39] A century before Richard, they made possible the gradual diffusion of this new method of knightly combat. It would be going too far to claim that the origins of chivalry can be ascribed to this new method of fighting alone. It can at least be claimed, however, with

some confidence, that it was specific to chivalry and helped give it many of its most characteristic features.

Until the late eleventh century there was little difference between the fighting methods of mounted soldiers and foot soldiers. Both used swords in the same way and continued to do so. The spear, too, was used in a similar fashion by men on foot and on horseback: it was either thrown (like a javelin), a technique widely used at the Battle of Hastings by both Saxons and Normans, or used to stab (like a pike). In the latter case three types of blow might be struck, all of them shown on the Bayeux Tapestry. For the first, a downwards thrust, the lance-pike had to be held firmly, near the middle, or, rather, a third of the way down, the arm raised bent above the head, as when preparing to throw a javelin. But in this case the weapon was not thrown; its point was embedded in the body of the adversary by a diagonal downwards movement of the arm. For the second, the lance was again held a third of the way along (to ensure a proper balance), with the arm and forearm forming a right angle and the elbow at waist level, and used to strike a direct forwards blow by a sudden straightening of the arm; the third, which was particularly difficult when on horseback, was to strike a blow both forwards and downwards, as if slashing with a knife.

In all three cases the technique was the same on horseback and on foot. Mounted combat was simply a transposition of fighting on foot. There was little or no advantage in being mounted, apart from the lesser fatigue of the march to the battlefield. It could even be a disadvantage. The effectiveness of the lance depended on the strength of the warrior's arm and the speed of delivery of the blow. The horse played only a minor role, bringing the rider closer to his enemy to enable him to deliver the desired blow. In the case of a head-on collision the speed of the animal could even become a handicap because it was difficult to aim with any precision or deliver thrusts with the lance without checking the animal's speed at the last moment. Further, if the warhorse was moving at full gallop at the moment of impact, the rider's arm was at considerable risk of suffering serious damage in the form of torn ligaments or a dislocated shoulder.

The new method of fighting, on the other hand, was specific to the knights and could be employed only on horseback; it avoided the problems of the old method while hugely increasing the power and possibly the accuracy of the blow. As the Syrian prince Ousama observed about 1119, it involved placing the shield in front of the body at the start of the charge, lowering the lance, held in a horizontal position throughout the assault, wedged firmly under the armpit and held fast against the body by the forearm; the hand served only to aim the point of the lance at the

enemy to be killed, and then to spur on the horse and launch it at full gallop until the moment of impact.[40] Strength of arm was now needed only to keep the lance steady, in a horizontal position, held slightly diagonally, from right to left (for the right handed), above the horse's head or a little left of it. The power and efficacy of the blow were wholly dependent on the precision of the rider's hand and the speed of the warhorse. Lance, rider and horse formed a single unit launched at top speed against the enemy, and have been compared to a 'human projectile' of unprecedented power.

This new method clearly gave those who adopted it a considerable advantage, especially when it was employed for a coordinated charge by a large number of knights accustomed to fighting together, massed tightly together, in *conrois*. The penetrative power of such a group launched at the gallop was certainly formidable and it had made a deep impression on the Greeks by the end of the eleventh century. The power of the lance thrust is brought out in the many descriptions of these charges with which jongleurs and poets liked to enliven their works, many of which were certainly known to and appreciated by Richard the Lionheart. They tell of furious assaults, of wooden shields smashed to smithereens by the impact of the lance, and of the rings bursting out of hauberks holed by the point which often penetrated the chain mail, sometimes piercing the enemy right through, lifting him out of the saddle and throwing him to the ground.

This very special new technique of mounted combat required a specific intensive training which was now completely unlike that for fighting on foot. You could no longer suddenly become a 'knight' simply by knowing how to get on your horse and fight. You needed time to get a training in tournaments, those true stylised wars which proliferated during this very period and which soon became immensely popular with the aristocratic public that participated in or watched them.

THE KNIGHTS JOIN THE ARISTOCRACY

The adoption of this method of fighting led, in a variety of ways, to a strengthening of the aristocratic features of knighthood, which had previously been quite separate from the nobility, but which was now increasingly reserved by the nobles for their own sons. This trend began to gather pace at the time of Richard I.

There were purely economic reasons for this development. Fighting on horseback, as we have seen, now required an assiduous training that needed the free time available only to the idle rich or to the 'professionals

of war'. Equally necessary were increasingly ample financial means, because it required well-fed and highly trained horses, accustomed to the clamour of battle and capable of performing the manoeuvres demanded by this new form of combat. The price of a warhorse of this type, called a destrier, varied, inevitably, according to region and period, but was always high, double or triple that of a palfrey (a parade horse), and four times that of a rouncey (a work horse). The warhorse had to be strong enough to bear the weight of the knight's armour, which was in itself becoming heavier.[41]

At the beginning of the twelfth century, armour consisted of a conical helmet with projecting nasal, the *helme* of the *chansons de geste*, worn on top of the mail coif; facial plates were added at the time of Richard I, and the closed helm was beginning to appear. It was worn, for example, by William Marshal: when his helmet was dented during a tournament, he was unable to take it off and a smith had to be summoned to release his head from its 'prison'.[42] From the tenth or eleventh centuries, the body was protected by an iron coat of mail, the hauberk, a pliable garment worn over a tunic that prevented the links from irritating or tearing the skin. In the twelfth century, the hauberk extended to the knees and was slit front and back to form two panels that were worn over the thighs when on horseback. The penetrative power of the blow of a lance delivered at charge led inevitably to the strengthening of the hauberk. Double hauberks appeared, as attested by Ousama, and even triple hauberks (*treslis*), at least according to the *chansons de geste* and a handful of other texts.[43] A simple hauberk of the twelfth century weighed between twelve and fifteen kilograms. Two hauberks worn one on top of the other, several instances of which are documented, entailed a considerable increase in weight; so did the appearance and development, at the end of the twelfth and in the thirteenth centuries, of rigid metal plates reinforcing the hauberk at the weakest points, the breast, shoulders and joints. Here, too, the new fighting technique led to an increase in the weight of the protective armour (though this should not be exaggerated) and to a considerable increase in its cost. At the time of Richard I, a hauberk cost roughly as much as fifteen oxen and required more than a hundred hours' work on the part of a smith. The shield protecting the knight was of wood covered with leather, sometimes reinforced with metal strips, and painted with the arms of the knight's lord; like the other weapons, it was carried in time of peace by a squire, so called because he was his *scutifer* (shield-bearer) or *armiger* (arms-bearer).

The offensive weaponry was less heavy but no less costly, particularly the sword, the 'chivalric' weapon par excellence, even though it was less specific to knights than the lance. The sword was about a metre in length

and weighed between one and two kilograms, and it, too, needed more than a hundred hours' work on the part of a specialised smith. It was used to cut rather than to thrust, and it was sharp enough to sever with a single blow the neck of a camel, or even the trunk of a man, if, that is, the knight's arm was sufficiently strong. This feat was attributed to several epic or historical heroes including Roland, Godfrey de Bouillon and Richard the Lionheart. Such swords could be extremely expensive. A lance was also required and, thanks to the new method of fighting, it grew both longer and heavier. Overall, the cost of the full equipment of a knight in the age of Richard I may be estimated at about that of fifty oxen. Equipment like this was obviously not within the means of all, not even of all 'nobles'. As a result, by the end of the twelfth century, we see a very marked reduction in the number of dubbings marking entry to knighthood, a tendency even clearer in the next century. In any case, knighting ceremonies were in themselves becoming increasingly lavish, honorific and costly, further strengthening the aristocratic character of chivalry.

Nevertheless, at the time of Richard and Philip Augustus, not all knights were necessarily of noble birth, as they would be half a century later, in the absence of a royal dispensation. Because of the cost of the equipment, and the onerous, lavish and declaratory ceremony of dubbing, however, all the knights were recruited by princes, selected by the nobility, commanded by aristocrats and employed in the service of lords. For the nobility, dubbing increasingly became a filter which allowed only some to pass through to enter the increasingly elitist and restricted body of knights.[44] This body, in the eleventh century a sort of 'noble guild of elite mounted warriors', tended, in the age of Richard and even more after him, to become the 'confraternity of noble knights of the social elite'. In the generation preceding that of Richard, all lay nobles were knights, but not all knights were nobles, far from it. In the generation after Richard, the trend was reversed. The nobility closed off access to knighthood, which was in future defined uniquely by birth. You could be a noble without necessarily being a knight. Many sons of the aristocracy no longer opted to be dubbed. They were known as *damoiseaux*. Knighthood became aristocratic, thinned its own ranks and first merged with the nobility then split off from it once again to form its elite and its cutting edge.

The age of Richard was therefore in this respect a true 'period of transition', inasmuch as this expression, much loved by historians, has any real meaning. It was a period in which knights admired and imitated the customs of the seigneurial and princely courts, adopted the aristocratic ideology and tended to merge with the nobility. It was also, conversely, an age when princes were no longer reluctant to call themselves knights

or to emphasise the old, purely warrior virtues of knighthood and the companionship of war. The word *miles*, or knight, no longer primarily evoked a lowly social level, distrusted by the nobility.[45] The function had become honourable and the nobility claimed it for its own.

THE 'POOR' KNIGHTS

The literature of the age repeatedly mentions the existence of 'poor knights'. Clearly, we should not see these men as poverty-stricken. For the most part, they were warriors from the lesser nobility, sometimes significantly less well off than household knights, the armed servants of princes, who formed their escort and their permanent guard. These 'poor knights' obviously pleaded their cause and emphasised the duty incumbent on kings and princes 'to maintain chivalry'; by this they meant their duty to recruit and support these same impoverished knights, who were forced to frequent tournaments to make a living, and were avid for booty and raiding, their only means of assuring their survival, as is clear from most literary works of the age of Richard I and Philip Augustus.[46] William Marshal refers to them in connection with Henry the Young King: from a love of splendid feats of arms and from solidarity with the knights, he 'retained' them, hiring them and providing them with the means to pursue their careers; in this way he saved them from the vagrant life of a 'knight errant', more likely to lead to misfortune and death than glory, whatever the romances said. In so doing, Henry 'saved chivalry', which, says William, adopting the cliché of a past Golden Age, had been on the point of dying out:

> Then I tell you that the young king,
> Who was good and handsome and courtly
> Acted so nobly afterwards in his life
> That he revived chivalry
> Which was then nearly dead.[47]

In fact, he adds, Henry set about recruiting and assembling *bachelers*, young warriors,[48] imitated in this by the other princes, his brothers, who, in their turn, surrounded themselves with knights who were paid, honoured and socially and ideologically elevated.

THE ARCHETYPE OF THE 'ROI-CHEVALIER'

Richard the Lionheart, perhaps even more than his brother Henry, surrounded himself with knights, at least in wartime, and, like his Angevin

ancestors, demonstrated his solidarity with them as companions in arms.
More than any other king, he identified with chivalry, making the values of
warriors and knights his cardinal virtues. His conduct was so imbued with
them that one may suspect that he felt more knight than king, or to be more
precise, that he wanted to incarnate chivalric ideology, and put into action
the dream that there could be no good prince who was not a knight, nor
good king except surrounded by knights; in fact to make chivalry a principle of government. Richard, in other words, from taste or policy, identified
himself with chivalry and fully adopted and exalted its values, perhaps in
imitation of the heroes of the romances of his day. In so doing, he created
a new model of kingship, the archetype of the 'roi-chevalier'.

This identification is clearly visible in many of the stories surrounding
Richard's death. I will quote just one, a fairly late one, written more than
fifty years after the events described, by the Minstrel of Reims, inventor
of the story of Blondel finding the King of England during his captivity
in Germany thanks to his talents as a troubadour. The way in which the
author presents King Richard as he succeeds his father on the throne of
England, at the beginning of the account of his life, is significant in this
regard: the King is presented as above all a knight, incarnating knightly
virtues, for which he is praised by all:

> [I] will tell you of King Richard his son, who came into this land. And he was
> a valiant man, and bold and courtly and bountiful, and a fine knight; and he
> came to tourney on the marches of France and of Poitou; and he so stayed so
> long taking part in them that everyone spoke well of him.[49]

This is a king identified with chivalry. It comes as no surprise, therefore,
to find the author emphasising, at the moment of Richard's death, the
irreparable loss it represented for chivalry. The King himself, sensing the
approach of death, was concerned for its future; with him gone, it could
not but decline and sink into ruin. Its golden age was over:

> Alas! King Richard, will you then die? O Death, how bold you are, who have
> dared to attack King Richard, the most perfect knight and the most courtly
> and most generous in the world. Oh, Chivalry, how will you fade away! Alas,
> poor ladies, poor knights, what will become of you? Who will now uphold
> chivalry, generosity and courtesy?[50]

Is this attitude a consequence of the relatively late date of this work? Is
it the result of the reinterpretation of facts through the distorting prism
of time, at a period when chivalry, invested with all the virtues by its identification with a nobility anxious to sing its own praises, may, in a sense,
have appropriated the image of King Richard for its own benefit? It is
possible, but hardly an adequate explanation. Many of these same fea-

tures are found in a poem composed very soon after Richard's death, while still feeling the shock of the event, by an Occitanian troubadour, Gaucelm Faidit:

I. It is very cruel that it should fall to me to tell and recapitulate in song the greatest unhappiness and the greatest grief that I, alas, have ever experienced, and that I must now, weeping, lament . . . For he who was the head and father of Valour, the mighty and valiant Richard, King of the English, is dead. Alas! O God! What a loss and what a blow! What a cruel word, and what a hard word to hear! Hard is the heart of him who can bear it . . .

II. The King is dead, and a thousand years have passed since there lived or was seen such a valiant man, and never again will there be a man like him, so generous, so powerful, so bold, so prodigal, and I believe that Alexander, the king who vanquished Darius, did not give or spend as much as he; and never Charlemagne or Arthur had more valour; because, in truth, he knew how to make himself feared by some and loved by others.

III. I would be amazed, seeing the world full of trickery and trumpery, if there remained in it one wise and courteous man, since fine words and glorious exploits count for nothing, and why should one bother, more or less, since now Death has shown us what it is capable of, by all at once taking the best in the world, all honour, all joys, all good things; and since we see that nothing can save them from death, much less should we fear dying!

IV. Alas, valiant lord king, what will happen now to arms and to the rough and tumble of tournaments, to rich courts and fine gifts, since you will no longer be there, you who were the master and head? And what will they do, those doomed to fare ill, who had put themselves in your service and waited for their reward? And what will those do, who now ought to kill themselves, who you introduced to wealth and to power?

V. A long sadness, a wretched life and perpetual mourning, that will be their lot. And Saracens, Turks, pagans and Persians, who feared you more than any other man born of mother, will arrogantly see their forces so increase, that the Holy Sepulchre will not be conquered for a long time yet. But this is God's will . . . For if he had not allowed it, and if you, sire, had lived, without any doubt, you would have made them flee Syria.

VI. Henceforth there is no hope that the kings and princes who might recover it will ever go there! However, all those who will be in your place ought to ponder how you loved Valour and Reputation, and what were your two brave brothers, the Young King and the courteous Count Geoffrey . . . And he who will be in your place ought to derive from the three of you great courage, the firm intention to accomplish valiant exploits, and a liking for feats of arms.

VII. O, Lord God! You who truly pardon, true God, true Man, true Life, mercy! Pardon him, he is in great need of it; and do not consider his sin, but bear in mind how he went to serve You![51]

After giving vent to his emotion, the writer emphasises Richard's 'chival-ric' virtues: his prowess, comparable to that of the ancient heroes of history and legend, which were then confused: Alexander the Great, Charlemagne and Arthur. He stresses Richard's largesse, his generosity and courtesy, too. In future, with him dead, what will happen to his knights, who had put their trust in and served him? What will become of chivalry, tournaments and arms? What will become of Christendom, of which he had made himself the champion? Who will now honour those who deserve glory and praise, as Richard and his brothers, Henry and Geoffrey, had done? One senses behind this last evocation a discreet appeal, though with no illusions, to Richard's as yet unknown successor. Lastly, the poet ends his lament with an appeal to God to pardon the sinful king: of this, it is conceded, he had great need! Let the King of Heaven not dwell on his sins, which could not be denied (a point to which we will return), but on the value of his service in His cause. The writer is thinking here, of course, of Richard's commitment to the crusade.

It is all there. Richard combined in his person the worldly virtues of chivalry, lauded by the literature of the twelfth century, and those which the Church had long inculcated in kings and princes, and which, for just over a century, it had tried to instil into the knights as a class, in parti-cular through the liturgical formulae of the ceremony of dubbing, marking the solemn entry into knighthood.

In mourning the death of the King of England, therefore, the poet is also lamenting the premature death of a 'roi-chevalier', the champion of Christendom but also and above all the incarnation of chivalric values. It remains for us to ask if Richard, in his actual behaviour, really was this model of chivalry, and if so, in what ways or, on the contrary, in what ways he deviated from it. We must also look at what impelled Richard to behave as a knight and to wish to project the image of being one, and even more closely, perhaps, at the motives which led the chroniclers to reflect, magnify and embellish that image.

NOTES

1. William of Newburgh, pp. 280ff.; see also, for Henry II, Ralph of Coggeshall, p. 25.
2. Ralph of Coggeshall, pp. 93–4.
3. See on this aspect, Ralph of Diceto, pp. 106ff.; Ralph of Coggeshall, pp. 56–7; Matthew Paris, *Chronica Majora*, II, pp. 395–6.
4. Gerald of Wales, *De Principis Instructione*, pp. 313–14.
5. Ibid., III, p. 30.

6. Matthew Paris, *Chronica Majora*, II, pp. 452–3. I am using here the French translation in A. Huillard-Breholles, vol. 2, pp. 301ff.; that of Arbellot ('Mort de Richard Cœur de Lion', pp. 49ff.) differs slightly. Matthew Paris records other epitaphs and commentaries on the King's death.

7. Baldwin, J., 'La Décennie Décisive: les Années 1190–1203 dans la Règne de Philippe Auguste', *Revue Historique*, 266 (1981), pp. 311–37; Gillingham, *Richard Cœur de Lion*, pp. 279–81. See also Baldwin, *Philip Augustus*, pp. 34ff., 49ff.; Nortier, M. and J. Baldwin, 'Contribution à l'Etude des Finances de Philippe Auguste', *Bibliothèque de l'Ecole des Chartes*, 138 (1980), pp. 5–33; Holt, J. C., 'The Loss of Normandy and Royal Finance', in Gillingham and Holt, *War and Government*, pp. 65–85.

8. M. Pastoureau, *Traité d'Héraldique* (Paris, 1933).

9. Jones, 'Grim to Your Foes'.

10. Jean de Marmoutier, *Historia Gaufredi Ducis*, in *Chroniques des Comtes d'Anjou*, p. 180.

11. *Gesta Henrici*, I, p. 42.

12. 'Le veissiez tanz Turs acorre/Droit à la baniere al lion': Ambroise, lines 11526–7 (p. 184 of Ailes translation); *Itinerarium*, VI, 22.

13. 'Scripsit B. Iterii feria sexta vigilia S[ancti] Johannis Baptistae quod ipso anno obiit Ricardus congnominatus Cor Leonis': Arbellot, 'Mort de Richard Cœur de Lion', p. 61.

14. 'Le preuz reis, le quor de lion': Ambroise, line 2310.

15. 'Unde et unus dictus est agnus a Grifonibus, alter leonis nomen accepit': Richard of Devizes, p. 17.

16. Matthew Paris, *Chronica Majora*, II, pp. 387–9.

17. 'Et sicut rebellibus leo fuit imperterritus, sic modestis agnus fuit mansuetus, leo superandis, agnus superatis': ibid., III, pp. 216–17.

18. *Der mittelenglische Versroman über Richard Löwenherz*, ed. K. Brunner (Vienna, 1913), lines 880–1100. See also Prestwich, J. O., 'Richard Cœur de Lion: Rex Bellicosus', in Nelson, *Richard Cœur de Lion*, pp. 1ff.; Gillingham, 'Legends of Richard the Lionheart', ibid., pp. 51–69. Gillingham emphasises that this legend must still have been popular in the sixteenth century as Shakespeare drew on it in King John (Act 1, Scene 1).

19. Ralph of Coggeshall, p. 45: 'hostes in plateis glomeratos, velut leo ferocissimus, invadendo prosternit, prostratos interfecti'.

20. Bertran de Born, ed. Gouiran, pp. 615ff.

21. Norgate, *Richard the Lion Heart*, p. 321.

22. Modern French translation in Lepage, Y., 'Richard Cœur de Lion et la Poésie Lyrique', in *Et c'est la Fin pour Quoy Sommes Ensemble*, vol. 2, pp. 893–910.

23. See on this point Flori, 'L'Idéologie Aristocratique'; and, more recently, Flori, 'Noblesse, Chevalerie et Idéologie Aristocratique'.

24. Matthew Paris, *Chronica Majora*, III, p. 213: 'quia, cum esset visu quasi speciosissimus hominum, quandoque tamen terribilis videbatur'.

25. The three descriptions are in Letters 66, 14 and 41 of Peter of Blois, *Opera Omnia*, ed. J. A. Giles (Oxford, 1846–7), 4 vols., 1, pp. 293, 50ff. and 125; also the dialogue with the abbot of Bonneval, ibid., 3, pp. 289ff. For the latter, the new edition by R. B. C. Huygens is preferable.

26. Petit-Dutaillis, *Feudal Monarchy*, p. 109.

27. Gerald of Wales, *De Principis Instructione*, III, 8; *Expugnatio Hibernica*, pp. 198–9.

28. William of Newburgh, p. 306.

29. Ralph of Coggeshall, pp. 93ff.

30. Geoffrey of Vinsauf, *Nova Poetria*: text in Arbellot, 'Mort de Richard Cœur de Lion', p. 251. For the poems attributed to Geoffrey of Vinsauf, see Faral, E., *Les Arts Poétiques du XIIe et XIII Siècle* (Paris, 1924), pp. 197–262, 18–27.

31. Ambroise, lines 1607ff. (p. 53 of Ailes translation); *Itinerarium*, II, p. 33.

32. Though with, it is true, a slight implication of public service; see Flori, *Chevaliers et Chevalerie*, pp. 64ff.

33. For the meaning of the Latin words relating to chivalry and the evolution of their connotations, see Van Winter, '*Cingulum militiae*'; Flori, J., 'Les Origines de l'Adoubement Chevaleresque: Etude des Remises d'Armes dans les Chroniques et Annales Latines du IXe au XIIIe Siècle', *Traditio*, 35 (1979), 1, pp. 209–72; Flori, '*Principes* et *Milites*'; Flori, J., 'Lexicologie et Société: les Dénominations des *Milites* Normands d'Italie chez Geoffrey Malaterra', in H. Débax (ed.), *Les Sociétés Méridionales à l'Age Féodal (Espagne, Italie et Sud de la France) (Hommage à Pierre Bonnassie)* (Toulouse, 1999), pp. 271–8.

34. This is the exact opposite, it seems to me, of the evolution described by G. Gougenheim, 'De "Chevalier" à "Cavalier" ', in *Mélanges E. Hoepffner*, pp. 117–26.

35. For the study of the terms in Old French relating to chivalry and the evolution of their connotations, see Flori, 'Chevalerie dans les Chansons de Geste'; Flori, 'Sémantique et Société Médiévale'; Flori, J., 'Les Ecuyers dans la Littérature Française du XIIe Siècle; Pour une Lexicologie de la Société Médiévale', in *Et c'est la Fin pour Quoy Sommes Ensemble*, vol. 2, pp. 579–91.

36. See, in particular, Burgess, 'The Term "Chevalerie" '; Flori, 'Chevalerie dans les Romans de Chrétien de Troyes'.

37. See on this point, Flori, 'Encore l'Usage de la Lance'.

38. For all these points see Flori, *Chevaliers et Chevalerie*, pp. 89ff., 109ff.; Flori, *La Chevalerie en France*.

39. See the illustrations collected and discussed in Flori, J., *Brève Histoire de la Chevalerie* (Gavaudun, 1998). See also, with a few necessary corrections, the voluminous iconographical dossier collected in the nineteenth century by E. Viollet-le-Duc, *Dictionnaire Raisonné du Mobilier Français de l'Epoque Carolingienne à la Renaissance* (Paris, 1874), and the new

edition: Viollet-le-Duc, E., *Encyclopédie Médiévale*, 2: *Architecture et Mobilier* (Tours, 1996).

40. Ousama Ibn Munqidh, *Enseignements de la Vie*; see also Miquel, A., *Ousama, un Prince Syrien face aux Croisés* (Paris, 1986), p. 26.
41. See Gaier, *Armes et Combats*; Gaier, C., 'Armement Chevaleresque'; Gaier, C., 'L'Evolution de l'Armement Individuel en Occident aux XIIe au XIIIe Siècles', in Rey-Delqué, *Les Croisades*, pp. 209–13.
42. *Guillaume le Maréchal*, lines 3104ff.
43. See on this point, with caution, the sceptical opinion of M. D. Legge in 'Osbercs Dublez, the Description of Armour in Twelfth-Century Chansons de Geste', in *Société Rencesvals. Proceedings of the Fifth International Conference* (Oxford, 1970), pp. 132–42. Adalbero of Laon speaks of the triple coat of mail (*lorica triplex*): *Carmen ad Rodbertum Regem*, ed. C. Carozzi (Paris, 1979), p. 10.
44. Here, at least as regards the twelfth century, I agree with A. Barbero, *Aristocrazia*, pp. 70ff.
45. See Van Winter, J. M., 'Uxorem de Militari Ordine sibi Imparem . . .', in *Miscellania . . . J. F. Niermeyer* (Groningen, 1967), pp. 113–24.
46. Flori, 'Noblesse, Chevalerie et Idéologie Aristocratique'.
47. *Guillaume le Maréchal*, lines 2637–42.
48. For the meaning of this word, see Flori, 'Qu'est-ce qu'un *Bacheler*?'.
49. *Ménestrel de Reims*, §27, pp. 13–14.
50. Ibid., §132.
51. Gaucelm Faidit, ed. J. Mouzat, *Les Poèmes de Gaucelm Faidit, Troubadour du XIIe Siècle* (Paris, 1965), no. 50, Planh, Complainte sur la Mort de Richard: 'Fortz chausa, es que tot la major dan', pp. 415ff., French translation pp. 423ff. The poem must have been composed soon after Richard's death, since the author does not yet know who will succeed him.

12

Chivalry Imagined before Richard

⌐~

THE THREE ORDERS

Georges Duby drew on the research of the best historians brilliantly to describe the distant origins and development of the theory of the three orders, in tandem with what he called 'feudalism imagined'.[1] Little more needs to be said on the subject here. We need simply to recall that the binary schema which dominated the thinking of scholars until about the year 1000 had long distinguished two categories (*ordines*) of person, the clergy (*clerici*) and the laity (*laici*). This distinction was based on ritual purity, moral dignity and the obligations these entailed. The clergy, dedicated to the worship of God, were required to detach themselves from earthly things and to aspire to things of the spirit; they had to reject the ties of marriage, the pollution of sex, the taint of bloodshed, the wealth of this world and the search for earthly glory in order to labour by their pure deeds and prayers for the establishment of the kingdom of God. These dictates, which accompanied the development of sacramentalism in the Church, especially from the fifth century on, gave expression to the split within the Church which now separated the clergy from the mass of the faithful. A more 'sanctified' behaviour was expected of the former than of the latter; it was reasonable to ask more of the clergy because their rewards would be greater and their salvation more assured if, having chosen the sovereign and apostolic way, they were able to avoid the stains of this world. The result was the creation of a hierarchy of ritual, moral and religious purity, which, within orders that were now distinct, put monks and nuns above secular priests, and the chaste and widows above the married.

Not long before the year 1000, Abbo of Fleury was still separating humanity into two orders, the clergy and the laity. But, as he described the harmonious society which would prevail if everyone fulfilled their role in the station in which he or she had been placed by God, he introduced into the second order a new distinction, based on *function* and no longer only on *kind*:

Of the first order of men, that is, laymen, it must be said that some are farmers (*agricolae*), others are fighters (*agonistae*); the farmers, in the sweat of their brow, work the fields and in other ways labour in the countryside . . . as for the fighters, who should content themselves with their military pay (*stipendiis militia*), let them not make war within their mother's bosom [that is, within the Church, or Christendom], and turn their efforts rather to extirpating the enemies of the holy Church of God.[2]

This, in outline, is the classification first sketched out by the school of Auxerre a century earlier, more clearly articulated by Gerard of Cambrai and Adalbero of Laon about 1030, and then repeated a century later by most authors discussing the 'estates of the world'.[3] In 1000, nevertheless, the classification was unrealistic. This was not only because of the private wars in which the armed bands of rival lords fought each other, but also, and perhaps even more so, because of the pillaging practised by the warriors of this period (the *milites*, a word which cannot yet be translated as 'knights'). Abbo of Fleury, like Abbo of Saint-Germain a century before him, denounced the intolerable behaviour of the *milites*, who dared to pillage churches and use the proceeds of their plunder to make offerings to God. It was hardly surprising that pagans were victorious over Christians! This was God's just punishment for their sins.[4]

In an attempt to limit these acts of violence against ecclesiastical establishments, churches and monasteries, the Church tried, at the end of the tenth century, to institute the Peace of God. This consisted, in the first place, of obtaining from princes and lords (and so from the warriors under their command) a commitment not to attack, kill, abduct or ransom the *inermes*, the people who did not practise the trade of arms: monks, priests, clerics of all ranks, women, children, pilgrims, peasants and merchants.[5] A little later, at the beginning of the eleventh century, the Church tried to impose temporal limits on the depredations of soldiers by forbidding the use of arms during certain periods of the week or year: on Friday in memory of the Passion of Christ, on Saturday in memory of his time in the tomb during the Sabbath day of rest, on Sunday in memory of his resurrection, and also during the principal liturgical seasons and on the feasts of major saints. It hoped, by these means, to create within the military world of feudal disorder (a disorder that was real enough, though it should not be exaggerated) a few islands of peace and order.

To ensure that these precepts were respected, the Church relied on excommunication and interdict. These were serious threats in a period when the sacraments played such an important role in the 'economy of salvation', and when to die deprived of the viaticum or, even worse, of

a Christian burial, doomed the guilty to eternal punishment. But such measures were not enough. As we are constantly told today, you have to be 'tough on crime, tough on the causes of crime'. There would have to be a change in mental attitudes, which required a more sophisticated, more protracted, many-faceted and persistent campaign. The formation of the chivalric ideal was the result of this slow and patient effort.

THE ORDER OF THE *MILITES*

The first and fundamental plank in this programme was to establish the lawful nature of the military function and recognise its worth, on certain conditions. For this, it was necessary first to distinguish within the lay world, like Abbo of Fleury, between those who fought and those who ploughed, toiled and sweated, backs bent, to cultivate the land. This distinction would be made on the basis of recognised functions that no-one should usurp. Everyone should remain in their station, in the rank ordained by God. The supporters of the Peace of God, who were mostly monks, tried to intervene in the political and military spheres through their public meetings and the solemn oaths which the *milites* were made to swear on the relics of saints. For Adalbero and Gerard of Cambrai, around 1025, it was not the job of monks but of the king, instructed by the bishops, to ensure peace and to constrain the warriors, so that they did not misuse their arms but instead fulfilled their function as protectors:

> In fact there are two rulers: the king and the emperor, and under their command the State remains strong. There are others that no power constrains if they abstain from the crimes that are repressed by the sceptres of kings: they are the warriors, protectors of churches. They defend the great and the small, they protect everyone and themselves at the same time.[6]

Nevertheless, by their tripartite schema, they, too, recognised the existence, within the old order of the laity, of an 'order of warriors' (*ordo militum*) distinct from that of those who tilled the soil:

> The house of God is thus triple, though seemingly one. Here below, some pray, others fight and yet others labour. These three are joined together and are not separated; so the labour of two rests on the function of one, each in its turn brings relief to all. It is simple, this triple liaison.[7]

In Adalbero's time, a programme based on a royal power that imposed peace, order and discipline on the turbulent bands of warriors was unrealistic. This was a time when the lords, sometimes emancipating themselves even from the power of the counts, much closer to home,

were imposing their own social and economic domination on the surrounding peasantry and making their own order (or disorder) prevail
in their castellanies. They relied on their own fortresses and their
own *milites*, when, that is, they were able to keep the latter's own aspirations to autonomy in check; some of these *milites* freed themselves
from this tutelage and became pillagers or brigands on their own
account. It was with extreme difficulty, in the eleventh century, that the
precepts of the Peace of God managed to curb all this criminality, but
they at least had the merit of establishing rules of conduct, if mostly
negative ones: *not* to attack unarmed people, *not* to pillage churches,
not gratuitously to burn mills and houses, *not* to extort but to be
content with one's pay, and so on. These rules constituted the first, rudimentary elements of the future and still distant chivalric ethic. The
second plank in the programme could not be implemented until, in both
France and England, the monarchy had succeeded in reasserting itself
once more, and the 'feudal' lords had been brought to heel. This was
the age of Henry II and Louis VII, and of Philip Augustus and Richard
the Lionheart.

The very fact of the proliferation of assemblies of peace during the
eleventh century and beyond is evidence of their ineffectiveness. The
Council of Clermont, in 1095, well illustrates this: by preaching the crusade, Pope Urban II diverted the violence of pillaging knights away from
Christendom, turning it against the Turks, now masters of Jerusalem.
Clermont was above all a council of peace; like so many others, its
purpose was to find a way of maintaining within the Christian West the
peace disturbed by the *milites* – whom we can now call knights – themselves. It is true that the preaching of the crusade was not just the cynical
expression of a papal desire to purge the West of its most troublesome
elements; those who took the cross were for the most part pious men,
even if the brutal and violent form their piety assumed tends (thank
God!) to shock us today. Piety and repentance can touch even the
hardest of hearts. The claims of Bernard of Clairvaux, with reference to
the creation of the order of the Templars, those permanent crusaders,
cannot therefore be applied without qualification to those who took
the cross:

> For to cap it all, in this multitude rushing to Jerusalem, there were relatively
> few who had not been criminals and ungodly, abductors and blasphemers,
> murderers, liars and adulterers. Their departure was the cause, therefore, of
> a twofold joy, which corresponded to a twofold advantage: their families
> were happy to see them leave; happy also were those who saw them coming
> to their aid.[8]

It remains the case that, in the context of a council of peace, Urban II contrasted two types of fighting: in the first – fatal for the soul – the knights of the West fought against each other within Christendom or, as it were, within the Church, which led to their ruin and their eternal damnation; in the second – beneficial – the same knights committed themselves to the armed reconquest of the Holy Sepulchre, which earned them spiritual rewards as it substituted for all other forms of penance and so led to the remission of confessed sins. This type of war was even able to procure a martyr's crown for those who died in so holy a combat.[9] There can be no doubt that it was the desire of the pope to export war to the land of the infidel and to turn the knights who were the cause of so much trouble within the Christian West into soldiers of Christ, liberating his heritage.

It is by no means certain, of course, that the departure of the crusaders made for greater security in the West. In fact, the opposite seems much more likely; for this to have been the outcome, it would have to have been only the most sinful robber knights who left. But it was in any case probably one of the pope's aims, and perhaps explains his decision to make the crusade a substitute penance.

We come here to a crucial point in the formation of the future chivalric ethic: the definition of the mission, seen by some as essential, to defend Christendom and in particular the Holy Places. Richard the Lionheart, a century later, inherited this already highly developed aspect of the 'external' mission of chivalry. It was indeed by no means negligible, but it was never, despite the Church's best efforts, a fundamental or inherent duty of knighthood.[10] In other words (and Urban II was insistent on this point), the crusaders were called on to abandon the *militia* of this world, which, he said, repeating an old play on words, was only *malitia* (wickedness), to become soldiers of Christ (*milites Christi*). The very formulation of his appeal reveals that chivalry and crusading were very different, even antinomic, in his eyes.

Raoul of Caen provides even clearer proof when he describes his hero, the future crusader Tancred, as torn between two opposing ideals: that of the Gospels, preaching love and peace, teaching that you should not take your revenge or resist the wicked, but rather turn the other cheek and offer your tunic to those who wanted to take your mantle, and instructing the *milites* to be content with their pay, and not to pillage, extort or ransom; and that of chivalry (*militia*), which required, on the contrary, that you avenge yourself, even attack first, that you accumulate booty and take ransoms, and that you seize both tunic and mantle alike. The papal message, he wrote, freed Tancred from his inner conflict by

showing him that he could reconcile the two ideals by fighting, sword in hand, as a member of the *militia Christi*, the crusader army, sanctified by its objective, the liberation of the Sepulchre of Our Lord.[11]

The crusade, as is generally accepted today, was an expression of an attempt on the part of the papacy to put the knights firmly in the service of the Church, in an 'external' enterprise. This had not previously been the case.[12] The popes also tried, in a variety of ways, to make use of the *ordo militum* within Christendom, thereby increasing the status of that order's function.

THE CHURCH AND CHIVALRY UP TO THE TWELFTH CENTURY

To defend itself against pillaging knights, or simply against its enemies, the precepts of the Peace of God, as we have shown, proved inadequate for the Church in the eleventh century. Ecclesiastical establishments therefore resorted to two other methods of ensuring their protection.

The first was to recruit warriors directly to fight under the banner of their patron saint. The great monasteries and bishoprics had their own *milites* from the tenth century on.[13] The Church of St Peter's in Rome, in particular, recruited soldiers of this type under Gregory VII in the second half of the tenth century.[14] The second method was to entrust this defensive function to a lay lord, an 'advocate' (*advocatus*), who, in return for payment, was required to use his own troops to protect the abbey or church in question. The recruitment of these advocates, defenders or *milites* of churches, gave rise, in the eleventh century, to investiture ceremonies that imitated both vassalic enfeoffments and coronation rituals. Since the lands, property and persons to be defended (against other *milites*, it should be noted in passing) belonged to churches, true ecclesiastical lordships, it was natural for these ceremonies of investiture to take place in the church in question, for the officiant to be a cleric and for the high moral nature of the mission to be emphasised, that to protect churches, monks, clergy and other unarmed groups, the peasants, defenceless women, widows and orphans living on these lands.

This mission had for a long time been incumbent on kings, who were reminded in liturgical blessings during their sacring and coronation ceremonies of this duty to protect the churches and the populations of the country entrusted by God to the princes being enthroned. An examination of the fullest of these rituals of investiture as defenders of churches, that of Cambrai (eleventh century), shows that the majority of the formulas of blessing used for this purpose were borrowed from the coronation liturgies of the Western Frankish kings and express, obviously, the

duties of the monarch. The Church simply transferred the previous royal ethic to the advocates it recruited.[15]

This is a point of great importance to my argument. These rituals were the link between the liturgies of royal sacring and those of the dubbing ceremonies of knights, the first evidence of which dates from the end of the twelfth century, that is, from the age of Richard I. The prayers said on these occasions, as knights were solemnly presented with their various arms, were borrowed from the rituals of the blessing of kings, then princes, during their coronation and anointing, by way of the earlier investiture rituals. In this way the Church urged those it saw as invested by God with the function of governing men to rule justly and in the interests of the faith. In re-using these formulas, with their strong ethical content, for blessing knights during dubbing ceremonies, which were increasing in solemnity during the twelfth century, the Church was trying to transfer to the knights *as a whole* what had formerly been the royal function of protecting the country, the Church and the weak.[16]

THE ETHIC AND FUNCTION OF CHIVALRY IN RICHARD'S DAY

The increasingly aristocratic nature of chivalry, in the second half of the twelfth century, and the production by the Church of didactic works promoting identical values and ideals, helped to increase the sense of there being a function, even a mission, reserved for knighthood.[17] The theory of the three orders, which had rather slipped from view since Adalbero, resurfaced in the writings of a few moralists and a number of works appeared, principally in the Plantagenet empire, devoted to the theme of chivalry and its role in society.

The principal and perhaps one of the earliest of these theoreticians was John of Salisbury.[18] In his *Policraticus*, written in 1159, he established the principles which made a man a genuine knight (*miles*). He must be chosen and recruited by the prince on the basis of physical and moral criteria (strength of mind and body, courage, loyalty and so on), and he must have sworn the military oath (*sacramentum militiae*) by which he promised to obey the prince, be loyal to him, fight valiantly under his command and neither desert the ranks nor flee in battle, but stand firm with his companions. These are the fundamental virtues of a soldier in the classical exposition, inspired by Frontinus and Vegetius, of the professional code imposed on all armies. The knights were, John said, the 'mailed fists of the prince', at his service so as to keep order internally and assure the security of the country against external enemies. John of

Salisbury was writing at the time when the conflict between Henry II and Thomas Becket, the English chancellor to whom he dedicated his book, was brewing and, as a good churchman, he emphasised that kings and princes had a duty to rule according to the precepts of the Church, instructed and guided by the bishops. They were simply the repositories of the public power conferred by God, who alone disposed of true authority. This was why, when they ceased to follow the path traced by the King of heaven and deviated from it too openly, these earthly princes, previously legitimate, ceased to be so and became tyrants; it then became lawful to kill them. This highly original doctrine of tyrannicide derived from a statist and clerical (but not lay) conception of the authority of the prince.

Turning to the warriors, John of Salisbury applied the same principle: the *milites* served God by obeying the prince who was himself the image of God (*imago Dei*), as long as he remained faithful to Him.[19] The king enjoyed a power conferred by God by receiving his sword from the hands of ecclesiastical officiants (an obvious allusion to the ceremony of sacring);[20] in the same way, the new *miles*, after receiving the *cingulum militiae*, sign of his new armed function in the service of what might be called the state, proceeded to the church where, on the altar, lay the sword symbolising this function, which would be girded on him.[21] In receiving it, the knight was bound to understand the nature of his duty: to protect the weak and above all the Church against evil doers:

> The function of the ordained knighthood (*militia ordinata*) is to protect the Church, to fight treachery, to venerate the priesthood, to defend the weak (*pauperes*) from injustices, to cause peace to reign in the country and – as their oath instructs – to shed blood on behalf of their brothers and to give up their lives for them if necessary.[22]

Nevertheless, John of Salisbury observes that in his day, too many knights were still attacking and looting churches and disturbing the internal order of Christendom. They had forgotten that it was their duty to serve the Church, even if they had not sworn an oath specifically binding them to do so; in fact they should see in the sword placed on the altar as a prelude to their knighting the sign of obedience they owed to God and the Church, through the obedience explicitly sworn to the prince who had recruited them.

As long as they acted within the framework of this twofold loyalty, each reinforcing the other, the knights were assured of saving their souls. John went even further: if their prince kept the faith (which it was not for them

to judge), the knights served God through him, and by this fact would become 'saints'.[23] This is a clear and very powerful expression of the way in which chivalry was sacralised by the performance of its function in the service of the state, even if it was a state conceived more as a community, a geographical and human rather than a political entity, ruled over by a prince guided by God and instructed by the ecclesiastical authorities. It is clear, nevertheless, that 'lay' chivalry, that of kings and princes, was being given a sacred character.

A few years later, about 1176, Stephen of Fougères, Bishop of Rennes, wrote in Old French one of the first 'estates of the world', adopting for the purpose the traditional trifunctional schema.[24] Like John of Salisbury, he subordinates the whole of society to the Church, whose bishops had the duty of directing princes, even of resisting them if they became tyrants.[25] It was the task of kings to set an example of virtue and to make justice and peace prevail. The lower orders would then be able to fulfil their mission to feed and to protect. Stephen summarises in a quatrain the respective functions of the three orders:

> The clergy should pray for all,
> The knights, with no holding back,
> Should defend and honour them,
> And the peasants should plough the land.[26]

Chivalry is here allotted a role in the divine plan. Like every moralist, Stephen of Fougères emphasises both the ancient nature and dignity of this order, and its present moral decadence, too much influenced by worldly manners:

> Chivalry was a noble order,
> But now it is given to trickery.
> [Knights] are too fond of dance and frolick
> And living like young bloods.[27]

The knight, notes Stephen, must be free, born of a free mother,[28] before being 'ordained'. Admittedly, the word ordo, in Latin as in Old French, designates an estate as much as a status.[29] But in this case we are clearly dealing with an order which the knights joined by the ceremony of dubbing. This marked their entry into a function which consisted of using the sword to punish wrongdoers and so assure order and justice:

> The other sword will be given
> To the knights, by which will be cut off
> The feet and hands of malefactors
> Who have wrongfully ill-treated people.[30]

The knights are once again the auxiliaries of princes. As such, they serve God indirectly and so can assure their own salvation in their own estate, if they are loyal and shun treachery:

> He can save himself in his order
> If he gives no cause for complaint.[31]

To emphasise the necessity of the knight's submission to the Church, Stephen also refers to the sword taken from the altar during the dubbing ceremony. It gave him an opportunity to summarise the knight's mission, the function he would fulfil as long as he lived:

> He should take the sword from the altar
> To defend the people of Jesus,
> And to the altar, let him understand,
> He should return it before he dies.[32]

The overall view reflected by the poet-bishop of Rennes is essentially very similar to that of John of Salisbury. As a bishop and champion of the Church, he was trying to portray contemporary Christian society as a body governed by princes who disposed of armed forces, but who were primarily directed by the clergy. Knights were recruited by the princes they served, but they also had duties to the Church.

Peter of Blois, a contemporary of Richard I and close to the Plantagenet court, was greatly influenced by John of Salisbury, whose disciple he was. He, too, castigated the lack of military discipline and the 'unworthy' conduct of some knights, who vied with each other in pride (*superbia*), constantly denigrated the *ordo* of the clergy and ridiculed the Church. In the past, he said, new recruits swore an oath not to flee the battlefield and to put the common good before their own safety. In his day, they received their sword from the altar, recognising by this rite that they were sons of the Church and should honour the clergy, protect the poor, punish wrong-doers and maintain the freedom of their homeland. In practice, however, they did exactly the opposite.[33] Once again, the global mission of the knights is related to the symbolism of the knighting ceremony, though this is all he says about it.[34]

Helinand of Froidmont, once a highly regarded trouvère at the court of Philip Augustus, withdrew from the world in 1182 to become a Cistercian monk. He repeats John of Salisbury, sometimes word for word, when describing the mission and ethic of the knights.[35] He, too, connects their moral obligations towards the Church to the fact of their having received their sword from the altar. He is the first to refer to the existence 'in some regions' of the vigil of arms: in the church, on the eve of the dubbing ceremony, the future knight must remain standing all night in prayer.[36] This statement reveals a clear strengthening of the religious character of the ceremony in the regions where this practice had become customary, although Helinand tells us nothing else about when or where this ritual occurred.

This, briefly summarised, is the tenor of the didactic writings of ecclesiastical origin on the subject of knighthood and its function, which Richard may have known, directly or indirectly, through quotations or oral accounts. This is particularly likely in the case of works whose authors frequented the court of Henry II or were close to Eleanor of Aquitaine. We have already referred to Richard's meeting with Joachim de Fiore and their discussion about the end of time; it is clear that, although a layman, Richard was curious about at least some aspects of ecclesiastical teaching. He may well have been interested in the way the moralists and theologians of his day saw the function of princes and their warriors. It is more likely, however, that he took his conception of chivalry from the literature in Romance rather more than from the Latin works of churchmen.

SECULAR AND LITERARY IMAGES OF CHIVALRY

At this same period, the *chansons de geste* and romances were spreading the idea of a more 'secular' chivalry, worthy and honourable in itself, to a far wider audience. In fact, the knight is the principal hero of all the literary works of the twelfth century, from the appearance of the earliest *chansons de geste*.

Do they reveal a real awareness of the existence of chivalry as an order (*ordo*), as in the works of ecclesiastical origin? Not yet, at least in the *chansons de geste*. The expression *ordene de chevalerie* appears only exceptionally (two occurrences in a very large corpus comprising the majority of epics written before Richard's death) and means something very different from what would later generally be understood by 'order of chivalry'. In the *Moniage Guillaume*, it is applied to the military orders, Templars or Hospitallers.[37] In *Aspremont*, a unique and late case, it certainly refers to entry into the order of chivalry, marked by the presentation of the sword, but the words are spoken by a Muslim warrior evoking the moment when he 'received knighthood'; they can hardly have had an ethical Christian connotation.[38]

This would seem to corroborate the idea that, for the knights of the second half of the twelfth century, the religious dimension of chivalry and dubbing remained minor. For them, 'chivalry' meant the body of elite warriors as a whole, without any obvious religious connotation or ethic. This accords with the sources for the First Crusade which say that only the Turks (Muslims) and the Franks (in the wide sense of the word) could call themselves 'knights', because only they had the chivalric qualities of valour and skill in mounted warfare. The Turkish knights, they emphasise, would have been without equal if they had adhered to the Christian faith, as God would then have been on their side and made them victorious.[39]

After Richard, it was rumoured that the Emperor Frederick I, too, had negotiated with the infidel and that he had even made a Muslim prince a knight, to the immense shock and horror of contemporary ecclesiastics.[40] A similar accusation was in due course made about Richard himself, suspected of being too friendly towards Saladin and his brother. By the end of the twelfth century, and even more in the next, Saladin himself became a model of chivalry for the West, in spite of his religion, and his legend explains this innate quality in a variety of ways:[41] for some he had travelled in the West, fallen in love with a Christian woman and been made a knight on Christian territory; for others, he had French ancestors and a secret leaning towards Christianity; for yet others, such as the Minstrel of Reims, in 1260, Saladin had enjoyed a romantic liaison with Eleanor of Aquitaine, 'a very evil woman', during the Second Crusade. Seduced by his chivalric qualities, his valour, his prowess and his largesse, she had made a vain attempt to flee and join him.[42] Later still, it was believed that Saladin had been knighted and even that he had been baptised on his deathbed.

This 'appropriation' of Saladin, which is extremely revealing with regard to the chivalric mentality in the West, was therefore effected in two stages. The first reflects the conception of a 'secular' chivalry which still prevailed at the end of the twelfth and very beginning of the thirteenth centuries. It saw him as no more than a valiant warrior and outstanding cavalryman, amply provided with all the physical and moral qualities of a Western knight; it was not averse to adopting him as a model, regretting only that he was not a Christian, which would have made even more certain the victory to which his valour might justly aspire. The second, more deeply marked by religiosity, developed during the thirteenth century and intensified subsequently. It reveals the growing influence of clerical ideology on chivalry conceived as an 'order'. It had become impossible to accept that a non-Christian could be a knight, because, for these later writers, chivalry had become an order impregnated with rituals and with Christian and Western ideology. It was therefore necessary to, as it were, 'baptise' Saladin, which explains the emergence of legends making him a descendant of Christians, a future Christian or a knight actually dubbed in the West, in fact a man 'predestined' to chivalry.

The origin of this legend is probably to be found in a very interesting text that can be dated to the beginning of the thirteenth century, the *Ordene de Chevalerie*. It tells of the curious request made by Saladin to one of his Christian prisoners, Hue de Tabarie (Hugh of Tiberias), that he would make him a knight. This was an opportunity for the author to describe the dubbing ceremony and explain its significance in some detail. J. Tolan has interpreted this scene, wrongly in my view, as evidence of the secularisation of this ritual, which is here wholly lay because, according to him, it lacked either a priest or any reference to the obligation to defend the Church and the clergy.[43] It seems to me that, on the contrary, the *Ordene de Chevalerie* reflects a very clerical conception of knighting and accentuates both the ethical and religious and the honorific and social aspects of chivalry.[44] The story is as follows: Hue de Tabarie, Saladin's prisoner, first firmly refuses to dub Saladin a knight for the sole reason, decisive in his eyes, that he was not a Christian:

> The holy order of chivalry
> Would be ill served by you,
> For you are deficient in the way
> Of goodness, baptism, and faith. (vv. 83–5)

The description that follows of the various stages in the ceremony provided him with an opportunity to set out the duties of knights, which are deeply impregnated with religion: the bath, likened to that of baptism, signifies that the knight should be steeped in honesty, courtesy and goodness; the bed on which the future knight reposes symbolises Paradise, to be won through his 'chivalry' (vv. 132ff.);[45] the white sheet evokes the purity for which the knight must strive (vv. 144ff.); the scarlet robe which he dons expresses the fact that the knight must shed his blood 'for God and in defence of his law' (v. 155); the gilded spurs recall that the knight must serve God all his life (v. 200); the sword with two edges – loyalty and justice – signifies that he must protect the poor against the harassment of the rich (v. 215), and so on. As for the moral duties of chivalry, they consist of not being party to any injustice or treason, of giving assistance to ladies and damsels in distress, of fasting on Fridays and of hearing mass every day. Most of these precepts are, of course, fairly general in nature and applied to all Christians. The *Ordene* still reflects a conception of chivalry much more tinged with religion and clericalism than all the works which preceded it, especially those written in the vernacular. It is very clearly the work of a cleric who stresses the

social status of the knights, whom all should honour precisely because they protect the clergy and defend its interests, as is emphasised by the 'us' in these few lines:

> For they defend the Holy Church
> And for us uphold justice
> Against those who seek to do us harm. (vv. 433–5)

The knights also protect the Church against unbelievers, heretics and Saracens (vv. 443ff.); so it is only proper that they should have the right, for example, to enter churches armed; also that they should be honoured above all men (vv. 455ff., 478ff.). If he faithfully performs his mission, according to 'his order', the knight can expect to go 'straight to Paradise' (v. 475). The role of chivalry is here clearly defined, and the notion of social status which is its corollary is enunciated.

We find the same clerical vision (or at least one deeply imbued with ecclesiastical values) around 1230 in the prose romance, *Lancelot du Lac*, or to be more precise, in a single passage in which the author provides a definition of chivalry and its mission, put into the mouth of the Lady of the Lake. Before having Lancelot dubbed, the Lady reminds him that chivalry is no 'light matter', but a heavy responsibility which involves duties. Chivalry, she tells him (anticipating Raymond Lull),[46] was created long ago by election: the weak chose the strongest and set them above them so that they would defend, protect and rule them justly. Chivalry was instituted, she goes on, to protect the Holy Church.[47] She demonstrates this in her turn by the symbolism of arms, before concluding:

> In this way you can know that the knight should be the lord of the people and the sergeant of God. He should be the lord of the people in all things. But he must be the sergeant of God, because he must protect, defend and maintain the Holy Church, that is to say, the clergy, by whom the Holy Church is served, widows, orphans, tithes and alms, which are assigned to the Holy Church. And just as the people support him physically and provide him with all that he needs, so the Holy Church must support him spiritually and earn for him life without end.[48]

This text is admittedly quite isolated in the work, which elsewhere scarcely mentions this aspect of the chivalric ethic, but it is nonetheless quite explicit and reflects the ideal which, in its final, very complex and complete form, the Church attempted, throughout the twelfth century, to inculcate into the knights: the mission to protect the clergy and the weak, in particular widows and orphans, with the intention of making the knights into an order with a predominantly religious ideology.

But this author was writing, it should be emphasised, a generation after the death of Richard I. No *chanson de geste* or romance, or any work in the vernacular written before this period, comes close to expressing a religious ethic as developed as this. The texts from later than 1200 previously quoted, far from expressing a secularisation of the chivalric ideal or of dubbing, reflect, on the contrary, the concentrated effort to Christianise this ideal, through the liturgy, didactic treatises and even literature of Celtic origin, in which the steady Christianisation of themes and motifs, such as the Grail, and of the whole Arthurian cycle, has often been noted.[49]

The image of chivalry is much more secular, worldly, professional and aristocratic in the romances of Antiquity and in courtly romances and, indeed, in those of Chrétien de Troyes. Yet dubbing duly features in them, and it is probably in Chrétien that the word *adouber* assumes for the first time its predominant, even exclusive, meaning of 'knighting', that is, of promoting and giving access to an order.[50] But the dubbing described by Chrétien de Troyes has few religious features. The essential element, here and elsewhere, is the solemn presentation of the sword, sometimes accompanied by a *colée* (a light blow) and the buckling on of one or two spurs. The ceremony is sometimes preceded by a bath that is more utilitarian than symbolic,[51] and there is no reference to any liturgy of dubbing that would confer a spiritual or moral character on entry into chivalry or make knights into men bound to the Church by specific duties.

Could it be said, therefore, that knights are described in these works simply as a body of elite warriors without any ethic at all? This, in my view, would be going too far,[52] because, for the first time in a vernacular text, knighthood is conceived as an 'order' with professional, social, cultural or moral aspects. This emerges clearly in the dubbing – albeit wholly lay – of Perceval by Gornemant de Goor:[53]

> And the gentleman took the sword, girded it on him, and kissed him and said that in giving him the sword he had conferred on him the highest order that God had set forth and ordained: that is, the order of knighthood, which must be maintained without villainy.[54]

Chivalry is here an 'order', even the most worthy and most noble order, which imposed on its members a specific ethical behaviour, which the 'gentleman' goes on to explain. It consisted of four main points:

1. Do not despatch in cold blood a defeated and unarmed adversary who begs for mercy.
2. Speak sparingly so as not to spread malicious gossip.

3. Assist with your advice those in need of it.
4. Go willingly to pray in church.[55]

Only the first of these precepts is specific to chivalry; and it had both a moral and an economic purpose, as Georges Duby observed.[56] The third precept could, at a pinch, prefigure the 'courtly' behaviour of coming to the rescue of ladies and damsels in distress as practised by the heroes of Chrétien de Troyes.[57] The other two simply complement those which Perceval's mother had already lavished on her son, then totally ignorant of the usages of polite society, unaware even of what a church was. They are not in any way 'chivalric'.

In other words, the ethic offered by the text still seems to be embryonic and scarcely marked by social or religious morality. There is no sign of a notion of chivalry linked to the Church by specific moral obligations, either in the descriptions of dubbing or elsewhere in the work, though it is by no means lacking in didactic elements. Here romance and a purer historiography converge.[58] And there is similar agreement in the case of the fundamental meaning assumed by the presentation of the sword in most literary texts up to the beginning of the thirteenth century.

This is the conception of chivalry that was known to Richard the Lionheart. Serving the Church, particularly in the *chansons de geste*, amounted in practice to crusading or, to be more precise, waging Holy War against the infidel. Again, this was not a duty specific to knights.

For the rest, the values of chivalry adopted and exalted by Richard were still, at this period, too secular and too profane in character for the Church to accept or praise them. It was to be the principal task of the Church after Richard's time to try, by means of the liturgy, didactic and even literary texts, to further the Christianisation of the chivalric ideal and make the key themes of the chivalric romances more clerical in nature. In this it was only partly successful.

NOTES

1. 'L'imaginaire du féodalisme': Duby, *The Three Orders*.
2. Abbo of Fleury, *Apologeticus ad Hugonem et Rodbertum Reges Francorum*, PL 139, col. 464 (translation from Duby, *The Three Orders*, p. 90).
3. For the origins of this schema, see Ortigues, 'Elaboration de la Théorie des Trois Ordres'; Iogna-Prat, D., 'Le "Baptême" du Schéma des Trois Ordres Fonctionnels: l'Apport de l'Ecole d'Auxerre dans la Seconde Moitié du IXe Siècle', *Annales E.S.C.* (1986), pp. 101–26.
4. Abbo of Saint-Germain, *Sermones*, ed. U. Onnerfors, *Abbo von Saint-Germain-des-Prés 22 Predigten, Kritische Ausgabe und Kommentar*

(*Latienische Sprache und Literatur des Mittelalters*, Bd. 16) (Frankfurt–Berne–New York–Nancy, 1985), sermo 6, p. 64 and sermo ii, pp. 113ff.

5. This is no more than a brief summary. For the debate among historians about the interpretation of the precepts of the Peace of God, see Flori, *Chevaliers et Chevalerie*, pp. 181ff.

6. Adalbero of Laon, *Carmen ad Rodbertum Regem*, ed. and trans. C. Carozzi (Paris, 1979), p. 21.

7. Ibid., p. 23.

8. Bernard of Clairvaux, *De Laude Novae Militiae*, §10, p. 77. The formulation is extreme, like so many of the arguments of this author.

9. On this controversial point, see Riley-Smith, J., 'Death on the First Crusade', in D. Loades (ed.), *The End of Strife* (Edinburgh, 1984), pp. 14–31; Cowdrey, H. E. J., 'Martyrdom and the First Crusade', in P. W. Edbury (ed.), *Crusade and Settlement* (Cardiff, 1985), pp. 47–56; Flori, J., 'Mort et Martyre des Guerriers vers 1000; l'Exemple de la Première Croisade', *Cahiers de Civilisation Médiévale*, 34 (1991), 2, pp. 121–39.

10. Flori, J., 'Croisade et Chevalerie; Convergence Idéologique ou Rupture?', in *Femmes, Mariages, Lignages . . . Mélanges Offerts à Georges Duby*, pp. 157–76.

11. Raoul of Caen, *Gesta Tancredi*, RHC Hist. Occ. III, pp. 603–20.

12. See on this point Robinson, I. S., *The Papacy, 1073–1198. Continuity and Innovation* (Cambridge, 1990); Flori, J., 'L'Eglise et la Guerre Sainte, de la Paix de Dieu à la Croisade', *Annales E.S.C.* (1992), 2, pp. 88–99.

13. See, for example, Evergates, T., 'Historiography and Sociology in Early Feudal Society: the Case of Hariulf and the Milites of Saint-Riquier', *Viator*, 6 (1975), pp. 35–49.

14. Semmler, J., 'Facti sunt Milites Domini Ildebrandi Omnibus . . . in Stuporem', in *Ritterbild in Mittelalter*, pp. 11–35.

15. For an edition and discussion of this ritual, see Flori, J., 'A Propos de l'Adoubement des Chevaliers au XIe Siècle: le Pretendu Pontifical de Reims et l'*Ordo ad Armandum* de Cambrai', *Frühmittelalterliche Studien*, 19 (1985), pp. 330–49.

16. See on this point Flori, 'Chevalerie et Liturgie'; Flori, 'Du Nouveau sur l'Adoubement des Chevaliers'; Flori, J., 'Les Origines de l'Adoubement Chevaleresque: Etude des Remises d'Armes dans les Chroniques et Annales Latines du IXe au XIVe Siècle', *Traditio*, 35 (1979), pp. 209–72. I essentially stick to my opinion in spite of the (excessively) critical remarks of D. Barthélémy: 'Note sur l'Adoubement'.

17. See on this point Flori, 'Eglise et Chevalerie au XIIe Siècle'.

18. For what follows see Flori, 'La Chevalerie selon Jean de Salisbury'.

19. John of Salisbury, *Policraticus*, IV, 7, p. 258; VIII, 17, p. 345.

20. Ibid., IV, 3, p. 239.

21. Ibid., VI, 10, p. 25. Despite its brevity, this is one of the clearest descriptions of the dubbing ceremony in the twelfth century.
22. Ibid., VI, 8, p. 23.
23. John of Salisbury, *Policraticus*, VI, 8, p. 23.
24. See on this point Batany, 'Du Bellator au Chevalier'; Flori, J., *L'Idéologie du Glaive; Préhistoire de la Chevalerie* (Geneva, 1983), pp. 158ff.
25. Stephen of Fougères, *Livre des Manières*, lines 289ff., 457ff.
26. Ibid., lines 673–6.
27. Ibid., lines 585–8.
28. Ibid., line 589; it should be emphasised that only the mother, who transmitted legal status, is mentioned here. Nothing is said about male descent; in particular, there is no mention of the need to have a 'noble' or knightly father.
29. It then becomes possible to differentiate the order of the rich and that of the poor, that of the old and that of the young, that of the married and that of the unmarried, and so on. See on this point Batany, J., 'Abbon de Fleury et les Théories des Structures Sociales vers l'An Mil', *Etudes Ligériennes d'Histoire et d'Archéologie Médiévales* (1975), pp. 9–18; Batany, J. et al., 'Plan pour l'Histoire du Vocabulaire Social de l'Occident Médiéval', in *Ordres et Classes. Colloque d'Histoire Sociale de Saint-Cloud* (Paris, 1973), pp. 87–92.
30. Stephen of Fougères, *Livre des Manières*, lines 649–52.
31. Ibid., lines 621–2. In contrast, perfidious knights, who betrayed their role, were to be 'disordained': they were to have their spurs cut off and their swords removed from them, and be expelled from knighthood: ibid., lines 625–8. This is the oldest and clearest allusion to a possible 'demotion' of knights.
32. Ibid., lines 617–20. We should note the ambiguity of the expression 'people of Jesus'. Does it refer to the clergy only, or to Christian society as a whole?
33. Peter of Blois, 'Letter to the Archdeacon', in *Epistola* 94, PL 207, col. 294. Further on, Peter, like Bernard of Clairvaux and John of Salisbury before him, deplores the 'worldliness' of the knights, their frivolous liking for fine clothing, decorations on their armour, games and so on.
34. Is he even speaking here of all knights? We should note in passing that the nephews of the archdeacon about whom Peter was complaining had entered the *militia* in the train of the advocate of Béthune; the possibility cannot therefore be ruled out that this was an ecclesiastic complaining about some *milites ecclesiae* who were unfaithful to their specific mission of defending the Church, if not simply as knights, at least as knights of the church that had recruited them.
35. Helinand of Froidmont, *De Bono Regimine Principis*, bc. 23, PL 212, cols 743–4. This text is very similar to John of Salisbury, *Policraticus*, VI, 9, p. 23.

36. Helinand of Froidmont, *De Bono Regimine Principis*, col. 744; this new element clearly strengthened the religious nature of this form of knighting ceremony and increased moral obligations towards the Church.

37. *Le Moniage Guillaume*, ed. W. Cloetta, 2nd edn (Paris, 1896), line 640.

38. See *Aspremont*, line 5915, ed. L. Blandin (Paris, 1970). This is proof, as later in the work which bore this name, that the knights accepted the existence of an 'order of chivalry' in Muslim society, imagined as a replica of the Christian world.

39. L. Bréhier (ed. and trans.), *Histoire Anonyme de la Première Croisade* (Paris, 1964), p. 51. See also Guibert of Nogent, III, 11, *Dei Gesta per Francos*, ed. R. B. C. Huygens, CCCM 127A (Turnhout, 1996), or RHC Hist. Occ IV, p. 162.

40. The same accusation appears in Joinville, *Vie de Saint Louis*, §196, pp. 96–7.

41. See on this point Tolan, 'Mirror of Chivalry'; Gillingham, J., 'Some Legends of Richard the Lionheart: their Development and their Influence', in Nelson, *Richard Cœur de Lion*, pp. 51–69.

42. *Ménestrel de Reims*, p. 4.

43. Tolan, 'Mirror of Chivalry', p. 32; it is perhaps hardly surprising that these things are not mentioned at Saladin's court.

44. *Ordene de Chevalerie*, ed. K. Busby (Amsterdam, 1983). See on this point Flori, *Chevaliers et Chevalerie*, pp. 215ff.

45. It is by no means certain that the expression is not here an allusion to a 'heroic' moral conduct, the exercise of virtue suggested to all Christians, rather than the warlike exploits of knights.

46. For the notion of chivalry in Raymond Lull, see Aurell, 'Chevaliers et Chevalerie chez Raymond Lulle'.

47. See on this point Baumgartner, 'Remarques sur la Prose du Lancelot'; Frappier, J., 'L'Institution de Lancelot dans le *Lancelot en prose*', in *Mélanges Hoeffner*, pp. 263–78.

48. *Lancelot du Lac*, ed. E. Kennedy (Paris, 1991), p. 405. See on this point Flori, 'L'Epée de Lancelot'.

49. Flori, 'Eglise et Chevalerie au XIIe Siècle'; Frappier, J., 'Le Graal et la Chevalerie', *Romania*, 75 (1954), pp. 165–210, repr. in Frappier, *Autour du Graal*, pp. 89–128; Frappier, 'Le Graal et ses Feux Divergents'.

50. See Flori, 'Pour une Histoire de la Chevalerie'.

51. I hold to my opinion on this, despite the unconvincing observations of Sargent-Baur: 'Knighthood in . . . Chrétien de Troyes'.

52. See Burgess, G. S., 'The Term "Chevalerie" '; Flori, 'Chevalerie dans les Romans de Chrétien de Troyes'.

53. B. N. Sargent-Baur ('Knighthood in . . . Chrétien de Troyes') accuses me of underestimating the religious aspect of dubbing by failing to mention that the gentleman makes the sign of the cross over the young Perceval; but the 'blessing' is not part of the knighting; it is only after the dubbing, when

Perceval is leaving him, that the gentleman blesses, in a farewell gesture: Chrétien de Troyes, *Le Roman de Perceval ou le Conte du Graal*, ed. W. Roach (Geneva, 1959), lines 1693ff., trans. William W. Kibler in *Chrétien de Troyes. Arthurian Romances*, Penguin Books (1991), revised edn 2004, p. 402.

54. Chrétien de Troyes, *Perceval*, lines 632–8; p. 402 of Penguin translation.
55. Ibid., lines 1640ff.
56. Duby, *Dimanche de Bouvines*, pp. 137ff.
57. It should be noted that this precept is expressed in the form of advice (*consilium?*) to all who are in need of it, men and women.
58. See Flori, *Essor de la Chevalerie*.

13

Richard and the Three Orders

⟨∾⟩

Educated persons at the time of Richard the Lionheart, as we have seen, conceived of society as made up of three functional categories, summarised around 1176 by Stephen of Fougères in the following way: the clergy, whose role was to pray for the salvation of all men and women; the peasants, whose role was to labour to feed them; and the knights, who were responsible for their protection.[1] This is a cursory classification and Stephen himself, copying John of Salisbury in particular, went on to clarify the position of each of his categories and its place in the hierarchy.

The order whose labour fed the others had originally consisted of those who worked on the land, hence Stephen's choice of the word 'peasants', corresponding to the *laboratores* or *agricultores* of the Latin texts; but this category had diversified as a consequence of the economic and demographic growth which, from the eleventh century, had transformed the medieval West. The 'class' of workers on the land, the peasantry, was no longer alone, as in the days of Adalbero, in providing the other two orders with food and material life. With the growth of towns and their associated trade, many professions had emerged: merchants, no longer itinerant but based in towns, with shops in the suburbs, and artisans, manufacturers and repairers, from goldsmiths to menders of old clothes. There were already even a few industrial trades, in particular in cloth manufacture (weavers and dyers); by the time of Richard I, they were on the verge of constituting a sub-proletariat of workers of both sexes exploited by a rapidly expanding urban patriciate. This patriciate may already feature in some romances, including those of Chrétien de Troyes, who came from a town renowned for its fair and well placed to observe its emergence.[2] We should also include all the many people who practised trades linked to intellectual, artistic and cultural life, itself also on the increase, at least in the persons of jongleurs, while poets, artists and writers were closer to the aristocratic courtly world and its chivalric lifestyle than to that of the mass of the workers.

This proliferation of 'crafts', and even more the perception of it by learned men, led some to distinguish the activities of the various groups

comprising each of the three orders. John of Salisbury, for example, observed of the third order that it was they who supported and provided for the social body as a whole, that is, were its feet. He used the word 'centipede', so many and so varied were these useful trades, which he listed; he distinguished them from those which, as a man of the Church and a moralist, he regarded as reprehensible: the *histriones*, the actors, jongleurs and singers, not to speak of the swindlers, moneychangers and dealers who, in contravention of all morality, traded in or lent money at interest.[3]

The rise of the bourgeoisie is one of the principal social characteristics of the period under consideration here. It led to a transformation of mental attitudes among people accustomed to argue on the basis of simple social categories and immutable and long-established hierarchies. The money which was now circulating increasingly freely disrupted these categories; it made the fortunes of some (the bourgeoisie, kindling their ambition and their desire for social promotion and hunger for honour and dignity), but brought about the gradual impoverishment of others. Chief among these were the lesser nobility, who lacked sufficient land, property and men to be able to produce and sell on the market, and so benefit from economic growth and rising prices, from which, consequently, they only suffered. The 'ordinary' knights were in this category. And it was they, even more than the upper nobility, who put up the strongest defence of their positions and their rank; they erected barriers against the rise of the bourgeoisie, closed off entry to knighthood and developed an aristocratic ideology which aligned them more closely with the masters they served by their arms, in the socially worthy profession they were determined to keep to themselves.

Traces of this aristocratic ideology can be found in most of the literary works of the late twelfth century; they glorify knights and express contempt for the bourgeois commoners, valued solely in terms of the services rendered to the former by providing hospitality or giving them whatever they needed, whether it be money, horses or even the loving care and attention of their wives or daughters, assumed always to be ready to succumb to knightly prestige.[4] Andrew the Chaplain, like the majority of authors of pastourelles, ranks peasant women and shepherdesses lower still since he accepts the rape of young country girls, unsuited to courtly love, as normal, even legitimate. They sometimes consoled themselves, however, by playing tricks on the knight in question,[5] and we see the first signs of a popular literature of 'class', which reacted by parodying, caricaturing and ridiculing the nobility, making jokes at its expense. Many branches of the *Roman de Renart*, fabliaux, pastourelles, *chansons de*

toile ('women's songs') and *chansons de reverdie* ('spring songs'), a few *chansons de geste*, like those of Audigier, and even romances testify to this nascent literature, though its rise was still masked by the major artistic productions that remained predominantly aristocratic in tone.[6]

THOSE WHO WORK

The third order, that of the peasants and merchants, is often ignored or given little prominence in the literature that was popular in the aristocratic and chivalric world. There are echoes of this in the attitudes of Richard I, who seems, like the chroniclers who record his activities, to have felt a certain contempt for the common people, together with a very real anti-Semitism.

Traces of this can occasionally be detected in his actions as reported by the chroniclers; however, sharing the same social prejudices, they clearly did not usually regard the common people as worthy of mention. The various taxes instituted by Richard to pay first for his crusade and then for his ransom were the subject of vigorous protests because they weighed on the powerful and on churchmen. The heavy carucage instituted in 1198 on cultivated land, however, merited only a few lines and virtually no comment, even though it was eventually levied at the rate of five shillings per carucate or hide and assessed in each county by a representative of each of the other two orders, a knight (*miles*) and a cleric. All the peasants (*rustici*) had to pay this tax, and those who attempted to evade it suffered the loss of their best ox.[7]

We should also note the way in which the workers were differentiated from the clergy and the knights in the regulation of games of chance during the sea voyage to the Holy Land. The kings could play freely, the clergy and the knights were subject to some restrictions, but servants and sailors had to abstain altogether; if they contravened the prohibition, and were unable to pay the fine, they were harshly punished, the former given the bastinado and the latter keel-hauled three days running. Similarly, servants and sailors who left their masters during the course of the pilgrimage were severely punished, whereas it was accepted that the clergy and the knights could change household.[8]

Another example of this disdain comes in the account of an incident which took place in Mileto, in southern Italy, on 22 September 1190. Richard, riding through the village in the company of only a single knight, heard the cry of a bird of prey (probably a falcon) coming from inside a house. Presumably assuming that here, as in his own lands, possession of such a bird was an aristocratic privilege denied to a common

villager, Richard entered the house without further ado and seized the bird. The villagers saw things differently and surrounded him threateningly, some of them brandishing sticks. Richard at first refused to return the bird, but one of the peasants got out his knife. The King struck him with the flat of his sword, which broke under the impact, and threw stones at the others to drive them away, finally managing to escape. This inglorious episode seems indicative of the King's attitudes.[9]

Another episode, this time not involving the King, reveals the contempt felt by some of the chroniclers, even more 'aristocratic' than the lay nobility, for the common people, particularly when they dared to rebel. It emerges in their interpretation of the social tensions that flared up in England in April 1196: William FitzOsbert, nicknamed 'Longbeard', presented himself as the defender of the poor, oppressed by taxes which, he pointed out, weighed most heavily on the humble and spared the rich. One chronicler spoke of a vast conspiracy, born in London out of 'the hatred of the poor for the insolence of the rich'. FitzOsbert was said to have assembled more than 50,000 conspirators of low birth, who had holed up in houses, after arming themselves with weapons of every sort, and dared to resist the nobles. Richard was then in Normandy, and FitzOsbert had at one point considered crossing the Channel to appeal to him against the injustice of the authorities. But Archbishop Hubert Walter, custodian of the kingdom in the King's absence, took hostages from among the common people and sent two 'citizens' of the town, with an armed escort, with orders to take advantage of a moment when the rabble-rouser was unarmed and unguarded to seize him. FitzOsbert struck back, killing with a hatchet blow one of the men attempting to seize him; one of his companions killed the other. Both men then took refuge in a church, a place of sanctuary. The Archbishop of Canterbury promptly set fire to the church, forcing them to flee the smoke-filled building.

As they left, the son of the man FitzOsbert had killed knifed him in the stomach to avenge his father's death. FitzOsbert was seized, summarily condemned, butchered, quartered and hanged, on 6 April. The chronicler notes that the populace dared to honour him as a martyr after his death, and that 'false miracles' were performed on his tomb. But, he insists, the 'errors' he had been forced to confess before his death were sufficient proof that he could not have been either a saint or a martyr. The Archbishop then had to intervene and punish the priest who had dared to spread such foolish tales and place guards round the tomb to prevent a crowd from gathering.[10] The whole tone of the account reveals the deep hostility of the author to the common people. There may also have been an element of racial prejudice, as the majority of the rebels

were Anglo-Saxons who complained of the oppression of the powerful, almost all of whom were of Norman origin.

This is perhaps why Matthew Paris, describing the same events, is much more favourable towards FitzOsbert, who is again presented as the defender of the poor against the exactions of the mighty, but with some justification. Matthew Paris describes him as a man of good birth who was well-regarded in the city, 'tall, vigorous and intrepid', and he emphasises that the scheme hatched to arrest him was dishonourable. He describes FitzOsbert defending himself with a knife but is careful not to call his action murder. His motives seemed legitimate to Matthew Paris; all he wanted, by resisting the iniquitous decisions of the powerful, was to demand an equal burden for all: taxation according to means. But his arguments were ignored, and they dared to set fire to a church, forcing him to flee half-choked; he was then seized, stripped and bound, his feet were shackled, and he was tied to a horse's tail to be dragged to prison. The trial of the troublemaker, even summary, is missing from this account, in which the Archbishop merely orders that he be once more dragged behind a horse to his place of execution. Matthew concludes with this highly favourable judgement:

> Thus was delivered to an unworthy death, by his fellow citizens, William, nicknamed Longbeard or the Bearded One. He died for having come to the defence of truth and embraced the cause of the poor. If it is the rightness of the cause that makes a martyr, no-one more than he and with greater justification can be called a martyr.[11]

Whichever version one prefers, the episode testifies to the tensions then present in the kingdom and to the resistance to taxes that were seen to weigh too heavily on the poor.

The chroniclers appear equally unmoved by the fate of the Jews. As we have seen, Philip Augustus had expelled them from his kingdom, a measure that was approved by most of the chroniclers, in particular Rigord; in his eyes it was justified by their excessive wealth, accumulated at the expense of Christians, and by the arrogance that went with it. But Rigord also displays a hatred that can properly be described as racist, fuelled by stories of the 'infamous' rites traditionally attributed to the Jews. Philip Augustus, he says, unlike his father, Louis VII, who had protected the Jews (and here there is a parallel with Richard and his father, Henry II), had 'learned' at a very young age that the Jews, every year, made a human sacrifice of a Christian child. He decided, therefore, to take firm action against them, but out of respect for his father (a respect Rigord deemed excessive), acted only after his coronation. He then had the Jews

arrested as they emerged from their synagogues and expelled from the kingdom, after being stripped of their wealth. Rigord heartily approved this measure; he saw Philip Augustus as a pious king who 'protected the Church against its enemies and defended it by exterminating the Jews, enemies of the Christian faith, and by spurning heretics who were mistaken about the Catholic faith'. Commenting on the laws of spoliation passed against the Jews two years later, in 1182, Rigord justifies them on two grounds.

The first focuses on the illegitimate and scandalous wealth of the Jews. It had come to a point, he says, where they owned half of Paris; many Christians were indebted to them, and they even kept Christian men and maidservants in their houses, who they forced to 'Judaise' with them. The King's piety, with the advice of the holy hermit Bernard of Brie, had caused him to issue an edict by which all Christians were discharged of their debts to Jews; the King merely demanded a fifth for himself. One could be pious without forgetting the financial interests of the kingdom.

Rigord's second reason concerns the contempt of Jews for the Christian religion. They owned chalices and other sacred vessels and utensils that had been pawned or sold to them by ecclesiastics (though Rigord is not shocked by this), and used them to drink out of, so profaning them in a way that was quite intolerable. Worse still, when they knew that their houses were going to be searched by royal officials, they dared to hide these sacred treasures in disgusting places. One of them, who owned various cups, a gold cross and a gospel bound with gold and precious stones, had the idea of putting his treasures in a sack and hiding them in a cesspit. But, 'by divine revelation', they were eventually found and restored to their churches – once the King had taken his fifth.[12]

Rigord enjoyed justifying and describing the 'wise measures' adopted by Philip Augustus against the Jews, who were for him, like heretics and Muslims, 'enemies of God and the Christian faith'. He praised the King for not having given in to their promises or prayers, and for having confirmed his edict, so compelling the Jews to sell their movable goods in great haste before fleeing the country; their landed property devolved on the royal treasury, while their synagogues were 'purified' and turned into churches.

To justify these measures, Rigord also invoked prophesy, and he offers in passing an interesting interpretation of the end of the world and of the role to be played in it by Jews and Muslims. He evoked the ancient measures of Dagobert, to whom Heraclius had written urging the extermination of the Jews, 'which was done', Rigord notes, with evident satisfaction if little regard for accuracy. He gives the

reasons: a prophecy had announced that his kingdom would be destroyed by the people of the circumcised. The King had believed, wrongly, that this referred to the Jews. In fact the prophesy foretold the arrival of the Agarenians, otherwise called the Saracens. History, says Rigord, has since provided proof

> because we know that the empire was subsequently seized by these Saracens, and totally devastated by them, and that this will happen again, at the end of time, according to Methodius: they are the Ismailites, who descend from Ismail.[13]

He then cites the text of Pseudo-Methodius announcing the end of the world, the coming of the Antichrist, the profanation of the Holy Sepulchre and the turning of churches into stables, arguments which had served as a basis for crusading propaganda as early as 1095, and in the days of Urban II. The story reveals the presence of eschatological preoccupations among the chroniclers; some of them linked the last days and the appearance of the Antichrist to the Arab conquest rather than to the conversion of the Jews, like several popular preachers during the First Crusade.[14]

The persecution and expulsion of the Jews from France in 1182 caused many of them to flee to neighbouring countries. Some took refuge in the lands of the Plantagents, in particular England,[15] where, as we have been, there were 'spontaneous' disturbances reflecting the same anti-Semitic attitudes, based on the same malicious stories and motives.[16] The English pogroms of 1189 are in part linked to the religious exaltation and fanaticism which accompanied all the large-scale departures on crusade, and they were probably encouraged by inflammatory preaching against the 'enemies of Christ'. Matthew Paris, for example, notes that in Norwich and York the crusaders, before leaving for Jerusalem, 'resolved first to make war on the Jews. All the Jews they found in their houses in Norwich were massacred'.[17]

Other English chroniclers, like Rigord in France, justified the massacre of the Jews by the abominable crimes they were supposed to have perpetrated. Ralph of Coggeshall, for example, mentions several murders of Christian children that had been committed earlier, in 1144 and 1181.[18] He also refers to blasphemies and to the increasing boldness of the Jews, not forgetting what he considered their excessive wealth, before concluding that, all in all, these cruel massacres of Jews by Christians were not undeserved.[19] Richard of Devizes reveals a similar anti-Semitic prejudice in his comments on the massacres: they had begun in London, where the population began to 'sacrifice the Jews to their father the devil', and continued more or less everywhere, with

Christians 'sending to hell with the same devotion these blood-suckers and the blood on which they had gorged themselves'; there had been one exception, the town of Winchester, which had 'spared the vermin it had nurtured'.[20]

William of Newburgh was no more sympathetic to the Jews, and provides useful details regarding the motives for the pogroms and the reactions of Richard the Lionheart. He notes first, as a cause for rejoicing, that the destruction of 'that heretical people' coincided with the first days of the glorious reign of the King and reflected the 'new confidence of the Christians against the enemies of the Cross of Christ'. In fact, he said

> the death of this people added lustre to the day and the place of the royal sacring at the very beginning of his reign, the enemies of the Christian faith began to fall and be slain very close to him.[21]

The equation of the Jews with the 'enemies of Christ' was traditional, and a motif developed before every crusade. In describing the origins of these massacres, that is, the intolerable insolence of the Jews who, in spite of the royal prohibition, wanted to take part in the coronation banquet and festivities, William described Richard's reaction on learning of it in some detail, and his account repays close scrutiny. The King was angry because the disturbances took place during the festivities:

> The new king, who had a noble and proud disposition, was filled with indignation and grief that such events had occurred in his presence, during the festivities surrounding his coronation and at the very beginning of his reign.[22]

What should he do? Richard hesitated. Should he shut his eyes and behave as if nothing had happened? But to let such deeds go unpunished would only encourage similar affronts to his royal majesty! Should he arrest those guilty of the massacres and the looting? Impossible, they were too numerous! In the event, says the chronicler, all the nobles and all their vassals came running, and almost the whole town, out of 'hatred of the Jews and the hope of plunder . . . had united in the performance of the work . . . it was therefore necessary to connive at that which could not be punished'.[23] William of Newburgh took consolation from the fact that it must have been divine Providence that had willed this. In York, he says, the inhabitants could not bear to observe the wealth of the Jews when they themselves, the nobles included, as they prepared to set out to liberate the Holy Sepulchre, were in financial distress. They were motivated by the desire for booty while also 'thirsting for their perfidious blood'. But, after the massacres in London, Richard had instituted a law guaranteeing the security

and peace of the Jews. The second wave of pogroms was therefore damaging both to his authority and to his treasury:

> He was indignant and enraged on account of the affront to his royal majesty and of the great loss sustained by his treasury; for everything owned by the Jews, who, as everyone knows, are the king's creditors, is of concern to the treasury.[24]

An enquiry was instigated but the massacre went unpunished.

Matthew Paris is also interesting on Richard's attitude after the first pogroms perpetrated in London. The mob had taken advantage of the disturbances that had followed the attempt of several Jews to participate in the royal festivities. They had been rudely rebuffed by the royal officials responsible for keeping order and the ensuing scuffles had served as a pretext for the crowd to beat up the Jews, burn and loot their houses and, of course, destroy the recognisances of debt they found there. Next day, Richard heard about this and Matthew Paris emphasises that he took it to heart as if he himself had been the victim of the attacks. The rest of his account reveals, however, that the punishment of the culprits was both limited and selective:

> [Richard] had three of the culprits, who had distinguished themselves by their behaviour during the rioting, seized and hanged: one was hanged because he had stolen from the house of a Christian, the other two because they had set fire to a building in the city, and this fire had consumed several houses belonging to Christians.[25]

Roger of Howden makes the same observation, in identical words.[26]

When we put together all the information about these pogroms in the chronicles, it is difficult to avoid the conclusion that anti-Semitism was widespread at that time, that it was further exacerbated on the eve of the crusade and that it was shared by almost all the chroniclers and probably also the clergy. Many people saw these massacres as a normal prelude to the crusaders' action against the enemies of Christ; they were not unduly shocked by them, they invariably justified them and often approved of them, if sometimes denouncing their excesses; only exceptionally did they criticise them. Ralph of Diceto alone condemns them.

Did Richard share these anti-Semitic feelings? There was a rumour, according to some chroniclers, that Richard himself had ordered all the Jews to be exterminated.[27] Others, however, were careful to present the King as indignant and anxious to ensure the safety of the Jews, promulgating edicts which protected them and ordering enquiries so that the guilty could be punished. Nevertheless, if we are to believe these accounts, his main concern was the way the disturbances constituted

an affront to his royal authority and dignity and even threatened his finances. His intention to arrest the culprits was stillborn given the scale of the participation in the pogroms of both nobility and common people. Ralph of Diceto, the chronicler most hostile to these activities and most anxious to disassociate Richard from them, says that they happened without the King's knowledge and that he later took his revenge by punishing those responsible for these crimes.[28] But the chroniclers mention the exemplary punishment of only three of the culprits. It is surely significant that all three, as the account of Matthew Paris cited above makes plain, had wronged Christians, not Jews: the first had taken advantage of the general pillaging to rob a Christian; the other two, by setting fire to Jewish houses, had started a conflagration which had unfortunately also burned Christian houses. The massacres of Jews and the burning and looting of their houses went unpunished, amid almost universal indifference.

Should Richard be criticised for having subscribed to some extent to the prevailing intolerance and anti-Semitism? Such attitudes were the norm. Sixty years later, in France, St Louis, a canonised king, urged Christians in the strongest possible terms not to debate the faith with Jews. The king had told Joinville about the debate between Jews and Christians that had taken place at Cluny. An old knight, hobbling on crutches, had obtained permission from the abbot to open the debate. He at once asked the most learned of the Jewish doctors if he believed in the Virgin Mary, mother of God. The Jew, naturally, said no. Even before he could explain himself, the old knight retorted that he was a fool, therefore, to have entered a church. Then, raising his crutch, he struck the Jew above the ear, knocking him to the ground. His fellow Jews fled, carrying their wounded companion with them. Telling this story, Louis IX approved of the knight's actions and drew from them this lesson: unless you are a very learned clerk, you should not get into an argument with Jews. The layman who heard anyone speak ill of the Christian faith should seek to defend it only with his sword, 'which he should drive into the belly as far as it would go'.[29]

Should we expect Richard to have been more judicious in this matter than St Louis?

THOSE WHO PRAY

Richard's relations with the clergy merit a longer discussion than is possible in this book. I will restrict myself to presenting a few aspects that are in some way indicative of his attitude, in which respect mingled with anticlericalism. Here, he acted above all as a ruler, as a politician and

a monarch concerned for the interests of his kingdom, consistent in his decisions and in his appointments of bishops and archbishops.

We have already noted his extremely critical attitude towards the pope, with whom he was often at odds, as a result of the pope's reluctance to appoint the King's relatives, friends or allies to bishoprics or archbishoprics, or of the compensatory financial demands to which these diplomatic manoeuvres gave rise. These disagreements led Richard to avoid a meeting with the pope when he passed very close to Rome during his journey to Sicily and the Holy Land and also to view Clement III as the Antichrist who, before the end of time, would seize the apostolic throne, according to the prophetic interpretation of Joachim of Fiore.[30] His relations with the higher clergy, though never approaching the degree of tension of the quarrel between his father and Thomas Becket, were not always amicable, and we have seen how unpopular were the financial decisions he took to procure the money he needed to organise his crusade. Most chroniclers criticise him for having infringed the privileges of the Church and its property. Ralph of Coggeshall was expressing the general sentiment when he said that Henry II, before Richard, had used the Saladin Tithe as an excuse to plunder Church treasures and squander them on his knights (*milites*) and salaried officials, and that this soon incurred a punishment from God: the ending of the peace between the two kings.[31] Matthew Paris describes this tax, camouflaged under the name of alms, as an 'act of true rapacity'.[32] It was certainly partly due to this new tax, levied on the clergy as well as the people, and to the 'forced loans' from the churches, that the King's reputation among the clergy was so low. We have also seen that Richard had no hesitation in seizing the treasures of churches and monasteries when he needed money to pay his troops of mercenaries, sometimes promising their return at a later date (which rarely happened); but in this he was, of course, no different from the Young Henry and most other princes.[33]

While deploring these methods, which were treated as serious extortions visited on the Church, the chroniclers did not forget to praise Richard as a defender of the faith and of Christendom in the Holy Land, using his sword for once as befitted someone of his order. All of them note that Richard was the first prince to wish to take the cross, 'with deep piety', as soon as Saladin's capture of Jerusalem was known, 'to avenge the insult done to Christ', in the words of Gerald of Wales, and that he took the cross without seeking or awaiting the advice of his father.[34] The notion of 'vengeance' was one of the motives which, beginning with the First Crusade, drove knights to go to the East to take back from the infidel the Holy Land, seen as the legitimate heritage of their lord Jesus Christ. Urban II had not shrunk from appealing to this eminently feudal value,

which was an integral part of the chivalric ethic. The *faide*, that is, vengeance taken by the vassals of an offended lord against the entourage of the offender, was regarded as a virtuous act, and it was virtually part of feudal obligations. Richard himself refers to it in a letter to the Abbot of Clairvaux, in which he tells of his crusade and his decision to join those who had placed the sign of salvation on their foreheads and shoulders in order to 'avenge the insults to the Holy Cross' and 'defend the places of the death of Christ, consecrated by his precious blood, which the enemies of the cross of Christ had till then profaned in a shameful fashion'.[35]

Nevertheless, as we have seen, this premature decision was deferred for a number of reasons. Richard had rebelled against his father, and so had first to obtain absolution from the clergy.[36] His repeated conflicts with Philip Augustus, before and after his father's death, also made him postpone his departure, to the point where he was criticised by the troubadour Gaucelm Faidit. While recalling the great honour due to Richard for having been first to take the cross, Gaucelm emphasises that it would only be by putting to sea that it would really be earned, and he deplored his procrastinations. He also reproached Richard for not having kept his word and for his failure to send him the material assistance he had promised, which would have allowed him, too, to go to the Holy Land.[37] Once again, the reasons were financial; before his departure, Richard needed to amass considerable sums, and we have seen some of the obstacles he encountered in doing this.

THOSE WHO FIGHT

Richard's interest in the crusade was obvious, however, and he was sincere in his wish to participate, simply from a desire to fight for God's cause. Like many knights of his day, and of the preceding age, he was both impetuous and violent, capable of serious sins but also of deep repentance, concerned about his own salvation, and therefore attracted by the indulgences attached to the crusade. Those who set out on a crusade were assured at least the remission of their confessed sins. This had been said by Urban II at the Council of Clermont before the First Crusade, in 1095, and Eugenius III had repeated the promise in the same words at the time of the Second Crusade, in 1146:

> We grant them finally, by the authority of Almighty God and by that of St Peter, prince of the apostles, which has been given us by God, the remission and absolution of their sins, just as they have been instituted by our predecessor: so that, whoever will devoutly undertake a pilgrimage so holy, and accomplish it, or who dies in accomplishing it, will obtain absolution from

all his sins, provided that he has confessed them with a contrite and humble heart. And he will receive from He who gives to all their recompense the fruit of eternal reward.[38]

Bernard of Clairvaux, who preached the Second Crusade, went further, claiming that, unlike the knights of this world who fought against their brethren, thereby endangering their souls, the knights of Christ ran no such risk in killing the infidel:

For the knights of Christ, on the contrary, it is in total safety that they fight for their Lord, without need of being afraid of sinning by killing their enemies, or of perishing if they should themselves be killed. Whether they suffer death, or give it, it is always a death for Christ: there is no crime in, it is most glorious. On the one hand, they do it to serve Christ; on the other, it allows them to attain Christ himself: for He permits, in order to avenge Him, the killing of an enemy, and He gives Himself even more readily to the knight to console him. So, as I said, the knight of Christ metes out death without having anything to fear; but he dies in even greater security: it is he who benefits from his own death, and Christ from the death he inflicts.[39]

Bernard was thinking of the Templars, those full-time knights of Christ, when he wrote these lines, but they are equally applicable to all crusaders. Richard had probably been reared on such conceptions of the crusade, in which the knight fighting for the recovery of the Holy Land was a soldier of God labouring for his own salvation, sword in hand, as was appropriate for his order.

Yet in the thinking of Urban II, Raoul of Caen, and even more of Bernard of Clairvaux, the crusade was the result of a conversion, a sort of rejection of ordinary chivalry. It was not one of the moral obligations incumbent on every knight simply because he was a knight. The bishop and poet Marbod of Rennes, soon after the First Crusade, was one of the few to suggest that every knight, to be worthy of the name, ought to go and fight the infidel,[40] but his remained a lone voice.

In spite of his sincere commitment to the crusade, Richard's actions in the Holy Land seem not to have won him the unanimous approval of the clergy. There was criticism of his role in Outremer. He was reproached for having been primarily concerned with his own glory, and for dissipating his efforts in operations designed to enhance his own prestige and further his own personal interests, in Sicily, Cyprus and sometimes even the Holy Land, though to no great effect. His diplomatic and personal relations with Saladin, his brother and the Saracens in general were also said to have been too amicable. The French, in particular, even accused him of colluding with the enemy.[41] Ambroise felt the need to defend him on this

count on several occasions, testifying in passing to the low opinion of his activities in this sphere prevalent in at least part of the army. Ambroise points out, for example, that even during the diplomatic negotiations marked by mutual visits and exchanges of gifts, Richard had continued to fight the Saracens and cut off enemy heads which he then exhibited in the Christian camp. Nor did the presents he received from the Saracens do anyone any harm, unlike the activities of certain Christians who 'plundered his purse', and but for whom, he claimed, in defiance of all the evidence, Richard would have reconquered the whole of Syria.[42]

Richard's dithering and his reluctance to press ahead with the march on Jerusalem when all the crusaders, including those in his own camp, were desperate to 'recover' the Holy City and the Sepulchre, were seen as over-cautious; they were heavily criticised and greeted with blind incomprehension. Even his most faithful supporter, Ambroise, shared this reaction with the French, more often the butt of his sarcasm. Richard's decision was the cause, as we have seen, of fierce dissension among the crusaders. Hugh of Burgundy composed a 'bad song', mocking this less than glorious attitude on the part of the King of England, to which Richard replied with a song of the same sort ridiculing the Duke. Ambroise, wholly devoted to the cause of the King of England, inveighed against such attitudes; how could God give victory, as in the First Crusade, to an army so divided and so little concerned for His cause?[43] Throughout his account, he tries to counteract the poor image of the crusaders, attaching not only to Philip Augustus, who had returned home to his kingdom to conspire with John Lackland against Richard, but to Richard himself, whose inconsistent decisions and meagre achievements were much emphasised. Ambroise himself reveals this when, right at the end of his account, he explains his motives for writing: his prime aim had been to exonerate the crusaders who had suffered so much for God and experienced such tribulations, not only in Syria but on their return voyage, when many of them had perished at sea, in shipwrecks:

> But many ignorant people say repeatedly, in their folly, that they achieved nothing in Syria since Jerusalem was not conquered. But they had not inquired properly into the business. They criticise what they do not know and where they did not set their feet. We saw it who were there; we saw this and knew it, who had to suffer, we must not lie about others who suffered for the love of God, as we saw with our own eyes.[44]

Ambroise is not the only chronicler to record these defamatory rumours about the crusaders. Ralph of Coggeshall also refers to and even repeats them; worse still, he makes them his own. For him, all the tribulations

they had suffered on their return journey, the shipwrecks, the separations, the ambushes and the various traps and even captures, including that of Richard himself, were the result of divine vengeance against these 'deserters of God', who had not completed the task He had entrusted to them; it had been God's plan to deliver Jerusalem and the Holy Land to them, and they would have conquered the country if only they had faithfully persevered instead of giving up the fight. For Ralph, the death of Saladin and the ensuing disputes between his heirs were proof.[45] The notion of immanent justice remained, at this period, one of the fundamental components of the medieval mentality. Failure and misfortune were the result of God's displeasure and His punishment.[46]

The committed account of the jongleur and trouvère Ambroise can reasonably be seen as a work of propaganda primarily designed to restore the image of the crusaders and in particular that of Richard I. Nevertheless, it is the chivalric virtues of the King of England on which he dwells. They were employed in the service of God's cause and of Christianity in the Holy Land, admittedly, but the way they were glorified reveals the extent to which they were integral to Richard's personality; even and above all on crusade, he was primarily perceived as the model of the 'roi-chevalier'.

What were the virtues which won such general praise and which came ultimately to be expected of every member of the still nascent order of chivalry? They are best reflected in literature of the age. The *chansons de geste*, in the persons of Roland, Oliver, Aiol, William of Orange, Girard de Roussillon, Garin de Monglane and Renaud de Montauban, exalt above all prowess and military valour, the physical and moral virtues that made the hero a formidable warrior. The romances, without in any way playing down these purely military qualities, which are still the main features of their heroes, add other more courtly virtues. The Church tried quickly to Christianise them, or rather to reorient and channel them into conformity with its own doctrines, as it had earlier tried to do in the case of war, through the crusade.

This process of development and appropriation was gathering pace in Richard's day and it is still too soon to apply to the knighthood of his period the idealised image conveyed by the romances of the early thirteenth century; this is even more the case with the description given by Raoul de Houdenc, around 1210–20, in his *Roman des Eles*, that 'catechism of the perfect knight' in the phrase of a renowned expert in the field, Alexandre Micha.[47] By this date, 'prowess' was no longer simply a synonym for warrior bravery; it was beginning to signify valour, proof of the renown which elevated a man. According to Raoul de Houdenc, it lifted the knight, symbol of *gentillesse* (nobility), above the common

run, and implied, he said, a certain dignity of behaviour. The two 'wings' evoked in the title of his poem are Largesse and Courtesy.

Largesse taught how to give well, open-handedly, without calculation or aim of receiving anything in return; Courtesy how to behave well in society, avoiding pride, boastfulness, haughtiness, malicious gossip and envy, instead loving joy, song and the company of ladies. The author then embarks on a long essay on love, its pleasures and pains, its joys and perils, comparing it to the sea, to wine and to the rose.[48]

This little manual of good conduct essentially extolled, as we see, the mental qualities and the types of behaviour which, under the influence of the poets and romance writers, gradually came to prevail, making the knight the model of the ideal aristocrat, civilised, affable and courteous, knowing how to live and to love, how to drink, sing and pay court to ladies. It is surprising to find in the work of a man so imbued with a clerical education only a single fairly brief reference to the mission which the Church had tried for so long to inculcate in knights. They should honour and protect it, he wrote, because it was for this that chivalry had long ago been instituted; a similar formulation would soon be put into the mouth of the Lady of the Lake who educated Lancelot. To Raoul de Houdenc, the finest 'courtesy' was to honour the Holy Church.

But how? Of this, he says nothing, and this furtive mention (only fifteen lines out of a total of six hundred and sixty) seems little more than a sort of concession to the obligatory deference due to religion. The rest of the poem is effectively devoted to exalting the wholly secular values of courtly chivalry, those values which Richard, too, in the literary milieu of the court, had probably already learned to know and perhaps to revere.

Prowess, largesse and courtesy are the cardinal virtues of chivalry at the end of the twelfth century. It was not by chance that Ambroise justified in these very terms one of his stories about the King of England, at the time of his landing at Acre to act in the service of God: the 'corteisie e la proesce . . . e la largesce' that he showed there 'should be recounted'.[49]

NOTES

1. See above pp. 244ff.
2. See on this point the sometimes controversial views of Jonin: 'Vie Sociale au XIIe Siècle'.
3. For this important contribution, see Flori, J., 'La Chevalerie selon Jean de Salisbury', *Revue d'Histoire Ecclésiastique*, 77, 1/2 (1982), pp. 35–77.
4. See, for example, Spencer, 'Argent dans Aiol'; Flori, 'L'Idéologie Aristocratique dans Aiol'. More generally, for the literature of the late

twelfth century and the formation of the aristocratic ideology, see Flori, 'Noblesse, Chevalerie et Idéologie Aristocratique'.

5. Flori, 'Le Chevalier, la Femme at l'Amour'.
6. See the contradictory but revealing remarks of J.-C. Payen ('Idéologie Chevaleresque'), who sees the *Roman de Renart* as essentially the ideological affirmation of the lesser knights under threat, and of J. Dufournet, who emphasises the parody of the chivalric world: 'Littérature Oralisante et Subversion: la Branche 18 du Roman de Renart, ou le Partage des Proies', *Cahiers de Civilisation Médiévale* (1981), pp. 321–35. For the fabliaux, see Nykrog, P., *Les Fabliaux*, 2nd edn (Geneva, 1973), who emphasises that the knights are here primarily represented as victors, whereas M.-T. Lorcin (*Les Fabliaux*) sees the fabliaux as reflecting a variety of outlooks; J. Ribard ('Si les Fabliaux n'étaient pas des "Contes à Rire"?') ascribes to them a more serious and deeper ethical significance and intent than P. Ménard: *Les Fabliaux, Contes à Rire du Moyen Age* (Paris, 1983).
7. Roger of Howden, IV, p. 46.
8. Ibid., III, pp. 60, 68.
9. Ibid., pp. 54–5; see also *Gesta Henrici*, II, p. 125.
10. William of Newburgh, pp. 466ff. Roger of Howden gives a more sober and relatively neutral account: IV, pp. 5–6.
11. Matthew Paris, *Chronica Majora*, II, pp. 418–19.
12. Rigord, §12, pp. 24–7.
13. Ibid., §19, p. 32.
14. See Flori, J., *Pierre l'Ermite et la Première Croisade* (Paris, 1999), pp. 221ff., 251ff.
15. Gervase of Canterbury says that by 1168 the King of England was getting money from Jews persecuted in France: I, p. 205.
16. See above, pp. 81ff.
17. Matthew Paris, *Chronica Majora*, II, pp. 357–8.
18. Ralph of Coggeshall, p. 12 (1144): 'Puer Willelmus crucifixus est a Judaeis apud Norwic'; ibid., p. 20 (1181): 'Puer Robertus a Judaeis crudeliter occiditur apud Sanctam Aedmundum.'
19. Ibid., p. 28: 'Unde non immerito tam crudelis persecutio a Christianis eis illata est.'
20. Richard of Devizes, pp. 3ff.
21. William of Newburgh, pp. 297ff.
22. Ibid.
23. Ibid.
24. Ibid.
25. Matthew Paris, *Chronica Majora*, II, p. 350.
26. Roger of Howden, III, p. 12; *Gesta Henrici*, II, pp. 88ff.
27. William of Newburgh, p. 295: 'Interea rumor gratissimus, quod scilicet rex omnes Judaeos exterminari jussisset, totas incredibili celeritate percurrit Lundinias.'

28. Ralph of Diceto, II, p. 68.
29. Joinville, *Vie de Saint Louis*, pp. 27–9.
30. *Gesta Henrici*, II, pp. 151ff.; Roger of Howden, III, pp. 75ff.
31. Ralph of Coggeshall, pp. 24–5.
32. Matthew Paris, *Chronica Majora*, II, p. 356.
33. Gerald of Wales, *De Principis Instructione*, p. 239; Ralph of Diceto, II, p. 50; William of Newburgh, p. 271; Richard of Devizes, pp. 7ff.
34. See Riley-Smith, J., 'Crusading as an Act of Love', *History*, 65 (1980), pp. 177–92; Riley-Smith, J., 'An Approach to Crusading Ethics', *Reading Medieval Studies*, 6 (1980), pp. 3–19; Flori, J., *La Première Croisade. L'Occident Chrétien Contre Islam* (Brussels, 1992) (2nd edn 1997), pp. 37ff.; Flori, *Pierre l'Ermite*, pp. 192ff., 201ff.
35. Roger of Howden, III, p. 130.
36. Ralph of Diceto, pp. 67, 73.
37. *Gaucelm Faidit*, ed. J. Mouzat, *Les Poèmes de Gaucelm Faidit, troubadour du XIIe Siècle* (Paris, 1965), no. 52, pp. 436ff. (French translation on p. 444) and no. 54, strophe V, pp. 455ff.
38. Quoted from Richard, J., *L'Esprit de la Croisade* (Paris, 1969), p. 69.
39. Bernard of Clairvaux, *De Laude Novae Militiae*, §4, p. 58 (based on the French translation in Richard, *L'Esprit de la Croisade*, p. 141).
40. 'Debet enim plane, nisi nomen gestat inane/contra gentiles pugnare deicola miles': Marbod of Rennes, *Carmina Varia*, col. 1672.
41. Rigord, §81, p. 116.
42. Ambroise, lines 7360ff.
43. Ambroise, lines 10652ff.
44. Ambroise, lines 12224ff. (p. 192 of Ailes translation).
45. Ralph of Coggeshall, pp. 52–7.
46. See on this point the pioneering and still useful research of P. Rousset, 'Justice Immanente'; Rousset, P., 'Un Problème de Méthodologie: l'Evénement et sa Perception', in *Mélanges R. Crozet*, pp. 315–21.
47. Micha, A., 'Une Source Latine du Roman des Ailes', *Revue du Moyen Age Latin*, 1 (1945), p. 305.
48. Houdenc, Raoul de, *Le Roman des Eles*, ed. K. Busby, in *Raoul de Houdenc: Le Roman des Eles; the Anonymous Ordene de Chevalerie* (Amsterdam–Philadelphia, 1983).
49. Ambroise, lines 4572ff.

14

Chivalric Prowess

⚭

A MILITARISED ARISTOCRATIC SOCIETY

The prime function of the knight was to fight. It should come as no surprise, therefore, to find that in the majority of literary works of the Middle Ages, the qualities singled out for praise are those expected of any soldier: bravery and physical and moral courage. These purely military virtues were adopted, in a sense appropriated, by the aristocracy when its members began to see themselves as warriors, though at a level appropriate for them, that is, as leaders, rulers and masters.

Yet this development was not an obvious one and it is not found in all societies. It reveals the emergence of a common mentality in a specific society, that of the aristocracy in the West, where, once the social structures generally designated by the useful but inappropriate term 'feudalism'[1] had been put in place, it was precisely these warlike qualities that were valued. They had become necessary in a militarised society where the focus of political, administrative, judicial and even economic power was the castle, and where authority was exercised at the local level by the castellans and maintained by their warriors, their *milites*, at once the defenders, protectors and sometimes oppressors of the unarmed population.

The distant Germanic origins of this value system are not in doubt. It is already briefly described in Tacitus; as a good Roman, respectful of social rank and the civil hierarchy, he was surprised to find that these 'barbarian' peoples honoured almost exclusively warlike virtues, and even more surprised to find that, in battle, their leader vied in daring with his companions, who were totally devoted to him and regarded it as a disgrace not to fight as bravely as he.[2] It is now generally accepted among historians that this sense of fellowship, this personal devotion and this cult of warrior might at the heart of the Germanic *comitatus* were transmitted to medieval society in the West. They provided it with its foundation and its value system, even if somewhat modified and toned down, thanks in part to the influence of the Church. But Franco Cardini is right

to emphasise that 'there was no hiatus between the Germanic warrior and the medieval knight: only a cultural leap'.[3]

It can be argued that the high regard for these virtues already present in the Merovingian and Carolingian world was even accentuated by what was still, not long ago, generally known as the 'mutation' or 'revolution' of the year 1000, but which has more recently divided historians into separate camps; it is a subject on which some, sadly, have lost all sense of proportion, preferring anathema to argument.

This is not the place to take up this debate.[4] All historians, whether 'mutationists' or not, are at least agreed on the increasing role in eleventh-century society of castles and knights: for the 'anti-mutationists', the knights were occupying their 'normal' place in the system of government of the princes to whom they remained overwhelmingly subordinate – in which case they were forces for order; for the 'mutationists', on the contrary, they were at the centre of a veritable political, social and economic revolution, as a result of which the castellanies became largely autonomous, escaping a central power in decline – in which case they act as fomenters of political and social disorder and economic tyranny at the local level. There were, it should be recognised, in any case, significant regional variations, depending on the degree to which the kings or counts were able to maintain their power over the knights; in fact the latter, as John of Salisbury would claim in the middle of the twelfth century, were in any case the mailed fist of princes and indispensable to the imposition of their law.

It is, at all events, from the eleventh century on that these warrior virtues are extolled with the greatest clarity and frequency. Was this a 'revelation' rather than a 'revolution'? Are we simply seeing the effects at this period because Latin culture and writing, while remaining in ecclesiastical hands, were taking more interest in the laity, beginning with princes, surrounded by their *familia*, their kin and their warriors? Or is it because the Church, which was in dire need of knights, was paying greater attention to their values and becoming more amenable to the glorification of these values, both oral and written? It could accept the *chansons de geste*, for example, because they recounted the exploits of Christians against the 'pagans', the infidel Saracens. There is a grain of truth in all these explanations. It remains the case, nevertheless, that these phenomena are in themselves evidence of the ideological advance of the values revered by the lay aristocracy, and that these values were military. Most highly prized, for a variety of reasons which need not detain us here, was 'prowess', the chivalric quality *par excellence*, described in every possible manifestation in epics, *lais*, verse chronicles and romances.

THE EPIC HERO

The *Song of Roland* offers the prototype, at the beginning of the twelfth century, in the person of Roland, a model epic hero, ever ready to draw his blade, eager for the fine blows with the lance or sword that would attract the love of his king,[5] bring him fame and assure him glory by a demonstration of courage beyond the norm (indeed, even beyond all reason, since Roland went so far as to refuse to sound his horn to call for aid, thereby bringing about the defeat and extermination of the Christians in the rearguard he commanded).[6] Why did he act in this way? As has frequently been pointed out, it was not so much in the hope of procuring a martyr's crown as of avoiding incurring the worst accusation of all, that of cowardice, from which it was impossible to recover. Such a disgrace would lead to 'evil songs' being composed, stigmatising not only the coward himself but his family, his kin and his lineage, who would be dishonoured for ever. To avoid this shame, the knights of the epics and romances were, in a sense, condemned to heroism. The expression 'shame culture' has been used to describe this value system, which, by the social and moral pressure it exerted, drove knights to extremes in their quest for telling feats of arms.[7] It still survived at the end of the thirteenth century, if toned down and modified by two centuries of debate. Joinville, for example, reports the anxieties of Erart de Sivry, who had been wounded in the face and lost many of his men at the Battle of Mansourah:

> 'Sir, if you think that neither I nor my heirs will be blamed for it, I will go and seek assistance from the Count of Anjou, whom I see over there in the fields.' And I said to him: 'My lord Everard, it seems to me that you will do yourself a great honour if you go to seek aid to save our lives, for your own is also in danger' . . . he asked the advice of all our knights that were there, and all gave him the same advice as I had done.[8]

This fear of dishonour sometimes went with a formalistic respect for a personal commitment, a vow made to God, as in the case of Vivien in the *Chanson de Guillaume*, who has sworn an oath never to retreat so much as a foot before the Saracens on the battlefield. Like most epics, this same song contrasts the fearless behaviour of a hero beyond reproach with the cowardice of the anti-heroes. Thibaut of Bourges, for example, with his sidekick Esturmi, follow their bragging before the battle with cowardice as it approaches, shameful desertion on the battlefield itself and the abandonment of their comrades, thereby exposed to even greater danger, adding to the moral stain of their own fear the physical sullying it produces.[9] Here, through literary variations on the theme of the hero in

battle, we come to the nub of the problem of chivalry. Yet what is at issue, it should be emphasised, is no more than the first duty of the soldier in every army in the world: not to flee in battle, not to desert the battlefield, not to 'break ranks' without having received the order and not to abandon one's comrades. This is central to all rules of war and the major element in all military codes, and not a quality specific to chivalry.

Yet knights, precisely because it was so much easier for them to flee than for the infantry, were more tempted to do so and more strongly obliged to respect this same rule. Around 1130 Orderic Vitalis tells of an episode in which both aspects are combined. He describes the inordinate and imprudent desire for prowess of a young knight, Waleran de Meulan, at the Battle of Bourgtheroulde, in 1124. Against the advice of Amaury de Montfort, the young Waleran, eager for a feat of arms that would make his name,[10] wanted to attack on foot the enemy troops, ranged in a defensive position. He almost felt he had already defeated them. But Amaury warned him off; the enemy knights had dismounted, he pointed out, so they were intending to fight to the death; a knight who made himself a foot soldier would not 'fly from the field' but 'either die or conquer'.[11] But there were others who despised these enemies proposing to fight like vulgar infantrymen, dismissing them as a ragbag of 'country bumpkins' and servants, incapable by definition of offering a convincing opposition to the flower of the French and Norman chivalry.[12] So Waleran went into battle first, with a band of forty knights. But he lost his horse, killed under him by an arrow, and others suffered the same fate even before they had been able to charge. Waleran, with eighty knights, was taken prisoner and the majority of his comrades took flight.

In 1141, at the battle of Lincoln, many knights, including nobles of high rank whose names are recorded by Orderic, succumbed to panic and fled. However, King Stephen and his enemy Ranulf of Chester dismounted to do battle alongside their foot soldiers, reassuring them by this demonstration of their determination to fight to the end.[13]

History records numerous examples of the whole-scale flight of knights, abandoning their infantry to a total rout and almost certain death. Richard of Devizes describes the strict rules applicable in such cases, and the punishments awaiting the guilty: loss of their baldric (and thus of their 'estate') in the case of the mounted soldier, amputation of a foot for the foot soldier.[14]

The desertion of a standard bearer was even more serious, as it could give the mistaken impression of an order to withdraw or of a defeat, so causing a general flight and the loss of a battle. William of Newburgh tells of the misfortune suffered by Henry of Essex, standard bearer of

Henry II, during a battle fought in Wales. Thinking, mistakenly, that the King had been killed, he lowered the standard that was the rallying sign and took flight, spreading the false news of the King's death. Consequently, he was accused of treason by Robert de Montfort, challenged to a judicial duel and, having been defeated in single combat, found guilty and condemned to death. His punishment was commuted by Henry II himself, but he was forced to enter a monastery, there to end his days, all his possessions confiscated.[15] Yet his offence had not been deliberate cowardice, simply an error of judgement.

The flight, or more accurately withdrawal, of Stephen of Blois at Antioch during the First Crusade, is well known, when he may well have felt that the situation of the crusaders was hopeless, surrounded by the huge Muslim army of Karbuqa which he found besieging Antioch. Stephen left the town for a while for medical reasons, but his defection was viewed so badly that it was said that he had deliberately simulated the illness to get away from the army and prepare his desertion. His 'cowardice' was widely vilified and his wife, Adela, a descendant of William the Conqueror, could not bear the disgrace. A worthy heiress of her grandfather, she made it plain to her husband, himself too wise to be a hero, that it was his duty to return to the Holy Land to erase the stain. Stephen joined the second expedition of 1101; this time he suffered a glorious death, and so was rehabilitated.[16]

It was not, therefore, unthinkable for knights to flee, and it may be for this very reason that flight was so strongly condemned in the chivalric ethos, and why epics made their heroes noble knights immune to fear.[17] It may also be why writers are almost unanimous in celebrating the prowess and the courage of the Western knights while criticising the pusillanimity, even cowardice, of Eastern warriors, in particular the Greeks. Geoffrey Malaterra, at the end of the eleventh century, Geoffrey of Monmouth, forty years later, and the chroniclers of Richard's reign at the end of the twelfth century invariably describe them as an effeminate people, unsuited to war, cowardly and given to treachery and flight.[18]

Was this much-lauded valour of the Frankish knights a reality? Why was there such emphasis on this virtue and what is its significance when it is attributed to the 'great'? Philippe Contamine has justly observed that even the most cursory examination of the epics, chronicles, biographies, romances and other narrative sources

> leads to the conclusion that courage was conceived above all as an aristocratic, noble form of behaviour, linked to race, blood and lineage, and as an individual trait arising from ambition and the desire for temporal goods, honour, glory and posthumous renown.

It was vital to avoid the shame that would be brought down on oneself and one's family by pusillanimity, sloth or cowardice.[19]

THE INDIVIDUAL IN THE CROWD

The insistence on individual prowess, Contamine goes on, can give the impression that medieval warfare consisted of a series of duels; the reality was very different. We know, thanks most recently to the work of J. F. Verbruggen, that the medieval cavalry was primarily effective because of its cohesion:[20] the knights were grouped into *conrois*, in serried ranks, to charge in a body in which there was little opportunity for individual initiative but in which the military tactics were considerably more elaborate than used to be thought. In these conditions, the solidarity of the unit was the prime virtue. It was acquired in training and tournaments and cemented by class consciousness and the desire for booty. Further, since the individual counted for less in reality than the literary sources suggest, fear and courage need to be reinterpreted in the light of this criterion of cohesion. What the knights feared most of all was being deprived of the protection of this sort of anonymous collective body, of no longer being fused into the compact mass of cavalry, whose power, speed, defensive weaponry and solidarity assured them almost total protection. Their overriding fear was of being separated from the mass, of being captured and unseated, and falling into the hands of the enemy infantry who, caring little for the 'chivalric code', would not hesitate to kill them.

This picture, though its overall validity is not in doubt, needs some qualification. First, the individual-group opposition should not be pushed too far. Medieval battles were for too long described almost exclusively on the basis of the documents which describe them most often and best: the *chansons de geste* and romances. These literary works inevitably put the emphasis on the individual action of their heroes, which made it easier for them to paint a physical and moral portrait of them to which their readers or hearers could relate; in this way they responded to the expectations of their audience while at the same time assuring their own success. The cavalry charge, even in chivalric warfare, was indisputably collective, and medieval battles were not a series of duels between knights. Indeed, battles were rare and sieges and raids designed for pillage and destruction were far more common. Further, even in the relatively rare battles or simply clashes, it was not always the cavalry that played the most important role. This was only the case in stories, which concentrate on the elite warriors, the warrior aristocracy, the cavalry and even more, within it, on individuals, particularly the great men, the lords and princes.

Conversely, however, it may also be observed that if the narrative sources put so much emphasis on the personal action of certain knights, usually, though not always, lords of high rank, it is because it was believed that such action was, or at least could be, truly important and decisive. If, in reality, some knights were vilified for their lack of courage and others praised for their valour (as was the case), it is because the conduct and military virtues of individuals were identifiable in the throng, in spite of the collective nature of the activity. Further, even in the compact charge, the individual did not disappear entirely, any more than he or she disappears in team sports today. Victory, it is true, was generally the result not of the sum of individual actions but rather of the subordination of self and the unity of all, in joint, collective action. But it remains true that a team composed of brilliant individuals has every chance of defeating a bunch of mediocrities, even if the latter are a more cohesive group (though it is unclear why the mediocrity of its members should increase the likelihood of its cohesion). In a collective charge, lastly, however massive (which it had to be, let us repeat, to achieve maximum effect), each knight saw himself as confronting a single opponent. In the enemy mass, at the moment of impact, it was another individual he faced and, in the ensuing mêlée, it was one enemy at a time that he tried to kill with his lance or sword. The vital necessity of initial cohesion in no way detracted from the individual valour of each of the knights comprising the group.

In other words, personal worth, the valour and the prowess of each individual, as long as not employed against the common interest (and this was what was most important), contributed to the common victory and so played a fundamental role.

Real life provides proof. In the mêlées that were tournaments, as in the wartime encounters to which they can still be compared in the age of Richard I, the combatants, at the conclusion of the general encounter, had no difficulty in distinguishing the respective merits of each of the warriors who had taken part, and chose from among them those who had shown most valour. They 'carried off the prize', in tournaments as in the real fighting of wars; they were called 'good knights'. This was still the case in the time of Louis IX, as Joinville reveals; he knew the names of several great men who had shown themselves cowards in battle, but chose not to divulge them so as not to besmirch their memory, since they were now dead.[21] Equally, there were certain knights who, from a desire for personal glory, showed no respect for discipline and wanted to charge too early, so as to be in the forefront of the battle and strike the first blow, then a coveted and urgently sought-after honour.

This evidence from real life should warn us against too systematic an opposition between the individual and the group. The valour of each single knight was valuable to the knights as a body; it was praised, consequently, if it was employed in the common interest and criticised, though often discreetly, if it might harm it. This can be seen in the Rule regulating the knights of the Temple, whose exemplary cohesion and discipline were almost universally admired, despite a few dangerous breaches on the part of some of them. It emerges not only that cowardice was strongly condemned, but that an excess of prowess was punished with equal severity. The brother who abandoned the battlefield to save his life (flight 'from fear of the Saracens') was permanently excluded from the order ('loss of the house'); he who charged or broke ranks without authorisation was temporarily excluded ('loss of the habit'); if he was a standard bearer, he was put in irons and lost his post. One departure from this rule might on occasion be acceptable: if a knight saw a Christian in danger of death because he had 'become isolated through his rashness', he might obey his conscience and go to his rescue; this was permissible, but he must immediately afterwards resume his place in the ranks.[22]

This was a dispensation in the statutes of the Knights Templar. 'Ordinary' knights, in contrast, regarded the duty of assistance to a comrade in peril as paramount. Not to do this was shameful. During Richard I's crusade, in 1191, at the battle of Arsuf, the count of Dreux was heavily criticised for failing in this duty. Conversely, Ambroise records a failure of discipline on the part of the Hospitallers during this same battle: Richard gave the order to bear patiently the harassment and provocation of the Saracens, but the Hospitallers balked at what they saw as an act of cowardice and eventually charged without having received the order:

> My lords, let us charge them! We are being taken for cowards! Such shame has never been seen, nor was our army ever put under such reproach by the infidel![23]

On another occasion, in June 1192, during the Turkish attack on the Christian camp at Beit-Nuba, a Hospitaller knight, Robert de Bruges, recklessly went ahead of his order's standard; charging a Turk, he ran him through with his lance. The Master of the Hospital wanted to punish him for this breach of discipline, but the nobles, the 'grandees', interceded on his behalf, requesting that he be pardoned because of his valour.[24]

Nor was praise of 'gratuitous' prowess or of an unconditional refusal to abandon the battlefield whatever the circumstances, in imitation of Roland or Vivien, automatic, even in the epics of the twelfth century. At

a quite early date the whole question was posed of the honourable withdrawal when all resistance was futile and insane and when it made more
sense, in the general interest, to save one's life and keep open the possibility of a future victory designed to avenge what had become an
inevitable defeat, or for some other equally valid reason. This is the case
in the *Chanson de Guillaume*, for example, when the epic hero, sole survivor of a massive Saracen attack, decides to make his way home by crossing the enemy lines disguised as an infidel so that he can tell his wife
Guibourc of the death of his nephews, assemble new troops to go in
search of their bodies and, hopefully, avenge their death. On numerous
occasions, the poet is careful to spell out that, in abandoning the battlefield to the pagans, William does not flee, but withdraws. It is a further
indication of the emergence of a new problematic which, distancing itself
a little from the act itself, began to switch the emphasis onto its motives,
which might alter its moral character. These new elements played a part
in the gradual formation of a chivalric ethic.[25]

THE 'BEST KNIGHTS IN THE WORLD'

Another necessary qualification concerns fear. It seems to me unhelpful,
in this case, to oppose the epic and romance heroes who are immune to
fear and real-life knights who must, in contrast, have frequently been terrified. The regularity with which literary works insist on the prowess of
their heroes, men capable of confronting more numerous and more
powerful enemies, at risk to their lives, and of fighting, sometimes to the
death, though more often to victory, undoubtedly emphasised an ideal,
desirable, if impossible to achieve in its full intensity and perfection; but
it also offered a model, and it was not something wholly unknown or
alien to the personal experience of real knights. It simply surpassed them,
through hypertrophy or sublimation, not because they were immune to
fear (in which case they would have been extraterrestrials), but because
they were capable of overcoming it and of acting in spite of it. A few
special cases apart, comical by their very unreality (Rainouart, for
example, possessed of Herculean strength, capable of overwhelming and
slaughtering a whole squadron while armed only with his *tinel*, a massive
beam so heavy that the combined efforts of many men were not enough
to lift it), epic heroes operate in the habitual world of the knights whose
feelings and fears they express. Their values are similar; only their scale is
different, and their intensity far greater.

   For this reason, the epic, despite its propensity to hyperbole and cari-
cature (and perhaps thanks to them), retains a level of realism which

tends to get lost in the romances. In the latter we are rather in a dream world, one of fairies, charms and philtres, of magicians and talismans, of covenants and secrets, where on the strength of a word or a silence, a formula, a vow or a challenge, one enters a different world, a looking-glass world, where one becomes effective or, on the contrary, ineffectual. In the *chansons de geste*, the heroes are superhuman because they surpass themselves without ceasing to be men; they feel the same anguish and the same fears and cultivate the same virtues. And it is precisely by their total fidelity to these values (which are thereby exalted) that they manage to conquer their fear, and so become plausible models for the knights of real life.[26]

And models they were: at the battle of Hastings, in 1066, a jongleur urged on the Norman warriors about to face Harold's army by singing of the exploits of Roland at Roncevaux;[27] during the First Crusade, before 1100, the prowess of the valiant knights was likened to that of Roland and Oliver; so, a few decades later, were the brave deeds of Richard the Lionheart. The model was present in the collective memory, a spur to imitation and sublimation.

Was this all in an imagined world? Or was it, at least in part, reality? The eleventh- and twelfth-century descriptions of knightly exploits themselves tend to a certain bombast. But they laud the same types of behaviour and so testify to a veritable osmosis between the world of epic heroes and that of knights, who, in any case, enjoyed the *chansons de geste* all the more precisely because they could imagine themselves as characters in them and be inspired by them.

The exaltation of valour and courage, even of daring and fearlessness, was not taken to the same lengths, clearly, in the Latin sources, more imbued with Christian religiosity. It became widespread, nevertheless, in the chronicles of the eleventh and even more the twelfth century. More significant still, princes and kings are increasingly often represented in them as knights, and not only as war leaders or strategists. They mingled with the combatants, exhorting them to fight bravely by word and example.

The case of William the Conqueror has already been mentioned. His panegyrist, William of Poitiers, begins the story of his reign by depicting him as a knight who, in arms since his accession to ducal power, soon made his neighbours tremble. At the Battle of Hastings, he portrays William in the middle of his soldiers, as does the Bayeux Tapestry which follows his text, using the same weapons as them, and claims he was more formidable with the broken shaft of his lance than those brandishing long javelins; he claims that William was in all things superior to Caesar because he was both *dux* (general) and *miles* (warrior). During

another engagement, at the siege of Domfront (about 1050), William sent young noble scouts to Geoffrey Martel to sound out his plans; Geoffrey made it known through his heralds that he would next morning be 'wakening William's sentries'; he stuck out his chest, determined to show that he was not in the least afraid at the prospect of a personal confrontation: 'he made it known in advance which would be his horse, his shield and his arms in the battle'; he could then be recognised and confronted, in a sort of single combat in the very middle of the mêlée.[28]

The aristocracy adopted chivalry, or at least its values, at this period. Princes no longer disdained to refer to themselves as *milites* and had themselves depicted as knights on their coins and their tombs, like Geoffrey Plantagenet, as we have already noted, on his enamel funerary plaque (now in Le Mans). They adopted this same image for their seals, like many lords in the eleventh century, and like Richard himself in the twelfth. They wanted to be seen sword in hand, but this was no longer the sword of justice, with which they sat in majesty, but the sword of the mounted warrior, or the lance embellished with a banner, revealing the pride they felt in fighting as knights.

From this point, it is clear that these leaders felt bound to possess the same virtues of courage as those under their command. If necessary, these virtues would be ascribed to them by the chroniclers employed to sing their praises, who sometimes compared them to the 'best knights in the world'. This is the title given by Ambroise to Richard I, but William Marshal had already prided himself on it in the reign of Henry II, and Gislebert de Mons had used it of Gilles de Chin, in about 1137, on account of his reputation for prowess and largesse, won in tournaments and war; once, in Outremer, he had killed a lion, not with arrows but armed only with a lance and a shield, a true knight indeed.[29]

The obsessive fear of the censure directed against the pusillanimous and besmirching their whole lineage with cowardice must have acted as a stimulus to the warlike ardour of knights. Another spur was the favour of ladies, at least if we are to believe the texts of all types which habitually associate love and prowess, in the ideal as well as in the real world. According to the chronicler Lambert of Ardres, Arnoul of Guisnes, in 1084, succeeded in winning the hand of the daughter of Baldwin of Alost through his exploits in tournaments, tales of which had reached and deeply impressed him. A century later, his namesake, knighted by his father in 1181, assiduously frequented jousts and tournaments and, thanks to his exploits, won the love of Ida of Boulogne.[30] History provides many such examples, and literature even more. The theme of the poor knight whose victorious sword won him the love and the hand of

a young lady of high rank features prominently in them, and undoubtedly sustained the dreams, fantasies, hopes and valour of knights of modest rank, sons of impoverished families or landless younger sons. For Bertran de Born, as for William IX of Aquitaine before him, a lady would only grant her favours to a knight who had demonstrated his prowess, largesse and courtesy. Provocative as ever, Bertran went so far as to claim that the lady, by taking such a lover, would obtain the remission of all her sins:

> Love wants a knightly lover, good with his weapons and generous in serving, sweet-tongued and a great giver, who knows what is right to do and say, outdoors or in, for a man of his potency. He should be amusing company, courtly and pleasing. A lady who lies with a stud like that is clean of all her sins.[31]

There are many examples of this connection between love and chivalry in the romances contemporary with Richard the Lionheart.[32] Chrétien de Troyes himself enunciated the principle already laid down by Richard's maternal ancestor, the troubadour prince, William IX of Aquitaine: a lady worthy of the name would grant her love and her favours only to a valiant knight. Thus, to deserve the love of the object of his affections, the daughter of his lord (who would never otherwise grant her love), the squire Melians de Lis must get himself knighted and demonstrate his valour in a tournament organised by his beloved's father. She herself explains the two reasons for this: by performing his exploits the knight will prove his love and show 'what price he put on her', while his warlike valour will demonstrate that he deserves her.[33]

This second reason is open to different interpretations. The first complements the notion we have just discussed: valour kindled love in the hearts of young ladies. This was also argued by the supporters of the knights in their debate with the clergy on this subject. The second interpretation is more utilitarian: warlike valour was necessary to assure the protection of the lady and her lands, that is, the estate she brought her husband by granting him her hand.[34] It was sometimes necessary to put this valour to the test, because the praise heaped on prowess might turn some knights into braggarts, or at any rate lead them to exaggerate their merits.

In Richard's day, the romance-writer Gautier d'Arras reveals how widespread this idea had become when, in his *Eracles*, he criticises those ladies who prefer the chattering of the clever talker to the sobriety of the good knight. Such an attitude, he says, makes knights into jongleurs, because each tries to be whatever is pleasing to his beloved. Ladies, therefore, had a responsibility to be attentive to the true chivalric virtues, promote them and so elevate and improve the knight.[35]

We find the same idea in Geoffrey of Monmouth, repeated by Wace, in the founding text of Arthurian legend and ideology. Here prowess is associated with another value fundamental to the chivalric ethic, even though of aristocratic rather than military origin: largesse. At Arthur's court, it is linked to prowess in the person of the King himself, who is consequently surrounded by the best knights in the world. At his court, no proper lady would dream of granting her love to a knight who had not 'proved' himself three times in battle. This moral rule, says Geoffrey, had a twofold advantage: the ladies 'became chaste and the knights more noble, as they were spurred on to excel themselves for love of the ladies'.[36]

The interest of ladies in the exploits of knights emerges in many ways, including their increasingly frequent presence at tournaments. In the time of Richard I, these were still for the most part codified wars taking place in an open space, not in an enclosure fitted out with stands and lists. This did not mean that ladies were absent, and literature, like iconography, especially after the end of the twelfth century, shows them at the top of castle towers or on town walls. It was often they who awarded the knight deemed the best fighter the prize which marked his victory and assured him praise and glory.

Chrétien de Troyes was the first to try and solve in his romances some of the many problems posed by the relationship between love and chivalry, and to try to give the latter a more elevated ideal than simply the quest for warlike feats.[37] In *Erec et Enide*, for example, he portrays the conflict which could make love inimical to prowess, when the complete satisfaction of love within marriage led a lord into *recreance*, that is, made him abandon the perpetual quest for exploits necessary to maintain his renown as a knight. William Marshal confined himself to saying, in connection with Young King Henry, bored by an England lacking both wars and tournaments, that too long a period of inactivity brought shame on young nobles:

> For know well, this is the heart of it,
> Idleness shames a young man.[38]

Chrétien de Troyes spells out the reasons for the inactivity of his hero, Erec: his conjugal felicity made him forget to practise his 'chivalry', by which we should understand his warrior valour.[39] He did not neglect largesse, as this great lord continued to 'retain' knights, that is, support them, shower them with gifts and provide them with both necessities and little extras, so that they could maintain their rank and take part in tournaments. But he himself, too absorbed in the happiness and pleasures of

the love he enjoyed with his wife, Enide, neglected tournaments. This hedonistic behaviour was frowned on, and rumours of his newfound pusillanimity began to circulate. The champion was on the downward slope! Was conjugal love, therefore, an obstacle to the indispensable chivalric valour? Unlike most romance writers, Chrétien de Troyes tried to show that this was not the case, and to rehabilitate love within marriage. Marie de France, during the same period, adopted an even more original standpoint, making the feeling that I have elsewhere called 'true love' the driving force of all noble and worthy action; the fact that this love might evaporate in the context of marriage, or even outside it, mattered little in her eyes, since the social conventions sometimes made marriage the enemy of true love, the one value underpinning all else. Chivalry and marriage did not always make good bedfellows, but chivalry and 'true love', on the other hand, should go hand in hand.[40]

The problem is resolved in an extremely subversive manner by the French adaptors of the Celtic legends relating to Tristan and Iseult.[41] They laid the foundations of a chivalric love that incites to valour by the omnipotence of love, usually adulterous, for social and psychological reasons to which we will return. Chrétien de Troyes himself seems to have worked this seam, though in an original way, in his romance *The Knight of the Cart*. Here, the adulterous love of the hero for Queen Guinevere leads him into every sort of exploit but also into every sort of submission, even every sort of shame, accepting dishonour, in defiance of the specifically chivalric values, a sense of honour and a concern for reputation. At the explicit request of the Queen, and for no other reason than to please her, he agrees to say goodbye to his reputation and all hope of prowess by promising to fight as badly as possible, at risk to his life. The Arthurian romances elaborated further on the theme of the adulterous love that incites to valour, and this provoked an ecclesiastically inspired poetic reaction; it is perhaps already hinted at in the unfinished *Conte du Graal* of Chrétien de Troyes, who tried to spiritualise the themes of the Arthurian quest and the person of its principal characters.[42]

In spite of this reaction, it is the association between prowess and adulterous love that prevailed at the time of Richard I. At the beginning of the thirteenth century, Gervase of Tilbury deplored such morals, which he regarded as perverse; to condemn adultery, he held up as an example to the young nobles, who delighted in amorous jousts and fine feats of arms, the fidelity of swans; it was an age, he said, when 'debauchery attracts praise, adultery is a sure sign of the valiant knight, and the favours extorted furtively from the ladies or demoiselles stimulate the ardour of an eminent nobility'.[43]

Richard the Lionheart, at the courts of Henry II and of Eleanor of Aquitaine, would certainly have come into contact with these issues, if not with the poets and jongleurs who explained the ideas. Like the knights of his day, he cultivated the values lauded by epics, romances and the majority of the works intended for the laity and produced by authors whose mental attitudes they shared.

NOTES

1. The term is incorrect in that it puts the emphasis on the fief (*feodum*), which is only one of the elements on which relations between men were then based; it was probably neither the first nor the principal element. The terms recently used by specialists in the social and economic history of the period (*incastellamento, encellulement, châtellenisation*) are more precise, undeniably, but too technical, hardly elegant and not very evocative.
2. Tacitus, *Germania*, cc. 13–14.
3. Cardini, *Alle Radici della Cavalleria Medievale*.
4. Flori, *La Chevalerie*, pp. 45ff., 73ff.
5. 'For such blows the Emperor loves us': *Song of Roland*, line 1376 (p. 73 of Penguin edn, trans. Glyn S. Burgess, Penguin Books: Harmondsworth, 1990). See also lines 1013ff., 1053ff.
6. The question of Roland's 'desmesure' has provoked a notably immoderate debate. See, among others, Foulet, 'Is Roland Guilty of Desmesure?'; Burger, A., 'Les Deux Scènes du Cor dans la Chanson de Roland', in *Technique Littéraire des Chansons de Geste*, pp. 105ff.; Renoir, 'Roland's Lament'; Guiette, R., 'Les Deux Scènes du Cor dans la Chanson de Roland et les Conquêtes de Charlemagne', *Le Moyen Age*, 69 (1963), pp. 845ff.; Le Gentil, 'A Propos de la Démesure de Roland'.
7. Jones, *Ethos of the Song of Roland*.
8. Joinville, *Vie de Saint Louis*, §226, p. 111.
9. *La Chanson de Guillaume*, ed. and trans. P. E. Bennett (London, 2000).
10. Waleran was 'adolescens militiae cupidus'; Marjorie Chibnall translates *militia* more directly as 'knighthood' ('anxious to prove his knighthood'): *Orderic Vitalis*, ed. Chibnall, vol. 6, p. 350.
11. Ibid., p. 350: 'Bellicosus eques iam cum suis pedes factus non fugiet, sed morietur aut vincet'. It should be noted that here Orderic uses the word *eques* and not *milites*.
12. Ibid., p. 350: 'hos pagenses et gregarios'. According to P. Guilhiermoz (*Essai sur l'Origine de la Noblesse en France au Moyen Age* (Paris, 1902), p. 340) the expression was a contemptuous reference to knights of very lowly status. According to R. A. Brown ('The Status of the Norman Knight', in Gillingham and Holt, *War and Government*, p. 24) it was simply an insult without precise social implications. To me it suggests the plausible existence

of just such a category of knights, as opposed to the 'flower of chivalry' ('Ecce militaris flos totius Galliae et Normanniae hic consistit').

13. *Orderic Vitalis*, ed. Chibnall, vol. 6, p. 542.

14. Richard of Devizes, pp. 21–2: 'Sit lex seruata sine remedio. Pedes pleno pede fugiens pedem perdat. Miles priuetur cingulo.'

15. William of Newburgh, I, p. 108.

16. J. A., Brundage ('An Errant Crusader: Stephen of Blois', *Traditio*, 16 (1960), pp. 380–95, repr. in Brundage, J. A., *The Crusades, Holy War and Canon Law* (London, 1991)) is harder on Stephen than P. Rousset: 'Etienne de Blois, Fuyard, Croisé, Martyr', *Geneva*, 9 (1963), pp. 163–95. For a re-evaluation of the circumstances of his defection and probable intentions, see Flori, J., *Pierre l'Ermite et la Première Croisade* (Paris, 1999), pp. 360ff.

17. See on this point Benton, 'The Enculturation of a Warrior Class'.

18. Geoffrey Malaterra, *De Rebus Gestiis Rogerii Calabriae et Siciliae Comitis et Roberti Guiscardi Ducis Fratris Eius*, ed. E. Pontieri (Bologna, RIS, V, 1, 1924), I, 10, p. 132; I, 14, p. 15; III, 39, p. 81 etc; Geoffrey of Monmouth, *Historia Regum Britanniae*, §169.

19. Contamine, *War in the Middle Ages*, p. 253.

20. Willard and Southern, *Warfare in Western Europe*.

21. Joinville, *Vie de Saint Louis*, §227.

22. *Règle du Temple*, §§162–3, p. 124; §168, p. 153; §242, p. 157; §243, p. 163.

23. Ambroise, lines 6396ff., 6651 (p. 119 of Ailes translation).

24. Ambroise, line 9905; *Itinerarium*, VI, 51, p. 371.

25. See Flori, 'Le Héros Epique et sa Peur'.

26. For a discussion of the problem of fear, see Barbero, A., 'Il Problema del Coraggio e della Paura nella Cultura Cavalleresca', in *L'Imagine Riflessa*, pp. 193–216.

27. William of Malmesbury, *Gesta Regum Anglorum*, vol. 2, p. 302.

28. William of Poitiers, *passim*, especially pp. 40–1.

29. Gislebert de Mons, *Chronicon Hanoniense*, ed. L. Vanderkindere, in *La Chronique de Gislebert de Mons* (Brussels, 1904), p. 59.

30. Lambert of Ardres, *Chronicon Ghisnense et Ardense*, ed. G. de Godefroy-Menilglaise (Paris, 1855), c. 123; c. 93.

31. 'E domna c'ab aital drut jaç/Es monda de toç sos peçaç', Bertran de Born, ed. Gouiran, strophe VII, p. 742, French translation p. 741 (p. 342 of Paden translation).

32. See on this point Flori, 'Noblesse, Chevalerie et Idéologie Aristocratique en France d'Oïl'.

33. Chrétien de Troyes, *Le Conte du Graal ou le Roman de Perceval*, ed. and trans. C. Méla (Paris, 1990), lines 4856–60.

34. M. Stanesco (*Jeux d'Errance*, pp. 79–80) sees only the former, that is, the glory of arms stirring love.

35. Gautier d'Arras, *Eracles*, ed. G. Raynaud de Lage (Paris, 1976), line 2527.

36. Geoffrey of Monmouth, *Historia Regum Britanniae*, ed. Wright (pp. 137–8 for the Arthurian part); see also E. Faral (ed.), *La Légende Arthurienne* (Paris, 1929); this text was repeated by Wace, *Le Roman de Brut*, lines 10508–20; see also lines 10765–72.
37. Payen, J.-C., 'Les Valeurs Humaines Chez Chrétien de Troyes', in *Mélanges Rita Lejeune*, vol. 2, pp. 1087–1101; Maranini, L., 'Cavalleria e Cavalieri nel Mondo di Chrétien de Troyes', in *Mélanges Jean Frappier*, vol. 2, pp. 731–51.
38. *Guillaume le Maréchal*, lines 2401ff.
39. Chrétien de Troyes, *Erec et Enide*, ed. M. Roques (Paris, 1981); trans. C. W. Carroll in *Chrétien de Troyes. Arthurian Romances*, Penguin Books (1991, repr. 2001).
40. See on this point Flori, 'Mariage, Amour et Courtoisie dans les Lais de Marie de France'; Caluwé, J. de and J. Wathelet-Willem, 'La Conception de l'Amour dans les Lais de Marie de France; Quelques Aspects du Problème', in *Mélanges P. Jonin*, pp. 139–58; Wind, B., 'L'Idéologie Courtoise dans les Lais de Marie de France', in *Mélanges M. Delbouille*, vol. 2, pp. 741–8.
41. See on this point Payen, J.-C., 'Lancelot contre Tristan: la Conjuration d'Un Mythe Subversif (Réflexions sur l'Idéologie Romanesque au Moyen Age)', in *Mélanges Pierre le Gentil*, pp. 617–32; Flori, J., 'Amour et Chevalerie dans le Tristan de Béroul'.
42. For J. Ribard (*Chrétien de Troyes*) this spiritualisation is already present in the first romances of Chrétien de Troyes. Ribard develops this attractive but problematic thesis in his *Du Mythique au Mystique*.
43. Gervase of Tilbury, *Oti Imperiala*; partial edn by Duchesne, A., *Le Livre des Merveilles (Divertissement pour un Empereur, Troisième Partie)* (Paris, 1992), p. 157.

15

The King of England's Prowess

⌒

... I can tell you of my lord for he is the best knight in the world and the best warrior, and he is generous and talented.[1]

In painting this brief portrait of Richard, Ambroise clearly sets out the qualities which characterised his king in his eyes, as in those of the majority of his contemporaries. In his *Estoire*, which is, of course, primarily concerned with the crusade, his main emphasis is on the military virtues of the King of England, his talents as a commander, as a leader of men and a strategist, but most of all as a knight. Among these qualities the most highly ranked by far is prowess. What did Ambroise understand by it? And what precise meaning should we attach to this word?

THE VOCABULARY OF PROWESS

An analysis of the vocabulary Ambroise employs is extremely revealing. The adjective *preux* appears eighty-four times in his *Estoire de la Guerre Sainte*. Its meaning, it should be emphasised, was not exclusively military, since it is several times applied to women in a wholly peaceful context, in particular to Richard's young wife, Berengaria.[2] In a study of this word based on nearly 800 occurrences in a corpus of more than 700,000 lines, half of them in Old French,[3] Théo Venckeler has shown that the word *proz* does not usually refer to courage or bravery in war but rather, in a much more general way, to conduct that was highly regarded and that conformed to the accepted meaning of honour and reputation. Contrary to received opinion, the adjective did not indicate an aspect of character or a physical quality, but rather a social and intellectual one; it expressed the high value put on an attitude or type of behaviour, judged according to the moral criteria then in force. To translate this adjective with total accuracy, it would therefore be necessary to resort to such clumsy expressions as 'careful of one's reputation', 'conscious of one's duty' or 'concerned for perfection'.[4]

The observation is valid. Nevertheless, in the context in which the word is used in the *Estoire* of Ambroise, and in most other accounts in

which military action takes pride of place, the adjective *proz* usually, indirectly but quite clearly, has the meaning of warrior valour, not in itself but in relation to the person whose worth it is in this way intended to emphasise. Its very frequent use in connection with knights performing their function reintroduces by that very fact the strictly military virtues which were specific to knights. In other words, the phrase *proz chevalier* certainly has the primary sense of 'a knight who is respected and worthy of respect', but the qualities which justify this favourable judgement are in this case so obviously military ones that the subsequent and much narrower meaning of the modern French word *preux* ('brave') is reintroduced and predominates. This is the case, most of the time, in Ambroise, when he is speaking of the King of England: *proz* is employed primarily to describe Richard's conduct as a valiant warrior.[5]

The military meaning is even more obvious in the case of the word *proesce*, to indicate the act which merited such praise. Here the word almost always refers to an exploit performed weapon in hand and in circumstances in which individual action could be distinguished, even if the individual so praised was not always as isolated as might appear; as we have seen, he was often at the head of a group of knights of whom he was the leader, but making an active, even telling, contribution. The desire of Ambroise to make Richard a model of valour is more obvious still in this case, since the word *proesce*, which appears thirty-four times in this account, is applied to the King twenty times.

We can go further: the occurrences of *proz* and *proesce* applied to Richard I become increasingly numerous as the story progresses, even when this is scarcely justified by events. This is particularly the case in the very last section,[6] that is, roughly speaking, the last 2,000 lines out of the total of 12,500. This final section records the last three months of Richard's time in the Holy Land, from 4 July to 9 October 1192. This was when the King had already announced his decision to return to England. It is as if Ambroise, conscious of the criticisms being voiced of the crusade and of the very limited success of the expedition, was seeking to defuse them by presenting Richard as an exemplary warrior. There is an obvious intention to achieve the ideological glorification of the King of England, who is invested with the principal virtues of chivalry, a sure sign of the prestige it enjoyed.

AN EXEMPLARY WARRIOR

Ambroise was not alone in emphasising these military virtues in the King of England. The majority of chroniclers refer to them, in which case it

may seem surprising that the knighting of Richard (by the King of France, admittedly, in 1173) is mentioned only briefly, and without comment, by Roger of Howden alone.[7] In connection with the dubbing of Richard's brother Geoffrey by Henry II, in July 1178, Roger notes that all the King of England's sons desired military glory, but that in this sphere, Geoffrey was surpassed by his two brothers:

> He tried all the harder to perform warlike feats because he knew his two brothers, Henry the Young King and Richard Count of Poitou, were more celebrated for their warrior exploits. They all had only one thought in their heads: to outshine the others in arms. They knew that you did not master the art of fighting at the opportune moment if you did not practice it in advance.[8]

Gerald of Wales, too, describes all Henry II's sons as remarkable knights, with the exception of John.[9] Many chroniclers refer to Richard's qualities as a strategist: he 'understood better than anyone else the affairs of war', he knew how to draw up his armies in marching and battle order, organise them into fighting units, allocate their respective roles and so on.[10] With regard to events in Messina, Richard of Devizes observes that the King of England 'knew better than anyone else how to conduct sieges of fortified places and to storm castles'. In building the castle of Mate-Grifons, to dominate and overlook Messina, he gave proof, says the chronicler, of his great military mastery.[11] William of Newburgh, at the time when Richard was preparing to leave for the Holy Land, emphasises, though without approval, that Richard had by then long experience as a warrior, so much so that it was said that he was 'broken and exhausted by the premature and excessive practice of the art of war, to which he had devoted himself to an unreasonable degree since he was a boy'.[12]

Matthew Paris gives as an example of Richard's military valour his successful attack on the castle of Taillebourg, in 1180, when the young Duke of Aquitaine demonstrated his qualities of daring, strategy and prowess during the siege, the initial manoeuvres and the assault itself:

> About the same time, Richard, Duke of Aquitaine and son of King Henry, assembled knights from all parts, in order to avenge the affronts of the arrogant Geoffrey de Rancon, and laid siege to Taillebourg, a stronghold which belonged to this same Geoffrey. It was a most desperate enterprise which none before him had ventured to attempt, because until this time this castle had resisted all attacks. It was in fact surrounded by a triple ditch and a triple enceinte of walls . . . but when the duke, bolder than a lion, came armed into the region, he seized the provisions from the farms, cut down the vines, burned the villages, destroyed and razed every building and finally pitched his camp near the castle. Here he established his engines to break down the walls,

and vigorously attacked the besieged who had not expected anything like it . . . [soon after, the defenders attempted a sortie but Richard repulsed them, acting as a knight] . . . The duke, rapidly arming himself, then set an example to his men, and forced the besieged to turn tail; he pursued them in their retreat and a furious battle began between the two camps, at the gates. There, the combatants were subjected to everything that could be inflicted by horses, lances, swords, bows and crossbows, shields, breastplates, pikes and maces . . . the intrepid Richard rushed into the town, and threw himself into the middle of his enemies, who could find no refuge anywhere.[13]

At Acre, twelve years later, Richard of Devizes shows us the King of England in his role as war leader and strategist: immediately after his arrival, he had the wooden tower that had been built under his super-vision in Sicily (Mate-Grifons) reassembled and re-erected and then himself took charge of the assault; he encouraged the sappers and the men manning the perrieres and exhorted the foot soldiers, running from one to the other, so that, said the chronicler, 'the fine deeds of each ought to be attributed to him'.[14] A little later, at Jaffa, he demonstrated these same qualities once again. He arranged his men in a triangle, tightly wedged together, all on foot because they had lost all their horses, leaving no space through which the enemy could penetrate during the assault. In front of each man he placed a piece of wood to give some protection, and he made them drive their lances into the ground, points turned towards the enemy; when their opponents charged, his men stood firm, grouped solidly together, showing no sign either of retreat or flight, an attitude which greatly discouraged the enemy. Once again, the credit was all due to Richard.[15] Ambroise says that, during this same battle of Jaffa, the King, expecting a Saracen attack, had hidden, beneath the shields and between two warriors, a crossbowman and a second man whose job was to prepare a second bow while his companion fired the first, so allowing the host to resist.[16]

WAR, JOUSTING AND TOURNAMENTS

Richard had gained all this experience on the ground, in the very many conflicts in which, as we have seen, he had fought against his father and sometimes his brothers. Unlike the latter, he seems not to have been an assiduous frequenter of tournaments, although they were hugely popu-lar in his day. They were prohibited in England, but there is no evidence of Richard's presence at any continental gathering of this sort.[17] Where-as Henry the Young King, in his zeal to take part in tournaments, travel-led far and wide throughout the regions bordering the principalities dependent on the kingdom of France, particularly to the north-west, as part of a team of knights led by William Marshal; William had been made responsible for looking after the young king and had often got him out of tight corners. Instructed by such a master, and surrounded by excellent knights, Henry the Young King soon acquired a solid reputation as a tourneyer. In one of his poems, Bertran de Born seems to contrast the behaviour and renown of the two brothers, Richard in war, Henry in tournaments.[18] On the death of the Young King, however, in 1183, he still lavished praise on the warlike qualities of his hero, whom he saw as the 'father of the young', supporter of arms and love, the warrior of the highest merit since Roland; no-one had loved war as much as he or obtained so much glory in this world, but it was above all in jousts that it had been earned:

> Lord, in you there was nothing to change: the whole world had chosen you for the best king who ever bore a shield, and the bravest one and the best knight in a tourney.[19]

In another poem, Bertran de Born is more overtly critical of those lords who preferred tournaments to war:

> As for rich tourneyers, they can never please my heart even though they spend freely, they are such tricksters. A rich man who, to take money, touts tournaments fixed to victimise his own vassals - honour and courage are not for him.[20]

The chroniclers also emphasise this difference in the behaviour of the two princes, both valiant, but in complementary disciplines.[21] Ralph of Diceto tells how the Young Henry had got his father's permission to leave England, where he had grown bored, to spend three years participating in tournaments in France. He did not approve of this behaviour on the part of a young prince, 'putting aside his royal dignity to turn himself into a knight'.[22] Matthew Paris, who based himself on Diceto, is of the same opinion, though he emphasises the glory the Young King acquired in these tournaments, for which he had been congratulated by his father:

> In the year of our lord 1179, the Young Henry, King of England, crossed the sea and passed three years in warlike jousting in France, on which he spent enormous sums. There he put aside the royal majesty, transformed himself totally from king to knight, set his horse prancing into the arena, carried off the prize for various passages of arms and acquired a great reputation wherever he went. Then, as his glory was complete, he returned to his father, and was received by him with honour.[23]

Reading the accounts of the chroniclers, it is impossible to escape the conclusion that Richard was probably not the son of Henry II most renowned for his prowess. He was almost certainly, at least as a knight, outclassed by his older brother Henry, whose eminently chivalric virtues they all emphasised. On the death of the Young King, Robert of Torigny lauded his qualities of largesse and prowess and described him as 'without equal in his military function', and feared by all as a result.[24] Gerald of Wales was particularly lavish in his praise in this regard, calling him the 'splendour, glory, light' of chivalry, worthy of comparison with Julius Caesar in military genius, Hector in valour, Achilles in strength, Augustus in conduct and Paris in beauty. Like Hector, with a weapon in his hand, he was invincible.[25]

It is almost as if, on Henry's death, Richard inherited his brother's chivalric prestige, as if the chroniclers saw it as essential for the designated heir to the throne to be the embodiment of chivalric values; or perhaps even more, as if the knights had chosen the Plantagenet heir as torchbearer for their order. In this, the chroniclers were following in a long tradition which, from Dudo of Saint-Quentin to Benoît de Sainte-Maure, by way of William of Jumièges, William of Poitiers and Wace, had portrayed the dukes of Normandy as valiant knights, in war and in tournaments.[26]

Though not himself participating in them (perhaps because he knew that in this sphere he was inferior to his brother), Richard was not wholly without interest in jousts, but his interest was essentially political and utilitarian. In 1194, as is well known, he authorised the holding of tournaments in his kingdom in certain clearly specified and closely supervised locations, in return for payment of a tax. He came to this decision having realised that their persistent popularity, in spite of the Church's prohibition,[27] was leading knights to leave England for France, where they could indulge in their favourite sport, and that this might encourage assemblies of knights hostile to his policies, in locations far removed from all supervision. This is how William of Newburgh explains his decision:

> Those military practices, that is to say, exercises in arms, which are commonly called tournaments, began to be celebrated in England; and the king, who established them, demanded a small sum of money to be paid by each person who wished to join the sport . . . in the times of the kings before him, and also in the time of Henry II who succeeded Stephen, these knightly exercises were altogether forbidden in England; and those who, perchance, sought glory in arms, and wished to join these sports, crossed over the sea, and practised them at the very ends of the earth. The illustrious King Richard, therefore, considering that the French were more expert in battle, from being more trained and instructed, chose that the knights of his own kingdom should be exercised within his own territory, so that from warlike games they might

previously learn the real art and practice of war, and that the French should not insult the English knights as unskilful and uninstructed.[28]

Diceto, while justifying Richard's decision on many other grounds, nevertheless condemned tournaments, which the Church considered immoral:

> At this period, the king of England ordered that the knights of England, on certain conditions and in return for payment of an appropriate tax, might meet in specified places and in order to exercise their powers in tournaments. He was led to this by this consideration that, if he decided to wage war on the Saracens or against his neighbours, or if the peoples of the neighbouring countries dared to attack him, [his knights] would thereby be better trained, more agile and more valiant in combat.[29]

But he deplored the fact that these assemblies were also occasions for dubious festivities and for displays of wealth, and indulgence in luxury and even lust.[30] They also affected the attitudes of the knights, encouraging them to capture their enemies in order to ransom them, and allowing their victims to amass their own ransom by means of the increasingly common practice of being freed on parole, so 'softening' chivalric customs:

> Wielding light lances certainly makes them more agile, but the luxury of their feasts makes them even more accustomed to foolish expense . . . thus, these young men, eager for glory and not for money, do not cruelly keep in close confinement those they have vanquished in combat, nor do they compel them by refined tortures to pay inordinate ransoms, but they allow those they have captured by right of war to depart freely, simply on the promise that they will return when they are summoned.[31]

Though he appears not to have taken part in official tournaments of this type in France before his departure on crusade, Richard was still appreciative of the glory of victory in warlike exercises. He could not bear, however, to be beaten. This was made very clear during the improvised joust in which he was pitted against William des Barres, in Sicily.[32]

If Richard's surprising and excessive animosity towards William was not due in part to the latter's flight when once, long ago, he had taken him prisoner, it is difficult to see what there was to reproach him for in this joust, other than his refusal to let himself be unseated by the King by means of clinging to the neck of his horse to stop himself falling off, a manoeuvre which had never been regarded as underhand.

The Minstrel of Reims goes further; wrongly locating this joust in the Holy Land (unless he was imagining a continuation of it, in the form of

another quarrel between the two men), he unequivocally makes William des Barres the unquestioned victor in the encounter: a highly skilled knight, he knew how to avoid the charge and grasp his adversary firmly with both arms and unseat him:

> And it happened one day that my lord William of Barres was riding through the middle of Acre, and King Richard also; and they met. And King Richard was holding the broken shaft of a great lance, and he charged William with the intention of unseating him . . . William held himself fast, for he was a proved knight, and as the English king tried to ride by him, he seized him by the neck, and spurred his horse and dragged him by the strength of his arms out of the saddle; and let go of him.[33]

Richard was thrown to the ground and seems to have fainted, while the triumphant William returned to his lodgings. This is almost certainly a fabrication. So what really happened at Messina? It seems likely that Richard was enraged to find that he had almost been thrown to the ground by William, in his first assault, 'because his saddle had slipped', or so Roger of Howden would have us believe.[34] We may take this with a pinch of salt.

According to Roger, the King of England several times suggested replacing a battle with a single combat, in which he, more knight than king, would be the champion, or at least one of the champions. This would imply considerable confidence in his own abilities, if, that is, there had been the slightest possibility of the proposals being accepted by his adversaries. In 1194, for example, during a conflict with Philip Augustus, the King of France, wishing to avoid the bloodshed of a general engagement, proposed to substitute for the battle a single combat between five champions from each camp, the outcome to be accepted as a judgement of God. According to Diceto, Richard first applauded this proposal but then attached a condition to his acceptance: the two kings had to be included among the five champions.[35]

The combat never took place. Why? Many explanations can be suggested. Perhaps Philip feared the superior warlike valour of his rival? Perhaps he feared his hatred even more? Or, more simply, perhaps the King of France, unlike Richard, did not see this as an appropriate role for a king.

Well before the crusade, in spite of his repeated failures and his always doubtful victories, Richard had already acquired a reputation as a warrior as Duke of Aquitaine. Ambroise, in particular, makes a point of this, summarising the feats already accomplished by his hero before his arrival in Acre, in an attempt to explain the enthusiasm of the Christian

population at his coming.[36] Yet Richard had by no means always shone during this period, often achieving success only thanks to the assistance of his father's army, as we have already noted.[37]

Further, there were a couple of episodes which did nothing to enhance his glory. When he was pursuing his father, Henry II, for example, after forcing him to leave Le Mans, Richard was forced to abandon his pursuit when a knight killed his horse with a thrust of his lance. This knight, as we have seen, was William Marshal, who loudly and very probably correctly proclaimed that, had he wanted to, he could have slaughtered his enemy as easily as his horse.[38] On another occasion, during the siege of Châteauroux, in July 1188, Richard was attacked by numerous French knights and thrown from his horse; he was in grave danger until he was saved by, of all people, a butcher.[39] These inglorious episodes apart, the chroniclers provide us with few details of the supposed prowess of the Duke of Aquitaine. It is not unreasonable to wonder why.

It is above all the exploits performed by Richard after his coronation that are lovingly described by the chroniclers. It would be impossible to mention all of them here; I will recall only a few of the most important, mentioned by every chronicler, occurring during important engagements, first in Sicily and then in Cyprus; I will then discuss a few feats of arms performed by the King on his return from captivity. His exploits in the Holy Land, both more numerous and more significant, will be dealt with in the next chapter.

The first example of Richard's 'prowess' was at the expense of his own troops, on 3 October 1190. The inhabitants of Messina, after a few 'ill deeds' committed against the English, had entrenched themselves in their town, after closing its gates. Richard's men were furious and wanted to launch into an assault on the city, but the King, who was anxious to keep the peace, mounted a speedy charger and rode through his army, striking his soldiers right and left, to prevent them reaching the walls.[40] It was only when the insults and acts of violence of the inhabitants continued that Richard eventually decided to act. This is how Ambroise describes his hero's victorious assault:

> The King of England mounted and went there to break up the disturbance, but as he went the people of the town hurled insults after him and reviled him and the king hastened to arm himself and had them attacked from all sides, by sea and by land, for there was not another such warrior anywhere in the world . . . I do not think that he had twenty men with him at the beginning. The Lombards left off their threats as soon as they saw him and turned and fled and the noble king pursued them. Ambroise witnessed this when it

happened, for when they saw the king come they would have reminded you of sheep fleeing the wolf; as the oxen strain against the yoke so did they strain to reach the postern on the Palermo side. He forced them forward, cutting down I do not know how many of them.[41]

Describing the same events, Richard of Devizes tells of the personal action of the King of England, who took part in the battles and marched at the head of his troops behind his much-feared dragon banner; his soldiers followed him, to the sound of trumpets, and entered the town, where they seized Tancred's palace.[42]

No other exploits of Richard in Sicily are described by the chroniclers with the exception of the highly dubious one involving William des Barres, already discussed, in which his conduct was neither measured nor glorious nor chivalrous.

En route between Sicily and Cyprus, Ambroise describes an act of 'prowess' on Richard's part. His account offers another example of the way this word was used. The King, he tells us, was always inclined to good deeds, and this is what he did while at sea:

He had the custom of having on his ship a great candle in a lantern, lit at night. It threw a clear light and burned all through the night to show others the way. He had with him able seamen, worthy men, who knew their work well. All the other ships followed the king's flame keeping it in near view, and if the fleet ever moved away he would willingly wait for them. In this way he led the proud fleet, as the mother hen leads her chicks to food. This was both *proesce* and natural [on his part].[43]

Here 'prowess' has to be understood in the initial sense of an act worthy of high praise; in this case the word has few if any military connotations.

Once on the island, against the Greeks of the 'emperor' Isaac Comnenus, Richard won victories and performed deeds that came closer to what we now call prowess. One such came at the very moment of landing. Richard of Devizes, who describes the Cyprus campaign only very briefly, says that the King leaped fully armed from his galley and struck the first blow in the war. But, he goes on, three thousand men were at his side before he had time to strike the second.[44] Ambroise goes into greater detail on this point. Richard's men, he says, sailors and crossbowmen, had already begun the landing, in the face of baying and arrows from the Greeks, but were struggling; they had already managed, however, to force the Greeks back by the time that Richard leapt from his landing craft, followed by the rest of his men.[45]

Next day, the King flushed out a band of Greeks from an olive grove and pursued them as far as their camp. Isaac's warriors counter-attacked.

With some fifty knights, and ignoring the advice to retreat offered by an overly cautious cleric, who was sharply rebuffed, Richard put them to flight:

> . . . there were not with the king at that time more than forty, or at the most fifty, knights. The noble king, who would wait no longer, rushed upon his enemies, faster than a bolt of lightning, as alert as a hobby going after a lark. (Anyone who saw the attack admired it greatly.) He struck into the press of hostile Greeks, so that they became perforce in disarray, and he so disordered them that they could not remain together.[46]

Other chroniclers enable us to see this exploit in a slightly different perspective. Roger of Howden reports the speech Richard gave to his men before the landing; it is full of expressions like: 'Do not fear them, because they are *inermes* [does this mean without armour, disarmed, or not warriors?], more likely to flee than to fight, whereas we, for our part, are well-armed.' The Greeks who were driven back and conquered by Richard and his men on the beach, he goes on to say, were not, for the most part, warriors; many were unarmed and in his opinion 'unskilled in fighting'.[47] And the victory won the next day by Richard over the camp of the Greek emperor, we learn, took place at night. The King and his knights had made a surprise attack on the Greek camp when their enemies were sleeping; they became rigid with terror, 'as if dead', not knowing what to do. These details, omitted by Ambroise, highlight the King's strategic skill, certainly, but rather diminish the scale of his personal prowess as a warrior. The booty seized in the camp, on the other hand, where the emperor's treasury was found, would certainly have increased his renown among his own men.

Ambroise relates two other anecdotes relating to Richard's battles against Isaac Comnenus. They show the King behaving like any knight of his day. In the first, he emerges as anxious to prove his personal valour in general mêlées, just like the heroes of epics and romances, by personal challenges. After his warriors had landed, all on foot, the Greeks fled before them and before the hail of arrows from the English crossbowmen. Richard and his men followed, still on foot, but the King managed to get hold of a horse that enabled him to catch up with the emperor and challenge him (fruitlessly, of course!) to a single combat:

> Both Greeks and Armenians fled before the brave Latins; they were chased as far as the fields so fiercely that they pressed the emperor, who fled. The king gave pursuit after him until he soon acquired a pack-horse or beast of burden, I do not know which, with a bag strapped to the saddle, and stirrups of thin cord. He leapt from the ground into the saddle and said to the false

and perfidious emperor, 'Emperor, come, joust!' But the emperor did not
fancy jousting.[48]

Are we to believe this obviously 'second-hand' account of Ambroise,
clearly intended to exalt the King's prowess, in which he pursues, alone,
a Greek army in full flight, with the emperor left isolated among the
stragglers? It is surely much more likely that Richard, the only one to
have laid hands on a chance mount, simply made a show of pursuit,
essentially pointless but enough for him to be able to hurl after their
retreating figures a challenge to a joust which the fleeing Greeks (and
even less the emperor) would hardly have been able to hear. In other
words, was it not simply a piece of ritual sabre-rattling?

The second anecdote is very similar, but it also allows us a glimpse of
the seething anger and impatience of knights in marching order, attacked
without warning by an enemy practising the Eastern style of harassment
that consisted of successive waves of horsemen throwing javelins and
shooting arrows; in this situation, knights were always tempted to break
ranks and launch into pursuit, so falling into the trap set by the enemy.
This particular episode happened when the emperor, after his defeat and
the loss of his camp, his treasure and his standard, had fled into the mountains. Richard, we are told, could not pursue him because he did not know
the country. A little later, however, he marched with his men towards
Nicosia. To protect his army's rear, the King stayed at the back. Isaac, who
had laid an ambush, suddenly rushed out, with seven hundred horsemen,
in front of the first contingents of the vanguard, discharging arrows and
javelins; they then rode rapidly along the full length of the marching army,
hurling large numbers of projectiles at its flanks, finally reaching the rearguard, where Richard was. Seeing him, Isaac shot two poisoned arrows,
which greatly angered the King; he broke ranks and set off in pursuit of
the emperor to avenge himself for this insult. According to Ambroise, he
would have been successful if the emperor had not mounted Fauvel, a
horse that was as swift as a stag (and which Richard later seized). It was
then impossible to catch him and the King had to abandon his vengeance
for the time being.[49] This was once again virtual prowess.

Richard's personal exploits in Cyprus were, it seems, strictly limited.
Ambroise was his panegyrist; he made the most of them in an attempt to
endow the King with a warrior's glory on a scale to match the considerable renown he had won by the highly lucrative but relatively easy conquest of the emperor's treasures and of the island itself, which was not
only wealthy but of considerable strategic value, as it gave the Christians
of the West a convenient staging post on the sea route to the Holy Land.

The chroniclers emphasise most of all, obviously, Richard's deeds of arms during his crusade. We will examine these and attempt to assess their ideological significance in the next chapter.

The year 1198 saw a revival of the clashes between the kings of France and England, and this gave rise to many accounts of battles in which Richard won fame as a knight. After losing Courcelles, on 27 September 1198, Philip Augustus fled towards Gisors, followed by Richard and his knights. Here, according to Roger of Howden, 'the king of England felled three knights with a single lance'.[50] What are we to understand by this? Did the King run three knights through simultaneously? This seems implausible. It is more likely, surely, that he brought down these three adversaries, one after the other, with the same lance, before it broke. However that may be, the exploit was notable because the King himself boasted of it in a letter to the Bishop of Durham, in which he named his three unfortunate adversaries; they were not, it emerges, dead, but his prisoners, which would seem to support the second hypothesis.[51]

Richard, as we see, was here making his own propaganda as a 'roi-chevalier', emphasising his personal role, not only at the head of his warriors but in their midst, as one of them; he was by the same title glorifying the chivalry with which he identified and whose values he wished to incarnate; chief among these was prowess in the manner of Roland, Gawain and Lancelot, and surpassing that of King Arthur, whose exploits and chivalry he had probably heard extolled throughout his childhood.

Why was there this insistence on his virtues as a knight? Three explanations may be suggested. Richard may in reality have been a king who behaved like a warrior of exceptional valour; or he may have been seeking, by imitating his literary heroes, to present himself in this light; or, under the influence of this same literature (or at least of the ideology underpinning it), the knights wanted to see him as their standard bearer, and so helped to forge this reputation for him.

It is not impossible that these three elements combined to make of Richard a model knight, the fine flower of chivalry.

NOTES

1. Ambroise, lines 12134ff. (p. 191 of Ailes translation).
2. For the adjective *proz* applied to a woman, see Ambroise, lines 819, 994, 1110, 1140.
3. That is, an average frequency of just over one occurrence per thousand lines. In Ambroise, with 84 occurrences in 12,353 lines, the frequency is 6 times greater, making an analysis of his vocabulary even more significant.

4. Venckeler, T., *Rollant li proz. Contribution à l'Histoire de Quelques Qualifications Laudatives en Français du Moyen Age* (Lille, 1975); Venckeler, T., 'Faux Topos ou Faux Exemple? (Roland, 1093). De l'Interprétation en Sémantique Historique', in *Le Monde des Héros dans la Culture Médiévale*, pp. 309–19.

5. *Proz* is used in sixteen out of the eighty-four instances to describe the King of England, particularly in the last two thousand lines describing events subsequent to his decision to leave the Holy Land (eight out of sixteen). Richard is well ahead of James of Avesnes (four instances) and Andrew de Chauvigny and the Earl of Leicester (three cases each).

6. Eight occurrences of the word *proz* (out of sixteen) and nine of the word *proesce* (out of twenty), used of Richard, come between lines 10,353 and 12,353.

7. Roger of Howden, II, p. 55: 'Eodem anno Lodowicus rex Francorum fecit Ricardum filium Henrici regis Angliae militem.'

8. Ibid., p. 166.

9. Gerald of Wales, *De Principis Instructione*, p. 308.

10. Ambroise, line 6137.

11. Richard of Devizes, pp. 24–5.

12. William of Newburgh, p. 306.

13. Matthew Paris, *Chronica Majora*, II, pp. 315ff.

14. Richard of Devizes, p. 44.

15. Ralph of Coggeshall, pp. 41ff.

16. Ambroise, line 11345. For Richard's skill as a strategist, see Gillingham, J., 'Richard I and the Science of War in the Middle Ages', in Gillingham and Holt, *War and Government*, pp. 78–91, repr. in Gillingham, *Richard Cœur de Lion*, pp. 211–26.

17. For tournaments in England and for English participation in tournaments abroad, see Barker, *Tournament in England*, pp. 9ff., 17ff., 112; Barker, J. R. V., and M. Keen, 'The Medieval English Kings and the Tournament', in Fleckenstein, *Das ritterliche Turnier im Mittelalter*, pp. 212–18; Coss, *The Knight in Medieval England*.

18. Bertran de Born, ed. Gouiran, pp. 11–35, chanson no. 1: envoi, lines 67–71, French trans. on p. 26: 'Sailor, you have honour, and we have changed a lord who was a good warrior for a tourney-goer.' (p. 202 of Paden translation).

19. Ibid., no. 13, pp. 240ff. (p. 220 of Paden translation).

20. Ibid., chanson no. 8, pp. 123ff. (p. 262 of Paden translation).

21. Gerald of Wales, *De Principis Instructione*, III, p. 8; *Expugnatio Hibernica*, p. 198: 'Martiis ille ludis, addictus, hic seriis.'

22. Ralph of Diceto, I, p. 428: '. . . totus est de rege translatus in militem'.

23. Matthew Paris, *Chronica Majora*, II, p. 308.

24. Robert of Torigny: 'In officio militari tantus erat, ut non haberet parem, sed principes et comites et etiam reges eum timerent.'

25. Gerald of Wales, *De Principis Instructione*, p. 174 (p. 23 of translation); *Expugnatio Hibernica*, pp. 193–4: 'Militiae splendor, gloria, lumen, apex.'
26. See on this point Flori, *Essor de la Chevalerie*, pp. 304ff.
27. See on this point Carlson, D., 'Religious Writers and Church Councils on Chivalry', in Chickering and Seiler, *Study of Chivalry*, pp. 141–71; and most of all Barker and Keen, 'Medieval English Kings and the Tournament'; Barker, *The Tournament in England*; Dolcini, C., 'Riflessioni sul Torneo nella Canonistica (sec. XII–XIV)', in *Gioco e Giustizia nell'Italia di Comune*, ed. G. Ortalli (Rome–Trevisa, 1993), pp. 145–8.
28. William of Newburgh, pp. 422ff. (p. 625 of Stevenson translation).
29. Ralph of Diceto, II, p. 120; see also Matthew Paris.
30. For the sins occasioned by tournaments, see the slightly later exposé in Jacques de Vitry, *Exempla*, sermon 141, pp. 62–3 (wrongly given as CLXI); this same text is referred to as 'Sermon 52 Ad potentes et milites' in Le Goff, J., 'Réalités Sociales et Codes Idéologiques au Début du XIIIe Siècle; un *Exemplum* de Jacques de Vitry sur les Tournois', in Le Goff, *Imaginaire Médiéval*, pp. 248–64; Le Goff edited the sermon on the basis of a transcription by M.-C. Gasnault from MS BN lat 17509 and Cambrai BM 534, pp. 11–112.
31. Ralph of Diceto, II, p. 121.
32. See above, pp. 104–5ff.
33. *Ménestrel de Reims*, §§ 57–8.
34. Roger of Howden, III, pp. 393ff.
35. Ralph of Diceto, II, p. 121.
36. Ambroise, lines 9553ff.
37. See pp. 58ff. below.
38. Gerald of Wales, *De Principis Instructione*, pp. 259ff., 283ff.; *Guillaume le Maréchal*, lines 8836ff.
39. Gervase of Canterbury, I, p. 434: 'sed cujusdam beneficio carnificis robusti valde liberatus evasit'; perhaps 'carnifex' should be translated not as 'butcher' but as 'routier'.
40. *Gesta Henrici*, II, pp. 127–9.
41. Ambroise, lines 721ff., French translation p. 343 (pp. 40–1 of Ailes translation).
42. Richard of Devizes, p. 14.
43. Ambroise, line 1185, French translation on p. 349 (p. 48 of Ailes translation, where *proesce* is translated as 'worthy'); H. Legohérel, *Les Plantagenêts* (Paris, 1999), describes Richard as possessing 'astonishing ability as a sailor and as commander of a squadron'.
44. Richard of Devizes, pp. 36–7.
45. Ambroise, line 1485; *Itinerarium*, II, p. 32.
46. Ambroise, lines 1607ff., French translation pp. 352–3 (p. 53 of Ailes translation).

47. 'Pauci illorum erant armati, et fere omnes indocti ad praelium'; Roger of Howden, III, pp. 106–8; *Gesta Henrici*, II, pp. 164ff.
48. Ambroise, lines 1551ff. (p. 53 of Ailes translation).
49. Ambroise, lines 1907ff.
50. 'Ricardus rex Angliae tres milites una lancea prostravit': Roger of Howden, IV, pp. 57–9.
51. 'Nos autem ibi cum una lancea prostravimus Mathaeum de Montemorenci, et Ianum de Rusci, et Fulconem de Gilerval, et captos detinuimus': ibid., p. 58. See also Ralph of Diceto, II, p. 164; Ralph of Coggeshall, p. 83.

16

Prowess in Outremer

In Outremer, even more than in Cyprus, Richard was to be confronted by an enemy cavalry whose fighting techniques had thoroughly disoriented Western knights during the First Crusade. They had become accustomed to using the massive head-on charge followed by the mêlée, that is, fighting at close quarters, in hand-to-hand combat. The Turks, in contrast, were more lightly armed and trusted to speed; they avoided close combat but made good use of ambushes, surprise attacks, simulated flight and, above all, fighting at a distance, using projectiles such as javelins and arrows. These last had been disdained by the Western knights since they had adopted the couched lance, before the end of the eleventh century. The Turkish horsemen used bows even when in flight, twisting round to let fly deadly arrows at the enemy. All the chroniclers of the First Crusade emphasise the strangeness of their tactics and the difficulties they caused the Christians.[1]

Almost a century later, the crusaders of Richard had similar experiences, as observed by Ambroise:

> When the Turk is followed he cannot be reached. Then he is like an annoy-
> ing venomous fly; when chased he flees; turn back and he follows. So did the
> cruel race harass the king; he rode and they fled; he turned back and they fol-
> lowed. At one point they suffered; at another they had the upper hand.[2]

It was in Palestine that Richard performed most of the exploits ascribed to him by those who wrote his history. They are in general agreement that they took place on a few main occasions, which they all emphasise, but to differing degrees, revealing their intentions.

THE CAPTURE OF THE EGYPTIAN SHIP

The first of these exploits, described by all the chroniclers, made a deep impression on the crusaders and greatly enhanced the fame and popularity of the King of England. Richard's fleet, sailing towards Acre, encountered a large Egyptian vessel which was bringing assistance to the city's

citadel, which had been besieged by the Christians for many months. Too
heavy to escape, and not helped, in any case, by a very light wind, the ship
was stormed by Richard's sailors, who sank it after seizing part of its
cargo. This capture, which was, in the last analysis, a fairly routine affair
and not particularly glorious (what chance did one becalmed vessel stand
against a fleet of some fifty speedier galleys?), was the subject of successive embellishments which are themselves of interest.

The French chronicler Rigord, unsurprisingly, gives us the most sober
account. He still speaks, however, of a ship that was 'marvellously armed',
containing flasks of Greek fire, ballistae, bows and other arms, and also
of the very valiant soldiers all killed by the King of England, as the broken
ship foundered. Anxious not to allow too much glory to Richard alone,
he is careful to add that the French seized another ship of Saladin's, near
Tyre, an episode which attracted little attention from other chroniclers.[3]

Ralph of Coggeshall is scarcely more loquacious on the subject and says
nothing about any exploits on Richard's part. He describes a ship that was
loaded with riches and held seven hundred brave young men; attacked and
rammed by the galleys, its hull pierced, it sank and eighty men were taken
alive. Richard's fleet then landed 'joyfully' at Acre.[4] William of Newburgh
is even more laconic; he, too, fails to credit Richard with any role in the
affair and generally makes little of it, mentioning only the fierce defence
of the ship by the Saracens before it sank, its hull pierced.[5]

Ralph of Diceto, too, is fairly brief. According to him, the dromon
was spotted by chance on 6 June 1191. It was carrying 1,500 men, jars
containing Greek fire and snakes that were intended to be thrown into
the Christian camp at Acre. The galleys launched an attack; one of the
rowers swam up to the Egyptian vessel and pierced its hull with a drill,
before returning safe and sound. Before the dromon sank, Richard captured the men; he had 1,300 of them drowned in the sea and kept 200
as prisoners.[6]

Matthew Paris largely repeats this account. He describes the ship,
loaded with riches and carrying 1,500 warriors, surrounded by the
Christian galleys. Richard armed his soldiers and a fierce battle began,
while the ship, becalmed, remained immobile. One of Richard's rowers,
a skilled diver, then swam under water and pierced the hull in several
places; the ship was then captured and Richard had 1,300 men drowned,
keeping only 200 for the sake of their ransoms. Unable to show prowess,
Richard demonstrated his largesse, distributing the foodstuffs among the
famished army in Acre.[7]

Richard of Devizes credits the King of England with a more active role
in the capture of this 'marvellous boat, the largest since Noah'. According

to him, Richard personally entered the fray, and was even in the front rank, because he always enjoyed demonstrating his valour. Bringing his galleys alongside, he was the first to storm the ship, before it sank like lead, for which the chronicler offers no explanation.[8]

Ambroise, naturally, concentrates on the person of Richard and the part he played in the episode, which he describes at length. Richard's role was, nevertheless, modest. According to Ambroise, this great ship, manned by eight hundred Saracens and covered with green felt on one side and yellow on the other, seemed to be the work of fairies, and was seeking to pass as a Genoese vessel (we should note in passing that the text says *engleis* (English), which I have corrected to 'Genoese' following the Latin translation). But one of Richard's sailors recognised it as a Saracen ship and warned the King:

> He said to the king, 'My lord, listen. May I be killed or hanged if this is not a Turkish vessel!' The king said, 'Are you sure of this thing?' 'Yea, sir, certain. Send at once another galley after them, which will not greet their people; see what they do and to what faith they belong.' The king gave his commands; another boat went towards them, but they did not greet them. The enemy having no business with them, began to shoot upon them with Damascus bows and with crossbows. The king was nearby and the people were ready. They attacked them forcefully when they saw them shoot upon our people. The enemy defended themselves very well, shooting and drawing bow against us, arrows raining down like hailstones. On both sides there was general fighting. The ship sailed with but little wind and they often reached it, but did not dare to board, nor could they overcome them. The king swore at that time that he would hang the oarsmen if they relaxed their efforts or if the Turks escaped them. They launched themselves forward, like a storm, dived in [to the water], heads and bodies, passing under the ship, going to and fro [under the ship]. They fastened ropes to the rudder of the ship belonging to the vile and filthy race, in order to dominate and destroy them and bring the ship low. They clambered up and moved forward enough to throw themselves on to the ship.[9]

In spite of this threat, enough to make any sailors and soldiers perform feats of bravery, the King's men were repelled. Richard then ordered the galleys to ram the ship and sink it:

> The Saracens made such efforts that they forced the oarsmen to retire to the galleys to begin the assault again. The king told them that they should ram the boat until it sank. They launched themselves forward, colliding with it so that it gave way in several places; because of these holes the vessel foundered. Then was the battle finished.[10]

Ambroise goes on to emphasise the importance of this prize. The ship, he says, contained eight hundred Turkish warriors, all picked men,

provisions, flasks of Greek fire and two hundred 'dark and ugly' snakes (according to the man who had helped to load them). But for Richard, he concludes, the ship would have re-provisioned the besieged garrison and Acre would never have been taken by the Christians:

> If the ship had arrived at Acre then the city would never have been taken, such means of defence would have been brought. This was the work of God, who cares for his people, and of the good and strong king of England, a keen fighter of battles.[11]

Ambroise does not, we should note, put particular stress on the personal role of the King in this capture, other than as the commander issuing orders. In Roger of Howden, the role played by the King assumes much greater importance. It was he, and not one of the sailors, who unmasked the deception of this Saracen vessel attempting to pass as a vessel of the King of France, whose standard it flew from its masthead, or so its sailors claimed to the messengers sent by the King of England. But Richard was not deceived and replied: 'They lied! The king [of France] has no vessel of this type!'[12] He then gave the order to attack and sink the ship. After the victory, and when most of the Saracens had been drowned, the King acted generously towards his sailors and distributed among them all the goods that had been seized.

One cannot but be struck both by the divergences and the similarities in these various accounts. The former are mostly to do with the identification of the ship and the role of Richard, which was in all probability limited to giving the order to attack, threatening his sailors with harsh punishment if they allowed it to escape and rewarding them with a share of the booty after its capture; in this way he was demonstrating largesse, as was expected of a war leader and even more of a king. On shore, however, the victory was inevitably attributed to this leader, who was accustomed to ride out at the head of his squadrons of knights. From that to making him play a decisive role in what was, when all is said and done, a very unequal naval battle was only a short distance, which some chroniclers travelled, one step at a time.

The glory of the victory, at all events, redounded to his credit and he received a triumphal welcome in Acre. Did the chroniclers exaggerate the importance of this prize? Probably, but it has to be said that the Arab writers, too, loudly lamented this loss. According to Imad ad-Din, however, it was the captain of the Saracen ship who, seeing his vessel immobilised and his sailors defeated, chose to scupper it, sending his vessel to the bottom and his passengers to death by drowning, hence to paradise.[13]

THE SIEGE OF ACRE

The arrival of Richard's fleet was certainly decisive because of the reinforcements in men and provisions it carried, and perhaps even more in the psychological comfort provided by his long-awaited arrival, triumphal entry and immediate largesse. All this is undeniable. Some chroniclers, in particular Ambroise, add some personal exploits. They emphasise, for example, Richard's skill in sieges and in the use of war machines, and also his forethought: had he not wisely, while in Sicily, constructed a collapsible tower that was opportunely re-erected at Acre? Had he not taken the precaution, again while in Sicily, of loading enormous round pebbles which were then used as ammunition for his perrieres?[14] In his determination to outdo Philip Augustus, Richard, though sick, like Philip, had himself carried close up to the walls, not only in order to direct the siege, but also to take part in it as an archer. Ambroise first attributed this exploit to the King of France:

> The King of France had a cat made at great cost and expense and a richly covered cercleia from which resulted great loss. The king himself would sit under the cercleia and often fired his crossbow at the Turks who came to defend the walls.[15]

The King of England could not bear to be outdone, even on this score. Besides, notes Roger of Howden, Richard 'loved archers and paid them well'; consequently they were brave and skilled, and feared on that account by Saladin and his army.[16] The King, carried up to the ramparts so that he could shoot alongside them, performed a notable deed, killing a Turk, on 6 June 1191:

> King Richard still lay ill, as I have told you; but he wished that the city of Acre should be attacked under his command. So he caused a cercleia dragged to the ditches, a richly wrought construction. His crossbowmen, who carried out their work well, were in it. He himself, as God bears witness, had himself carried to the cercleia in a great silken quilt to [personally] work against the Saracens. With his ever-ready hand, he shot many bolts against the Tower, which his catapults were attacking and where the Turks shot back . . . One Turk had arrayed himself richly in the arms of Aubery Clément and that day he took too great a risk. King Richard struck him with a bolt square in the chest, which killed him instantly.[17]

This interest in archery, as we know, was to prove fatal to Richard at Châlus. At this point, it was lauded by the chroniclers, who saw the King as a bold and enterprising crusader.

Nevertheless, it was not as an archer but as a knight that Richard

performed his most noteworthy feats of prowess. Ambroise records them all. Thus in August 1191, after the Christian victory at Acre against Saladin, previously regarded as invincible, the King marched with the crusader army, in an order he himself had decided; he was at the front, the Templars on this occasion bringing up the rear. The Saracens, as was their custom, began to harass the host as it marched. Richard charged them with ardour and would have won a decisive victory if only the other knights had been as brave as he:

> That day the king of England, who should be much praised for this, spurred on and would have done great deeds of valour had it not been for the laziness [of others]. For the king and his men pursued [the enemy], but there were others whose lethargy brought them much blame at evening and rightly so, for he who would have followed the king would have had a fine passage of arms.[18]

A little later, two days before the battle of Arsuf, Richard was wounded in the side by a javelin, but the wound was not serious, as he himself wrote in a letter;[19] nevertheless, says Ambroise, he 'quickly turned on them'.[20]

After these few isolated exploits, the chroniclers concentrate on three major feats of arms, the first at Arsuf, the second not far from Jerusalem, during the capture of a great caravan, and the last at Jaffa.

THE BATTLE OF ARSUF

This was without doubt Richard's greatest victory over Saladin. Yet the battle had begun badly thanks to the indiscipline of two men, the Marshal of the Hospital and Baldwin le Caron. These two, seeing the host harassed by Saladin's men, could not restrain themselves and charged, in defiance of the King's orders, taking many knights in their train and gravely endangering them as a result. Appreciating the situation, Richard gave the signal for a general charge, and himself rushed to their rescue, so performing his first exploit. James of Avesnes was killed in the battle; this 'valiant martyr' was found dead, surrounded by the bodies of the fifteen Saracens he had slaughtered before himself dying, like Roland long ago at Roncevaux:

> As soon as the troubled king saw that the army was disordered and had broken rank, he spurred his horse to the gallop without waiting any longer and let it run at speed, to help the first of the divisions. Faster than the bolt from a crossbow with his valiant and well-tried entourage he came to a division of pagans on the right, a group of them, striking them indiscriminately so hard that they were stunned, because of the valiant men they encountered

there, who made them quit their saddles. Then you would have seen them lying on the ground, as thick as sheaves of corn. The valiant king of England came after them and came down upon them. He did such deeds that time that all around him, above and below, behind and beside were the bodies of Saracens, who fell dead, so that others fled. The line of the dead lasted for half a league.[21]

The epic exaggeration is clear in this passage, as is the conscious imitation of the *Song of Roland*. Essentially, in his account of this battle, Ambroise emphasises, in addition to the feats of arms of the heroic martyr, James of Avesnes, those of two men who went to his assistance with equal valour: Richard of England and William des Barres. Thanks to his prowess on this occasion, the latter was reconciled with the king, his sworn enemy.

THE CAPTURE OF THE CARAVAN

The substantial booty won by Richard during the attack on a large caravan, on 23 June 1192, was the subject of a number of divergent accounts. Ralph of Diceto dismisses it in a line, and gives few details.[22] According to Ralph of Coggeshall, Richard captured a caravan making its way from Cairo to Jerusalem, seizing 7,000 camels loaded with a variety of riches.[23] Roger of Howden saw the episode as a great victory for the King of England: with 15,000 men, he had defeated the 11,000 Muslim warriors who were escorting the caravan; he also seized 3,000 camels and countless horses and mules and distributed the booty among his knights.[24] Matthew Paris says that a group of merchants were travelling from Cairo to Jerusalem 'with 7,000 camels loaded with every type of wealth and especially provisions' and led by five (or more likely five hundred or even five thousand) warriors from Saladin's army. The King of England, accompanied by a few men-at-arms (he is no more specific) rushed out to meet it, attacked it and seized camels and riches, which Richard generously distributed among his army, in particular the Normans.[25]

Ambroise describes the episode in great detail, highlighting the personal courage of the King of England. Richard, learning that a large caravan would shortly be travelling nearby, agreed with the Duke of Burgundy, in return for the promise of a third of the booty, to launch an attack at the head of 500 knights armed at his own cost. A Saracen spy warned Saladin and the Jerusalem garrison, who sent 2,000 mounted warriors and many foot soldiers as reinforcements for the caravan. Richard and his men marched by night and arrived near the place indicated by a spy, which was suitable for an ambush, and pitched camp.

The King ordered his soldiers not to think of the booty but only of trouncing the enemy; he first sent Turcopoles to harass the caravan, then made his appearance at the head of one of the two units of his army. This is how Ambroise goes on to describe Richard's dazzling intervention:

> Do not think that I undertake to flatter him here for so many men saw his fine blows that they make me dwell on them. There you would have seen the king chasing the Turks, his sword of steel in his hand that those whom he caught as he pursued them, no armour would protect from being split to the teeth so that they fled him as sheep who see a wolf.[26]

The booty was considerable: 4,700 camels and innumerable mules and donkeys. Once again, as with the capture of the Saracen ship, accounts of the episode differ. There is a marked tendency on the part of Ambroise to exalt the prowess of the King of England, whereas the other chroniclers choose rather to emphasise the virtue of largesse in the King's distribution of the booty to his valiant warriors.

THE ASSAULT ON JAFFA

The last important occasion for remarkable feats by Richard was the capture of Joppa (Jaffa) on 1 August 1192. In fact, Richard retook the town, which had fallen into the hands of Saladin the previous day. Diceto describes the event in a few words, adding that Richard then gave a demonstration of his prowess: learning that the King of England was present, the Saracens threw themselves on him in an attempt to take him alive, but he resisted and felled many with his sword.[27] This is all Diceto says. Roger of Howden is even less effusive on the subject of the personal exploits of the King: Richard came to the rescue of the besieged citadel and repulsed the Saracens, killing many of them.[28]

Ralph of Coggeshall, in contrast, describes the episode in almost epic style. Richard, learning that Saladin was besieging Jaffa, and having tried in vain to persuade Hugh of Burgundy to join him in bringing assistance to the Christians, decided to proceed alone with his troops. When the King landed at Jaffa, Saladin had already taken the town and slaughtered all who remained, sick or wounded. The Christian soldiers, who had taken refuge in the citadel, were on the point of surrender when the patriarch (who moved freely from one army to the other) warned them that they would lose their lives whatever happened, because Saladin's soldiers had sworn to kill them all in order to avenge their friends and relatives, massacred without pity by the King of England on various occasions.

The garrison was in despair when Richard's ship arrived, and the King leaped into the water to come to their aid:

> At once, with an agile bound, he jumped fully armed from his ship with his men and, like a furious lion, laying about him to clear a path, he launched boldly into the midst of the enemy battalions, which were occupying the shore in serried ranks and harrying with javelins and arrows those who arrived in the port. The Turks did not resist this lightning attack; they believed that the king had brought a large army and, fleeing as fast as their legs would carry them, they abandoned the siege.[29]

Saladin was ashamed of the behaviour of his men. He had them counted, and discovered they numbered 62,000! How could so many warriors have shamefully fled before such a tiny band of Christians? He urged them to return to the fray, at night, and capture Richard. Woken from his sleep, the King fought like a lion, especially as all flight was impossible:

> He took with him six brave knights who scorned death, and he marched on the town, brandishing the royal banner, and, like a ferocious lion, he attacked the enemy massed in the squares, clearing a passage with his lance and his sword; by his assault, he felled them and killed them. [The Saracens then fled] like little beasts before the pitiless lion driven by hunger to devour whatever chance has put in his path. In the end, the pagans were repulsed and put to flight by the astonishing and incomparable bravery of the glorious king.[30]

It was a miracle; no Christian was wounded in this assault, although one cowardly knight, fleeing, met the death he feared. Later on, Ralph of Coggeshall summarises the whole of this battle, marvelling yet again at the bravery of this glorious king, and at this incredible feat of arms, impossible without divine intervention. Had there ever before been a town liberated by a mere six knights? Matthew Paris, openly basing himself on Ralph of Coggeshall, tells very much the same story; he too compares Richard to a lion, though he gives him eleven companions rather than six.[31]

Ambroise makes an even greater point of the King's valour. When, in his ship, Richard was wondering how best to proceed, a priest from Jaffa threw himself into the water and came to beg him to intervene as quickly as possible to save the Christians, whose throats were already being cut by the Saracens. At once, Richard leapt into the water, before anyone else, so setting an example, and he was in the thick of the action, in the front rank, using a crossbow as well as a sword:

> And so soon as the king heard how it was he tarried no longer. Then he said. 'God brought us here to endure and suffer death, and since we must die may he be shamed who does not come.' Then he had his galleys advanced and,

with his legs unprotected, he jumped into the sea, [only] waist-deep – fortunately for him – and came by force to dry land, first or second, as was his custom. Geoffrey du Bois and the noble Peter of Préaux, a companion of the king, leaped in after him; they reached the Turks who filled the strand and the king himself attacked them with his crossbow and his valiant bold and everready men, followed him along the shore. The Turks fled before the king, not daring to draw near him. He took his sword in his hand and rushed upon them, harrying them, so that they had no opportunity to defend themselves. They did not dare await him and his experienced company, who hit the Turks like madmen, who struck them and pressed them until they freed the strand of Turks, forcing them all back.[32]

'The boldest king in all the world' was then the first to enter the town, where he rallied the Christians' courage:

There he was the first to enter, forcing his way into the town where he found more than three thousand Saracens pillaging the castle and carrying everything off. As soon as Richard, the boldest king in all the world, was up on the wall he had his banners unfurled and shown on high to the Christians so that they would see them. As soon as they noticed them they cried 'Holy Sepulchre', took their arms and armed themselves without delay.[33]

The Turks fled the town. But Richard's exploits did not end there. Ambroise shows him again, later that same day, and the following days, pursuing the Saracens, more redoubtable than Roland at Roncevaux:

The king came out after them, having carried out such deeds that day and having then only three horses. Never, even at Roncevaux, did any man, young or old, Saracen or Christian, conduct himself so well.[34]

In the end, the Saracens struck back, after a harangue from Saladin. Three days later, their vigorous attack endangered another brave knight, the Earl of Leicester, who was toppled from his horse. Richard rushed to his rescue; as soon as they saw the royal banner, the Turks fell on the King, but he, being invincible, cut them to pieces. Next he went to the aid of another knight being led away by the Turks, and rescued him from their grasp. That day, Richard performed countless feats of prowess, more than any man before, as the jongleur-poet insists:

Then did the king look round and saw to his right the noble earl of Leicester fall, his horse struck from under him. He fought well until the king came to his rescue. There you would have seen so many Turks rush towards the Lion Banner! There was Ralph of Mauléon taken prisoner by the Turks; the king spurred on his valuable horse until he had delivered him from their hands. The powerful king was in the press, against the Turks and the Persians. Never did one man, weak or strong, make in one day such efforts. He threw himself against the Turks, splitting them to the teeth.[35]

Ambroise ends his account of this momentous day by relating one last exploit of Richard's: isolated after a charge, but completely unperturbed, under a hail of arrows, he hacked his way through the Saracens who surrounded him, even slicing one of them in two with a single blow from his sword, inspiring terror in the infidel:

> Then did he undertake a daring charge. Never was the like seen. He charged into the accursed people, so that he was swallowed up by them and none of his men could see him, so that they nearly followed him, breaking their ranks, and we would have lost all. But [the king] was not troubled. He struck before and behind, creating such a pathway through [the Turks] with the sword he was holding that wherever it had struck there lay either a horse or a corpse, for he cut all down. There, I believe, he struck a blow against the arm and head of an emir in steel armour whom he sent straight to hell. With such a blow, seen by the Turks, he created such a space around him that, thanks be to God, he returned without harm. However, his body, his horse, his trappings were so covered with arrows which that dark race had shot at him that he seemed like a hedgehog. In this way did he return from the battle which lasted all the day from morning till night, a battle so cruel and fierce that if God had not supported our people evil would have come of it.[36]

However indisputable the warlike valour and courage of Richard, on this as on many other occasions, one cannot but be struck by the insistence of certain chroniclers, in particular Ambroise, on presenting him not as a strategist, a leader or king commanding his armies, but as the embodiment of chivalric virtues, the chief among them being valour pushed to extremes, even to recklessness.

RICHARD THE RECKLESS

It was this excessive ardour in battle, this ill-considered thirst for the feat of arms, which most impressed itself on many observers, in both the Christian and the Muslim camps.

In the case of the battle of Arsuf, for example, Ambroise himself records the unease provoked by the King's recklessness when he abandoned his role as king in favour of that of a simple knight. Such reservations were vain, he emphasises, because as soon as there was a fight, Richard was incapable of holding back. And God was with him, protected him and gave him victory, so silencing the fears of his entourage and bringing honour on the King himself:

> 'Lord, for the sake of God, do not do this! It is not for you to go on such spying expeditions. Protect yourself and Christianity. You have many good

people. Never again go alone on such business. When you want to damage the Turks, take a large company, for in your hands is our support, or our death, should harm come to you – for when the head of the body falls, the limbs cannot survive alone, but will soon fail and fall and misadventure then comes.' In this way many worthy men took great pains and put much effort into rebuking him but always, this is the sum of it, when he saw any skirmishes, very few of which were hidden from him, he would go against the Turks and bring things to a conclusion and he would always finish the business so that some were killed and so that the greatest honour was his. God always brought him out of the greatest dangers of that hostile race.[37]

Richard never hesitated, as we have seen, to throw himself into the fray to come to the assistance of his knights in peril. Here, too, he was often told that this was not his role, as king, because he was risking his life and so endangering the whole army, even the sacred cause of Christendom. But the King had a 'chivalric' conception of kingship, as Ambroise emphasised in connection with Richard's prowess at Arsuf, when he rushed to the assistance of his men:

The struggle was in full force when the warrior King Richard arrived and saw our people in the middle of the hostile pagans. He had few men with him but his company was in fine order. Then some of them began to say to him, 'In faith, sir, it could do much harm for you to go on, nor will you be able to rescue our men. It is better that they should suffer alone without you than that you should suffer there. For this reason it is good that you should turn back, for if harm comes to you Christianity will be killed. The king's colour changed. Then he said, 'When I sent them here and asked them to go, if they die there without me then would I never again bear the title of king.' He kicked the flanks of his horse and gave him free rein and went off, faster than a sparrow-hawk. Then he galloped in among the knights, right into the Saracen people, breaking through them with such impetus that if a thunderbolt had fallen there there would have been no greater destruction of their people. He pierced the ranks and pursued them; he turned and trapped them, hewing off hands and arms and heads. They fled like beasts. Many of them were exhausted, many killed or taken. He chased them so far, following and pursuing them, until it was time to return. This is how that day went.[38]

This recklessness, unconcern in the face of danger and determination to act like an ordinary knight meant that he was often in difficulties and several times narrowly escaped death or capture. Once, as we have seen, he was saved by William de Préaux who, to distract the Saracens' attention, pretended to be the King and was captured in his place.[39] This

eminently chivalric gesture meant that Richard took it upon himself to pay William's huge ransom before his departure. This is how the Muslim chronicler Imad ad-Din described this episode:

> The king of England went out in disguise, followed by his knights, to protect the men sent out foraging and collecting firewood. Our men attacked him from their ambush; this accursed man engaged them, and there was a mighty battle, our men fighting nobly; the king was nearly taken and mortally wounded, his chest pierced by a blow from a lance; but one of his knights sacrificed himself on his behalf: through the beauty of his raiment, he attracted the attention of the man attacking the king, so that he left the king alone and took the knight prisoner; in this way the accursed king, escaping, covered his traces; many of his knights were killed or captured; the rest were put to flight, after this attack that achieved nothing.[40]

Richard's fame as a warrior, according to a curious passage in Richard of Devizes, had already reached Muslim ears well before his arrival in the Holy Land. This was as a result of the exploits he had performed while still Count of Poitou, fighting against his father and against the King of France, and then against Tancred in Messina. They both feared and admired him as a result.[41] Ambroise echoes this, and describes a reputation further enhanced by the unprecedented behaviour of this 'roi-chevalier', sword in hand. He relates (or rather imagines) the flattering comments of the Muslims in the account they gave to Saladin of their defeat, due to the incredible valour of the King of England:

> What is to be even more wondered at is a Frank who is one of them, who kills and maims our men. You never saw anyone like him; he will always be at the front; he will always be found at the place of need, as a good and tested knight. It is he who cuts so many of us down. They call him Melec Richard, and such a melec should hold land, conquer and dispense wealth.[42]

There can be no doubt that the Muslims were impressed by the warlike fury of the King of England and by his indomitable character. Many accounts testify to this. Richard of Devizes puts this flattering judgement into the mouth of Saladin's brother, a great admirer of the King of England:

> Nevertheless, although we are his enemies, we found nothing in Richard to which we could take exception save his bravery, nothing to hate save his skill in arms.[43]

Richard's reputation for warrior valour lived on after his departure from the Holy Land. Some fifty years after his death, the Continuator of

William of Tyre reveals that the name of Richard could still arouse fear in the Saracens:

> King Richard's renown terrified the Saracens so much that when their children cried their mothers would scare them with the king of England and say, 'Be quiet for the King of England!' When a Saracen was riding a horse and his mount stumbled at a shadow, he would say to him, 'Do you think the king of England is in that bush?', and if he brought his horse to water and it would not drink, he would say to it, 'Do you reckon the king of England is in the water?'[44]

Later still, Joinville tells very similar stories, probably drawn from the same source:

> King Richard performed such feats of arms overseas at that time that when the Saracens' horses were frightened of a bush, their masters would say to them: 'Do you think it's the King of England?' And when the Saracens' children used to bawl, the women would say to them, 'Hush, hush, or I'll go and get King Richard who'll kill you.'[45]

We should remember that the King of England, the mortal enemy of Philip Augustus, was to Joinville a model for St Louis. We may see this as a consequence of the total success of the promotion of the image of the 'roi-chevalier' which Richard set out to embody.

Ambroise reports, in this connection, an interesting conversation which he represents as taking place in Jerusalem between the Bishop of Salisbury and Saladin himself, just before Richard's departure from the Holy Land. During the course of this courteous exchange, the Muslim sovereign asked the Bishop for his opinion of himself, Saladin, and of the King of England. The bishop at once emphasised the 'chivalric' qualities of his king, his largesse and his prowess, which made him, in his eyes, the best knight in the world. Saladin agreed, echoing the praise of his largesse, but nevertheless emphasising Richard's lack of moderation, his foolhardy rashness, which he did not envy; for himself, as a prince, he preferred a wiser and more measured attitude. In his report of the carefully considered judgement of Saladin, an expert in chivalry, Ambroise neatly summarises the image Richard projected of himself in the East and probably also in the West, that of prince who was more knight than king:

> He began to ask about the King of England, about his qualities and what we Christians thought of those who were with him. The bishop replied, 'My lord, I can tell you of my lord for he is the best knight in the world and the best warrior, and he is generous and talented. I say nothing of our

sins but if one were to take your qualities and his together then we will say that nowhere in all the world would ever two such princes be found, so valiant and so experienced.' The sultan listened to the bishop and said, 'I know indeed that the king has great valour and boldness, but he rushes into things so foolishly! However high a prince I should be I would prefer to exercise generosity and judgement with moderation, than boldness without moderation.'[46]

Ambroise was not alone in presenting such a picture of the King. The Arab historians, too, testify to the reputation which the King acquired in the Holy Land for largesse and for prowess. The Arab chronicler Abu al-Fida says that the Muslims had never had an opponent or an enemy more valiant, braver or less wily than the King of England.[47] Another, Baha ad-Din, paints a picture of him that would certainly have been pleasing to Richard, in that it placed him above his feudal overlord in the scale of chivalric values:

> The King of England was a very powerful man among the Franks, a man of great courage and spirit. He had fought great battles and was especially bold in war. His kingdom and standing were inferior to those of the King of France, but his wealth, reputation and valour in battle were greater.[48]

NOTES

1. See on this point the discussion of J. Flori, 'Chevalerie Chrétienne et Cavalerie Musulmane; Deux Conceptions du Combat Cheveleresque vers 1100', in Buschinger, *Monde des Héros*, pp. 99–113 (reprinted in Flori, *Croisade et Chevalerie*, pp. 389–405).
2. Ambroise, lines 5648ff., French translation p. 394 (p. 110 of Ailes translation).
3. Rigord, §75, pp. 109–10.
4. Ralph of Coggeshall, p. 32.
5. William of Newburgh, p. 352.
6. Ralph of Diceto, pp. 93–4.
7. Matthew Paris, *Chronica Majora*, II, pp. 373–4.
8. Richard of Devizes, p. 38.
9. Ambroise, lines 2141ff. (pp. 63–4 of Ailes translation).
10. Ibid. (p. 64 of Ailes translation).
11. Ibid., French translation p. 359 (p. 64 of Ailes translation).
12. *Gesta Henrici*, II, p. 168; see also Roger of Howden, III, p. 112.
13. Imad ad-Din, *Conquête de la Syrie*, p. 299.
14. Ambroise, lines 4795ff.
15. Ambroise, line 4891, French translation, p. 385 (p. 99 of Ailes translation).
16. *Gesta Henrici*, II, p. 186.

17. Ambroise, lines 4927ff., 4966ff., French translation, p. 387 (pp. 100–1 of Ailes translation).

18. Ibid., lines 5945ff., French translation, p. 397 (pp. 113–14 of Ailes translation); *Itinerarium*, IV, 14.

19. Roger of Howden, III, pp. 129–33: 'Two days before the rout of Saladin, we were wounded in the left side by a javelin. But, thanks be to God, we are already healed.'

20. Ambroise, line 6059; *Itinerarium*, IV, 15.

21. Ambroise, lines 6360ff., French translation, p. 403 (p. 120 of Ailes translation). For this battle, see Smail, *Crusading Warfare*, pp. 161ff.; Gillingham, *Richard the Lionheart*, pp. 188–91. Richard's prowess emerges less clearly in the *Gesta Henrici*, II, pp. 190–2; Ralph of Diceto, p. 95; even less in William of Newburgh, p. 361; or even in the letter from Richard reproduced in Roger of Howden, III, pp. 129ff.

22. Ralph of Diceto, II, p. 104.

23. Ralph of Coggeshall, p. 38.

24. Roger of Howden, III, p. 182.

25. Matthew Paris, *Chronica Majora*, II, p. 383.

26. Ambroise, lines 10329ff. (p. 171 of Ailes translation); *Itinerarium*, VI, pp. 4–5.

27. Ralph of Diceto, II, p. 104.

28. Roger of Howden, III, p. 182.

29. Ralph of Coggeshall, p. 41 (based on the modern French translation in *Richard Cœur de Lion*, ed. Brossard-Dandré and Besson, p. 199).

30. Ralph of Coggeshall, pp. 45–6.

31. Matthew Paris, *Chronica Majora*, II, pp. 387–9.

32. Ambroise, lines 11095ff. (p. 179 of Ailes translation); *Itinerarium*, VI, p. 15.

33. Ambroise, lines 11095ff., French translation p. 452 (p. 179 of Ailes translation).

34. Ibid. (p. 180 of Ailes translation).

35. Ambroise, lines 11526–7, French translation p. 455 (p. 184 of Ailes translation).

36. Ambroise, line 11596, French translation p. 456 (pp. 184–5 of Ailes translation).

37. Ambroise, lines 7150ff., French translation p. 410 (p. 129 of Ailes translation).

38. Ambroise, line 7327, French translation p. 412 (p. 131 of Ailes translation); *Itinerarium*, IV, p. 30.

39. Roger of Howden, III, p. 133; Ambroise, line 12263.

40. Imad ad-Din, *Conquête de la Syrie*, p. 347; see also Ambroise, lines 7086ff.

41. Richard of Devizes, pp. 75–6.

42. Ambroise, lines 6830ff., French translation p. 406 (p. 124 of Ailes translation).

43. Richard of Devizes, p. 78.
44. *Continuation de Guillaume de Tyr*, p. 150 (pp. 119–20 of Edbury translation).
45. Joinville, *Vie de Saint Louis*, p. 276.
46. Ambroise, lines 12115ff., 12146–52 (p. 191 of Ailes translation).
47. See Abdul Majid Nanai, 'L'Image du Croisé dans le Sources Historiques Musulmanes', in *De Toulouse à Tripoli*, pp. 11–39.
48. Baha ad-Din (Gabrieli, *Arab Historians*, p. 213; translation slightly amended).

17

Royal Largesse

∽

WHAT IS LARGESSE?

In his *Roman des eles*, Raoul de Houdenc visualised Prowess (in the sense of commendable behaviour worthy of renown) as borne by two wings, one called Largesse and the other Courtesy. For him, it was by the practice of these two virtues that one could increase one's worth. We should note in passing that Raoul totally ignores prowess in the military sense of the term, as discussed in the preceding chapters. This consisted, as we have seen, of a purely military virtue; it pertained to the professional code of the soldier, which was appropriated in turn by lords, princes and kings as the growing militarisation of the society known as feudal drew them into a much closer involvement with their knights. This in turn gave rise to a sort of soldierly freemasonry between them and their men, which was cultivated in tournaments as well as in war.

This sense of fellowship did not, however, abolish the hierarchies. Chivalry, which tended to form itself into a guild of elite warriors during the twelfth century, was far from egalitarian. Like all the guilds and corporations created after it, around other, less elevated professions, it had its masters or patrons (the princes and lords), its journeymen (the knights), its apprentices (squires, valets 'in arms', *bachelers*, young aristocrats serving a relative or friend of the family 'to learn arms'),[1] its rite of passage (dubbing), its patron saints (the military saints George, Mercury, Demetrius, Martin and Theodosius) and its characteristic tools of the trade (the weapons deemed 'chivalric', described above). Like all these other guilds, but well in advance of them, chivalry tended to close ranks, to recruit only from amongst its own members and to reserve dubbing for the sons of the aristocracy, so turning itself into a caste.

It was towards the end of the thirteenth century that the other corporations began to close themselves off. In the case of knighthood, this shift started almost a century earlier. This is hardly surprising, as it was no ordinary profession, but an armed function which fell to the elite, and which was symbolised by dubbing. The latter became increasingly

honorific, ritualised by the aristocracy even more than by the Church, though the latter tried to infuse it with its own values, making it the sign of a dignity which it further increased. Dubbing, which became increasingly aristocratic in character during the twelfth century, acted as a public declaration of recruitment, officially sanctioning the bearing of arms in the legitimate service of the princes who were the recruiters.[2] This social evolution led, as we have said, to the transformation of chivalry, a noble corporation in the old and socio-professional sense of the term (though a worthy and respected profession), into a confraternity of nobles in the socio-juridical sense of the term (in other words, a noble caste). The latter sense was eventually to prevail, inconveniently making us, these days, forget the former.

In Richard I's time, however, this trend was still in its very early stages, its first signs alone being visible. It then becomes clear why the warlike prowess discussed above, essentially humble and lowly in origin (since consisting of the qualities required of soldiers since the Roman period, if not from all time), was in a sense introduced by chivalry, as it developed, into the aristocratic and noble milieus from which knights were increasingly recruited. In a word, prowess was a quality of the common soldier which became, at this period, a virtue of the noble knight.

Largesse, on the other hand, followed an opposite trajectory. It was the princes who were originally its dispensers, and the warriors its beneficiaries. It was the slow propagandist and ideological rise of chivalry (to say nothing here of its probable but debatable social promotion)[3] that made it possible for the aristocratic value of largesse to be turned into a chivalric value.

The extolling of largesse in the literature of the twelfth century, both by the troubadours of the South and the trouvères of the North, and by the jongleurs as well as by the poets and romance writers, has been interpreted in sociological terms by fine medievalists, both literary specialists and historians (if such a distinction deserves to exist for the Middle Ages, where it is hardly possible to do worthwhile historical research without paying close attention to literature, or to understand the literature without deep historical knowledge). Eric Köhler, a specialist in romance literature, largely followed by Georges Duby, saw this praise of largesse as the ideological affirmation of what amounted to a 'social class', that of the impoverished lesser nobility, claiming membership of the aristocracy. Largesse then became a feudal virtue *par excellence*, necessary to ensure the maintenance of the social order through the redistribution of wealth within the aristocratic world. This economic necessity, which required the king (or prince) to provide for the needs of the 'poor knights', was thus

idealised, transformed into an ideology, a value common to the aristocratic chivalric world as a whole. According to Köhler, this largesse, a
generosity which was indistinguishable from prodigality, was useful to
the great vassals and the monarch as a way of ensuring the loyalty of
the knights. This quality defined, therefore, a common ideal, removing the
tensions between lower nobility and great feudal lords, promoting the
maintenance of the status quo. The courtly equilibrium was largely based
on this virtue, which had originated among the lower nobility before
being adopted, for reasons of convenience, by the high aristocracy. It was
logical, therefore, for largesse to be generally regarded as an eminent
virtue and for its principal beneficiaries to come from the lower fringes
of the nobility.[4]

This interpretation, which was once widely accepted, has recently
been criticised on the basis of close study of the very texts on which it
had originally itself been based, that is, the Arthurian romances.[5] Here,
according to the literary specialist Dominique Boutet, the largesse practiced by King Arthur performed a political rather than an economic function, or function of social redistribution, as Köhler had argued. It
originated not at the level of the lesser nobility or the knights, but at the
highest level, that of kings. The poor knights subsequently adopted this
notion and turned it to their own advantage for social and economic
reasons, a sign that the principle was already firmly entrenched. The
theme is also found, furthermore, well before the twelfth century, in the
authors of the 'mirrors of princes' of the Carolingian period. Boutet sees
it as originating in the Indo-European ideology transmitted by the Anglo-
Saxon writers, drawing on the Celtic heritage.

Whatever its distant origins, it would certainly seem that the virtue (or
duty) of largesse was primarily the privilege of the powerful, lauded in
princes by those close to them who were its accustomed beneficiaries,
that is the ecclesiastics and the courtiers. I myself see largesse as heir to
two antinomic ancestors, of which it retained certain features: on the one
hand 'charity' (caritas), Christian and ecclesiastical in origin, on the
other aristocratic ostentation (close to superbia).

Charity, extolled by the Church from its beginnings, resulted from the
contempt for the riches of this world professed by Jesus and his disciples.
This world passes; naked we come into it and naked we leave it. The
kingdom of heaven belongs to the poor. Over the centuries, this ideal of
poverty, or at least of indifference to wealth, had undergone some modi-
fications. The growing separation between the clergy and the ordinary
believers had led the Church to weaken, for the latter, evangelical requirements that had themselves been modified with the passage of time. It was

soon only the clergy, in the first place, and then increasingly the monks, who were required, by the vows pronounced in accord with the rules of the monastic orders, to shun the stain of shedding blood, the pleasures of sex and possession of worldly goods. In any case, these vows of individual poverty taken by monks had long been seen as perfectly compatible with the very real collective wealth of their order, which periodically led to abuse and criticism that encouraged the birth of a new, more demanding, order. In the twelfth century, this demand was incarnated by the Cistercians.

It was particularly visible between the mid eleventh and mid thirteenth centuries, when the economic and demographic growth of Western Europe produced both more wealth and more people in a position to distance themselves from the obsessive, permanent and precarious search for life or survival, to reflect on the individual destiny of humankind. The aspiration to poverty then gradually gained ground in social circles previously largely indifferent to it, even among the laity, that is, artisans, merchants, townspeople and knights. St Francis and the Waldensian and Cathar 'heresies' owed at least part of their success to this new aspiration.[6]

Hitherto, these lay men and women, by the simple fact of exercising their trade or their status, were stained by sin. They needed to redeem themselves. This was particularly the case with the lay lords, triply threatened by the three sins mentioned above. Alms-giving performed this function. It could be done directly, by a few gifts to the poor, for example the beggars stationed at church doors or castle gates. More often it was done indirectly, by charitable donations, offerings made to God and his poor, that is, to his Church, which was responsible for redistributing them. By its insistent condemnation of the insane practice of putting one's trust in wealth (*fol dives*), ecclesiastical preaching doomed to hell the rich layman who hoarded his treasure and was miserly with his possessions, while lauding the generosity of the powerful towards the Church, even though it was itself rich, powerful and a hoarder of treasure. Alms-giving redeemed many sins. Donations were even more effective, as testified by charters, all of which emphasise this very point.

But largesse was not alms-giving. Its motives, recipients and practices were quite different. Its purpose was not to procure a place in the other world by giving humbly to the poor, so that one's wealth was forgotten, but rather to publish it, to proclaim it by a prodigality intended to attract favour among men in this world, even at the risk of incurring ecclesiastical disapproval. Not unreasonably, the Church often likened this extravagant expenditure to a display of pride (*superbia*). It was during this period, it has been observed, that, for the first time, pride came before

avarice in the list of vices condemned by the Church.[7] The aristocracy remained unmoved, however, and ostentatiously practiced largesse. In the epic, it was criticised by monks, but it was 'natural to great men', praised by jongleurs and knights because it gladdened the humble and bound them to the great.[8]

Largesse served many purposes – economic, political, religious, social and ideological. Only the last is of direct concern to us here. In a society where money was circulating ever more rapidly and becoming increasingly necessary, it made it possible for the chivalric body to become aware of its solidarity, not as a class (because, as we have seen, it did not constitute a social class), but as an order, or more precisely, a functional status.[9] Kings and princes needed knights to establish, consolidate and affirm their power; knights needed kings and princes to be able to practise their profession, since they neither tilled the soil nor engaged in trade, nor produced any wealth, but only consumed it.

They all, in fact, in their own way, lived as predators, from the booty seized from enemies when successful in time of war, from the fruits of the toil of the *laboratores* in time of peace, or through taxes accepted as legitimate or exactions that were tolerated, levied by the powerful, and particularly by kings and princes as, in the twelfth century, states began to develop their administrative systems. The praise of the ideal of largesse, the condemnation of the hoarding of wealth and the lofty professions of disdain for money can then be seen as an expression of the disarray of the most vulnerable sector of the warriors of feudal society, but also, and even more confidently, as a reflection of the development of an aristocratic and noble ideology that gathered behind kings and great princes all those who lived by the sword.[10] Many literary works in the second half of the twelfth century, from the romances of Chrétien de Troyes to *Aiol* or *Partonopeu de Blois*, contain increasingly clear signs of this chivalric and violently anti-plebeian ideology.[11]

It was particularly strongly expressed, perhaps, by the poets and romance writers of the kingdom of France, so as to stigmatise and denounce the increasingly important economic and political role played by the bourgeoisie at the courts of Louis VII and Philip Augustus. But it can also be argued that the works which expound this aristocratic ideology and place the perfect realisation of this ideal at the court of King Arthur were seeking to influence the Plantagenet court. Its adoption by this court served its political interests by rallying the aristocracy and the knights to its cause against Philip Augustus, regarded (or rather disregarded) as a bourgeois king, betraying the interests and ideals of chivalry. This is the thesis advanced by Eric Köhler and Georges Duby, which I accept

in part, with numerous qualifications, since it cannot explain all these works, though it remains valuable for many of them, particularly the most important.

Did these works have any influence on the behaviour of Richard the Lionheart? It would be surprising if they did not, given the relations existing between the Plantagenet court and the authors of these major works. Wace, for example, or Benoît de Sainte-Maure, openly praised the exemplary largesse of Richard's ancestors, the dukes of Normandy; Duke Richard, in particular, had been generous to his barons, raising (that is, bringing up and educating) their sons and often making them knights, rewarding them well and offering them generous gifts in addition. This laudatory portrait is thrown into greater relief by contrast with the totally negative one given of Raoul Torta, his adversary, who took money from all and sundry, was a stingy employer to the people of his household and rewarded his knights meanly, never giving them a penny more than their wages.[12] According to Wace, Duke Richard II wisely confined his largesse to 'noble knights', who received clothes and gifts every day.[13] A few years later, Bertran de Born, a poet but also a knight, urged the lords of his day to make war, because this made even the most miserly show largesse towards the knights.[14] It is reasonable to conclude, therefore, that this ideology found its expression both in literature and in reality, both products of a shared mentality, each serving as a model for the other, and so strengthening and reinforcing each other.

RICHARD'S LARGESSE

The point has recently been made that, to be a warrior king (*bellicosus*), Richard first needed to be rich (*pecuniosus*); money was necessary not only to recruit mercenaries but also to pay, by one means or another, the lords who agreed to serve under his command, whether in the West or in the Holy Land.[15] It was not only the mercenaries who sold their services. In their case, service was at a fixed rate, specified in a sort of contract. It was different in the case of the princes or lords of high rank, who commanded their own troops, paying them in cash if they were mercenaries, in land or property if their service was 'feudal' in nature; these great men served according to a variety of arrangements that are often obscure, but in which material interest, while not always all-important, was never totally absent. Thus, from top to bottom of the social scale, kings and princes were obliged to demonstrate their generosity, for short-term interest or from a more general desire to raise or maintain their prestige.

Largesse towards princes

The main reasons for largesse towards kings and princes were political or diplomatic. The solemn festivities which accompanied the main occasions of social life, such as coronations, marriages, knightings, receptions or visits, were intended to strengthen, by displays of splendour and gifts, the cohesion of the family in the broadest sense of the term, that of lineage, or 'house', while at the same time affirming its power by the opulence and expenditure that characterised such gatherings. The chroniclers highlight these great displays of extravagance without really explaining their significance, as we have seen in the case of the coronation festivities for Richard I, though these were too specific in nature wholly to fit into this category, however large the expenditure they required.

The significance of other, more ordinary, festivities is more obvious. Ambroise was a witness to one such occasion, marked by gifts and a variety of ostentatious displays. It took place at Messina, at a time when Richard was trying to dazzle and ingratiate himself with the King of France while also making himself popular with the crusader knights and refugees from Outremer. This is how Ambroise describes this lavish occasion, taking care to emphasise the various beneficiaries of royal largesse:

> The knights who had been there during the summer moaned and complained and grumbled at the expense they incurred. The complaints spread among high and low and reached King Richard who said that he would give each one enough money that he would be able to congratulate himself. Richard – who is not mean or miserly – gave them such great gifts of silver chalices and gilded cups, brought to the knights according to their station, that all men praised him for his fine gifts, those of high, middle and low degree and he did them such honour that even he that went on foot had one hundred sous from him; to the disinherited ladies who had been ejected from Syria, to the ladies and to the girls, he gave great gifts at Messina. Similarly the king of France also gave generously to his people . . . I was present at the feasting . . . I have not, it seems to me, seen so many rich gifts given at once time as King Richard gave then, handing over to the king of France and to his people vessels of gold and silver.[16]

Other displays of princely largesse had an even more specific purpose, intended, for example, to contract an alliance, win the support of a lord of some importance, retain a vassal, earn the 'friendship' of a prince or simply buy his military assistance for a while. There were many such occasions during the Christian expedition to the Holy Land, during which the King of England was often forced to go in for displays of largesse to rally to his cause some hesitant or impoverished princes. For example, in

Cyprus, on the eve of his marriage to Berengaria, the King of England honoured Guy of Lusignan, who had come to support his cause: in a gesture 'both courteous and wise', he opened his treasure chest, offering him two thousand silver marks and twenty precious cups, two of fine gold, which, observes Ambroise, was 'no mean gift'.[17] A little later, at Acre, the King lent the Duke of Burgundy 5,000 marks from his treasury; and at the time of Philip Augustus's departure, in order to retain the services of the French, Richard 'obtained from his treasury large amounts of gold and silver, which he gave most freely to the French, to encourage them where there had been only discouragement'.[18]

On his arrival in Acre, the Count of Champagne, who was short of money, appealed to Philip Augustus, but all he was offered was 100,000 *livres* on condition he surrendered Champagne as security. The offended count then declared he would go to whoever would accept him and show himself 'ready to give more than to receive'. He turned to the King of England, who gave him 4,000 measures of corn and 4,000 *livres* in silver. At the news of this largesse, lords and warriors from every nation flocked to Richard to serve him and take him as their leader.[19] William of Newburgh also describes this largesse on the part of Richard, who, 'opening up his own treasury, offered generous sums to persuade a large number of nobles and princes to remain with their knights in the army of the Lord'.[20] Among them were many French, but also the Duke of Austria, who was later to forget the King of England's generosity.

Richard also demonstrated largesse towards the King of France, according to Ambroise. As he was preparing to leave the Holy Land, Philip Augustus asked the King to lend him two galleys:

> So they set off for the port where they gave him two fine boats, well equipped and swift, given freely and poorly rewarded.[21]

These acts of largesse were certainly gifts, but they were not, for all that, money wasted; in medieval aristocratic society, every gift called for a gift in return, attracting gratitude, consideration and even, as we have seen, service.[22] The line between largesse and payment, even corruption, was a fine one. This was the case, for example, with the expenditure required to entice away one of the enemy's vassals and gain his support. Thus, in 1197, to strengthen his arm against Philip Augustus, Richard managed, by his largesse, to obtain the alliance of many princes of the kingdom of France, notably those of Champagne, Flanders and Brittany, who were won over to his side by his generous gifts. The Count of Flanders, for example, received 15,000 silver marks not to make peace with the King of France.[23]

Largesse to dependants

In the case of dependants, vassals or mercenaries, knights, sergeants and foot soldiers, largesse served also as pay, a reward and an encouragement to do a good job. We see this on the occasion of the capture of the large caravan already frequently referred to, when the King of England added largesse to prowess by distributing the booty acquired to everyone who had been involved, directly and indirectly, with due regard, of course, to the hierarchies:

> The king distributed the camels, which were as fine as ever seen, both among the knights protecting the army and those who had gone out. Similarly, he distributed the mules and asses among them generously. He had the donkeys given to the men-at-arms, both great and small.[24]

Another example of royal generosity to the general advantage came when the army was badly hit by shortages, causing a rise in the price of foodstuffs, in particular meat, including that from slaughtered horses. Richard issued a proclamation to the effect that anyone who gave his dead horse to the soldiers would receive a live one in exchange. From that moment on, horses were abundant, prices fell and the soldiers had plenty to eat.[25] This episode reveals in passing that there had not been real shortages, but simply speculation according to the laws of the market. In promising a ready supply of live horses in exchange for dead, Richard 'prompted' the speculators to hand over their animals, so increasing the supply and lowering the price. But this operation was, in the end, entirely supported by him and put a heavy strain on his treasury.

On his arrival in Acre, on the other hand, the King of England raised the stakes by proposing to recruit knights at a higher rate than Philip Augustus; the King of France paid three gold besants a month for the service of a knight, which, notes the chronicler, was the going rate. Richard offered four, with the success already described. This greatly displeased the King of France, who, not unreasonably, saw it as an insult to his honour as suzerain.[26] Ralph of Coggeshall claims that Philip's decision to leave was partly due to this eye-catching gesture of Richard's. Thanks to his victories in Sicily and Cyprus, he had access to much greater wealth than the King of France, so he was in a position to spend more and gather behind him a greater number of knights, sergeants and soldiers of every sort, so eclipsing him in glory.[27] Richard also recruited archers, at a lower rate, admittedly, but high enough to rally them to his banner. When about to launch an attack on Saladin, Richard summoned all his archers and paid them generously to encourage them.[28]

Richard also displayed largesse in his dealings with the technicians in siege warfare, men whose services were invaluable but who were generally held in low esteem, for example the sappers and others of similarly humble rank. After the sappers had made a breach in a tower at Acre, in July 1191, the King had it cried through the camp that he would give two gold besants, then three and later four, to anyone who pulled a stone from the tower; soldiers flocked from all sides and set to work, many of them being wounded.[29] On the occasion of the capture of the Egyptian ship before its arrival in Acre, Richard was even generous to the sailors, generally looked down on and despised.[30]

Admittedly, Richard was not alone in his displays of largesse. Rigord notes that Philip Augustus did the same, at Christmas, in Messina (perhaps thanks to the money he had received from Richard), making large gifts to the 'poor knights of his land' who had lost everything in the storm. Rigord does not name all of them, but records as among the beneficiaries of this largesse the Duke of Burgundy, who received 1,000 marks, the Count of Nevers (600 marks), William des Barres (400 marks) and several others less generously treated, none of whom could exactly be regarded as 'poor knights'.[31] The majority of sources, however, attest to the fact that Richard surpassed everyone else in largesse. Indeed he went too far, in the eyes of some, especially with regard to knights. According to Ralph of Coggeshall:

> The king, however, gradually saw his treasury melt away; he had distributed it, without much thought and with a generous hand, among his knights; he saw the army of the Franks and all the foreigners who, for more than a year, he had commanded and kept at his side, at a very high cost, decide, after the death of the Duke of Burgundy, to return home.[32]

This excessive generosity soon left Richard impoverished, in spite of the enormous wealth at his disposal at the time of his arrival. He therefore had to resign himself to returning, all the more so because the political situation in England and France demanded his presence and the French were no longer in cooperative mood. But he promised to return as soon as he could assemble an even more powerful army, in other words, when he had found the money necessary for effective recruitment.

Derogations from largesse

If Richard is seen as an irreproachable model of prowess (and no source criticises him on this score), the same is not true in the case of largesse. Roger of Howden, for example, sometimes criticised the King for

a degree of avarice that was completely at variance with the virtue expected of him. This was the case at Acre, where, he says, after the town had been taken, the two kings of France and England kept for themselves the booty that had been won and chose not to distribute it to the counts and barons, who, as a result, threatened to return home. Faced with this prospect, Richard and Philip promised to give them their share of the booty, but kept putting it off, playing for time, obviously reluctant to keep their word; a number of knights were reduced to such desperate straits that they were forced to sell their arms to survive.[33] Richard himself gave nothing to his men, who then became unwilling to follow him because they had no more horses and nothing to eat, drink or wear. But such a violation of convention on Richard's part could only be temporary, as Roger of Howden admits; the King eventually noted the destitution of his men and took pity on them, providing them with whatever they needed.[34]

Another refusal of largesse on Richard's part was more excusable. This was when he rejected a new demand by the Duke of Burgundy, who had run out of money to pay the French knights and men-at-arms, who were demanding their wages. Harsh words were exchanged between the King and the Duke, but Richard refused to open up his treasury; as a result, the Christian host lost more than 700 knights, says Ambroise, who deplored the fact, though he dared not criticise Richard for avarice.[35]

Matthew Paris was bolder. Referring to the presents which the King had frequently and secretly received from Saladin, which were, as we have seen, the subject of much comment in the army, particularly, we may be sure, among the French, he reports Richard's servants as saying, to apologise for his greed: 'Let him squander in prodigality what belongs to him.'[36]

Such criticism is infrequent; it is probably to be explained by the disappointment felt by the crusaders at the disputes which too often divided the kings and princes, their leaders, for political and ideological reasons, certainly, but also, more mundanely, over vulgar questions of money.

Richard was often hard up. Was this because he was so prodigal? Perhaps his frequent and excessive generosity was, in the end, the chief obstacle to his own virtue of largesse, at least during his stay in the Holy Land, when occasions to spend lavishly were legion. This is what Matthew Paris seems to be saying when he describes Richard's arrival in Acre, as a splendid prince, surpassing his 'rival', Philip Augustus, in every sphere, by his prowess and his largesse, thereby making himself hugely

popular with the crowds, including the crusaders already on the spot. Philip Augustus was well aware of this and took umbrage:

> Every day the reputation of his rival grew greater. Richard was richer in treasure, more liberal in distributing presents, accompanied by a larger army and more eager to attack the enemy.[37]

His meticulously stage-managed arrival, ostentation and carefully planned liberality, preceded by rumours of the victories and riches he had acquired in Sicily and Cyprus, and further enhanced by the spectacular seizure of the great Egyptian ship, won the King of England huge popularity in the eyes of all. Richard of Devizes testifies to this, even if, in comparing Richard's arrival to that of Christ returning to earth at the end of time, he might have been slightly overdoing the enthusiasm of the Christian masses:

> The king . . . came to the siege of Acre and was received by the besiegers with as much joy as if he had been Christ Himself returning to earth to restore the kingdom of Israel.[38]

The King of France, he adds, had also enjoyed great success on his arrival, but with the coming of the King of England, the glory of Philip Augustus was eclipsed 'even as the moon loses its light at sunrise'.

Was this an instance of cleverly orchestrated propaganda or a natural expression of Richard's generous temperament? It was a bit of both, probably. We find a similar sort of display at the time of the King's departure. According to Roger of Howden, the King

> lavishly distributed his treasure to all the knights and squires in the army, and there were many who said that none of his predecessors had ever given away in a year what he gave in a single month.

Roger praises this attitude, which, he says, also won him the favour of the Lord, 'because God loves him who gives with a smile'.[39] This virtue of largesse, so favourable to the knights who were dependent on it, seems to have reached its apogee in the second half of the twelfth century, at least according to the literary and historical sources; it then just as rapidly declined, at the end of the twelfth and in the early thirteenth centuries. Was it only to conform to the tradition of praising times past that Guiot de Provins, a few years after Richard's death, lamented the disappearance of this virtue, once practised by all princes in all courts?

> Now weep the fine houses
> For the good princes and good barons,

> Who kept great courts in them
> And gave fine gifts.[40]

At the same period, the author of *Perlesvaus* points up the disappearance of this virtue even from the court of King Arthur, previously the model of chivalry and largesse. The result was predictable: the knights of his household drifted away; whereas once they had numbered 370, now they were only 25.[41] Huon de Méry, a few years later, tried to revive the practice. He gave a high position to this virtue in his allegory of the *Tournoi de l'Antichrist*, in which he describes the battle between the virtues and the vices, in imitation of Prudence. Opposed to Avarice, Largesse unseats her adversary, who is remounted by the Lombards. Avarice then cuts off her right hand, and the minstrels bemoan their fate: if Largesse disappeared, they would die in poverty! Nor were they the only ones to complain; what would become of the poor but worthy knights whom Largesse was in the habit of clothing? Who, in future, would give them fabrics of Tyre and cloths from Outremer? Courtesy and Prowess wept, because 'Prowess without Largesse is dead'.[42] Happily, however, the virtues finally won the victory and the booty, which they handed over to their knights, providing a banquet for all-comers.

In 1227, Jean Renart made a disillusioned comment common at this period: chivalry was dying. In the past, in the time of King Conrad, princes had set more store by being surrounded by knights than by furniture! They had treated them generously, supported them and preferred them to the bourgeoisie and the common people.[43] Around 1230, the author of the prose *Lancelot* also emphasised the merits of the largesse of kings and princes towards their knights. It was praiseworthy but it was also beneficial:

> No one is lost by largesse, only by avarice: you should take care to give without ceasing: the more you give, the more will you have to give, because what you give will remain in your lands and it will attract wealth from other lands.[44]

This virtue, however, was tending to fall into disuse. William Marshal, too, saw the age of Richard the Lionheart as the golden age of chivalry and largesse. But he gave most of the credit to Richard's brother Henry, who loved chivalry, and 'revived' it by engaging many household knights and treating them generously. In fact, the Young King

> Who was good, handsome and courteous,
> Acted so meritoriously
> That he revived chivalry
> Which was at that time close to death.

Henry's example was followed, as we know, by many other princes who, in their turn, vied with each other in largesse to the knights they recruited:

> And the great men of the land
> Who wanted to win honour
> Sought and kept
> The *bachelers* they knew to be good.
> And they freely gave them
> Horses, arms and money
> Or land or fine equipment.

But on the death of the Young King, chivalry and largesse were, he said, in mourning:

> O Lord! What will Largesse do now,
> And Chivalry and Prowess
> Which used to dwell within him?
> . . .
> In Martel died, it seems to me,
> The one who embodied within himself
> All courtesy and worth
> Breeding and largesse.[45]

Was Richard surpassed not only in prowess but also in largesse by his brother in the chivalric imagination?

NOTES

1. For the prospects of squires becoming knights, see Flori, J., 'Les Ecuyers dans la Littérature Française du XIIe Siècle; Pour une Lexicologie de la Sociétée Médiévale', in *Et c'est la Fin pour Quoy Sommes*, vol. 2, pp. 579–91. For the 'young', see Köhler, 'Sens et Fonction du Terme "Jeunesse" '; Duby, 'Les "Jeunes" dans la Société Aristocratique'; for the bachelors, see Flori, 'Qu'est-ce qu'un *Bacheler*?'.

2. On this point, see Coss, *The Knight in Medieval England*, pp. 31ff.

3. Flori, *Essor de la Chevalerie*; for a contrary view, see Barbero, *Aristocrazia*, and even more Barthélémy, D., 'Note sur le "Titre Chevaleresque" en France au XIe Siècle', *Journal des Savants* (Jan–June 1994), pp. 101–34; Barthélémy, D., 'Qu'est-ce que la Chevalerie en France au Xe et XIe Siècles', *Revue Historique*, 290, 1 (1994), pp. 15–74; for a recent discussion and attempt at a conciliatory synthesis, see Flori, *Chevaliers et Chevalerie*.

4. Köhler, 'Observations Historiques'; Köhler, *Aventure Chevaleresque*, pp. 9ff., 16ff., 35ff., etc; Duby, G., 'Problèmes d'Economie Seigneuriale dans la France du XIIe Siècle', in *Problème des 12. Jahrhunderts* (Stuttgart, 1968), pp. 161–7.

5. Boutet, 'Origine et Sens de la Largesse Arthurienne'.
6. Vauchez, A., *La Spiritualité du Moyen Age Occidental* (Paris, 1975); Vauchez, A., *Les Laïcs au Moyen Age: Pratiques et Expériences Religieuses* (Paris, 1987).
7. Little, L. H., 'Pride Goes Before Avarice; Social Change and the Vices in Latin Christendom', *American Historical Review*, 76 (1971), pp. 16–49.
8. See Cloetta, W. (ed.), *Le Moniage Guillaume* (Paris, 1906), lines 290ff., 883ff., 907ff., 1017ff., 1035ff., 5964ff.
9. For this important qualification, see Batany, 'Le Vocabulaire des Catégories Sociales'.
10. See Batany, 'Du Bellator au Chevalier'.
11. See on this point, for Chrétien de Troyes, Flori, 'Chevalerie dans les Romans de Chrétien de Troyes'; for *Aiol*, Spencer, 'Argent dans Aiol'; Flori, J., 'Sémantique et Idéologie; un Cas Exemplaire: les Adjectifs dans Aiol', in *Essor et Fortune de la Chanson de Geste*, pp. 55–68; Flori, 'L'Idéologie Aristocratique dans Aiol'. For *Partonopeu de Blois* and many other romances of the time of Richard I, see Flori, 'Noblesse, Chevalerie et Idéologie Aristocratique en France d'Oïl'.
12. For the largesse of Duke Richard, see Benoît de Sainte-Maure, *Chronique*, lines 19566ff., 19644ff., 24729ff.; for praise of the largesse of Robert of Normandy, see Batany, J., 'Les Trois Bienfaits du Duc Robert: un Modèle Historiographique du Prince Evergète au XIIe Siècle', in R. Chevalier (ed.), *Colloque Histoire et Historiographie 'Clio'* (Paris, 1980), pp. 263–72.
13. Wace, *Le Roman de Rou*, lines 780ff.
14. Bertran de Born, ed. Gouiran, no. 28, p. 501; no. 37, p. 735.
15. Prestwich, J. O., 'Richard Cœur de Lion: Rex Bellicosus', in Nelson, *Richard Cœur de Lion*, pp. 1–16.
16. Ambroise, lines 1054ff., French translation p. 347 (p. 46 of Ailes translation).
17. Ambroise, lines 1701ff. (p. 55 of Ailes translation).
18. Ambroise, lines 5360ff. (p. 106 of Ailes translation).
19. Richard of Devizes, p. 42.
20. William of Newburgh, p. 360.
21. Ambroise, lines 5245ff. (p. 105 of Ailes translation).
22. See on this point Frappier, 'Le "Don Contraignant"'.
23. Roger of Howden, IV, pp. 19–20.
24. Ambroise, line 10505, French translation p. 445 (pp. 172–3 of Ailes translation). There is a similar hierarchic distribution ibid., lines 10313ff.
25. Ibid., lines 6075ff.
26. Ibid., lines 4569ff.
27. Ralph of Coggeshall, p. 33.
28. *Gesta Henrici*, II, p. 185.

29. Ambroise, lines 4054ff., 4927ff. In 1099, during the assault on Jerusalem, Raymond de Saint-Gilles had made a similar promise to all who brought a stone to help fill the ditch which faced them.
30. Roger of Howden, III, p. 106.
31. Rigord, §72, p. 106.
32. Ralph of Coggeshall, pp. 51–2.
33. *Gesta Henrici*, II, p. 181.
34. Ibid., pp. 187ff.
35. Ambroise, lines 8170ff.
36. Matthew Paris, *Chronica Majora*, II, p. 368.
37. Ibid., p. 375.
38. Richard of Devizes, p. 39.
39. Roger of Howden, III, pp. 93–5.
40. Guiot de Provins, *La Bible Guiot*, ed. J. Orr (Paris–Manchester, 1951) (repr. Geneva, 1974), lines 102ff.
41. *Le Haut Livre du Graal, Perlesvaus*, ed. W. A. Nitze and T. A. Jenkins (New York, 1972), lines 64–76, p. 26.
42. Huon de Mery, *Li Tornoiement Antecrit*, ed. G. Wimmer, trans. S. Orgeur (Orleans, 1994).
43. Renart, Jean, *Le Roman de la Rose ou de Guillaume de Dole*, ed. F. Lecoy (Paris, 1979), lines 569–99 (modern French translation by J. Dufournet and others (Paris, 1988)).
44. *Lancelot du Lac*, ed. E. Kennedy (Paris, 1991), pp. 767–8.
45. *Guillaume le Maréchal*, lines 2679ff., 3643ff., 6985ff.

18

Chivalric Conduct

Prowess and largesse, eminently chivalric virtues, were above all the expression of an intense desire for glory, which could lead to pride (*superbia*), arrogance and an aristocratic hauteur close to contempt for others, and also to boastfulness and self-promotion, by means of every method then known, in order to publicise the glory striven for.[1] The ardent and immoderate temperament of the King of England naturally inclined him towards this darker side of chivalric behaviour; eminently sympathetic and honourable though some aspects of chivalry were, it should not be idealised. It had other, less attractive, features.

SUPERBIA

This tendency to ostentation has already been noted in connection with the arrival of Richard and his fleet wherever he was expected by his rivals (whom he invariably kept waiting), in Sicily and in Acre. The King of England did everything in his power to see that he appeared as a saviour, an all-powerful king, suffering no comparison with his rivals, especially Philip Augustus, whom he outshone in pomp, prestige and physical presence. The King of France, blind in one eye and introverted, not given to spectacular displays, was no match for Richard in this sphere. It is possible that the King of England, from the very beginning of his crusade, had been planning to promote his image by taking with him historiographers and jongleurs, in particular Ambroise, ever eager to sing his praise. This would have been nothing new. Roger of Howden records (and criticises) a similar procedure, not on Richard's part, but on that of William Longchamp, Bishop of Ely, who also made use of this type of publicity:

> In order to increase his fame and glorify his name, he had flattering poems and adulatory songs written; with presents he had enticed singers and entertainers from the kingdom of France, so that they would sing his praises in the streets.[2]

Fiercely anti-French, Roger is strongly critical of the use of jongleurs, which he regarded as a typically continental practice. The same criticism

was levelled against William Marshal, accused of paying a herald-at-arms to proclaim his name loudly at tournaments and comment favourably on his exploits.[3] But Richard, we should not forget, was above all 'French', a lover of epic compositions and of songs with a propaganda purpose; had he not himself composed (or had composed within his entourage) songs against the Duke of Burgundy, who had employed the same methods against him? It would hardly be surprising if the King drew on the services of such eulogists to glorify his deeds and actions in the Holy Land or elsewhere.

Though so determined to spread the news of his own renown, Richard proved notably quick to take offence and seems to have been reluctant to recognise the renown of others. We need only recall the animosity verging on hatred he displayed towards William des Barres, guilty of having dared to try to outdo him in some trivial joust in Sicily. The King did not hesitate to ridicule his rivals, in particular Philip Augustus, as we have frequently seen. We should also remember the humiliation he inflicted on the Duke of Austria, whom he prevented from joining the 'victors' at the triumphal entry into Acre; yet the Duke had been besieging the town since the spring of 1191, well before the arrival of Richard, to whom he had rallied and whose royal largesse he had accepted. Richard of Devizes recalls how long he had been involved in the siege before describing the episode in this way:

> With his banner carried before him, he appeared to claim for himself a part of the triumph. If not at the order at least with the consent of the offended king, the duke's banner was cast into the dirt and trampled upon as an insult to him by people set to ridicule him. The duke, though fearfully enraged against the king, had to swallow an offence that he could not avenge.[4]

Rigord offers no explanation for Richard's behaviour, content simply to report the episode, which he places in a different context. Richard, he says, had seized the standard of the Duke of Austria from 'a prince', near Acre, and to shame the Duke, had it broken and thrown into a deep cesspit.[5] Matthew Paris, who was rabidly anti-Norman, tells a rather different story. According to him the conflict between the two princes dated back to the time when Duke Leopold, on his way to the Holy Land, had sent his officials on ahead to prepare his lodgings. There, his men had clashed with a Norman knight from the household of the King of England, who, 'with the foolish and hot-headed vanity of the natives of that country', claimed a prior right to the rooms on the grounds that he had been first to arrive and already reserved them. An argument ensued, which degenerated into insults. Richard, 'whose biased spirit was strongly disposed to find in

favour of the Norman', flew into a violent rage against the Duke's men: 'forgetting all good manners, he precipitately ordered that the Duke's banner, raised as a signal above the building, should be thrown into a sewer'. The Duke, expelled from his lodgings, went to the King to complain, but was ridiculed for his pains. He then appealed to God, asking him to avenge such a deep insult and humble this proud man; after which he went home. What followed, and the role played by the humiliated Duke in the arrest of the King of England, is well known. Matthew Paris notes in conclusion that 'Richard later felt ashamed of his anger, when he was fiercely criticised for it'.[6] Whatever the real motives for this quarrel, the anger and pride displayed by Richard cannot be glossed over. He was clearly intent on humiliating his partner. He was to pay dearly for this flaw in his character.

Let us look at another example of Richard's arrogance, verging on vanity, which no doubt helped to establish his reputation as a worthy knight, but which may also have alienated those who, not unreasonably, saw it as self-importance. The episode, which is recounted only by Gerald of Wales (much given to similar 'historical sayings' and other edifying but possibly fabricated anecdotes), took place in 1197, shortly after Richard had embarked on the construction of the formidable fortress of Château-Gaillard, reputed from the first to be impregnable. Before his men, who were admiring the fortifications, the King of France professed himself delighted to see such a formidable castle, even wishing that the walls were made of iron, so confident was he that when he had subdued the whole of Normandy, as he had subdued Aquitaine, he would annex it to his own lands; which is, of course, exactly what happened after Richard's death, although Philip's claim might well, at the time, have seemed pretentious and something of a vain boast. When word of it reached Richard, he responded with another piece of bluster, even more provocative, the arrogance of which is emphasised by Gerald:

> When afterwards this speech had been related to King Richard, who was a man of too much arrogance and of immense courage, he burst forth into these words, in the hearing of many of his soldiers: 'By God's throat,' said he (for he was accustomed to swear by these and similar blaspheming oaths), 'if the whole of this fortress were made of butter, never mind of iron or stone, I should feel no doubt whatsoever that I could well and truly defend it against him and all his forces.' But since, by this insolent speech, he neither sought nor wished the help of God, but had rashly presumed to ascribe the whole defence to his own arm, and to his own powers alone, when a very few years had passed, the thing happened contrary to his own wish and haughty declaration, and King Philip prevailed over him and took possession of the place.[7]

Should we see these signs of pride and *superbia* as essential components of the king's chivalric behaviour? Probably yes; after all, like Cyrano de Bergerac, he had Aquitainian, if not Gascon, ancestors.

MERCY, GRACE AND PITY

Other aspects of the chivalric ethic, occasionally mentioned in chronicles and even more developed in literary works, in particular the Arthurian romances, have a more attractive side. Chrétien de Troyes, in his *Conte du Graal*, enunciates the principle in the form of a precept taught to Perceval during his dubbing by Gornemant de Goor: a knight should avoid killing a defeated or a disarmed enemy.[8] He even makes it one of the principal components of the chivalric ethic. In all his romances Chrétien invariably describes the practical application of this ethic: the victorious hero, except in rare cases which are properly made clear, spares his defeated enemy and takes him prisoner. Orderic Vitalis, describing the battle of Brémules (1119), may already be revealing the effects of this when he emphasises how this engagement, although involving many knights on both the French and English sides, led to relatively few deaths:

> In that battle of the two kings, in which about nine hundred knights were engaged, only three were killed. They were all clad in mail and spared each other on both sides, out of fear of God and fellowship in arms; they were more concerned to capture than to kill the fugitives.[9]

It is possible, of course, that Orderic is expressing his own monastic ideology rather than that of the knights and that he was trying to apply to this battle the Augustinian canons of the just war.[10] He also, it must be said, mentions other far bloodier confrontations, even between knights. But one cannot altogether dismiss the hypothesis that this ethic, involving the sparing of the defeated adversary – provided he was a knight – had penetrated the chivalric mentality. The reasons for doing so were even stronger when he was a noble, for whom the captor might hope to gain a substantial ransom, while also earning a degree of gratitude on the part of his unhappy adversary, perhaps even the expectation of similar treatment should he himself later be defeated by this adversary's own men. This ethic created a feeling of fellowship, a common ideology that can be seen as a sort of 'knightly freemasonry',[11] though I myself prefer to describe it as a sense of belonging to the elitist guild of chivalry.

More than the 'fear of God' evoked by Orderic Vitalis, it was probably the diffusion of these shared values that helped to spread the

practice of sparing a defeated enemy who cried 'Mercy'. It probably owed its success more to the clearly perceived self-interest of the knights than to any natural compassion they may have felt or to humanity on the part of the victors. It contributed nevertheless, over the long term, to the development of the future 'laws of war' and, in the short term, to the creation of the chivalric ethic, which retained only its honourable aspect. The omnipresence of this theme of 'mercy' in Arthurian romances suggests that we should accept at least a degree of correspondence with reality, if only through the influence exerted by romance heroes on knights in the real world.[12]

There were, however, limits to the application of this custom: it essentially concerned Christian knights fighting among themselves within Christendom. Heretics and 'infidels' were doubly excluded, as neither knights nor Christians. They could be massacred without fear or criticism. St Bernard called those who slew the infidel in battle in the Holy Land 'evil-killers', as opposed to 'man-killers'.

Nevertheless, it seems likely that, at a very early stage, during the First Crusade and increasingly in the twelfth century, the warlike valour of the Turkish horsemen and the respect they inspired in their opponents gave rise to the notion of a sort of universal chivalry, transcending frontiers of race and religion. The legend attached to Saladin, regarded as a model of chivalry although a Muslim, is one sign of this belief. But it is already suggested by the comments of the chroniclers of the First Crusade, who believed that only the Turks and the 'Franks' could claim the title of knight on account of their warlike qualities. In explanation, they invoked a common origin for the two races: both Franks and Turks were descended from the Trojans, ancestors of all chivalry.[13]

One example among many of the way in which this behaviour had penetrated the chivalric mentality in the age of Richard the Lionheart is provided by a particularly picturesque incident. In the *Chanson de Guillaume*, the hero, William, in battle, unseated the Saracen king Déramé by cutting off his thigh with a blow from his sword. When William's nephew, the youthful Gui, saw the fallen 'pagan' writhing on the grass, he drew his sword and cut off his head, for which he was reproved by his uncle, shocked at such a violation of the principles. He expressed his criticism in no uncertain terms, revealing the widespread acceptance of a code of honour that forbade the killing of a wounded opponent incapable of defending himself: 'You bloody brat, how dare you lay hands on a disabled man? You'll be reproached for it in noble courts.'[14] Without emotion and without scruple, the young man defended himself by invoking the common good: the Saracen may have lost a thigh, but he still had his

testicles and was quite capable of fathering a king who might, in his turn, have invaded Christian territory. This argument (which, we should note in passing, could equally well be applied to a Christian enemy, including a neighbour) appeared so convincing to William that he immediately praised the wisdom of so young a man and later had no hesitation in beheading another Saracen adversary cut down in identical circumstances. This has all the appearance of an attempt to justify the slaughter of Muslim 'knights', contrary to an earlier well-established tradition discouraging the killing of an unarmed and wounded knight. We know, for example, that William the Conqueror is supposed to have 'deprived of the baldric of the *militia*' a Norman knight who cut off the head of the wounded Harold at the battle of Hastings.[15]

Richard seems himself to have been a beneficiary of this aspect of the chivalric code. He was once seriously endangered, as we have seen, when pursuing his father Henry II. Just as he was about to catch up with him, William Marshal, loyal to the Old King and determined to protect him, turned and charged straight at the Count of Poitou. Richard was without his hauberk, having launched into the pursuit on impulse, not anticipating a battle. According to William Marshal, who recorded the incident, the future king was seriously worried and begged for mercy:

> He spurred straight on
> Towards Count Richard who was approaching.
> And when the Count saw him coming
> He cried out angrily
> 'By God's legs, Marshal,
> Do not kill me; that would be wrong.
> For I am totally unarmed.'
> And the Marshal replied:
> 'No indeed! Let the devil kill you!
> For I shall not.'[16]

Heeding Richard's request for mercy, William Marshal contented himself with killing his mount, so bringing the rider down and forcing him to abandon his pursuit. It is possible that this is why Richard, once king, confirmed William in his post and gave him the richest heiress in the kingdom as his wife.

Did Richard himself practise this sort of 'mercy'? No example is recorded. The few instances of the King's 'pity' mentioned by the chroniclers hardly fit into this context. The chroniclers note, for example, the 'pity' felt by the King for the daughter of Isaac Comnenus, the defeated 'emperor' of Cyprus, who, suspecting that his cause was lost, left his fortress and walked out to surrender to the King. Richard was content

to despatch the young girl to Queen Berengaria as a hostage, as had been laid down in the earlier agreements, which Isaac had broken.[17]

A later legend, transmitted by Matthew Paris, tells of a more significant example of Richard's *misericordia*, this time towards an exile. An English knight from the New Forest, who had long been in the habit of hunting illegally in the royal forests, was caught red-handed one day and condemned to exile by the royal courts. The law decreed by Richard to punish those guilty of poaching in the royal forest was more merciful than those of his predecessors. In the past, offenders had had their eyes put out, been castrated or lost a hand or a foot. But to Richard it seemed inhuman that men, for an offence concerning beasts, should mutilate in this way creatures made in God's image. He ordered, therefore, that the guilty should be punished only by prison, exile from England or Gascony, or even a fine. This *miles*, consequently, was banished, with his wife and children, and forced to beg for food. Deciding one day to approach Richard in Normandy and beseech his clemency, he found him in a church, hearing mass. He entered, trembling, but dared not approach the King because, due to his abject poverty, his appearance was barely human. Instead, he began to pray fervently to the crucifix for a reconciliation with the King. Richard heard his prayers and lamentations and saw that he was sincere in his devotion to the crucifix, which aroused his admiration. He summoned the knight and enquired who he was. The *miles* said he was his liege man, like his ancestors before him, and told his story, explaining the reason for his prayers. The King asked him: 'Have you in your lifetime done any other good thing than show this devotion to the crucifix?' The knight explained the origin of this particular devotion. It dated back to a long-ago event. His father and another knight had quarrelled, and the knight had killed his father when he himself was still only a boy (*puer*); the fatherless child had decided to avenge and kill this murderous *miles*, but without success since he was always on his guard. Eventually, one Easter, now himself a knight, he found him alone. He drew his sword to kill him, but the old knight ran away and took refuge by a roadside cross, as he was now past defending himself properly. He implored the young knight, in the name of the crucifix of Our Lord, not to end his days, and made a solemn promise to provide money for a chaplain to pray for the salvation of the soul of the deceased father. Moved, overcome by pity, the knight sheathed his sword and abandoned the idea of killing the old man; thus, thanks to his devotion for the crucifix, he had pardoned the murderer for his father's death. Richard was much impressed and loudly praised the young knight's conduct, saying: 'You acted wisely, because the Crucifix has also obtained your pardon.' He

summoned his chancellor and instructed him, by letters patent, to restore the *miles* to his lands and former estate. Matthew Paris concludes: 'And this act of mercy performed by the pious King Richard, with other works of this sort, we truly believe, delivered him from the peril of damnation and torments.'[18]

This story is primarily an exemplum honouring the crucifix, the cult of which had begun to spread at this period. It is revealing with regard to the morals and religious sensibilities which the Church was then seeking to instil, as also to the virtues of generosity and mercifulness attributed to Richard with a view to sparing him in the next world the punishments resulting from his sins.

Among the sins for which the King of England was criticised, alongside lust, those of pride, greed and cruelty loom large. Ralph of Coggeshall, describing his death in 1199, summarises in a few lines Richard's career and the vain hopes raised by his accession to the throne. Alas, he belonged to 'the immense cohort of sinners'; even his laudable desire to liberate Jerusalem was tainted by pride, pomp and vainglorious displays of wealth; having won every honour, he was unable to remain humble in victory, and fell even deeper into sin, his heart full of pride, greed, vicious insolence and cruelty:

> He did not understand that he owed his victory to the hand of God, he failed to show his Saviour the gratitude he owed him and he made no attempt to correct in his soul the dissolute morals he had adopted in his hot-headed youth. As he grew older, he was cruel to the point where his abusive harshness consigned to oblivion all the merits he had shown at the beginning of his reign.[19]

Happily, Ralph adds, a few good deeds (his pilgrimage to the tomb of St Edmund, his piety and assiduity in attending mass, his alms to the poor, and so on) and, above all, at the end of his life, his sincere confession and repentance for his past sins, might have earned him divine mercy and a mitigation of his deserved punishment.

Other chroniclers also criticised Richard for his needless cruelty. For Gervase of Canterbury, it was his extreme violence which had driven the barons of Aquitaine to rise against him and rally to the support of his brother Henry, and prevented Henry II from going on crusade.[20] Gerald of Wales admitted this fault but reckoned the accusation unjust because, he believed, Richard's rigour and his savagery disappeared once the troubles in Aquitaine were over; he then became mild and merciful, finding a just balance between excessive severity and excessive indulgence.[21] But it is the same Gerald who, describing the King's death, notes

that he died from a bolt from a crossbow, a weapon 'he had too often cruelly misused'.[22] It is far from clear to which events he was referring. The chroniclers report many instances of his cruelty when using this weapon which might explain this global judgement. It is unlikely it had anything to do with the treatment meted out to the Christian who had renounced his faith and been taken prisoner with twenty-four Turks; to punish this renegade, 'the king had him stood in front of some archers and pierced with arrows'.[23] But who would feel sorry for this renegade? Ralph of Coggeshall, followed by Matthew Paris, tells how a spy of Richard's had one night spotted envoys from Saladin on their way to the Duke of Burgundy, taking rich presents: five camels loaded with gold, silver and silks. The spy laid an ambush with a small band of knights, and they seized the Muslim envoys on their return and led them captive to the King of England. Under torture, one of them confessed what messages and gifts Saladin had sent to the Duke of Burgundy. Next day, Richard summoned the Duke and proposed they march together on Jerusalem, which the Duke refused. Richard then accused him of treachery and reproached him for receiving gifts from Saladin, which the Duke vehemently denied. Richard then had the spy and the captive messengers brought before them, and they told all, to the great shame of the Duke of Burgundy. The King then gave orders for his servants to shoot arrows at Saladin's envoys before the assembled army. The army, the chronicler adds, 'was greatly surprised at this act of cruelty, because no-one knew what the men had done or where they came from.'[24] But these were carefully limited 'massacres', and of 'infidels', carried out during the crusade; it seems unlikely that acts of this nature would provoke such strong criticism. Even less can they explain the accusation made against Richard at the time of his death. Although he himself made fairly frequent use of this weapon, there is nothing to suggest that it was he who was chiefly responsible for the generalised use of the crossbow in conflicts between Christians within western Europe – in spite of the formal prohibition on the use of the crossbow (together with the ordinary bow) in 1139 by the Second Lateran Council.[25]

THE TREATMENT OF PRISONERS

Perhaps the accusation of cruelty was based more on the massacre of Muslim prisoners which took place on the King's orders after the capture of Acre. Unsurprisingly, responsibility for this slaughter was attributed to Saladin by the Christian sources and to Richard by the Muslim sources, both accusing the enemy of failing to keep agreements. But they are all,

or nearly all, agreed in stating that it was the King of England who was the first to execute his prisoners. Saladin, later and in retaliation, dealt with his Christian captives in similar fashion. According to Richard of Devizes, the King of England had his Saracen captives beheaded, with the exception of one notable, because he was unable to obtain from Saladin the Holy Cross, which it had been agreed should be returned.[26] Matthew Paris says that the Saracens were supposed to return the Cross, liberate 1,500 Christian captives and make a payment of 7,000 gold besants. But, he goes on:

> When the day fixed for the restitutions arrived, Saladin fulfilled none of his promises. To punish him for this violation of the treaty, 2,600 Saracens had their heads cut off. Only the chief among them were spared, for the kings to dispose of as they pleased.[27]

Rigord gives a different version of events, but he, too, attributes responsibility for the massacre to the Saracens, who were unable to carry out the agreed conditions:

> But as they were effectively unable to do what they had sworn to do, the King of England, greatly incensed, had the pagan prisoners, to the number of 5,000 and more, led out of the city and beheaded, keeping back the most powerful and the most wealthy, for whom he received a huge sum of money in ransom.[28]

According to Ambroise, Saladin failed to observe the agreements and 'abandoned the hostages to perish, without rescue'. He 'acted in a false and treacherous manner when he did not redeem or deliver those who were condemned to death. Because of this he lost his renown, which was great'.[29] In the face of this bad faith, Richard decided to execute his prisoners: 2,700 Saracens were brought out of the town and put to death. Ambroise was jubilant and interpreted this as a grace of God, a vengeance taken on these impious men for the blows they had inflicted with sword and crossbow.

Roger of Howden reproduces a letter from the King of England in which he soberly sets out his own version of events. The men in the citadel of Acre, he says, realising that they could resist no longer, decided to surrender if they were given a guarantee that their lives would be spared, to which the King agreed. But the Saracens violated the agreement (how is not specified) and Richard resolved to 'do his duty':

> The citadel of Acre soon surrendered, to us and to the king of France; we spared the lives of the Saracens who had been sent there to guard and defend it. An agreement was even concluded and fully confirmed by Saladin, by which Saladin would return to us the Holy Cross and also 1,500 captives,

alive; he himself fixed the day for the implementation of these clauses. But when the agreed term expired, as the pact he had concluded had obviously been broken, we put to death about 2,600 Saracens from among those who were in our custody, as was right and proper. We kept a few nobles, nevertheless, hoping that the Holy Cross and some captive Christians would be returned as their ransom.[30]

Roger himself offers an explanation which is more detailed but still somewhat confused. According to him, Richard had threatened Saladin as early as 13 August that he would behead his prisoners unless he speedily implemented all the clauses of the agreement. Saladin replied with equal brusqueness: 'If you decapitate my pagans, I will decapitate your Christians.'[31] But he still dragged his feet, handing over neither the Cross, nor the captives nor even the money promised in exchange for the lives of his men. He requested a further delay, which Richard refused. Then, on 18 August, Saladin had his Christian prisoners beheaded and on the same day Richard ordered his army to prepare to attack the enemy camp. Learning of the massacre of the Christian prisoners, it was still only two days later, on 20 August, that Richard ordered the slaughter of the Muslims. This version is clearly an attempt to justify the King's action, which is presented simply as 'reprisals' for the earlier executions by Saladin. What is more, Richard was merciful enough not to bring forward the announced executions, sticking to the agreed date.

The Muslim chroniclers did not conceal the fact that Saladin had tried to gain time by delaying implementation of the agreed terms, but they still accuse the King of England of having shamefully gone back on his word. According to Imad ad-Din al-Isfahani, the Franks made unreasonable demands, asking first for the prisoners to be handed over, then for 100,000 dinars, also asking to see the Holy Cross, which should be returned to them. Saladin had little confidence in the Christians, but nevertheless paid the first instalment and showed them the Holy Cross, before which they prostrated themselves, accepting, at this point, that the agreement was being respected. But soon afterwards, Richard, out of perfidy, moved as if to attack the Muslim camp, keeping the captives tightly bound. Saladin's men, thinking that the Christians were arriving for a peaceful consultation, rode out to meet them, but 'these accursed men' threw themselves on the prisoners and slaughtered the lot of them, leaving their bodies where they fell. A battle ensued and the Muslims refused, from that moment, to carry out the agreement, handing over neither the prisoners (of whose fate he says nothing) nor the promised ransom, nor the Cross, which was returned to the Treasury, 'not to respect it but to humiliate it'.[32]

Baha ad-Din admits that Saladin procrastinated, but is even more emphatic about the treachery of the King of England, who, he says, deliberately broke his word:

> When the English King saw that Saladin delayed in carrying out the terms of the treaty he broke his word to the Muslim prisoners with whom he had made an agreement and from whom he had received the city's surrender in exchange for their lives. If the Sultan handed over all that had been agreed, they could go free with their possessions, wives and children, but if the Sultan refused they would be treated as prisoners. Now, however, the king broke his word and revealed the secret thought he had formed even before making the agreement, and put it into effect even after he had received the money and the prisoners [that is, the liberated Franks], as even his fellow Christians later reported.[33]

Imad ad-Din says that Richard was no stranger to such violations, from capriciousness or from treachery. This had already been demonstrated during an earlier negotiation, started on 8 November 1191:

> As for the correspondence of the king, it failed completely to achieve its aim, because he conducted himself with his habitual fickleness; [in fact] every time he made an agreement, he violated and broke it; every time he settled an affair, he twisted things and confused the issue; every time he gave his word, he went back on it; every time he was entrusted with a secret, he did not keep it; every time we said: 'he will be true', he betrayed us; when we thought he would improve, he got worse; and he revealed only villainy.[34]

The systematic massacre of prisoners had become rare in the West in the mid twelfth century, at least in the countries where chivalry had developed, with its specific ethic favouring the capture of an enemy and his liberation in return for a ransom. The barbaric custom persisted only in outlying regions, in particular on the borders of Richard's own kingdom, in the Celtic wildernesses of Scotland and Ireland. These allegedly savage peoples, unlike the Anglo-Norman knights who attacked them, generally fought on foot and for their freedom or their lives rather than for wages or some other reward; they were indifferent to the chivalric code or the fate of captives.[35] The practice of mutilating the garrisons of fortresses or of towns that had been stormed had also ceased to be customary and it was now frowned on, except as a punishment for rebellious vassals.[36]

Even in the West, however, many exceptions to this decreasing brutality are known.[37] During his campaigns of 'pacification' in Aquitaine, Richard and his routiers perpetrated a very large number of atrocities of this type, burning villages and crops, depopulating the countryside and mutilating or killing the garrisons of captured castles. Here, however, it

was a matter of punishing rebel vassals, in which case feudal law justified such conduct, although it was forbidden against 'ordinary' enemies.[38] Nevertheless, in Richard's struggle against Philip Augustus, particularly after his return from captivity, the chroniclers record a sharp increase in such acts of barbarism. Roger of Howden, for example, describes how, after the collapse of one of the innumerable truces between the two kings, they each invaded the lands of the other in order to depopulate them, carrying off booty and captives, burning villages, even massacring prisoners who had fought for the enemy.[39] In the course of his conflict with his brother Geoffrey, in Poitou, Richard also carried out various acts of cruelty and infringements of the normal practice of ransom. In 1183, for example, he ordered all the prisoners who were vassals of his brother to be killed, irrespective of rank, and himself supervised many of these executions.[40]

Such acts were even more common on crusade, where chivalric customs were not established and where massacres on both sides were by no means unknown. As we have seen, Richard had no scruples in ordering the drowning of the majority of the Saracens taken from the Egyptian ship sunk off Acre. According to Ambroise, during another naval battle off the same town, a Turkish galley was brought by force into the port and its occupants had their throats cut by the women from the Christian camp:

> Then would you have heard great celebration. Then would you have seen women coming, knives in their hands, taking the Turks by the hair, pulling them to their great pain, then cutting off their heads, bearing them to the ground.[41]

The risk of reprisals was obvious, as we have seen in the case of the general massacre at Acre, and this sometimes exercised a restraining influence. A Muslim chronicler notes, for example, that on 24 June 1191, the Christians burned a prisoner alive; the Muslims immediately did the same, and matters rested there.[42] Reciprocity did not always, however, operate in the direction of restraint. If we are to believe Matthew Paris (though the story is probably legendary), Saladin asked a Christian prisoner what treatment he would have inflicted on him if their roles had been reversed. The prisoner replied haughtily, even insolently:

> You would suffer the capital sentence at my hands; as you are the cruellest enemy of my God, no treasure could redeem you; and as you persist in your law which is good for dogs, I would cut off your head with my own hands.[43]

Saladin told him that he had pronounced his own death sentence and the prisoner, whose hands were tied behind his back, was beheaded, and

so made a martyr. Saladin, as we have seen, also ordered the beheading of the Templars and Hospitallers captured at the battle of Hattin in 1187. Such massacres were not, therefore, particularly unusual. The episode of the slaughter of the Muslim captives ordered by Richard was different, however, because it took place after an agreement, during a period of truce, and in real or apparent violation of a word given; this was clearly contrary to the chivalric code then in the process of formation.

WORD OF HONOUR

The expression 'word of honour' had not yet emerged at this date, but the idea itself existed. Respect for one's given word was one of the foundations of the chivalric code; it was indispensable to the conduct of negotiations for the ransom of captured knights. In both romances and real life many cases are known of defeated knights freed 'on parole', left unharmed on condition that they went to give themselves up to their captor's lord, or bound to surrender to him on a given date after going to alert their families to their situation and urge them to raise the sum agreed for their ransom. It is true that the ancient custom of taking hostages was still practised, a brother, son or other relative then serving as security, temporarily standing in for the prisoner in captivity. But manners became more refined during the twelfth century and hostages were increasingly treated as guests; in any case it made sense not to treat too harshly prisoners for whom it was hoped to obtain a good ransom. The costs of lodging and feeding them could be added to the ransom demanded. In the twelfth century, the weakening of the ties of the *familia*, the rise of individualism, as evidenced by the fashion for chivalric romances featuring individual heroes who were knights errant, the development of 'courtly morality' and other less well understood factors all helped to give increasing importance to the 'word of honour'.

This marked a profound shift in mental attitudes, a consequence of a certain secularisation of society. This 'word' was solemn, but was not accompanied by any religious ritual; it was not an oath pronounced over relics, with salvation at stake if it was broken. But it had an equal value, or almost, within aristocratic society. Respect for this word involved no more than the reputation of whoever gave it. It was sufficient in itself. But it could be accepted only if the individual who gave it received, as it were, the sanction of a recognised and respected body, a sort of legal entity, to which he belonged. This then amounts to an 'order' in both the socio-professional and moral sense, with strong ideological, even religious, connotations. This was the case with chivalry, which, in the second

half of the twelfth century, came of age. We can then (and only then, in my opinion) properly speak of chivalry, rather than of the heavy cavalry, however 'elite'.

In William Rufus, King of England at the beginning of the twelfth century, we can already see signs of this outlook emerging. In 1098, having taken prisoner a large number of knights from Poitou and Maine, he treated them honourably. They were released from their bonds so that they could eat more comfortably, once they had given their word that they would not take advantage to try to escape. To those of his followers (*satellites*) who expressed doubts as to the wisdom of this procedure, William brusquely replied: 'Far be it from me to believe that a true knight (*probus miles*) would break his sworn word (*fidem*). If he did so he would be despised for ever as an outlaw.'[44]

Admittedly these are words attributed to the King by a monk, and it may be argued that once again he was projecting his own monastic ethic onto the knights. But the writer, Orderic Vitalis, is on several occasions at pains to record violations of this moral code by numerous other individuals. Such criticism make sense only if these knights, though laymen, shared an ethic which was peculiar to them, here presented as self-evident. In fact by the end of the eleventh century, a sort of code of honour seems to have required that one kept one's word, even to an infidel. In 1086, in Spain, when King Alfonso VI was planning to break his sworn word to the Moroccan sultan, Youssouf, he was dissuaded by his entourage on the grounds that such conduct would be unbecoming.[45] It should be noted, however, that it was the conduct of a prince and financial and political matters that were at issue here, and not the specifically knightly practices of captivity and freeing on parole.

There were certainly violations of this ethic, but the simple fact that they are mentioned is in itself evidence that the ethic existed. Thus in 1198, according to several English chroniclers, William des Barres, who had been captured by Richard near Mantes, fled on a rouncey, while his captors were occupied with other prisoners, despite having given his word. William himself gave another version of his capture, which might explain this apparent lapse. According to him, the King of England had been unable to defeat him, so had killed his horse with his sword in order to capture him. This first act, hardly chivalric (though not prohibited), was the cause of the second, further evidence that the chivalric ethic was well on the way to being codified, if only in the knightly mentality; there was clearly no question of any legal redress, but the incident led to a lasting enmity between Richard and William, which degenerated into the brawl at Messina.[46] Many breaches of this ethic are known during the

crusades, primarily, like that involving Richard, when garrisons which surrendered were massacred in disregard of promises made. Saladin himself had few illusions on this score. During peace negotiations with Richard, he confided to his entourage that the agreements would soon be violated by the Christians, and a letter written soon after the signing of the agreement between Saladin and Richard describes the Westerners as habitually devious, because perfidy was built into their character.[47] But these cases involved Westerners and 'enemies of the faith', and not all Christians shared the moral rectitude of St Louis, who, to the astonishment of his entourage, insisted on paying the Saracens the 10,000 *livres* (out of 200,000) that had secretly been kept back when his ransom was paid.[48]

Jordan Fantosme, in his rhymed chronicle written at the end of the twelfth century, reveals the near-universal acceptance of this morality among knights. He refers to the prowess of a valiant knight, William de Mortemer, who, in battle, charged many adversaries, including a knight called Bernard de Balliol, whom he toppled from his horse. He at once made him a prisoner 'on parole', as, the author adds, 'one did with a knight', suggesting that this was the custom generally observed in his day, and by then characteristic of knightly conduct.[49]

This word of honour can be compared, as observed above, to a secular oath. It implied the same compulsion and could be equally formalistic; as with the oath, it was essential to respect scrupulously the letter of the exact words spoken. In this connection, we may compare the conduct of Richard the Lionheart to that of the adulterous queen in the romance *Tristan et Yseut*. Accused of illicit relations with Tristan by jealous courtiers of her husband, King Mark, the Queen was required to swear a solemn oath, in public, on the relics of the saints. The King and his court gathered to hear her in a meadow beside a river. Yseut, beforehand, told Tristan to wait on the opposite bank, near a ford, disguised as a leper. She herself then arrived by this route and openly asked the 'leper', in fact her lover, to carry her to the other side of the river, to join the court, so she would not get her gown wet. He carried her across piggyback and set her down on the shore where the court was waiting. Here Yseut shamelessly exonerated herself with an ambiguous oath which God could, however, only approve:

> 'My lords', she said, 'by the mercy of God I see holy relics here before me. Listen now to what I swear, and may it reassure the king: so help me God and St Hilary, and by these relics, this holy place, the relics that are not here and all the relics there are in the world. I swear that no man ever came between my thighs except the leper who carried me on his back across the ford and my

husband, King Mark. Those two I exclude from my oath; I exclude no-one else in the world. From two men I cannot exculpate myself: the leper and King Mark my lord. The leper was between my legs . . . if anyone wants me to do more, I am ready here and now.'[50]

Yseut's confident oath made a deep impression and convinced the whole court; had she not promised solemnly, before God, swearing on the relics of the saints, virtually inviting God to punish her on the spot if she had uttered a false oath? For her part, Yseut had no fear of divine anger; her words were literally and in every respect true. It remains, for all that, in our eyes, a downright lie and total deception. But it deceived only the evil *losengiers*, intent on the destruction of heroes; by this artifice, the poet makes common cause with his audience, who are all on the side of the lovers, establishing by means of this ambiguous oath a secret connivance between God and Yseut in which the audience is invited to join.

Without quite rising to this peak of duplicity, Richard, too, respected, in his own fashion, the promise made to the emperor in Cyprus, in May 1191. Defeated by the King, Isaac Comnenus was forced to surrender and beg for mercy; he asked to be spared the humiliation of being clapped in irons. Richard agreed to his request, though without relinquishing his vengeance: the emperor was loaded down with chains of precious metal.[51] Matthew Paris, belatedly joining in the fun, emphasises that Richard stuck faithfully to his word:

> Cursac [Isaac] had agreed with the king that he would not be put in chains of iron: the king, true to his word, had him put in chains of silver and shut up in a castle near to Tripoli.[52]

Ambroise brings out the funny side of the royal response:

> Before he came he sent word to the king, asking him that he would have pity on him, saying that he would surrender everything to his mercy, so that nothing would remain to him, of land, castles, houses but, for his in honour and as was right, he asked that the king would spare him on one count: that he would not be put in iron chains or fetters. Nor was he, but, on account of the protests of the people, he was put in bonds of silver.[53]

William of Newburgh goes even further. In his version, Isaac Comnenus, captured by Richard, told him he would not survive captivity; he would die if he was put in irons. To which the King replied: 'He speaks well, because he is noble, and I do not desire his death; but let him live without doing harm in silver chains.'[54] Richard of Devizes, lastly, tells the story laconically, with already typically British humour: '[Isaac] promised to surrender if only he would not be put in iron fetters. The king granted the suppliant's prayers and had silver shackles made for him.'[55]

Was Richard thinking, at this moment, of the ambiguous oath of Yseut before the court of King Mark? It is not impossible, as *Tristan et Yseut* was famous and widely known in the Plantagenet lands at that time. The episode is in any case evidence of a widespread mentality in the second half of the twelfth century, which was itself ambiguous. It is usually interpreted as a reflection of a purely formalistic and ritualistic conception of the oath. But it quite possible that there was already in this conception a hint of irony, a whiff of insolence, a faint irreverence, in fact a leaven of subversive secularism.

Richard was not always totally true to his word, however, if we are to believe several adverse comments found here and there in the chroniclers. Several examples have already been quoted. To these we may add the complaints of his troubadour friend Gaucelm Faidit, who, in 1189 or 1190, composed a poem reproaching the King of England for failing to provide the financial assistance he had solemnly promised, that would have made it possible for him to go on crusade.[56] But this was again a word given in a context that was more 'political' than chivalric. And in this regard, in spite of a few failures, Richard behaved with far greater correctness than his rival, Philip Augustus of France. He, it will be remembered, had pronounced on relics a solemn oath not to invade Richard's lands as long as he was on crusade, as Ambroise, a witness to the scene, in Acre, opportunely recalled:

> Richard wished that King Philip would reassure him and swear on the relics of saints that he would do no harm to his land, nor harm him at all while he was on God's journey and on his pilgrimage, and that when he returned to his land, that he would cause no disturbance or nor do him any harm, without warning him by his French [messengers] forty days before. The king made this oath.[57]

What eventually happened is well known. Yet the validity of this solemn oath had been confirmed by the pope, to whom Philip had appealed in vain to be released from it. It is understandable, therefore, that, in comparison with the King of France, the Duke of Austria or the Emperor, all to a greater or lesser degree perjurers or violators of accepted moral standards in such matters, Richard, despite the occasional lapse, once again incarnated the emergent ideal of chivalry.

Even in Ambroise, however, he was outstripped in the matter of chivalric deeds by some of the Muslims, in particular Saladin and his brother. Roger of Howden tells how, near Jaffa, Richard and his entourage, strolling in an orchard, were attacked by Muslim warriors. Richard leapt onto the first available horse and resisted as best he could, but was

forced eventually to flee; he was saved from capture by the devotion of William de Préaux, who distracted the attention of the Saracens by crying out that he was the King. In the skirmish, the King lost his rich belt of gold and gems. It was found by a Saracen who took it to Saladin's brother; he returned it to Richard, along with his horse, which had also been captured.[58]

Ambroise emphasises another highly chivalrous side of this brother of Saladin, called by him 'Saphadin of Arcadia'. According to Ambroise, he much admired Richard for his knightly exploits, and often visited him. During a battle at Jaffa, on 5 August 1192, seeing that the king had already had two warhorses killed under him, he sent him two more, in the thick of the battle. Ambroise wrote at length on the subject of this chivalrous gesture by a Saracen, which he describes in almost epic style:

> Then there came spurring up, apart from the other Turks, on a swift and speedy horse, a single Saracen. It was the noble Saphadin of Arcadia, a man of valiant deeds, kindness and generosity. As I said, he came galloping up with two Arab horses which he sent to the king of England, beseeching him and begging him, because of his valiant deeds, which he, Saphadin, knew and because of his boldness, that would mount one [of the horses] on condition that, if God brought him out of this safe and sound, that if he lived then Richard would ensure that he received some reward. He later received a large recompense. The king took them willingly and said that he would take many such, if they came from his most mortal enemy, such was his need.[59]

'Chivalric' behaviour was not, then, the exclusive preserve of Richard the Lionheart, and the chroniclers were quite prepared to credit such deeds even to the most determined of his opponents, enemies of Christendom. I see this as proof of the omnipresence of the chivalric ideal in the thinking of the chroniclers of the period; they were anxious to glorify, in the person of Richard but also in his most valiant adversaries, the real or supposed virtues of chivalry. There was here 'common ground', a shared value system, over and above differences of social status, race or religion. Or this, at any rate, is what they would have us believe, which is in itself not without importance. It attests to the enormous significance of the chivalric ideology in the age of Richard the Lionheart.

NOTES

1. In literary works dealing with the 'debate between the cleric and the knight', a common criticism made by the clergy is that, in their quest for glory and prowess, the knights are led into pride, boastfulness and vanity. See Oulment,

Débats du Clerc et du Chevalier, pp. 20ff. Ecclesiastical writers obviously emphasised this particular criticism.

2. *Gesta Henrici*, II, p. 7.
3. *Guillaume le Maréchal*, lines 5227, 5862; heralds-at-arms were originally jongleurs: see Flori, *Chevaliers et Chevalerie*, pp. 250–3.
4. Richard of Devizes, p. 46.
5. Rigord, §82, p. 118.
6. Matthew Paris, *Chronica Majora*, II, p. 384.
7. Gerald of Wales, *De Principis Instructione*, III, p. 25 (pp. 91–2 of translation, slightly amended).
8. Chrétien de Troyes, *Le Conte du Graal ou le Roman de Perceval*, ed. and trans. C. Méla (Paris, 1990), lines 2224ff., 1603ff.
9. *Orderic Vitalis*, ed. Chibnall, vol. 6, book 12, p. 241.
10. This is the thesis developed by John Gillingham in his 'Conquering the Barbarians', and adopted by Strickland in his *War and Chivalry*, p. 14.
11. The expression comes from Chibnall, *World of Orderic Vitalis*, p. 137.
12. M. L. Chênerie ('Motif de la Merci') accepts an even closer correspondence.
13. Anonymous, *Gesta Francorum et Aliorum Hierosolimitanorum*, ed. and trans. L. Bréhier, in L. Bréhier (ed. and trans.), *Histoire Anonyme de la Première Croisade* (Paris, 1964), c. 9, p. 21; Guibert of Nogent, RHC Hist. Occ IV, p. 162. For the Trojan origins, see Bossuat, 'Origines Troyennes'; Hiestand, R., 'Der Kreuzfahrer und sein islamisches Gegenüber', in *Ritterbild im Mittelalter*, pp. 51–68; and, more generally, Jung, *La Légende de Troie en France*.
14. *La Chanson de Guillaume*, ed. and trans. P. E. Bennett (London, 2000), p. 127.
15. William of Malemsbury, p. 303 (though it is not clear if it was for having killed Harold, mutilated him or deprived William of his capture).
16. *Guillaume le Maréchal*, lines 8834ff. For this episode, see Gillingham, *Richard the Lionheart*, p. 123; Duby, *William Marshal*, pp. 121ff.
17. Roger of Howden, III, pp. 110–11; Ambroise adds that Isaac's daughter, 'who was most beautiful and a very young girl' was sent to the Queen to 'be taught and instructed': lines 2065ff., p. 61 of Ailes translation.
18. Matthew Paris, *Chronica Majora*, III, pp. 213–15; identical text in Roger of Wendover, III, pp. 21–5; French translation in Arbellot, 'Mort de Richard Cœur de Lion', pp. 206ff.
19. Ralph of Coggeshall, pp. 90ff.
20. Gervase of Canterbury, I, pp. 82ff., 325.
21. Gerald of Wales, *Topographia Hibernica*, III, pp. 50–1; see also his *De Principis Instructione*, pp. 105–6, 197.
22. Ibid., III, p. 30.
23. Roger of Howden, III, pp. 180ff.
24. Ralph of Coggeshall, pp. 37–41; Matthew Paris, *Chronica Majora*, II, p. 385.

25. It should be emphasised that the prohibition did not apply solely to the use of the crossbow, as is so often claimed, but also to that of the bow: 'We forbid on pain of anathema that this murderous art, hateful to God, which is that of the crossbowmen and *of the archers* (author's italics), should be practised in future against Christians and Catholics': canon 29 of the second canon of the Lateran Council (text in *Conciles Œcuméniques*). An identical measure is found in the acts of a synod supposedly held at Rome in 1097–9: *Acta Pontificum Romanorum Inedita, II: Urkunden der Päpste (1097–1197)*, ed. J. von Pflugk-Harttung (Stuttgart, 1884) (repr. Graz, 1958), p. 168; but this is almost certainly an erroneous attribution, as this text clearly derives from the canon of Lateran II and cannot antedate it, as already noted by C. Hefele: Hefele, C. and H. Leclerq, *Histoire des Conciles* (Paris, 1911), vol. 5, pp. 454ff.
26. Richard of Devizes, p. 47: 'Cum in redibitionem sancte crucis nulla posset ethnicus supplicatione deflecti, rex Anglorum . . . omnes suos decapitavit . . .'
27. Matthew Paris, *Chronica Majora*, II, p. 374.
28. Rigord, §82, p. 117.
29. Ambroise, lines 5409ff. (pp. 107–8 of Ailes translation).
30. Roger of Howden, III, p. 131.
31. *Gesta Henrici*, II, p. 188; see also Roger of Howden, III, p. 127.
32. Imad ad-Din, *Conquête de la Syrie*, p. 328.
33. Baha ad-Din (Gabrieli, *Arab Historians*, pp. 223–4; translation slightly amended).
34. Imad ad-Din, *Conquête de la Syrie*, pp. 353–4.
35. See on this point Gillingham, 'Conquering the Barbarians'.
36. See on this point *Orderic Vitalis*, ed. Chibnall, vol. 6, pp. 352–4.
37. Strickland, *War and Chivalry*, pp. 198ff.
38. See, for example, Geoffrey of Vigeois, *Recueil des Historiens*, 18, p. 213; Matthew Paris, *Chronica Majora*, II, p. 659.
39. Roger of Howden, IV, p. 54.
40. *Gesta Henrici*, I, p. 293.
41. Ambroise, line 3309 (p. 79 of Ailes translation).
42. Imad ad-Din, *Conquête de la Syrie*, p. 303.
43. Matthew Paris, *Chronica Majora*, II, p. 391.
44. *Orderic Vitalis*, ed. Chibnall, book 10, vol. 5, pp. 244–5.
45. Abd'al Wah'id al-Marrakusi, *Histoire des Almohades*, trans. E. Fagnan (Algiers, 1893), p. 110.
46. *Gesta Henrici*, II, p. 46.
47. See the evidence of Ibn Saddad and d'al-Asfahani quoted by Abdul Majid Nanai, 'L'Image du Croisé dans les Sources Historiques Musulmanes', in *De Toulouse à Tripoli*, p. 29.
48. Joinville, *Vie de Saint Louis*, §387, p. 191.
49. 'Si l'ad mis par fiance, cum l'um fait chevalier': *Jordan Fantosme's Chronicle*, line 1864.

50. *Le Tristan de Béroul*, lines 4165ff. (pp. 141–2 of Penguin Classics edn, trans. Alan S. Fedrick, *The Romance of Tristan* (Penguin: Harmondsworth, 1970)).
51. *Gesta Henrici*, II, p. 167; Roger of Howden, III, p. 111.
52. Matthew Paris, *Chronica Majora*, II, p. 370.
53. Ambroise, lines 2044ff. (p. 60 of Ailes translation).
54. William of Newburgh, p. 351: 'Bene loquitur, quia nobilis est, et mori eum nolumus; sed ut vivat innoxius argenteis astringatur catenis.'
55. Richard of Devizes, p. 38.
56. Gaucelm Faidit, ed. J. Mouzat, *Les Poèmes de Gaucelm Faidit, Troubadour du XIIe Siècle* (Paris, 1965), no. 54: 'Mas la bella de cui mi mezeis temh', verse V, pp. 455ff.
57. Ambroise, lines 5300ff. (p. 105 of Ailes translation); see also Ralph of Coggeshall, p. 34.
58. Roger of Howden, III, p. 133.
59. Ambroise, lines 11545ff. (p. 184 of Ailes translation).

19

Richard and Women

∽

WHAT IS COURTESY?

Largesse and Courtesy are the two wings of Prowess, wrote Raoul de Houdenc. In other words, to win a good reputation, a noble knight must be both 'large-handed', that is, generous in the extreme, even prodigal or extravagant, and 'courteous'.

What did this mean in the age of Richard the Lionheart? The question has been much debated, since the word 'courteous' has many and varied connotations, especially if we include the notion of *amour courtois*, or 'courtly love', the many facets of which have already briefly been mentioned.[1]

One thing is clear: the modern meaning of the word does not wholly convey all its varied connotations in the Middle Ages. Today, to say of a man that he is 'courtly' or 'courteous' is primarily to emphasise his politeness, elegance, savoir-faire and consideration for others, especially the female sex. In the age of Richard, the word *corteis* (or *curteis*, derived from the Latin *curtis*, meaning 'court') was applied to behaviour that was laudable because it was 'courtly', that is, it conformed to the customs of the court. And so it was applied to a person who did not appear 'out of place' in this milieu but behaved in a seemly fashion, in accord with the accepted manners of the day. This first meaning can sometimes lead to statements that are, to us, surprising; in the *chansons de geste* (and sometimes even in the romances), there are actions described as 'courtly' which certainly no longer conform to our modern conception of the term, the pitiless slaughter of enemies, for example, the burning and destruction of their lands, or the use of stratagems in war that were effective but hardly 'chivalrous', still less 'courteous' in the modern sense of these words.[2] This is a sign of the persistence of the ancient mentalities which put most emphasis on military virtues.

The refinement of sensibilities and manners already noted, however, under the influence of a literature that was both a reflection of manners and a motor of their evolution, tended increasingly to prize the less

brutal aspects of this 'courtly' conduct. It is true that valour remained the chief virtue of a knight for many people, and a quality likely to attract the interest of princes and the admiration, favours and even love of ladies. At the end of the thirteenth century, Joinville could still tell this anecdote: with the count of Soissons and Pierre de Noville, he had been given the task of guarding for a day a little bridge over a branch of the Nile. Joinville and the few sergeants on duty with him had to endure a heavy barrage from the Saracen archers and assaults by their infantry. Joinville himself was hit by five arrows, his horse by fifteen. But between two charges, intended to relieve the sergeants and put the Saracens temporarily to flight, the knights found time to joke and look forward to the day when they would be able to tell their story to the ladies:

> The good Count of Soissons, in the plight in which we were, jested with me and said: 'Seneschal, let these curs howl; for by God's bonnet (which is how he used to swear) we'll speak of this day yet, you and I, in the company of ladies.'[3]

Military exploits remained, as we have seen, an excellent way of proving one's love for a lady; this is neatly shown in the dialogue in *Lancelot du Lac* which precedes the moment when Queen Guinevere receives from the mouth of Lancelot the avowal of his love and prepares to respond by giving herself to him:

> – Tell me, all these deeds of chivalry you have performed, for whom did you perform them?
> – My lady, for you.
> – Really! Do you then love me so much?
> – My lady, I love not myself as much, or any other.[4]

Warlike prowess, then, still retained all its prestige. But it was no longer the sole criterion of conduct. In the second half of the twelfth century, to be called 'courteous', a knight had to be more than just a valiant warrior capable of fine blows with his sword. He had to be able to take his place in mixed company, at the gatherings of the court, inside the castle in winter but out in the orchards in summer, the season when love springs afresh, in those 'pleasant places' in which literature situates the plots of its romances. He must shine, or at least hold his own, in conversations, games and dances and know how to turn a compliment, sing or even compose poetry. The word 'courteous' increasingly acquired all these values, associated with the company of the fair sex.

It is sometimes claimed that the twelfth century saw an improvement in the position of women. Georges Duby argued strongly, perhaps too strongly, against this, convinced it was an illusion.[5] He was surely correct

if what is meant is a profound shift in society which elevated the wife to the same level as her husband, a husband still referred to by such significant terms as sire, lord or baron. The 'vassalage of love' often quoted was probably essentially ludic, like courtly love in the form in which it was until recently imagined, complete with courts of love.[6] Yet the twelfth century saw the emergence of some significant female figures. Such women had existed before, certainly, but perhaps not of such stature, or in such numbers. Eleanor of Aquitaine is one, and enough has been said previously about the influence of this exceptional woman on the manners and thinking of her day. She was not alone, as Duby himself admitted. The role of women in animating courtly life, the crucible in which new mental attitudes were forged, was crucial, probably greater than that of the *iuvenes*, the landless and unmarried knights, so skilfully elucidated by Duby himself.[7] It was under their influence, even though exploited to the benefit of male ideology, that the chivalric mentality which is here our sole concern was modified and civilised.

The role of women, love and marriage was central to the intellectual debates which preoccupied educated men and women in the twelfth century as the whole of literature reveals. In spite of his excesses (in particular his insistence on the Cathar origins of courtesy), Denis de Rougemont was surely right in his assertion that love had not always existed, and that it was, in a sense, a 'French invention of the twelfth century'.[8] The troubadours of the *langue d'oc* did not have to be Cathars to be influenced by certain Cathar doctrines, in particular their criticism of the contemporary Church, with its formalistic and excessive sacramentalism, and of aristocratic marriage, conceived as a social contract, the union of two houses rather than of two persons, its prime purpose to assure peace though family alliances and its sole aim the procreation of an heir. They may have conceived or adopted the idea of romantic love, a love that was sensual, free, detached from social ties and arbitrary conventions and independent of marriage, because impossible within this restrictive institutional contract, since love could not be constrained. These ideas may have led them into a sort of eulogy of free love. This would inevitably have been popular with the 'young' (whoever they were), for whom such an attitude was highly convenient, deprived as they were, in a rigid and codified seigneurial society, of the wives and women (other than whores) they desired. It may also have been popular with women, including those in high society, usually unhappily married, themselves frustrated and longing for love and the union of hearts as well as bodies. This lies behind the emergence of a new code of conventions, which banned jealousy, and new 'courtly' rules which, as in a game, concealed their essential core, which

was the aspiration to a love that was sensual, romantic, extra-marital, even adulterous, and therefore contrary to the sacraments of the Church and to procreation, the bases of the feudal society rejected en masse by Cathar doctrines. But simply to articulate these ideas is in itself enough to show that it was quite possible for these new notions to develop outside Catharism, within feudal society itself, like a subversive leaven or a game, simply an 'idea', perhaps, but one of those which rule the world, or at least influence character and transform mentalities.

It was in the twelfth century, at all events, that the 'courteous' knight felt honour bound to know how to pay 'court' to ladies, and not only how to take them when they did not offer themselves, as in most *chansons de gestes*. The presence of women, rare or of secondary importance in the epic, came to be all-pervasive in the romance, and love now occupied an important, indeed prime, place in literature.

But what sort of love? In romances, as in the larger part of the poetic output of the twelfth century, it was very far from a disembodied or platonic sentiment, simply an idea. It was not the love expressed by Jaufré Rudel, who celebrated in song his *amor de lonh*, a disembodied and absolute passion for a distant princess (identified by some as the Countess of Tripoli) he had never met, symbol of a courtly love that deliberately fixed on a woman who was inaccessible, in his poems thanks to geographical distance, elsewhere to a social gulf.[9] It is true that many troubadours make the lady a married woman, the wife of a great lord, of whom the amorous knight is the vassal or at least social inferior. The love and 'courtesy' of the knight were then doomed to failure, or at least to remaining platonic, if binding conventions were observed. But this is precisely not the case with the poets and romance writers, who, on the contrary, take the part of love against social convention and vilify the *losengiers*, incarnations of jealousy. In many troubadours (beginning with the first, Duke William, Richard's ancestor) and in the majority of poets and romance writers, starting with Béroul, Marie de France and Chrétien de Troyes, and then in the whole tradition of Arthurian romances, love triumphs and achieves its aim, physical union; this was sometimes within marriage (which, as we have seen, was an attempt at rehabilitation on the part of Chrétien de Troyes) but more often outside it, in an adulterous affair of which the romance writers and their audience approved and which God himself did not condemn.

Should we see this as no more than a dream, a sort of safety valve without relation to reality, a convention, a game, a pure fiction? If this had been the case, the game would have been a dangerous one. Nor would the Church have fought against it with such virulence and on so many

fronts, if ultimately in vain. It is difficult to believe, furthermore, that such a high degree of unanimity in situations and themes did not reflect a social problem. According to Erich Köhler, this, too, as in the case of largesse, was a conscious elaboration of a class ideology, that of the lesser nobility, with whom the troubadours identified. In feudal society, these *iuvenes*, younger sons or members of the impoverished lesser nobility, were deprived of land, an inheritance and a means of existence worthy of their rank. They were deprived also of wives; the great men, the rich, the 'barons', heads of established families, well provided-for and married, monopolised the women, and the young had to wait with what patience they could muster for the death of a 'boss', their father or elder brother. In paying court to the lady, their lord's wife, or to some other lady, often married or betrothed, they tried to prove themselves in love and assuage their frustrations, but also to develop an ideology which excluded jealousy, deemed unworthy, a characteristic of the low-born, the bourgeois or the miser! A noble or a knight could not be jealous, because the woman one loved was not an object that was owned. The jealous husband who saw his wife as a thing, as his property, prevented her from participating in society and its 'improvement', and for that very reason deserved to be deceived. Jealousy was stigmatised as an anti-social, vulgar trait, in fact the ultimate betrayal of the chivalric ideal.

Köhler went further, but not without contradicting himself. He claimed, offering no evidence beyond his own claims to that effect, that the lesser knights saw themselves as the sole repositories of the courtly ideal, which they managed to impose with the help of the troubadours. But, he adds, the *iuvenes* lost out in the long run, because, while the barons took advantage of the courtly ideal to get hold of other men's wives, they continued to keep a close watch on their own, so jamming the system.[10]

Georges Duby refined this interpretation by supposing an ideological 'hijacking' of the courtly ideal by the prosperous barons. Within chivalry, the ritual became a factor promoting the maintenance of order and the status quo. The subversive value of the courtly myth was then exorcised by the master of the court using his wife like the queen in a game of chess. Through this training in self-control, a prime value of the courtly ritual, the upper nobility managed to allay social tensions within the household and tame the turbulence of the *iuvenes*. His thesis is well summarised in a few lines that deserve to be quoted:

> Within chivalry itself, ritual contributed in another and complementary way to the maintenance of order: it helped to control the element of turmoil and to tame 'the young'. The game of love was first and foremost an education in moderation. Moderation was one of the key words in its vocabulary. Urging

the repression of the impulses, it was in itself a factor promoting calm and cooling things down. But this game, which was an education, also encouraged rivalry. The aim was to surpass one's rivals and win the prize, which was the lady. And the *senior*, the head of the household, was content to place his wife at the centre of the competition, in an illusory, ludic situation of primacy and power. The lady refused her favours to one, granted them to another; but only up to a point: the code held out the hope of conquest as a mirage with the hazy boundaries of an artificial horizon . . . in this way the lady had the function of stimulating the ardour of the young knights and of wisely and judiciously evaluating the virtues of each of them. She presided over their permanent rivalries. She crowned the best man and the best man was whoever had served her best. Courtly love taught service, and to serve was the duty of the good vassal. In actual fact, it was the vassalic obligations which were transferred into a sort of gratuitous entertainment, but which were also, in a sense, made more painful since the object of the service was a woman, a naturally inferior being. To achieve greater mastery over himself, the pupil was constrained by a demanding, and therefore all the more effective, education to humiliate himself. The exercise that was demanded of him was submission. It was also fidelity, and selflessness.[11]

This brilliant analysis explains a number of features of both the historical reality and of the romances. It corresponds, but only in part, to the situations described by some (but not all) troubadours, for whom the love of the lady, wife of the lord, remains a dream and a fiction, and the courtly ritual only a game. It also corresponds to the situations found in romances of Celtic inspiration, those of *Tristan et Yseut* or the Arthurian cycle, in which the king (Mark or Arthur) seems to accept the love affairs of the queen (Yseut or Guinevere) with the best knight in the kingdom (Tristan or Lancelot), whose valour is indispensable to ensure its safety. Only the *losengiers*, the traitors and hypocrites, force the king, in each case, to open his eyes to the queen's conduct, so causing her loss and consequently endangering society as a whole. Nevertheless, the situation of the lady in these hugely successful romances was by no means illusory or ludic and love was far from a hypothetical exercise in self-control; it was, on the contrary, a devouring passion, demanding and imperious. 'Moderation' alone defined the rules of the game, but it was expressed in the lover's submission to the wishes expressed by the lady. It made Lancelot climb into the cart of infamy or fight *au noauz* (that is, as feebly as possible), suffer humiliations and wounds and constantly risk his life to liberate the Queen. But this oversteps the barrier evoked by Duby, because carnal, sensual love, total and excessive, triumphs, even if it ends in death through the villainy of the *losengiers*: Tristan and Yseut are clearly lovers in the full sense of the term, with or without love potion, as are Lancelot

and Guinevere. And they are without scruples or remorse, because for them, as for the poet and his audience, love is the true absolute value. This is even more marked perhaps, in Marie de France, who put love at the top of her list of values and disdained all social conventions.[12]

The courtly ideology of the twelfth century (or, to be more precise, the romantic ideal proposed by Tristan and Lancelot, emblematic figures of chivalry) was therefore deeply subversive, as Jean-Charles Payen, another great medievalist, clearly saw.[13] We can probably go further. It may well be that courtly love never amounted to an ideology or a codified system of behaviour. It is more likely that what we find in literature are intellectual debates, a range of meditations, expressing fantasies about love; not 'debates about courtly love', but rather 'a courtly discourse on love'; in which case the whole edifice of 'courtly love' is fiction and not necessarily, as argued by Köhler, an expression of the ideology of the lesser nobility or, for that matter, a means of domination utilised by the rich and powerful, as argued by Duby.

Courtly love may never have possessed the conceptual and ideological reality so often attributed to it, but it would be risky to proceed from this to argue that the 'courtly discourse' was detached from all contemporary social context. The very success of the romances is evidence that the problems they posed accurately corresponded to a range of issues raised by the society of the day. We should probably see this as a consequence of a range of developments, such as the emergence of the individual and the new desire to be free of existing structures; in the religious sphere, these gave rise to dissident, evangelical or heretical movements such as the Cathars, the Waldensians, the Poor of Lyons, eremitical movements and so on. More directly still, the success of these ideas led to protests against the restrictions feudal society imposed on marriage in its desire to limit the risk of the disintegration of patrimonies where there were too many heirs, before the widespread adoption of primogeniture among the aristocracy; it led also to a weakening of patriarchal authority over the wider family. The practice of frequenting tournaments, a form of 'errantry' which was stylised by the romances, promoted the emancipation of youthful spirits and increased their desire for independence and enjoyment, while at the same time increasing their chances of achieving them. It was not for nothing that the Church denounced tournaments as immoral free-for-alls and occasions for debauchery.

This immediately raised the even more acute question of the relationship between marriage – a social institution sanctioned by the Church – and love – a personal feeling now valued for its own sake. Was love possible within marriage as it was then conceived? What was to be done if

love was in conflict with marriage? Should the true value (love) take account of the social contract or not? These are the real themes around which revolves almost all literature from the age of Richard the Lionheart on. They were not purely fictitious or artificial 'academic' debates; they were addressing real existential problems, arising from the profound changes taking place in minds, ideas and morals as the twelfth century drew to a close.

RICHARD'S 'COURTESY'

If 'courtesy', as has frequently been asserted since Köhler, was the ideological expression of the knights of the lesser nobility, the obvious indifference towards it of Richard the Lionheart is understandable. As a prince, Count of Poitou, then King of England, son of one of the most powerful sovereigns in Europe and descendant, into the bargain, of colourful characters with rich and turbulent love lives, he hardly had to contend with the sort of problems described above. He was unlikely to be deprived of women. Yet, as we have observed throughout this book, he seems to have paid little attention to them, either before or after his marriage. His conduct, so close to the chivalric ideal in the spheres of prowess, largesse and some of its other major manifestations as lauded in literature, is here markedly at odds with the romance models. We do not find Richard fighting in tournaments sporting the sleeve or colours of his lady, paying court to queens and princesses or even composing poems for them. In spite of his patronage of troubadours, the handful of sirventes attributed to him do not deal with love or ladies. Richard here seems closer to the knights of the epics than to those of Arthurian romances, modelling himself more on Roland than on Lancelot, Gawain or even King Arthur himself.

Was this because he was a king? Was it regarded as unseemly to present a sovereign imitating a knight engaged in serving his lady or embarking with her on an affair that might well be adulterous? It seems unlikely. As we know, the chroniclers were hardly reticent in evoking the extra-marital affairs of his parents, Henry II and Eleanor. Indeed, they even raked over the escapades of his remote ancestors, such as those two notorious womanisers, Geoffrey Plantagenet and William of Aquitaine, always on the lookout for women to sleep with, married or not. Unlike Lancelot, the best knight in the world, they did not hesitate 'courteously' to screw the queen in the chambers of the royal palace. And this is exactly the accusation made against another 'best knight in the world', William Marshal, suspected of having once been the lover of Margaret of France, wife of

the Young Henry. Here, as in the romances, it was the *losengiers* who
sought to discredit him: they 'resented the wealth and the good life of the
Marshal and the love he bore for his lord'.[14] So they went in search of one
of the Young King's close friends and asked him to tell him of the
Marshal's misconduct:

> But that is the pure truth,
> That he is screwing the queen.
> And it is a great shame and great scandal.
> If the king knew of his madness
> We should be well avenged on him . . .
> That is why we beseech you, dear lord,
> To show him this outrage,
> This wickedness and shame
> Which sullies us all
> Whereby the king is shamefully duped.[15]

Reality here comes very close to situations portrayed in the chivalric
romances. We also get a glimpse of the risks and dangers of what is known
as 'courtly love' when its object was a lady of such eminence!

COURTLY LOVE: A LOVE BETWEEN MEN?

It has recently been suggested that, when paying court to the lady, it was
really the husband that the knight was aiming to seduce. This is clearly
true in the sense that it was a professional necessity for a knight to belong
to the household of a powerful lord. Pleasing the lady might involve, as
we have seen, performing warlike exploits calculated also to attract the
attention of the master of the household; the knight might then be
recruited by him and so provided with a secure career or at least a temporary home. The same might be the case where the knight who loved a
lady wished to live close by her, to which end he needed to win the
approval of the lord, become a member of his personal guard and live in
the castle or at least have easy access to it. This is the situation of many
heroes of romances, including Tristan. But it is not what was meant by
Georges Duby, in this case too strongly influenced by an article by
Christiane Marchello-Nizia, who saw courtly love as a cover for and a
transposition of homosexual love.[16] Duby wrote:

> We are led to ponder the true nature of relations between the sexes. Was the
> woman any more than an illusion, a sort of veil, a screen, in the sense Genet
> gave to this word, or rather an interpreter, an intermediary, the mediator . . .
> was courtly love, in this military society, not really a love between men?[17]

A few years later, discussing the *Histoire de Guillaume le Maréchal*, Duby returned to this theme; he spoke of 'manly friendship at its peak' in connection with the relationship binding William Marshal to John of Earley, a relationship which John, in his history, calls 'love'; he notes the unimportance of women in the *Histoire* and again emphasises the frequency with which the word 'love' is used to describe these 'manly friendships'. Of the accusation against William previously referred to, he writes:

> Thus, the entire episode turns on love, but let there be no mistake: it is the love of men among themselves. This no longer surprises us; we are beginning to discover that courtly love, the love celebrated, after the troubadours, by the trouvères, the love that the knights devoted to the chosen lady, may have masked the essential – or rather projected into the realm of sport the inverted image of the essential: amorous exchanges between warriors.[18]

I am not, for once, wholly convinced by my revered master and friend. I do not doubt that chivalry nurtured many homosexual passions. A specifically masculine and warrior corporation, which valued virility, physical qualities and the virtues of companionship, was surely particularly likely (along with the clergy, against whom similar accusations were already being made) to have given rise to such relationships, further encouraged by the enforced intimacy of drill halls and camps. Nevertheless, in studying the texts, we must be careful not to read into them more than is there.[19]

We must be cautious, first, about the meaning of the words. The word 'love', so generally used to describe a friendship between men in twelfth-century texts, did not in the Old French of the period have the 'amorous' and sensual, even sexual, resonance so emphasised today. Its first meaning is affection, a sentimental tie, of friendship or vassalage.[20] To speak of the love of a knight for his master was no more ambiguous than to speak of the love of a subject for his king or a believer for his God. There is no ambiguity when the poet says that Roland loved Oliver, or, with all due respect to the modern scandalmongers and addicts of malicious gossip, when the evangelist John describes himself as 'the disciple Jesus loved'. One can even turn the conclusion on its head: the medieval word 'love' described primarily friendship pure and simple, whereas to speak of one's *amie*, friend or beloved, and even of friendship, was more ambivalent.

We must also take into account the situations and themes dealt with in literary works. Homosexuality scarcely appears, unless one indulges in exegetical acrobatics. Its presence has not unreasonably been suggested in the extraordinary male friendship between Lancelot and Galahad in the prose *Lancelot*.[21] Elsewhere, however, traces of it are few and

questionable. Above all, it is generally fiercely denied. Let us look, for
example, at some dialogue in the *Lai de Lanval* of Marie de France. Once
again, a queen has fallen in love, in this case with Lanval, who is 'generous and courtly'; in fact he has infinite wealth at his disposal thanks to the
love of his mistress, a fairy with magical powers, and his splendour and
valour win all hearts. Lanval at first politely rejects the Queen's advances
when she offers her love (*drüerie*) by quoting feudal morality:

> I have no desire to love you, for I have long served the king and do not want
> to betray my faith. Neither you nor your love will ever lead me to wrong my
> lord.

Humiliated by this rejection, the Queen becomes angry and accuses
Lanval of preferring boys to women:

> 'Lanval,' she said, 'I well believe that you do not like this kind of pleasure.
> I have been told often enough that you have no desire for women. You have
> well-trained young men and enjoy yourself with them. Base coward, wicked
> recreant, my lord is extremely unfortunate to have suffered you near him.
> I think he has lost his salvation because of it!'

Lanval is distressed by this allegation, which he finds deeply insulting. He
replies in the same coin, though careful first to deny the accusation:

> 'Lady, I am not skilled in the profession you mention, but I love and I am
> loved by a lady who should be prized above all others I know. And I will tell
> you one thing: you can be sure that one of her servants, even the very poorest
> girl, is worth more than you, my lady the Queen, in body, face and beauty,
> wisdom and goodness.'[22]

It may, of course, be observed that this *lai* is attributed to a woman,
Marie de France, perhaps more predisposed than other poets to criticise
sexual relations between men. The fact remains: courtly discourse on
love, as a whole, nearly always avoids referring to homosexuality and the
rare references made to it are resolutely hostile.

WAS RICHARD HOMOSEXUAL?

The relaxation of morals that began after the Second World War and has
advanced so rapidly in recent years has led to a renewed interest in this
matter, particularly with reference to Richard the Lionheart. It has been
suggested that the rarity of references to women in connection with him
in the chronicles, his evident reluctance to marry Alice, the indifference
he seems to have felt towards his wife, the lack of a legitimate heir and
a few allusions to his 'sin' (more specific and certainly more frequent than

the references in the contemporary literature previously noted) are to be explained by the King of England's homosexuality.

John Gillingham, who has made a detailed study of this issue, has pointed out that this thesis is extremely recent; no historian seems to have openly claimed that Richard was homosexual before 1948.[23] Yet his homosexuality is now fairly generally accepted by contemporary historians, not entirely immune to fashion.[24] There would be little point in rehearsing the debate here, especially given its thorough treatment by Gillingham. I will confine myself to commenting on some of the arguments and conclusions.

What are the grounds for the claim that Richard the Lionheart was homosexual? A few elements are worth singling out.

The first is what might be called the 'Alice affair'. It may be recalled that the kings of France and England, Henry II and Louis VII, planned to marry Alice to Richard, perhaps as early as 1161; in 1169, when scarcely nine years old, she was entrusted to the care of the King of England with this end in view. As we know, the marriage never took place, and it seems clear that the principal reasons for this were her treatment, first by Henry, and then by Richard. For a long time Henry II seems to have put obstacles in the way of the marriage, so many times demanded by Louis VII and so frequently postponed by the King of England; Henry was seeking to hold on to Alice's dowry, in particular Gisors, without actually concluding the union. Richard, meanwhile, seems to have been in no hurry; as we have seen, he promised on many occasions, in official treaties, to go through with the marriage, but it was repeatedly postponed and finally abandoned. He was equally hostile to the proposal to marry Alice to his brother John, probably for political reasons; such a marriage would have supplanted him to the benefit of his brother in the French alliance and been tantamount to recognition of John as heir to the throne.[25] Eventually, at Messina, in February 1191, Richard managed to get Philip Augustus to agree to release him from his betrothal, and soon after he married Berengaria. Alice was returned to her brother and, in 1195, she was married to John, Count of Ponthieu.[26] Is this prolonged bachelorhood (Richard was thirty-four, hardly unusual, except for a king who needed to assure his succession) and refusal to marry his betrothed proof of prejudice on the part of the King of England against women in general? It is possible, but far from certain.

It is possible that Richard felt a more localised, specific repulsion for Alice herself, like Philip Augustus for his young wife Ingeborg of Denmark, with whom he seems to have been unable to consummate his marriage. In Alice's case, there were rumours at a very early stage of

guilty relations with Henry II. Many chroniclers refer to them. In the thirteenth century, the Minstrel of Reims was familiar with the main lines of the story, though he confused Richard with his brother and saw the 'misdeed' of Alice and the 'faithless' Henry II (who debauched the little girl when his son was in Scotland) as the cause of the Young King's death:

> But during this period, the faithless King Henry took such advantage of the little girl that he knew her carnally. But when Henry Curtmantle had returned and learned the truth of this, his was so angry that he took to his deathbed, and he died of it. And the little girl was sent back again to this side of the sea, and she landed in the county of Ponthieu, where she stayed for a long time; because she dared not show herself to her brother, King Philip, because of her misdeed.[27]

According to Gerald of Wales, Henry II seduced the daughter of his suzerain, still a little girl, when she was in his care and this misconduct contributed to the hatred between him, Eleanor and his sons. After the death of his 'official' mistress, Rosamund Clifford, in 1176, Gerald asserts that Henry had planned to divorce Eleanor, marry Alice and have children by her, which would mean he could more effectively disinherit his rebellious sons.[28] We cannot take on trust everything recounted by this scandalmonger with a predilection for 'spicy' stories, with which he liked to illustrate his moralising assertions. But other chroniclers, without being so specific, also refer to Henry's behaviour with the child in a way which effectively presents him as a paedophile. Richard of Devizes simply alludes in veiled terms to the 'suspect custody' provided by the king,[29] but the usually well-informed Roger of Howden is very specific about how Richard, at Messina, finally gave Philip Augustus his reasons for not marrying his sister:

> The king of England answered that it was quite impossible for him to marry his sister because his father, the king of England, had slept with her and had a son by her; and he brought forward numerous witnesses who were ready to prove it in many ways.[30]

It is easy to believe that Richard felt a certain repugnance about marrying Alice, who had been his father's mistress, just as it is easy to understand why Eleanor exerted herself to find another wife for her son as soon as the risk of a rupture with the King of France, thanks to Richard's failure to honour his promise, seemed to have been averted. Their joint participation in the crusade might well appear a propitious moment. In fact, the 'Alice affair' is evidence of the lasciviousness of Henry II, but not of the homosexuality of his son.

Richard's relatively late marriage to Berengaria can partly be attributed to the same cause. He was first obliged to extricate himself from his
promise to the King of France. Politically, his marriage to Berengaria was
by no means a bad move and it proved its worth in the alliance it procured with the house of Navarre. We should not, however, take too seriously the thesis that it was Eleanor personally, who, despite her great age,
arranged this marriage, almost forcing Richard's hand to see that he was
at last provided with a wife.[31] The Continuator of William of Tyre claims
that Eleanor was the sole instigator of the marriage, and that she was
anxious at all costs to prevent a union between her son and a daughter
of Louis VII, because of her hatred and resentment of the King of France
and his children.[32] Ambroise, on the other hand, attributes the initiative
to Richard, who had long loved Berengaria and desired her when he was
still Count of Poitou:

> He went with the king of France on his galleys, then made his way beyond
> the straits, straight to Reggio whence news had been sent to him that his
> mother had arrived there bringing to the king his beloved. She was a wise
> maiden, a fine lady, both noble and beautiful, with no falseness or treachery
> in her. Her name was Berengaria; the king of Navarre was her father. He had
> given her to the mother of King Richard who had made great efforts to bring
> her that far. Then was she called queen and the king loved her greatly. Since
> the time when he was count of Poitiers she had been his heart's desire. He
> had brought her straight to Messina with her female attendants and his
> mother. He spoke to his mother of his pleasure and she to him, without
> keeping anything from him. He kept the girl, whom he held dear, and sent
> back his mother to look after his land that he had left, so that his honour
> would not decrease.[33]

Ambroise is the only chronicler to insist on the long duration and
strength of Richard's love for Berengaria. Subsequently, however, the
King seems to have paid little attention to his young wife; not only were
there no children of the marriage (though we do not know why), but he
seems often to have preferred to be apart from her. He usually sailed in
a different boat from Berengaria on the way to the Holy Land. This separation of the young spouses may be explained by fear of the loss of both
the King and any heir carried by the mother in one accident, but there
was never any sign of an heir. It makes no more sense to explain the separation in terms of 'moral purity' during a crusade. Indeed William of
Newburgh praises Eleanor for having, by giving Richard Berengaria,
'a young girl celebrated for her beauty and goodness', provided her son
with a way of avoiding fornication; Richard, he says, was a young man,
and his long practice of pleasures inclined him to vice.[34] He does not,

unfortunately, say what pleasures or what vice he had in mind, though sexual relations are obviously implied.

Was the chaste and prudent Berengaria a sufficient remedy for her husband? It is doubtful, as they seem rarely to have been in each other's company after the wedding, either in the Holy Land or during the return journey, when they again travelled in different ships. After the long years of separation as a result of the King's captivity, Berengaria was still absent from Richard's second coronation. Nor do we know if she really was beautiful. Contrary to the other chroniclers, Richard of Devizes describes her as 'more wise than beautiful'.[35] Was this lack of affection due to some quality in Berengaria, incapable of arousing her royal husband, or to his homosexuality?

A third point relates to acts and conduct which some historians of today have perhaps rather hastily ascribed to Richard's homosexuality, most of which have already been mentioned. I refer, for example, to his prohibition of the presence of women (and Jews) at his coronation feast; this proves very little and may be explained at least in part by the absence of a queen at these festivities. Must we, John Gillingham has asked, conclude from this measure that all the kings of England were homosexual, since such a prohibition was traditional?[36] Without being wholly inadmissible *a priori*, this thesis is in my view unjustified, though not for the reasons advanced by Gillingham. His analysis of the passages in Geoffrey of Monmouth on which his conclusion is based is open to question. In chapter 35, Geoffrey evokes the Trojan origins of certain customs which, he says, the Britons had inherited; he mentions three, including the rule of primogeniture and the separation of the sexes at banquets (separation, not prohibition). Later, in chapter 157, he gives a description of the ceremonies of sacring and coronation of the mythical King Arthur which might well apply to those of King Richard. After these ceremonies, he says, the King 'went off with the men to feast in his own palace and the queen retired with the married women to feast in hers'. To justify this custom, unfamiliar to his readers and likely to surprise them, Geoffrey explains: 'For the Britons still observed the ancient custom of Troy, the men celebrating festive occasions with their fellow-men and the women eating separately with the other women.'[37]

To Geoffrey, then, this was an ancient tradition still in force at the time of Arthur (the sixth century) but which had fallen into disuse, and was therefore strange and incomprehensible to his readers in the middle of the twelfth century, and which he thus felt it necessary to explain. We might just as well turn the thesis on its head and suggest that it was Geoffrey's story that influenced Richard: if the King wished to take inspiration from

this Arthurian custom, newly popularised by Geoffrey of Monmouth, the absence of the Queen would in itself have justified abolishing the women-only banquet, in which case the prohibition would not have been misogynistic in nature. But no chronicler suggests this, and the explanation put forward by Matthew Paris, invoking the risks of magical practices linked to the presence of Jews and women, is hardly an argument in its favour. We have to conclude that Richard, for reasons of his own, chose to exclude women and Jews from these festivities, when this was neither traditional nor accepted practice. This double exclusion must, therefore, be significant; it proves a degree of misogyny and an undeniable anti-Semitism. It is not, however, sufficient grounds on which to assert that Richard was homosexual.

Also insufficient as evidence are the demonstrations of affection or grief noted without comment by the chroniclers. Historians in the West today have been too quick to see them as evidence of homosexuality; contemporary Western society has become unused to the spontaneity and exuberance of the displays of emotion still common today between men in, for example, Muslim or even Mediterranean countries, without there necessarily being any question of homosexual tendencies. Thus, describing the cordial atmosphere of the several meetings at which the kings of France and England were reunited at Messina, Richard of Devizes notes that Richard and Philip spent many pleasurable days together, surrounded by their men, and that 'the kings separated, tired but not sated' to return to their own quarters.[38] This was a literary echo; the chronicler is using a phrase from Juvenal, who was referring to lust. But was Richard of Devizes really trying to imply an element of sensuality in the encounter between the two kings? It is possible, but it is far from certain.

We may draw the same conclusion (or rather lack of conclusion) from Roger of Howden's account of the alliance and friendship already existing between Philip and Richard when the latter went to the French court to oppose his father, before their final conflict, in 1187.

> Once peace had been made, Richard, Duke of Aquitaine, son of the king of England, concluded a truce with Philip, King of France, who had long shown him so much honour that they ate everyday at the same table, from the same plate, and that, at night, the bed did not separate them. The King of France cherished him like his own soul; and they bore such love for each other that, because of the intensity of this affection which existed between them, the lord King of England [Henry II], dumbfounded, wondered what it signified. As a precaution against whatever might come of it, he postponed his decision to return to England, which he had previously taken, until he could discover what had brought about so sudden a love.[39]

Love is certainly referred to here, but what sort of love? Had the two princes already been lovers in 1187, which would explain the emotion of their reunion at Messina and the passage just quoted? Yet again, the conclusion is too hasty, based, as it is, on too 'modern' an interpretation of the facts recounted. It was not the intention of the chronicler to emphasise the moral or sentimental significance of the demonstrations of affection between the two princes, but rather their political implications. What worried Henry II was the prospect of a strategic alliance between his son and his enemy, not a romantic homosexual affair, which remains possible, of course, but is far from proven. Sharing the same table, or even the same bed, did not have the sensual connotations it has today.[40] Are we, for example, to accuse Henry II and Henry the Young King of incestuous relations simply because, according to some chroniclers, father and son, reconciled after one of their many quarrels, shared the same intimacy as Richard and Philip Augustus?

> In the year 1176, the two kings of England, the father and the son, arrived in England; every day they ate at the same table and enjoyed in the same bed the tranquil repose of night.[41]

Similarly, are we to assume a homosexual love between Philip Augustus and Richard's brother, Geoffrey, simply from the fact that, on the young man's death, according to Gerald of Wales, the King of France loudly protested a grief that we see as excessive, even threatening to throw himself into the open grave?

> King Philip was afflicted with such deep sorrow and despair at his death, that, in proof both of his love for him and of the honour in which he was held, the count was ordered by him to be buried before the high altar in the cathedral church of Paris, which is dedicated to the blessed Virgin; and at the end of the funeral service, when the body was being lowered into the grave, he would have thrown himself into the gaping tomb with the body, if he had not been forcibly restrained by those who were around him.[42]

In interpreting such descriptions, we need to allow for literary bombast, and even more for a mentality, long lost today in the West, that required the ostentatious demonstration of feelings by means of gestures, cries, tears or physical contact. Such attitudes might well be ambiguous in Western society at the beginning of the twenty-first century, but this was not the case in the twelfth century, nor is it the case in all contemporary societies.

A fourth and weightier argument is based on the accusations of immorality made against Richard and the accounts of his repentances and the penances he imposed on himself. Such accusations hung even

more heavily over Richard than over his father, though the latter seems the more culpable in contemporary eyes. Many chroniclers, as we have seen, allude to Richard's debauched life, his bad habits and 'the dissolute habits he had adopted in his hot-headed youth'.[43] On his death, his faults were recalled and it was generally agreed that he would be required to spend several years at least in purgatory (a concept only recently invented) on account of his numerous sins.[44] The King himself, furthermore, admitted his guilt, sometimes publicly, and his confession led to repentance and penance on at least two occasions. Both confessions concerned his sexual behaviour.

The first, already discussed, took place in Sicily, before his marriage to Berengaria, in an atmosphere of spirituality, repentance and eschatological expectations.[45] Roger of Howden says that the king then remembered the 'vileness' (*foeditas*) of his past life and realised that 'the prickings of lust' had until now pervaded his whole being. But, inspired by the Holy Spirit, he was impelled to repent and 'realised the full extent of his sin'. During an expiatory ceremony, described at some length, the king had himself solemnly whipped by the bishops after confessing the 'the ignominy of his sins'. Then, emphasises the chronicler, the king 'abjured his sin' and, from that hour, began to fear God; nor did he fall back into 'his iniquity'. References simply to Richard's 'sins' would certainly be too vague to serve as the basis for any conclusions, but the chronicler's insistence on using the singular – 'his sin', 'his iniquity', 'his lust' – makes it clear that he was referring to a moral failing of a sexual nature that was specific to Richard and habitual. Should we assume fornication, sexual relations outside marriage, inevitable and unlikely to be much criticised in a king who was at that stage unmarried? The same chroniclers, well acquainted with the far more culpable sexual activities of his father, Henry II, who was both married and the father of a family, were nowhere near as exercised about them. The severest critic of Henry's promiscuity was probably William of Newburgh, who described him as 'addicted to certain vices especially unbecoming in a Christian prince. He was prone to debauchery, and with no respect for the laws of marriage . . . in pursuit of pleasure, he fathered many bastards.'[46] Nevertheless, in spite of his justified and proven reputation as a lecherous adulterer and probable paedophile, the chroniclers were relatively discreet on the subject. They make no reference to pressing appeals to penitence for all this adulterous copulation; it was commonplace in sovereigns and tolerated by churchmen as long as they did not flaunt their mistresses too openly, although Henry II, it must be said, did exactly that. Richard, on the other hand, did not violate the laws of marriage and we

know of no liaisons on his part with women. It is then only a short step, and a tempting one, to conclude that the sin (in the singular) for which Richard was criticised was of a very different nature than the traditional pre-marital affairs, though still sexual.

Was it, in fact, an allusion to his homosexuality? The second account of a penance tends to support this. It happened in 1195, after his captivity, in the fourth year of his marriage to Berengaria:

> In that year, a hermit came to find King Richard and, preaching the words of eternal salvation, said to him: 'Remember the destruction of Sodom and abstain from illicit acts (*ab illicitis te abstine*), for if you do not God will punish you in fitting manner.' But the king desired the things of this world more than those that come from God and he could not so quickly turn his soul away from the forbidden acts (*ab illicitis revocare*).[47]

So Richard had not changed his life, as Roger of Howden claimed, after his penitence at Messina. This time, in spite of the hermit's warning, he waited for a sign from God. It came not long after, on the Monday of Holy Week, 4 April 1195, when he fell gravely ill and saw this as the hand of God, anxious to bring him back to Him:

> That day, the Lord struck him by sending him a serious illness; then the king had religious men summoned to his presence and was not ashamed to confess to them the ignominy of his life;[48] after doing penance, he received his wife, with whom he had not slept for a long time. Rejecting illicit couplings (*abjecto concubitu illicito*) he joined with his wife, and they were both one flesh; the Lord restored health to his body as well as his soul.[49]

Here, everything seems to point to a grave fault of a sexual nature: Richard had abandoned the bed of his wife in favour of 'forbidden relations'. The reference to Sodom and Gomorrah lends force to the idea that these relations were homosexual.

John Gillingham, however, rejects such a conclusion and accuses those who draw it of being too swayed by fashion and deficient in knowledge of the Bible:

> In the last forty years it has apparently become impossible to read the word 'Sodom' without assuming that it refers to homosexuality. This tells us a lot about the culture of our own generation: its unfamiliarity with the Old Testament and its wider interest in sex. In fact, however, the magnificent maledictions of the Old Testament prophets are rarely complete without a reference to the destruction of Sodom and, more often than not, this phrase carries no homosexual implications. It refers not so much to the nature of the offences as to the terrible and awe-inspiring nature of the punishment.[50]

Being myself not entirely without knowledge of the Bible, I feel able to challenge both Gillingham's argument and his conclusions. So as to dissociate the reference to Sodom from any obligatory allusion to homosexual, or even sexual, practices, he puts forward two arguments: first, he says, the majority of biblical references to the destruction of Sodom are intended solely to evoke a punishment of God and contain no allusion to homosexuality; second, and conversely, the condemnation of homosexuality in the Bible is usually made without reference to Sodom.

SODOM AND GOMORRAH

There are in the Bible some twenty references to Sodom and its destruction by God. Most of them are primarily intended to put the audience of the prophets on guard before the prospect of a punishment of God on sinners. The argument relies on a reminder of divine interventions in history, described in the Bible and known to all: remember the Flood, when God wiped out humanity because of its sins. True, God had promised (the rainbow was proof) never again to cause the ruin of the whole of humanity, but a more selective (though still terrible) punishment was not excluded: for proof, see the destruction of Sodom and Gomorrah. It is therefore not surprising to find in the Bible allusive references to these two towns simply as a call to order. It is quite true that a reference to the destruction of Sodom did not in itself imply that the sins targeted by the prophet were homosexual in nature or even simply sexual.

We should not, however, push this too far. There remains always, in the background, for anyone with even a superficial knowledge of the Bible, the memory of the reasons why God destroyed these towns. And these reasons are explicit, unarguably linked to sexual relations considered unnatural. The first book of the Bible clearly states that 'the men of Sodom were wicked and sinners before the Lord exceedingly' (Genesis 13: 13). This was why God decided to destroy the city and sent two 'angels' (in human form) to warn Lot and his family, the only righteous people there. God himself warned Abraham, Lot's uncle, that he had no alternative but to destroy Sodom and Gomorrah, because 'their sin is very grievous'(Genesis 18: 20). Meanwhile, the two envoys from God arrived at Sodom and lodged with Lot. Soon, the whole male population of the town gathered outside the house and demanded that Lot hand the two young men over to them, so that they could have with them sexual relations that the biblical language describes in its own fashion, without the least ambiguity for anyone who knows the meaning to be given to the verb 'to know' in the Bible: 'Bring them out unto us, that we may know

them' (Genesis 19: 5). Horrified at these suggestions, which seemed to
him not only against nature but against God's law and the laws of hospitality, Lot negotiated, even offering to hand over instead his two daughters, still virgins. It was no good. The townsmen even threatened to inflict
the same fate on Lot himself if he did not comply with their demand. Only
the forceful intervention of the envoys from God prevented them from
breaking down the door of the house to get their way. This was too much;
this time the sin was extreme and God destroyed the town.

An allusion to the destruction of Sodom, therefore, conveys two messages. One recalls God's punishment of sinners, which might be terrible.
The other evokes the reasons for that punishment, that is, the sins of men,
and particularly what we call sodomy and what the Bible denounces as
an abominable crime: to 'lie with mankind, as with womankind'.[51] The
fact that this biblical condemnation in its starkest form does not actually
mention Sodom is not, as Gillingham argues, proof that the compilers (or
even more the readers) of the Bible did not remember it. Proof comes in
the account in the book of Judges of a situation very similar to that of
Lot and his guests in Sodom, but this time in the middle of the land of
the sons of Israel: a Levite lodged one night with his concubine at the
house of an old man, at Gibeah, in the land of Benjamin; the inhabitants
of the town, who were 'perverse', also ordered the old man to hand over
his guest. The old man was indignant and made them the same offer as
Lot, for the same reasons:

> Nay, my brethren, nay, I pray you, do not so wickedly; seeing that this man
> is come into my house, do not this folly. Behold, here is my daughter a maiden,
> and his concubine; them I will bring out now, and humble ye them, and do
> with them what seemeth good unto you; but unto this man do not so vile a
> thing.[52]

The close similarity between the two accounts and the nature of the proposed solution leave no doubt. Yet the author of Judges makes no reference to Sodom. Whatever the reasons, the readers of the Bible would
clearly have made the obvious connection themselves.

Gillingham is correct, therefore, to emphasise that references to Sodom
in the Bible do not always imply an allusion to homosexuality; in over half
the cases the prophet simply refers to the destruction of the city as an
example familiar to all and so having the value of a universal warning.[53]
But he is wrong to go on to claim that the sin of Sodom is rarely mentioned, and even less so its sexual or homosexual nature. In many cases,
the emphasis is clearly put on the sins of Sodom, to which the faults of
those to whom the warning was addressed were compared.[54] Sometimes

the prophet emphasises a particular aspect of the sins of these cities: Isaiah, for example, condemns the impudence of the sinners of his day who, like the inhabitants of Sodom, no longer hid to commit their sins, and openly declared their crimes instead of concealing them.[55] In at least two cases, the nature of the sin of Sodom is even more explicit. The Second Epistle of Peter quotes the destruction of Sodom as prefiguring the final destruction: just as God destroyed Sodom but spared Lot and his family, so, at the end of time, a few would survive and be saved. The Epistle spells it out: God spared Lot because Lot was 'shocked by the dissolute habits of the lawless society in which he lived'.[56] Similarly, on Judgement Day, the wicked would be punished like the inhabitants of Sodom, but above all 'those who follow their abominable lusts'. The reference to the sexual practices of the Sodomites is clear.

It is even clearer in the Epistle of Jude, which evokes the sin of the inhabitants of Sodom and Gomorrah and the neighbouring towns, 'who committed fornication and followed unnatural lusts', and whose punishment was 'an example for all to see', so they would not be imitated.[57]

The practice of homosexual sodomy was therefore clearly in the background of these references when they were not simply reminders of a possible punishment by God, but refer to a specific sin, usually of a sexual nature. This connection was clearly established in Richard's day by Gerald of Wales, when he declared that the 'vice of Sodom' was of Trojan origin (hence transmitted by the Franks who were their heirs) and still unknown to the Welsh.[58] This was also the case with the hermit who, as we have seen, asked Richard to remember the punishment of Sodom and Gomorrah and give up 'illicit acts'. Yet Richard would not yet comply or agree to deprive himself of these 'forbidden pleasures'. What follows clearly shows that they were sexual in nature and it becomes highly probable, if not certain, that what the hermit meant to condemn in Richard were the sodomitic practices which God had long ago forbidden and chastised. If what had been at issue here were adulterous relations, as Gillingham seems to be suggesting, the hermit would almost certainly have chosen another exemplum, for example that of David and Bathsheba. The Bible is not short of instances of adulterous kings condemned by the prophets in more or less forceful terms – less rather than more, it must be said, in the case of kings.

A LECHER KING?

Is this to say that Richard was exclusively and unremittingly homosexual? It would appear not. Reference has already been made to the

complaint of certain Poitevin barons about the sexual licence of their count, who was accused of debauching not female serfs or maidservants, but the wives and daughters of free men:

> In fact they said that they did not wish to hold their land of Richard any more, claiming that he was bad for everyone, worse than his men, worse still for himself. Because he carried off by force the wives, daughters and kinswomen of free men and made them his concubines; and when he had slaked his lecherous passions with them, he passed them on to his *milites* as whores. He afflicted his people with these and many other wrongs.[59]

Richard did not, therefore, disdain sexual relations with women. Roger of Howden says he had a natural son, called Philip (in memory of Philip Augustus?), to whom he gave the castle of Cuinac and who, after his father's death, avenged him by killing the Viscount of Limoges.[60] But this last story may be legendary. So, probably, is the story told by the Dominican Stephen of Bourbon in the mid thirteenth century: Richard was inflamed with desire for a nun of Fontevraud and threatened to burn down the monastery if she was not surrendered to him. The nun asked the King what it was about her that so attracted him. 'Your eyes,' replied the King, at which the modest and faithful nun took up a knife, cut out her eyes and sent them to the king who so desired them.[61] A similar story appears in Peter the Chanter, who died two years before Richard, this time attributed simply to an unspecified 'king of England'.[62] Gillingham has suggested that Stephen of Bourbon, who says he had heard the sermons of Peter the Chanter, may have got the anecdote from him; Peter would have known that the king was Richard but chose prudently not to refer to him by name.[63] But this seems unlikely as, in Richard's lifetime, any reference to an incident of this sort would immediately have been recognisable if the story was indeed true. However, the fact that such a story could be told about Richard in the mid thirteenth century is evidence that he was then regarded as dissolute, but keener on nuns than on young boys.

At the same period, recalls Gillingham, a chronicler spelt out the reasons for the death of the king before Châlus. Contemporaries, as we have seen, deplored the fact that the King took no notice of the advice of his doctors to behave with moderation.[64] This can be interpreted in many ways: rejection by the King of any diet or other alimentary prohibitions, refusal to abstain from wine or other alcoholic drinks, refusal to take complete bed rest, and so on. Walter of Guisborough, a century after the King's death, says very clearly that Richard, on his deathbed, against the advice of his doctors, still demanded that he be provided with women.[65] In the

same spirit, the author of an English romance of the late thirteenth century presents Richard as possessed of an irresistible charm which enabled him to seduce the daughter of his gaoler in Germany.[66] There is no doubt that the legend of Richard was at this period inclined to see him as a hetero-sexual seducer. But could it, at this period, have done anything else?

Can we draw any certain conclusions on such a controversial subject, on the basis of documents and evidence which mostly speak in veiled terms? Rather than an out-and-out and exclusive homosexual, Richard seems to have been, like his father and his ancestors before him, above all a hedonist; almost certainly less of a paedophile than his father, but probably bisexual; in a word, a versatile lecher. His legend, anticipated by his ancestors and nurtured by Richard himself, does not dwell on this side of his personality, even though sometimes, as well as praising his chivalric virtues, it refers to other scabrous aspects about which Richard himself dared to boast.

NOTES

1. See above, pp. 3ff.
2. For example, in the lifetime of Richard the Lionheart, in 1188, William Marshal advised Henry II to make it look as if he had decided not to attack and had laid off his army, then, when the enemy soldiers had dispersed, attack and ravage his lands. This ruse was approved by the King's council, which described it as a *mult curteis*: *Guillaume le Maréchal*, lines 7782ff.; about 1175, Jordan Fantosme attributes similar advice to Philip of Flanders: *Jordan Fantosme's Chronicle*, lines 437ff. Yet these were two heroes renowned for their 'chivalry'. On the subject of pillage as wholly acceptable to chivalric customs, see Strickland, *War and Chivalry*, pp. 129, 285.
3. Joinville, *Vie de Saint Louis*, §242, p. 121.
4. *Lancelot du Lac*, ed. E. Kennedy (Paris, 1991), pp. 886–7.
5. For example, in several articles collected in his *Mâle Moyen Age*; see in particular pp. 40ff., 74ff.
6. For this conception, see Wind, B., 'Ce Jeu Subtil, l'Amour Courtois', in *Mélanges Rita Lejeune*, vol. 2, pp. 1257–61. For a more recent conception of courtly love as discourse, see Schnell, R., 'Amour Courtois'.
7. Witness this passage in *Mâle Moyen Age* (p. 195): 'But it came also, it should not be forgotten, from women. Everything suggests that their participation in scholarly culture was more precocious and more widespread than that of the men of the lay aristocracy . . . it was in their presence that young men wished to shine . . . did they not constitute one of the essential intermediaries between the Renaissance and lay high society?' This well expresses the crucial role of women in the development of custom and mentalities that is our prime concern here.

8. Rougemont, *L'Amour et l'Occident*.

9. Jaufré Rudel, song no. VI, ed. A Jeanroy, *Les Chansons de Jaufré Rudel* (Paris, 1915); synoptic edition of all the versions in Pickens, R. T., *The Songs of Jaufré Rudel* (Toronto, 1978). The literature on this particular poem is abundant. See, above all, Monson, Don A., 'J. Rudel et l'Amour Lointain: les Origines d'une Légende', *Romania*, 106 (1985), pp. 36–56; Bec, P., ' "Amour de Loin" et "Dame Jamais Vue". Pour une Lecture Plurielle de la Chanson VI de J. Rudel', in *Mélanges A. Roncaglia* (Modena, 1989), vol. 1, pp. 101–8.

10. Köhler, E., 'Toubadours et Jalousie', in *Mélanges Jean Frappier*, vol. 1, pp. 543–59; Köhler, 'Observations Historiques', pp. 27–51.

11. Duby, G., 'A Propos de l'Amour que l'On Dit Courtois', in *Mâle Moyen Age*, pp. 80–1.

12. See on this point Flori, 'Amour et Société Aristocratique'; Flori, 'Mariage, Amour et Courtoisie'; Flori, 'Amour et Chevalerie dans le Tristan de Béroul'.

13. See, for example, Payen, J.-C., 'Lancelot contre Tristan: la Conjuration d'un Mythe Subversif (Réflexions sur l'Idéologie Romanesque au Moyen Age)', in *Mélanges Pierre le Gentil*, pp. 617–32; Payen, J.-C., 'Ordre Moral et Subversion Politique dans le Tristan de Béroul', in *Mélanges . . . Offerts à Mademoiselle Jeanne Lods*, pp. 473–84; Payen, J.-C., 'La Crise du Marriage à la Fin du XIIIe Siècle d'Après la Littérature Française du Temps', in Duby and Le Goff, *Famille et Parenté*, pp. 413–26; Payen, *La Rose et l'Utopie*.

14. *Guillaume le Maréchal*, lines 5127ff.

15. Ibid., lines 5243ff.

16. Marchello-Nizia, 'Amour Courtois'.

17. Duby, *Mâle Moyen Age*, pp. 81–2.

18. Duby, *William Marshal*, pp. 35, 46–7, 51ff., 59.

19. Thus it is in my view quite mistaken to deduce from the story of the games King Stephen, who held him prisoner, played with William, then still a little boy, that 'tender relations' existed between them, and ask: 'Should we exclude from the attitudes natural to these warriors love for little boys?' Of course we should not exclude them, but no more should we deduce them from accounts which in no way suggest them.

20. Flori, *Chevaliers et Chevalerie au Moyen Age*, pp. 241ff.

21. See, for example, *Lancelot du Lac*, ed. Kennedy, vol. 1 (trans. F. Moses), pp. 842ff.; vol. 2 (trans. M.-L. Chênerie) (Paris 1993), p. 17. We should note in passing that in pp. 899ff., 907, 909ff. and 911, the story has two women (Guinevere and the lady of Malehaut) and two men (Lancelot and Galehaut) coming together every night to enjoy their mutual conversation and 'other types of pleasure'. All alike love Lancelot. The ambiguity of the scene seems here deliberate, even if everything is ultimately subordinated to the love of the Queen and of Lancelot: Galehaut bows before the omnipotence of this

love, like the lady of Malehaut, and Guinevere 'gave' this woman to the knight Galehaut.

22. Marie de France, *Le Lai de Lanval*, lines 273ff., 279ff., 292ff., ed. K. Warnke, trans. L. Harf-Lancner, in *Lais de Marie de France* (Paris, 1990), pp. 148–9. The English translation used here is that of Glyn S. Burgess and Keith Busby, *The Lais of Marie de France*, Penguin Books, revised edn (Harmondsworth, 1999), pp. 76–7.

23. J. H. Harvey, *The Plantagenets, 1154–1485* (London, 1948), pp. 33ff. See Gillingham, J., 'Richard I and Berengaria of Navarre', in Gillingham, *Richard Cœur de Lion*, pp. 119–39, especially pp. 136ff. In fact, an allusion to Richard's homosexuality occurs in Richard, *Histoire des Comtes de Poitou*, vol. 2, p. 130; see also Gillingham, J., 'Some Legends of Richard the Lionheart: their Development and their Influence', in Nelson, *Richard Cœur de Lion*, pp. 51–69.

24. Among others, Brundage, *Richard Lionheart*, pp. 38ff., 88ff., 202ff., 212ff., 257ff.; Runciman, *History of the Crusades*, vol. 3, pp. 41ff. The thesis has been enthusiastically adopted by J. Boswell, *Christianity, Social Tolerance and Homosexuality*, pp. 231ff.

25. Roger of Howden, III, p. 204; *Gesta Henrici*, II, p. 236.

26. See above, p. 183.

27. *Ménestrel de Reims*, §19, p. 10.

28. Gerald of Wales, *De Principis Instructione*, III, 2, p. 232.

29. Richard of Devizes, p. 26.

30. Roger of Howden, III, p. 99; see also *Gesta Henrici*, II, p. 160.

31. See above, pp. 107–8.

32. *Continuation de Guillaume de Tyr*, p. 110.

33. Ambroise, lines 1135ff. (p. 47 of Ailes translation).

34. William of Newburgh, pp. 346–7.

35. Richard of Devizes, pp. 25–6.

36. Gillingham, *Richard Cœur de Lion*, p. 182.

37. Geoffrey of Monmouth, *Historia Regum Britanniae* (p. 229 of Thorpe translation).

38. Richard of Devizes, p. 16.

39. *Gesta Henrici*, II, 7; the Latin words are 'Rex Franciae eum dilexit . . . se mutuo diligebant . . . propter dilectionem inter illos . . . donec sciret quid tam repentinus amor machinaretur.'

40. The fact remains, even if the example quoted by Gillingham (with an incorrect reference) in support is inconclusive: 'Richard I and Berengaria of Navarre', p. 135, note 71. The text of the *Histoire de Guillaume le Maréchal* (lines 8980–4) says only that William managed to convince a sick Henry II to rest and made him lie down on a bed, without any suggestion that William shared this bed.

41. Matthew Paris, *Chronica Majora*, II, p. 297.

42. Gerald of Wales, *De Principis Instructione*, p. 176.

43. Ralph of Coggeshall, pp. 90ff.
44. According to a vision of Bishop Henry of Rochester, Richard would be able to leave Purgatory thirty-three years after his death, that is, on Saturday 27 March 1232: Matthew Paris, *Chronica Majora*, III, p. 212.
45. *Gesta Henrici*, II, pp. 146ff.; see also above pp. 100ff.
46. William of Newburgh, pp. 280ff.
47. Roger of Howden, III, pp. 288ff.
48. 'Coram se viris religiosis vitae suae foeditatem confiteri non erubuit', an expression very close to that used in connection with the penitence at Messina.
49. Roger of Howden, III, pp. 288–9.
50. Gillingham, 'Richard I and Berengaria of Navarre', p. 134.
51. Leviticus 18: 22: 'Thou shalt not lie with mankind, as with womankind; it is an abomination'. See also Leviticus 20: 13; Romans 1: 26–7.
52. Judges 19: 23–4.
53. For example: Deuteronomy 29: 23; Isaiah 1: 9 and 13: 9; Jeremiah 49: 18 and 50: 40; Sophonia (Zephaniah) 2: 9; Amos 4: 11; Matthew 11: 23; Luke 17: 29 etc.
54. See, for example, Jeremiah 23: 14; Ezekiel 16: 48–9; Lamentations 4: 6.
55. Isaiah 3: 9.
56. 2 Peter 2: 7 and 10.
57. Jude: 6–7.
58. Gerald of Wales, *Itinerarium Kambriae* and *Descriptio Kambriae*, vol. II, 7 (pp. 196–7 of Everyman edn).
59. *Gesta Henrici*, I, pp. 291–3.
60. Roger of Howden, IV, p. 97; see also *Archives Historiques du Poitou*, 4, pp. 21–2.
61. Stephen of Bourbon, *Anecdotes Historiques*, ed. A. Lecoy de La Marche (Paris, 1877), pp. 211ff., 431.
62. Baldwin, *Peter the Chanter and his Circle*, vol. 1, p. 245; vol. 2, pp. 183ff.
63. Gillingham, 'Richard I and Berengaria of Navarre', p. 136.
64. See above, p. 199ff.
65. *Chronicle of Walter of Guisborough*, ed. H. G. Rothwell (London, 1957), p. 142, quoted by Gillingham, 'Richard I and Berengaria of Navarre', p. 136, note 77.
66. *Der mittelenglische Versroman über Richard Löwenherz*, ed. K. Brunner (Vienna, 1913).

20

Richard and his Legend

It will by now be clear to readers of this book that Richard the Lionheart was a man who liked to be talked about, who cultivated his publicity and who created his own legend. This was one of the manifestations, it seems to me, of an important aspect of his character: his desire to dominate, his ambition to stand out from the crowd and to triumph in any activity in which he took part. He wanted, in a word, to be exceptional, even extraordinary; not only in his titles of count or king, which he obtained only belatedly and with difficulty thanks to the family disputes I have recorded, but also in himself, as a man.

AN EXTRAORDINARY FAMILY

This ostentation was accompanied by a large dose of provocation, many examples of which have been noted in the preceding pages. Furthermore, Richard did not hesitate, in his own lifetime, to contribute to the creation of his legend by incorporating disturbing elements, sulphurous or ambiguous, freely confusing mythology and his own and his family's history.

An anecdote about the fairy Melusine, told by Gerald of Wales, illustrates this aspect of Richard's character. It tells the story of a long-ago countess of Anjou, 'of remarkable beauty' but unknown origin, for the Count had married her for her looks alone. The couple lived happily together, except that the Count was disturbed by the fact that she rarely went to church and, when she did, 'manifested very little or no devotion'. She never remained for the consecration of the host, always leaving immediately after the gospel. This aroused his suspicions so, one day, he ordered four of his knights to detain her as she left the church, as was her invariable custom, with her four children. But when the knights approached, she slipped off her robe, left the two children on her right where they were, tucked the other two under her arm and flew out through a window, in full view of the congregation. She was never seen again. Richard liked to tell this story, says Gerald, and quote it so that he

could claim a supernatural origin for himself and his family; quite without shame, he said that this explained why the fathers and sons were forever fighting each other and tearing each other apart. 'For . . . they all had come of the devil, and to the devil they would go.' Gerald recalled other ancestral vices, including the conduct of Richard's mother Eleanor who, in addition to her affair with her uncle at Antioch, had been the mistress both of Geoffrey Plantagenet and of his son, before eventually marrying him. 'When, therefore,' Gerald concluded, 'the root was in every way so corrupt, how was it possible that the branches from such a stock could be prosperous or virtuous?'[1]

The secret indiscretions of his father, Henry II, with Alice, and his public affair with Rosamund Clifford, added extra spice to the scabrous reputation of a family already celebrated in this sphere. Richard's maternal ancestor William IX, as we have seen, had delighted in scandalising the moralists by openly appearing with his mistress, la Maubergeonne, and had even dared to have her painted naked on his shield. It was hardly surprising, said Gerald, that such a lineage had been struck by God with a variety of ills or that so many of its sons had died without heirs.

Richard was not the only one to blame the internal conflicts which rent his family on an accursed heritage. His brother Geoffrey did the same, according to Gerald, openly saying as much to an envoy sent by his father, Henry II, when he was trying to heal the breach between himself and his sons:

> Are you ignorant that this is a natural property, engrafted and inserted in us by hereditary right, as it were, by our fathers and forefathers; that no-one of us should love the other, but that the brother should always oppose his brother with all his might, and the son the father? Do not, therefore, deprive me of my hereditary right, nor labour to expel my nature from me.[2]

The belief in a divine curse pronounced on the Plantagenets seems already to have been established in the family well before Richard's time. Henry II had the revolt of his sons portrayed in allegorical form on a fresco in his palace at Winchester, as if it was a mythological subject, and he saw it as the fulfilment of a prophecy. During this revolt, he often told the Bishop of Lincoln that a hermit had once reproached William IX for his adultery, prophesying that the progeny of this illicit union would never bear fertile fruit. For Henry, the rebellion of his sons was this prediction come true.[3]

Richard seems to have been no more eager than his ancestors to cultivate virtue. The chroniclers often criticise him for his 'debauchery' and

his 'lustfulness'. Ralph of Coggeshall interpreted the King's arrest and captivity in Germany as a punishment from God:

> This lamentable misfortune, we must accept, did not happen against the will of Almighty God, even if his will escapes us; perhaps it was to chastise the sins that the king himself had committed in his years of debauchery or to punish the sins of his subjects, or even more so that the detestable wickedness of those people who persecuted the king in the situation he was in should be known all over the world and should leave to their descendants the stain attached to such a crime.[4]

The anecdote reported above is not the only one to refer to the links between the Plantagenets and the forces of darkness. William of Newburgh, for example, on the subject of the King's second repentance in 1197, says that the devil had been extremely disappointed by Richard's 'conversion'. A demon had made himself known to a pious man and told him that, in the past, he had been able to manipulate the King through his hold over him and over several other princes of this world. It was he, he claimed, who had accompanied the two kings on crusade and sown discord between them so that the expedition would be a failure; it was also he who had had Richard arrested in Germany; and it was he, lastly, who had prompted him into cupidity since his return, frequently standing beside the King's bed, like a trusted servant, and watching carefully over his treasury at Chinon. But he had been forced to leave the sovereign when he repented, decided that his bed would in future be chaste and took generous alms from his treasury for the poor.[5] In this anecdote we see Richard accused not only of conniving with the devil and of a culpable tendency to the lust or indecency discussed in the last chapter, but also of avarice.

Another anecdote, told this time by Roger of Howden, emphasises the three main faults attributed to Richard: pride, cupidity and lust, while at the same time demonstrating the cavalier and even humorous way in which Richard, by a clever retort, could turn a tricky situation to his own advantage. It also suggests a certain anticlericalism on his part, several examples of which we have already noted. Such an attitude would not have been displeasing to the knights who were his companions. The incident took place in 1198 and concerned the (hypothetical) meeting between Richard and Fulk of Neuilly, preacher of the crusade. Fulk apparently reproached the King for his unworthy conduct and concluded his speech with a parable culminating in a warning and an appeal to repentance:

> 'I order you, in the name of Almighty God, to marry as soon as possible the three wicked daughters you have, so that you do not suffer a greater ill' . . .

the king responded: 'Charlatan, you lie, I have no daughters'. To which Fulk replied: 'Assuredly I tell no lie; you have, as I have told you, three very wicked daughters: the first is called Pride, the second Cupidity and the third Lust.' The king then summoned all the counts and barons who were nearby and said to them: 'Listen to the words of this hypocrite; he says I have three very wicked daughters, Pride, Cupidity and Lust, and orders me to marry them. So I give my daughter Pride to the proud Templars, Cupidity to the monks of the Cistercian order and Lust to the prelates of the churches.'[6]

The Templars had not yet acquired the detestable reputation for corruption, heresy, avarice and homosexual lust that they enjoyed a century later. All they were accused of in Richard's day was their 'superiority complex', their lofty dignity. The accusation of greed levelled against the Cistercians may surprise, given that the order had been created out of a desire to break with the ostentatious wealth of the Church, and in particular that of Cluny. But its very success, recently enhanced by the prestige of St Bernard, had attracted a flood of donations, and its thrifty management only added to its wealth, all the more so because its expenses were minimal, as the labour was performed by the monks themselves.

The accusation of lust, which the King turned against the prelates, is unsurprising at this period, including its association with homosexuality, as is perhaps the case here. We need only recall, for example, that the Bishop of Ely, William Longchamp, one of Richard's trusted servants, who governed England in his absence, was notorious for his 'horror of women' and his homosexual relations. Roger of Howden said that the bishop never tried to do good, but 'practised evil in his bed where he slept with servants of evil or with his favourites'. Pursued by the mob, he tried to flee disguised as a woman, exchanging his clerical gown for the robe of a harlot. This amazed the chronicler who mocked this knightly prelate who had always before shown such hostility to the fair sex. 'What is so surprising,' he wrote, 'is that he should have become so effeminate and chosen to disguise himself as a woman, he who was accustomed often to wear the armour of a knight'.[7] At the same period those irreverent clerical poets, the goliards, were poking fun at such behaviour, common amongst the prelates. A satirical song composed in the middle of the twelfth century, for example, mocks a lecherous bishop who demands the sexual services of a *bacheler* whom he was to dub knight the next morning 'for his merits'.[8] However justified, Richard's stinging reply nevertheless drew attention to the nature of the vices for which he himself was criticised.

The King of England was probably far from discontented with this sulphurous reputation. John Prestwich has rightly emphasised that, like all

great captains, Richard knew the value of legends as a means of impressing his soldiers and intimidating his enemies. He would probably not have been displeased to know that on the (premature) news of his liberation from captivity, Philip Augustus remarked to his accomplice, John: 'The devil has been let loose.'[9] Nor did he hesitate, as we have seen, to flaunt his membership of an Angevin dynasty that was on good terms with the devil, fairies and enchanters.

RICHARD AND ARTHURIAN LEGEND

This belief was further strengthened by interpretations of the 'prophecies' attributed by Geoffrey of Monmouth to Merlin, further confusing shadowy Celtic mythology and the history of the Plantagenet family.[10]

Had Richard really been impressed from childhood by this 'curse', worthy of the Atreids, and these vestiges of Celtic mythology? It is by no means impossible, given the importance attached by the Plantagenet court to the literature inspired by the Arthurian myth. Without accepting all the often extravagant claims of Jean Markale, we must agree with him on the profound influence of Celtic traditions on these courtly milieus and the poets who frequented them. As well as an undeniable atmosphere of magic and pagan spirituality, these Celtic traditions, which were drawn on by the romance writers, transmitted values alien to Christian society in the West; they did not reject the homosexuality of heroes and they also emphasised the role of women in the transmission of royal power (hence the central importance of the figure of Guinevere), so justifying the minor role and strange behaviour of King Arthur.[11]

Richard's personal interest in these traditions (and perhaps also his desire to turn them to political advantage) manifested itself in the searches conducted in his reign to find the tomb of King Arthur. Many chroniclers highlight the 'discovery', in 1191 or 1192, of the tomb of the mythical British king, to whom contemporaries, including the educated, attached great ideological importance and ascribed real historicity; the success of Geoffrey of Monmouth, reworked by Wace and the romance writers responsible for the Arthurian cycle, testifies to this. The chroniclers describe the discovery, close to Glastonbury, of the remains of the famous King of Britain, Arthur, who lay in a sarcophagus alongside two ancient pyramids bearing a worn inscription in 'an ancient barbarian language'. On the sarcophagus, they said, was a cross of lead on which were written these words: 'Here lies the illustrious king of the Britons, Arthur, buried in the Isle of Avalon';[12] this site, surrounded by marshland, had, in fact, formerly been called the Isle of Avalon, or the Isle of Apples.

This 'discovery' had a real political significance. It put a stop to the almost messianic expectations of the Celts or Britons who, in their mute resistance to the Norman invaders, had projected onto Arthur the nostalgic memory of their ancient liberties, but also the incarnation of their hopes; they had cultivated the legend of a king who was not dead but who, like the emperor of the last days, lived on in hiding and would assume the leadership of his loyal followers in his final victorious battle against the invader. Further, the strong interest displayed by the Plantagenets in these legends (and their increasingly chivalric orientation) made members of their family, owners of Excalibur, the legitimate descendants of the Arthurian power and monarchy; they were heirs to the ideal he represented, that of a body of knights united and gathered around the King, 'first among equals', as it were, in a society in which chivalry occupied its rightful place, at the top. It was an ideal that could unite Britons, Anglo-Saxons and Normans behind the emblematic figure of a 'roi-chevalier' who was heir to the mythical King Arthur. Richard was certainly alive to this consideration, which attracted attention to the court of England, designated as heir to ancient traditions, culmination of a long migration which had led from Troy to the Arthurian court. These traditions, successively transmitted by the Greeks and the Romans, were knowledge and valour, 'clergy and chivalry' as they were called by Geoffrey of Monmouth, Wace and Benoît de Sainte-Maure, all seeking to associate the crown of England with the heroes of Graeco-Latin Antiquity. Other writers, perhaps inspired by Richard's crusade, would soon establish yet another link, between earthly and celestial chivalry, a further example of the Christianisation of a chivalric myth.

The discovery of the tombs of Avalon was probably, it is now thought, a 'pious invention' of the monks of Glastonbury, but many people believed in it;[13] others, perhaps fewer in number, only pretended to believe, entering into the game. Richard was probably among the latter. In acting as a 'roi-chevalier', or an Arthurian hero, sometimes imitating King Arthur in certain actions, he in a sense 'appropriated' some of the prestige then attached to all things Arthurian, not only in the Celtic world but also much further afield, wherever people were influenced by the dissemination of the romance, that is, almost all over the Western world. It is noteworthy, for example, that when Richard set out on his crusade he took the sword Excalibur with him. John Gillingham sees this as proof that he was deliberately associating himself with the heroic Arthurian world.[14] While I fully accept this interpretation, I find it surprising that the King of England should then have given a sword so rich in the symbolism of royal dignity, and bearing such an ideological weight, to Tancred; can Richard really

have seen him as so important a figure in the diplomatic sphere? True, Tancred was offering Richard substantial material advantages in return: 20,000 ounces of gold, the return of the dowry of his sister Joan and the promise of a further 20,000 ounces of gold to be handed over on the occasion of the proposed marriage of his daughter to Richard's nephew, Arthur of Brittany, whose name alone testifies to the influence of the Arthurian legends on the Plantagenet court.[15] Did Richard for once prefer the substance to the shadow?

RICHARD AND CHIVALRIC MYTH

It was not only the Arthurian world that influenced Richard's conduct and, perhaps even more, the choice of themes to define his legend. His panegyrists, official or occasional, also compared him to the heroes of Graeco-Roman mythology. Gerald of Wales took up the notion of a transmission of values (and not only of knowledge, as is usually claimed) from East to West which, beginning with Troy, culminated at the court of the King of England. Gerald put the king of this court at the end of a long line of which he was a worthy successor, that of Priam, Hector, Achilles, Titus and Alexander;[16] we should note that Gerald is referring here not to knowledge but to chivalry and warrior valour. Further, the king in question is not Richard but his elder brother Henry.[17] Richard seems here to have been only a substitute for his brother, required, as it were, to do as well as he. Walter Map tells the story of a young man who wanted 'to gain . . . instruction in arms', so went to the court of Count Philip of Flanders because, he wrote, he was in this age 'the most valiant in war . . . since the passing of the Young King Henry, the son of Henry, our King, who hath – God be thanked – no peer among living men'.[18] He makes no mention of Richard. It was also the Young Henry who was compared by Bertran de Born to Roland, in laudatory terms, at the time of his death:

> Lord, in you there was nothing to change: the whole world had chosen you for the best king who ever bore a shield, and the bravest one and the best knight in a tourney. Since the time of Roland, and even before, no-one ever saw so excellent a king or one so skilled in war, or one whose fame so spread through the world and gave it new life, or one who sought fame from the Nile to the setting sun, looking for it everywhere.[19]

After the death of his brother, unanimously recognised as a model of chivalry, Richard, in his turn, was compared to Roland. Never, declared Ambroise, even at Roncevaux, had a knight acquitted himself as valiantly

as Richard at Jaffa, when he had almost single-handedly routed the Saracens.[20] But Richard was not the only one of whom such comparisons were made. Ambroise says the same about several valiant knights who distinguished themselves in the Holy Land. Of Geoffrey de Lusignan, for example, he remarks: 'Everywhere resounded so to the sound of his blows that not since Roland and Oliver had there been such a praiseworthy knight.'[21]

Was Richard really a model knight and was he generally recognised and glorified as such amongst knights in general? Or is this how he wished to appear, so as to meet expectations? Perhaps he was the designated champion of the knights simply as heir to the throne of Arthur, bearer of a standard that had been intended for Henry the Young King, or even Geoffrey, and which he had inherited only in their absence. It is impossible, reading the chroniclers, to avoid the impression that the story of his exploits corresponds to a sort of double 'horizon of expectations', to use the phrase made fashionable by some recent literary theorists: on the one hand, the desire of the King of England to see his fine deeds as a knight celebrated; on the other, that of the knights to make him not only their standard bearer, leader and most eminent representative, but also the defender and patron of their order and the embodiment of their values and interests; it might even be said, the saviour of chivalry. The conjuncture of these two sets of expectations resulted, as we have seen, in the development of a 'legend' which was beginning to emerge even in Richard's lifetime, and to which he himself contributed both by his own attitude and by the more or less romanticised accounts made out of it.

We should not distinguish, therefore, the historical Richard from the Richard of the legend, for two reasons: on the one hand, Richard probably tried in real life to behave like a character in a legend; on the other, the stories through which we know him were also, from the beginning, full of fabrications which the King himself disseminated. The legend of Richard developed after his death, certainly, in the ways we have already described, making him conform even more closely to the ideal knight as he was then conceived, from the thirteenth century on: a valiant knight, brave, intrepid, indomitable, generous and courteous, a poet and full of charm. Nevertheless, the majority of these traits, with the possible exception of the last, were already part of the image which Richard, in his own lifetime, wanted to present of himself to his contemporaries before transmitting it to posterity.

One example will illustrate what I mean. By the end of the thirteenth century, an English romance embroidered on several of the elements we

have emphasised. It placed Richard in the lineage not only of Alexander and Charlemagne (that is, ancient history romanticised) but also of Arthur and Gawain (that is, myth historicised). Hero of the true faith, the King of England had to confront the champion of error, Saladin, who was able, obviously, in that capacity, to call on magic and occult forces (so bringing in religious history). In spite of this, Richard succeeded in triumphing over evil spells, as the French romance on which the English one was based, *Le Pas Saladin*, had already said, more soberly, half a century before.[22] This Saladin, a true model knight (except as regards the faith) was compelled to recognise the chivalric superiority of the King of England. True, the devil had not spoken his last word and Richard was treacherously imprisoned in Germany, where his noble bearing, haughty and chivalric, irritated his gaoler but seduced his daughter; she fell in love with him, became his mistress and provided him with the means of escape from the jaws of the lion which was meant to end his days.[23] Our hero demonstrates all the chivalric virtues, but hardly differs (if we except the seduction of the lady) from the image of himself that Richard had tried to convey in his lifetime.

Why did he do this? What were his motives in cultivating this image? One possible answer has already been suggested. His eternal enemy, the King of France, Philip Augustus, was a king regarded as a realist, down-to-earth, relying on his 'good towns', surrounding himself with plebeian advisers and favouring the bourgeoisie; the response of the Plantagenet kings – Henry II first and then Richard even more so – was to present themselves as the natural defenders of the nobility and the knights. The moralists and poets say as much: these kings 'restored chivalry', when it was 'almost dead'. Could they have been referring here to the restoration of the *fyrd* and of chivalry by Henry II in the Assize of Arms of 1181, which decreed that all noble and free men must own a set of military equipment and swear to put it at the King's service, and which defined in some detail the obligation of armed service on all who held a knight's fee?[24] It is unlikely, because something very different from an obligation was meant; it was rather a conferring of value, a method of government that glorified the nobility and its prime activity, war. This explains the extolling of chivalry which is visible in all the works composed at the Plantagenet court, designed to win over the feudal princes hostile to the policies of the King of France. It also explains why the kings of this lineage were so anxious to acquire a reputation as knights. This, in essence, is the thesis put forward by the literary scholar Eric Köhler and the historian Georges Duby, who constructed an overall theory based on certain comments and studies of their predecessors.[25] In other words,

the Plantagenet court (particularly in the person of Richard) made the chivalrous image of its king into a sort of system of government appropriating the prestige of the aristocratic, corporatist and elitist Arthurian court, symbolised by the Round Table. The figure of Arthur, model for the Plantagenet world, here counterbalances that of Charlemagne, claimed by the kings of France. The thesis is solid and certainly contains a large element of truth. But it is not the whole truth and is even open to certain objections and the accusation of internal contradictions. Below I give some to which a totally satisfying response has not yet, to my mind, been given.

Why, for example, if this was the case, has Henry II not preserved for posterity the image of 'roi-chevalier' which he seems to have possessed at the time of his seduction of Eleanor? Perhaps this was because of his extramarital escapades or, more likely, his role in the murder of Thomas Becket. Yet, as we have seen, the majority of chroniclers judged his reign more favourably than that of his son. It is more likely that it is because this king, in spite of his many military campaigns, lacked the personal valour and, even more to the point, the taste for spectacular acts and feats of prowess developed by his son.[26]

A second question: it may well be the case that the chivalric ideal was exalted by the poets of the Plantagenet court, or at least in its lands, but this high praise was not exclusive to them. There is no shortage of romances originating in the kingdom of France which exalt the very same aristocratic and chivalric values. It would seem, therefore, that the reasons for this praise must be more social than political and must reflect a general trend in the second half of the twelfth century. Richard is more likely to have shared than to have created this mentality.

A third question: if the Plantagenet court wanted to appear as the refuge and natural defender of the nobility and chivalry, why did it, perhaps more than any other court of its time, recruit mercenaries on such a large scale? These routiers, Flemings, cotereaux and Brabançons, were particularly numerous in the armies of Henry II and in the immediate entourage of Richard I, most notably in the person of Mercadier, who accompanied him everywhere and was present at his death. This was surely an ideological inconsistency. It can be argued, admittedly, that the necessities of war required leaders to recruit routiers in time of need and dismiss them as soon as hostilities ended or a truce was agreed; they were then let loose in the countryside, where they lived 'on' the inhabitants, as predators, looters, brawlers, robbers and rapists, spreading terror and attracting universal reprobation. Perhaps this was a useful way of dissociating chivalry from these rough elements; on many

occasions, obedient to the precepts of the Church, which granted indulgences to those who took up arms against them, the knights on both sides 'purged' the countryside of their presence;[27] but only for a while, as they were recruited again as soon as necessity called. And nothing obliged Richard to be so closely and so publicly associated with Mercadier and his routiers.

For all these reasons, it seems to me, we have to add to his undeniable political motives a purely personal interest, a motivation of a psychological nature resulting from an individual choice: Richard wanted to be seen as a model knight because he felt like a knight, in his own innermost being. He seems to have been at ease in the company of warriors, of foot soldiers and archers, with whom he sometimes mixed, but even more in that of knights, amongst whom he had grown up, sharing their games and exercises, their training and their battles, their tastes and possibly their vices. The chroniclers (men of the Church, of course) reproached him for this. Well before he became king, they said, he was broken by the premature and excessive exercise of the trade of arms.[28] Like Bertran de Born, he loved war, fine blows with the sword and lance, headlong charges to the sound of war cries and the clatter of arms, amidst the shimmering colours of shields, and banners streaming in the wind. Identifying with the knights was probably more than a political calculation; for Richard, it was a natural choice. He not only *presented* himself as one of them; he *was* one of them.

Recognising this, the knights loved and admired him all the more and, in return, bestowed on him all the prestige of chivalry, already established by a literature which inspired Richard and which he may also have inspired. His legend as 'roi-chevalier', rooted in reality but strengthened by his own propaganda, compared him to the heroes who were glorified ad nauseam in the literature of his age. In this sphere, Richard was unequalled, streets ahead of his rivals, kings and princes alike, all less brilliant knights than he, at least after the death of his brother.

His campaign in the Holy Land, despite its relative failure, further contributed to the growth of his prestige in this sphere. As we have seen, the chroniclers, and in particular Ambroise (principal eyewitness, but also almost unconditional panegyrist of the crusader king), transformed this semi-failure into an epic by their constant lauding of the warlike exploits of the valiant King of England, constantly hampered by the permanent treachery of his perfidious partners. Faced with a reputedly invincible Saladin, Richard became the sole true defender of Christendom, champion of the faith. The other princes either abandoned or betrayed him, employing against him infamous practices wholly at

variance with the chivalric ethic. Some, like Philip Augustus and the Duke of Burgundy, fled the field of battle out of cowardice or vile personal interest. Others resorted to lies and calumny, unjustly accusing him of attempting to assassinate the Marquis of Montferrat and even the King of France; it was the Saracens, more chivalrous than these ignoble Christians, who had to exonerate him by letters written by their leader, the Old Man of the Mountain, chief of the Assassins. Worse, the King of France himself, according to witnesses quoted by the chroniclers, had sought to have Richard assassinated.[29] These same traitors, the Duke of Burgundy for example, dared to accuse this hero of cowardice and write 'evil songs' about him, to which Richard replied with both the pen and the sword. Others, at the instigation of the French, and particularly Philip of Beauvais, that deceitful knight-bishop who kept standing in Richard's way, spread all sorts of malicious rumours about the King of England, stirring up hatred against him, so much so that he was delivered into the hands of Duke Leopold and then thrown into the gaols of the perfidious emperor. His ignoble capture and his unjust detention may have been interpreted by some clerical chroniclers as a divine punishment but they were seen by many, in particular among the laity and the nobility, as an anomaly and an insult to aristocratic morality.

His prestige was only further enhanced, fuelled by the censure and indignation provoked by the ignoble behaviour of his enemies. Richard soon began to appear as the sole defender of the Holy Land, a 'knight of God'. Was he not, furthermore, the only conqueror of Saladin, whose earlier reputation, assiduously built up by Ambroise, only enhanced the prestige of that great knight Richard, who surpassed him in everything, even winning his admiration? The glorification of Saladin only served further to increase the renown of the King of England.

Both the historical and the literary sources provide proof: Richard's battle against the Muslims is symbolically represented on the enamelled tiles of Chertsey Abbey, where the King, as a knight, charges a Muslim horseman, probably Saladin himself; by the mid thirteenth century this episode has been transformed into a mythical combat in the work mentioned above, *Le Pas Saladin*; better still, St Louis on his own crusade, also in the thirteenth century, made constant references to King Richard.

His image already served as a model, and St Louis tried to imitate it. It has already been noted that Richard never actually made the unarmed pilgrimage to Jerusalem authorised by the treaty concluded with Saladin. He even, according to one Arab chronicler, asked the Sultan to forbid entry to the Holy City to all those who had not received his own safe conduct. His intention was clear; he wanted to avoid a situation where

the completion of the pilgrimage might make people forget the true purpose of the Holy War: the reconquest of Jerusalem:

> The king of England had corresponded with the sultan and had asked him to prohibit the Franks from visiting the church, except for those who arrived with a letter or an envoy from that king; he was very anxious that the sultan respond to his request and agree to his demand. What he wanted, it was said, was that those people, having returned home regretting that they had never visited the church, would remain favourably inclined to the war and the turmoil, whereas those who made the visit found their hearts calmed and their anxiety relieved.[30]

Perhaps Richard, too, wanted to preserve intact in his heart the desire to return to the Holy Land and successfully complete the reconquest of the Holy Sepulchre. Yet if we are to believe William of Newburgh, he did not make this pilgrimage himself, but sent a substitute, Hubert of Salisbury:

> It is reported that he visited for himself, and for the prince, the sepulchre of the King of Kings; and pouring out there a deluge of pious tears, and performing mass, he accomplished equally his own and the king's vows, to whom he returned.[31]

Richard of Devizes offers a more chivalric explanation of Richard's abandonment of this project. Hubert visited the Sepulchre, he says, and then, on his return, pressed the King, too, to make the journey. But Richard, with dignity, refused and uttered these haughty words: he had no wish to receive, as a privilege granted by the pagans, what he had not been able to obtain as a gift from God.[32]

Some fifty years later, St Louis found himself in a very similar position. At Jaffa, he was informed by his entourage that the sultan would agree to give him a safe conduct so that he could make the pilgrimage to Jerusalem. The King consulted his advisers who said he should refuse the offer, because it would be tantamount to accepting the Muslim status of the Holy City. To strengthen their case, they told him how Richard had once acted, not after the treaty with Saladin but before, during an expedition intended to seize the town: the Christians had been on the point of reaching it when the Duke of Burgundy ordered his troops to turn back, impelled by hatred and jealousy, so that it could never be said that the English had taken Jerusalem. This is how Richard's noble attitude was reported to St Louis by his council:

> As they were speaking, one of his knights called out to him: 'Sir, Sir, come here and I will show you Jerusalem.' And when the king heard this, he put his surcoat over his eyes and wept and said to Our Lord: 'Fair Lord God, I pray

that you suffer me not to see your Holy City, since I may not deliver it from the hands of thine enemies'.[33]

Richard's renown as God's royal knight (in other words, crusader) could only emerge strengthened from the comparisons that it was impossible to avoid between him and his predecessors and rivals. No sovereign, we should remember, had taken part in the First Crusade, the only one to be truly successful. In the Second Crusade, King Louis VII of France had failed lamentably and his wife Eleanor had conducted herself so imprudently with her uncle at Antioch that later legend could even accuse her of an affair with Saladin himself. In any case, cuckolded or not, it was at this point that the King of France, more monk than knight in shining armour, decided to have his marriage annulled. Eleanor promptly married Henry II, so once again the Angevin dynasty scored over that of France, in love as in war. The German sovereigns, meanwhile, with the exception of Frederick II (who was excommunicated and has been very harshly judged), could derive little glory from the crusades. Frederick Barbarossa had drowned while crossing a river and his scattered army played only a very minor role in the crusade. Henry VI discredited himself by imprisoning Richard. In fact, Saladin was the sole adversary worthy of him and their respective legends elevated them even further above the common run, turning them into myths in their own lifetimes. From this perspective, it is easier to understand the tide of praise which, in the contemporary literature, exalted Saladin and made him into a nigh-perfect model knight: a Muslim equivalent for Richard, if not a foil for him, a sort of mirror of the chivalric virtues of the Christian king, as he would be, much later, in Sir Walter Scott's *The Talisman*.[34]

By the thirteenth century Richard the Lionheart appeared in history as the ideal crusader, knight and king, combining in his person all the virtues of these three functions. Even St Louis, emblematic figure of the Capetian monarchy, admitted Richard's superiority over his own grandfather, Philip Augustus, and referred to it in the Holy Land.

This image was destined never to fade. The perfect illustration came during the festivities which, on Sunday 20 August 1389, marked the entry into Paris of Charles IV and Isabella of Bavaria. They played out, once again, *Le Pas Saladin*, that mythical combat which, near Jaffa, had pitted Richard the Lionheart against his Muslim rival. Men dressed up as Richard and his companions mimed a 'battle' in the Rue St-Denis:

Next, outside the Church of the Trinity, a raised platform had been set up overlooking the street. On it was a castle, and disposed along the platform was the tournament of King Saladin, with all the participants, the Christians

at one end and the Saracens at the other. There were men impersonating all the famous knights who had fought at Saladin's tournament equipped with the arms and armour which were used at the time. A little way from them was a person representing the King of France, with the twelve peers of France round him all wearing their arms. As the Queen's litter came opposite the platform, King Richard stepped forward from among his companions, went up to the King of France, and asked permission to attack the Saracens. When it had been given, he went back to his twelve companions who drew up in battle order and immediately moved to the attack of Saladin and his Saracens. A fierce mock battle took place, which lasted for some time and delighted the spectators.[35]

This dramatisation may well contain a desire to show the King of England as owing allegiance to the King of France, his suzerain; Richard, it should be noted, asks the latter for permission to lay into the Saracens. But it was on Richard that the glory redounded. He was the standard bearer of Christendom, the flower of chivalry in the West. We may also detect in it another allegory, more in line with modern interpretations of the reigns of Richard and of Philip Augustus. While the King of France governed and ruled in his kingdom, the King of England was far away, fighting the Saracens. This is how Richard has often been presented by English historians, who have tended to see him as a knight in search of adventure, a poor king and a mediocre ruler, improvident and unstable, a utopian lone rider forever tilting at windmills. John Gillingham has refuted this accusation. Richard was very far from being a mediocre king, but his main interest lay in his continental domains, the heart of the Angevin empire, and he showed little affection for England. It is easy to conclude that the decline of the Plantagenets should be blamed not on Richard but on his successor. This is neatly symbolised by the fate of Château-Gaillard: this castle, which Richard had boasted of being able to defend against Philip Augustus even if its walls were made of butter, fell into the hands of the King of France in 1204. It fell, as Philip had prophesied it would, and with it fell the whole of Normandy; his men-at-arms had managed to penetrate it by cunning, through the latrines, which was hardly chivalric but undeniably effective. Great victories like this had eluded Philip Augustus in Richard's time. Richard was not a bad king who neglected the realities of his role as sovereign in favour of the utopia of chivalry.

It is for his reputation for chivalry, however, that Richard was primarily renowned, and this remains true today. It was this dominant characteristic which impressed his contemporaries, friends or foes, as the judgement passed on him by Saladin shows. Sixty years after his

death, it was these chivalric virtues as a whole which were emphasised by the Minstrel of Reims at the beginning of his account, to justify its existence:

> [I] will tell you of King Richard his son, who came into this land. And he was a valiant man, and bold and courteous and bountiful, and a fine knight; and he came to tourney on the marches of France and of Poitou; and he stayed so long taking part in them that everyone spoke well of him.[36]

His reputation as a knight in search of adventure was not undeserved. It could even be said that he inaugurated a new way of ruling, on horseback and sword in hand, of which he would forever be the model.

Richard was truly a 'roi-chevalier': he was a knight who was also a good monarch; he was a king who was and wanted to be a model of chivalry. In this he succeeded and this he remains. The image of Richard which has survived to this day may be inaccurate, schematic, incomplete, extreme and exaggerated, but it is not necessarily false.

NOTES

1. Gerald of Wales, *De Principis Instructione*, pp. 299–301 (p. 98 of translation).
2. Ibid., p. 302 (p. 99 of translation).
3. Ibid., pp. 295, 298 (p. 95 of translation)
4. Ralph of Coggeshall, p. 57.
5. William of Newburgh, p. 434.
6. Roger of Howden, IV, pp. 76–7.
7. *Gesta Henrici*, II, 7.
8. Hugh of Orleans (or Primat?) (c. 1145–6): 'Or est venu li moines ad episcopum', in Dobiache-Rojdesvensky, O., *Les Poésies des Goliards* (Paris, 1931), p. 115; Contamine P., et al., *L'Europe au Moyen Age*, vol. 2: *Fin IXe s.–Fin XIIIe S.* (Paris, 1969), p. 311.
9. Roger of Howden, III, pp. 216–17. For this aspect, see Prestwich, J. O., 'Richard Cœur de Lion: Rex Bellicosus', in Nelson, *Richard Cœur de Lion*, p. 2.
10. For the prophecies of Merlin applied to the Plantagenets, see *Gesta Henrici*, I, 42; Matthew Paris, *Chronica Majora*, II, pp. 293–4, 342–3, 346; Richard de Poitiers, addenda, pp. 418–21; Ralph Diceto, II, p. 64; Roger of Howden, II, pp. 46–7; *Gesta Henrici*, I, p. 42, referring to Geoffrey of Monmouth, VII, 3.
11. See, on this point, in between some veritable rants, the many pertinent remarks of J. Markale, *Le Roi Arthur*; also Markale, *Lancelot*, in particular pp. 44ff., 76ff.
12. Matthew Paris, *Chronica Majora*, II, 379; Ralph of Coggeshall, p. 36. For

the impact of the legend, see Wace, *Le Roman de Brut*, lines 13275–98; and Cassard, J. C., 'Arthur est vivant! Jalons pour une enquête sur le messianisme royal au Moyen Age', *Cahiers de Civilisation Médiévale*, 32 (1989), pp. 135–46.

13. See on this point Grandison, A., 'The Growth of the Glastonbury Traditions and Legends', in *Journal of English History*, 27 (1976), pp. 337–58; Keen, *Chivalry*, pp. 113ff.

14. Gillingham, J., 'Some Legends of Richard the Lionheart: their Development and their Influence', in Nelson, *Richard Cœur de Lion*, p. 52.

15. Ambroise, lines 976ff.

16. Gerald of Wales, *De Principis Instructione*, p. 173.

17. Ambroise also compares James of Avesnes to Achilles and Hector: lines 2884ff.

18. Walter Map (*Master Walter Map's Book*, pp. 177–8).

19. Bertran de Born, ed. Gouiran, song no. 13, p. 235: 'Mon chant fenis ab dol et ab maltraire', strophe IV, p. 243 (p. 262 of Paden translation).

20. Ambroise, lines 11231ff.

21. Ambroise, lines 4657ff., French translation p. 384 (p. 96 of Ailes translation).

22. See on this point Loomis, 'Richard Cœur de Lion . . . in Medieval Art'.

23. *Der mittelenglische Versroman über Richard Löwenherz*, ed. K. Brunner (Vienna, 1913).

24. 'Assize of Arms, A.D. 1181', in *Select Charters and Other Illustrations of English Constitutional History*, ed. W. Stubbs (Oxford, 1913), 9th edn, pp. 181–4.

25. See, for example, Köhler, *Aventure Chevaleresque*, pp. 7ff., 69ff., 82ff., etc; Duby, *The Three Orders*, pp. 293ff.

26. Though Henry II is signalled as a valiant knight in many sources; see, for example, Walter Map: *Master Walter Map's Book*, p. 178; and Ralph Niger (p. 336) describes him as 'miles strenuus, sed minus pius'. But the majority of chroniclers tend rather to emphasis his desire for peace.

27. In particular Lateran III (1179): see *Conciles Œcuméniques*, canon 27, p. 482. For Richard's actions against routiers, see, for example, Geoffrey of Vigeois, *Chronicon* (extracts), *Recueil des Historiens*, 18, p. 213.

28. William of Newburgh, p. 306.

29. For the origin of the accusation that Richard murdered first Conrad and then Philip Augustus, see Rigord, §87, pp. 120–1; Roger of Howden, III, p. 181; Ralph of Coggeshall, p. 35; William of Newburgh, p. 458; Ibn al Athir, XVIII, p. 51 (Gabrieli, *Arab Historians*, p. 239). For the supposed assassination attempt on Richard by men of Philip Augustus at Chinon in 1195, see Roger of Howden, III, p. 283.

30. Imad ad-Din, *Conquête de la Syrie*, p. 394.

31. William of Newburgh, p. 378 (p. 604 of Stevenson translation).

32. Richard of Devizes, p. 84: 'Ut [quod] de Dei dono non poterat, de gratia gentilium consquerentur.'

33. Joinville, *Vie de Saint Louis*, §556, p. 276.

34. See on this point Jondot, J., 'Le Même et l'Autre dans Le Talisman de Sir Walter Scott', in *De Toulouse à Tripoli*, pp. 191–209; in the French translation, the book has the title of *Richard en Palestine*. For the later image of Richard in English literature, see, for example, de Laborderie, O., 'L'Image de Richard Cœur de Lion dans La Vie et La Mort du Roi Jean de William Shakespeare', in Nelson, *Richard Cœur de Lion*, pp. 141ff. The same volume has several other articles on the development of Richard's myth in Western literature, which I have not attempted to address here. See also Irwin, R., 'Saladin and the Third Crusade. A Case Study in Historiography and the Historical Novel', in M. Bentley (ed.), *Companion to Historiography* (London, 1997).

35. Froissart, *Chronicles* (p. 353 of Penguin Froissart).

36. *Ménestrel de Reims*, §27, pp. 13–14.

Bibliography

I. SOURCES

A. Principal sources and abbreviations

Ambroise, *L'Estoire de la Guerre Sainte*, ed. G. Paris (Paris, 1897) trans. E. N. Stone in *Three Old French Chronicles of the Crusades*, University of Washington Publications in the Social Sciences, vol. 10, October 1939, pp. 9–160 (Seattle, 1939), and, more recently, Marianne Ailes, with Notes by Marianne Ailes and Malcolm Barber, *The History of The Holy War. Ambroise's Estoire de la Guerre Sainte* (Woodbridge, 2003).

An Anglo-Norman jongleur-poet from the region of Evreux who accompanied Richard on crusade, Ambroise was an eyewitness to the facts he so eloquently describes. The relationship between his text and that of the *Itinerarium Regis Ricardi* has been endlessly debated, but it seems that the earlier source is the *Estoire* of Ambroise, subsequently translated into Latin, then expanded by Richard, Prior of the Holy Trinity, London, between 1216 and 1222.

Benoît de Sainte-Maure, *La Chronique des Ducs de Normandie par Benoît*, ed. C. Fahlin (Uppsala, 1951–4).

A continuation of the work of Wace, the chronicle of Benoît de Sainte-Maure (also author of the *Roman de Troie*) was begun about 1170 on the instructions of Henry II (who had by that date dismissed Wace, who had gone out of fashion). Though without either the interest or historical value of the work of his predecessor, it is informative as to the way in which a panegyrist of Henry II could write his history.

Bernard Itier, *Chronique*, ed. and trans. J.-L. Lemaître (Paris, 1998); *Extraits de la Chronique de Saint-Martial de Limoges*, *Recueil des Historiens des Gaules et de la France*, 18, pp. 223ff.

The marginal notes in his own hand of this librarian-monk of the abbey of Saint-Martial, Limoges, a contemporary of Richard the Lionheart, are, though brief, of great interest, thanks to the precision of this fine witness to the events taking place in these troubled regions.

Bertran de Born, *Chansons*, ed. C. Appel, *Die Lieder Bertrans von Born* (Halle, 1932); ed. and trans. G. Gouiran, *L'Amour et la Guerre. L'Oeuvre de Bertran de Born* (Aix–Marseille, 1985); ed. and trans. W. P. Paden, T. Sankovitch and P. H. Stablein as *The Poems of the Troubadour Bertran de Born* (Berkeley] c. 1986).

Sire of Hautefort, this troubadour-lord, a great lover of war, observed at first hand the quarrels of the barons of Aquitaine. Originally a supporter of Henry the Young King against Richard, then rallying to Richard's cause, he is an excellent example of the chivalric mentality of the period.

The Crusade and Death of Richard I, ed. R. C. Johnson (Oxford, 1961).
An Anglo-Norman chronicle based on Roger of Howden, Roger of Wendover, Matthew Paris and a lost prose Anglo-Norman chronicle.

Geoffrey of Vigeois, *Chronica Gaufridi*, ed. P. Labbe, in *Novae Bibliothecae Manuscriptorum Librorum*, II (Paris, 1657); and in part in *Recueil des Historiens des Gaules et de la France*, ed. Dom Bouquet, 12, 18.
One of the best chroniclers of events in Aquitaine up to 1184, the probable year of his death.

Gerald of Wales, *De Principis Instructione*, ed. G. F. Warner (1891); trans. as *Concerning the Instruction of Princes* (Felinfach, Dyfed, 1991) (reprint of trans. Joseph Stevenson) (London, 1858).

Gerald of Wales, *Expugnatio Hibernica*, *Itinerarium Kambriae* and *Descriptio Kambriae*, in *Giraldi Cambrensis Opera*, ed. J. F. Dimock, Rolls Series (London, 1868) (Kraus Reprint, 1964); trans. as *The Itinerary through Wales and The Description of Wales*, Everyman edn (London, 1908, repr. 1912), also Penguin Classic (1978, reprint 2004).
Born about 1147 and dead in 1223, this Welsh student of Peter Comestor dedicated his *Expugnatio Hibernica* to Richard, then Duke of Aquitaine; but, perhaps disappointed in the King, he was highly critical of and even malicious about him in his *De Principis Instructione*.

Gervase of Canterbury, *The Historical Works of Gervase of Canterbury*, ed. W. Stubbs, 2 vols, Rolls Series (London, 1879–80).
A monk of the abbey of Christ Church, Canterbury, who died in 1210, his chronicle is useful in spite of his prejudice against Richard, guilty in his eyes of failing to support his monastery in its disputes with the Archbishop of Canterbury.

Gesta Regis Henrici Secundi Benedicti Abbatis, followed by *Gesta Regis Ricardi*, ed. W. Stubbs, *The Chronicle of the Reigns of Henry II and Richard I*, 2 vols, Rolls Series (London, 1867).
Long attributed to a monk by the name of Benedict of Peterborough, this very valuable chronicle is today generally accepted as the work of Roger of Howden. It is one of the best historical sources for this period.

Histoire de Guillaume le Maréchal, ed. P. Meyer, 3 vols (Paris, 1891–1901); ed. and trans. A. J. Molden, S. Gregory and D. Crouch as *History of William Marshall*, ANTS Occasional Publications 4, vol. 1 (2002), with two further volumes forthcoming.
A verse account in Old French of the life of William Marshal, one of the best knights of his day, close to Henry II, Henry the Young King and Richard I and often a player in the principal events of their reigns. Composed about 1230 by his friend John of Early after William's death

(1217), the *Histoire* offers invaluable insight into the chivalric mentality of the period.

Itinerarium Peregrinorum, ed. H. E. Mayer (Stuttgart, 1962).

Itinerarium Peregrinorum et Gesta Regis Ricardi, in *Chronicles and Memorials of the Reign of Richard I*, ed. W. Stubbs, Rolls Series (London, 1864); trans. H. E. Nicholson as *The Chronicle of the Third Crusade* (Crusade Texts in Translation, no. 3) (Ashgate, 1997).

The Itinerary of King Richard I, with Studies on Certain Matters of Interest Connected with his Reign, ed. L. Landon, Pipe Roll Society, NS, 13 (London, 1935).
A very useful research tool, supplying references to charters and documents relating to Richard's reign.

John of Salisbury, *Policraticus*, ed. C. I. Webb (London, 1909); *Policraticus I–IV*, ed. K. S. B. Keats-Rohan (Turnhout, 1993); ed. and trans. C. J. Nederman (Cambridge–New York, 1990); *Letters of John of Salisbury*, ed. W. J. Miller and C. N. L. Brooke (Oxford, 1979).
John (1115–80) was a student of Abelard, William of Conches and Gilbert de la Porée in Paris. He was successively secretary to the Archbishop of Canterbury, advisor to Pope Hadrian IV and secretary to Thomas Becket before becoming Bishop of Chartres in 1176. His *Policraticus*, dedicated to Thomas Becket, provides very useful reflections of the relations between politics and religion and a remarkable ideological interpretation of the state and of chivalry.

Jordan Fantosme, *Jordan Fantosme's Chronicle*, ed. and trans. R. C. Johnson (Oxford, 1981)

Matthew Paris, *Chronica Majora*, ed. H. R. Luard, 7 vols, Rolls Series (London, 1872–84); trans. J. A. Giles, 3 vols (1852) (repr. New York, 1968); *Historia Anglorum sive . . . Historia Minor*, ed. F. J. Madden, 3 vols, Rolls Series (London, 1866–9).

Peter of Blois, *De Hierosolymitana Peregrinatione Acceleranda*, Patrologiae Cursus Completus . . . Series Latina Prima, 207, cols 1057–70; *Dialogus inter Regem Henricum Secundum et Abbatem Bonevallis*, ed. R. B. C. Huygens, *Revue Bénédictine*, 68 (1958), 1–2, pp. 87–112.
After a spell at the court of Henry II, Peter (1135–1204) became the King's secretary, then chancellor of the Archbishop of Canterbury. His great learning and proximity to the court mean that his writings are important sources for this book.

Ralph of Coggeshall, *Chronicon Anglicanum*, ed. J. Stevenson, Rolls Series (London, 1875).
Ralph, Abbot of Coggeshall, provides very detailed information about Richard.

Ralph of Diceto, *Radulphi de Diceto Decani Londiniensis Opera Historica*, ed. W. Stubbs, 2 vols, Rolls Series (London, 1876).
After studies in Paris, Ralph became archdeacon then dean of St Paul's, and

played a public role at the first coronation of Richard I, about whom he was well-informed, in 1189.

Récits d'un Ménestrel de Reims au Treizième Siècle, ed. N. de Wailly (Paris, 1876); trans. E. N. Stone in *Three Old French Chronicles of the Crusades*, University of Washington Publications in the Social Sciences, vol. 10 (October, 1939), pp. 249–366 (Seattle, 1939).

This romanticised version of the life of Richard I illustrates the development of his legend in the thirteenth century.

Richard Cœur de Lion (*rotrouenge* attributed to Richard), in Bec, P., *La Lyrique Française au Moyen Age* (Paris, 1978), vol. 2, pp. 124–5; sirventes, Provençal text and translation in Lepage, Y., 'Richard Cœur de Lion et la Poésie Lyrique', in *Et c'est la Fin pour Quoy Sommes Ensemble*, vol. 2, pp. 904ff.

Richard Cœur de Lion, texts trans. and presented by M. Brossard-Dandré and G. Besson (Paris, 1989).

A useful collection of texts in French translation. The references, unfortunately, are so badly placed and difficult to distinguish as to be virtually unusable; they are in any case often incorrect.

Richard of Devizes, *The Chronicle of Richard of Devizes of the Time of King Richard the First*, ed. and trans. J. T. Appleby (London, 1963).

A Benedictine monk from St Swithun's Abbey, Winchester, Richard appears well-informed about the actions and deeds of Richard for the period with which he deals (3 September 1189 to October 1192), except for the crusade. He is favourably inclined towards Richard and lauds his chivalric virtues with already typically British humour. He is extremely anti-French. His chronicle was written about 1198.

Rigord, *Gesta Philippi Regis*, ed. H.-F. Delaborde (Paris, 1882).

A monk at St-Denis and doctor and historiographer to King Philip Augustus of France, his account counterbalances that of the English historiographers, and vice-versa.

Robert of Torigny, *Chronica*, ed. C. Bethmann, Monumenta Germaniae Historia, Scriptores 6, pp. 475–535; also in *Chronicles and Memorials of the Reigns of Stephen, Henry II and Richard I*, ed. R. Howlett, vol. 4, Rolls Series (London, 1889).

Abbot of Mont-Saint-Michel from 1154 on and one of the best chroniclers for the period between 1135 and 1186, the year of his death.

Roger of Howden, *Chronica*, ed. W. Stubbs, 4 vols, Rolls Series (London, 1868–87).

Born at Howden, Yorkshire, a clerk at the English court and well-informed thanks to the documents he was able to consult and the people he met. One of the most reliable sources. His *Chronicle* and the *Gesta Henrici* often overlap, but each describes different events. Died c. 1201.

Roger of Wendover, *Flores Historiarum*, ed. H. G. Hewlett, 3 vols, Rolls Series (London, 1886–9).

A monk at St Albans and a good source for the early thirteenth century. With

regard to Richard, he was dependent on earlier chronicles which he interpreted with great care.

'Le Roman de Richard Cœur de Lion', *Romania*, 26 (1897), pp. 353–93.
A good source for the development of the legend of Richard the Lionheart.

Wace, *Le Roman de Brut*, ed. I. Arnold, 3 vols (Paris, 1978–80); *Le Roman de
Rou*, ed. A. J. Holden, 2 vols (Paris, 1970–1).
Although written in Anglo-Norman verse, the works of Wace have some
documentary value; they provide an invaluable mirror of the times.

Walter Map, *De Nugis Curialium, Courtiers' Trifles*, ed. and trans. M. R. James,
C. N. L. Brooke and R. A. B. Mynors (Oxford, 1983); trans. F. Tupper and
M. B. Ogle as *Master Walter Map's Book De Nugis Curialium (Courtiers'
Tales)* (London, 1924).
Born in Wales about 1140, Walter first studied in Paris and then entered the
service of Henry II; he became chancellor at Lincoln and then archdeacon at
Oxford. A good observer of court affairs, which he describes with humour
tinged with irony.

William the Breton, *Gesta Philippi Augusti* and *Philippidos*, ed. H. F. Delaborde,
in *Œuvres de Rigord et de Guillaume le Breton* (Paris, 1882).
Chaplain to Philip Augustus, he continued his history after the death of
Rigord, up to 1222. Interesting on account of his prejudice in favour of the
King of France.

William of Newburgh, *Historia Rerum Anglicarum*, ed. R. Howlett, in *Chronicles
and Memorials of the Reigns of Stephen, Henry II and Richard I*, vols 1 and 2,
Rolls Series (London, 1884–5); trans. J. Stevenson, in *The Church Historians
of England*, vol. 4, part 2 (London, 1856) (repr. Felinfach, Dyfed, 1996); and
trans. in part (Book 1) P. G. Walsh and M. J. Kennedy, *The History of English
Affairs* (Warminster, 1988).
An Augustine canon at Newburgh (1136–98), his chronicle is particularly
detailed for the reigns of Henry II and Stephen.

B. *Other sources used*

In order to shorten the bibliography, I have omitted the majority of the literary
works of the twelfth century (*chansons de geste*, romances, *lais*, fabliaux, pastourelles, and so on) even though they are of great interest to the historian of
mentalities.

Aelred of Rievaulx, *Relatio de Standardo*, ed. R. Howlett, *Chronicles and
Memorials of the Reigns of Stephen, Henry II and Richard I*, vol. 3, Rolls
Series (London, 1886), pp. 181–99.

Andrew the Chaplain, *Traité de l'Amour Courtois*, trans. C. Buridant (Paris,
1974).

Bernard of Clairvaux, *De Laude Novae Militiae*, ed. and trans. P.-Y. Emery
(Paris, 1990) (SC no. 367).

Chrétien de Troyes, *Le Chevalier de la Charrette*, ed. M. Roques (Paris, 1981); ed.

and trans. C. Méla (Paris, 1992) (Lettres Gothiques); trans. William W. Kibler as 'The Knight of the Cart' in *Chrétien de Troyes. Arthurian Romances*, Penguin Books (1991, repr. 2001).

Chroniques des Comtes d'Anjou et des Seigneurs d'Amboise, ed. L. Halphen and R. Poupardin (Paris, 1913).

Les Conciles Œcuméniques: les Décrets, vol. 2, 1: *Nicée à Latran V*, text and trans. A. Duval et al. (Paris, 1994).

The Conquest of Jerusalem and the Third Crusade, Sources in Translation, trans. P. W. Edbury (Aldershot, 1996).

La Continuation de Guillaume de Tyr, ed. M. R. Morgan (Paris, 1982); translated in *The Conquest of Jerusalem and the Third Crusade*.

Coutumiers de Normandie, ed. E. J. Tardif (Rouen, 1881).

Eadmer of Canterbury, *Historia Novorum in Anglia et Opuscula Duo de Vita Sancti Anselmi et Quibusdam Miraculis Eius*, ed. M. Rule, Rolls Series (London, 1884).

English Historical Documents, vol. I (500–1042), ed. D. Whitelock, 2nd edn (London, 1979); vol. II (1042–1189), ed. D. C. Douglas, 2nd edn (London, 1981); vol. III (1189–1327), ed. H. Rothwell (London, 1975).

Eracles, ed. P. Paris (Paris, 1879).

Li Estoire de Jérusalem et d'Antioche, RHC Hist. Occ. V, p. 623ff.

Frequenter Cogitans, ed. M. Edelstand du Meril, *Poésies Populaires Latines du Moyen Age* (Paris, 1847), pp. 129ff.

Gabrieli, F. (ed.), *Arab Historians of the Crusades* (London, 1969).

Geoffrey of Monmouth, *Historia Regum Britanniae*, in N. Wright (ed.), *The 'Historia Regum Britanniae' of Geoffrey of Monmouth, I: Bern Burgerbibliothek MS 568* (Cambridge, 1984); trans. L. Thorpe as *The History of the Kings of Britain* (Harmondsworth: Penguin Books, 1996).

Gervase of Tilbury, *Otia Imperiala*, Monumenta Germaniae Historia. Scriptores 27.

Guernes de Pont-Sainte-Maxence, *Vie de Saint Thomas Becket*, ed. E. Walberg (Paris, 1936).

Henry of Huntingdon, *Historia Anglorum*, ed. T. Arnold, Rolls Series (London, 1979); trans. D. Greenaway, *Henry, Archdeacon of Huntingdon: Historia Anglorum: The History of the English People* (Oxford, 1996).

Ibn al Athir, ed. Tornberg (Leiden, 1853–64).

Ibn al Qalanisi, *Histoire de Damas*, trans. R. Le Tourneau, *Damas de 1075 à 1154* (Damascus, 1952).

Imad ad-Din al-Isfahani, *Conquête de la Syrie et de la Palestine par Saladin*, trans. H. Massé (Paris, 1972).

James of Vitry, *The Exempla (Sermones)*, ed. T. F. Crane (London, 1890).

James of Vitry, *Lettres*, ed. R. B. C. Huygens (Leiden, 1960), pp. 86–9.

John of Worcester, *Chronicon*, ed. J. R. H. Weaver (Oxford, 1908).

Joinville, *Vie de Saint Louis*, ed. and trans. J. Monfrin (Paris, 1995); trans. J. Evans, *History of St Louis* (Oxford, 1938).

Magna Carta, ed. J. C. Holt (Cambridge, 1992).

Marbod of Rennes, *Carmina Varia*, Patrologiae Cursus Completus . . . Series Latina Prima, 171.

Orderic Vitalis, ed. and trans. M. Chibnall, *The Ecclesiastical History of Orderic Vitalis*, 6 vols (Oxford, 1965–78).

Ousama Ibn Munqidh, *Des Enseignements de la Vie*, trans. A. Miquel (Paris, 1983).

The Peterborough Chronicle, 1070–1154, ed. C. Clark (Oxford, 1970).

Peter of Blois, *Passio Reginaldi Principis Olim Antiocheni*, Patrologiae Cursus Completus . . . Series Latina Prima, 207, cols 957–76.

Philippe de Beaumanoir, *Coutumes du Beauvaisis*, ed. A. Salmon, 2 vols (Paris, 1899–1900).

Ralph Niger, *Chronica Universalis* (extracts), Monumenta Germaniae Historia. Scriptores 27, pp. 331ff.

Raymond Lull, *Livre de l'Ordre de Chevalerie*, trans. P. Gifreu (Paris, 1991).

La Règle du Temple, ed. H. de Curzon (Paris, 1886).

Richard of Poitiers (Le Poitevin), *Chronicon*, *Recueil des Historiens des Gaules et de la France*, 12.

Stephen of Fougères, *Le Livre des Manières*, ed. R. A. Lodge (Geneva, 1979).

The Waltham Chronicle, ed. L. Watkiss and M. Chibnall (Oxford, 1994).

William of Malmesbury, *Gesta Regum Anglorum*, ed. W. Stubbs, 2 vols, Rolls Series (London, 1877–89).

William of Malmesbury, *Historia Novella*, ed. K. R. Potter (London, 1955), revised edn, ed. E. King (Oxford, 1988).

William of Poitiers, *Gesta Guillelmi Ducis*, ed. and trans. R. Foreville, *Histoire de Guillaume le Conquérant* (Paris 1952).

William IX of Aquitaine, see Payen, *Prince d'Aquitaine*.

William of Tyre, *Willelmi Tyrensis Archiepiscopi Chronicon*, ed. R. B. C. Huygens (Turnhout, 1986).

William the Conqueror, *Consuetudines et Iustitiae*, ed. H. Haskins, *Norman Institutions* (New York, 1960).

II. STUDIES

A. *On Richard the Lionheart*

Arbellot, F., 'Mort de Richard Cœur de Lion', in *Récits de l'Histoire du Limousin* (1885).

Archibald, J. K., 'La Chanson de la Captivité du Roi Richard', *Cahiers de Civilisation Médiévale*, 1 (1974), pp. 149–58.

Bridge, A., *Richard the Lionheart* (London, 1989).

Broughton, B. B., *The Legends of King Richard I Cœur de Lion. A Study of Sources and Variations to the Year 1600* (The Hague–Paris, 1966).

Brundage, J. A., *Richard Lionheart* (New York, 1974).

Choffel, J., *Richard Cœur de Lion* (Paris, 1985).

Cloulas, I. and A., Denieul *Bérangère et Richard Cœur de Lion, Chronique d'Amour et du Guerre* (Paris, 1985).

Et c'est la Fin pour Quoy Sommes Ensemble (Hommage à Jean Dufournet) (Paris, 1993), vol. 2.

Gillingham, J., *The Life and Times of Richard I* (London, 1973).

Gillingham, J., *Richard the Lionheart*, 1st edn (London, 1978), 2nd edn (1989).

Gillingham, J., 'Conquering Kings. Some Twelfth-Century Reflections on Henry II and Richard I', in T. Reuter (ed.), *Warriors and Churchmen in the High Middle Ages. Essays Presented to Karl Leyser* (London, 1992), pp. 163–78.

Gillingham, J., *Richard Cœur de Lion. Kingship, Chivalry and War in the Twelfth Century* (London, 1994).

Henderson, P., *Richard Cœur de Lion. A Biography* (London, 1958).

Kessler, U., *Richard I. Löwenherz. König, Kreuzritter, Abenteurer* (Graz–Vienna–Cologne, 1995).

Lepage, Y.-G., 'Blondel de Nesle et Richard Cœur de Lion. Histoire d'une Légende', *Florilegium* (Ottawa), 7 (1985), pp. 109–28.

Loomis, R. S., 'Richard Cœur de Lion and the Pas Saladin in Medieval Art', *Publications of the Modern Language Association of America*, 30 (1915), pp. 509–28.

Martindale, J., 'Eleanor of Aquitaine', in Nelson, *Richard Cœur de Lion*, pp. 17–50.

Needler, G. H., *Richard Cœur de Lion in Literature* (Leipzig, 1890).

Nelson, J. L. (ed.), *Richard Cœur de Lion in History and Myth* (London, 1992).

Nicolin, R., *Richard Cœur de Lion, le Roi Chevalier du XIIe Siècle* (Chambray-lès-Tours, 1999).

Norgate, K., *England under the Angevin Kings*, 2 vols (New York, 1887).

Norgate, K., *Richard the Lion Heart* (London, 1924).

Pernoud, R., *Richard Cœur de Lion* (Paris, 1988).

Poole, A. L., 'Richard the First's Alliances with the German Princes in 1194', in *Studies in Medieval History Presented to F. M. Powicke* (Oxford, 1948), pp. 90ff.

Riccardo Cuor di Leone nella Storia e nella Legenda (Colloque Italo-Anglais, Accademia Nazionale dei Lincei) (Rome, 1981).

Richard, A., *Histoire des Comtes de Poitou, 778–1204*, 2 vols (Paris, 1903).

Spetia, L., 'Riccardo Cuor di Leone tra Oc et Oïl', *Cultura Neolatina*, 46 (1996), 1–2, pp. 101–55.

Turner, R. V., 'Eleanor of Aquitaine and her Children: an Enquiry into Medieval Family Attachment', *Journal of Medieval History*, 14 (1988), pp. 321–35.

B. On the historical context (twelfth century)

Appleby, J. T., *Henry II. The Vanquished King* (London, 1962).

Appleby, J. T., *England Without Richard, 1189–1199* (London, 1965).

Arbellot, R., *Les Chevaliers Limousins aux Croisades* (Paris, 1881).

Aubé, P., *Thomas Becket* (Paris, 1988).

Audouin, E., 'Sur l'Armée Royale au Temps de Philippe Auguste', in *Le Moyen Age*, 26 (1913), pp. 1–41.

Aurell, M., *La Vielle et l'Epée: Troubadours et Politique en Provence au XIIIe Siècle* (Paris, 1989).

Aurell, M., *La Noblesse en Occident (Ve–XVe Siècle)* (Paris, 1996).

Baldwin, J. W., *Masters, Princes and Merchants. The Social View of Peter the Chanter and his Circle*, 2 vols (Princeton, 1970).

Baldwin, J. W., *The Government of Philip Augustus: Foundations of French Royal Power in the Middle Ages* (Berkeley–London, 1986).

Baldwin, J. W., 'Five Discourses on Desire: Sexuality and Gender in Northern France around 1200', in *Speculum*, 66 (1991).

Baldwin, J. W., *The Language of Sex: Five Voices from Northern France around 1200* (Chicago–London, 1994).

Bancourt, P., 'De l'Imagerie au Réel: l'Exotisme Oriental d'Ambroise', in *Images et Signes de l'Orient dans l'Occident Médiéval* (Aix–Marseilles, 1982), pp. 29–39.

Barber, M. (ed.), *The Military Orders. Fighting for the Faith and Caring for the Sick* (London, 1994).

Barber, M., *The New Knighthood: a History of the Order of the Temple* (Cambridge, 1995).

Barber, R. and J. Barker, *Tournaments, Jousts, Chivalry and Pageants in the Middle Ages* (Woodbridge, 1989).

Barlow, F., 'Roger of Howden', *English Historical Review*, 65 (1950), pp. 352ff.

Baume, A., 'La Campagne de 1189: Richard Cœur de Lion et la Défense du Vexin Normand', *Etudes Archéologiques*, 19–20 (1985), pp. 3–8.

Bautier, R.-H. (ed.), *La France de Philippe Auguste. Le Temps des Mutations* (Paris, 1982).

Beech, G. T., *A Rural Society in Medieval France: the Gatine of Poitou in the Eleventh and Twelfth Centuries* (Baltimore, 1964).

Beeler, J. H., 'The Composition of Anglo-Norman Armies', *Speculum* (1965), pp. 398–414.

Beeler, J. H., *Warfare in England, 1066–1189* (Ithaca–New York, 1966).

Beeler, J. H., *Warfare in Medieval Europe, 730–1200* (London, 1971).

Benjamin, R., 'The Angevin Empire', in N. Saul (ed.), *England in Europe, 1066–1453* (London, 1994), pp. 65–75.

Bisson, T. N., 'The Organised Peace in Southern France and Catalonia, ca. 1140–ca. 1233', *American Historical Review*, 82 (1977), pp. 290–311.

Bisson, T. N., 'Nobility and Family in Medieval France: a Review Essay', *French Historical Studies*, 16 (1990), pp. 597–613.

Blair, C., *European Armour c. 1066 to c. 1700* (London, 1970) (1958).

Bloch, M., *Seigneurie Française et Manoir Anglais*, 5th edn (Paris, 1960).

Bloch, M., *La Société Féodale* (Paris, 1968), trans. L. A. Manyon, *Feudal Society* (London, 1961).

Bongaert, Y., *Recherches sur les Cours Laïques du Xe au XIIIe Siècle* (Paris, 1949).

Boswell, J., *Christianity, Social Tolerance and Homosexuality* (Chicago, 1980).

Bouchard, C. B., 'The Origins of the French Nobility. A Reassessment', *American Historical Review*, 86 (1981), pp. 501–32.

Bournazel, E., *Le Gouvernement Capétien au XIIe Siècle, 1108–1180. Structures Sociales et Mutations Institutionnelles* (Paris, 1975).

Boussard, J., *Le Comté d'Anjou sous Henri II Plantagenêt et ses Fils (1151–1204)* (Paris, 1938).

Boussard, J., 'Les Mercenaires au XIIe Siècle. Henri II Plantagenêt et les Origines de l'Armée de Métier', *Bibliothèque de l'Ecole des Chartes* (1945–6), pp. 189–224.

Boussard, J., 'La Vie en Anjou aux XIe et XIIe Siècles', *Le Moyen Age*, 56 (1950), pp. 29–68.

Boussard, J., 'L'Enquête de 1172 sur les Services de Chevalier en Normandie', in *Mélanges C. Brunel* (Paris, 1955), pp. 193–208.

Boussard, J., *Le Gouvernement d'Henri II Plantagenêt* (Abbeville, 1956).

Boutruche, R., *Seigneurie et Féodalité*, 2 vols (Paris, 1968–70).

Bradbury, J., 'Battles in England and Normandy, 1066–1154', *Anglo-Norman Studies*, 6 (1983), pp. 1–12.

Bradbury, J., *The Medieval Archer* (Woodbridge, 1985).

Bradbury, J., *The Medieval Siege* (Woodbridge, 1992).

Brooke, C., *Thomas Becket. Collected Essays* (London, 1971).

Brown, R. A., *Castles, Conquest and Charters: Collected Papers* (Woodbridge, 1989).

Brown, S. D. P., 'Military Service and Monetary Reward in the 11th and 12th Centuries', *History*, 74, 240 (1989), pp. 20–38.

Bruguières, M.-B., 'A Propos des Idées Reçues en Histoire: le Divorce de Louis VII', *Mémoires de l'Académie des Sciences, Inscriptions et Belles-Lettres de Toulouse*, 140, 9 (1978), pp. 191–216.

Brunel-Lobrichon, G. and C. Duhamel-Amado, *Au Temps des Troubadours, XIIe et XIIIe Siècles* (Paris, 1997).

Buschinger, D. (ed.), *Littérature et Société au Moyen Age* (Amiens, 1978).

Buschinger, D. (ed.), *Cours Princières et Châteaux* (Greifswald, 1993).

Cardini, F., *La Culture de la Guerre, Xe–XVIIIe S.* (Paris, 1982).

Cartellieri, A., *Philipp II. August König von Frankreich*, 4 vols (Leipzig, 1899–1921).

Chatelain, A., *Châteaux Forts et Féodalité en Ile-de-France du XIe au XIIIe Siècle* (Paris, 1983).

Chazan, R., 'Emperor Frederick, the Third Crusade and the Jews', in *Viator*, 8 (1997), pp. 83–93.

Chédeville, A., *Chartres et ses Campagnes, XIe–XIIIe Siècle* (Paris, 1973).

Chibnall, M., 'Feudal Society in Orderic Vitalis', *Anglo-Norman Studies*, 1 (1978), pp. 35–48.

Chibnall, M., *The World of Orderic Vitalis* (Oxford, 1984).

Chibnall, M., *The Empress Matilda, Queen Consort, Queen Mother and Lady of the English* (Oxford, 1991).

Cine, R. H., 'The Influence of Romances on Tournaments in the Middle Ages', *Speculum*, 20 (1945), pp. 204–11.

Cingolani, S. M., 'Filologia e Miti Storiografici: Enrico II, la Corte Plantageneta e la Letteratura', *Studi Medievali*, 32 (1991), pp. 815–32.

Clanchy, M., *From Memory to Written Record, England, 1066–1307* (London, 1979).

Contamine, P., *La Guerre au Moyen Age* (Paris, 1980); trans. M. Jones, *War in the Middle Ages* (Oxford, 1984).

Contamine, P. and O. Guyotjeannin (eds), *La Guerre, la Violence et les Gens au Moyen Age*, vol. 1: *Guerre et Violence*, vol. 2: *La Violence et les Gens* (Paris, 1996).

Coss, P. R., *Knighthood and Locality. A Study in English Society c. 1180–c. 1280* (Cambridge, 1991).

Crouch, D., *William the Marshal: Court, Career and Chivalry in the Angevin Empire, 1147–1219* (London–New York, 1990).

Debord, A., *La Société Laïque dans les Pays de Charente, Xe–XIIe Siècle* (Paris, 1984).

De Toulouse à Tripoli, Itinéraires de Cultures Croisées (Toulouse, 1997).

Devailly, G., *Le Berry, du Xe S. au Milieu du XIIIe S.* (Paris, 1973).

Dronke, P., 'Peter of Blois and Poetry at the Court of Henry II', in *Medieval Studies*, 38 (1976), pp. 185–235.

Dubois, M.-M., *La Littérature Anglaise du Moyen Age (500–1500)* (Paris, 1962).

Duby, G., *La Société aux XIe et XIIe s. dans la Région Mâconnaise*, 1st edn (Paris, 1953), 2nd edn (Paris, 1971).

Duby, G., 'Au XIIe Siècle: les "Jeunes" dans la Société Aristocratique', *Annales, E.S.C.* (1964), pp. 835–46.

Duby, G., *Le Dimanche de Bouvines* (Paris, 1973).

Duby, G., *Hommes et Structures du Moyen Age* (Paris, 1973).

Duby, G., and J. Le Goff (eds), *Famille et Parenté dans l'Occident Médiéval* (Rome, 1977).

Duby, G., *Les Trois Ordres ou l'Imaginaire du Féodalisme* (Paris, 1978), trans. A. Goldhammer, *The Three Orders. Feudal Society Imagined* (Chicago–London, 1980).

Duby, G., *Le Chevalier, la Femme et le Prêtre* (Paris, 1984), trans. Barbara Bray, *The Lady, the Knight and the Priest. The Makings of Modern Marriage in Medieval France* (Harmondsworth, 1984).

Duby, G., *Guillaume le Maréchal ou le Meilleur Chevalier du Monde* (Paris, 1984), trans. R. Howard, *William Marshal, Flower of Chivalry* (London, 1986).

Duby, G., *La Société Chevaleresque* (Paris, 1988), trans. Cynthia Postan, *The Chivalrous Society* (London, 1977).

Duby, G., *Mâle Moyen Age. De l'Amour et Autres Essais* (Paris, 1988).

Duby, G., *Enquête sur les Dames du XIIe Siècle* (Paris, 1995), trans. Jean Birrell, *Women of the Twelfth Century*, 3 vols (Cambridge, 1997–8).

Edwards, J. G., 'The Itinerarium Regis Ricardi and the "Estoire de la Guerre Sainte" ', in Edwards, J. G., V. H. Galbraith and F. Jacobs (eds), *Historical Essays in Honour of James Tait* (Manchester, 1933), pp. 59–77.

Evergates, T., *Feudal Society in the Baillage of Troyes under the Counts of Champagne, 1152–1284* (Baltimore, 1975).

Farmer, H., 'William of Malmesbury. Life and Works', *Journal of Ecclesiastical History*, 13 (1962), pp. 39–54.

Flahiff, G. B., 'Deux non vult. A Critic of the Third Crusade', *Medieval Studies*, 9 (1947), pp. 162–79.

Flori, J., 'La Chevalerie selon Jean de Salisbury', *Revue d'Histoire Ecclésiastique*, 77, 1/2 (1982), pp. 35–77.

Flori, J., *L'Essor de la Chevalerie, XIe–XIIe Siècles* (Geneva, 1986).

Flori, J., *Croisade et Chevalerie* (Brussels–Paris, 1998).

Flori, J., 'Châteaux et Forteresses aux XIe et XIIe S. Etude sur le Vocabulaire des Historiens des Ducs de Normandie', *Le Moyen Age*, 103, 2 (1997), pp. 261–73.

Foreville, R., *L'Eglise et la Royauté en Angleterre sous Henri II Plantagenêt (1154–1189)* (Paris, 1943).

Foreville, R., 'Les Institutions Royales et la Féodalité en Angleterre au Milieu du XIIe Siècle', *Revue Historique du Droit Français et Etranger* (1946–7), pp. 99–108.

Foreville, R. (ed.), *Thomas Becket* (Paris, 1975).

Forey, A. J., 'The Emergence of the Military Orders in the 12th Century', *Journal of Ecclesiastical History*, 36, 2 (1985), pp. 175ff.

Forey, A. J., *The Military Orders from the 12th to the Early 14th Century* (London, 1992).

Fossier, R., 'Remarques sur l'Etude des Commotions Sociales aux XIe et XIIe Siècles', *Cahiers de Civilisation Médiévale*, 16 (1973), pp. 45–51.

Fossier, R., *Enfance de l'Europe* (Paris, 1982).

France, J., *Western Warfare in the Age of the Crusades, 1000–1300* (London, 1999).

Gaier, C., *Les Armes* (Turnhout, 1979).

Gaier, C., *Armes et Combats dans l'Univers Médiéval* (Brussels, 1995).

Garaud, M., *Les Châtelains du Poitou at l'Avènement du Régime Féodal (XIe et XIIe Siècle)* (Poitiers, 1967).

Gaudemet, J., 'Le Dossier Canonique du Mariage de Philippe Auguste et

d'Ingeburg de Danemark (1193–1213)', *Revue Historique du Droit Français et Etranger* 62.

Gauthier, M.-M., 'A Propos de l'Effigie Funéraire de Geoffoy Plantagenêt', *Académie des Inscriptions et Belles-Lettres (Compte Rendu des Séances, Janv.–Mars 1979)*.

Geary, P., 'Vivre en Conflit dans une France sans Etat; Typologie des Mécanismes de Règlement des Conflits (1050–1200)', in *Annales E.S.C.*, 41 (1986), pp. 1107–33.

Génicot, L., 'Noblesse ou Aristocratie. Des Questions de Méthode', *Revue d'Histoire Ecclésiastique*, 85 (1990), pp. 334ff.

Gillingham, J., 'The Introduction of Knight Service into England', *Proceedings of the Battle Conference on Anglo-Norman Studies*, 4 (1981), pp. 53–64.

Gillingham, J. and J. C. Holt (eds), *War and Government in the Middle Ages. Essays in Honour of J. O. Prestwich* (Cambridge, 1984).

Gillingham, J., 'Conquering the Barbarians: War and Chivalry in Twelfth-Century Britain', *Haskins Society Journal*, 4 (1992), pp. 68–84.

Gillingham, J., 'The Travels of Roger of Howden and his View of the Irish, Scots and Welsh', *Anglo-Norman Studies*, 20 (1997), pp. 151–69.

Goody, J., *The Development of the Family and Marriage in Europe* (Cambridge, 1983).

Graboïs, A., 'De la Trêve de Dieu à la Paix du Roi; Etude sur les Transformations du Mouvement de Paix au XIIe Siècle', in *Mélanges R. Crozet*, pp. 585–96.

Graboïs, A., 'Anglo-Norman England and the Holy Land', *Anglo-Norman Studies*, 7 (1984), pp. 132–41.

Graboïs, A., 'The Crusade of Louis VII, King of France: a reconsideration', in P. W. Edbury (ed.), *Crusade and Settlement* (Cardiff, 1985), pp. 94–104.

Graboïs, A., 'La Royauté Sacrée au XIIe Siècle: Manifestation de la Propagande Royale', in *Idéologie et Propagande en France* (Paris, 1987), pp. 31–41.

Graboïs, A., 'Louis VII, Pèlerin', *Revue d'Histoire de l'Eglise de France*, 74 (1988), pp. 5–22.

Gransden, A., *Historical Writing in England, c. 550–1307* (London, 1974).

Green, J. A., *The Aristocracy of Norman England* (Cambridge, 1997).

Hamilton, B., 'The Elephant of Christ: Reynald of Châtillon', *Studies in Church History*, 15 (1978), pp. 97–108.

Harper-Bill, C. and R. Harvey (eds), *The Ideals and Practice of Medieval Knighthood*, II (Woodbridge, 1988); III (Woodbridge, 1990); IV (Woodbridge, 1992).

Harvey, S., 'The Knight and the Knight's Fee in England', *Past and Present*, 49 (1970), pp. 3–43.

Henri II Plantagenêt et son Temps (Actes du Colloque de Fontevraud, 29 Septembre–1 Octobre 1990).

Hollister, C. W., *The Military Organization of Norman England* (Oxford, 1965).

Holt, J. C. and R. Mortimer, *Acta of Henry II and Richard I. Hand-List of*

Documents Surviving in the Original in Repositories in the United Kingdom (London, 1986).

Kedar, B. Z., *Crusade and Mission. European Approaches Towards the Muslims* (Princeton, 1984).

Kedar, B. Z. (ed.), *The Horns of Hattin* (Jerusalem, 1992).

Kellog, J. L., 'Economic and Social Tensions Reflected in the Romance of Chrétien de Troyes', *Romance Philology*, 39 (1985), pp. 1–21.

Kelly, A. R., *Eleanor of Aquitaine and the Four Kings* (Harvard, 1950).

Kenaan-Kedar, N., 'Aliénor d'Aquitaine Conduite en Captivité. Les Peintures Murales Commémoratives de Sainte Radegonde de Chinon', *Cahiers de Civilisation Médiévale*, 41 (1998), pp. 317–30.

Kennedy, E., 'Social and Political Ideas in the French Prose Lancelot', *Medium Aevum*, 26, 2 (1957), pp. 90–106.

Kibler, W. W. (ed.), *Eleanor of Aquitaine. Patron and Politician* (London, 1973).

Klein, K. W., 'The Political Message of Bertran de Born', *Studies in Philology*, 65 (1968), pp. 610–30.

Labande, E.-R., 'Pour une Image Véridique d'Aliénor d'Aquitaine', *Bulletin de la Société des Antiquaires de l'Ouest et des Musées de Poitiers*, 3 (1952), pp. 175–234.

Leclercq, J., *Le Mariage Vu par les Moines au XIIe Siècle* (Paris, 1983).

Legge, M. D., 'The Influence of Patronage on Form in Medieval French Literature', in *Stil- und Formproblem in der Literatur* (Heidelberg, 1959), pp. 163ff.

Legge, M. D., *Anglo-Norman Literature and its Background* (Oxford, 1963).

Lejeune, R., 'Le Rôle Littéraire de la Famille d'Aliénor d'Aquitaine', *Cahiers de Civilisation Médiévale*, 1 (1958), pp. 319–36.

Le Patourel, J., 'The Plantagenet Dominions', *History*, 1 (1965), pp. 289ff.

Le Patourel, J., *The Norman Empire* (Oxford, 1976).

Lewis, A. W., *Le Sang Royal. La Famille Capétienne et l'Etat, France, Xe–XIVe S.* (Paris, 1986).

Lewis, B., *Les Assassins, Terrorisme et Politique dans l'Islam Médiéval* (Brussels, 1984).

Lewis, S., *The Art of Matthew Paris in the Chronica Majora* (Aldershot, 1987).

Lobrichon, G., *La Religion des Laïcs en Occident, Xe–XIVe S.* (Paris, 1994).

Lodge, A., 'Literature and History in the Chronicle of Jordan Fantosme', *French Studies*, 44 (1990), pp. 257–70.

Luchaire, A., *La Société Française au Temps de Philippe Auguste* (Paris, 1909).

Markale, J., *Aliénor d'Aquitaine* (Paris, 1979).

Marshall, C., 'The Use of the Charge in Battles in the Latin East, 1192–1292', *Historical Research*, 63, 152 (1990), pp. 221–6.

Marshall, C., *Warfare in the Latin East, 1192–1291* (Cambridge, 1991).

Martin, J.-M., *Italies Normandes, XIe–XIIe Siècle* (Paris, 1994).

Martindale, J., 'The French Aristocracy in the Early Middle Ages: a Reappraisal', *Past and Present*, 75 (1977), pp. 5–45.

McCash, J., 'Marie de Champagne and Eleanor of Aquitaine: a Relationship Reexamined', *Speculum*, 54 (1979), pp. 698–711.

McLoughlin, 'The Language of Persecution: John of Salisbury and the Early Phase of the Becket Dispute (1163–1166)', *Studies in Church History*, 21, *Persecution and Toleration* (1984), pp. 73–87.

Morillo, S., *Warfare Under the Anglo-Norman Kings, 1066–1135* (Woodbridge, 1994).

Mortimer, R., *Angevin England, 1154–1258* (Oxford, 1994).

Nicolle, D., *Arms and Armours of the Crusading Era, 1050–1350*, 2 vols (White Plains, New York, 1988).

Norgate, K., 'The Itinerarium Peregrinorum and the Song of Ambroise', *English Historical Review*, 25 (1910).

Orme, N., *From Childhood to Chivalry. The Education of the English Kings and Aristocracy, 1066–1530* (London–New York, 1984).

Owen, D. D. R., *Eleanor of Aquitaine. Queen and Legend* (Oxford, 1993).

Pacaut, M., *Louis VII et les Elections Episcopales dans le Royaume de France* (Paris, 1957).

Pacaut, M., *Louis VII et son Royaume* (Paris, 1964).

Pacaut, M., *Frédéric Barberousse*, 1st edn (Paris, 1967) (Paris, 1991).

Painter, S., *William Marshal, Knight-Errant, Baron and Regent of England* (Baltimore, 1933).

Paris, G., 'La Légende de Saladin', *Journal des Savants* (1893), pp. 284–99, 354–65, 428–38, 486–98.

Partner, N., *Serious Entertainments. The Writing of History in 12th-Century England* (Chicago–London, 1977).

Pastoureau, M., *La Vie Quotidienne en France et en Angleterre au Temps des Chevaliers de la Table Ronde* (Paris, 1976).

Pastoureau, M., 'L'Apparition des Armoiries en Occident. Etat du Problème', *Bibliothèque de l'Ecole des Chartes* (1976), pp. 281–300.

Paterson, L. 'Great Court Festivals in the South of France and Catalonia in Twelfth- and Thirteenth-Century Occitania', *Medium Aevum*, 55 (1986), pp. 72–84.

Payen, J.-C., *Le prince d'Aquitaine. Essai sur Guillaume IX et son Œuvre Erotique* (Paris, 1980).

Pernoud, R., *Aliénor d'Aquitaine* (Paris, 1965).

Petit-Dutaillis, C., *La Monarchie Féodale en France et en Angleterre, Xe–XIIIe Siècles*, 1st edn (Paris, 1933), 2nd edn (Paris, 1971); trans. E. D. Hunt, *The Feudal Monarchy in France and England: from the Tenth to the Thirteenth Century* (London, 1936).

Phillips, J., *Defenders of the Holy Land. Relations between the Latin East and the West, 1119–1187* (Oxford, 1996).

Poly, J.-P. and E. Bournazel, *La Mutation Féodale* (Paris, 1980).

Powicke, F. M., *The Loss of Normandy (1189–1204)*, 2nd edn (Manchester, 1961).

Powicke, F. M., *Military Obligation in Medieval England. A Study in Liberty and Duty* (Oxford, 1962).

Pringle, R. D., 'King Richard I and the Walls of Ascalon', *Palestine Exploration Quarterly*, 116 (1984), pp. 133–47.

Reynolds, S., *Fiefs and Vassals* (Oxford, 1994).

Richard, J., *Le Royaume Latin de Jérusalem* (Paris, 1953); trans. J. Shirley, *The Latin Kingdom of Jerusalem*, 2 vols (Amsterdam–New York–Oxford, 1979).

Richard, J., 'Le Transport Outre-mer des Croisés et des Pèlerins (XIIe–XVe Siècle)', in *Croisades et Etats Latins d'Orient*, Variorum, VII (1992), pp. 27–44.

Richard, J., *Histoire des Croisades* (Paris: Fayard, 1996); trans. J. Birrell, *The Crusades, c. 1071–c. 1291* (Cambridge, 1999).

Richard, J., 'La Vogue de l'Orient dans la Littérature Occidentale du Moyen Age', in *Mélanges R. Crozet*, pp. 557–61.

Richardson, H. G., 'The Letters and Charters of Eleanor of Aquitaine', *English Historical Review*, 74 (1959), pp. 193ff.

Riché, P., 'L'Instruction des Laïcs au XIIe Siècle', in *Mélanges Saint Bernard* (Dijon, 1953), pp. 212–17.

Riley-Smith, J., *The Crusades. A Short History* (London, 1987).

Rouse, R. H. and M. A. Rouse, 'John of Salisbury and the Doctrine of Tyrannicide', *Speculum*, 42 (1967), pp. 693–700.

Rousset, P., 'La Sens du Merveilleux à l'Epoque Féodale', *Le Moyen Age*, 72 (1956), pp. 25–37.

Rousset, P., *Histoire des Croisades*, 1st edn (Paris, 1957), 2nd edn (Paris, 1978).

Rousset, P., 'Recherches sur l'Emotivité à l'Epoque Féodale', in *Cahiers de Civilisation Médiévale*, 2 (1959), pp. 53–67.

Rousset, P., 'La Notion de Chrétienté aux XIe et XIIe Siècles', *Le Moyen Age*, 69 (1963), pp. 191–203.

Runciman, S., *A History of the Crusades*, 3 vols (Cambridge, 1951–5) (vol. 3 is 1954, but repr. with corrections 1955).

Sassier, Y., *Louis VII* (Paris, 1991).

Schamitzer, M., *Crusaders and Muslims in Twelfth-Century Syria* (Leiden, 1993).

Schlight, J., *Monarchs and Mercenaries. A Reappraisal of the Importance of Knight Service in Norman and Early Angevin England* (New York, 1968).

Setton, K. M. (ed.), *A History of the Crusades*, vol. 1: *The First Hundred Years* (Philadelphia, 1955); vol. 2: *The Later Crusades* (Philadelphia–London, 1962); vol. 5: *The Impact of the Crusades on the Near East* (Madison, 1985); vol. 6: *The Impact of the Crusades on Europe* (Madison, 1989).

Sheils, W. J. (ed.), *Studies in Church History*, 20, *The Church and War* (1983).

Siberry, E., *Criticism of Crusading, 1095–1274* (Oxford, 1985).

Sigal, P.-A., *L'Homme et le Miracle dans la France Médiévale (XIe–XIIe Siècles)* (Paris, 1985).

Smail, R. C., *Crusading Warfare (1097–1193)*, 2nd edn (Cambridge, 1976).

Southern, R. W., 'Peter of Blois, a Twelfth-Century Humanist?', in R. W. Southern, *Medieval Humanism and Other Essays* (Oxford, 1970), pp. 105–32.

Southern, R. W., 'Peter of Blois and the Third Crusade', in *Studies in Medieval History Presented to R. H. C. Davis* (London, 1985), pp. 207–18.

Stenton, D. M., 'Roger of Howden and Benedict', *English Historical Review*, 68 (1953), pp. 374–82.

Strickland, M. (ed.), *Anglo-Norman Warfare* (Woodbridge, 1992).

Strickland, M., *War and Chivalry. The Conduct and Perception of War in England and Normandy, 1066–1217* (Cambridge, 1996).

Tabacco, G., 'Su Nobiltà e Cavalleria nel Medioevo. Un Ritorno a Marc Bloch?', in *Studi di Storia Medievale e Moderna per E. Sestan* (Florence, 1980), vol. 1, pp. 31–55.

Tûrk, E., *Nugae Curialum, le Règne d'Henri II Plantagenêt (1145–1189) et l'Ethique Politique* (Geneva, 1977).

Tyerman, C., *England and the Crusades, 1095–1588* (Chicago, 1988).

Van Winter, J.-M., *Riottertum, Ideal und Wirklichkeit* (Bussum, 1969).

Vaughan, R., *Matthew Paris*, 1st edn (Cambridge, 1958), 2nd edn (Cambridge, 1979).

Verbruggen, J. F., 'La Tactique Militaire des Armées de Chevaliers', *Revue du Nord*, 29 (1947), pp. 161–80.

Warren, *Henry II* (London, 1973).

Wilks, M., *The World of John of Salisbury* (Oxford, 1984).

Willard, S. and S. C. M. Southern, *The Art of Warfare in Western Europe during the Middle Ages, from the Eighth Century to 1340*, 2nd revised edn (Woodbridge, 1997), translation of J. F. Verbruggen, *De Krijskunst in West-Europa in de Middeleeuwen (IX tot begin XIVe Eeuw)* (Brussels, 1954).

C. *On chivalry and the chivalric ideology*

Accarie, M., 'Une Lance est une Lance; Critique et Fascination de la Chevalerie dans le Conte du Graal', in *Hommage à Jean Richer, Annales de la Fac. des Lettres et Sciences Humaines de Nice*, 51 (1985), pp. 9–19.

Arnold, B., *German Knighthood, 1050–1300* (Oxford, 1985).

Aurell, M., 'Chevaliers et Chevalerie chez Raymond Lulle', in *Raymond Lulle et le Pays d'Oc* (Cahiers de Fanjeaux, 22) (1987), pp. 141–68.

Balard, M. (ed.), *Autour de la Première Croisade (Actes du Colloque de Clermont-Ferrand, 22–25 Juin 1995)* (Paris, 1996).

Baldwin, J. W., 'Jean Renart et le Tournoi de Saint-Trond: une Conjonction de l'Histoire et de la Littérature', *Annales E.S.C.* (1990), 3, pp. 565–88.

Bancourt, P., 'Sen et Chevalerie. Réflexion sur la Tactique des Chevaliers dans Plusieurs Chansons de Geste des XIIe et XIIIe Siècles', in *Actes du VIe Congrès International de la Société Rencesvals* (Aix, 1973), pp. 621–37.

Barber, R., *The Knight and Chivalry* (London: Woodbridge, 1995).

Barbero, A., 'Nobiltà e Cavalleria nel XII Secolo: Walter Map e il "De Nugis Curialum" ', *Studi Medievali*, 25 (1984), pp. 721–43.

Barbero, A., *L'Aristocrazia nella Società Francese del Medioevo* (Bologna, 1987).

Barker, J. R. V., *The Tournament in England (1100–1400)* (Woodbridge, 1986).

Barthélémy, D., 'Note sur l'Adoubement dans la France des XIe et XIIe Siècles', in *Les Ages de la Vie au Moyen Age (Actes du Colloque de Provins, 16–17 Mars 1990)* (Paris, 1992), pp. 108–17.

Bartlett, R., 'Technique Militaire et Pouvoir Politique, 900–1300', *Annales E.S.C.*, 41 (1986), pp. 1135–59.

Batany, J., 'Des Trois Fonctions aux Trois Etats?', *Annales E.S.C.* (1963), pp. 933–8.

Batany, J. and J. Rony, 'Idéal Social et Vocabulaire des Statuts; le "Couronnement de Louis" ', *Langue Française*, 9 (1971), pp. 100–18.

Batany, J., 'Le Vocabulaire des Catégories Sociales Chez Quelques Moralistes Français vers 1200', in *Ordres et Classes. Colloque d'Histoire Sociale de Saint-Cloud* (Paris, 1973), pp. 59–72.

Batany, J., 'Du Bellator au Chevalier dans le Schéma des "Trois Ordres"; Etude Sémantique', in *Actes du CIe Congrès National des Sociétés Savantes* (Lille, 1976, Paris, 1978), pp. 23–4.

Baumgartner, E., 'Remarques sur la Prose du Lancelot', *Romania*, 105 (1984), pp. 2–15.

Beinhauer, M., *Ritterliche Tapferkeitsbegriffe in den altfranzösischen Chansons de geste des 12. Jhdts* (Cologne, 1958).

Bell, D. M., *L'Idéal Ethique de la Royauté en France au Moyen Age* (Geneva, 1962).

Beltrami, P. G., 'Chrétien, l'Amour, l'Adultère: Remarques sur le "Chevalier de la Charrete" ', in *Actes du 14e Congrès International Arthurien* (Rennes, 1984), pp. 59–69.

Bender, K. H., 'Un Aspect de la Stylisation Epique: l'Exclusivisme de la Haute Noblesse dans les Chansons de Geste du XIIe Siècle', *Studia Romanica*, 14 (1969), pp. 95–105.

Bennett, M., 'La Règle du Temple; or, "How to Deliver a Cavalry Charge" ', in *Studies in Medieval History Presented to R. Allen Brown* (Woodbridge, 1989), pp. 7–20.

Bennett, P. E., 'La Chronique de Jordan Fantosme: Epique et Public Lettré au XIIe Siècle', *Cahiers de Civilisation Médiévale*, 40 (1997), pp. 37–56.

Benson, L. D. and J. Leyerle, *Chivalric Literature; Essays on Relations between Literature and Life in the Middle Ages* (Kalamazoo, 1981).

Benton, J., 'Nostre Franceis n'unt Talent de Fuir: the Song of Roland and the Enculturation of a Warrior Class', *Olifant*, 6 (1979), pp. 237–58.

Bezzola, R. R., 'Guillaume IX et les Origines de l'Amour Courtois', *Romania*, 66 (1940–1), pp. 232–4.

Bezzola, R. R., *Le Sens de l'Aventure et de l'Amour: Chrétien de Troyes* (Paris, 1947).

Bezzola, R. R., *Les Origines et la Formation de la Littérature Courtoise en Occident*, vol. 2: *La Société Féodale et la Transformation de la Littérature de Cour* (Paris, 1960); vol. 3, 1: *La Cour d'Angleterre comme Centre Littéraire sous les Rois Angevins (1154–1190)* (Paris, 1963) and vol. 3, 2: *Les Cours de France, d'Outremer et de Sicile au XIIe Siècle* (Paris, 1963).

Bloch, R. H., *Medieval Misogyny and the Invention of Western Romantic Love* (Chicago–London, 1991).

Boase, R., *The Origin and Meaning of Courtly Love* (Manchester, 1977).

Borst, A., *Das Rittertum im Mittelalter* (Darmstadt, 1976).

Bossuat, A., 'Les Origines Troyennes: Leur Rôle dans la Littérature Historique du XVe S.', *Annales de Normandie* (1958), pp. 187–97.

Bouchard, C. B., *Strong of Body, Brave and Noble. Chivalry and Society in Medieval France* (Ithaca–London, 1998).

Boutet, D., 'Sur l'Origine et le Sens de la Largesse Arthurienne', *Le Moyen Age*, 89 (1983), pp. 397–411.

Boutet, D., *Charlemagne et Arthur, ou le Roi Imaginaire* (Paris, 1992).

Boutet, D. and A. Strubel, *Littérature, Politique et Société dans la France du Moyen Age* (Paris, 1979).

Bouzy, O., 'Spatha, Framea, Ensis. Le Vocabulaire de l'Armement aux VIIIe–XIIIe Siècles', *Le Moyen Age*, 105 (1999), pp. 91–107.

Braun, W., *Studien zum Ruodlieb. Ritterideal, Erzälstruktur und Darstellungsstil* (Berlin, 1962).

Brucker, C., ' "Prudentia", "Prudence" aux XIIe–XIIIe Siècles', *Romanische Forschungen*, 83 (1971), pp. 464–79.

Brundage, J. A., ' "Allas! That evere love was synne": Sex and Medieval Canon Law', *Catholic Historical Review*, 72, 1 (1986), pp. 1–13.

Brundage, J. A., *Law, Sex and Christian Society in Medieval Europe* (Chicago, 1987).

Bumke, J., *Studien zum Ritterbegriff im 12. und 13. Jhdt* (Heidelberg, 1964).

Bumke, J., *The Concept of Knighthood in the Middle Ages* (New York, 1982).

Burgess, G. S., *Contribution à l'Etude du Vocabulaire Pré-Courtois* (Geneva, 1970).

Burgess, G. S., ' "Orgueil" and "Fierté" in Twelfth Century French', *Zeitschrift für Romanische Philologie*, 89 (1972), pp. 103–22.

Burgess, G. S., 'Chivalry and Prowess in the Lays of Marie de France', *French Studies*, 37, 2 (1983), pp. 129–42.

Burgess, G. S., 'The Theme of Chivalry in Ille et Galeron', *Medioevo Romanzo*, 14 (1989), pp. 339–62.

Burgess, G. S., 'Chivalric Activity in the Anonymous Lays', in G. Angeli and L. Formisano (eds), *L'Imaginaire Courtois et son Double* (Salerno, 1992), pp. 271–91.

Burgess, G. S., 'The Term "Chevalerie" in the 12th-Century French', in P. R. Monks and D. D. R. Owen (eds), *Medieval Codicology, Iconography, Literature and Translation*, (Leiden, 1994), pp. 343–58.

Busby, K. and E. Kooper, *Courtly Literature, Culture and Context* (Amsterdam, 1990).

Buschinger, D. (ed.), *Tristan et Iseut, Mythe Européen et Mondial* (Göppingen, 1987).

Buschinger, D. (ed.), *La Croisade: Réalités et Fictions* (Göppingen, 1989).

Buschinger, D. and W. Spiewok (eds), *Le Monde des Héros dans la Culture Médiévale* (*Wodan*, 35) (Greifswald, 1994).

Buttin, F., 'La Lance et l'Arrêt de Cuirasse', *Archaeologia*, 99 (1965), pp. 77–178.

Caluwé, J. de, 'La Conception de l'Amour dans le Lai d'*Eliduc* de Marie de France', *Le Moyen Age*, 77 (1971), pp. 53–77.

Caluwé, J. de, 'La Jalousie, Signe d'Exclusion dans la Littérature Médiévale en Langue Occitane', *Senefiance*, 5 (1978), pp. 165–76.

Cardini, F., 'La Tradizione Cavalleresca nell'Occidente Medievale', *Quaderni Medievali*, 2 (1976), pp. 125–42.

Cardini, F., 'La Cavalleria: Una Questione da Riproporre?', *Annali dell'Istituto di Storia*, 2 (1980–1), pp. 45–137.

Cardini, F., *Alle Radici della Cavalleria Medievale* (Florence, 1982).

Charlemagne et l'Epopée Romane (Actes du VIIe Congrès International de la Société Rencesvals, Liège, 28 Août–4 Sept. 1976) (Paris, 1978), vol. 1.

Chênerie, M.-L., ' "Ces Curieux Chevaliers Tournoyeurs . . .", des Fabliaux aux Romans', *Romania*, 97 (1976), pp. 331ff.

Chênerie, M.-L., 'Le Motif de la Merci dans les Romans Arthuriens des XIIe et XIIIe Siècles', *Le Moyen Age*, 83 (1977), 1, pp. 5–52.

Chênerie, M.-L., 'L'Episode du Tournoi dans Guillaume de Dole, Etude Littéraire', *Revue des Langues Romanes*, 83 (1979), pp. 40–62.

Chênerie, M.-L., *Le Chevalier Errant dans les Romans Arthuriens en Vers des XIIe et XIIIe Siècles* (Geneva, 1986).

Chickering, H. and T. H. Seiler (eds), *The Study of Chivalry* (Kalamazoo (Michigan), 1988).

Chocheyras, J., 'Lecture Critique de Tristan et Iseut', in *Le Désir et ses Masques* (Grenoble, 1981), pp. 15–24.

Cirlot, V., 'Techniques Guerrières en Catalogne Féodale; le Maniement de la Lance', *Cahiers de Civilisation Médiévale* (1985), pp. 35–43.

Clerc au Moyen Age (Le), *Senefiance*, 37 (1995).

Combarieu Du Grès, M. de, 'Le Goût de la Violence dans l'Epopée Médiévale', *Senefiance*, 1 (1976), pp. 35–67.

Combarieu Du Grès, M. de, *L'Idéal Humain et l'Expérience Morale Chez les Héros des Chansons de Geste, des Origines à 1250* (Aix–Marseille, 1979).

Combattant au Moyen Age (Le), in *Actes du XVIIe Congrès de la Société des*

Historiens Médiévistes de l'Enseignement Supérieur Public (Saint-Herblain, 1991).

Coss, P., *The Knight in Medieval England, 1000–1400* (Stroud, 1993).

Crouch, D., *The Image of Aristocracy in Britain. 1000–1300* (London–New York, 1992).

Cuozzo, E., *Normanni. Nobiltà e Cavalleria* (Salerno, 1995).

Davis, R. H. C., 'The Medieval Warhorse', in F. M. L. Thompson (ed.), *Horses in European Economic History* (London, 1983).

Davis, R. H. C., *The Medieval Warhorse: Origin, Development and Redevelopment* (London, 1989).

Davis, R. H. C., 'Did the Anglo-Saxons have Warhorses?', in *Weapons and Warfare in Anglo-Saxon England* (Oxford, 1989), pp. 141–4.

Devries, K., *Medieval Military Technology* (Peterborough, 1992).

Dubuis, R., 'La Notion de Druerie dans les Lais de Marie de France', *Le Moyen Age*, 98 (1992), pp. 391–413.

Duby, G., 'Lignage, Noblesse et Chevalerie au XIIe Siècle dans la Région Mâconnaise: une Révision', *Annales E.S.C.* (1972), 4–5, pp. 803–23.

Duby, G., 'La Diffusion du Titre Chevaleresque sur le Versant Méditerranéen de la Chrétienté Latine', in *La Noblesse au Moyen Age. Essais à la Mémoire de Robert Boutruche* (Paris, 1976), pp. 39–70.

Dufournet, J. (ed.), *La Mort du Roi Arthur ou le Crépuscule de la Chevalerie* (Paris, 1994).

Essor et Fortune de la Chanson de Geste dans l'Europe et dans l'Orient Latin (Actes du 9e Congrès International de la Société Rencesvals) (Modena, 1984).

Faral, E., *Recherches sur les Sources Latines des Contes et Romans Courtois du Moyen Age* (Paris, 1913).

Faral, E., (ed.), *La Légende Arthurienne*, vol. 1 (Paris, 1929).

Fasoli, G., 'Lineamente di Una Storia dells Cavalleria', in *Studi di Storia Medievale e Moderna in Onore di E. Rota* (Rome, 1958), pp. 83–93.

Faulkner, K., 'The Transformation of Knighthood in the Early Thirteenth Century', *English Historical Review*, 111 (1996), pp. 1–23.

Fées, Dieux et Déesses au Moyen Age (Lille, 1994).

Femmes, Mariages, Lignages (XIIe–XIIIe Siècles), Mélanges Offerts à Georges Duby (Brussels, 1992).

Flandrin, J.-L., *Le Sexe et l'Occident. Evolution des Attitudes et des Comportements* (Paris, 1981).

Flandrin, J.-L., *Un Temps pour Embrasser. Aux Origines de la Morale Sexuelle Occidentale (VIe–XIe Siècle)* (Paris, 1983).

Fleckenstein, J., 'Zum Problem der Abschliessung des Ritterstandes', in H. Baumann (ed.), *Historische Forschungen für Walter Schlesinger* (Cologne–Vienna, 1974), pp. 252–71.

Fleckenstein, J. (ed), *Das ritterliche Turnier im Mittelalter* (Göttingen, 1985).

Fleckenstein, J. (ed.), *Curialitas: Studien zu Grundfragen der höfischritterlichen Kultur*, (Göttingen, 1990).

Fleckenstein, J., 'Friedrich Barbarossa und *das Rittertum*', in *Festschrift für Hermann Heimpel* (Göttingen), vol. 2, pp. 1023–41.

Flori, J., 'Qu'est-ce qu'un *Bacheler*?', *Romania*, 96 (1975), pp. 290–314.

Flori, J., 'La Notion de Chevalerie dans les Chansons de Geste du XIIe Siècle. Etude Historique de Vocabulaire', *Le Moyen Age*, 81, 2 (1975), pp. 211–44; 3/4, pp. 407–44.

Flori, J., 'Sémantique et Société Médiévale: le Verbe Adouber et son Evolution au XIIe Siècle', *Annales E.S.C.*, 31 (1976), pp. 915–40.

Flori, J., 'Chevalerie et Liturgie; Remise des Armes et Vocabulaire Chevaleresque dans les Sources Liturgiques du IXe au XIVe Siècle', *Le Moyen Age*, 84 (1978), pp. 247–78; 3/4, pp. 409–42.

Flori, J., 'Pour une Histoire de la Chevalerie: l'Adoubement chez Chrétien de Troyes', in *Romania*, 100 (1979), pp. 21–53.

Flori, J., 'L'Idéologie Aristocratique dans Aiol', *Cahiers de Civilisation Médiévale*, 27 (1984), pp. 359–65.

Flori, J., 'Le Origini dell'Ideologia Cavaleresca', *Archivo Storico Italiano*, 143, 2 (1985), pp. 1–13.

Flori, J., 'Du Nouveau sur l'Adoubement des Chevaliers (XIe-XIIe S.)', *Le Moyen Age*, 91 (1985), pp. 201–26.

Flori, J., '*Principes* et *milites* chez Guillaume de Poitiers, Etude Sémantique et Idéologique', *Revue Belge de Philologie et d'Histoire*, 64 (1986), 2, pp. 217–33.

Flori, J., 'Seigneurie, Noblesse et Chevalerie dans les Lais de Marie de France', *Romania*, 108 (1987), pp. 183–206.

Flori, J., 'Encore l'Usage de la Lance ... La Technique du Combat Chevaleresque vers 1100', *Cahiers de Civilisation Médiévale*, 31, 3 (1988), pp. 213–40.

Flori, J., 'Le Chevalier, la Femme et l'Amour dans les Pastourelles Anonymes des XIIe et XIIIe Siècles', in *Mélanges J.-C. Payen* (1989), pp. 169–79.

Flori, J., 'Mariage, Amour et Courtoisie dans les Lais de Marie de France', in *Bien Dire et Bien Aprandre*, 8 (1990), pp. 71–98.

Flori, J., 'Aristocratie et Valeurs Chevaleresques dans la Seconde Moitié du XIIe Siècle', *Le Moyen Age*, 106, 1 (1990), pp. 35–65.

Flori, J., 'Pur Eshalcier Sainte Crestïenté; Croisade, Guerre Sainte et Guerre Juste dans les Anciennes Chansons de Geste Françaises', *Le Moyen Age*, 97, 2 (1991), pp. 171–87.

Flori, J., 'Amour et Société Aristocratique au XIIe Siècle; l'Exemple des Lais de Marie de France', *Le Moyen Age*, 98, 1 (1992), pp. 17–34.

Flori, J., 'Le Héros Epique et sa Peur, du Couronnement de Louis à Aliscans', *Pris-Ma*, X, 1 (1994), pp. 27–44.

Flori, J., *La Chevalerie en France au Moyen Age* (Paris, 1995).

Flori, J., 'L'Epée de Lancelot. Adoubement et Idéologie au Début du XIIIe Siècle', in *Lancelot/Lanzelet, Hier et Aujourd'hui (Mélanges Offerts à Alexandre Micha)*, (Wodan, 51) (Paris, 1995), pp. 147–56.

Flori, J., 'Amour et Chevalerie dans le Tristan de Béroul', in A. Crépin and W. Spiewok (eds), *Tristan-Tristrant. Mélanges en l'Honneur de D. Buschinger à l'Occasion de son 60e Anniversaire* (*Wodan*, 66) (Griefswald, 1996), pp. 169–75.

Flori, J., 'La Notion de Chevalerie dans les Romans de Chrétien de Troyes', *Romania*, 114 (1996), 3–4, pp. 289–315.

Flori, J., 'Eglise et Chevalerie au XIIe Siècle', in D. Buschinger and W. Spiewok (eds), *Les Ordres Militaires au Moyen Age* (*Wodan*, 67) (1996), pp. 47–69.

Flori, J., 'L'Idée de Croisade dans Quelques Chansons de Geste du Cycle de Guillaume d'Orange', *Medioevo Romanzo*, 21, 2–3 (1997), pp. 476–95.

Flori, J., *Chevaliers et Chevalerie au Moyen Age* (Paris, 1998).

Flori, J., *La Chevalerie* (Paris, 1998).

Flori, J., 'Noblesse, Chevalerie et Idéologie Aristocratique en France d'Oïl (XIe–XIIIe Siècle)', in *Renovación Intelectual del Occidente Europeo, Siglo XII (XXIV Semana de Estudios Medievales, Estella, 14 a 18 de Julio de 1997)* (Pamplona, 1998), pp. 349–82.

Foulet, A., 'Is Roland Guilty of Desmesure?', *Romance Philology*, 10 (1957), pp. 145–8.

Frappier, J., 'Le Caractère et la Mort de Vivien dans la Chanson de Guillaume', in *Coloquios de Roncesvalles* (Zaragoza, 1956), pp. 229–43.

Frappier, J., 'Vues sur les Conceptions Courtoises dans les Littératures d'Oc et d'Oïl au XIIe Siècle', *Cahiers de Civilisation Médiévale*, 2 (1959), pp. 135–56.

Frappier, J., 'Le Motif du "Don Contraignant" dans la Littérature du Moyen Age', *Travaux de Linguistique et de Littérature*, 7, 2 (1969), pp. 7–46.

Frappier, J., 'Le Graal et ses Feux Divergents', *Romance Philology* (1971), pp. 373–440.

Frappier, J., *Chrétien de Troyes et le Mythe du Graal* (Paris, 1972).

Frappier, J., 'Sur un Procès fait à l'Amour Courtois', *Romania*, 93 (1972), pp. 141–8.

Frappier, J., *Amour Courtois et Table Rond* (Paris, 1973).

Frappier, J., *Autour du Graal* (Geneva, 1977).

Gaier, C., 'L'Armement Chevaleresque au Moyen Age (IXe au XVe Siècle)', in *Châteaux-Chevaliers en Hainaut au Moyen Age* (Brussels, 1995), pp. 199–214.

Gaier, C., 'La Cavalerie Lourde en Europe Occidentale du XIIe au XVIe S.: un Problème de Mentalité', in Gaier, *Armes et Combats*, pp. 300–10.

Gallais, P., 'Bleheri, la Cour de Poitiers et la Diffusion des Récits Arthuriens sur le Continent', in *Actes du VIIe Congrès National de la Société Française de Littérature Comparée* (Paris, 1967), pp. 47–79.

Gallais, P., *Perceval et l'Initiation* (Paris, 1972).

Gallais, P., *Genèse du Roman Occidental: Essai sur Tristan et Iseut et son Modèle Persan* (Paris, 1974).

Gaucher, E., 'Entre l'Histoire et le Roman: la Biographie Chevaleresque', *Revue des Langues Romanes*, 97 (1993), pp. 15–23.

Gautier, L., *La Chevalerie* (Paris, 1884).

Génicot, L., 'La Noblesse dans la Société Médiévale', *Le Moyen Age*, 71 (1965), pp. 539–60.

Génicot, L., 'La Noblesse Médiévale. Encore!', *Revue d'Histoire Ecclésiastique* (1993), pp. 137–201.

Gosman, M., 'Le Roman d'Alexandre et les Juvenes: une Approche Socio-historique', *Neophilologus*, 66 (1982), pp. 328–39.

Gosman, M., 'Le Roman de Toute Chevalerie et le Public Visé: la Légende au Service de la Royauté', *Neophilologus*, 72 (1988), pp. 335–41.

Gougenheim, G., 'Le Sens de "Noble" et de ses Dérives Chez Robert de Clari', in *Etudes de Grammaire et de Vocabulaire Française* (Paris, 1970), pp. 328–9.

Graböis, A., '*Militia* and *Malitia*: the Bernardine Vision of Chivalry', in M. Gervers (ed.), *The Second Crusade and the Cistercians* (New York, 1992), pp. 49–56.

Green, R. B., ' "Fin" Amors dans Deux Lais de Marie de France: Equitan et Chaitival', *Le Moyen Age*, 81 (1975), pp. 265–72.

Guidot, B., *Recherches sur la Chanson de Geste au XIIIe Siècle (d'Après Certaines Œuvres du Cycle de Guillaume d'Orange)*, 2 vols (Aix–Marseille, 1986).

Hanning, R. W., 'The Social Significance of Twelfth-Century Chivalric Romance', *Medievalia et Humanistica* (1972), 3, pp. 3–29.

Harvey, R., 'Marcabru and the Spanish Lavador', *Forum for Modern Language Studies*, 22, 2 (1986), pp. 123–44.

Hattoa, A. T., 'Archery and Chivalry: a Noble Prejudice', *Modern Language Review*, 35 (1940), pp. 40–54.

Imagine Riflessa (L'), 12, vol. 1 (Genoa, 1989).

Jackson, W. H. (ed.), *Knighthood in Medieval Literature* (Woodbridge, 1981).

Jackson, W. H., *Chivalry in 12th-Century Germany* (Cambridge, 1994).

Jaeger, C. S., *The Origins of Courtliness, Civilising Trends and the Formation of Courtly Ideals, 939–1210* (Philadelphia, 1985).

Jones, G. F., 'Grim to Your Foes and Kind to Your Friends', *Studia Neophilologica*, 34 (1962), pp. 91–103.

Jones, G. F., 'Roland's Lament: a Divergent Interpretation', *Romanic Review*, 53 (1962), pp. 91–103.

Jones, G. F., *The Ethos of the Song of Roland* (Baltimore, 1963).

Jonin, P., 'Le Vassalage de Lancelot dans le Conte de la Charrette', *Le Moyen Age*, 68 (1952), pp. 281–98.

Jonin, P., 'Aspects de la Vie Sociale au XIIe Siècle dans Yvain', *L'Information Littéraire*, 2 (1964), pp. 47–54.

Jung, M. R., *La Légende de Troie en France au Moyen Age* (Basel–Tübingen, 1996).

Keen, M., *Chivalry* (London, 1984).

Keen, M., 'War, Peace and Chivalry', in B. P. McGuire (ed.), *War and Peace in the Middle Ages* (Copenhagen, 1987), pp. 94–117.

Kelly, D., 'Courtly Love in Perspective: the Hierarchy of Love in Andreas Capellanus', in *Traditio*, 24 (1968), pp. 119–47.

Kelly, T. E., 'Love in Perlesvaus: Sinful Passion or Redemptive Force?', in *Romanic Review*, 66 (1975), pp. 1–12.

Köhler, E., 'Le Rôle de la "Coutume" dans les Romans de Chrétien de Troyes', *Romania*, 81 (1960), pp. 67–82.

Köhler, E., 'Quelques Observations d'Ordre Historico-Sociologique sur les Rapports entre la Chanson de Geste et le Roman Courtois', in *Chansons de Geste und Höfischer Roman* (Heidelberg, 1963), pp. 21–63.

Köhler, E., 'Observations Historiques et Sociologiques sur la Poésie des Troubadours', *Cahiers de Civilisation Médiévale*, 7 (1964), pp. 27–51.

Köhler, E., 'Sens et Fonction du Terme "Jeunesse" dans la Poésie des Troubadours', in *Mélanges R. Crozet*, vol. 1, pp. 567–83.

Köhler, E., 'Die Pastorellen des Troubadours Gavaudan', in *Esprit und arkadische Freiheit: Aufzätze aus der Welt der Romania* (Frankfurt–Bonn, 1966), pp. 67–82.

Köhler, E., *L'Aventure Chevaleresque* (Paris, 1970).

Lachet, C., 'Les Tournois dans les Roman de Flamenca', *Le Moyen Age*, 98 (1992), pp. 61–70.

Laffont, R., *Le Chevalier et son Désir* (Paris, 1992).

Lazar, M., *Amour Courtois et Fins Amor dans la Littérature du XIIe Siècle* (Paris, 1964).

Lefèvre, Y., 'L'Amour, c'est le Paradis; Commentaire de la chanson IX de Guillaume IX d'Aquitaine', *Romania*, 102 (1981), pp. 289–304.

Le Gentil, P., 'A Propos de la Démesure de Roland', *Cahiers de Civilisation Médiévale*, 11 (1971), pp. 203–9.

Le Goff, J., 'Mélusine Maternelle et Défricheuse. Le Dossier Médiéval', *Annales E.S.C.*, 26 (1981), pp. 587–603.

Le Goff, J., *L'Imaginaire Médiéval* (Paris, 1985); trans. A. Goldhammer, *The Medieval Imagination* (Chicago–London, 1988).

Legros, ' "Seignur Barun", "Vavassur Onuré", le Discours Mobilisateur dans la Chanson de Guillaume', *Le Moyen Age*, 89, 1 (1983), pp. 41–62.

Lénat, R., 'L'Adoubement dans Quelques Textes Littéraires de la Fin du XIIe Siècle; Clergie et Chevalerie', in *Mélanges Ch. Foulon* (Paris, 1980), vol. 1, pp. 195–203.

Le Rider, P., 'Le Dépassement de la Chevalerie dans le Chevalier de la Charrette', *Romania*, 112, pp. 83–99.

Le Rider, P., *Le Chevalier dans le Conte du Graal* (Paris, 1978).

Loomis, R. S., *Arthurian Tradition and Chrétien de Troyes* (New York, 1949).

Lorcin, M.-T., *Façon de Sentir et de Penser: les Fabliaux* (Paris, 1979).

Mancini, M., *Societa Feudale e Ideologie nel Charroi de Nîmes* (Florence, 1992).

Mandach, A. de, *Chanson de Roland. Transferts de Mythes dans le Monde Occidental et Oriental* (Geneva, 1993).

Marchello-Niza, C., 'Amour Courtois, Société Masculine et Figures du Pouvoir', *Annales E.S.C.* (1981), pp. 969–82.

Markale, J., *L'Epopée Celtique d'Irlande* (Paris, 1971).

Markale, J., *Le Roi Arthur et la Société Celtique* (Paris, 1976), 4th edn (Paris, 1982).

Markale, J., *Lancelot et la Chevalerie Arthurienne* (Paris, 1985).

Marx, J., *La Légende Arthurienne et le Graal* (Paris, 1952).

Marx, J., 'Quelques Observations sur la Formation de la Notion de Chevalier Errant', *Etudes Celtiques*, 11 (1964–5), pp. 344–50.

Matarasso, P., *The Redemption of Chivalry. A Study of the 'Queste del Saint Graal'* (Geneva, 1979).

Maurer, F., 'Das ritterliche Tugendsystem', in *Deutsches Vierteljahreszeitschrift für Literaturwissenschaft und Geistesgeschichte*, 23 (1949), pp. 252–85 and 24 (1950), pp. 274–85, 526–9.

Méla, C., *La Reine et le Graal. La Conjointure dans les Romans du Graal* (Paris, 1981).

Mélanges de Langue et de Littérature du Moyen Age Offerts à Teruo Sato, I (Nagoya, 1973).

Mélanges de Littérature du Moyen Age au XXe Siècle, Offerts à Mademoiselle Jeanne Lods (Paris, 1978).

Mélanges E. Hoeffner (Paris, 1949).

Mélanges Jean Frappier (Geneva, 1970).

Mélanges Maurice Delbouille, vol. 2, *Philologie Médiévale* (Paris or Gembloux, 1964).

Mélanges Pierre le Gentil (Paris, 1973).

Mélanges P. Jonin (Senefiance, 7) (Paris–Aix-en-Provence, 1979).

Mélanges R. Crozet (Poitiers, 1966).

Mélanges Rita Lejeune (Gembloux, 1969).

Meyer, P., *Alexandre le Grand dans la Littérature Française du Moyen Age*, vol. 1: *Texte* (Paris, 1886); vol. 2: *Histoire de la Légende* (Paris, 1886).

Micha, A., 'Le Mari Jaloux dans la Littérature Romanesque des XIIe et XIIIe Siècles', *Studi Medievali*, 17 (1951), pp. 303–20.

Micha, A., *Essais sur le Cycle du Lancelot-Graal* (Geneva, 1987).

Morgan, G., 'The Conflict of Love and Chivalry in *Le Chevalier de la Charrette*', *Romania*, 102 (1981), pp. 172–201.

Morris, C., '*Equestris Ordo*, Chivalry as a Vocation in the Twelfth Century', in D. Baker (ed.), *Religious Motivations: Bibliographical and Sociological Problems for the Church Historians* (Oxford, 1978), pp. 87–96.

Nelli, R., *L'Erotique des Troubadours* (Gap, 1963).

Newman, F. X. (ed.), *The Meaning of Courtly Love* (New York, 1967).

Noble, P., 'L'Influence de la Courtoisie sur le Tristan de Béroul', *Le Moyen Age*, 65 (1969), pp. 467–77.

Noble, P., 'Attitudes to Social Class as Revealed by Some of the Older Chansons de Geste', *Romania*, 94 (1973), pp. 359–85.

Noble, P., 'Le Roi Marc et les Amants dans le Tristan de Béroul', *Romania*, 102 (1981), pp. 221–6.

Oakeshott, R. E., *A Knight and his Armour* (London, 1961).

Oakeshott, R. E., *A Knight and his Weapons* (London, 1964).

Oakeshott, R. E., *The Sword in the Age of Chivalry* (London, 1964).

Ordinamenti Militari in Occidente nell'Alto Medioevo (Spoleto, 1968), vol. 2.

Ortigues, E., 'L'Elaboration de la Théorie des Trois Ordres chez Haymon d'Auxerre', *Francia*, 14 (1986), pp. 27–43.

Oulment, C., *Les Débats du Clerc et du Chevalier dans la Littérature Poétique du Moyen Age* (Paris, 1911).

Owen, D. D. R., 'From Grail to Holy Grail', *Romania*, 89 (1968), pp. 31–53.

Painter, S., *French Chivalry, Chivalric Ideas and Practices in Medieval France* (Baltimore, 1940).

Paravicini, W., *Rie ritterlich-höfische Kultur des Mittelalters* (Munich, 1994).

Paterson, L., 'The Concept of Knighthood in the 12th Century Occitan Lyric', in *Chrétien de Troyes and the Troubadours* (Cambridge, 1984), pp. 112–31.

Payen, J.-C., 'La Destruction des Mythes Courtois dans le Roman en Vers après Chrétien de Troyes', *Revue des Langues Romanes*, 78 (1969), pp. 213ff.

Payen, J.-C., 'Structure et Sens du Roman de Thèbes', *Le Moyen Age*, 76 (1970), pp. 493–513.

Payen, J.-C., 'Structure et Sens du Chevalier au Barisel', *Le Moyen Age*, 77 (1971), pp. 239–62.

Payen, J.-C., ' "Peregris". De l'Amor de Lonh au Congé Courtois. Notes sur l'Espace et le Temps de la Chanson de Croisade', *Cahiers de Civilisation Médiévale*, 17 (1974), pp. 247–53.

Payen, J.-C., *La Rose et l'Utopie* (Paris, 1977).

Payen, J.-C., 'L'Idéologie Chevaleresque dans le Roman de Renart', *Marche Romane*, 38, 3–4 (1978), pp. 33–41.

Payen, J.-C., 'Le Peuple dans les Romans Français de "Tristan": la "Povre Gent" chez Béroul, sa Fonction Narrative et son Statut Idéologique', *Cahiers de Civilisation Médiévale*, 23 (1980), pp. 187–98.

Peirce, I., 'The Knight, his Arm and Armour, c. 1150–1250', *Anglo-Norman Studies*, 15 (1992), pp. 251–74.

Pollmann, L., *Die Liebe in der Hochmittelalterlichen Literatur Frankreichs* (Frankfurt-am-Main, 1966).

Pulega, A., *Amore Cortese e Modelli Teologici. Guglielmo IX, Chrétien de Troyes, Dante* (Milan, 1995).

Renoir, A., 'Roland's Lament; its Meaning and Function in the Chanson de Roland', *Speculum*, 35 (1960), pp. 572–83.

Reuter, H. G., *Die Lehre vom Ritterstand*, 2nd edn (Cologne, 1975).

Rey-Delqué, M. (ed.), *Les Croisades. L'Orient et l'Occident d'Urbain II à Saint Louis, 1096–1270* (Milan, 1997).

Rey-Flaud, H., *La Névrose Courtoise* (Paris, 1983).

Ribard, J., *Chrétien de Troyes, le Chevalier de la Charette, Essai d'Interprétation Symbolique* (Paris, 1972).

Ribard, J., 'L'Ecriture Romanesque de Chrétien de Troyes d'après le Perceval', *Perspectives Médiévales*, 1 (1975), pp. 38–52.

Ribard, J., 'Et si les Fabliaux n'étaient pas des "Contes à Rire"?', *Reinardus*, 11 (1989), pp. 134–43.

Ribard, J., *Du Mythique au Mystique. La Littérature Médiévale et ses Symboles* (Paris, 1995).

Das Ritterbild in Mittelalter und Renaissance (Düsseldorf, 1985).

Rocher, D., 'Chevalerie et Littérature Chevaleresque', *Etudes Germaniques* (1966), 2, pp. 165–79; (1963), 3, pp. 345–57.

Rocher, D., 'Lateinische Tradition und ritterliche Ethik', in *Ritterliches Tugentsystem* (Darmstadt, 1969), pp. 452–77.

Roques, M., 'L'Attitude de Héros Mourant', *Romania*, 64 (1940), pp. 355ff.

Ross, D. J. A., 'L'Originalité de Turoldus: le Maniement de la Lance', *Cahiers de Civilisation Médiévale*, 6 (1963), pp. 127–38.

Ross, D. J. A., 'Breaking a Lance', in W. Van Emden and P. E. Bennett (eds), *Guillaume d'Orange and the Chanson de Geste. Essays Presented to D. McMillan* (Reading, 1984), pp. 127–35.

Rougemont, D. de, *L'Amour et l'Occident* (Paris, 1971) 3rd edn.

Rousset, P., 'La Croyance en la Justice Immanente à l'Epoque Féodale', *Le Moyen Age*, 54 (1948), pp. 225–48.

Rousset, P., 'La Description du Monde Chevaleresque Chez Orderic Vital', *Le Moyen Age*, 65 (1969), pp. 427–44.

Rousset, P., 'Saint Bernard et l'Idéal Chevaleresque', *Nova et Vetera*, 45, 1 (1970), pp. 28–35.

Rousset, P., *Histoire d'une Idéologie: la Croisade* (Lausanne, 1983).

Rousset, P., 'Note sur la Situation du Chevalier à l'Epoque Féodale', in *Littérature, Histoire et Linguistique. Recueil d'Etudes Offerts à B. Gagnebin* (Lausanne, 1973), pp. 189–200.

Ruiz-Domenec, J. E., 'L'Idea della Cavalleria Medievale come una Teoria Ideologica della Società', *Nuova Rivista Storica* (1981), pp. 341–67.

Ruiz-Domenec, J. E., 'Littérature et Société Médiévale: Vision d'Ensemble', *Le Moyen Age*, 88, 1 (1982), pp. 77–113.

Ruiz-Domenec, J. E., *La Caballeria o la Imagen Cortesana del Mundo* (Genoa, 1984).

Sargent-Baur, B. N., '*Dux Bellorum/Rex Militum*/Roi Fainéant; la Transformation d'Arthur au XIIe Siècle', *Le Moyen Age*, 90, 3/4 (1984), pp. 357–73.

Sargent-Baur, B. N., 'Love and Rivalry in Beroul's Tristan', *Romania*, 105 (1984), pp. 291–311.

Sargent-Baur, B. N., 'Promotion to Knighthood in the Romances of Chrétien de Troyes', *Romance Philology*, 37, 4 (1984), pp. 393–408.

Scaglioni, A., *Knights at Court* (Berkeley, 1991).

Schnell, R., *Causa Amoris. Liberskonzeption und Liebesdarstellung in der mittelalterlichen Literatur* (Bern–Munich, 1985).

Schnell, R., 'L'Amour Courtois en tant que Discours Courtois sur l'Amour', *Romania*, 110 (1989), pp. 72–126, 331–63.

Schuchard, B., *Valor, zu seiner Wortgeschichte im lateineschen und romanischen des Mittelalters* (Bonn, 1970).

Schwinges, R. C., *Kreuzzugsideologie und Toleranz. Studien zu Wilhelm von Tyrus* (Stuttgart, 1977).

Shippey, T. A., 'The Uses of Chivalry: "Erec" and "Gawain" ', *Modern Language Review*, 66 (1971), pp. 241–50.

Spencer, R. H., 'Le Rôle de l'Argent dans Aiol', in *Charlemagne et l'Epopée Romane*, pp. 653–60.

Stanesco, M., 'Le Héraut d'Arme et la Tradition Littéraire Chevaleresque', *Romania*, 106 (1985), pp. 233–53.

Stanesco, M., *Jeux d'Errance du Chevalier Médiéval* (Leiden, 1988).

Subrenat, J., 'Sur le Climat Social, Moral, Religieux du Tristan de Béroul', *Le Moyen Age*, 82 (1976), pp. 219–61.

Technique Littéraire des Chansons de Geste (La) (*Actes du Colloque de Liège, 1957*) (Paris, 1959).

Tolan, J. V., 'Mirror of Chivalry: Salah Al Din in the Medieval European Imagination', in D. R. Banks (ed.), *Images of the Other: Europe and the Muslim World before 1700*, Cairo Papers in Social Science, vol. 19, 2 (1996), pp. 7–38.

Tomaryn-Brukner, M. T., 'Fiction in the Female Voice: the Women Troubadours', *Speculum*, 67 (1992), pp. 865–91.

Trotter, D. A., 'La Mythologie Arthurienne et la Prédication de la Croisade', in L. Harf-Lancner and D. Boutet (eds), *Pour une Mythologie du Moyen Age* (Paris, 1988), pp. 155–71.

Turner, R. V., 'The "*Miles Literatus*" in 12th and 13th Century England', *American Historical Review*, 83 (1978), pp. 928–45.

Van Dijk, H. and W. Noomen (eds), *Aspects de l'Epopée Romane: Mentalités, Idéologies, Intertextualités* (Groningen, 1995).

Van Hoecke, W. and A. Welkenhuysen, *Love and Marriage in the 12th Century* (Louvain, 1981).

Van Winter, J.-M., *Rittertum, Ideal und Wirklichkeit* (Bussum, 1969).

Van Winter, J.-M., '*Cingulum militiae*, Schwertleite en *miles*-terminologie als spiegel van veranderend menselijk gedrag', in *Tijdschrift voor Rechtgeschiedenis* (1976), pp. 1–92.

Venckeler, T., 'Faut-il Traduire *Vassal* par Vassal? Quelques Réflections sur la Lexicologie du Français Médiéval', in *Mélanges de Littérature et de Philologie Médiévales Offerts à J. R. Smeets* (Leiden, 1982), pp. 303–16.

Vinay, G., 'Il *De Amore* di Andrea Capellano nel Quadro della Letteratura Amorosa e della Rinascita del Sec. XII', *Studi Medievali*, 17 (1951), pp. 203–76.

Vreede, F., *L'Idéal Chevaleresque et Courtois dans la Littérature du Moyen Age* (Djakarta–Groningen, 1965).

Waard, R. Van, 'Le Couronnement de Louis et le Principe de l'Hérédité de la Couronne', *Neophilologus*, 30 (1946), pp. 52–8.

Waltz, M., *Rolandslied, Wilhelmslied, Alexiuslied* (Heidelberg, 1966).

Waltz, M., 'Spontanéité et Responsabilité dans la Chanson de Geste: Raoul de Cambrai', *Studia Romanica*, 14 (1969), pp. 194–202.

Wathelet-Willem, J.,'La Fée Morgane dans les Chansons de Geste', *Cahiers de Civilisation Médiévale* (1970), pp. 209–19.

Whitehead, F., 'Ofermod et Demesure', *Cahiers de Civilisation Médiévale*, 3 (1960), pp. 115–17.

Whitehead, F., 'L'Ambiguïté de Roland', in *Studi in Onore di Italo Siciliano* (Florence, 1966), vol. 2, pp. 1203–12.

Zaganelli, G., 'Béroul, Thomas e Chrétien de Troyes (Sull'Amore, la Morte, la Gioa)', in *Le Forme e la Storia* (1992), 1–2, pp. 9–46.

Zink, M., *La Pastourelle, Poésie et Folklore au Moyen Age* (Paris, 1972).

Zink, M., 'Les Chroniques Médiévales et le Modèle Romanesque', *Mesure*, 1 (January, 1989), pp. 33–45.

Zumthor, P., 'Notes en Marge du Traité de l'Amour de André le Chapelain', *Zeitschrift für Romanische Philologie*, 63 (1943), p p. 178–91.

Zumthor, P., 'Le Roman Courtois, Essai de Définition', *Etudes Littéraires* (1971), 1, pp. 75–90.

Index

Abbo of Fleury, 244–6
Abbo of Saint-Germain, 245
Achard of Châlus 205
Adalbero of Laon, 235n, 245–6, 250, 264
Adela of Champagne, wife of Louis VII, 6, 25, 47–8
  Adela, sister of Henry I, wife of Count of Blois, 2
Ademar of Angoulême, 175, 182, 191
Adso of Montier-en-Der, 103
  Alice, daughter of Louis VII and Eleanor of Aquitaine, 5, 10–11
Alice, daughter of Louis VII and Constance of Castile, 6, 25, 28, 35, 44, 58, 60–2, 64, 67–70, 72, 78, 85–6, 97–8, 106–7, 163, 183, 185, 380–2, 398
Alice of Blois, 10
Alice of Maurienne, 35
Aimar of Angoulême, 65
Aimar of Limoges, 42, 44, 48, 50–1, 54, 58, 61n, 181, 191, 198, 201–2, 206, 211, 213–14
Alexander III, Pope, 25, 27, 44
Alfonso II of Aragon, 45, 51, 88
Alfonso VI of Castile, 362
Alfonso VIII of Castile, 1, 22, 86, 183–4
Amaury of Lusignan, 118, 145
Ambroise, chronicler, 64n, 86, 89, 95, 98–9, 113–15, 117–18, 121–2, 125–7, 133–6, 139–40, 142–3, 145–9, 225–6, 276–9, 289, 292, 299–300, 302,

306–10, 315, 317–29, 338–9, 342, 348, 357, 360, 364–6, 383, 403–4, 407–8
Andrew the Chaplain, 265
Andrew of Chauvigny, 142, 300n
Arnoul of Guisnes, 292
Arthur, legendary king, 10, 105, 239–40, 294, 311, 334, 336, 344, 375, 377, 384, 401–2, 404–6
Arthur of Brittany, 84–5, 99, 180, 186, 191, 403

Baha ad-Din, chronicler, 134, 141, 156n, 329, 359
Baldwin IV of Jerusalem, 60
Baldwin, Archbishop of Canterbury, 63, 79, 80, 116
Baldwin Carew, 138
Baldwin le Caron, 320
Baldwin of Alost, 292
Baldwin of Béthune, 77, 158
Baldwin of Boulogne, 9
Baldwin of Flanders, 189–91
Baldwin of Hainault, 47, 187
Becket, Thomas, 22–3, 26–31, 33, 35, 46, 80, 93, 176, 177, 222, 251, 406
Bela II of Hungary, 60, 64
Benoît de Sainte-Maure, 10, 304, 337, 402
Berengaria of Navarre, 65, 86, 88, 97, 100, 105, 107–8, 113–14, 117–18, 140, 157, 178, 181, 299, 354, 381, 383–4, 387–8
Bernard of Clairvaux, 21, 247, 276